QUILTERS DREAM BATTING®

"Quilts Like a Dream"

QUILTERS DREAM ANGEL™

Heavenly Batting made 100% from Flame Retardant Fibers

Flame Retardant Fibers are needlepunched creating a soft cozy breathable batting with a natural look and feel. Specially engineered fibers. The perfect batting for the ones you love!

QUILTERS DREAM POLY®

You Won't Believe It's Polyester!

Dream Poly is not polyester as usual. An exclusive blend of soft silky fine denier polyester microfibers. Developed to imitate the softness, drape and breathability of natural fibers. Available in white and midnight black. Also available in Fusible!

QUILTERS DREAM WOOL

"Shear-ly B'ewe'" Wool Batting

A beautiful consistent batting made with a blend of fine Domestic & Merino wool. No scrim or resins. May be machine-washed and dried with no shrinkage. Light and luxurious with a lovely drape and wonderful warmth.

QUILTERS DREAM PUFF

Light as a Feather yet Warmer Than Down!

Lusciously light and lofty batting that imparts volume and definition without adding weight. Dream Puff's soft, silky fibers offer superior insulation that is 1.5 times warmer than down! Stitches up to 10" apart. Excellent for hand and machine quilting, trapunto, garments, comforters and tied quilts.

QUILTERS DREAM 80/20

Perfectly Blended Batting 80% Dream Cotton & 20% Fine Dream Poly Microfibers

Quilters Dream Batting will donate 10% of our Dream Pink sales to Metastatic Breast Cancer Research. Available in Natural, White, Pink and Fusible.

QUILTERS DREAM GREEN™

Earth-Friendly Soft Polyester Batting Made 100% From Recycled Plastic Bottles!

QUILTERS DREAM® FOR MACHINES Blend™

"Soft to hug, yet takes the tug!"

70% natural cotton and 30% silky fine denier poly microfibers blended in perfect harmony and needlepunched through an ultralight scrim base. Developed especially for machine quilters. Stitches up to 12" apart. Soft and drapeable, yet strong and stable.

QUILTERS DREAM® COTTON

100% Pure Cotton Batting

Available in four wonderful lofts in both natural and white. No scrim or resins. Stitches may be up to 8" apart. No prewashing. Minimal shrinkage. Drapes softly and imparts a beautiful look and feel to your quilts. Also available in Fusible!

QUILTERS DREAM® ORIENT

East Meets West in this Luxurious Natural Batting made from an Exotic Blend of BAMBOO, SILK, TENCEL®, and COTTON

Quilters Dream Batting is Available in Fine Specialty Quilt Shops

www.QuiltersDreamBatting.com   757-463-3264

Please join us for the Hopes & Dreams Quilt Challenge for ALS (Lou Gehrig's Disease)
"Making Hopes & Dreams come true, one quilt at a time"

Table of Contents

Product Ads . . . . Pg. 1 and 3 thru 9
Credit Page and About Us. . . . Pg. 10
Exclusive Pattern from *Quilt In A Day* . . . . Pg. 12
Exclusive Pattern from *Pacific Rim Quilt Company*. . . . Pg. 14
Exclusive Pattern from Trackside Quilting. . . . Pg. 18
Quilt Show Ads . . . . Pg. 21 thru 31
Retreat Facility Ads . . . . Pg. 32 thur 41

U.S. Shops

	Featured Ads	Index
Alabama	42	44
Alaska	45	49
Arizona	50	54
Arkansas	56	59
California	61	70
Colorado	77	84
Connecticut	87	88
Delaware	89	89
District of Columbia	90	90
Florida	91	99
Georgia	102	105
Hawaii	107	108
Idaho	109	111
Illinois	112	128
Indiana	132	143
Iowa	146	155
Kansas	158	165
Kentucky	167	172
Louisiana	174	177
Maine	178	181
Maryland	183	188
Massachusetts	190	193
Michigan	196	207
Minnesota	212	219
Mississippi	223	225
Missouri	226	238
Montana	242	247
Nebraska	249	255
Nevada	257	260
New Hampshire	261	263
New Jersey	265	266
New Mexico	268	272
New York	273	282

	Featured Ads	Index
North Carolina	287	291
North Dakota	294	296
Ohio	297	308
Oklahoma	312	315
Oregon	317	322
Pennsylvania	326	332
Rhode Island	336	336
South Carolina	337	339
South Dakota	340	343
Tennessee	344	352
Texas	355	362
Utah	367	368
Vermont	370	372
Virginia	373	378
Washington	381	385
West Virginia	388	390
Wisconsin	391	401
Wyoming	405	408

Canadian Shops

	Featured Ads	Index
Alberta	—	409
Atlantic Provinces		
New Brunswick	411	412
Newfoundland	—	412
Nova Scotia	—	413
Prince Edward Island	—	413
British Columbia	414	416
Manitoba	418	418
Northwest Territory	419	419
Nunavut	—	—
Ontario	420	422
Quebec	—	426
Saskatchewan	—	427
Yukon Territory	—	427

Journal Pages 428

Look for the entire listing of shows at
www.quilterstc.com or crafterstc.com

GRANDMA'S SECRET PRODUCTS®

GRANDMA'S SECRET MIRACLE MOISTURIZER®

Grandma's Original Recipe for Soft Skin Brings a Trusted Solution To a New Generation.

Simply apply a small amount to re-hydrate skin. Greaseless, Stainless and Fragrance Free.

GRANDMA'S SECRET SPOT REMOVER®

Gradma's Wipes Out a Wide Range of Stains: Food, Grease, Blood and Many More!

Fast working and easy to use. Convenient, take-along size is perfect at home or on the go.

One Bottle Lasts Up To a Year!

GRANDMA'S SECRET WRINKLE REMOVER®

Just a Spray and You're On Your Way!

If you have Wrinkles but don't have time to iron, Grandma can help. Lightly mist garment and smooth with your hands.

GRANDMA'S SECRET GOOEY REMOVER®

Spray It On and Your Sticky Mess Is Gone!

Can remove chewing gum to candle wax. Watch it easily disappear.

No Gooey Mess Is Too Much for Grandma!

GRANDMA'S SECRET JEWELRY CLEANER®

Don't Just Clean Your Jewelry, Make It Sparkle!

With everyday exposure to soaps, lotions, body oils and perspiration, your Jewelry has lost its twinkle.

Safe Enough To Use Everyday!

1-800-605-SOAP (7627)
www.GrandmasSecretProducts.com
All of Grandma's Products are Biodegradable, Non-Toxic, Eco-Friendly and Made In The USA.

Tour our US and Canadian Certified Shops...It's time to check this adventure off your bucket list!

CERTIFIED SHOPS

1 **A STITCH OF COUNTRY**
Fernley, NV

2 **THIMBLE TOWNE**
Bakersfield & Visalia, CA

3 **ALWAYS QUILTING**
San Mateo, CA

4 **JANNILOU CREATIONS**
Philomath, OR

5 **STITCH N' SNIP**
Garden Valley, ID

6 **GLACIER QUILTS**
Kalispell, MT

7 **AROUND THE BLOCK**
Beaverlodge, AB Canada

8 **BACKDOOR QUILT SHOPPE**
Billings, MT

9 **QUILTER'S STASH**
Windsor, CO

10 **SEW-CIETY**
Castle Rock, CO

11 **CANTON VILLAGE QUILT WORKS**
Mesa, AZ

12 **THE QUILTER'S MARKET**
Tucson, AZ

13 **FABRIC FANATICS**
Plano, TX

14 **STITCHIN' HEAVEN**
Mineola, TX

15 **CROSSROADS QUILTING**
Cameron, MO

> ❝ It is rewarding to be able to offer our customers exclusive patterns and teach them how to achieve amazing results using Judy's techniques. ❞
>
> Back Door Quilt Shoppe

Our Certified Shops are exclusive dealers of the our *Technique of the Month Programs* which means they're trained teachers of Judy's techniques, authorities on our product line, they have living galleries of completed quilts, and are committed to kitting to meet your needs. The States and Provinces with quilts displayed below have Certified Shops in them!

CERTIFIED SHOPS

BATIKS PLUS 16
St. Louis, MO

PEDDLER'S WAY QUILT CO 17
Washington, IL

QUILTERS QUEST 18
Woodridge, IL

PARK BENCH QUILT SHOP 19
Midland, MI

SEW MANY THINGS 20
Clinton Township, MI

THE COTTON CUPBOARD QUILT SHOP 21
Bangor, ME

APPLETREE FABRICS 22
Auburn, MA

QUILT BASKET 23
Pawling, NY

QUILTER'S CORNER 24
Midlothian, VA

THREADS RUN THRU IT 25
Phenix, VA

BATIKS ETC & SEW WHAT FABRICS 26
Wytheville, VA

TENNESSEE QUILTS 27
Jonesborough, TN

SEW MUCH FUN 28
Columbus, GA

QUILTING BY THE BAY 29
Panama City, FL

BOUTIQUE 4 QUILTERS 30
West Melbourne, FL

Being a Certified Shop allows us to educate our students with a truly fabulous method of paper piecing, that results in stunning designs!

Canton Village Quilt Works

SCAN THE CODE FOR MORE INFORMATION ABOUT THE FEATURED CERTIFIED SHOPS LISTED ABOVE AND MANY MORE NEAR YOU!

The Country Register®

Available across the U.S.A. & Canada

A Complimentary Guide to Specialty Shopping and Events

Get your Name Out There! We can help!

Effective & Affordable Advertising!
For Quilt Shops, Fabric Stores, Needlework shops
Tea Rooms, Gift Shops, Plus Much More!
Please contact your local publisher for more information

USA
*Arizona: (602) 942-8950
*Arkansas: (405) 470-2597
*California and N. Nevada: (602) 942-8950
 Colorado: (719) 749-9797
*Connecticut: (919) 661-1760
*Delaware: (888) 616-8319
*Florida: (866) 825-9217
*Georgia: (706) 340-1049
*Idaho (N): (605) 722-7028
*Idaho (S): (602) 942-8950
*Illinois: (405) 470-2597
*Indiana: (888) 616-8319
 Iowa: (641) 751-2619
*Kansas: (866) 966-9815
*Kentucky: (443) 243-1118
*Maine: (207) 324-7482
*Maryland: (888) 825-9217
*Massachusetts-RI: (919) 661-1760
 Michigan: (989) 793-4211
*Minnesota: (763) 754-1661
*Missouri: (405) 470-2597
*Montana: (605) 722-7028
*Nebraska: (602) 942-8950
*Nevada (N): (800) 349-1858
*Nevada (S): (702) 523-1803
 New Hampshire: (603) 571-1822

*New Jersey: (888) 616-8319
 New Mexico: (719) 749-9797
*New York: (866) 825-9217
*North Carolina: (602) 942-8950
*North Dakota: (605) 722-7028
*Ohio: (937) 652-1157
*Oklahoma: (405) 470-2597
*Oregon: (602) 942-8950
*Pennsylvania: (866) 825-9217
*Rhode Island: (919) 661-1760
*South Carolina: (602) 942-8950
*South Dakota: (605) 722-7028
*Tennessee: (443) 243-1118
*Texas: (405) 470-2597
*Utah: (602) 321-6511
 Vermont: (603) 571-1822
*Virginia: (866) 825-9217
*Washington - E. OR: (602) 942-8950
*West Virginia: (866) 825-9217
*Wisconsin: (715) 838-9426
*Wyoming: (605) 722-7028

Canada
*Alberta: (780) 889-3776
 British Columbia: (250) 494-4275
*Manitoba & Saskatchewan: (306) 736-2441
*Ontario: (613) 612-8465

* Indicates these editions are available on-line at www.countryregister.com

Visit us online at www.countryregister.com

Quilters Haven
PO Box 11823
Fort Mohave, AZ 86427

Less Than Traditional by "Charlie"

A Fast and Fun, Quick and Easy Way
to get beautiful Circle Quilts!
Easy enough for a beginners first quilt project
while fast and fun for any skill level.
Each "Kit" contains the pattern, templates
and rulers needed for all of our projects.
Additional books and patterns available to
give you lots of different looks.

Sunflower Table Runner: Made using Large Kit and Flowers Book #3

Ryan's Puzzle:
Made using Large Kit & Book #2

www.quiltershaven.net

Kits available in 4 sizes:
Large starts with a 13" square of fabric
Medium starts with a 10" square of fabric
Small starts with an 8" square of fabric
Extra Small starts with a 4" square of fabric

Each Kit contains:
Step by step instructions with diagrams
2 pc template set (the key to our patterns)
Ruler and Cutting Arc appropriate to the size

(Large Kit Pictured)

Got Scraps:
Made using Small Kit
Our most popular pattern!

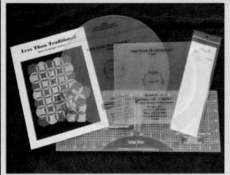

We also sell all the best notions
including our line of *easy to read*
square ups and rulers!
Laser etched on
fluorescent acrylic the lines will
never rub off!

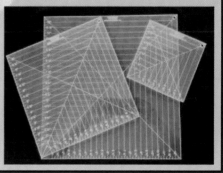

Quilting in the Mountains, Valley, Desert, or by the Sea, if Quilting with my Girlfriends it's the perfect place to be!

Quilting in the Desert...

Quilting by the Sea...

Quiltmobile

Gifts & Projects for Quilters!

- Fabric Art Panels
- T-Shirts
- Magnets
- Zipper Charms
- Patterns
- Greeting Cards

Lots of fun for Quilters, Quilt Retreats, Shop Hops and so much More!

Three 6" x 12" Art Panels, Three Zipper Charms and Instructions for Jody's Shoulder Tote

Finished Size Approximately 12.5" x 13.5" x 4"

Three Quilter's Wisdom 6" x 12" fabric Art Panels

Coordinating Zipper Pull Charms One inch in Diameter

JodyHoughtonDesigns.etsy.com

JodyHoughtonDesigns.etsy.com

Notes

Quilters' Travel Companion and Crafters' Guide

Quilting, Yarn, Needlepoint and Cross Stitch

15th Edition
2018-2020

Edited By:

Kyle Heath
Samuel Heath

Special Thanks:
Ruth & George Heath
Jamieson Ramsey

Cover Design By:

Jody Houghton

chalet Since 1992
Publishing

PO Box 370
Depoe Bay, OR 97341

Local: 719-685-5041

kyle@quilterstravelcompanion.com

www.crafterstc.com
www.quilterstc.com

You can find lots of valuable information on our website:

Your one stop for shops, shows and retreats.

www.quilterstc.com or www.crafterstc.com

1. Unfortunately, shops do move, change or go out of business.
   We are constantly *updating* this information on our website.
   In addition, we provide an *Up-to-Date Newsletter* to help you keep track of
   these changes; this is *free* when you provide us with your e-mail address!
   If you know about new shops or changes needed, please *contact us*;
   we strive to have the most up-to-date and accurate information possible.

2. The website also includes updates and new information on *quilt shows*.
   Please let us know about additions or corrections!

3. We also include a nice group of *quilt retreat facilities* so you
   and your friends can plan a great getaway.

Making Quarter Square Triangles

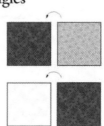

1. Lay out four 4½" squares.
    (2) 1646 – 40 Lace Green
    (1) 1646 – 07 Lace Cream
    (1) 1647 – 60 Bubble Violet

2. Flip right sides together.

3. Stack pairs with medium on top.

4. Layer cut on both diagonals.
    Do not open.

5. Pick up first quarter stack with stiletto.

6. Sew first pair.

7. Assembly-line sew second pair.

8. Continue to assembly sew remaining
    stacks. Clip apart every two.

Clip

9. Open and turn.

10. Flip right sides together and lock cen-
    ter seam.

11. Push top seam up and underneath
    seam down.

12. Assembly-line sew.

13. Unsew stitches in seam allowance.

14. Flip patch over and unsew stitches in
    seam allowance.

15. Lay flat wrong side up. Swirl seam
    clockwise.

16. Open center into Four-Patch and flat-
    ten.

17. Place quarter-square triangles on rotat-
    ing mat.

18. Place 3½" Fussy Cut Ruler on patch
    and trim on four sides.

Homestead Stars Quilt
Yardage for One Quilt

Fussy Cut Fabric	¼ yd each	
1641 – 84 Rosette Aqua		
1641 – 66 Rosette Purple		
1641 – 07 Rosette Cream		
1646 – 07 Lace Cream	⅓ yd	
1647 – 02 Bubble Pink	⅓ yd	
1646 – 40 Lace Green	⅓ yd	
1645 – 80 Buds Teal	⅓ yd	
1646 – 02 Lace Pink	⅓ yd	
1644 – 10 Winter Sweet Red	¼ yd	
1644 – 22 Rose	⅓ yd	
1645 – 22 Rose Bud Rose	⅓ yd	
1647 – 60 Bubble Violet	¼ yd	
1648 – 80 Border Teal/Beige	1⅓ yd	
Binding 1644 – 10	½ yd	
Backing	1½ yd	
Batting	44" x 52"	

Sewing Block Together

1. Lay out block.

2. Flip middle vertical row to left vertical row, right sides together.

3. Assembly-line sew.

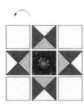

4. Open. Flip right vertical row to middle vertical row, right sides together. Assembly-line sew.

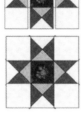

5. Turn. Sew remaining rows, locking seams and pressing seams away from quarter square triangles.

6. Press seams away from middle row.

Sewing Columns of Stars

1. Cut four 10" squares for Side Triangles in half on one diagonal.

2. Cut two 11" squares for Corner Triangles in fourths on both diagonals.

3. Place Triangles with Stars and sew together, matching square ends. Trim tips. Press seams away from Stars.

Making Square in a Square Cornerstones for Border

1. Fussy cut cream rosette fabric into four 3¼" squares.

2. Cut eight 3½" squares of 1645 dark red in half on one diagonal.

3. Place Fussy Cuts with two stacks of triangles.

4. Flip and center Triangles right sides together to Rosette.

5. Assembly-line sew.

6. Press open. Trim tips.

7. Place remaining triangles.

8. Flip, center, and assembly-line sew triangles.

9. Press open.

10. Square up with 4½" Fussy Cut Ruler.

Sewing Top Together

1. Pin and sew 4½" Center Border strip between Stars. Press seams toward Border. Trim straight.

2. Measure width. Cut Top and Bottom strips to size.

3. Pin and sew Outside Border strips to Stars. Press seams toward Borders.

4. Sew Square in a Square Cornerstones to ends of Top and Bottom strips. Press seams toward Borders.

5. Pin and sew Borders. Press seams toward Borders.

6. Layer, quilt, and bind.

1955 Diamond St. San Marcos, CA, 92078   www.quiltinaday.com

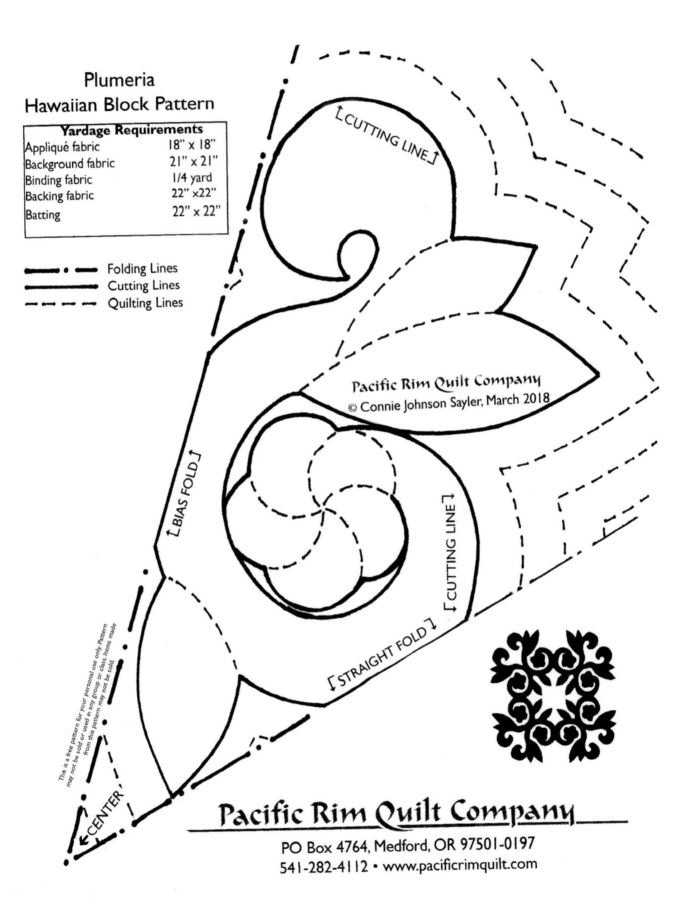

Plumeria
Hawaiian Block Pattern

Yardage Requirements	
Appliqué fabric	18" x 18"
Background fabric	21" x 21"
Binding fabric	1/4 yard
Backing fabric	22" x 22"
Batting	22" x 22"

— - — - — Folding Lines
————— Cutting Lines
– – – – – Quilting Lines

⌐ CUTTING LINE ⌐

Pacific Rim Quilt Company
© Connie Johnson Sayler, March 2018

⌐ BIAS FOLD ⌐

⌐ CUTTING LINE ⌐

⌐ STRAIGHT FOLD ⌐

← CENTER

Pacific Rim Quilt Company

PO Box 4764, Medford, OR 97501-0197
541-282-4112 • www.pacificrimquilt.com

Plumeria Hawaiian Quilt Block Pattern
Instructions

Instructions copyrighted by Pacific Rim Quilt Company 1/2018.
Do not make copies without prior written permission of copyright owner.
www.pacificrimquilt.com

1. **SELECT FABRIC & THREAD.** Most people are happier with two fabrics that have strong contrast, and that read as solids, or near solids. Batiks and hand dyed fabrics are particularly good choices. Buy the best fabric you can afford. It takes time to make a Hawaiian quilt, and you want the quilt to last a long time. Select thread to match the appliqué fabric.

2. **WASH** the fabric to preshrink, and remove excess dye.

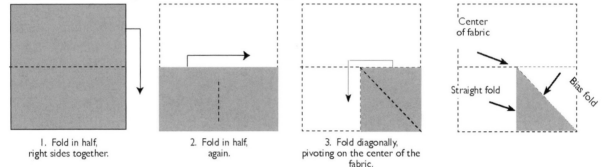

1. Fold in half, right sides together.

2. Fold in half, again.

3. Fold diagonally, pivoting on the center of the fabric.

3. **FOLD and PRESS** both the appliqué and background fabrics into eighths, right sides together, pivoting around the center of the fabric, as illustrated below.

    Fold and press both the appliqué fabric and the background fabric identically, but separately. Press in TEMPORARY fold guidelines using a warm (not hot), dry iron. When pressing on the bias fold (created with the 3rd fold), be sure to lift the iron and firmly place on the fold, rather than sliding the iron along the fold. Leave fabrics folded until instructed to open them in later steps.

    The folds in the background fabric will be used in Steps 9-11 as registration marks to help position the appliqué fabric.

4. **TRACE THE APPLIQUÉ PATTERN** onto another piece of paper to preserve the master pattern. Trace only the solid cutting lines. Transfer key words "center," "straight fold," and "bias fold" onto the traced paper pattern. Cut out the traced paper pattern.

5. **PLACE THE PATTERN ON FOLDED APPLIQUÉ FABRIC.**
    It is very important to align the center, straight edge, and bias edge of the pattern with the center, straight fold and bias edge of the fabric. If you do not, the pattern very likely will not fit on your fabric.

    Once the pattern is in place, pin the pattern to the fabric. You only need enough pins to hold the pattern in place while you draw around it. Pinning through just one or two layers of fabric is fine at this point.

6. **DRAW THE PATTERN ONTO THE APPLIQUÉ FABRIC.** Draw around the edge of the traced paper patterns. Do not add seam allowances. A 3/16" seam allowance has already been added to the original pattern. Since you are tracing the cutting line, you can use a pencil, permanent fabric marker, or other marking tool that will show on the appliqué fabric. Do not use a ball point pen.

7. **UNPIN and REMOVE** the paper pattern. **RE-PIN** through all eight layers of fabric to hold it securely in place. Now, use lots of pins, and place pins only on the 'inside' of the design. This will help you know what to cut and what not to cut in the next step.

8. **CUT FABRIC.** Using sharp scissors, cut along lines, through all eight layers of fabric. Leave the pins in until instructed to remove them later.

9. **UNFOLD THE BACKGROUND FABRIC** and lay it right side facing up on a table. Find the section in the background fabric that has three "down" folds together (on the straight, the bias, and the straight). This is the section where you will begin to lay out the appliqué fabric (Section A). Place that section close to you and lightly tape the background fabric to the table to avoid shifting.

10. **PLACE THE APPLIQUÉ** in Section A, pins facing up. Remove the pins, but leave the appliqué folded for now. Carefully align the center, straight folds, and bias folds of the appliqué fabric with the folds of the background fabric. Notice that the bias fold has more bulk than the straight folds, so position the bias fold of the appliqué slightly inside the bias fold of the background fabric. When the appliqué fabric is unfolded this bias fold will fall into the fold on the background fabric.

    The appliqué fabric needs to be in its most natural, relaxed position (no ripples in the edges, nothing stretched out of shape, no overlapping pieces). The appliqué was cut out of a single, flat piece of fabric, so it must lay flat again. Before you proceed make sure the bottom layer is in its relaxed position, gently rub your fingers along any parts of the appliqué which need to be coaxed into position.

11. **PIN THE BOTTOM LAYER** after the appliqué is in its proper position. Pin the bottom layer *only*. Only the bottom layer remains in this position, the other seven layers will open up and be placed elsewhere on the background fabric. Add pins where you can easily get them in the appliqué fabric. You will get to add more pins once the appliqué is entirely opened up.

12. **UNFOLD THE APPLIQUÉ.** Once the bottom layer is pinned, unfold the top FOUR layers of fabric. These will open along the bias fold. Position the appliqué in this section, and pin the bottom layer. Then unfold the top TWO layers of fabric. Position this quarter of the design in place, and pin the bottom layer. Unfold the top single layer, position this half of the design aligning with the folds of the background fabric, and pin.

    Once the entire appliqué is fully opened and in position, add enough pins so the fabric will not shift while you thread baste it in place.

13. **BASTE.** Using a thread which contrasts in color to the appliqué fabric, thread-baste around the entire appliqué fabric. Keep basting stitches at least 1/2" inside the cut edge so the basting stitches will not interfere with the appliqué process. Remove the pins as you baste.

14. **IRON.** Using a hot iron (with steam if necessary), iron out all the temporary fold lines.

15. **APPLIQUÉ** as desired. We recommend the needleturn method, using approximately a 3/16" turn-under seam allowance.

16. **JOIN THE BLOCKS** together (if you have more than one block) with or without sashing, as you prefer.

17. **SANDWICH THE LAYERS.** The backing fabric and batting should be a few inches larger than the quilt top. Use masking tape to secure the backing fabric (right side down) on a surface suitable for basting. Position the batting on top of the backing fabric and lightly tape it down. Center the quilt top, right side up, on the batting and lightly tape it down.

18. **BASTE THE LAYERS TOGETHER.** Using an ugly colored thread will encourage you to keep quilting just so you can pull out the ugly basting thread as you quilt. To keep the edges of your quilt from fraying as you quilt, turn the edges of the backing fabric over the batting and quilt top to enclose the edges, secure using a long whip stitch.

19. **CHOOSE QUILTING THREAD.** Old Hawaiian quilts were quilted with white thread because that was what was available. We now have colored quilting thread available, so choose the thread color(s) you prefer to enhance your quilt.

20. **QUILT.** Begin quilting in the center and work your way out to the edge of the quilt. Quilt "in the ditch" around the appliqué as you quilt from the center out.

    Suggested quilt lines are shown as dashed lines on the pattern page. These are only suggestions, you may vary the quilting as you like. Echo quilting lines on a quilt this size are spaced approximately 1/2" apart.

21. **BIND**, add a **LABEL**, and a **SLEEVE** or make into a lovely pillow. Then enjoy your Hawaiian Quilt with pride for many, many years.

United we Stand
Finished size 54" x 63"

Fabric Requirements:
- If using upcycled jeans as the denim – you will need 8 – 10 pairs, depending on the size and condition of the jeans.
- If using denim yardage: you will need ½ yard of 4 different shades of blue denim and ½ yd. of a very dark blue for the stars.
- ¼ yd. of Cream tonal flannel
- ⅓ yd. of 3 different shades of red flannel
- Twin size batting or 60" x 70" piece
- 3 ½ yds. Binding/Backing fabric
- Creative Grids 4-in1 Half square triangle ruler

Cutting Instructions:

Cream Flannel
- cut 2 - 3 ½" x WOF strips
  - Sub-cut 4 – 3 ½" squares

Red Flannels
- Color 1 Red – cut 3 – 3 ½" x WOF strips
  - Sub-cut into these lengths, 2 –18 ½", 1 - 12 ½", 1 – 30 ½", and 1 – 15 ½"
- Color 2 Red – cut 2 - 3 ½" x WOF strip
  - Sub-cut into 2 – 15 ½", and 1 – 18 ½", 1 - 12 ½" lengths
- Color 3 Red – cut 2 3 ½" x WOF strips
  - Sub-cut into 2 – 18 ½", and 2 – 21 ½" lengths

Denim

If using jeans cut the usable parts into 3 ½" strips – get as much as you can out of each pair minus seams, pockets, waistband etc.

If using denim yardage, cut into 3 ½" strips x WOF
- From the darkest Denim cut 16 – 3 ½" squares for stars

Sewing Instructions: All seams are pressed open due to bulk unless otherwise stated.
- Place 1 – 3 ½" strip of the darkest denim and 1 – cream tonal flannel, right sides together. Using method 2 on your 4-in1 Half square triangle ruler cut 16 sets of triangles

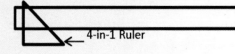

4-in-1 Ruler

- Sew these sets together to make 16 half square triangles. Press to the flannel side. Clip dog ears (points) Half square triangles measure 3 ½"
- Lay out your stars so that you are sure they
- are in 3 rows with the points in the correct position .
- Make 4 sets of each row of stars. These units measure 3 ½" x 9 ½".

Star top

Star Middle

Star Bottom

As I laid out the rows, I had to consider what I had in the way of different colors of denim since I used upcycled jeans for my background. All denim is cut into 3 ½" strips and I just cut the lengths as I went, using what I had and digging for more if I needed another color. Before cutting the denim to size, make sure you look at what will be next to each other by way of the color pieces you have. I just went row by row and cut the first piece from one strip of denim and then looked for a different color and cut the next size piece from that etc.

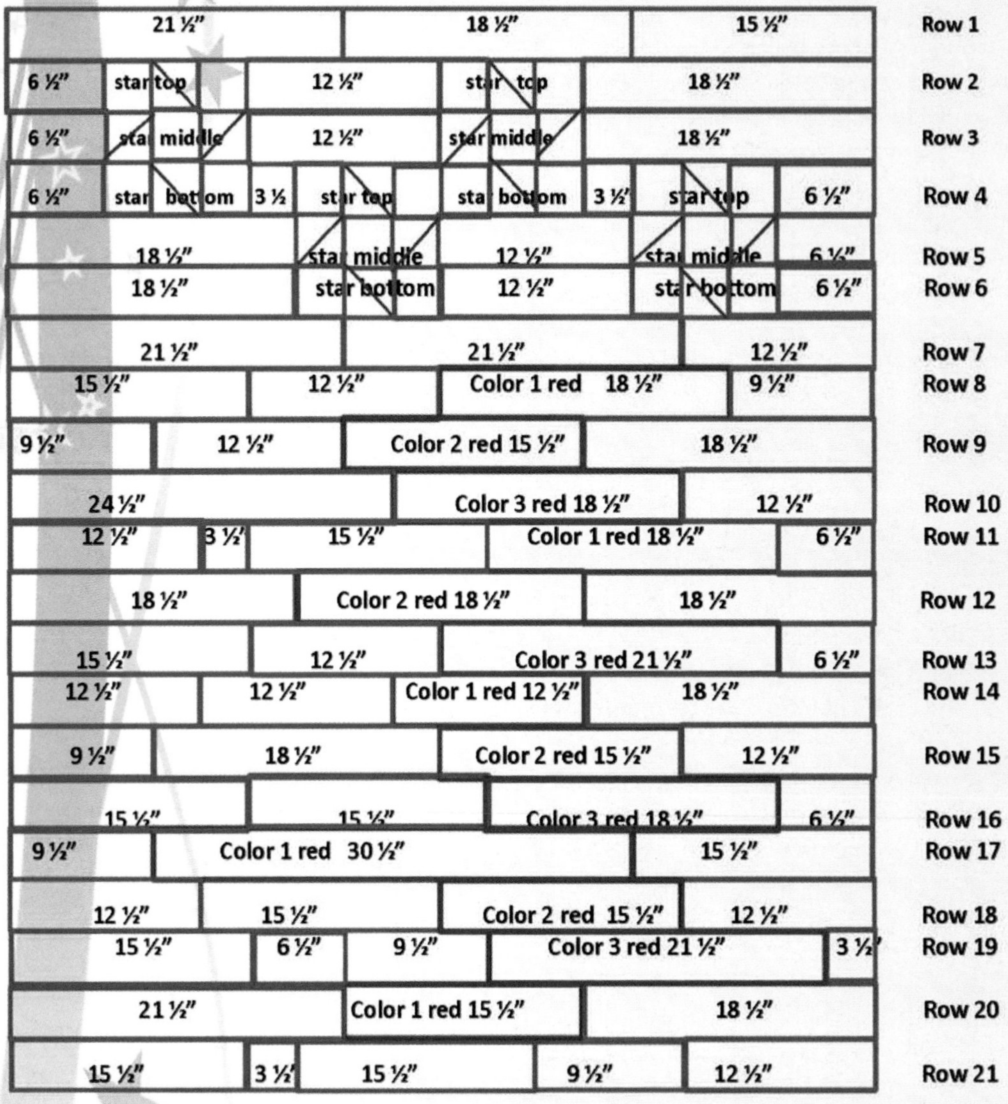

Row	Pieces (left to right)
Row 1	21 ½" 18 ½" 15 ½"
Row 2	6 ½" star top 12 ½" star top 18 ½"
Row 3	6 ½" star middle 12 ½" star middle 18 ½"
Row 4	6 ½" star bottom 3 ½ star top star bottom 3 ½" star top 6 ½"
Row 5	18 ½" star middle 12 ½" star middle 6 ½"
Row 6	18 ½" star bottom 12 ½" star bottom 6 ½"
Row 7	21 ½" 21 ½" 12 ½"
Row 8	15 ½" 12 ½" Color 1 red 18 ½" 9 ½"
Row 9	9 ½" 12 ½" Color 2 red 15 ½" 18 ½"
Row 10	24 ½" Color 3 red 18 ½" 12 ½"
Row 11	12 ½" 3 ½ 15 ½" Color 1 red 18 ½" 6 ½"
Row 12	18 ½" Color 2 red 18 ½" 18 ½"
Row 13	15 ½" 12 ½" Color 3 red 21 ½" 6 ½"
Row 14	12 ½" 12 ½" Color 1 red 12 ½" 18 ½"
Row 15	9 ½" 18 ½" Color 2 red 15 ½" 12 ½"
Row 16	15 ½" 15 ½" Color 3 red 18 ½" 6 ½"
Row 17	9 ½" Color 1 red 30 ½" 15 ½"
Row 18	12 ½" 15 ½" Color 2 red 15 ½" 12 ½"
Row 19	15 ½" 6 ½" 9 ½" Color 3 red 21 ½" 3 ½"
Row 20	21 ½" Color 1 red 15 ½" 18 ½"
Row 21	15 ½" 3 ½ 15 ½" 9 ½" 12 ½"

Designed by Sue Hanson©
Trackside Quilting
109 E Main, Laurel, MT 59044
www.tracksidequilting.com
406-628-7051

United States Shows

There is 1 show in Canada in Decoste Centre, Picton, Nova Scotia

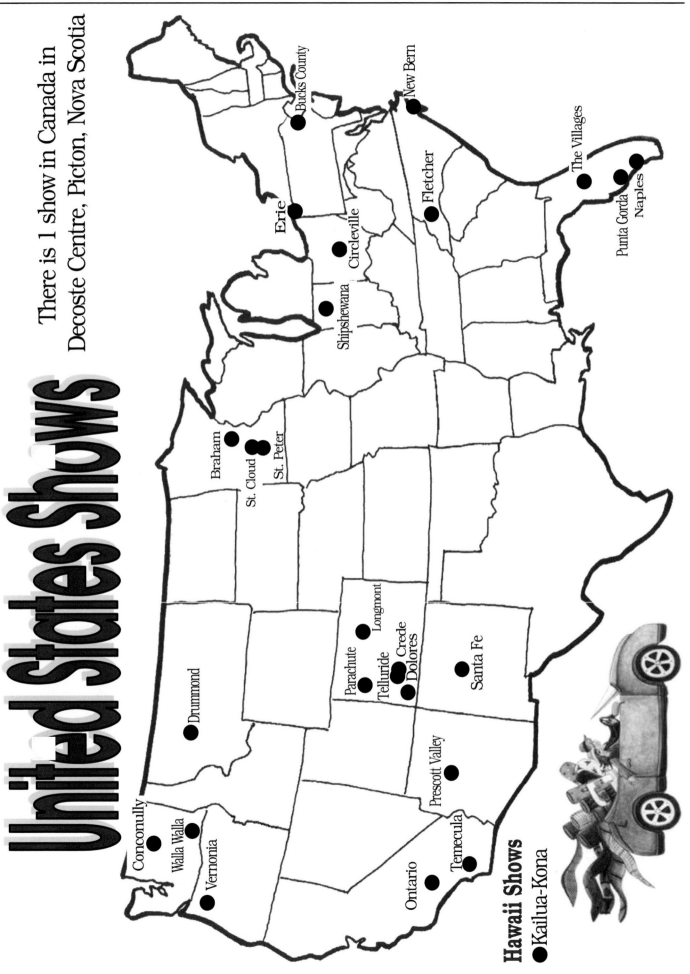

Bucks County

New Bern

Fletcher

The Villages

Punta Gorda

Naples

Erie

Circleville

Shipshewana

Braham

St. Cloud

St. Peter

Longmont

Parachute

Telluride

Crede

Dolores

Santa Fe

Drummond

Prescott Valley

Conconully

Walla Walla

Vernonia

Ontario

Temecula

Hawaii Shows
● Kailua-Kona

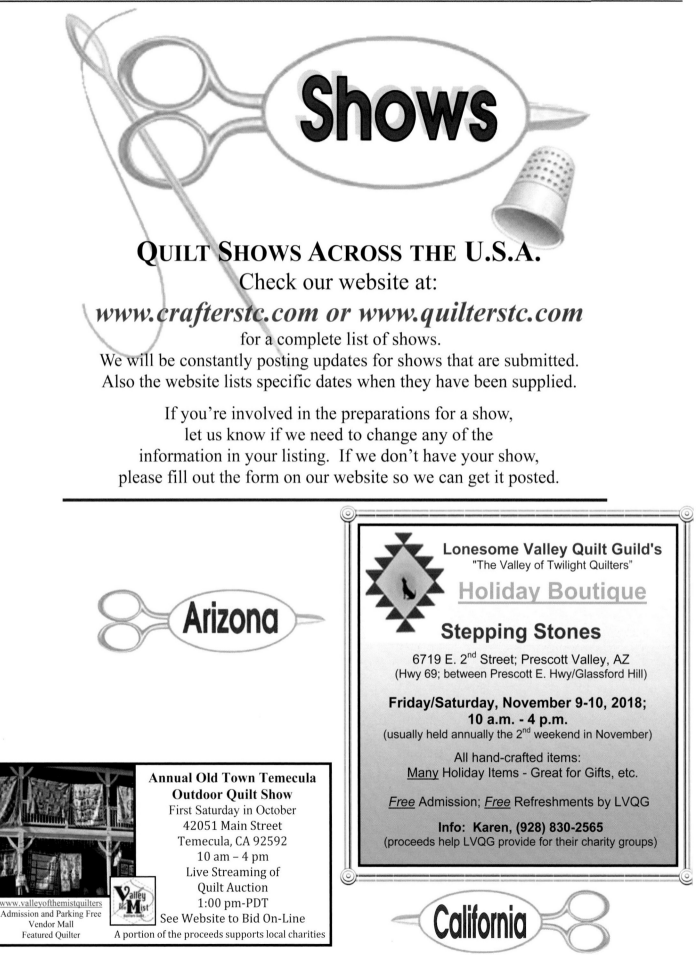

QUILT SHOWS ACROSS THE U.S.A.

Check our website at:

www.crafterstc.com or www.quilterstc.com

for a complete list of shows.
We will be constantly posting updates for shows that are submitted.
Also the website lists specific dates when they have been supplied.

If you're involved in the preparations for a show,
let us know if we need to change any of the
information in your listing. If we don't have your show,
please fill out the form on our website so we can get it posted.

Arizona

Lonesome Valley Quilt Guild's
"The Valley of Twilight Quilters"

Holiday Boutique

Stepping Stones

6719 E. 2nd Street; Prescott Valley, AZ
(Hwy 69; between Prescott E. Hwy/Glassford Hill)

**Friday/Saturday, November 9-10, 2018;
10 a.m. - 4 p.m.**
(usually held annually the 2nd weekend in November)

All hand-crafted items:
Many Holiday Items - Great for Gifts, etc.

Free Admission; *Free* Refreshments by LVQG

Info: Karen, (928) 830-2565
(proceeds help LVQG provide for their charity groups)

**Annual Old Town Temecula
Outdoor Quilt Show**
First Saturday in October
42051 Main Street
Temecula, CA 92592
10 am – 4 pm
Live Streaming of
Quilt Auction
1:00 pm-PDT
See Website to Bid On-Line

www.valleyofthemistquilters
Admission and Parking Free
Vendor Mall
Featured Quilter
A portion of the proceeds supports local charities

California

Canada

Colorado

catch the bug!

Quilt Show

Colorado

Florida

Quilt Show

Florida

Hawaii

Indiana

Minnesota

4th Biannual
Ewenique Quilt Show

October 12 & 13, 2019
Saturday 9am to 5pm, Sun 12n to 4pm

Sunrise Assembly of God Church Hall
722 Sunrise Drive, St. Peter, MN 56082

150+ Quilted items on display plus Guest Speakers,
Venders, Demonstrations and Door Prizes.
Boutique items for sale.
Plus much more!

Minnesota Quilters, Inc.
Quilt Show & Conference

June 14 to 16, **2018** in St Cloud, MN
June 13 to 15, **2019** in Rochester, MN
June 11 to 13, **2020** in St Cloud, MN
June 10 to 12, **2021** in Rochester, MN

Come enjoy quilting heaven! Hundreds of judged and non-judged Quilts
on display, Vendors, Workshops, Lectures, Special Exhibits and more.
MQ is a membership organization of quilters. We have monthly
meetings with speakers, workshops, monthly newsletter and discounts
on the Show and events.
See www.mnquilt.org for information.

www.brahampieday.com

Braham City Hall
201 South Broadway Ave.
Braham, MN 55006
August 3, 2018 ~ 10am-6pm
Annual Event - Always the first Friday of August
Pie Day Office: 320-396-4956
Sponsored by:
Hands All Around Quilt Guild

SHOW OF SMALL QUILTS (PERIMETER 180 INCH or LESS)

Missouri

Lee's Summit Quilters' Guild
Annual Quilt Show

October 19 & 20, 2018
(Always third weekend of October)
9:00 am – 4:00 pm Daily

Woods Chapel Church
4725 NE Lakewood Way
Lee's Summit, MO 64064

$3 Admission
www.LSQG.blogspot.com

Triple Creek Quilt Guild Quilt Show

Drummond High School – Old Gym
108 West Edwards St.
Drummond, MT

October 6-7, 2018
October 5-6, 2019
Annual: Always the first full weekend in October
Saturday 10:00-5:00, Sunday 10:00-4:00
Entry $2 – Raffle items $2 per ticket or $5 for three

Sponsored by the Triple Creek Quilt Guild
www.triplecreekquiltguild@gmail.com
PO Box 6, Drummond, MT 59832

Montana

Quilt Fiesta Santa Fe
October 19-20, 2018

$7 Admission
10am-5pm

Santa Fe Convention Center

200+ Quilts on display | Vendors
Gift Shop | Quilts for Sale

QuiltFiestaSantaFe.org

Presented by the Northern New Mexico Quilt Guild

New Mexico

Fabricologist:
/fa-bric-'ă-lə-jist/
n:/one who has perfected the art
of stashing fabric.

North Carolina

Twin Rivers Quilters Guild Presents 2018 Bee by the River
"Seasons for Quilts"
Biannual Quilt Show

Friday October 26, 2018 9:00 - 5:00
Saturday October 27, 2018 9:00 - 4:30
(Next Show October 2020)

New Bern Convention Center
203 S. Front St, New Bern, NC 28560

www.twinriversquiltersguild.com

AQG

Show is held annually on last weekend in September

ASHEVILLE QUILT GUILD

Date: September 28-30, 2018
Location: 765 Boylston Hwy, Fletcher, NC
WNC Ag Center, Davis Building

www.ashevillequiltguild.org

Over 300 Quilts, Demonstrations, Vendors,
Gift Shop, Raffle Quilt, Quilts for Sale,
Group Discounts.

Ohio

THE GOODTIME QUILTERS GUILD
Circleville, OH

NEW DATE
August 2 - 4, 2018
2019 to be Announced
Admission: $6.00
$10.00 for multiple days.

FEATURING
150 Plus Quilts,
Demonstrations,
Venders & More.

LOCATION
Ohio Christian University
1476 Lancaster Pike
Circleville, OH

For more info: www.goodtimequilters.org

St. Mary's 48th Annual Quilt & Crafts Fair

SEPT 20, 21, 22, 2018
THURSDAY–SATURDAY 10 AM – 4 PM

(3 DAYS ONLY)
Starts on the 3rd Thursday of September every year

MANY BEAUTIFUL QUILTS & CRAFTS FOR SALE

Lunch Served Daily at 11:00 a.m.

"Star of Bethlehem" Raffle Quilt Tickets: $1.00 each or 6 for $5.00

St. Mary's Catholic Church
960 Missouri Avenue
Vernonia, OR 97064

503-429-8841

maryscatholicchurch@frontier.com

2019 DATES:
Sept. 19, 20, 21

Oregon

Pennsylvania

Eureka Toilet Pins

Quilts were made by hand,
with a needle and thread
until using a sewing machines became
popular in the mid 1800's.

Washington

Originally, the Chinese and Egyptians were the first to sew three layers of fabrics together to form the quilt..

Annual Quilt Show
September 14 - 16, 2018
Walla Walla, WA

Fri-Sat 10-5 & Sun 10-3
Admission: $6.00 (good all 3 days)

Beautiful Quilts - Hourly Demonstrations
Vendors Mall - Silent Auction
2018 Quilt Challenge: Booville
Cash Prizes: 1st, 2nd & 3rd

Featured Quilter:
Teresa Silva

Walla Walla Fairgrounds
360 Orchard Street, Walla Walla, Washington

www.wallawallaquiltfestival.org

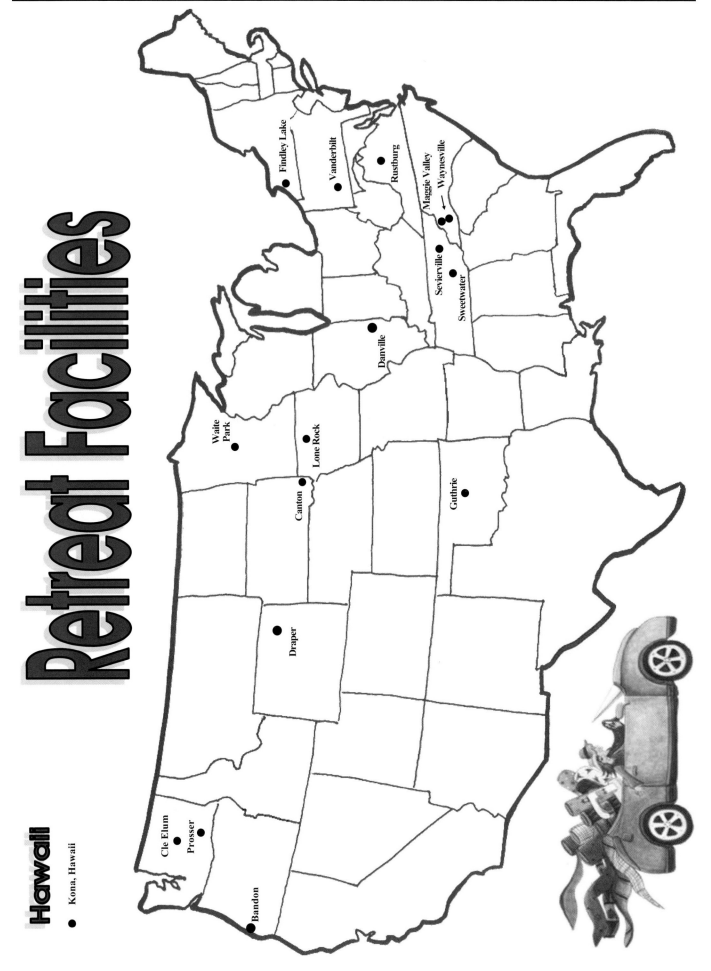

Retreat Facilities

Hawaii
- Kona, Hawaii

Findley Lake

Vanderbilt

Rustburg

Maggie Valley ← Waynesville

Sevierville

Sweetwater

Danville

Waite Park

Lone Rock

Canton

Guthrie

Draper

Cle Elum

Prosser

Bandon

Retreats
QUILT RETREATS
ACROSS THE U.S AND CANADA

Hawaii

Iowa

Threads and Beds
Retreat Center

www.threadsandbedsretreat.com

207 S. Buchanan St.
Danville, IL 61832
1-217-431-9202
reservations@threadsoftimefab.com

Welcome to Threads and Beds Retreat Center! Our unique facility allows you to relax, explore your creativity, and have a fantastic time sewing with friends and fellow crafters. Our goal is to provide you with the most spacious and gracious accommodations you can find -- a facility specifically designed for artistic endeavors of sewing, quilting, and textile arts.

We look forward to hosting you and providing for your artistic needs, both in our retreat center and in the fabulous attached quilt shop, Threads of Time, with more than 4,000 bolts of fabric, hundreds of the newest notions, books, patterns, and fabulous displays.

- 10,000 sq. ft. of retreat area
- Three large sewing areas with sewing tables and chairs
- Sewing space for 42 sewists at a time
- Maximum of 36 overnight sewers
- Horn cutting tables, irons, and ironing-boards
- 7 Large Design Walls (8' x 6')
- Totally handicapped accessible, one-level facility with no stairs
- 7 individual restrooms, 4 shower rooms
- 3 Large kitchens & dining rooms
- Refrigerators, microwaves, toaster ovens & coffee pots
- Wireless Internet in dining areas
- Connected to Threads of Time, the region's premier quilt shop
- Online Registration

"For the times of your life and the fabric of the times..."

Minnesota

North Carolina

New York

Notes

Oklahoma

Oregon

Pennsylvania

Virginia

Washington

Retreat Facilities

Next time you're planning a retreat consider one of these facilities.
Bold listings in this index are for ads in this retreat section.

USA Retreat Facilities

AK	Skagway	The White House	8 & Main St.	(907) 983-9000	
AL	Crane Hill	Red Rooster Retreats	2140 Couty Rd. 870	(256) 747-4295	
AR	Eureka Springs	The Retreat at Sky Ridge	637 County Rd. 111	(479) 253-9465	
AZ	Lakeside	Pinetop Star	103 W. Yeager Ln.	(928) 367-1709	
CA	Big Bear Lake	Inspiration at Big Bear Lake	425 Conklin Rd.	(909) 866-8081	
CA	Buellton	The Creation Station	252 E Hwy. 246 Unit A	805-693-0174	
CA	San Marcos	Lake Arrowhead Retreats	425 Landmark Ct.	(760) 208-5514	
CO	Black Hawk	Quinberry Lodge	26 Paradise Valley Pkwy.	(303) 819-9720	
CO	Black Hawk	Pineberry Lodge	220 Timber Rd.	(303) 819-9720	
CO	Buena Vista	Liars' Lodge B&B	30000 CR 371	(719) 395-3444	
CO	Colorado Springs	The Hideaway	3805 Walker Rd.	(719) 481-2083	
CO	Estes Park	A Picture Perfect Place	540 Laurel Ln. #1D	(970) 284-6603	
CO	Golden	The Silk Pincushion	1523 Ford St.	(303) 278-8813	
CO	Granby	Snow Mountain Ranch	1101 Country Rd. 53	(970) 887-2152	
FL	Rockledge	The Quilt Place	575 Barton Blvd.	(321) 632-3344	
GA	Trenton	Home Harvest Retreat	1047 Grant Rd.	(706) 657-4296	
HI	**Kona**	**Quilting on the Beach**	**Courtyard King Kemehameha's Kona Beach Hotel**		
				(808) 329-7475	**Pg. 33**
IA	Jesup	Merry's Stitchins	1923 Baker Rd.	(319) 827-6703	
IA	**Lone Rock**	**The Quilted Steeple**	**2605 90th Ave.**	**(515) 570-9625**	**Pg.33**
IA	Mt. Pleasant	Quilter's Paradise	120 N. Main St.	(319) 385-1749	
IA	Oelwein	Lou Ann's Quilt Garden	21 E. Charles St.	(319) 283-5165	
ID	Kamiah	Quilt House Bed & Breakfast	247 Flying Elk Dr.	(208) 935-7668	
IL	Big Rock	Esther's Place	201 W. Galena St.	(630) 556-9665	
IL	**Danville**	**Threads of Time**	**207 S. Buchanan**	**(217) 431-9202**	**Pg. 34**
IL	Oblong	The Village Stitchery	108 E. Main St.	(618) 592-4134	
IL	Orangeville	Memory Lane Crafting Retreat	10006 N. Rote Rd.	(815) 868-2363	
IL	Princeton	Quilter's Garden	527 S. Main St.	(815) 879-3739	
IN	Batesville	Hickory Road Inn	20116 Hickory Rd.	(812) 933-0335	
IN	Twelve Mile	Kathy's Kaptured Moments	8050 E. State Rd. 16	(574) 664-5833	
KS	Hoxie	Cressler Creek Log Cabin	1302 N. Road 80 E.	(785) 675-1295	
KS	Manhattan	All About Quilts	8651 E. US Hwy. 24	(785)539-6759	
KS	Sylvia	Prairie Oaks Inn	35810 W. Greenfiield Rd.	(620) 486-2962	
KS	Valley Falls	The Barn Bed & Breakfast Inn	14910 Bluemound Rd.	(785) 945-3225	
MD	Wenona	Pieceful Cottage B & B	23120 Manokin Ct.	(410) 784-2150	
ME	Rangeley	Threads Galore Quilt Shop	27 Pleasant St.	(207) 864-5752	
MI	Chesaning	Creative Passions	203 Pearl St.	(989) 845-2159	
MI	Frankenmuth	The Front Porch Quilt Shop	305 S. Franklin St.	(989) 652-8050	
MI	Hillman	Thunder Bay Reso	27800 M-32	(989) 742-4732	
MI	Pinconning	Bittersweet Vintage Retreat	216 E. Fifth St.	(989) 879-1900	
MN	Anoka	Millie P's Quilt Shop	219 E Main St	(763) 421-0367	
MN	Cushing	Campfire Bay Resort	31504 Azure Rd.	(800) 677-7263	
MN	Hampton	Kelwood Retreat House	23560 Lillehei Ave.	(651) 437-4414	
MN	Meadowlands	Lady Slipper Retreat House	10853 Hwy. 133	(218) 721-4307	
MN	New Prague	The Getaway at Cedar Lake	72 Cedar Lake Court	(651) 755-4048	
MN	Princeton	Norwegian Wood Retreat	30440 US. Hwy. 169	(651) 335-3449	
MN	Spring Valley	Glad Gatherings Retreat	310 N. Broadway St.	(507) 346-2023	
MN	Staples	The Landmark Inn	631 3rd Ave. NE	(218) 894-4444	
MN	**Waite Park**	**Gruber's Quilt Shop**	**310 4th Ave. NE**	**(320) 259-4360**	**Pg. 35**
MO	Brunswick	Sew Sweet Quilt Shop	207 E. Broadway St.	(660) 548-3056	
MO	Kingsville	Liberty Homestead	115 SW 1991 Rd.	(816) 597-9402	
MO	St. Charles	Lococo House	1309 N. 5th St.	(636) 946-0619	
MT	Bozeman	Quilting in the Country	5100 S. 19th Rd.	(406) 587-8213	
MT	Deer Lodge	Mountain View Retreat	1525 Valley View Lane	(406) 846-1521	
MT	Gallatin Gateway	Nine Quarter Circle Ranch	5000 Taylor Fork Rd.	(409) 995-4276	
NC	**Maggie Valley**	**Summit Sew & Quilt Retreat**	**388 Summit**	**(704) 682-9567**	**Pg. 35**
NC	**Waynesville**	**Ponderosa Quilt Retreat**	**184 Park Dr.**	**(704) 682-9567**	**Pg. 35**
NE	Brock	Quilt Retreat	73402 628th Ave.	(402) 264-3345	
NE	Cedar Rapids	Plum Center Retreats	3404 240th St.	(402) 942-2624	
NE	Gretna	The Quilted Moose	109 Enterprise Dr.	(402) 332-4178	
NE	Newman Grove	Crystal Key Inn	314 S. 4th St.	(877) 335-2772	
NE	North Platte	Knoll's Country Inn B & B	6232 S. Range Rd.	(308) 368-5634	
NE	Red Cloud	Red Cloud B & B	909 N. Seward St.	(402) 746-3989	
NH	East Madison	Purity Spring Resort	1251 Eaton Rd. Rt. 153	(603) 367-8896	

State	City	Name	Address	Phone	Page
NY	Hamilton	Bridle Creek Bed & Breakfast	5519 Hill Rd.	(315) 824-1962	
NY	Inlet	Black Bear Lodges	114 Rt. 28	(352) 628-4240	
NY	Lockport	Brickhouse Quilting	8206 Tonawanda Creek Rd.	(716) 542-5146	
NY	Palmyra	Milkhouse Wool Shop	993 Cornwall RD.	(315) 597-6742	
NY	Penn Yan	Weaver View Farms	386 State Rt. 14	(315) -781-2571	
NY	**Sherman**	**Fabric Outlet Barn& Needle in a Haystack Retreat**			
			3141 N. Rd.	**(814) 882-0411**	**Pg. 36**
OH	Archbold	Sauder's Village Retreat	22611 State Rt. 2	(800) 590-9755	
OH	Whipple	The Quilted Work	320 Stanleyville Narrows Rd.	(740) 373-0579	
OK	Barnsdall	Red Barn Quilting	99 CR 2285	(918) 847-2544	
OK	Cookson	Chicken Creek Hen House	20188 W. Chicken Creek Rd.	(918) 457-3307	
OK	Fletcher	Looney Cloon's Quilt'n Farm	300 West Rd.	(580) 549-6604	
OK	Guthrie	Treasured Antiques	103 W. Oklahoma Ave.	(405) 282-8101	
OK	**Guthrie**	**Seven10 LLC**	**710 E. Warner Ave.**	**(833) 738-3610**	**Pg. 37**
OK	Miami	Hidden Lane Retreat Center	11153 South 652 Rd.	(918) 212-6022	
OK	Tahlequah	Camp Egan Retreat Center	28633 Hwy. 62	(918) 456-6489	
OR	**Bandon**	**Forget-Me-Knots**	**640 2nd St. SE Hwy. 101**	**(800) 347-9021**	**Pg. 37**
OR	Boring	Fagan's Haven Bed & Breakfast	14024 SE Hollyview Terrace	(503) 658-2010	
OR	Gleneden Beach	Beachcombers Haven	7045 NW Glen	(800) 428-5533	
PA	Bird-in-Hand	Amish View Inn	3125 Old Philadelphia Pike	(866) 735-1600	
PA	Coudersport	Miller's Mountain Retreat	222 Buffalo Rd.	(814) 331-3866	
PA	Gettysburg	The Lodges at Gettysburg	685 Camp Gettysburg Rd.	(717) 642-2500	
PA	Johnstown	Schrader's Fabrics by Barb	2078 Bedford St.	(814) 266-3113	
PA	**Vanderbilt**	**Seams Like Home Quilt**	**2010 Emerald Valley Rd.**	**(724) 984-1399**	**Pg. 37**
SD	**Canton**	**Canton Quilt Retreat**	**200 E. 3rd St.**	**(605) 987-9059**	**Pg. 38**
SD	Howard	Olsen House Inn	203 E. Farmer Ave.	(605) 772-5632	
TN	Franklin	Butterfly Meadows Inn & Farm	6775 Bethesda Arno Rd.	(877) 671-4594	
TN	Morrison	The Cottage	879 Tom Grissom Rd.	(931) 668-2100	
TN	**Sevierville**	**The Lodge at Douglas Lake**	**1280 Flat Creek Rd.**	**(615) 268-7781**	**Pg. 38**
TN	**Sweetwater**	**Whistlestop Quilt Retreat**	**134 Head of Creek Rd.**	**(423) 271-6380**	**Pg. 38**
TX	Camp Wood	Suzie Q Quilts	508 S. Nueces St.	(830) 597-6310	
TX	Cedar Hill	The 1890 House - A Quilters Retreat	455 E. F.M. 1382 Ste. 3-189	(972) 291-0472	
TX	Fredericksburg	Emilie's Quilt Haus	455 Seven Falls Dr.	(512) 789-3320	
TX	Gainesville	LE Retreat House	412 E. Pecan	(940) 668-2607	
TX	Granbury	Houston St. Mercantile	126 N. Houston St.	(817) 279-0425	
TX	Joshua	Batiks Galore	7301 County Rd. 912	(817) 556-2200	
TX	Mineola	Stitchin' Heaven	1118 N. Pacific St.	(800) 841-3901	
TX	Wolfforth	Red Barn Ranch	18311 County Rd. 1640	(806) 863-2276	
UT	**Draper**	**The Quilter's Lodge**	**12214 S. 900 E.**	**(801) 576-0390**	**Pg. 38**
VA	**Rustburg**	**Back Porch Retreats by Threads Run Thru It**			
			40 Exchange Dr.	**(434) 821-3000**	**Pg. 39**
VT	Vergennes	Strong House Inn	94 W. Main St.	(802) 877-3337	
WA	Camano Island	Over the Rainbow Retreat Lodge	668 Hawthorne Ln.	(425) 418-2862	
WA	**Cle Elum**	**Ruby's Store**	**116 E. 1st St.**	**(509) 674-2296**	**Pg. 39**
WA	Cle Elum	Crazy For Quilts	208 W. 5th St.	(475) 417-7808	
WA	Ephrata	The Fabric Patch	220 10th Ave. SW	(509) 754-8280	
WA	Leavenworth	Dee's Country Accents	917 Commercial St.	(509) 548-5311	
WA	Lind	Crazy Quilter	316 N. I St.	(509) 677-3335	
WA	Poulsbo	Quilter's Cottage	5201 NE Falcon Ridge Ln.	(360) 710-5536	
WA	**Prosser**	**The Sewing Basket & The Quilted Country Inn**			
			1108 Wine Country Rd.	**(509) 786-7367**	**Pg. 39**
WA	Woodinville	Knit & Live	22703 78th Ave. SE	(425) 481-2455	
WI	Cashton	Country Pleasures Bed & Breakfast	1075 Weister Creek Rd.	(608) 839-4915	
WI	Downsville	Woodland Ridge Retreat	4620 E. County Rd. C	(715) 664-8220	
WI	Eau Claire	Bridge Creek Cottage	415 Southwood Ct.	(320) 420-0250	
WI	Fennimore	Quilt Peddler	4420 US Hwy. 18 E	(608) 822-6822	
WI	Foster	Foster Retreat Center	10725 County Rd. HH	(715) 563-6680	
WI	Hillpoint	Homestead Cabin Retreat	E 3957 Prouty Rd.	(608) 986-4154	
WI	Lac du Flambeau	Dillman's Bay Resort	13277 Dillman's Way	(715) 588-3143	
WI	Mishicot	Fox Hills Resort	250 W. Church St.	(800) 950-7615	
WI	Mt. Horeb	A Place To Sew	206 Oak Tree Court	(608) 335-9694	
WI	Poynette	Cattail Retreat	W9110 County Rd. CS	(608) 592-4139	
WI	Sparta	Quilt Corner	219 N. Water St.	(608) 269-1083	
WI	Spring Green	Country Sampler	133 E. Jefferson St.	(608) 588-2510	
WI	St. Croix Falls	Pins "N" Needles	126 N. Washington	(715) 483-5728	

Canadian Retreat Facilities

State	City	Name	Address	Phone	Page
AB	Canmore	Lady Macdonald Country Inn	1201 Bow Valley Tr.	(403) 678-3665	
AB	Canmore	Creekside Country Inn	709 Benchlands Tr.	(866) 609-5522	
AB	Carseland	Bow Bench Retreat	Range Rd. 260	(403) 934-3491	
AB	Pincher Creek	Bloomin' Inn	1037 Bev McLachin Dr.	(403) 627-5829	
ON	Bracebridge	Quilters Mis Bee Haven	2095 Hwy. #141	(705) 645-3987	

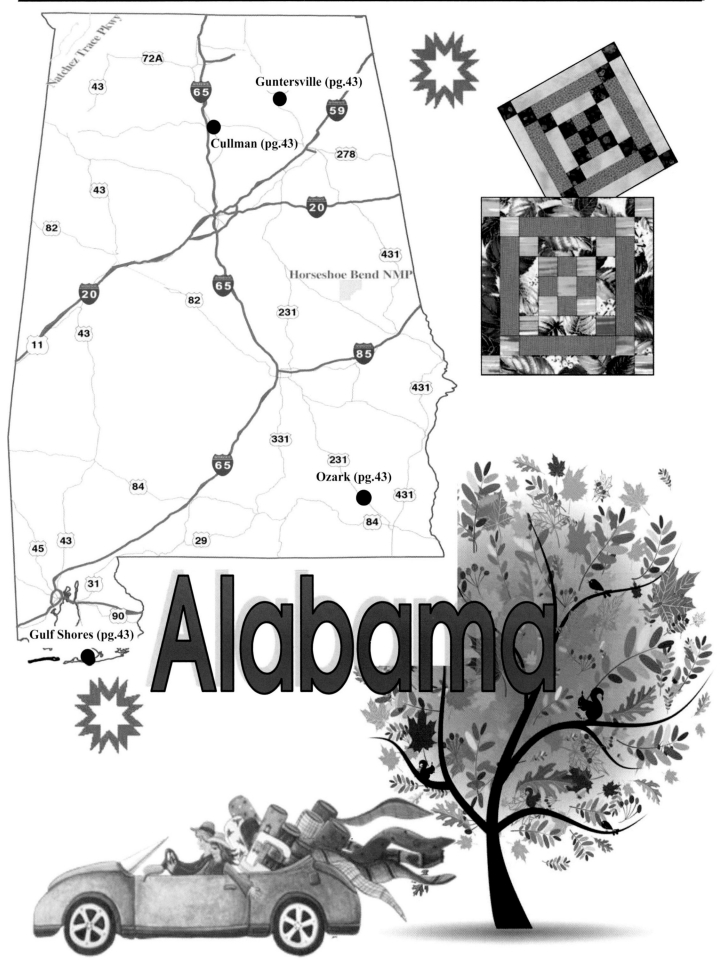

Guntersville (pg.43)

Cullman (pg.43)

Horseshoe Bend NMP

Ozark (pg.43)

Gulf Shores (pg.43)

Alabama

The Tutwiler

Established in 1914, the Tutwiler is a national historic landmark in the heart of Birmingham. Featuring 149 guestrooms with expansive windows for views of the cityscape, the hotel sits within minutes of the Birmingham Civil Rights Institute, Birmingham Museum of Art, Iron City, Regions Field and Railroad Park.
The Tutwiler Bar and Grill is located on the lobby level and is said to have a resident ghost!

2021 Park Place, Birmingham, Alabama, 35203 – (205) 322-2100
www. hamptoninn3.hilton.com/en/hotels/alabama/hampton-inn-and-suites-birmingham-downtown-tutwiler-BHMDNHX/index.html

Alabama Shops

Q-Quilting ~ Y-Yarn ~ N-Needlework ~ R-Retreats ~ M-Museum

Alberta	Gee's Bend Quilters Collective	14570 County Rd. 29	(334) 573-2323	
Albertville	Sew Irresistible	212 N. Broad St. #B	(256) 878-0023	
Alexandria	Yvie's	7534 US Hwy. 431	(256) 225-7986	
Andalusia	Andalusia Sewing Center	128 Convington Mall	(334) 222-4124	
Ashville	Ashville House Quilt Shop	35 3rd St.	(205) 594-7046	
Athens	3 Hens & A Chick Quilt Shop, LLC	1114 US Hwy. 31 S, #B	(256) 771-2040	
Auburn	Stitch Therapy	555 Opelika Rd #1	(334) 821-7781	
Birmingham	In the Making	4232 Dolly Ridge Rd. #100	(205) 298-1309	
Birmingham	Needleworks, LLC	2810 Crescent Ave.	(205) 870-5191	
Birmingham	The Sewing Room	1040 Inveness Corners	(205) 980-1112	
Birmingham	Zig Zag Sewing Studio	5479 Hwy. 280 #117	(205) 290-5062	
Boaz	Out of the Box	103 S. Main St.	(256) 840-0059	
Boaz	Wilson Fabric Outlet	1524 US HWY 431 N.	(256) 593-6501	
Clanton	Sew Charming	9 Village Square	(205) 903-4133	
Cullman	**Quilted Treasures**	**1430 4th St. SW**	**(256) 339-0980**	**Pg. 43**
Cullman	Kenziebe Fabrics	1430 4th St. SW	(256) 339-3781	
Decatur	The Cross Stitch Peddler	124 14th St. SW, Suite D-1	(256) 350-7780	
Decatur	Yarn Boutique by Mitsie	518 14th St. SE	(256) 580-5510	
Dothan	Dothan Sewing Center	2797 Ross Clark Cir.	(334) 794-3177	
Dothan	Smock Shoppe	1445 Westgate Pkwy. #1	(334)793-8233	
Double Springs	Fine Yarns on Main	25215 AL-195	(205) 489-8009	
Fairhope	The Yarn Cottage	9 N. Church St.	(251) 928-4046	
Florence	Calico Rose Quilt Shop	1707 Darby Drive	(256) 760-8227	
Florence	Thread	213 N. Court St.	(256) 275-7112	
Florence	Unraveled Yarn and Gifts	215 N. Court St.	(256) 349-2533	
Foley	Clara's Loom	7518 Riverwood Dr.	(251) 943-2960	
Gadsden	Sew Irrestible	2104 Rainbow Dr.	(256) 459-5355	
Gadsden	The Taming of the Ewe	532 Broad St.	(256) 546-9090	
Gardendale	Our Sewing Nook	841 Odum Rd. #117	(265) 285-5091	
Gulf Shores	**S.E.A. Quilt Shoppe**	**22131 Cotton Creek Dr.**	**(251) 968-7327**	**Pg. 43**
Guntersville	**Stitchers Haven**	**1600 Gunter Ave.**	**(256) 582-8234**	**Pg. 43**
Hartselle	In the Loop Yarn Shop	410 Main St. W.	(256) 318-3423	
Harvest	Little Barn, Inc.	173 McKee Rd.	(256) 755-0129	
Headland	Quilted Creations	24 S. Main St.	(334) 693-5808	
Huntsville	Barb's Sewing Center	2310-A Whitesburg Dr. S.	(256) 539-2414	
Huntsville	Creative Sewing	8415-R Whitesburg Dr.	(256) 883-4414	
Huntsville	Fiber Art Work	817 B Regal Dr.	(256) 656-0163	
Huntsville	Hunstville Sew & Vac	200 Oakwood Ave. NE Unit K-L	(256) 536-3757	
Huntsville	Patches & Stitches	603 Humes Ave. NE	(256) 533-3886	
Huntsville	Threaded Needle Too	1847 University Dr. NW	(256) 585-1339	
Jacksonville	Yarns by HomePlace Farm	402 Pelham Rd. N. #4	(256) 452-5206	
Jasper	Sew Simple	215 Hwy. 195 N.	(205) 295-2229	
Mobile	All About Sewing	590 Schillinger Rd. S. #D	(251) 634-3133	
Mobile	Mobile Yarn	4318 Downtowner Loop N.	(251) 308-2257	
Monroeville	Susie's LLC	38 W. Claborne St.	(251) 743-2589	
Montgomery	Needle Bug	7020 Vaughn Rd.	(334) 270-0064	
Montgomery	Sew Bernina	51 N. Burbank Dr.	(334) 274-0887	
Opelika	Opelika Sewing Center	3305 Pepperell Parkway	(334) 749-9522	
Opelika	Yarnhouse Studio	115 S. 8th St.	(334) 745-7300	
Owen Cross Roads	A Stitch Above	2729 Whistler Ln.	(256) 533-0213	
Oxford	Wilson Fabric	832 Snow St. #E	(256) 831-8804	
Ozark	**Front Porch Quilt Shoppe**	**199 N. Hwy 231**	**(334) 445-3521**	**Pg. 43**
Ozark	Fabric Bin	120 N. Court Square	(334) 443-0658	
Pelham	Zig Zag Sewing Studio	2156 Pelham Pkwy. #C	(205) 624-4647	
Rainbow City	Tomorrows Treasures, LLC	3805 Rainbow Dr. #C	(256) 442-1290	
Theodore	Susan's Heirloom	6851 Old Pascagoula Rd.	(251) 653-7784	
Trussville	SEWBIZZ	1110 N. Chalkville Rd. #160	(205) 655-7060	
Tuscaloosa	Serendipity Needleworks	412 Queen City Ave.	(205) 758-0108	
Tuscaloosa	Sew Delightful	1875 McFarland Blvd. Ste. 200	(205) 752-1700	
Vestavia Hills	In The Making: A Knit Shop	4232 Dolly Ridge Rd.	(205) 298-1309	

Alaska

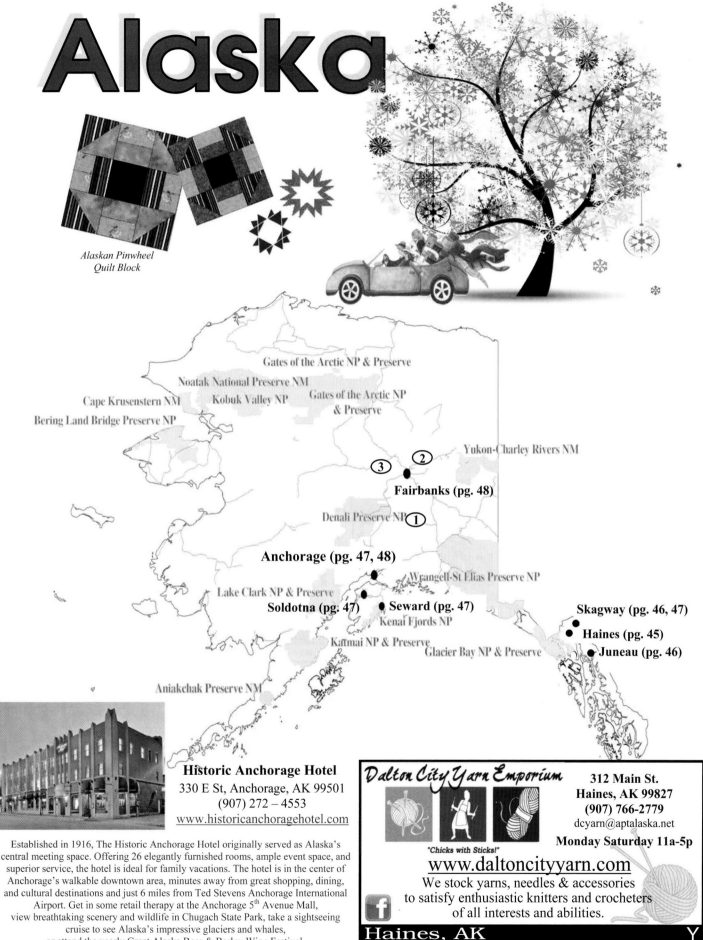

*Alaskan Pinwheel
Quilt Block*

Gates of the Arctic NP & Preserve

Noatak National Preserve NM

Cape Krusenstern NM   Kobuk Valley NP   Gates of the Arctic NP
                                                       & Preserve

Bering Land Bridge Preserve NP

Yukon-Charley Rivers NM

③   ②

Fairbanks (pg. 48)

Denali Preserve NP ①

Anchorage (pg. 47, 48)

Wrangell-St Elias Preserve NP

Lake Clark NP & Preserve

Soldotna (pg. 47)   **Seward (pg. 47)**

Kenai Fjords NP   **Skagway (pg. 46, 47)**

Katmai NP & Preserve   **Haines (pg. 45)**

Glacier Bay NP & Preserve   **Juneau (pg. 46)**

Aniakchak Preserve NM

Historic Anchorage Hotel
330 E St, Anchorage, AK 99501
(907) 272 – 4553
www.historicanchoragehotel.com

Established in 1916, The Historic Anchorage Hotel originally served as Alaska's
central meeting space. Offering 26 elegantly furnished rooms, ample event space, and
superior service, the hotel is ideal for family vacations. The hotel is in the center of
Anchorage's walkable downtown area, minutes away from great shopping, dining,
and cultural destinations and just 6 miles from Ted Stevens Anchorage International
Airport. Get in some retail therapy at the Anchorage 5th Avenue Mall,
view breathtaking scenery and wildlife in Chugach State Park, take a sightseeing
cruise to see Alaska's impressive glaciers and whales,
or attend the yearly Great Alaska Beer & Barley Wine Festival.

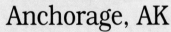

Alaska Shops

Q-Quilting ~ Y-Yarn ~ N-Needlework ~ R-Retreat ~ M-Museum

Anchorage	**The Quilt Tree**	**341 E. Benson Blvd. #5**	**(907) 561-4115**	**Pg. 47**
Anchorage	**The Quilted Raven**	**415 G St.**	**(907) 278-3521**	**Pg. 48**
Anchorage	**The Wooly Mammoth**	**416 G St.**	**(907) 278-3524**	**Pg. 48**
Anchorage	Far North Fibers	3200 E. 15th Ave.	(907) 279-0332	
Anchorage	Far North Yarn Co.	2636 Speanrd Rd. #6	(907) 258-5648	
Anchorage	Quilt Zone	510 W Tudor Rd. suite 2	(907) 561-2020	
Anchorage	Seams Like Home, LLC	2153 E. 88th Ave.	(907) 677-8790	
Chitina	Timberberry Farm	44.5 McCarthy Rd.	(907) 253-7170	
Cooper Landing	Bearly Threaded Quilting	Mile 47.5 Sterling Hwy.	(907) 631-8129	
Cordova	The Net Loft	140 Adams St.	(907) 424-7337	
Delta Junction	The Calico Cow	1407 Grizzly Ln.	(907) 895-5210	
Denali Park	Northern Heart Originals	190 George Parks Hwy.	(907) 683-1221	
Eagle River	The Quilt Cache	12812 Old Glenn Hwy. #A2	(907) 622-7858	
Eagle River	The Tangled Skein	11753 Celestial St.	(907) 622-9276	
Eagle River	Twisted Sisters' Quilty Pleasures	11401 Old Glenn Hwy. #101-A	(907) 694-8777	
Fairbanks	**Northern Threads**	**1875 University Ave. Ste. 2**	**(907) 455-0299**	**Pg. 48**
Fairbanks	A Weaver's Yarn	1810 Alaska Way	(907) 374-1995	
Fairbanks	That Old Sew and Sew	704 2nd Ave.	(907) 799-9031	
Fairbanks	The Material Girls	3065 College Rd.	(907) 474-8118	
Fairbanks	The Spinning Room	516 2nd Ave. #211	(907) 458-7610	
Haines	**Dalton City Emporian**	**312 Main St.**	**(907) 766-2779**	**Pg. 45**
Healy	Granma's Quilt Shop	4 Coal St.	(907) 683-2200	
Homer	CommuKnitty Stash	3581 B Main St.	(907) 299-0601	
Homer	Ulmer's Drug & Hardware	3858 Lake St. #5	(907) 235-8594	
Juneau	**Changing Tides**	**175 S. Franklin St. Ste. 203**	**(907) 523-6084**	**Pg. 46**
Juneau	Ben Franklin	233 Front St.	(907) 586-6762	
Juneau	Rain Tree Quilting	2213 Dunn St.	(907) 789-7900	
Juneau	Seaside Yarns	2 Marine Way #125	(907) 723-9227	
Kenai	Kenai Fabric Center	115 N. Willow St.	(907) 283-4595	
Ketchikan	Soft Goods and Green Things	2417 Tongass Ave. #219	(907) 225-3222	
Ketchikan	The Hive on the Creek	716 Totem Way #1	(907) 225-9161	
Ketchikan	The Point Art Café	25 Jefferson Way #102	(907) 225-2858	
Ketchikan	Whale's Tail Quilt Shop	5 Salmon Landing #204	(907) 225-5422	
Kodiak	Compass Rose Quilting	1315 Mill Bay Rd. #C	(907) 486-0416	
Kodiak	The Rookery	104 Center Ave. #100B	(907) 486-0052	
North Pole	Ben Franklin	301 N. Santa Claus Ln. #16	(907) 488-8544	
Palmer	Just Sew	579 S. Alaska St.	(907) 745-3649	
Palmer	Wild Hare Yarn Shop & Gifts	3465 S. Sandvik Cir.	(907) 745-2477	
Palmer	Windy Valley Muskox	9523 N. Wolverine Rd.	(888) 762-5830	
Seward	**Sew'n Bee Cozy**	**211 4th Ave.**	**(907) 224-7647**	**Pg. 47**
Seward	A Flyin' Skein	223 Fourth Ave.	(907) 224-5648	
Sitka	Abby's Reflection	231 Lincoln St.	(907) 747-3510	
Sitka	Knitting With Class	102 Lincoln St.	(907) 738-0957	
Skagway	**Aurora Yarns of Alaska**	**340 5th Ave.**	**(907) 983-3707**	**Pg. 46**
Skagway	**Rushin' Tailor's Quilt Alaska**	**370 3rd Ave.**	**(907) 983-2397**	**Pg. 47**
Soldotna	**Bearly Threaded Quilting Too**	**44332 Sterling Hwy. Ste. 8**	**(907) 262-3262**	**Pg. 47**
Soldotna	Black Sheep Yarn & Knitting Machines	222 N. Binkley St.	(907) 262-5817	
Wasilla	Sylvia's Quilt Depot	1261 S. Seward Meridian, #E	(907) 376-6468	

Index

Notes

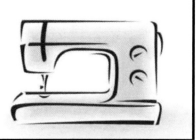

Lake Mead NRA

Grand Canyon NP

Canyon de Chelly NM

Lake Mead NRA

Grand Canyon NP

180

Wupatki NM

93

Kingman (pg. 51)

Flagstaff (pg. 51)

Petrified Forest NP

89

40

Cottonwood (pg. 51)

180

89A

Prescott (pg. 51)

Lakeside (pg. 51)

17

60

Glendale (pg. 52)

10

Phoenix (pg. 52)

Miami (pg. 53)

Mesa (pg. 51, 52)

60

Chandler (pg. 53)

70

8

89

Yuma (pg. 54)

Organ Pipe Cactus NM

Saguaro NM

Saguaro NM

Tucson (pg. 53)

Chiricahua NM

191

Sierra Vista (pg. 53)

Arizona

Coronado National Memorial NM

Phoenix Quilt Block

Did you know that Arizona is roughly the size of the country of Italy.

Arizona Biltmore, A Waldorf Astoria Resort

Established February 23rd, 1929, The Arizona Biltmore was
constructed in grand form and has been host to vibrant social events
for 89 years. Editor's Pick in Conde Nast Traveler's Gold List 2018,
the resort features championship golf, Spa Biltmore,
39 acres of gardens, 8 swimming pools, multiple restaurants,
and a variety of amenities.
2400 East Missouri Avenue, Phoenix, Arizona 85016 (602) 955-6600
www.arizonabiltmore.com

The Hotel Congress

Established in 1919, The Historic Hotel Congress is the longest
continuously running hotel in the state. The fully renovated and restored
Mission/Spanish Revival property is part hotel, part award-winning
restaurant and bar, and part world-renowned nightclub, all wrapped into
one. Located in Downtown Tucson, the hotel is within 2 miles of Rialto
Theatre, University of Arizona, and Arizona Stadium. Fox Theatre and
Children's Museum Tucson are also within 10 minutes.

311 East Congress Street, Tucson, AZ 85701
(520) 622-8848
www.hotelcongress.com

Arizona Shops

Q-Quilting ~ Y-Yarn ~ N-Needlework ~ R-Retreat ~ M-Museum

Index

Anthem	The Yarn Outlet Store	42212 N. 41st Dr. #106	(480) 894-1818	
Bullhead City	Marges Hobby House	1110 Hwy. 95	(928) 754-3313	
Casa Grande	Carlton's Quilters Corner	515 E. Florence Blvd.	(520) 421-2641	
Chandler	**35th Ave. Fabric World II**	**4939 W. Ray Rd. Ste. 27**	**(480) 961-7363**	**Pg. 53**
Chandler	Cutting Edge Quilts	64 S. San Marcos Pl.	(480) 857-3443	
Cottonwood	**Quilter's Quarters and Bernina too**	**51 Verde Heights Dr.**	**(928) 634-8161**	**Pg. 51**
Eagar	Quilter's Haven	41 W. 2nd Ave. Ste. A	(928) 333-2739	
Flagstaff	**Odegaard's Sewing Center**	**2109 N. Fourth St.**	**(928) 774-2331**	**Pg. 51**
Flagstaff	Purl In The Pines	2544 N. 4th St.	(928) 774-9334	
Ft. Mohave	Roxy's Quilt & Sew	5221 S. Hwy. 95 #6	(928) 788-2400	
Gilbert	Bolts & More	3133 S. Lindsay Rd.	(480) 899-4611	
Gilbert	Doro's Quiltworks & More	4502 E. Juanita Ave.	(623) 217-6081	
Gilbert	Patchwork Pieces Quilt Co.	1250 N. Sailors Way	(480) 545-7096	
Glendale	A Qulted Country Bear	5930 W. Greenway Rd. #20	(602) 368-2536	
Glendale	**Mulqueen Sewing Center**	**7838 N. 59th Ave.**	**(623) 934-0084**	**Pg. 52**
Glendale	Quilted Country Bear	5930 W. Greenway Rd. #21	(602) 368-2536	
Glendale	Sally Knits	6823 N. 58th Ave.	(623) 934-8367	
Globe	Hill Street Mall	383 S. Hill St.	(928) 425-0022	
Goodyear	Bearly Stitchin Sewing Center	14270 W. Indian School Rd. C-5	(623) 243-5552	
Holbrook	Painted Desert Quilts	206 Navajo Blvd. NE	(928) 524-5600	
Kingman	**Connie's Quilter's Hide-A-Way**	**310 E. Beale St.**	**(928) 753-9096**	**Pg. 51**
Kingman	Donna's Quilt Shop	310 E. Oak St.	(928) 718-5535	
Kingman	The Spinster	116 N 4th St.	(928) 753-3660	
Lake Havasu City	A Material Obsession	34 Lake Havasu Ave. N. # 11 & 12	(928) 505-3612	
Lake Havasu City	Fabrics Unlimited	2089 W. Acoma Blvd. #1	(928) 733-6331	
Lakeside	**Amazing Quilts**	**2964 W. White Mountain Blvd. Ste. 6**		
			(928) 368-5567	**Pg. 51**
Lakeside	Country Creations Quilt Shop	1663 W. White Mountain Blvd. #B	(928) 368-5482	
Lakeside	Pinetop Star	103 W. Yeager Ln.	(928) 367-1709	
Mesa	**A Quilters Oasis**	**9963 E. Baseline Rd. #105**	**(480) 354-4077**	**Pg. 51**
Mesa	**Mulqueen Sewing Center**	**3716 E. Main St.**	**(480) 545-0778**	**Pg. 52**

Q-Quilting ~ Y-Yarn ~ N-Needlework ~ R-Retreat ~ M-Museum

Mesa	"ETC"	2820 E. University Dr. # 111	(480) 854-2303	
Mesa	Attic Needlework	1837 W. Gaudalupe #109	(480) 898-1838	
Mesa	Cabbage Rose Quilt Shop	260 N. Dobson Rd.	(480) 733-5868	
Mesa	Mad B's Quilt & Sew	7415 E. Southern Ave. #108	(480) 964-8914	
Mesa	The Fiber Factory	216 W. Main St.	(480) 969-4346	
Miami	**Julie's Sewing Corner**	**600 W. Sullivan St.**	**(928) 473-7633**	**Pg. 53**
Overgaard	Rim Country Quilts & Paper Crafts	2381 Hwy. 260	(928) 240-1791	
Payson	The Copper Needle	201 W. Main St. #B	(928) 363-4036	
Payson	Village Wools	418 S. Beeline Hwy.	(928) 476-4710	
Peoria	You Can Quilt	9720 W. Peoria Ave. #111	(623) 594-2783	
Phoenix	**35th Ave Fabric World**	**3548 W. Northern Ave.**	**(602) 841-5427**	**Pg. 52**
Phoenix	**Modern Quilting**	**4649 E. Cactus Rd.**	**(602) 710-1771**	**Pg. 52**
Phoenix	3 Dudes Quilting	5053 E. Elliot Rd.	(480) 598-8601	
Phoenix	Bloomin' Stitches	7000 N. 16th St. Ste. 120 #404	(602) 944-4197	
Phoenix	Family Arts Needlework Shop	5555 N. 7th St. #144	(602) 277-0694	
Phoenix	Golden Needle Art	11220 N. 44th Pl.	(602) 996-6603	
Phoenix	Quiltz	21630 N. 9th Ave. #102	(602) 482-4141	
Phoenix	SWTC Inc. Yarn Outlet Store	2205 W. Lone Cactus Dr. #17	(480) 894-1818	
Phoenix	The Bernina Connection	4219 E. Indian School Rd.	(602) 553-8350	
Phoenix	The Olde World Quilt Shoppe	30855 N. Cave Creek Rd. Ste. 134	(480) 473-2171	
Phoenix	The Other Quilt Shop	4271 W. Thunderbird Rd.	(602) 843-1554	
Pinetop	Nana's By The Yard	1400 E. White Mountain Blvd.	(928) 367-1929	
Prescott	**Fiber Creek**	**1046 Willow Creek Rd. Ste. 123**	**(928) 717-1774**	**Pg. 51**
Prescott	Love it Again Fabrics N Fun Stuff	220 W. Goodwin #102	(928) 778-7080	
Prescott	Seams Sew Right Quilt Studio	220 W. Goodwin St. #4	(928) 771-1200	
Prescott Valley	ClothPlus Quilting	6479 E. Copper Hill Dr.	(928) 772-5010	
Prescott Valley	Quilt n' Sew Connection	6546 E. 2nd St. Ste. A	(928) 775-9580	
Safford	Cotton Clouds	5176 S. 14th Ave.	(928) 428-7000	
Safford	The Jack of Arts	417 W. Main St.	(928) 428-5225	
Scottsdale	BeStitched Needlepoint	8658 E. Shea Blvd. #180	(480) 991-0706	
Scottsdale	Jessica Knits	8660 E. Shea Blvd. #170	(480) 515-4454	
Scottsdale	Old Town Needlework	7128 E. 5th Ave.	(480) 990-2270	
Scottsdale	Quail Run Needlework	8320 N. Hayden Rd. #C112	(480) 551-1423	
Scottsdale	Scottsdale Quilts	15444 N. 76th St. #105	(480) 951-8000	
Scottsdale	Sewing Nuts	4250 N. Scottsdale Rd.	(480) 659-1222	
Sedona	Quilter's Store Sedona	3075 W. Hwy. 89A	(928) 282-2057	
Sedona	Sedona Knit Wits, LLC	2370 W. SR 89A #A3	(928) 282-3389	
Sierra Vista	**The Squirrel's Nest**	**4049 E. Camino Principal**	**(520) 417-1070**	**Pg. 53**
Snowflake	Arizona Embroidery & Quilting	121 N. 1st St. E.	(928) 243-2606	
Sun City	Sewin Asylum Fabric Boutique	10050 W. Bell Rd.	(623) 398-6235	
Sun City	Sun Valley Quilts	9857 W. Bell Rd.	(623) 972-2091	
Sun City West	Bob's Variety & Fabrics	13583 W. Camino Del Sol	(623) 584-2448	
Surprise	Arizona Quilts	12301 W. Bell Rd. Suite A-109	(623) 566-8878	
Surprise	Cactus Yarn	15170 W. Bell Rd. #109	(623) 537-9747	
Tempe	Quilters' Ranch	1721 E. Warner Rd #C-8	(480) 838-8350	
Tempe	Tempe Yarn & Fiber	1415 E. University Dr. #103	(480) 557-9166	
Tucson	**Cactus Quilt Shop**	**7921 N. Oracle Rd.**	**(520) 498-4698**	**Pg. 53**
Tucson	Birdhouse Yarns	2540 E. 6th St.	(520) 305-4187	
Tucson	Cathey's Vac & Sew	8700 N. Oracle Rd.	(520) 797-7177	
Tucson	Cathey's Vac & Sew	3906 N. Oracle Rd.	(520) 690-9144	
Tucson	Cathey's Vac & Sew	5701 E. Speedway Blvd.	(520) 721-4000	
Tucson	Eagles Wings Quilting	3921 E. 29th St. #309	(520) 790-7041	
Tucson	Grandma's Spinning Wheel	6544 E. Tanque Verde Rd. #150	(520) 290-3738	
Tucson	Quilt Basket, Inc.	6538 E. Tanque Verde Rd. #130	(520) 722-8810	
Tucson	The Quilter's Market	7601 E. Speedway Blvd.	(520) 747-8458	
Tucson	The West Inc.	5615 E. River Rd. Ste. 101	(520) 299-1044	
Tucson	Tucson Yarn Company	6330 N. Oracle Rd. #D-242	(520) 229-9276	
Valdez	Smiling Seal Sewing	354 Fairbanks Dr.	(907) 835-3222	
Wickenburg	Isabelle's Parlour - A Yarn Boutique	51020 Hwy. 60/89	(928) 684-4937	
Wilcox	World Wide Hobbies	100 S. Haskell Ave.	(520) 384-3197	
Winslow	Canyon Rose Quilt Company	212 W. First St.	(928) 289-2800	
Winslow	Loose Ends	209 N. Williamson Ave.	(928) 289-4800	
Yuma	**Grandma Jo's**	**5720 E. 32nd St.**	**(928) 314-0058**	**Pg. 54**
Yuma	Bonnie's Fabric on Wheels	3351 S. Ave. 4E	(541) 921-0125	

Index

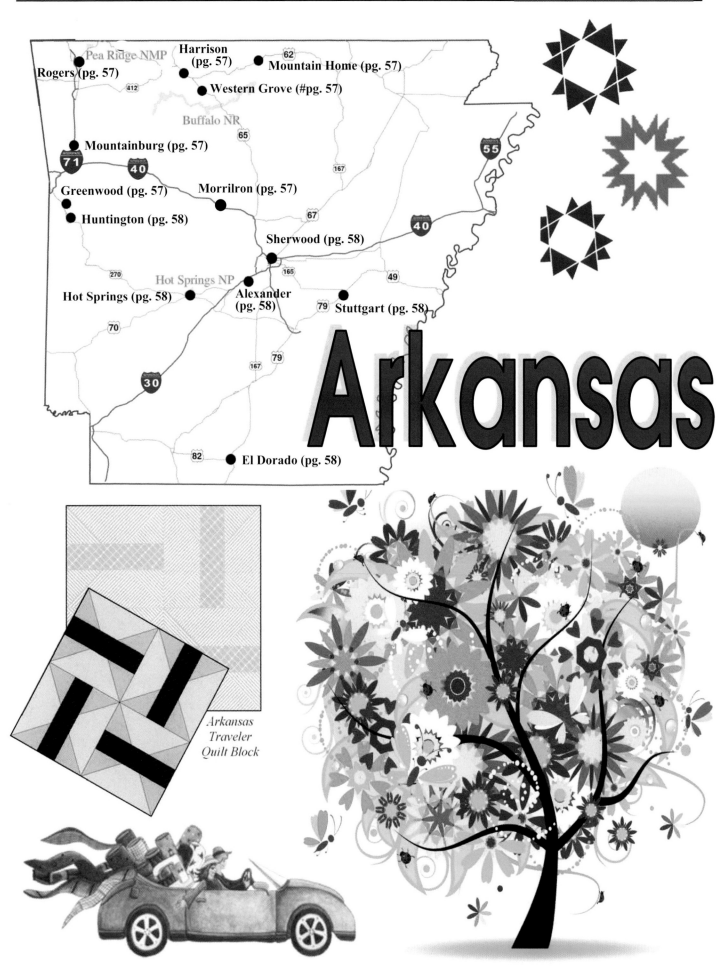

Pea Ridge NMP

Harrison (pg. 57)

Rogers (pg. 57)

Mountain Home (pg. 57)

Western Grove (#pg. 57)

Buffalo NR

Mountainburg (pg. 57)

Greenwood (pg. 57)

Morrilron (pg. 57)

Huntington (pg. 58)

Sherwood (pg. 58)

Hot Springs NP

Hot Springs (pg. 58)

Alexander (pg. 58)

Stuttgart (pg. 58)

El Dorado (pg. 58)

Arkansas

*Arkansas
Traveler
Quilt Block*

Arkansas Fun Facts:

Pivot Rock balances on a base 15 times smaller than its top.

Alma is claimed to be the Spinach Capital of the World.

The Ozark National Forest covers more than one million acres.

Arkansas Shops

Q-Quilting ~ Y-Yarn ~ N-Needlework ~ R-Retreat ~ M-Museum

City	Shop	Address	Phone	Page
Alexander	**Pinwheel Fabrics**	**7915 Hwy. 5 North**	**(501) 847-4177**	**Pg. 58**
Alpena	Rag Barn	307 E. Elm St.	(870) 437-2325	
Arkadelphia	Knit Unto Others	323 Main St.	(870) 245-2552	
Arkadelphia	Tye Quilts	105 S. 8th St.	(870) 617-7042	
Batesville	Marshall Dry Goods	310 W. Main St.	(870) 793-2405	
Batesville	Paper Chase Book and Yarn Shop	136 W. Main St.	(870) 793-4276	
Beebe	Calico Junction	210 W. Center St.	(501) 882-0333	
Benton	Bed-Warmer Quilt and Sew	17270 I-30 N.	(501) 860-6176	
Bentonville	Village Quilting	13020 Frontage Rd. #105	(479) 855-3800	
Bull Shoals	Gabriele's Flowers & Fibers	904 Central Blvd.	(870) 445-4273	
Cabot	Stitchery Sewist Shop	302 E. Main	(501) 286-8335	
Cave City	Quilt Rack	1094 Hwy 230	(870) 283-2429	
Conway	The Stitcher's Garden	1026 Van Ronkle St.	(501) 513-1851	
El Dorado	**MNM Quilt Shop**	**171 Pete Mason Rd.**	**(870) 862-0580**	**Pg. 58**
El Dorado	Fiber Arts Studio	617 E. 3rd St.	(870) 863-5086	
Elkins	Lonesome Pine Quilts	1910 Hwy. 18	(479) 601-6011	
Eureka Springs	Delightfully Sew & Quilt	51 Spring St.	(417) 671-2176	
Eureka Springs	Fleece 'N Flax	51 Spring St.	(479) 253-0711	
Eureka Springs	Red Scottie Fibers	51 Spring St.	(479) 253-0711	
Eureka Springs	The Quilter's Cottage	106 E. Van Buren	(479) 719-1412	
Fayetteville	Hand-Held - A Knitting Gallery	225 N. Block Ave.	(479) 582-2910	
Fayetteville	Sew in Heaven	3162 W. Milk Dr.	(479) 443-2445	
Flippin	Curiousity Shop	9084 Hwy. 62 E.	(870) 453-5300	
Gassville	R-Gems Inc.	5435 Hwy. 62 W.	(870) 430-5225	
Gentry	Gentry Quilts	213 E. Main	(479) 736-0050	
Glenwood	Fabric Creations	219 N. Bumble Bee Rd.	(870) 356-3142	
Green Forest	McKee Sewing Center	64 Sparrow Rd.	(870) 437-2862	
Greenwood	**Crooked Creek Quilts**	**1736 West Center St.**	**(479) 996-5808**	**Pg. 57**
Hardy	Ozark Rustic Charm	112 E. Main St.	(870) 856-2727	
Harrison	**Heart Quilt Shop**	**8874 Hwy. 62 W.**	**(870) 437-5400**	**Pg. 57**
Harrison	Country Corner Quilt Shop	10872 Hwy. 392	(870) 437-2299	
Harrison	Deb's Frames & Things	102 W. Stepenson Ave.	(870) 741-6070	
Heber Springs	Heber Sew N Vac/ Quilters Corner Fabric	207 W. Main St.	(501) 362-8612	
Horseshoe Bend	The Quilted Heart	3022 Hwy. 289 S.	(870) 670-4292	
Hot Springs	**Amy's Fun Fabric & More**	**2998 Park Ave.**	**(501) 318-2739**	**Pg. 58**
Hot Springs	**Cathy's Quiltin' Square**	**3256 Albert Pike**	**(501) 760-6099**	**Pg. 58**
Hot Springs	Knittin on the Corner	801 Central Ave. #11	(501) 623-2001	
Hot Springs	The Rocking Chair	1698 Higdon Ferry Rd.	(501) 525-8057	
Huntington	**Mama's Log House**	**3715 E. Clarks Chapel Rd.**	**(479) 928-1600**	**Pg. 58**
Jonesboro	Jana's Quilting & Décor	2005 E. Highland Dr.	(870) 972-5543	
Kirby	Vickie's Quilting Shack	3049 Hwy. 70 W.	(870) 398-4109	
Little Rock	Shepherd's Needle	11601 W. Markham #D	(501) 221-6990	
Little Rock	The Stitchin' Post	1501 Macon Dr.	(501) 227-0288	

Index

Little Rock	The Yarn Mart, LLC	5711 Kavanaugh Blvd.	(501) 666-6505	
Little Rock	Yarn Kandy	8201 Cantrell Rd. #201	(501) 508-5559	
Morrilron	**The Fabric Patch & More**	**204 W. Railroad Ave.**	**(501) 289-6512**	**Pg. 57**
Mountain Home	**Remember Me Quilt Shop**	**307 S. Main St. Ste. 5**	**(870) 425-7670**	**Pg. 57**
Mountain Home	Sew Unique	960 E. 9th St.	(870) 424-4739	
Mountain Home	Thus & Sew	2612 Hwy. 5 S.	(870) 424-3243	
Mountain View	Ritsy Rags Quilt & Antique Shop	112 Howard Ave.	(870) 269-2800	
Mountainburg	**Piece of Heaven Quilt Fabric**	**16864 Old Locke Rd.**	**(479) 369-4006**	**Pg. 57**
Mulberry	Cozy Quilts & Things	10017 Silver Maple Dr.	(479) 997-8366	
Paragould	Hancocks Fabric and Tuxedo	421 W. Kingshighway	(870) 236-7536	
Pea Ridge	Country House Quilting	16324 N. Hwy. 94	(479) 451-8978	
Pea Ridge	Sew N Sew Quilts	346 Lee Town Rd.	(479) 451-1685	
Prairie Grove	Daisies and Olives	129 E. Buchanan St.	(479) 846-1800	
Reyno	Fabrics and Quilts	272 W. 2nd St.	(870) 810-1485	
Rogers	**Rogers Sewing Center**	**1802 South 8th St.**	**(479) 636-8240**	**Pg. 57**
Rogers	Mockingbird Moon	315 N. 2nd	(479) 202-5640	
Rogers	Sew Graceful Quilting	14094 Pleasant Ridge Rd.	(479) 372-7403	
Rogers	The Busy Needle	205 N. 3rd St.	(479) 633-0113	
Russellville	Knit 2 Together	2300 W. Main St #6	(479) 968-5648	
Sherwood	**Sew Much More**	**2001 E. Kiehl Ave. Ste 1**	**(501) 753-6050**	**Pg. 58**
Siloam Springs	Sager Creek Quilts & Yarn Works	304 E. Central	(479)524-5244	
Springdale	The Sewing Shop	5320 W. Sunset Ave.	(479) 419-8989	
Stuttgart	**The French Seam**	**2015 S. Buerkle**	**(870) 673-8156**	**Pg. 58**
Western Grove	**White Chapel Fabrics**	**813 US. 65B Hwy.**	**(870) 429-5454**	**Pg. 57**

Notes

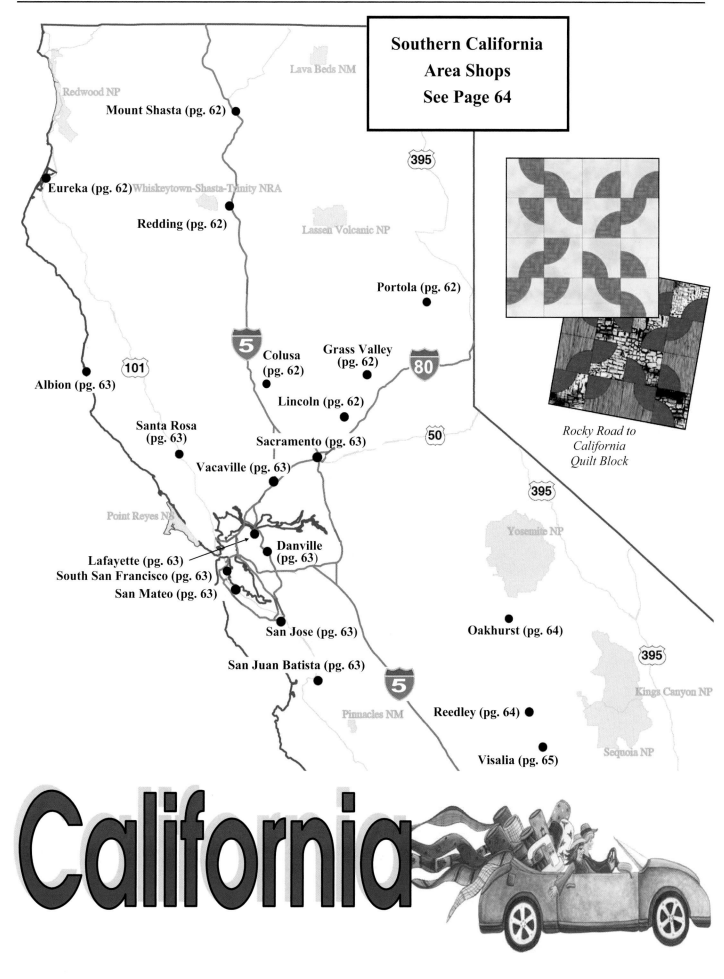

Southern California
Area Shops
See Page 64

Lava Beds NM

Redwood NP

Mount Shasta (pg. 62)

Eureka (pg. 62) Whiskeytown-Shasta-Trinity NRA

Redding (pg. 62)

Lassen Volcanic NP

395

Portola (pg. 62)

5

Colusa (pg. 62)

Grass Valley (pg. 62)

80

Lincoln (pg. 62)

Albion (pg. 63)

101

Santa Rosa (pg. 63)

Sacramento (pg. 63)

50

Vacaville (pg. 63)

Point Reyes NS

395

Yosemite NP

Lafayette (pg. 63)
South San Francisco (pg. 63)
San Mateo (pg. 63)

Danville (pg. 63)

San Jose (pg. 63)

Oakhurst (pg. 64)

395

San Juan Batista (pg. 63)

5

Kings Canyon NP

Pinnacles NM

Reedley (pg. 64)

Visalia (pg. 65)

Sequoia NP

Rocky Road to
California
Quilt Block

California

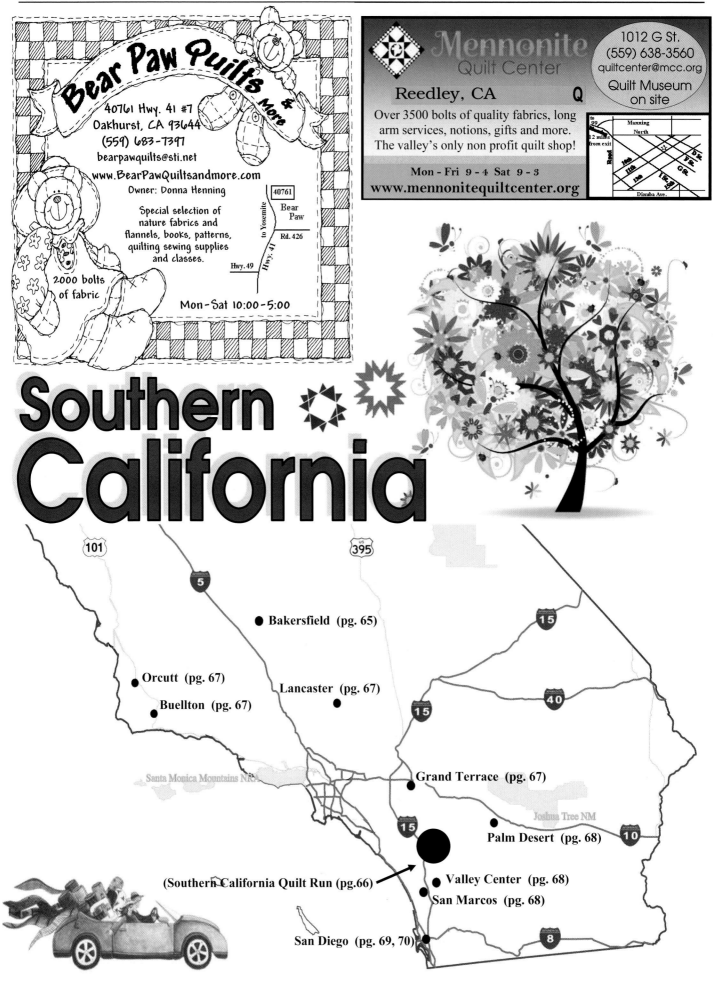

Southern California

Bakersfield (pg. 65)

Orcutt (pg. 67)

Buellton (pg. 67)

Lancaster (pg. 67)

Santa Monica Mountains NRA

Grand Terrace (pg. 67)

Joshua Tree NM

Palm Desert (pg. 68)

(Southern California Quilt Run (pg.66)

Valley Center (pg. 68)

San Marcos (pg. 68)

San Diego (pg. 69, 70)

Did you know?
California produces more than 17 million gallons of wine each year.

Did you know?
In 2012, Eleanor Burns was inducted into
The Quilters Hall of Fame.

ROSIE'S
Calico Cupboard Quilt Shop

7151 El Cajon Blvd. Suite 'F'
San Diego, CA 92115
(619) 697-5758
Fax: (619) 465-8298
rozgonzalez@cox.net
www.rosiescalicocupboard.com

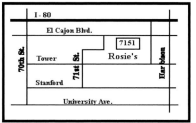

Hwy. 8 (East or West) — take 70th St. exit, travel south on 70th St. for 1/2 mile to El Cajon Blvd., turn left (east) onto El Cajon Blvd., travel for 1 1/2 blocks.
Hwy. 94 (East or West) — take the Mass. exit, travel north to University Ave., turn left, follow to 70th St., turn right, follow to El Cajon Blvd., turn right.
We are freeway close from all points of San Diego and the trolley stops ONE mile from our shop.

- Well stocked sale rack with values from 25 to 75% off suggested Retail Prices.
- New stock arriving daily.
- 1100 sq.ft. Classroom with a full calendar of Quilting & Crafting Classes year round.
- Mail Orders and Special Orders Welcome
- Visa, MC, Discover, ATM Cards

Offering over 8000 sq. ft. (stocked to the brim) with over 16,000 bolts of First Quality 100% Cotton Prints at everyday DISCOUNT prices. Books, Batting, Notions, Patterns, Quilting Thread and Machine Embroidery Thread, Machine Embroidery Designs, and Quilting and Crafting related Gift items. Authorized JANOME Sewing Machine Dealer -- Sales, Service, Repair, Janome Sewing Club, Janome Embroidery Club and Janome Sewing Machine classes, plus much much more.

Believe in Your Creativity
JANOME®

FLORIANI EMBROIDERY
Sewing & Quilting Products
Anita Goodesign™
EMBROIDERY DESIGNS · EVENTS · EDUCATION

Monday - Friday 9 - 5   Wednesday til 8
Saturday 8 - 5   Sunday 11 - 5

A Full Service Quilt Shop
Catering to Quilters and
Crafters Since 1990

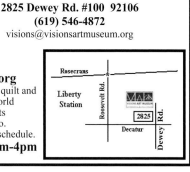

California Shops

Q-Quilting ~ Y-Yarn ~ N-Needlework ~ R-Retreat ~ M-Museum

City	Shop	Address	Phone	Page
Alameda	Alameda Yarn Co.	2002 Encinal Ave.	(510) 523-9003	
Alameda	Needle In A Haystack	2433 Mariner Square Loop	(510) 522-0404	
Albany	Avenue Yarns	1325 Solano Ave.	(510) 526-9276	
Albion	**Rainbow Resource**	**33875 E. Lane**	**(707) 937-0431**	**Pg. 63**
Albion	The Quilt Complex	30701 Middle Ridge Rd.	(707) 937-0739	
Anaheim	Mel's Sewing & Fabric Center	1189 N. Euclid St.	(714) 774-3460	
Anaheim	Newton's Knits	2100 E. Howell Ave. Ste. 211	(714) 634-9116	
Anaheim	Soft Expressions	1230 N. Jefferson St. #M	(714) 630-7414	
Anaheim Hills	Velona Needlecraft	5701-M Santa Ana Canyon Rd.	(714) 974-1570	
Anderson	Quilter's Paradise	16325 Tacoma Ln.	(530) 357-4864	
Antioch	Queen B's Quilt Shop	720 W. 2nd St.	(925) 978-4587	
Apple Valley	Fanciwerks Yarn Shoppe	21810 US Hwy 18, Ste. 2	(760) 961-0113	
Arcata	Daisy Drygoods	959 H St.	(707) 822-1893	
Arcata	Fabric Temptations	942 `G' St.	(707) 822-7782	
Atascadero	Quilter's Cupboard	5275 El Camino Real	(805) 466-6996	
Atascadero	Ranch Dog Knitting	5835 Traffic Way	(805) 464-4075	
Atascadero	Sew Fun	8775 El Camino Real	(805) 462-9739	
Atwater	Needle Nook	1299 Broadway Ave.	(209) 358-7853	
Auburn	Auburn Needlework Co.	839 Lincoln Way	(530) 888-0202	
Auburn	Whistle Stop Quilt Shop	13342 Lincoln Way	(530) 888-1882	
Avalon	Catalina Crafters	115 Sumner Ave.	(310) 510-3590	
Bakersfield	Cherry Berry Quilts	6433 Ming Ave.	(661) 282-8300	
Bakersfield	Classy Knits & Yarns	1839 F St.	(661) 325-7226	
Bakersfield	Strawberry Patches	6433 Ming Ave.	(661) 835-1738	
Bakersfield	**Thimble Towne**	**2841 Unicorn Rd. #103**	**(661) 399-5778**	**Pg. 65**
Bakersfield	Tod's Sew & Vac	905 19th St.	(661) 323-7504	
Banning	Knitting Nook	3158 W. Ramsey St. Ste. B	(951) 849-5340	
Barstow	Route 66 Quilt Shop	24525 W. Main St.	(760) 253-5307	
Bellflower	Stitches in Time	16525 Bellflower Blvd.	(562) 804-9341	
Benicia	Fiber-Frolics	637 First St.	(707) 747-9276	
Berkeley	Lacis Museum of Lace & Textiles	2982 Adeline St.	(510) 843-7290	
Berkeley	New Pieces	766 Gilman	(510) 527-6779	
Berkeley	Stonemountain & Daughter Fabrics	2518 Shattuck Ave.	(510)845-6106	
Big Bear City	Yarn Designers Boutique	439 W. Big Bear Blvd.	(909) 584-9715	
Big Bear Lake	Bear Country Quilts & Gifts	42139 Big Bear Blvd.	(909) 567-8766	
Big Bear Lake	Susan's Needlearts	42180 Moonridge Rd.	(909) 273-9874	
Bishop	Sierra Cottons & Wools	117 E. Line St.	(760) 872-9209	
Brea	We, of the Needle	2810 Imperial Hwy.	(909) 444-8325	
Buellton	**The Creation Station**	**252 E Hwy. 246 Unit A**	**(805) 693-0174**	**Pg. 67**
Burbank	Handmade, A Needlework Studio	2112 N. Glenoaks Blvd.	(818) 846-0346	
Calimesa	Busy Bee Quilt Shop	1007 Calimesa Blvd. Ste. J	(909) 795-2778	
Calimesa	Cherry Berry Quilts	1096 Calimesa Blvd. #B	(909) 795-9090	
Camarillo	A Thread Garden / BeadTime	5217 Verdugo Way #F	(805) 482-5256	
Camarillo	The Fabric Shoppe	2360-A Las Posas Rd.	(805) 383-7183	
Cambria	Ball & Skein & More	4210 Bridge St.	(805) 927-3280	

Cambria	Flying Fuzzies	719 Main St.	(805) 927-2649	
Cambria	Pine Tree Patchworks	815 Main St.	(805) 927-3869	
Campbell	Golden State Sewing Center	2435 S. Winchester Blvd.	(408) 866-1181	
Carmel	Knitting By The Sea	5th Ave. Near Junipro	(831) 624-3189	
Carmichael	Creative Sew & Vac	4141 Manzanita Ave. #150	(916) 483-1414	
Carpinteria	Roxanne's, A Wish and A Dream	919 Maple Ave.	(805) 566-1250	
Cedarville	Warner Mountain Weavers	459 S. Main St.	(530) 279-2164	
Chatsworth	Patches Fabrics	9749 Mason	(818) 709-2678	
Chester	Paper Stuff	425 Main St.	(530) 258-3966	
Chico	Cathy's Sew & Vac	2418 Cohasset Rd.	(530) 895-8055	
Chico	Heartstrings Yarn Studio	1909 Esplanade	(530) 894-1434	
Chico	Honey Run Quilters	2418 Cohasset Rd.	(530) 342-5464	
Chico	Rabbit Hole	2607 Esplanade	(530) 345-5015	
Chula Vist	Border Leather Corp	261 Braodway	(619) 691-1657	
Chula Vista	Quilter's Choice	417 3rd. Ave.	(619) 425-2545	
Citrus Heights	Runs With Scissors	7130 Auburn Blvd.	(916) 722-2500	
Claremont	Phebie's Needleart	532 W. 1st St. Unit 210	(909) 624-5250	
Cloverdale	Bolt Fabric & Home	219 N. Cloverdale Blvd.	(707) 894-2658	
Clovis	D & J Sewing Center	2700 Clovis Ave. #101	(559) 225-4927	
Colusa	**Friends Around the Block**	**211 8th St.**	**(530) 458-7467**	**Pg. 62**
Colusa	Sew N Things	157B Market St.	(530) 458-4474	
Concord	Beverly's Fabric & Craft	4677 Clayton Rd.	(925) 686-1886	
Corning	Quilt'n Thyme Sew & Vac	955 Hwy. 99 W. #115	(530) 824-4240	
Corona Del Mar	Jebba Needlepoint Designs	2628 E. Coast Hwy.	(949) 644-7904	
Costa Mesa	Knit Schtick	2915 Redhill Ave. #C108	(714) 557-4220	
Costa Mesa	Newport Needlepoint	369 E. 17th St. #6	(949) 650-8022	
Costa Mesa	Piecemakers Country Store	1720 Adams Ave.	(714) 641-3112	
Cottonwood	Emanations Jewelry and Fabric	19863 Freshwater Dr.	(530) 347-2455	
Covina	Garden Gate Needlepoint	236 N. Citrus Ave.	(626) 966-4141	
Crescent City	A Perfect Yarn	124 US. Hwy. 101 N.	(707) 464-1864	
Culver City	The Knitting Tree, LA	6285 Bristol Ave.	(310) 395-3880	
Cypress	Tranquility Quilts & Fabric Shop	10191 Valley View St.	(714) 952-8928	
Danville	**Wooden Gate Quilts**	**125-F Railroad Ave.**	**(925) 837-8458**	**Pg. 63**
Danville	A Yarn Less Raveled	730 Camino Ramon #186	(925) 263-2661	
Davis	Pincushion Boutique	1602 2nd St.	(530) 574-0271	
Dublin	Dublin Sewing Center	7367 Village Pkwy.	(925) 829-6511	
El Cajon	Cozy Creative Center	756 Jamacha Rd.	(619) 670-0652	
El Cajon	Memory Lane Quilt Shop	1626 N. Magnolia Ave.	(619) 562-2288	
Elk Grove	Country Sewing Center	9414 Elk Grove Florin	(916) 685-8500	
Elk Grove	Knitique	8739 Elk Grove Blvd.	(916) 714-7719	
Emerald Hills	Amazing Yarns	2559 Woodland Place	(650) 306-9218	
Encinitas	Claire's Collection	3461 Bumann Rd.	(858) 756-5718	
Encinitas	Common Threads	191 N. El Camino Real #201	(760) 436-6119	
Encinitas	The Black Sheep	1060 S. Coast Hwy. 101	(760) 436-9973	
Escalon	Purple Patch Quilting	2212 Arroya St.	(209) 838-7249	
Escondido	Annie's Quilting Den, LLC	1876 W. El Norte Pkwy.	(760) 747-4444	
Escondido	Stitchers Treasures	132 E. Grand Ave.	(760) 737-3113	
Eureka	**Ocean Wave Quilts**	**305 V St.**	**(707) 444-0252**	**Pg. 62**
Eureka	Bunny Hop Quilt Shop	1809 Albee St.	(707) 497-6356	
Eureka	Eureka Fabrics	412 2nd St.	(707) 442-2646	
Eureka	Lavender Rose Fabrics	301 W. Harris	(530) 945-2770	
Eureka	Northcoast Knittery	407 2nd St.	(707) 442-9276	
Eureka	Yarn	518 Russ St.	(707) 443-9276	
Fair Oaks	Babetta's Yarn and Gifts	4400 San Juan Ave.	(916) 965-6043	
Fair Oaks	Thistle Dew Quilt Shoppe	10127 Fair Oaks Blvd.	(916) 967-5479	
Fairfax	Rainbow Fabrics--Rose Tabor	50 Bolinas Rd.	(415) 459-5100	
Fallbrook	Jan's Village Yarn	39315 Daily Rd.	(760) 723-9276	
Fallbrook	Quilter's Cottage	131 E. Fig St. Ste. 6	(760) 723-3060	
Ferndale	Foggy Bottoms	561 Main St.	(707) 786-9188	
Ferndale	Stitch	385 Main St.	(707) 786-5007	
Ferndale	Stitch - Quilting Inspiration	385 Main St.	(707) 725-2823	
Folsom	Meissner Sewing Maching Co.	98 Clarksville Rd. #130	(916) 984-7071	
Fort Bragg	Navarro River Knits	167 Boatyard Dr.	(707) 964-9665	
Fort Bragg	Sew'n Sew	890-A N. Franklin St.	(707) 964-4152	
Fortuna	All Washed Up	685 Spring St.	(707) 725-9773	
Fortuna	Fortuna Fabrics & Crafts	2045 Main St.	(707) 725-2501	
Fortuna	Generations	906 S. Fortuna Blvd.	(707) 725-4293	
Fremont	Color Me Quilts	37495 Niles Blvd.	(510) 494-9940	
Fremont	Not Just Quiltz	37831 Niles Blvd.	(510) 797-6579	
Fresno	Authorized Vac & Sew	5351 N. Blackstone	(559) 439-2560	
Fresno	Janna's Needle Art	1085 E. Herndon Ave. #104	(559) 227-6333	

Fresno	Kiki's Quilt Shack	1732 W. Bullard Ave.	(559) 412-8233	
Fresno	Second Chance Fabrics	5322 W. Spruce Ave. #110	(559) 365-0132	
Fresno	Swatches	1764 W. Bullard Ave.	(559) 435-2813	
Garden Grove	Bear's Quilt Shop	10722 Trask Ave. #A	(714) 590-9209	
Garden Grove	Needlepoints, Ltd.	7707 Garden Grove Blvd.	(714) 894-5242	
Gilroy	The Nimble Thimble	7455 Monterey St.	(408) 842-6501	
Glendora	The Purlside	1200 E. Rte. 66 #109	(626) 914-3747	
Glendora	The Sew N Sew	160 N. Glendora Av. #E	(626) 852-2223	
Graeagle	Woolly Notions	7580 Hwy. 89, House 118	(530) 836-1680	
Grand Terrace	**Bluebird Quilts & Gallery**	**22320 Barton Rd. #A**	**(909) 514-0333**	**Pg. 67**
Grass Valley	**Ben Franklin Crafts**	**598 Sutton Way**	**(530) 273-1348**	**Pg. 62**
Grass Valley	A Star Alpacas	10521 Godfrey Ln.	(530) 274-8748	
Grass Valley	Humble Fabric & Crafts	1451 E. Main St.	(530) 575-9338	
Grass Valley	Sugar Pine Quilt Shop	452 S. Auburn St.	(530) 272-5308	
Gualala	The Loft	39225 S. Hwy. 1	(707) 884-4424	
Half Moon Bay	Elizabeth's Yarn Shop	80 Cabrillo Hwy. N. #O	(650) 712-9276	
Half Moon Bay	Fengari	415 N. Main St.	(650) 726-2550	
Hawthorne	Slipt Stitch	13737 Inglewood Ave.	(310) 322-6739	
Healdsburg	Fabrications	116 Matheson St.	(707) 433-6243	
Healdsburg	Purls of Joy	461 Healdsburg Ave.	(707) 433-5697	
Hesperia	Tops and Bobbins	15550 Main St.	(760) 881-4025	
Hilmar	Quilters Cabin	8177 Lander Ave.	(209) 427-2100	
Huntington Beach	California Yarn Sales	9542 Hamilton Ave.	(714) 965-0018	
Huntington Beach	Knit Nut	8566 Larkhall Circle, Ste. 808B	(714) 969-2199	
Huntington Beach	Moore's Fabric Shop	15041 Goldenwest	(714) 596-3999	
Inyokern	Quilted Patches	300 Mark Ct.	(760) 377-5378	
Jackson	Sewing Cottage	11984 W. State Hwy. 88 #2074	(209) 223-0393	
Jackson	The Hole Affair	46 Main St.	(209) 257-1793	
Joshua Tree	Knotty Knitters	7635 Vista Rd.	(760) 401-7084	
Julian	Kat's Yarn & Craft Cottage	2112 Fourth St.	(619) 246-8585	
Kelseyville	Bird Brain Designs	3925 Main St.	(707) 279-8787	
Kensington	Deep Color Studio	450 Colusa Ave.	(510) 528-8734	
King City	Meandering Threads	51460 White Oak Dr.	(831) 385-3434	
La Grange	Siri's of California	9910 Alamo Dr.	(209) 852-2762	
La Jolla	Fay's Needle Nook of La Jolla	7719 Fay Ave.	(858) 459-1711	
La Jolla	Needlepoint of La Jolla	5685 La Jolla Blvd.	(858) 454-0082	
La Mesa	The Country Loft	4685 Date Ave.	(619) 466-5411	
La Mesa	Two Sisters and Ewe	8874 La Mesa Blvd.	(619) 460-8103	
Lafayette	**The Cotton Patch**	**1025 Brown Ave.**	**(925) 284-1177**	**Pg. 63**
Lafayette	Busy Stix	3418 Mt. Diablo Blvd. #A	(925) 284-1172	
Lafayette	The Yarn Boutique	963-C Moraga Rd.	(925) 283-7377	
Laguna Hills	Sewing Party	23561 Ridge Route Rd. #F	(949) 716-7264	
Lancaster	**Bolts in the Bathtub**	**723 W. Lancaster Blvd.**	**(661) 945-5541**	**Pg. 67**
LaVerne	Make One Yarn Company	2127 Foothill Blvd. #A	(909) 593-8790	
Laytonville	The Fat Quail Quilt Shop	44550 N. Hwy. 101	(707) 984-6966	
Lemon Grove	Yarn N Thread Expressions	3568 Main St. #B	(619) 460-9276	
Lincoln	**Angel Quilter's Studio**	**6011 Nicolaus Rd.**	**(916) 645-8760**	**Pg. 62**
Little River	Mendocino Yarn Shop	7901 N. Hwy. 1	(707) 937-0921	
Livermore	In Between Stitches	2190 First St.	(925) 371-7064	
Lomita	AAA Sewing, Fabric & Vacuum Center	2365 Pacific Coast Hwy.	(310) 257-1744	
Long Beach	Alamitos Bay Yarn Co.	174 N. Marina Dr.	(562) 799-8484	
Long Beach	SewVac Ltd.	1762 Clark Ave.	(562) 498-6684	
Los Altos	Uncommon Threads	293 State St.	(650) 941-1815	
Los Angeles	Bea's Knit Shop	1930 Thayer Ave.	(310) 474-0605	
Los Angeles	FabricHotel.com	848 S. Wall St.	(213) 623-8081	
Los Angeles	Jennifer Knits	108 Barrington Walk	(310) 471-8733	
Los Angeles	Knit Café	8441 Melrose Ave.	(323) 658-5648	
Los Angeles	Knit Culture Studio	8118 W. 3rd St.	(323) 655-6487	
Los Angeles	Needlepoints West	6227 W. 87th St.	(310) 670-4847	
Los Angeles	Pina Francioso	1417 S. Robertson Blvd.	(310) 858-3779	
Los Angeles	Sew Modern	10921 W. Pico Blvd.	(310) 446-4397	
Los Angeles	The Altered Stitch	12443 Magnolia Blvd.	(818) 980-1234	
Los Angeles	The Little Knittery	3195 Glendale Blvd.	(323) 663-3838	
Los Banos	JMG Fabric & Crafts	1044 6th St.	(209) 827-1808	
Los Gatos	Natural Expressions of Los Gatos	18 N. Santa Cruz Ave.	(408) 354-5330	
Los Gatos	Very Knit Shop	24 N. Santa Cruz Ave. Floor 2	(408) 354-1434	
Los Gatos	Why Knot Stitch	140 W. Main St. #C	(408) 839-1414	
Los Gatos	Yarndogs	151 E. Main St.	(408) 399-1909	
Magalia	Seams To B	14543 Grinnell Ct.	(530) 873-2670	
Manhattan Beach	Twist...Yarns of Intrigue	226 S. Sepulveda Blvd.	(310) 374-7810	

Manteca	Ladybug's Quilts	1236 N. Main St. #A	(209) 824-0485
Maricopa	Maricopa Quilt Company	370 California St.	(661) 769-8580
Marysville	Sew-n-Piece	410 4th St.	(530) 713-3822
Mendocino	Ocean Quilts of Mendocino	45270 Main St.	(707) 937-4201
Menlo Park	Old World Designs	727 Santa Cruz Ave.	(650) 321-3494
Mill Valley	Once Around	352 Miller Ave.	(415) 389-1667
Milpitas	The Intrepid Thread	1709 S. Main St.	(408) 649-3844
Mission Viejo	Moore's Sewing and Fabric	25390 Marguerite Pkwy.	(949) 580-2520
Mission Viejo	Yarn del Sol	24471 Alicia Pkwy. #2	(949) 581-9276
Modesto	Knitters Square	899 W. Roseburg	(209) 566-9119
Modesto	The Urban Sheep	899 W. Roseburg Ave.	(209) 522-7400
Montrose	Needle in a Haystack	2262 Honlulu Ave.	(818) 248-7686
Montrose	Quilt 'n' Things, Inc.	2411 Honolulu Ave.	(818) 957-2287
Morgan Hill	Continental Stitch	16375 Monterey St. #J	(408) 779-5885
Morgan Hill	Madonna Needle Works	15750 Vinyard Blvd. Ste. 170	(408) 776-6857
Morgan Hill	Quilts & Things	16985 Monterey St. #316	(408) 776-8438
Morgan Hill	Sew Bee It Quilting	94 San Pedro Ave.	(408) 778-5058
Morro Bay	LINA G'-All the Trimmings	468 Morro Bay Blvd.	(805) 772-7759
Morro Bay	Morro Fleece Works	1920 Main St.	(805) 772-9665
Morro Bay	The Cotton Ball	2830 Main St.	(805) 772-2646
Mountain View	Custom Handweavers	2263 Old Middlefield Way	(650) 967-0831
Mt. Shasta	**Weston's Quilting and Crafts**	**414 Chestnut St.**	**(530) 926-4021** Pg. 62
Murrieta	Primitive Gatherings Quilt Shop	26855 Jefferson Ave. Unit D	(951) 304-9787
Napa	Yarns on First	1305 1st St.	(707) 257-1363
Newbury Park	The Quilters' Studio	1090 Lawrence Dr. #101	(805) 480-3550
Newport Beach	Sheared Sheep	1665 Westcliff Dr. #A	(949) 722-7977
Nipomo	Creative Patches and Sewing	136 A&B N. Thompson Rd.	(805) 929-3704
Norco	Sewn Together	1700 Hammer Ave. #112	(951) 479-5121
Northridge	Candy's Quiltworks	8549 Reseda Blvd.	(818) 349-7397
Oakdale	A Quilters Place	7450 River Rd. #4	(209) 844-5070
Oakhurst	**Bear Paw Quilts & More**	**40761 Hwy. 41 Ste. 5**	**(559) 683-7397** Pg. 64
Oakland	A Verb for Keeping Warm	6328 San Pablo Ave.	(510) 595-8372
Oakland	Piedmont Fabric	4009 Piedmont Ave.	(510) 653-8015
Oakland	Piedmont Yarn & Apparel, LLC	4171 Piedmont Ave. #102	(510) 595-9595
Oceanside	Aretoy Quilts	4749 Oceanside Blvd. #A	(760) 630-9234
Ojai	Artful Living	107 S Signal St.	(805) 640-0800
Ojai	Designer Yarns	811 Tico Rd.	(805) 646-9915
Orange	Fabric Land	936 E. Lincoln Ave.	(714) 974-1214
Orange	Moore's Sewing Center	2265 N. Tustin Ave.	(714) 279-6830
Orange	Orange Quilt Bee	628 E Katella Ave.	(714) 639-3245
Orcutt	**Old Town Quilt Shop**	**165-A West Clark Ave.**	**(805) 938-5870** Pg. 67
Oroville	Pieces of Love Quilt Shop	2216 5th Ave.	(530) 990-0699
Pacific Grove	Back Porch Fabrics	157 Grand Ave.	(831) 375-4453
Palm Desert	**Monica's Quilt & Bead Creations**	**77780 Country Club Dr. Ste. C & D**	
			(760) 772-2400 Pg. 68
Palm Desert	Harriets' Yarns	777-80 County Club Dr. Ste. F	(760) 772-3333
Palm Desert	Ralph's Sewing & Vacuum	73941 Hwy. 111	(760) 568-2226
Palm Desert	The Quilters Faire	34500 Gateway Dr. #110	(760) 328-8737
Palm Desert	The Yarn Company of Palm Desert	73661 Hwy. 111, Ste. 1	(760) 341-7734
Palo Cedro	Blue Iris Quilt Shop	9348 Deschutes Rd.	(530) 547-2228
Paradise	Debbie's Quilt Shop	6455 Skyway	(530) 877-8458
Paradise	Knit Wits	6311 Skyway	(530) 877-9276
Paradise	Zel's Stitchery	1863 Lillian Ave.	(530) 872-3357
Pasadena	Abuelita's Knitting & Needlepoint	696 E. Colorado Blvd. #2	(626) 799-0355
Pasadena	New Moon Textiles	1756 E. Colorado Blvd.	(626) 578-9432
Pasadena	Skein, A Fine Yarn Store	1101 E. Wanut St.	(626) 577-2035
Paso Robles	Birch Fabrics	1244 Pine St. Ste. D	(805) 239-8888
Paso Robles	The Quiltery	1413 Riverside Ave. # B	(805) 227-4561
Patterson	Village Yarn & Etc.	32 S. 3rd St.	(209) 892-3786
Petaluma	Knitterly	1 Fourth St.	(707) 762-9276
Petaluma	Quilted Angel	200 G St.	(707) 763-0945
Pine Grove	Joy's Yarn Country	20483 St. Hwy. 88	(209) 296-7400
Pinole	BiStitchual	2406 San Pablo Ave.	(510) 964-7053
Pismo Beach	A Fine Yarn	859 Oak Park Blvd.	(805) 668-2200
Pismo Beach	Quiltin Cousins	330 Pomeroy Ave.	(805) 773-4988
Pismo Beach	The Sewing Café	541 Five Cities Dr.	(805) 295-6585
Placentia	The Sewing Center of Orange County	1239 E. Imperial Hwy.	(714) 993-2739
Placerville	High Sierra Quilters	1444 Broadway	(530) 622-9990
Placerville	Kelsey's Needle Krafts	447 Main St.	(530) 622-6205
Placerville	Lofty Lou's Yarn Shop	585 Main St.	(530) 642-2270
Pleasanton	Knit This, Purl That!	205 Main St. Ste. A	(925) 249-9276

Index

Point Arena	Casari Ranch Mercantile	250 Main St.	(707) 882-1908	
Port Reyes	Black Mountain Artisans	11245 Main St.	(415) 663-9130	
Porterville	Calico Mermaid	122 N. Main	(559) 793-2510	
Portola	**Blue Petunia Quilts and Gifts**	**74631 Hwy. 70**	**(530) 832-4026**	**Pg. 62**
Poway	Bits & Pieces	12625 Danielson Ct. #111	(858) 679-5880	
Poway	Paradise Sewing Center	12639 Poway Rd.	(858) 679-9808	
Quincy	The Woolroom	390 Jackson St.	(530) 283-0648	
Ramona	Ramona's Country Yarn Store	638 Main St.	(760) 789-7305	
Rancho Cordova	Rita Traxler Designs	11345 Trade Center Dr. #150	(916) 376-7138	
Rancho Cucamonga	Richard's Fabrics	8663 Baseline Rd.	(909) 987-6061	
Red Bluff	Stitch by Stitch	340 Hickory St. #B	(530) 200-3110	
Redding	**The Sewing Room**	**2665 Park Marina Dr.**	**(530) 246-2056**	**Pg. 62**
Redding	Ewe-Baa Street Yarns	1725 Yuba St. #101	(530) 246-9276	
Redding	Hokema's Sewing Center	2736 Bechelli Ln.	(530) 223-1970	
Redding	Sew Simple	2223 Larkspur Ln.	(530) 222-1845	
Redding	Village Sewing Redding	2167 Hilltop Dr. #D	(530) 691-4047	
Redlands	Hands on Knitting Center	922 New York St. #A	(909) 793-8712	
Redlands	Redlands Sewing Center Inc.	422 E. State St.	(909) 792-3994	
Redondo Beach	Custom Handweaving	228 Ave. D	(310) 316-0910	
Redondo Beach	L'Atelier	1722 S. Catalina Ave.	(310) 540-4440	
Reedley	**Mennonite Quilt Center**	**1012 G St.**	**(559) 638-3560**	**Pg. 64**
Ridgecrest	Quilt 'N Home	425 E. Ridgecrest Blvd.	(760) 371-9060	
Ridgecrest	The Quilted Quail	901 N. Heritage Dr. #104	(760) 446-7420	
Riverbank	Riverbank Quilt Company	3300 Santa Fe St.	(209) 502-1957	
Riverside	Designer Hand Knits	6850 Brockton Ave. Ste. 102	(951) 275-9711	
Riverside	Moore's Sewing Center	10357 Magnolia Ave. #L	(951) 688-6254	
Riverside	Raincross Fiber Arts	3498 University Ave.	(951) 684-5647	
Riverside	The Quilter's Cocoon	9901 Indiana Ave. # 104	(951) 351-0346	
Rocklin	Meissner Sewing Machine Co.	6848 Five Star Blvd. #6	(916) 791-2121	
Roseville	Got Your Goat Yarn Studio	1850 Douglas Blvd. #910	(916) 899-5416	
Sacramento	**Quilter's Corner**	**9792 B Business Park Dr.**	**(916) 366-6136**	**Pg. 63**
Sacramento	Fabric Garden	2654 Marconi Ave. #155	(916) 483-2955	
Sacramento	Meissner Sewing Machine Co.	2417 Cormorant Way	(916) 920-2121	
Sacramento	Rumpelstiltskin	1021 R St.	(916) 442-9225	
San Anselmo	Atelier Marin	217 San Anselmo Ave.	(415) 256-9618	
San Clemente	Strands Knitting Studio	111 Avendia Granada	(949) 496-4021	
San Diego	**Rosie's Calico Cupboard**	**7151 El Cajon Blvd. Ste. F**	**(619) 697-5758**	**Pg. 69**
San Diego	**Visions Art Museum**	**2825 Dewey Rd. #100**	**(619) 546-4872**	**Pg. 70**
San Diego	Aranitas Yarns by Sofia	2925 Lincoln Ave.	(619) 674-8480	
San Diego	Needlecraft Cottage	870 Grand Ave.	(858) 272-8185	
San Diego	Sew Hut	4226 Balboa Ave.	(858) 273-1377	
San Diego	South Park Dry Goods Co.	3010 Juniper St.	(619) 550-5765	
San Dimas	Beautiful Quilt Fabric.com	237 W. Bonita Ave. #B	(909) 592-9571	
San Francisco	Atelier Yarns	1945 Divisadero St.	(415) 771-1550	
San Francisco	Carolina Homespun	455 Lisbon St.	(800) 450-7786	
San Francisco	Carolina Homespun	455 Lisbon St.	(415) 584-7786	
San Francisco	Elaine Magnin Needlepoint Design	3310 Sacramento St.	(415) 931-3063	
San Francisco	Fabric Creation	1846 26th Ave.	(415) 731-7539	
San Francisco	Greenwich Yarn	2073 Greenwich St.	(415) 567-2535	
San Francisco	Imagiknit	3897 18th St.	(415) 621-6642	
San Francisco	Needlepoint Inc.	275 Post St. 3rd Floor	(415) 392-1622	
S. San Francisco	**Cottage Yarns**	**607 W. Orange Ave.**	**(650) 873-7371**	**Pg. 63**
San Jose	**San Jose Museum of Quilts & Textiles**			
		520 South 1ST St.	**(408) 971-0323**	**Pg. 63**
San Jose	Green Planet Yarn	1702 Meridian Ave. #H	(408) 620-1042	
San Jose	Kim's Embroidery	3830 Charter Park Dr. #F	(408) 264-7518	
San Juan Bautista	**Family Threads Quilt Shoppe**	**107 D The Alameda**	**(831) 623-0200**	**Pg. 63**
San Luis Obispo	Betty's Fabrics	1229 Carmel St.	(805) 543-1990	
San Luis Obispo	Picking Daisies	570 Higuera St. #120	(805) 783-2434	
San Luis Obispo	SLO Creative Studio	3595 Sueldo St. #100	(812) 345-1552	
San Luis Obispo	Yarns At The Adobe	964 Chorro St.	(805) 549-9276	
San Marcos	**Quilt in a Day**	**1955 Diamond St.**	**(760) 591-0929**	**Pg. 68**
San Marcos	Grand Country Quilters	801 Grand Ave. #1	(760) 471-1114	
San Marcos	Yarning for You	1001 West San Marcos Blvd. # 180	(760) 744-5648	
San Marino	A Stitch in Time	2465 Huntington Dr.	(626) 793-5217	
San Mateo	**Always Quilting**	**4230 Olympic Ave.**	**(650) 458-8580**	**Pg.63**
San Mateo	City Needlework	61 E. 4th Ave.	(650) 348-2151	
San Mateo	Luv 2 Stitch	715 Bermuda Dr.	(650) 571-9999	
San Mateo	Scruffy Quilts	11 37th Ave.	(650) 274-0292	

San Rafael	Come To The Point	10 California Ave.	(415) 485-4942
San Rafael	Dharma Trading Co.	1604 4th St.	(415) 456-1211
Santa Ana	Ursula's Yarn Boutique	2441 N. Tustin Ave. Ste. D	(714) 834-1908
Santa Barbara	Cardigans - A Knit Shop	3030 State St.	(805) 569-0531
Santa Barbara	Loop & Leaf	536 Brinkerhoff Ave.	(805) 845-4696
Santa Clara	Exclamation Point	1055 Monroe St.	(408) 246-3800
Santa Clarita	Craft Creations Knitting Studios	24631 Arch St.	(661) 291-1228
Santa Clarita	Creative Ewe	17733 Sierra Hwy.	(661) 250-4600
Santa Clarita	Queen Anne Stitches	20655 Soledad Canyon Rd. #30	(661) 286-1248
Santa Cruz	Golden Fleece	303 Potrero St. Bldg. 29, Ste. 101	(831) 426-1425
Santa Cruz	Hart's Fabric Center	1620 Seabright Ave.	(831) 423-5434
Santa Cruz	Judy's Sewing Center	806 Ocean St.	(831) 464-8181
Santa Cruz	The Swift Stitch	402 Ingalls St. # 12	(831) 427-9276
Santa Maria	Betty's Fabrics	1627 S. Broadway	(805) 922-2181
Santa Maria	Santa Maria Sewing	127 E. Main St.	(805) 922-1784
Santa Monica	Aristela Needlepoint	200 26th St.	(310) 260-6330
Santa Monica	Compatto Yarn Salon	112 Wilshire Blvd.	(310) 453-2130
Santa Monica	Sewing Arts Center	3330 Pico Blvd.	(310) 450-4300
Santa Monica	Wild Fiber	1453-E 14th St.	(310) 458-2748
Santa Rosa	**Village Sewing Center**	**1455 Santa Rosa Ave.**	**(707) 544-7529** Pg. 63
Santa Rosa	Cast Away	100 4th St.	(707) 546-9276
Santa Rosa	Renee Yarns	4801 Montgomery Dr.	(707) 538-1519
Sausalito	Bluebird Yarn & Fiber Crafts	325 Pine St.	(415) 331-9276
Sebastopol	Yarnitudes	3598 Gravenstein Hwy. S	(707) 827-3618
Simi Valley	Quilty Pleasures	1742 E. Los Angeles Ave.	(805) 581-1577
Solvang	Rasmussen's	1697 Copenhagen Dr.	(805) 688-6636
Solvang	Thumbelina Needlework	1683-A Copenhagen Dr.	(805) 688-4136
Solvang	Village Spinning & Weaving Shop	425 Alisal Rd. Ste. B	(805) 686-1192
Sonoma	Broadway Quilts	20525 Broadway	(707) 938-7312
Sonora	Bearly Quilting	13769 Mono Way #E	(209) 694-0226
Sonora	By Hand Yarn	106 S. Washington St.	(209) 694-8161
Sonora	Quail's Nest Quilt Company	14675 Mono Way	(209) 288-2392
Stockton	Quilters' Hollow	8807 Thornton Rd. #C-1	(209) 477-5253
Studio City	La Knitterie Parisienne	12642 Ventura Blvd.	(818) 766-1515
Studio City	Lani's Needlepoint	12416 Ventura Blvd.	(818) 769-2431
Sunnyvale	Eddie's Quilting Bee	480 S. Mathilda Ave.	(408) 830-9505
Sunnyvale	Purlescence Yarns	564 S. Murphy Ave.	(408) 735-9276
Sunnyvale	The Granary	1326 S. Mary Ave.	(408) 735-9830
Susanville	Country Pines Quilt Shop	704-395 Richmond Rd. E.	(530) 257-4071
Tarzana	NeedleHearts	18900 1/2 Ventura Blvd.	(818) 344-6277
Tarzana	Zoe Zeynep Knit Studio	18596 Ventura Blvd.	(818) 881-9637
Tehachapi	5 Heart Quilts	104 W. Tehachapi Blvd.	(661) 822-8709
Tehachapi	Debbie's Fabrics Etc.	112 E. Tehachapi Blvd.	(661) 823-7114
Temecula	Moore's Sewing Center	26490 Ynez Rd. #F&G	(951) 297-3796
Temecula	Needle in a Fabric Stash	43049 Margarita Rd. #A102	(951) 587-8274
Temecula	Temecula Quilt Co.	33353 Temecula Pkwy.	(951) 302-1469
Temecula	The Wool Lady	28690 Old Town Front St. #310	(951) 699-2900
Thousand Oaks	Cotton & Chocolate Quilt Company	1724 Avenida de los Arboles, Ste. E	(805) 241-0061
Thousand Oaks	Eva's Needlework	1321 E. Thousand Oaks Blvd. Ste. 120	(805) 379-0722
Thousand Oaks	Jackie's Gifts & Things	2087 Truett Circle	(805) 492-8658
Toluca Lake	Sit 'N Stitch	10154 Riverside Dr.	(818) 760-9330
Torrance	Concepts In Yarn & Needlepoint	24520 Hawthorne Blvd. Ste. 100	(310) 791-3800
Torrance	Maddie Made It	2929 Rolling Hills Rd.	(424) 263-5282
Torrance	Momen Plus	1323 El Prado Ave.	(310) 328-0500
Tracy	Roxy's Quilt & Sewing Oulet	1005 E. Pescadero Ave. Ste. 171	(209) 597-5989
Turlock	Cloth & Quilts	625 E. Main St.	(209) 632-3225
Tustin	Flying Geese Fabrics	307 El Camino Real	(714) 544-9349
Tustin	Mel's Sewing & Fabric Center	600 E. First St.	(714) 669-0583
Ukiah	Heidi's Yarn Haven	180 S. School St.	(707) 462-0544
Ukiah	Village Sewing of Ukiah	1252 Airport Park Blvd.	(707) 467-9383
Upland	Needles & Niceties	1655 N. Mountain Ave. #116	(909) 985-6264
Upland	Upland Vac & Sew	113 N. 2nd Ave.	(909) 949-4884
Vacaville	**A Quilted Heart**	**878 Alamo Dr.**	**(707) 447-9000** Pg. 63
Vacaville	The Loom Room	273 Markham Ave.	(707) 448-5869
Vallejo	Keeping You In Stitches	231 Ramsgate Way	(707) 649-2881
Valley Center	**Inspirations Quilt Shop**	**27350 Valley Center Rd. #B**	**(760) 751-9400** Pg. 68
Van Nuys	A-Major-Knitwork	6746 Balboa Blvd.	(818) 787-2659
Ventura	Anacapa Fine Yarns	4572 Telephone Rd. Ste. 909	(805) 654-9500
Ventura	Quilt Ventura	4572 Telephone Rd. Ste. 908	(805) 658-9800
Ventura	superbuzzy	1794 E. Main St.	(805) 643-4143
Visalia	**Thimble Towne**	**400 W. Caldwell Ave. #F**	**(559) 627-5778** Pg. 65

Index

Index

Vista	Fat Quarters Quilt Shop	728 Civic Center Dr.	(760) 758-8308
Weaverville	Sweet Sheep	515 Main St.	(530) 623-8650
Whittier	The Yarn Garden	7648 Painter Ave. #B	(562) 698-1593
Willows	Quilt Corral	245 W. Wood St.	(530) 934-8116
Winters	Cloth Carousel	9 Main St.	(530) 795-2580
Winters	Cloth Carousel Quilt Shop	14 Main St.	(530) 794-6114
Woodland Hills	The Quilt Emporium	4918 Topanga Canyon Blvd.	(818) 704-8238
Yorba Linda	Velona Needlecraft	22435 La Palma Ave. #A	(714) 692-2286
Yuba City	Sew So Shop	787 Plumas St.	(530) 742-7626
Yucca Valley	Mimi's Quilt	55922 29 Palms Hwy.	(760) 365-1744
Yucca Valley	Quilting Between Friends	7379 Hopi Tr.	(760) 365-4519

Notes

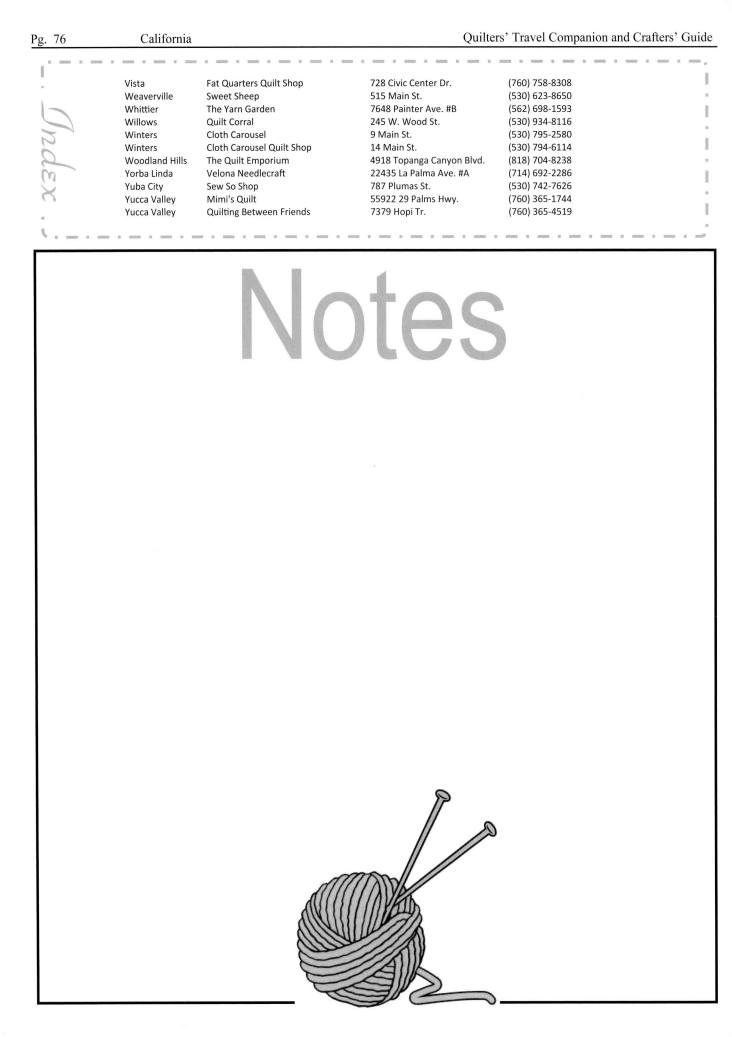

Colorado

Did you know that Pikes Peak
is 14,114 feet in elevation?

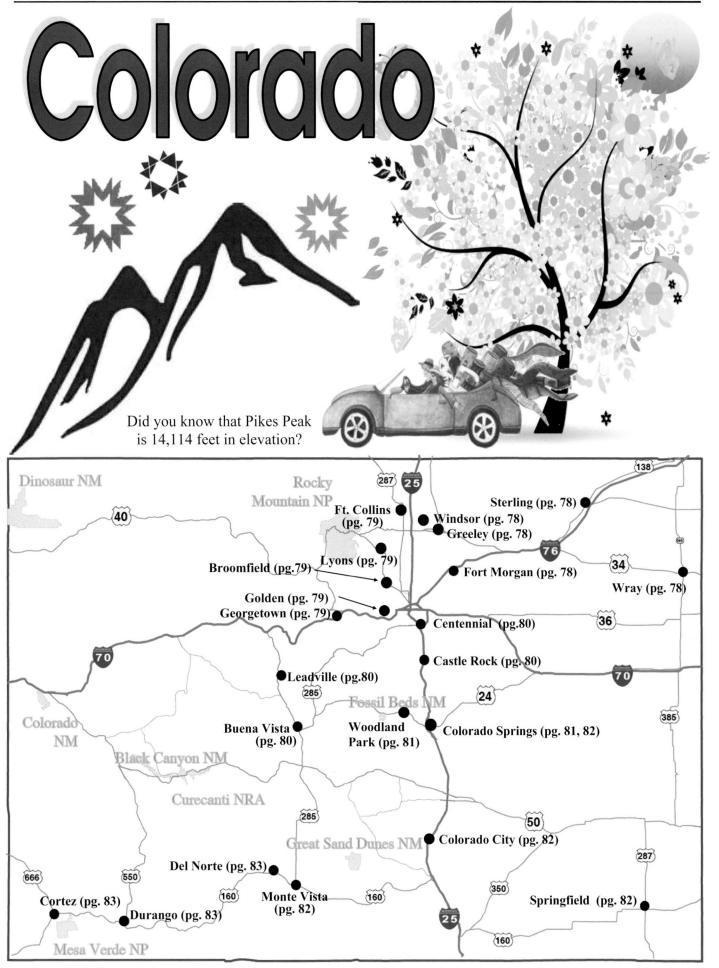

Dinosaur NM

Rocky
Mountain NP

Sterling (pg. 78)

Ft. Collins
(pg. 79)

Windsor (pg. 78)
Greeley (pg. 78)

Broomfield (pg.79)

Lyons (pg. 79)

Fort Morgan (pg. 78)

Wray (pg. 78)

Golden (pg. 79)
Georgetown (pg. 79)

Centennial (pg.80)

Castle Rock (pg. 80)

Leadville (pg.80)

Colorado
NM

Fossil Beds NM

Black Canyon NM

Buena Vista
(pg. 80)

Woodland
Park (pg. 81)

Colorado Springs (pg. 81, 82)

Curecanti NRA

Great Sand Dunes NM

Colorado City (pg. 82)

Del Norte (pg. 83)

Cortez (pg. 83)

Durango (pg. 83)

Monte Vista
(pg. 82)

Springfield (pg. 82)

Mesa Verde NP

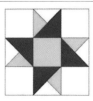

Did you know?
Colorado's southwest corner borders Arizona, New Mexico and Utah
the only place in America where the corners of four states meet.

The Colorado Rockies play at the 50,000 seat Coors Field, located in downtown Denver.

Did you know?
The headwater on twenty rivers begins in Colorado, with the Continental Divide directing each river's course.

Woodland Park, CO   Q

Nuts 'n Bolts
N E E D L E W O R K S

200 S. Chestnut St.
Woodland Park, CO. 80863
719-687-2272
marsha.mccain@gmail.com
www.nutsnboltsneedleworks.com

A Beautiful Mountain Drive to a fun and
welcoming quilt shop that is geared
towards wild animals. Cross Stitch and
Floss also available.

Monday-Saturday
10:00-5:00

Nuts N Bolts
To Colorado Springs
HWY. 67
U.S. 24
Gold Hills Shopping Center

Nanas Quilt Cottage

Established 2010 in Historic Old Colorado City.
Come see patterns, books, quilting notions,
kits, samples, and beautiful fabric in our
bright and cheerful shop!
Row by Row Participant!

"Get Creative at Nanas!"

Colorado Springs, CO   QN

www.nanasquiltcottage.com
35 S. 26th St. Colorado Springs, CO 80904
(719) 634-9500
Monday - Saturday 10am - 5pm

Nana's in the Old Colorado City Historic District
Febras
Colorado Ave.
26th St.
U.S. 24
Auto Parts
Exit 141
I-25
Approx. 2 miles from I-25

Husqvarna   **VIKING**

RUTH'S Stitchery

4440 Austin Bluffs Pkwy. Colorado Springs, CO 80918
Toll Free **(888) 591-8803** or (719) 591-1717
Owners: Catherine Culp & Beth Spillane
RStitchery@pcisys.net

www.ruthsstitchery.com

Better Homes & Gardens
Quilt Sampler
TOP SHOP

- ◆ Hand & Machine Quilting
- ◆ Beginning to Advanced Quilting
- ◆ Cross Stitch Supplies
- ◆ Over 7000 Bolts
- ◆ Book and Patterns
- ◆ Visit our Web Site to View our Class Schedule

Handi Quilter
Designed by a Quilter, for Quilters.

Designer **EPIC**

Authorized Husqvarna Viking Sewing Machine / Serger
Dealer and Service center for Colorado Springs area.

"New neighbors…WOODCRAFT has moved in next door!"

Monday-Saturday 9:00-6:00,
Sunday 12:00-5:00

Old Chicago
Academy Blvd.
Ruth's Stitchery
Restaurants
4440
Austin Bluffs Pkwy.
Barnes

The Broadmoor Hotel
A luxury resort with a spirit of adventure

Since first opening their doors nearly a century ago, the Broadmoor has
offered guest an incredible way to experience the unique beauty of the
American West. Today, that tradition is met with warm, genuine hospitality
and an unmatched selection of programs and activities that
celebrate their magnificent surroundings. For the active guest, they offer 54
holes of legendary golf, a world-renowned tennis program, hiking,
horseback riding, mountain biking, archery, canoeing, fly fishing, rock
climbing, falconry and more. For a more tranquil retreat they have
multiple resort pools, a Forbes Travel Guide Five-Star Spa, and several
restaurants, including Colorado's only Forbes Five-Star,
AAA Five-Diamond restaurant. There is always something new
and exciting to discover at "the most unique resort in the world."

1 Lake Ave, Colorado Springs, CO 80906 (855) 634-7711
www.broadmoor.com

Did you know?
Colorado's first and oldest military post, Fort Garland was established in 1858 and
commanded by the legendary frontiersman Kit Carson.

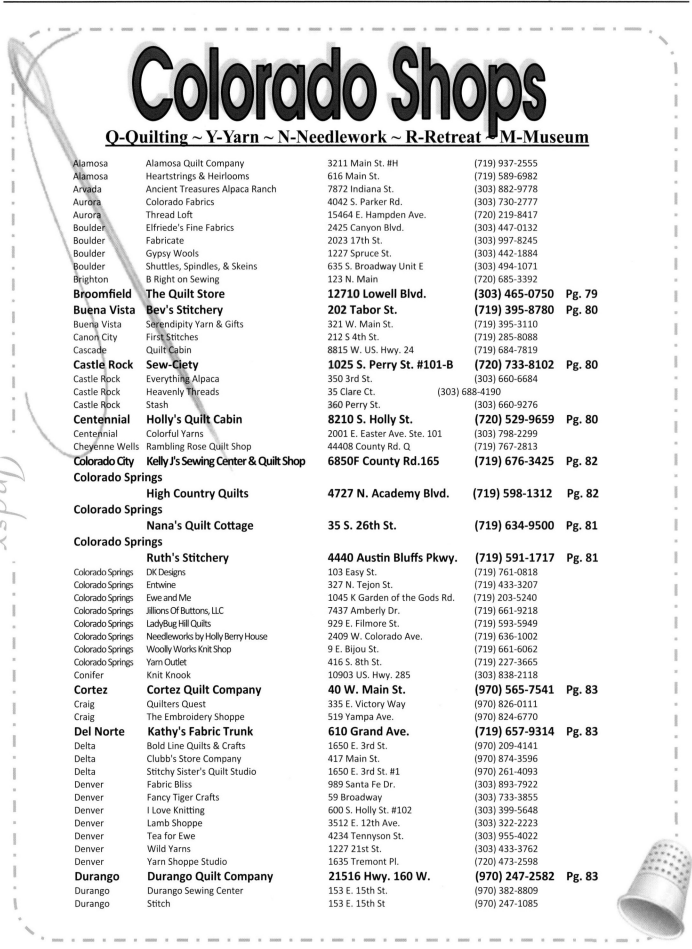

Colorado Shops

Q-Quilting ~ Y-Yarn ~ N-Needlework ~ R-Retreat ~ M-Museum

City	Shop	Address	Phone	Page
Alamosa	Alamosa Quilt Company	3211 Main St. #H	(719) 937-2555	
Alamosa	Heartstrings & Heirlooms	616 Main St.	(719) 589-6982	
Arvada	Ancient Treasures Alpaca Ranch	7872 Indiana St.	(303) 882-9778	
Aurora	Colorado Fabrics	4042 S. Parker Rd.	(303) 730-2777	
Aurora	Thread Loft	15464 E. Hampden Ave.	(720) 219-8417	
Boulder	Elfriede's Fine Fabrics	2425 Canyon Blvd.	(303) 447-0132	
Boulder	Fabricate	2023 17th St.	(303) 997-8245	
Boulder	Gypsy Wools	1227 Spruce St.	(303) 442-1884	
Boulder	Shuttles, Spindles, & Skeins	635 S. Broadway Unit E	(303) 494-1071	
Brighton	B Right on Sewing	123 N. Main	(720) 685-3392	
Broomfield	**The Quilt Store**	**12710 Lowell Blvd.**	**(303) 465-0750**	**Pg. 79**
Buena Vista	**Bev's Stitchery**	**202 Tabor St.**	**(719) 395-8780**	**Pg. 80**
Buena Vista	Serendipity Yarn & Gifts	321 W. Main St.	(719) 395-3110	
Canon City	First Stitches	212 S 4th St.	(719) 285-8088	
Cascade	Quilt Cabin	8815 W. US. Hwy. 24	(719) 684-7819	
Castle Rock	**Sew-Ciety**	**1025 S. Perry St. #101-B**	**(720) 733-8102**	**Pg. 80**
Castle Rock	Everything Alpaca	350 3rd St.	(303) 660-6684	
Castle Rock	Heavenly Threads	35 Clare Ct.	(303) 688-4190	
Castle Rock	Stash	360 Perry St.	(303) 660-9276	
Centennial	**Holly's Quilt Cabin**	**8210 S. Holly St.**	**(720) 529-9659**	**Pg. 80**
Centennial	Colorful Yarns	2001 E. Easter Ave. Ste. 101	(303) 798-2299	
Cheyenne Wells	Rambling Rose Quilt Shop	44408 County Rd. Q	(719) 767-2813	
Colorado City	**Kelly J's Sewing Center & Quilt Shop**	**6850F County Rd.165**	**(719) 676-3425**	**Pg. 82**
Colorado Springs	**High Country Quilts**	**4727 N. Academy Blvd.**	**(719) 598-1312**	**Pg. 82**
Colorado Springs	**Nana's Quilt Cottage**	**35 S. 26th St.**	**(719) 634-9500**	**Pg. 81**
Colorado Springs	**Ruth's Stitchery**	**4440 Austin Bluffs Pkwy.**	**(719) 591-1717**	**Pg. 81**
Colorado Springs	DK Designs	103 Easy St.	(719) 761-0818	
Colorado Springs	Entwine	327 N. Tejon St.	(719) 433-3207	
Colorado Springs	Ewe and Me	1045 K Garden of the Gods Rd.	(719) 203-5240	
Colorado Springs	Jillions Of Buttons, LLC	7437 Amberly Dr.	(719) 661-9218	
Colorado Springs	LadyBug Hill Quilts	929 E. Filmore St.	(719) 593-5949	
Colorado Springs	Needleworks by Holly Berry House	2409 W. Colorado Ave.	(719) 636-1002	
Colorado Springs	Woolly Works Knit Shop	9 E. Bijou St.	(719) 661-6062	
Colorado Springs	Yarn Outlet	416 S. 8th St.	(719) 227-3665	
Conifer	Knit Knook	10903 US. Hwy. 285	(303) 838-2118	
Cortez	**Cortez Quilt Company**	**40 W. Main St.**	**(970) 565-7541**	**Pg. 83**
Craig	Quilters Quest	335 E. Victory Way	(970) 826-0111	
Craig	The Embroidery Shoppe	519 Yampa Ave.	(970) 824-6770	
Del Norte	**Kathy's Fabric Trunk**	**610 Grand Ave.**	**(719) 657-9314**	**Pg. 83**
Delta	Bold Line Quilts & Crafts	1650 E. 3rd St.	(970) 209-4141	
Delta	Clubb's Store Company	417 Main St.	(970) 874-3596	
Delta	Stitchy Sister's Quilt Studio	1650 E. 3rd St. #1	(970) 261-4093	
Denver	Fabric Bliss	989 Santa Fe Dr.	(303) 893-7922	
Denver	Fancy Tiger Crafts	59 Broadway	(303) 733-3855	
Denver	I Love Knitting	600 S. Holly St. #102	(303) 399-5648	
Denver	Lamb Shoppe	3512 E. 12th Ave.	(303) 322-2223	
Denver	Tea for Ewe	4234 Tennyson St.	(303) 955-4022	
Denver	Wild Yarns	1227 21st St.	(303) 433-3762	
Denver	Yarn Shoppe Studio	1635 Tremont Pl.	(720) 473-2598	
Durango	**Durango Quilt Company**	**21516 Hwy. 160 W.**	**(970) 247-2582**	**Pg. 83**
Durango	Durango Sewing Center	153 E. 15th St.	(970) 382-8809	
Durango	Stitch	153 E. 15th St	(970) 247-1085	

Durango	Yarn Durango	755 E. Second Ave.	(970) 259-9827	
Englewood	Blazing Star Ranch	3424 S. Broadway	(303) 514-8780	
Englewood	Diversions Needlepoint	1610 E. Girard Place #G	(303) 761-7766	
Englewood	Wooden Spools Quilting & More!	2805 S. Broadway	(303) 761-9231	
Erie	A Quilter's Corner	71 Erie Pkwy. #104	(720) 328-8181	
Estes Park	Cottage Bliss	870-A Moraine Ave. Hwy. 36	(970) 577-1557	
Estes Park	Neota Designs Studio & Gallery	156 Wiest Dr.	(970) 586-8800	
Estes Park	The Stitchin' Den	165 Virginia Dr.	(970) 577-8210	
Evergreen	Crafty Lady Quilts	28566 Clover Ln.	(303) 674-3126	
Fort Collins	**The Sewing Circle**	**2948 Council Tree Ave.**	**(970) 672-2147**	**Pg. 79**
Fort Collins	Lambspun of Colorado	1101 E. Lincoln Ave.	(970) 484-1998	
Fort Collins	My Sister Knits	1408 W. Mountain Ave.	(970) 407-1461	
Fort Collins	The Fig Leaf	2834 S. College Ave.	(970) 495-1766	
Fort Collins	The Loopy Ewe	2720 Council Tree Ave. #255	(970) 568-5290	
Fort Collins	The Presser Foot	1833 E. Harmony #1A	(970) 484-1094	
Fort Morgan	**Inspirations Quilt Shop**	**423 Main St. #300**	**(970) 542-0810**	**Pg. 78**
Fountain	Na-La's Quilt Shoppe	117 S. Main St.	(719) 382-6252	
Ft. Collins	Your Daily Fiber	4019 S. Mason	(970) 484-2414	
Georgetown	**The Quilted Purl**	**707 Taos St.**	**(303) 569-1115**	**Pg. 79**
Golden	**Golden Quilt Company**	**1108 Washington Ave.**	**(303) 277-0717**	**Pg. 79**
Golden	**The Rocky Mountain Quilt Museum**	**200 Violet St.**	**(303) 215-9001**	**Pg. 79**
Golden	Creative Crafts Group	741 Corporate Cir. Ste. A	(303) 215-5600	
Golden	The Craft Box	16399 S. Golden Rd. #A	(303) 279-1069	
Golden	The Recycled Lamb	2081 Youngfield St.	(303) 234-9337	
Granby	Fabric Nook	387 E. Agate Ave.	(970) 887-2005	
Granby	Lonesome Stone	946 County Rd. 60	(970) 887-9591	
Grand Junction	Busy Bea Quilter	527 Bogart Ln.	(970) 250-7071	
Grand Lake	Cabin Quilts & Stitches	908 Grand Ave.	(970) 627-3810	
Greeley	**Sew Downtown**	**3820 W. 10th #B**	**(970) 352-9230**	**Pg. 78**
Highlands Ranch	Highland Ranch String	9325 Dorchester St. Ste. 121	(720) 344-9276	
Holyoke	Creative Traditions	115 S. Interocean	(970) 854-3699	
Hotchkiss	Sew Many Quilts	29503 Hwy. 92	(970) 250-3362	
Hudson	Country Cottage Quilt Shoppe	14755 Imboden Rd.	(720) 257-5558	
Ignacio	Navajo Lake Alpacas	1060 County Rd. 329	(970) 883-3635	
Lafayette	Mew Mew's Yarn Shop LLC	2770 Dagny Way #108	(303) 665-5591	
Lakewood	Showers of Flowers Yarn Shop	6900 W. Colfax Ave.	(303) 233-2525	
Leadville	**Mtn. Top Quilts**	**129 E. Seventh St.**	**(719) 486-3454**	**Pg. 80**
Leadville	Fire on the Mountain	715 Harrison Ave.	(719) 486-2071	
Littleton	A Knitted Peace, LLC	5654-C S. Prince St.	(303) 730-0366	
Littleton	Craft Scraps	1500 W. Littleton Blvd. #113	(303) 798-2192	
Littleton	The Creative Needle	6905 S. Broadway #113	(303) 794-7312	
Longmont	Longmont Yarn Shoppe	454 Main St.	(303) 678-8242	
Longmont	Quality Sewing, Inc	1450 Main St.	(303) 651-7752	
Longmont	The Presser Foot	2430 Main St.	(303) 485-6681	
Louisville	Fingerplay Studio	901 Front St. #135	(303) 604-4374	
Loveland	Quilters Dream	517 N. Denver Ave.	(970) 461-3452	
Lyons	**Lyons Quilting**	**42 E. Main St.**	**(303) 823-6067**	**Pg. 79**
Merino	D & J Country Antiques	32093 County Rd. 31	(970) 842-5813	
Monte Vista	**Shades, Quilts, & Etc**	**129 Adams St.**	**(719) 852-2179**	**Pg. 82**
Montrose	Fabrics & More	341 N. 1st St.	(970) 240-6089	
Montrose	LadyBugz Quilt Company	330 S. 8th St	(970) 249-1600	
Monument	Frankie's Fabric Shoppe	252 Front St.	(719) 418-3614	
Monument	Peak Ranch Alpaca Boutique	19850 Beacon Lite Rd.	(719) 232-8509	
Palmer Lake	Sew Motion - Fabric Notions & More	862 Hwy. 105	(719) 481-1565	
Palmer Lake	Yarn Bird Fibers	790 Hwy. 105 #C	(719) 377-0403	
Paonia	Desert Weyr, LLC	16870 Garvin Mesa Rd.	(970) 527-3573	
Parker	High Prairie Quilts	18870 E. Plaza Dr.	(303) 627-0878	
Parker	Purls of Wisdom	18671 E. Main St. #E	(303) 805-3736	
Pueblo	Artisan Textile Co.	113 Broadway Ave.	(719) 744-6696	
Pueblo	Creative Sewing Design	2729 Elizabeth	(719) 562-0385	
Pueblo	Stitcher's Garden	308 S. Union Ave.	(719) 545-3320	
Rifle	The Fabric Store	160 E. 26th Ave.	(970) 618-9221	
Salida	Fringe	139 F St.	(719) 539-4006	
Springfield	**Justa Stitchin' LLC**	**1173 Main St.**	**(719)523-4985**	**Pg. 82**
St. Littleton	A Quilters Choice	5787 S. Gallup	(435) 229-2703	
Steamboat Springs	Sew Steamboat	929 Lincoln Ave.	(970) 879-3222	
Sterling	**Quilts-N-Creations**	**125 N. 2nd St.**	**(970) 522-0146**	**Pg. 78**
Sterling	Fiberspace	113 N. 2nd St.	(970) 521-9041	
Stratton	Benay's Country Quiltin'	32131 County Rd. HH	(970) 362-4650	

Index

Index

Walsenburg	Edla's Yarns	302 W. 7th St.	(719) 738-3318	
Windsor	**Quilter's Stash**	**1180 W. Ash St. Ste. 100**	**(970) 686-5657**	**Pg. 78**
Windsor	Mazown	36758 Weld County Rr. 15	(970) 689-4414	
Windsor	The Black Wool Shop	429 Main St.	(970) 460-9309	
Woodland Park				
	Nuts 'n Bolts Needleworks	**200 S. Chestnut St.**	**(719) 687-2272**	**Pg. 81**
Woodland Park	Nikki's Knots	301 US. 24	(719) 686-6424	
Wray	**Rainbow Fabrics and Crafts**	**409 Main St.**	**(970) 332-4343**	**Pg. 78**
Wray	You Keep Me In Stitches	355 W. 2nd St.	(970) 630-2856	

Notes

The Stanley Hotel

**Listed on the National Register of Historic Places and a member of Historic Hotels of America, The Stanley Hotel is famous for its old-world charm. Multiple renovations have restored this 140-room hotel to its original grandeur while offering over 14,000 square feet of sophisticated meeting and event space equipped with modern amenities.
Only an hour away from Denver, it is the ideal destination for your Colorado getaway!**

**333 Wonderview Ave, Estes Park, CO 80517   (970) 577-4000
www.stanleyhotel.com**

Vernon (pg. 87)

Berlin (pg. 87)

Connecticut

Connecticut Mosaic
Quilt Block

Connecticut Shops

Q-Quilting ~ Y-Yarn ~ N-Needlework ~ R-Retreat ~ M-Museum

Avon	Knit & Pearls	395 W. Avon Rd.	(860) 404-0694	
Avon	The Village Needlecrafts	19 E. Main St.	(860) 678-1882	
Berlin	**Lisa's Clover Hill Quilts**	**27 Webster Square Rd.**	**(860) 828-9325**	**Pg. 87**
Bethel	A Stitch in Time	276 Greenwood Ave.	(203) 748-1002	
Bethel	Homestead Quilts	101 Elizabeth St.	(203) 744-3118	
Bethlehem	Yarns for Ewe	22 Cowles Rd.	(203) 266-7062	
Bozrah	Mothers of Purl Yarns	441 Salem Tpke.	(860) 823-0434	
Branford	The Yarn Basket	288 E. Main St.	(203) 208-3288	
Bristol	New England Yarn and Spindle LLC	801 Terryville Ave.	(860) 516-4646	
Canterbury	Burgis Brook Alpacas	44 N. Canterbury Rd.	(203) 605-0588	
Colchester	Colchester Mill Fabrics	120 Lebanon Ave.	(860) 537-2004	
Danbury	Pieceful Acre Needlearts	66 Sugar Hollow Rd.	(203) 733-9772	
Danbury	Stitch in Time Sewing Center	19 Sugar Hollow Rd.	(203) 748-7283	
Danielson	The Velvet Tomato at Heart & Home	65 Main St.	(860) 774-2623	
Darien	House of Needlepoint	839 Post Rd.	(203) 655-9112	
Eastford	Still River Fiber Mill LLC	210 Eastford Rd.	(860) 974-9918	
Fairfield	Poster's Arts & Crafts	2353 Black Rock Tpke.	(203) 372-0717	
Glastonbury	Close to Home	2717 Main St.	(860) 633-0721	
Glastonbury	Thistle Needleworks	1005 Hebron Ave.	(860) 633-8503	
Granby	Marji's Yarncrafts	381 Salmon Brook St.	(860) 653-9700	
Haddam	Connecticut Yarn & Wool Co.	85 Bridge Rd.	(860) 575-9050	
Kent	Black Sheep Yarns	12 Old Barn Rd.	(860) 927-3808	
Madison	Cate's Sew Modern	266 Boston Post Rd.	(203) 421-6853	
Madison	Madison Wool	56A Wall St.	(203) 245-5921	
Middletown	Pamela Roose, Specialty Hand Knits & Yarn	88 Court St.	(860) 788-2715	
Monroe	The Bolt Quilt Shop	150 Main St.	(203) 445-2658	
Mystic	CT Quilt Works	27 Coogan Blvd. Bldg. 1C	(860) 245-0111	
Mystic	Driftwood Yarns	29 1/2 Broadway Ave.	(860) 415-8118	
Mystic	Mystic River Yarns, LLC	14 Holmes St.	(860) 536-4305	
Mystic	Needlepoint Nook of Mystic	2 Pearl St.	(860) 536-7380	
Naugatuck	Lula's Melange	26 Church St.	(203) 723-9276	
New Canaan	It's A Stitch	33 Stonehenge Dr.	(203) 972-3844	
New Hartford	Quilted Ewe	37 Greenwoods Rd.	(860) 379-3260	
New Haven	Knit New Haven	26 Whitney Ave.	(203) 777-5648	
Newtown	The Quilt Shop by Lois	12 Queen St.	(203) 270-0341	
North Franklin	Stitch Chicks Quilt Shop	43 Manning Rd.	(860) 642-8099	
Norwalk	Christie's Quilting Boutique	176 Main St.	(203) 807-8458	
Old Greenwich	The Village Ewe	244 Sound Beach Ave.	(203) 637-3953	
Old Saybrook	Coastal Sewing Machines & Fabrics	27 N. Main St.	(860) 388-1832	
Old Saybrook	My Friends and Me	1712 Boston Post Rd.	(860) 853-8601	
Old Saybrook	Saybrook Yarn	99 Main St.	(860) 388-3415	
Old Saybrook	Sudberry House	323 Boston Post Rd.	(860) 388-9045	
Orange	Close To Home	196 Boston Post Rd.	(203) 878-1654	
Ridgefield	Nancy O	23 Catoonah St.	(203) 431-2266	
Rocky Hill	Affordable Fabrics	2119 Silar Deane Hwy.	(860) 563-7647	
Scotland	Pins to Needles	6 Huntington Rd.	(860) 450-4440	
Seymour	Yankee Quilter	5 Klarides Village Dr.	(203) 888-9196	
Simsbury	Caroline's Quilts	542 Hopmeadow St. #119	(860) 658-4677	
Simsbury	Sew Inspired Quilt Shop	8 Wilcox St.	(860) 651-8885	
Somers	Knitting Criations	60 Springfield Rd.	(860) 749-4005	
South Woodstock	Whispering Hill Needlecraft	Rte. 169, 18 Castle Rock Rd.	(860) 928-0162	
Southington	Close to Home	995 Queen St.	(860) 793-6639	
Torrington	In Sheep's Clothing	10 Water St.	(860) 482-3979	
Vernon	**Quilting By The Yard**	**435-O Hartford Tpke.**	**(860) 896-1056**	**Pg. 87**
Vernon	Knit Two-Gether	435 K Harford Tpke.	(860) 870-3883	
Wallingford	Yankee Cloth	411 Center St.	(203) 265-1932	
Westport	Westport Yarns	582 Post Rd. E.	(203) 454-4300	
Wilton	The Enriched Stitch	196 Danbury Rd.	(203) 210-5107	
Windsor	Creative Fibers, LLC	645 A Poquonock Ave.	(860) 687-9931	
Woodbridge	The Yarn Barn	1666 Litchfield Tpke.	(203) 389-5117	

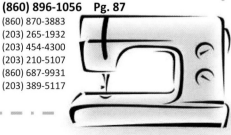

Delaware

Wilmington (pg. 90)

Dover (pg. 90)

Dover Quilt Block

Bethany Beach (pg. 89)

Dagsboro (pg. 89)

Did you know?
Delaware is the only state without a national park.

Delaware Shops

Q-Quilting ~ Y-Yarn ~ N-Needlework ~ R-Retreat ~ M-Museum

Bear	Milady Creates	152 Cornwell Dr.	(302) 983-5700	
Bethany Beach	**Sea Needles**	**780 Garfield Pkwy.**	**(302) 539-0574**	**Pg. 89**
Bridgeville	Terry Miller Designs	8010 Cannon Rd.	(302) 629-6329	
Dagsboro	**Serendipity Quilt Shop**	**31821 Cannon St.**	**(302) 732-6304**	**Pg. 89**
Dover	**Shady Lane Selections LLC**	**1121 B Victory Chapel Rd.**	**(302) 674-3623**	**Pg. 90**
Dover	Chicks -n- Stitches	1151 E. Lebanon Rd. #F	(302) 535-8438	
Dover	Delaware Sewing Center **	1716 S. Governors Ave.	(302) 674-9030	
Lewes	Mare's Bears Quilt Shop	528 E. Savannah Rd.	(302) 644-0556	
Middletown	Lil' Country Shoppe	551 Boyds Corner Rd.	(302) 378-5568	
Newark	Blue Hen Quilt Shop	73 Marrows Rd.	(302) 533-5215	
Newark	Stitches With Style	16-E Polly Drummond Shopping Center		
			(302) 453-8130	
Rehoboth Beach	Kitschy Stitch	413 Rehoboth Ave.	(302) 260-9138	
Seaford	Butler's Sewing Center, Inc.	1023 W. Stein Hwy.	(302) 629-9155	
Wilmington	**Hayes Sewing Machine Co.**	**4425 Concord Pike**	**(302) 764-9033**	**Pg. 90**

Hotel Du Pont

Once an architectural icon, an internationally renowned hotel, and the pride of Delaware, Hotel Du Pont has many stories to tell. Nestled in the heart of Wilmington, Delaware and the picturesque Brandywine Valley, one of the country's grandest hotels is as rich in history and tradition as it is in atmosphere. The twelve-story Italian Renaissance building debuted in 1913 after a two-and-a-half-year labor of love by French and Italian craftsmen who carved, gilded and painted this exceptional landmark to life. From the lavish splendor of the lobby to the shimmering majesty of the Gold Ballroom, every detail speaks to an eye for flawless style.

42 West 11th St, Wilmington, DE 19801 (302) 594-3100
www.hoteldupont.com

District of Columbia

| Washington | Looped Yarn Works | 1732 Connecticut Ave. NW #200 | (202) 714-5667 |
| Washington | Point Of It All | 5232 44th St. NW #1 | (202) 966-9898 |

Florida

Cumberland Island NS

Timucuan Ecological and Historical

Jacksonville (pg. 92)

Orange Park (pg. 92)

St. Augustine (pg. 93)

Ormond Beach (pg. 93)

Canaveral NS

Maitland (pg. 94)

Melbourne (pg. 94)

Sebastian (pg. 95)

Greenacres (pg. 98)

Boca Raton (pg. 98)

Fort Lauderdale (pg. 98)

Biscayne NP

Plant City (pg. 94)

Temple Terrace (pg. 95)

Sebring (pg. 95)

Everglades NP

Big Cypress N PRES

Key West (pg. 98)

Lake City (pg. 92)

Chiefland (pg. 93)

Brooksville (pg. 93)

Dade City (pg. 94)

Zephyrhills (pg. 93)

Clearwater (pg. 96)

St. Petersburg (pg. 97)

Palmetto (pg. 97)

Venice (pg. 98)

Tallahassee Quilt Block

Tallahassee (pg. 92)

Crestview (pg. 92)

Gulf Islands NS

Pensacola (pg. 92)

Did you know?
The United States city with the highest rate of lightning
strikes per capita is Clearwater.

Quilts on Plum Lane

Located in Dade City's Downtown Antique District. Large selection of Books & Patterns, notions, classes. New Brand-Name 100% Cottons, Flannels, Batiks & Kits.

14215 7th St.
Dade City, FL 33523
(352) 518-0003

Monday - Saturday
10am - 5pm
Thursday til 7pm
1st Saturday til 7pm

Fax: (352) 518-0022
plumlanedl@cs.com
Owner: Donna Lillibridge
Mgr. Carol Bradshaw
Est: 2003

Quilts on Plum Lane
7th St.
I-75
Meridian
Hwy. 301

www.quiltsonplumlane.net

Melbourne, FL   Q

quilts and lace
where it's always a... *Sweet Time Quilting*

7720 N. Wickham Rd. #111 Melbourne, FL 32940
(321) 622-8602
Authorized full-line retailer for Baby Lock, Brother, Koala, Anita Goodesign, Floriani and DIME. Quilting fabrics and supplies. Classes and events.
www.quiltsandlace.com
Mon, Wed, Fri 10:00-5:00, Tue 10:00-7:00, Sat 10:00-2:00

Inspire!
Quilting
Sewing

101 N. Collins Street
Plant City, FL 33563
(813) 704-4867
Monday-Friday
10:00-5:00
Saturday 9:00-4:00

www.inspirequiltingandsewing.com

Many full collections of fabrics from the top manufacturers. A huge assortment of solids and blenders. The newest notions and LOTS of patterns and books. An Anita Goodesigns Dealer. Classes for all skill levels.

brother. at your side

Plant City, FL   Q

Did you know ?
Key West has the highest average temperature in the United States.

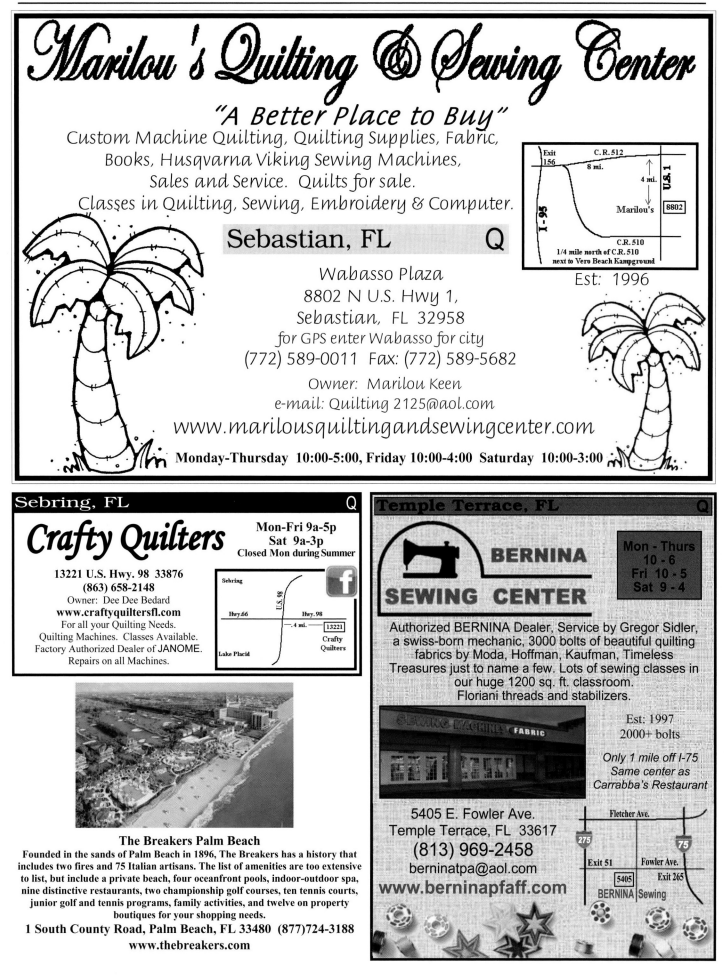

Marilou's Quilting & Sewing Center

"A Better Place to Buy"

Custom Machine Quilting, Quilting Supplies, Fabric,
Books, Husqvarna Viking Sewing Machines,
Sales and Service. Quilts for sale.
Classes in Quilting, Sewing, Embroidery & Computer.

Sebastian, FL　　　　　Q

Wabasso Plaza
8802 N U.S. Hwy 1,
Sebastian, FL 32958
for GPS enter Wabasso for city
(772) 589-0011 Fax: (772) 589-5682

Owner: Marilou Keen
e-mail: Quilting 2125@aol.com
www.marilousquiltingandsewingcenter.com

Monday-Thursday 10:00-5:00, Friday 10:00-4:00 Saturday 10:00-3:00

Map detail:
Exit 156　C.R. 512　8 mi.　4 mi.　U.S. 1　8802　I-95　Marilou's　C.R. 510
1/4 mile north of C.R. 510
next to Vero Beach Kampground

Est: 1996

Sebring, FL　　　　　Q

Crafty Quilters

Mon-Fri 9a-5p
Sat 9a-3p
Closed Mon during Summer

13221 U.S. Hwy. 98 33876
(863) 658-2148
Owner: Dee Dee Bedard
www.craftyquiltersfl.com
For all your Quilting Needs.
Quilting Machines. Classes Available.
Factory Authorized Dealer of JANOME.
Repairs on all Machines.

Map: Sebring　U.S. 98　Hwy. 66　Hwy. 98　.4 mi.　13221　Crafty Quilters　Lake Placid

The Breakers Palm Beach
Founded in the sands of Palm Beach in 1896, The Breakers has a history that
includes two fires and 75 Italian artisans. The list of amenities are too extensive
to list, but include a private beach, four oceanfront pools, indoor-outdoor spa,
nine distinctive restaurants, two championship golf courses, ten tennis courts,
junior golf and tennis programs, family activities, and twelve on property
boutiques for your shopping needs.
1 South County Road, Palm Beach, FL 33480 (877)724-3188
www.thebreakers.com

Temple Terrace, FL　　　　　Q

BERNINA SEWING CENTER

Mon - Thurs
10 - 6
Fri 10 - 5
Sat 9 - 4

Authorized BERNINA Dealer, Service by Gregor Sidler,
a swiss-born mechanic, 3000 bolts of beautiful quilting
fabrics by Moda, Hoffman, Kaufman, Timeless
Treasures just to name a few. Lots of sewing classes in
our huge 1200 sq. ft. classroom.
Floriani threads and stabilizers.

Est: 1997
2000+ bolts

*Only 1 mile off I-75
Same center as
Carrabba's Restaurant*

5405 E. Fowler Ave.
Temple Terrace, FL 33617
(813) 969-2458
berninatpa@aol.com
www.berninapfaff.com

Map: Fletcher Ave.　275　75　Exit 51　Fowler Ave.　Exit 265　5405　BERNINA Sewing

Enter as a stranger -- leave as a friend

A fully stocked
Quilt Shop --
4,000 bolts of quilter's
cotton and cotton
flannels. Friendly
service, notions, books
and patterns.
We carry a full line of
woven, felted wool that
includes wool yardage,
pennies, and fat
quarters in addition to
everything you would
need to complete
wool appliqué projects.
Also in stock are perle
cottons, embroidery floss
and
embroidery patterns.

1983 Drew Street   33765
(727) 461-4171
Owners: Marilyn & John Humphries
www.countryquiltsandbears.com

Monday - Saturday   10 - 4

Colorful, exciting fabrics
Helpful, friendly, knowledgeable staff
Experienced, enthusiastic teachers
Inspiring classes for all skill levels
Fun and happy atmosphere

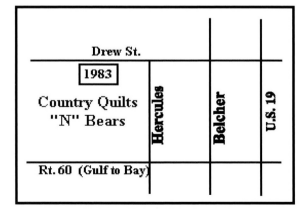

Clearwater, FL   Q

Est: 1986   3300 sq.ft.

The Fontainebleau Miami Beach

When it opened in 1954, Fontainebleau Miami Beach was the largest
and most luxurious hotel in South Florida. Over the years,
the Miami Beach oceanfront hotel has costarred in numerous major
Hollywood productions including, Goldfinger, The Bellboy, Scarface,
The Specialist and The Bodyguard. Situated on oceanfront Collins
Avenue in the heart of Millionaire's Row, Fontainebleau Miami Beach
is one of the most historically and architecturally significant hotels on
Miami Beach, Florida. Its iconic design is a spectacular blend of
Miami's glamorous golden era and stylish modern luxury. A revered
Miami Beach landmark for more than half a century,
the 22-acre oceanfront Miami Beach hotel features signature restaurants by award-winning chefs,
two chic nightlife venues, a two-story spa, a virtually endless poolscape, miles of pristine beach and
state-of-the-art conference and event facilities.

4441 Collins Ave, Miami Beach, FL 33140 (800)548-8886 www.fontainebleau.com

Florida Shops

Q-Quilting ~ Y-Yarn ~ N-Needlework ~ R-Retreat ~ M-Museum

City	Shop	Address	Phone	Pg.
Alachua	Julie's Pins and Needles	14911 Main St.	(904) 214-6633	
Altamonte Springs	Needle Orts	1002 W. State Rd. 436 #1024	(407) 869-0078	
Amelia Island	The Bristly Thistle	302 Ash St.	(904) 729-4020	
Apalachicola	Downtown Books and Purl	67 Commerce St.	(850) 653-1290	
Avon Park	Heart to Heart Fabrics & More	1103 W. Circle St.	(863) 453-3100	
Belleair Bluff	The Flying Needles	432 N. Indian Rocks Rd.	(727) 581-8691	
Boca Raton	**Stitch Craft**	**399 S. Federal Hwy.**	**(561) 447-4147**	**Pg. 98**
Boca Raton	Marion's Nimble Needle	23269 St. Rd. 7 #113	(561) 477-1219	
Boca Raton	Sew Much Fun	7491 N. Federal Hwy. C-11	(561) 999-9992	
Bradenton	Bits & Pieces Quilt Shop	1303 13th Ave. W.	(941) 932-5869	
Bradenton	Cross Stitch Magic	1834 Tamiami Tr.	(941) 746-4163	
Brandon	Gigi's Fabric Shop	706 W. Lumsden Rd.	(813) 661-9000	
Brooksville	**Nana's Quilt Shop**	**18851 Cortez Blvd.**	**(352) 796-0011**	**Pg. 93**
Cedar Key	The Salty Needle Quilt Shop	434 2nd St.	(352) 543-9779	
Chiefland	**Levy County Quilt Museum**	**11050 NW 10th Ave.**	**(352) 493-2801**	**Pg. 93**
Clearmont	Quilters Anonymous Inc.	9225 Pine Island Rd.	(352) 241-6768	
Clearwater	**Country Quilts "N" Bears**	**1983 Drew St.**	**(727) 461-4171**	**Pg. 96**
Clermont	Clearmont Sewing & Quilting	741 W. Montrose St.	(352) 243-4568	
Cocoa	Knit & Stitch Boutique	15 Stone St.	(321) 632-4579	
Coral Gables	The Giving Tree	248 Giralda Ave.	(305) 445-3967	
Coral Gables	The Knitting Garden	1923 Ponce De Leon Blvd.	(305) 774-1060	
Crestview	**Margie's Sew Much Fun**	**2014 Lacey Ln.**	**(850) 682-6920**	**Pg. 92**
Crestview	A Quilter's Place	757 N. Ferdon Blvd.	(850) 398-5566	
Crestview	Granny's Attic	337 N. Main St.	(850) 682-3041	
Crystal River	A White's Sewing and Fabric	979 N. Suncoast Blvd.	(352) 563-5338	
Dade City	**Quilts on Plum Lane**	**14215 7th St.**	**(352) 518-0003**	**Pg. 94**
Daytona Beach	The Sewing Garret	949 Beville Rd. Bldg. #2	(386) 767-3545	
Deland	Quilt Shop of Deland	115 W. Rich Ave.	(386) 734-8782	
Delray Beach	Knitters Nook	5195 W. Atlantic Ave. # J & K	(561) 495-1095	
Delray Beach	Stitches by the Sea, Inc.	710 E. Atlantic Ave.	(561) 865-5775	
Destin	Coastal Stitches, Inc.	225 Main St. #13	(850) 376-9405	
Destin	TJ's Fabrics	36074 Emerald Coast Pkwy.	(850) 598-9446	
Dunedin	Raspberries	728 Douglas Ave.	(727) 738-1477	
Dunnellon	Stitch Niche	20782 Walnut St.	(352) 465-8000	
Elkton	Adela's Yarn	5445 St. Ambrose Church Rd.	(904) 692-2101	
Fernandina Beach	Lollipops Quilt Shop	1881 S. 14th St. #5	(904) 310-6616	
Fort Walton Beach	Stitcher's Quest	745 Beal Plwy. NE Ste. 5	(850) 864-4555	
Fort Walton Beach	The Sewing Center	913 N. Beal Pkwy #F	(850) 243-8261	
Ft. Lauderdale	**Cross Stitch Cupboard**	**1600 NE 26th St.**	**(954) 563-8900**	**Pg. 98**
Ft. Lauderdale	Once Upon a Quilt	3404 Griffin Rd.	(954) 987-8827	
Ft. Lauderdale	Yarns and Arts	3330 NE 32nd St.	(954) 990-5772	
Ft. Myers	Flash. Sew and Quilt	6800 Shoppes at Plantation Dr.	(239) 288-4059	
Ft. Myers	Geez Leweez Needle Work	16876 McGregor Blvd.	(239) 395-2900	
Gainesville	Yarnworks	4113 NW 13th St.	(352)-337-9965	
Greenacres	**Quilt a Bit**	**2914 S. Jog Rd.**	**(561) 304-7211**	**Pg. 98**
Gulfport	FAB Fiber LLC	5708 Gulfport Blvd.	(727) 744-7051	
Gulfport	Fabric Smart	5401 Gulfport Blvd. S.	(727) 914-8850	
Haines City	Lollipops Shoppe	3393 US. Hwy. 17-92 W.	(863) 353-2621	
Holiday	A & A White Sew & Vac	3307 US. Hwy. 19	(727) 484-6560	
Holiday	A & A White Sewing Center	3307 US. Hwy. 19 N.	(727) 232-6718	
Homosassa	Winder's Fabric Outlet	6027 S. Suncoast Blvd.	(352) 628-0951	
Hudson	Quilt 'Til You Wilt & Embroidery Studio	9609 Fulton Ave.	(727) 862-6141	
Jacksonville	**Ladybug Quilt Shop**	**1400 Cassat Ave. #4**	**(904) 527-8994**	**Pg. 92**
Jacksonville	A Stitch In Time	5724 St. Augustine Rd.	904-731-4082	
Jacksonville	Cinnamon's Quilt Shoppe	4220 Hood Rd.	(904) 374-0532	
Jacksonville	Paula's Fine Fabrics	8358 Point Meadows Dr. #4	(904) 519-7705	
Jupiter	The Inspired Sewist	661 Maplewood Dr. #14	(561) 747-0525	
Key West	**Seam Shoppe**	**1113 Truman Ave.**	**(305) 296-9830**	**Pg. 98**
Key West	Island Needlework	527 Fleming St.	(305) 296-6091	
Kissimmee	Heartfelt Quilting & Sewing	401 S. John Young Pkwy.	(407) 846-7998	
Kissimmee	The Yarn Shack	204 E. Drury Ave.	(407) 978-6705	
Lady Lake	A Quilting Palette, LLC	732 S. US. Hwy. 441	(352) 751-0405	

Index

Lady Lake	The Sewing Studio	980 Bichara Blvd.	(352) 753-0219	
Lady Lake	The Yarn Lady	304 Oak St.	(352) 775-9974	
Lake City	**Fabric Art Shop**	**4136 W. US. Hwy. 90**	**(386) 755-0179**	**Pg. 92**
Lake Mary	Bernina Sewing Center	3593 Lake Emma Rd.	(407) 805-9300	
Lake Park	Needlepoint Alley	905 US. Hwy. 1 Unit K	(561) 691-3223	
Lake Placid	Granny Sue Quilts	115 Lake Shore Dr.	(863) 465-7236	
Lake Worth	Just Imaginknit	6663 Lake Worth Rd. Ste. B	(561) 433-3444	
Lakeland	Fabric Warehouse	3030 N. Florida Ave.	(863) 680-1325	
Largo	Criativity	720 9th Ave. SW	(727) 584-4191	
Largo	Keep Me In Stitches	10459 Ulmerton Rd.	(727) 648-2490	
Largo	The Crafty Framer	9204 Ulmerton Rd.	(727) 518-1400	
Lauderhill	Sheep Thrills	4701 N. University Dr.	(954) 742-1908	
Longwood	Knit!	900 Fox Valley Dr. Ste. 106	(407) 767-5648	
Lutz	Scrap and Sew	16541 Pointe Village Dr. #108	(813) 749-0888	
Lutz	Sweet Darling Quilts	26240 Wesley Chapel Blvd.	(813) 994-2994	
Maitland	**The Sewing Studio Fabric Superstore**	**9605 S. Hwy. 17-92**	**(407) 831-6488**	**Pg. 94**
Maitland	Rabbles	2090 Mohican Trail	(407) 628-4054	
Margate	Sunshine Sewing Co., Inc.	1821 Banks Rd.	(954) 971-4810	
Melbourne	**Quilts and Lace, LLC**	**7720 N. Wickham Rd. #111**	**(321) 622-8602**	**Pg. 94**
Melbourne	Boutique 4 Quilters	2945 W. New Haven Ave.	(321) 768-2060	
Miami	A Stitcher's Paradise	1365 NW 98th Ct. Ste. 1	(305) 629-8679	
Miami	Absolutely Needlepoint	2496 SW 28 Ln.	(305) 858-1212	
Miami	Elegant Stitches	8841 SW 132nd St.	(305) 232-4005	
Milton	Yarns & Things	5211 Dogwood Dr.	(850) 382-4670	
Miramar Beach	Destin Yarn Shop	12273 US. Hwy. 98 W. #109	(850) 650-0006	
Mt. Dora	Sew-Mini Things	3820 N. Hwy. 19A	(352) 483-0082	
Naples	Flash, Sew and Quilt	1575 Pine Ridge Rd. #13	(239) 304-8387	
Naples	Knitting With Nancy	3804 E. Tamiami Tr.	(239) 793-8141	
Naples	Needlepoint in Paradise	975 Imperial Golf Course Blvd. # 118	(239) 591-0654	
Naples	SEW Studio	2380 Immokalee Rd.	(239) 598-3752	
New Smyrna Beach				
	Seaside Sewing & Quilts	403 Mary Ave.	(386) 402-8995	
North Fort Myers	Quilt Lovers' Hangout	13494 N. Cleveland Ave.	(239) 995-0045	
North Fort Myers	Susie Q's Quilts	1890 N. Tamiami Tr.	(239) 656-2722	
Ocala	Brick City Cross Stitch	4901 E. Silver Springs Blvd. #606	(352) 629-2991	
Ocala	Tomorrow's Treasures Quilt Shop	6122 SW Hwy. 200	(352)-690-1915	
Odessa	Fiber Art Inc.	8727 Gunn Hwy.	813) 792-5999	
Orange Park	**Country Crossroads**	**799 Blanding Blvd. Ste. 3**	**(904) 276-1011**	**Pg. 92**
Orange Park	Calico Station, Inc.	1857 Wells Rd.	(904) 269-6911	
Orlando	The Black Sheep	1201 W. Fairbanks Ave.	(407) 894-0444	
Orlando	Wandering Stitches Quilting Studio	5818 Hoffner Ave. #905	(407) 658-4044	
Ormond Beach				
	Byrd's Nest Quilting	**156 E. Granada Blvd.**	**(386) 615-8789**	**Pg. 93**
Ormond Beach	The Ball of Yarn	156 W. Granada Blvd.	(386) 672-2858	
Oviedo	Wren's Nest Quilt Shop	320 N. Central Ave.	(407) 278-3030	
Palatka	Miss D's Quilts	305 St. Johns Ave.	(386) 385-5678	
Palm Bay	Knitting Closet	2901 Palm Bay Rd. #I	(321) 961-2801	
Palm Beach Gardens				
	Laura's Sewing and Fabric*	3966 Northlake Blvd.	(561) 799-5228	
Palmetto	**Quilters Haven & More**	**925 10th St. E.**	**(941) 729-0511**	**Pg. 97**
Panama City	Quilting by the Bay	2303 Winona Dr.	(850)-215-7282	
Panama City	Threads Unlimited Knits	3900 Marriott Dr.	(850) 588-7588	
Pembroke Pines	Raging Wool Yarn Shop	1850 NW 122 Terrace	(954) 385-0861	
Pensacola	**A & E Fabric**	**923 N. New Warrington Rd.**	**(850) 455-0112**	**Pg. 92**
Pensacola	King's Sewing & Knitting Center	2633 Creighton Rd.	(850) 377-8897	
Pensacola	Susan's Sew & Vac	8084 N. Davis Hwy. #C1	(850) 477-6093	
Plant City	**Inspire Quilting & Fabrics**	**101 N. Collins St.**	**(813) 704-4867**	**Pg. 94**
Port Charlotte	Charlottes Sewing Studio	1109 Tamiami Tr.	(941) 235-3555	
Port Charlotte	Golden Needle	1225 Tamiami Tr. #A3	(941) 743-4410	
Port Saint Lucie	Laura's Sewing & Fabric	1707 NW St. Lucie W. Blvd. #102	(772) 344-5229	
Port St. Lucie	Pam's Fabric Nook	8631 S. US. Hwy. 1	(772) 800-3019	
Punta Gorda	Gloria's Stash	1133 Bal Harbor Blvd. #1143	(941) 575-8900	
Rockledge	Quilting Folks Sewing Gallery, Inc.	6420 3rd St. #101	(321) 253-3882	
Rockledge	The Quilt Place	575 Barton Blvd.	(321) 632-3344	
Sanibel	Three Crafty Ladies, LLC	1628 Periwinkle Way	(239) 472-2893	
Sarasota	A Good Yarn	7418 S. Tamiami Tr.	(941) 487-7914	
Sarasota	A Quilter's Stash	6388 N. Lockwood Ridge Rd.	(941) 351-5559	
Sarasota	Alma Sue's Quilt Shop	3737 Bahia Vista St.	(941) 330-0993	
Sarasota	Picasso's Moon Yarn Shop	200 S. Washington Blvd. Ste. 11	(941) 932-0103	

Index

Sarasota	Sew Worth It!	5507 Palmer Crossing Cir.	(941) 924-5600	
Sarasota	The Modern Sewist	6585 Gateway Ave.	(941) 706-3846	
Sebastian	**Marilou's Quilting & Sewing Center**	**8802 N. US. Hwy. 1**	**(772) 589-0011**	**Pg. 95**
Sebring	**Crafty Quilters**	**13221 Hwy. 98 S.**	**(863) 658-2148**	**Pg. 95**
Sebring	The Fabric & Sewing Shop	1422 Prosper Ave.	(863) 382-1422	
Silver Springs	E T Yarns	5300 E. Silver Springs Blvd. Ste. E	(352) 236-3000	
Spring Hill	Bayside Stitches Quilting Shop	5164 Commercial Way	(352) 584-3743	
St. Augustine	**Fran's Knitting Boutique**	**2790 US. Hwy. 1 S**	**(904) 797-9951**	**Pg. 93**
St. Augustine	Bee's Quilt Shop and Studio	1690 US. Hwy. 1 S. #I	(904) 826-4007	
St. Augustine	Magrieta's Quilt Shop, LLC	142-C King St.	(904) 829-3137	
St. Petersburg	**Jay's Fabric**	**801 Pasadena Ave. S.**	**(727) 381-6600**	**Pg. 97**
St. Petersburg	Fiberologie	237 2nd Ave. S.	(727) 827-4911	
St. Petersburg	Silk Road Needle Arts	2887 22nd Ave. N.	(727) 327-5127	
Stuart	Needlepoint Land	3836 SE Dixie Hwy.	(772) 223-9700	
Summerfield	The Yarn Lady	16810 S. Hwy. 441	(352) 693-2065	
Tallahassee	**Bernina Connection**	**1400 Village Square Blvd. #4**	**(850) 386-7397**	**Pg. 92**
Tallahassee	Stitches of Love Quilting	414 E. 7th Ave. #2	(850) 329-7435	
Tallahassee	Yarn Therapy Inc.	1760 Thomasville Rd.	(850) 577-0555	
Tamarac	Cynthia's Fine Fabrics	8126 N. University Dr.	(954) 724-2900	
Tampa	Florida Quilting Center	13013 W. Linebaugh Ave.	(813) 855-2857	
Tampa	Happy Apple Quilts	13013 W. Linebaugh Ave.	(813) 925-9037	
Tampa	Keep Me In Stitches	4504 W. Kennedy Blvd.	(813) 282-1526	
Tampa	Keep Me In Stitches	14833 N. Dale Mabry Hwy.	(813) 908-3889	
Tampa	Knit 'N Knibble	4027 S. Dale Mabry Hwy.	(813) 837-5648	
Temple Terrace				
	Bernina Sewing Center	**5405 E. Fowler Ave.**	**(813) 969-2458**	**Pg. 95**
Titusville	Kathy's Quilt Studio	4527 S. Hopkins Ave.	(321) 529-0117	
Trenton	Suwannee Valley Quilt Shoppe	517 N. Main St.	(352) 463-3842	
University Park	Cotton Patch Quilt Shop	8480 Cooper Creek Blvd. #101	(941) 359-3300	
Venice	**Deborah's Quilt Basket**	**337 W. Venice Ave.**	**(941) 488-6866**	**Pg. 98**
Venice	The Knit N Stitch Shop	5115 State Rd. 776	(941) 408-7416	
Venice	The Knitting Place	258 Miami Ave. W. Ste. 4	(941) 486-1584	
Vero Beach	DragonFly Quilt Shop	1436 Old Dixie Hwy. #E	(772) 567-9600	
Vero Beach	Knitty Gritty Yarn Shop	1561 Old Dixie Hwy. #B	(772) 778-9199	
Vero Beach	Needle Nicely	1531 US. #1	(772) 567-6688	
Wildwood	Sharky's Vac n Sew	700 N. Main St.	(352) 330-2483	
Winter Garden	Nancy's Quilt Shop	121 W. Plant St.	(407) 614-8755	
Winter Haven	Four Purls	331 3rd St. NW	(863) 662-8288	
Winter Haven	Heart to Heart Fabrics & More	237 Ave. O SW	(863) 298-8185	
Winter Haven	Heartfelt Quilting & Sewing	355 5th St. SW	(863) 299-3080	
Zephyrhills	**Quilter's Quarters**	**4833 Allen Rd.**	**(813) 779-2615**	**Pg. 93**

Index

Notes

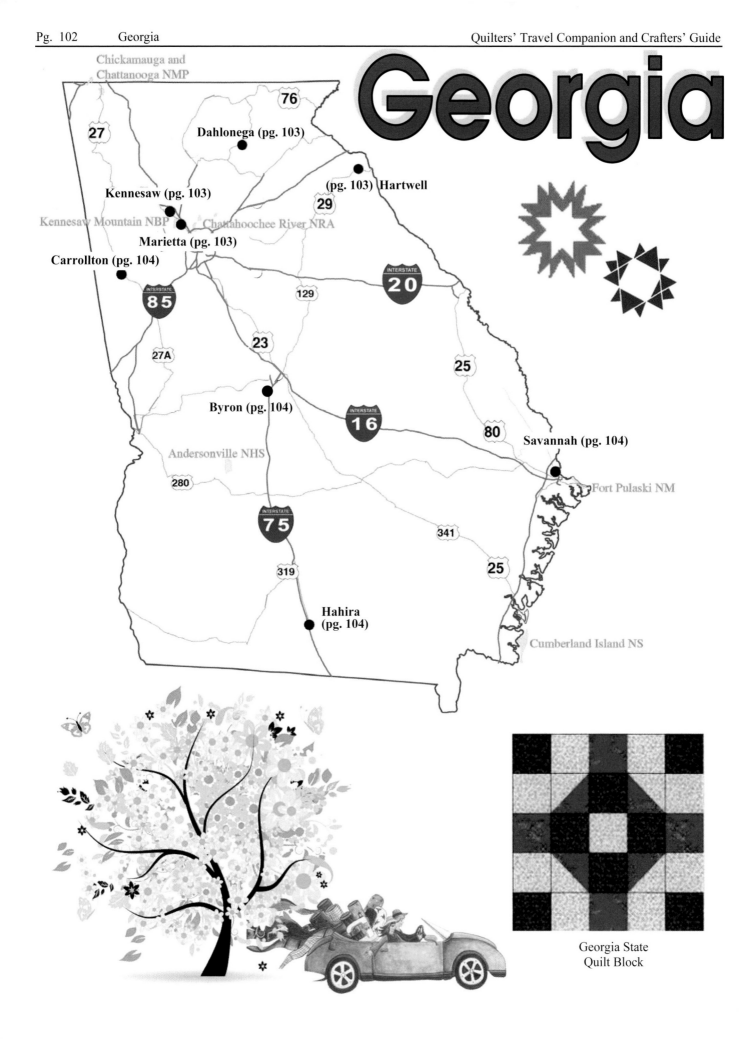

Georgia

Chickamauga and
Chattanooga NMP

76

27

Dahlonega (pg. 103)

Kennesaw (pg. 103)

(pg. 103) Hartwell

29

Kennesaw Mountain NBP

Chattahoochee River NRA

Marietta (pg. 103)

Carrollton (pg. 104)

INTERSTATE 20

129

INTERSTATE 85

27A

23

25

Byron (pg. 104)

INTERSTATE 16

Andersonville NHS

80

Savannah (pg. 104)

280

Fort Pulaski NM

INTERSTATE 75

341

319

25

Hahira (pg. 104)

Cumberland Island NS

Georgia State
Quilt Block

TINY STITCHES
A Gathering Place for Quilters

Est. 1992

Better Homes & Gardens
Quilt Sampler
TOP SHOP

The Gathering Place for the Quilting Community
We are a fully stocked quilt shop with over
7,000 Bolts of the highest quality quilting and sewing fabric.
Large selection of the newest notions & books.
Friendly, knowledgeable service.
Classes offered in quilting, sewing and accessories.

Monday-Saturday 9:30-5:30
Sunday 1:00-5:00

Follow us on Facebook

Be sure to check our website frequently for upcoming retreats and events.

2518 E. Piedmont Rd. Marietta, GA 30062
770-565-1113
We gladly ship both online and phone orders.
Visit our website: www.tinystitches.com

Handi Quilter
OFFICIAL RETAILER

*Just off I-75, Tiny Stitches is a convenient stop
for the traveling Quilter. Exit 269,
east onto Barrett Pkwy. This becomes E.
Piedmont. We are located at 2520 E. Piedmont.*

Dahlonega, GA   QN

The Common Thread

598 Grove St. N   30533
(706) 864-0740   Fax: Same
Est: 2008   1700 sq.ft.   5100 Bolts
thecommonthread@windstream.net
www.thecommon-thread.com

For all your quilting
and sewing needs.
Long-Arm Quilting Service.

Tue-Fri 10-5 and Sat 10-2

Hartwell, GA   Q

Annies Pretty Pieces
Quilt, Craft and Supplies

Tues - Sat
10 - 6

138 N. Forest Ave. #E   30643
(706) 337-3313   Est: 2011
anniesprettypieces@gmail.com
www.anniesprettypieces.com
Fabrics from Windham, Moda, Red Rooster,
RJR, Paintbrush Studios, and Windham.
108" wide backings in prints and colors.
Check out our special value section & class
schedule. Clubs and newsletter.

A Quilt Shop
You Can Call Home.

Cottontail Quilts

We want to be your favorite
quilting and sewing center!

www.cottontailquiltshop.com

A Unique quilt shop located in historic Downtown Kennesaw.
We offer a huge selection of
fabric, books, patterns, notions and classes.
Our friendly and knowledgeable staff will help you with your
quilting and sewing needs.

Monday-Saturday 9:30-5:00

**2259 Lewis St. NW
Kennesaw, GA 30144
678-355-6776**
info@cottontailquiltshop.com

Kennesaw, GA   Q

Did you know?
Georgia is the number one producer of peanuts, pecans, and peaches in the US.

Georgia Shops

Q-Quilting ~ Y-Yarn ~ N-Needlework ~ R-Retreat ~ M-Museum

Acworth	Yarn & Stuff	4442 S. Main St.	(770) 575-2152	
Atlanta	In Stitches	3137 E. Shadowlawn Ave. NE	(404) 816-4612	
Atlanta	Life's A Stitch, Inc.	857 Collier Rd. NW #14B	(404) 355-5797	
Atlanta	Needle Nook	2165 Briarcliff Rd. NE	(404) 325-0068	
Atlanta	The Nimble Needle	290 Hilderbrand Dr. NE #B-4	(404) 843-8687	
Atlanta	Yarning for Ewe	3220 Cobb Pkwy. #102	(678) 909-4963	
Augusta	Branum's Sewing & Vacuum Center	3230 Washington Rd.	(706) 860-5434	
Blairsville	Fabric Center & Quilt Shop	19 Cobalt St. Ste. G	(706) 745-6918	
Blairsville	Knitter's Knitch	64 Brackets Way #6	(706) 835-1078	
Blairsville	The Dogwood Patch	5305 Ford Mountain Rd.	(706) 745-9255	
Buford	Georgia Sewing & Quilting, Inc.	81 Maddox Rd.	(770) 831-7990	
Byron	**Birdhouse Quilts**	**103 Peach Wood Dr.**	**(478) 654-6880**	**Pg. 104**
Carrollton	**Southeastern Quilt & Textile Museum**			
		306 Bradley St.	**(770) 301-2187**	**Pg. 104**
Carrollton	Ewe Knit Yarn	815 Cedar St.	(770) 830-6480	
Cartersville	The King's Knit-Wit	12 S. Wall St.	(770) 883-9023	
Chickamauga	Memories & More	121 Gordon St.	(706) 375-5300	
Columbus	Sew Much Fun	7801 Veteran's Pkwy.	(706) 317-0024	
Covington	Patrick's	10285 Covington Bypass Rd.	(770) 786-3220	
Cumming	Fleece	1735 Buford Hwy. #210	(770) 886-5648	
Cumming	Thread Bear Fabrics, LLC	515 Sawnee Corners Blvd. #500	(770) 781-0001	
Dahlonega	**The Common Thread**	**598 Grove St. N.**	**(706) 864-0740**	**Pg. 103**
Dahlonega	Magical Threads	315 Church St.	(706) 867-8918	
Dawsonville	Sew Memorable Inc.	4055 Hwy. 53 E. #110	(706) 265-2121	
Decatur	Intown Quilters, Inc.	1058 Mistletoe Rd.	(404) 634-6924	
Duluth	Atlanta Sewing Center	2148 Duluth Hwy. NE #111	(770) 622-1880	
Ellerslie	Sunday Best Quiltworks	4517 Harris Rd.	(706) 569-7744	
Ellijay	Strings & Sticks Yarn Shoppe	449 Industrial Blvd.	(706) 698-5648	
Fayetteville	Quilt 'N' Fabric	935 W. Lanier Ave. #1016	(678) 817-7878	
Gainesville	Yarn Rhapsody	475 Dawsonville Hwy. #C	(770) 536-3130	
Griffin	Young at Heart	409 Airport Rd.	(678) 688-4373	
Hahira	**Sew Blessed Fabric**	**213 W. Main St. #B**	**(229) 794-0076**	**Pg. 104**
Hahira	**Sew Blessed Fabric**	**201 S. Church St.**	**(229) 794-1100**	**Pg. 104**
Hartwell	**Annies Pretty Pieces**	**138 N. Forest Ave. #E**	**(706) 377-3313**	**Pg. 103**
Hartwell	ElsieBee Originals	79 Depot St.	(706) 376-2787	
Hoschton	City Square Quilts	23 City Sq.	(706) 921-4958	
Hoschton	Yarn Junkees	25 City Sq.	(706) 921-4116	
Kennesaw	**Cottontail Quilts**	**2259 Lewis St. NW**	**(678) 355-6776**	**Pg. 103**
Kennesaw	Knitting Emporium	2803 S. Main St. NW	(770) 421-1919	
Lake Park	Sew Into Quilting	1250 Lakes Blvd.	(229) 412-2012	
Lawrenceville	Naked Sheep Yarn Shop	963 Buford Dr.	(404) 641-6292	
Lawrenceville	Yarn Garden Knit Shop	159 W. Pike St.	(678) 225-0920	
Mabelton	Stitch'n Quilt	5590 Mabelton Pkwy. Ste. 114	(770) 944-3356	
Macon	Couture Sewing Center	3755 Bloomfield Rd.	(478) 474-7224	
Macon	Creative Yarns	134 Speer Ave.	(478) 746-5648	
Macon	Cross Stitchers Ark	2370-B Ingleside Ave.	(478) 745-6080	
Macon	Magical Stitches	4126 Hartley Bridge Rd.	(478) 788-0555	
Madison	Sartoria Monica	232 W. Washington ST.	(706) 343-0000	
Marietta	**Tiny Stitches**	**2518 E. Piedmont Rd.**	**(770) 565-1113**	**Pg. 103**
Marietta	Atlanta Sewing Center	50 Barrett Pkwy. #4005	(770) 428-5522	
Marietta	Red Hen Fabrics	22 Trammell St. #B	(770) 794-8549	
Martinez	Jeff's Sewing & Vacuum Center	3833 Washington Rd.	(706) 863-0090	
Martinez	Memory Lane Quilting	Fury's Ferry Shoppes Shopping Center	(706) 496-8822	
McDonough	A Scarlet Thread	1601 McDonough Place	(678) 583-2296	
Mountain City	Fabric Station	2553 US. 441	(706) 746-7415	
Newnan	In Stitches	12 E. Broad St.	(770) 251-6009	
Newnan	Quilt Museum at the Male Academy	30 Temple Ave.	(770) 251-0207	
Peachtree City	Sugarfoot Yarns	100 N. Peachtree Pkwy.	(770) 487-9001	
Ringgold	It's Sew Time	7801 Nashville St.	(706) 937-3777	
Rocky Face	Sew 'n So Quilt Shop	600 LaFayette Rd.	(706) 519-4111	

Index

Rome	The Stitchery	9 Central Plaza	(706) 622-2345	
Roswell	Cast-On Cottage	1003 Canton St.	(770) 998-3483	
Savannah	**Sew Much More**	**4831-A Augusta Rd.**	**(912) 966-5626**	**Pg. 104**
Savannah	A Frayed Knot	6 W. State St.	(912) 233-1240	
Savannah	Fabrika Fine Fabrics	2 East Liberty St.	(912) 236-1122	
Savannah	A Fabric Parlor	311 Whitaker St.	(912) 209-0942	
Savannah	Unwind Yarn & Gifts	7710 Waters Ave.	(912) 303-3970	
Smyrna	Eat.Sleep.Knit	6400 Highlands Pkwy. #1	(770) 432-9277	
Springfield	Quarterdeck Quilts	490 Stillwell Rd.	(912) 754-1865	
St. Simons Island	Stepping Stones Quilts	226 Redfern Village	(912) 638-7128	
St. Simons Island	Stitchery of St. Simons	3411 Frederica Rd.	(912) 638-3401	
Statesboro	Deb-Bees Creations	17943 Hwy. 80 W.	(912) 764-5423	
Thomaston	Southern Stitches	1615 Hwy. 19 N.	(706) 647-9152	
Thomasville	Fuzzy Goat	223 W. Jackson St.	(229) 236-4628	
Tifton	Country Charm Quilt Shop	2072 US. Hwy. 82E.	(229) 238-2488	
Trenton	The Quilter's Garden	12695 N. Main St.	(423) 504-2422	
Tucker	Home Spice Décor	2615 Mountain Ind. Blvd. #6	(770) 934-4224	
Tunnel Hill	Janet's Place Quilt Shop	3525 Chattanooga Rd.	(706) 519-0200	
Valdosta	Pinwheels Quilting & Needlework	361 Northside Dr.	(229) 232-4531	
Valdosta	Sew and So Fabrics	601 E. Park Ave.	(229) 333-2594	
Woodstock	Sew Main Street	8816 Main St.	(678) 401-6126	
Woodstock	The Whole Nine Yarns	8826 Main St.	(678) 494-5242	

Index

Notes

Jekyll Island Club Resort

Established in 1947 on Georgia's Atlantic coast, Jekyll Island offers a tranquil getaway that doesn't skimp on luxurious offerings. Formerly home to a hunting and recreational club comprised of wealthy members from the Rockefeller and Vanderbilt families, the resort is a prime vacation spot for golfers, boaters, and nature enthusiasts.

901 Downing Musgrove Parkway, Jekyll Island, GA 31527
(912)635-3636   www.jekyllisland.com

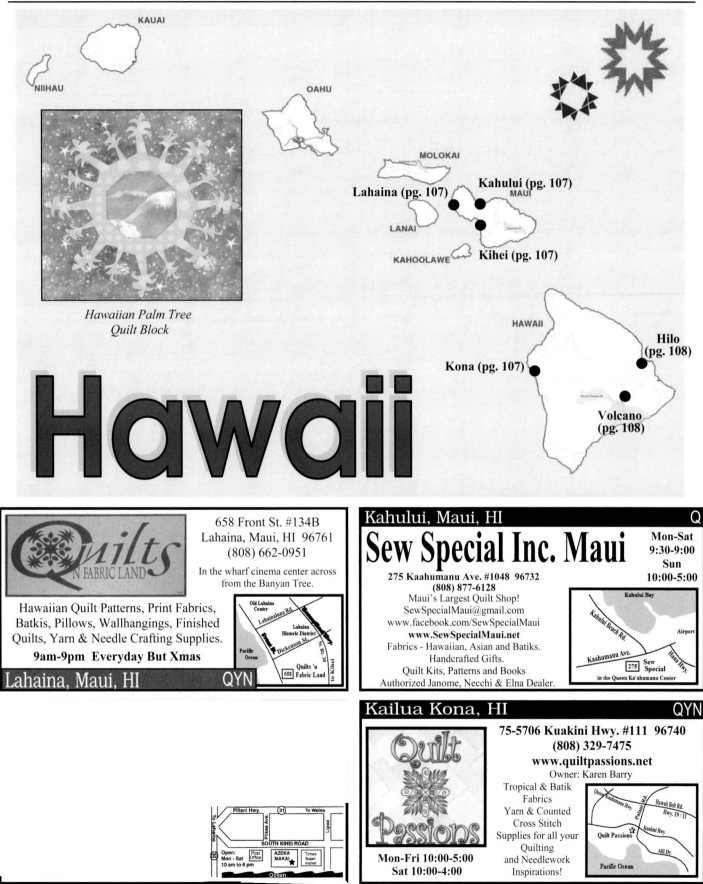

KAUAI

NIIHAU

OAHU

Hawaiian Palm Tree Quilt Block

MOLOKAI

Lahaina (pg. 107)

Kahului (pg. 107)

MAUI

LANAI

Kihei (pg. 107)

KAHOOLAWE

HAWAII

Hilo (pg. 108)

Kona (pg. 107)

Volcano (pg. 108)

Hawaii

Hawaii Fun Facts:

Hawaii's `Iolani Palace is the only royal residence in the United States of America.
More than one-third of the world's commercial supply of pineapples comes from Hawaii.

Hawaii Shops

Q-Quilting ~ Y-Yarn ~ N-Needlework ~ R-Retreat ~ M-Museum

City	Shop	Address	Phone	Page
Hanalei	Hanalei Strings	5-5190 Kuhio Hwy.	(808) 826-9633	
Hilo	**Kilauea Kreations II**	**680 Manono St.**	**(808) 961-1100**	Pg. 108
Hilo	Discount Fabric Warehouse	933 Kanoelehua Ave.	(808) 935-1234	
Hilo	Fabric Workshop	1348 Kilauea Ave.	(808) 933-1010	
Hilo	Strings Fabric and Needlework Shoppe	285 Kinoole St. #202	(808) 937-2160	
Hilo	The Yarn Basket	50 E. Puainako St. # 107	(808) 959-0034	
Honokaa	Topstitch	45-3599 Mamane St.	(808) 885-4482	
Honolulu	Fiddlesticks Too	620 Coral St.	(808) 533-4565	
Honolulu	Hawaii Fabric Mart	1631 Kalahaua Ave.	(808) 947-4466	
Honolulu	Hawaiian Fabric	3207 Martha St.	(808) 381-3909	
Honolulu	Hawaiian Style Quilts	1071 Luapele Dr.	(808) 487-3700	
Honolulu	Hidden Yardage	50 S. Beretania #C113	(808) 523-3330	
Honolulu	Isle Knit	1188 Bishop St. #1403	(808) 533-0853	
Honolulu	Kaimuki Dry Goods	1144 10th Ave.	(808) 734-2141	
Honolulu	Kuni Island Fabrics	2563 S King St.	(808) 955-1280	
Honolulu	Needlepoint Etc.	1134 S. King St.	(808) 591-0377	
Honolulu	The Calico Cat	1223 Koko Head Ave.	(808) 732-3998	
Honolulu	Viking & Singer Sewing & Vacuum	670 Auahi St.	(808) 521-7966	
Honolulu	YarnStory	1411 S. King St. #201	(808) 593-2212	
Kahului	**Sew Special**	**275 Kaahumanu Ave. #1048**	**(808) 877-6128**	Pg. 107
Kahului	Discount Fabric Warehouse	230 Hana Hwy.	(808) 871-6900	
Kailua	Fabric and Quilting Deights	74-5599 Luhia St. Unit D5	(808) 329-8177	
Kailua	Yarn & Needlecrafts Ltd.	46 Hoolai St.	(808) 262-9555	
Kailua Kona	**Quilt Passions**	**75-5706 Kuakini Hwy. #111**	**(808) 329-7475**	Pg. 107
Kailua Kona	Island Yarn & Art Supplies	73-5568 Olowalu St.	(808) 326-2820	
Kailua Kona	Kapa Fabrics	76-964 Hualalai Rd.	(808) 329-1880	
Kailua-Kona	Discount Fabric Warehouse	74-5605 Luhia St.	(808) 326-7474	
Kaneohe	Aloha Yarn	46-018 Kamehameha Hwy. Ste. 209	(808) 234-5865	
Kapaa	Vicky's Fabric Shop	1326 Kuhio Hwy. #4	(808) 822-1746	
Kihei, Maui	**The Maui Quilt Shop**	**1280 S. Kihei Rd.**	**(808) 874-8050**	Pg. 107
Lahaina	**Quilts 'n Fabric Land**	**658 Front St. #134B**	**(808) 662-0951**	Pg. 107
Lahaina	Ka Honu Gift Gallery	277 Wili Ko Pl. #40	(808) 661-0173	
Lihue	Discount Fabric Warehouse	3-3215 Kuhio Hwy.	(808) 246-2739	
Lihue, Kauai	The Kapaia Stitchery	3-3551 Kuhio Hwy.	(808) 245-2281	
Volcano	**Kilauea Kreations**	**19-3972 Old Volcano Hwy.**	**(808) 967-8090**	Pg. 108
Wahiawa	The Pineapple Patch	64-1550 Kamehameha Hwy.	(808) 622-3494	

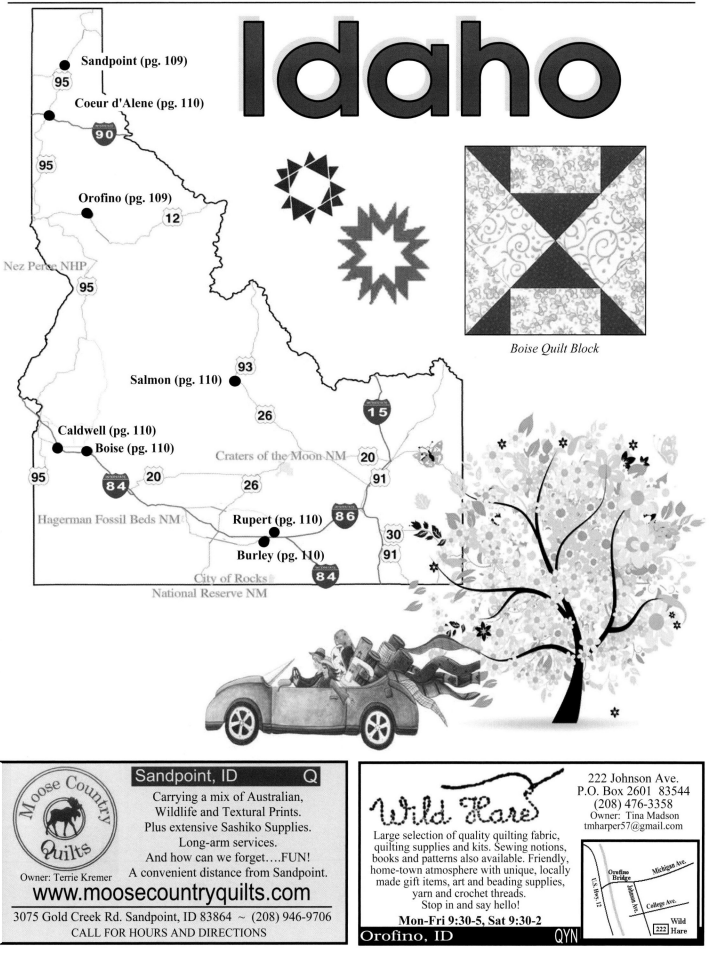

Idaho

Sandpoint (pg. 109)

95

Coeur d'Alene (pg. 110)

90

95

Orofino (pg. 109)

12

Nez Perce NHP

95

Salmon (pg. 110)

93

26

15

Caldwell (pg. 110)

Boise (pg. 110)

Craters of the Moon NM

20

95

84

20

26

91

Hagerman Fossil Beds NM

Rupert (pg. 110)

86

30

Burley (pg. 110)

91

City of Rocks

84

National Reserve NM

Boise Quilt Block

Idaho Shops

Q-Quilting ~ Y-Yarn ~ N-Needlework ~ R-Retreat ~ M-Museum

Blackfoot	Spools and Spindles	377 N. 460 W	(208) 680-5654	
Boise	**The Quilt Crossing**	**10959 W. Fairview Ave.**	**(208) 376-0087**	Pg. 110
Boise	Ideal Sew Shop	3845 Sumter Way	(208) 859-0160	
Boise	Twisted Ewe	1738 W. State St.	(208) 287-3693	
Bonners Ferry	A Little Comfort Quilting	7189 Main St. #641	(208) 267-9200	
Bonners Ferry	A Little Moore Quilting	7228 Main St.	(208) 267-9200	
Bonners Ferry	Alley Fabric Nook	6485 Harrison St. #102	(208) 267-6665	
Bonners Ferry	Callie's Niche	6429 Bonner St.	(208) 267-1583	
Buhl	Bobbins Quilt and Sew	1007 Main St.	(208) 543-0956	
Burley	**Mill End Fabrics**	**1358 Overland Ave.**	**(208) 878-5713**	Pg. 110
Burley	Sandy's Bernina Sales & Service	1234 Oakley Ave.	(208) 678-1573	
Caldwell	**Cindy's Quilt Shop**	**720 S. Kit Ave.**	**(208) 453-8228**	Pg. 110
Caldwell	Quilting Bliss & Sew Much More	6115 Cleveland Blvd. #102	(208) 402-5962	
Clark Fork	Affordable Quilting and Fabric Shop	419 W. 4th	(208) 255-6821	
Coeur d'Alene	**Bear Paw Quilting & Bernina**	**600 W. Kathleen Ave. unit 10**		
			(208) 664-1554	Pg. 110
Coeur d'Alene	Knit-N-Crochet	600 W. Kathleen Ave. #30	(208) 676-9276	
Garden City	Quilt Expressions	5689 Chinden Blvd.	(208) 338-8933	
Garden Valley	Stitch n' Snip	342 S. Middle Fork Rd.	(208) 462-4602	
Grace	Fabulous Fabrics	18 S. Main	(208) 425-3821	
Grangeville	Home Grown Quilts	207 W. Main St.	(208) 983-0254	
Grangeville	Quilt Treasures	120 W. Main St.	(208) 451-4909	
Hailey	Sun Valley Fabric Granary	122 S. Main St. Ste. B	(208) 788-1331	
Idaho Falls	Daydreams Quilt N Sew	802 Pancheri Dr.	(208) 227-8394	
Idaho Falls	Madsens Crafts & Framing	2125 W. Broadway	(208) 523-6074	
Idaho Falls	Porter's Craft and Frame	2455 E. 25th St.	(208) 522-5882	
Idaho Falls	The Blackbird Haven	140 S. Freemont Ave.	(208) 528-7879	
Idaho Falls	The Yarn Connection	415 Park Ave.	(208) 524-8256	
Ketchum	Sun Valley Needle Arts	351 Leadville Ave. N.	(208) 928-7620	
Kuna	Room to Learn	1703 N. Andrew Ln.	(208) 922-1601	
Lewiston	Becky's Fabrics & Bernina	1702 21st St.	(208) 743-4448	
Lewiston	Emerald Garden	2125 14th Ave.	(208) 743-1849	
Lewiston	Home Grown Quilts	556 Thain Rd.	(208) 743-0503	
Mackay	Lost River General Store	4372 W. Houston Rd.	(208) 588-2270	
Marsing	Sleepy Hollow Quilt Shop	107 Main St.	(208) 899-5623	
McCall	Granny's Attic	104 N. Third St.	(208) 634-5313	
McCall	Huckleberry Patches	136 E. Lake St.	(208) 634-4933	
McCall	Keep Me In Stitches	136 E. Lake St. #3	(208) 634-2906	
Meridian	Craft Warehouse	1160 N. Eagle Rd.	(208) 288-2039	
Meridian	The Calico Garden	6235 Joplin Rd.	(208 286-9509	
Moscow	Stitches & Petals	1016 W. Pullman Rd.	(208) 882-5672	
Moscow	The Yarn Underground	409 S. Washington St.	(208) 882-7700	
Nampa	Bluebird Quilt Studio	311 14th Ave. S.	(208) 467-4148	
Nampa	Nancy's Quilts	5310 W. Columbia Rd.	(208) 288-3294	
Nampa	Puffy Mondaes	200 12th Ave. S.	(208) 407-3359	
Oldtown	Ben Franklin Oldtown	201 E. 4th St. N.	(208) 437-4822	
Orofino	**Wild Hare**	**222 Johnson Ave.**	**(208) 476-3358**	Pg. 109
Orofino	Material Girls Quilting Etc.	10492 Hwy. 12	(208) 476-4646	
Pocatello	Mustard Seed Dreams	362 N. Main St.	(208) 233-1697	
Pocatello	Sages Creek Quilt Company	1625 N. 2nd Ave.	(208) 232-0709	
Preston	Fabric Farm & Quilts	1173 S. 1600 E.	(208) 852-1419	
Preston	Suppose Quilt Boutique	21 N. State St.	(208) 852-1449	
Rexburg	Porter's Craft & Frame	19 College Ave.	(208) 359-0786	
Rupert	**The Gathering Place**	**524 6th St.**	**(208) 436-0455**	Pg. 110
Rupert	Bed of Roses Machine Quilting	276 N. 125 W.	(208) 430-7144	
Salmon	**Copper Mountain Quilting**	**605 Lena St.**	**(208) 742-1758**	Pg. 110
Salmon	Sophie's Quilts and Fabric	527 Main St.	(208) 756-1547	
Sandpoint	**Moose Country Quilts**	**3075 Gold Creek Rd.**	**(208) 946-9706**	Pg. 109
Sandpoint	Blue Flag handweaving studio	1223B Michigan St.	(208) 263-4600	
Shelley	Ribbon Retreat	650 N. State St. Ste. 5	(208) 357-3887	
Shoshone	Karen's Place	115 S. Rail St. N.	(208) 358-5279	
Shoshone	Salli's Back Porch Fabrics	465 N. 150 W.	(208) 886-2022	
Teton	Sho Gun Crafts	3 W. Main	(208) 458-4912	
Weiser	Judy Ann's Quilting ETC	35 E. Commercial St.	(208) 405-5121	

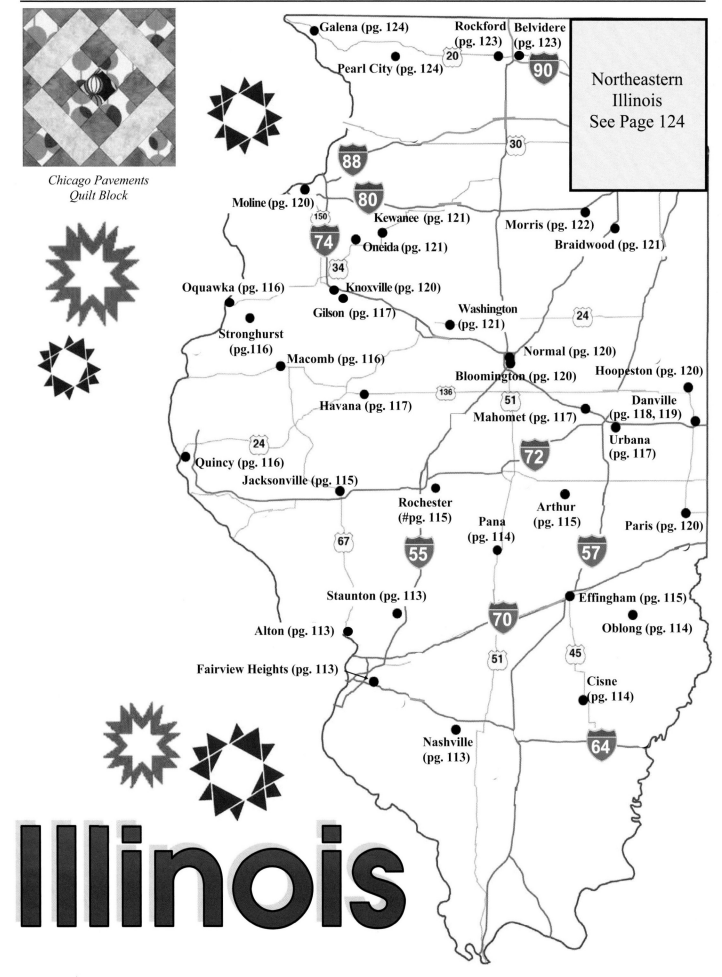

Chicago Pavements
Quilt Block

Galena (pg. 124)
Rockford (pg. 123)
Belvidere (pg. 123)
Pearl City (pg. 124)
20
90

Northeastern
Illinois
See Page 124

30

88

Moline (pg. 120)
80
Kewanee (pg. 121)
Morris (pg. 122)
150
74
Oneida (pg. 121)
Braidwood (pg. 121)
34

Oquawka (pg. 116)
Knoxville (pg. 120)
Gilson (pg. 117)
Washington (pg. 121)
24

Stronghurst (pg.116)
Macomb (pg. 116)
Normal (pg. 120)
Hoopeston (pg. 120)
Bloomington (pg. 120)
136
Havana (pg. 117)
51
Danville (pg. 118, 119)
Mahomet (pg. 117)

24
72
Urbana (pg. 117)
Quincy (pg. 116)
Jacksonville (pg. 115)

Rochester (#pg. 115)
Arthur (pg. 115)
Pana (pg. 114)
Paris (pg. 120)
67
55
57

Staunton (pg. 113)
Effingham (pg. 115)
70
Alton (pg. 113)
Oblong (pg. 114)
45
Fairview Heights (pg. 113)
51
Cisne (pg. 114)

Nashville (pg. 113)
64

Illinois

Did you know?
The world's first Skyscraper was built in Chicago in 1885.

Cisne, IL   Q

Your Quilting Stash

1722 CR 725 E. Cisne, IL 62823
(618) 835-2681
Owners: Cheryl & Rick Matthews
Est: 2009 1500 sq.ft. 2000+ bolts
cherylm2014@yahoo.com

We put a personal touch on everything.
Machine quilting available with
a Gammill Statler Stitcher.

Tuesday-Friday 9-5, Saturday 8-2

Show us this ad for 10% off regularly priced items!

Map:
U.S. 50
Salem
Johnsonville   Cisne   Rt. 161
Exit 109
I-57
Mt. Vernon   ☆ Your Quilting Stash   Approx 22 mi. from I-57
I-64

Pana, IL   Q

The Fabric Patch

www.thefabricpatchil.com
208 N. 2600 E. Rd. Pana, IL 62557
(217) 561-1157
Owners: Brenda & Mike Gelsinger
thefabricpatch@yahoo.com
HANDI QUILTER RETAILERS
Sales, Service and Education.
Try it before you buy it.

Monday
Wednesday
Friday
9:00-5:00
Saturday
9:00-12:00

f

Handi Quilter
OFFICIAL RETAILER

We specialize in service & inspiration!

The Village Stitchery

Quilt Shop & Retreat Center

Better Homes
Quilt Sampler
FEATURED SHOP 2016

108 E. Main St., Oblong, IL 62449 ~ 618-592-4134
Owner: Lisa Pinkston ~ thevillagestitchery@gmail.com

Visit our large shop and enjoy the charming atmosphere where numerous quilt and stitchery displays abound.
We offer a unique variety of books, patterns & notions as well as home decor items.
An abundance of fabric and kits are available from the industries best designers.
We invite you to stop by and visit our "Quilters Paradise"!

Oblong, IL   QR

Monday - Saturday
9:00am - 5:00pm
evenings by appointment

www.villagestitchery.com

We'd be delighted to host your RETREAT stay!

Sew, learn, dine, and relax with friends in our comfortable 12-bed/3-bath Retreat designed to inspire creativity.

The Retreat Center has four bedrooms - two w/2 twin beds and two w/4 twin beds.

Our two large sewing/crafting areas are designed with your comfort in mind.
For more photos of our Retreat please visit our website at www.villagestitchery.com.
Please call for bookings or more information.

The retreat center is open 365 days a years!

And did we mention it adjoins the A W E S O M E quilt shop!

The Palmer House

Though the first iteration of this landmark hotel burned down in the Great Chicago Fire just 13 days after opening in 1871 in the Great Chicago Fire, it has endured for over a century since. It was Chicago's first hotel with operating elevators, plus electric light bulbs and telephones in the guest rooms, and a $170 million renovation ensures its rich history of luxury is maintained.

17 E Monroe St, Chicago, IL 60603
(312) 726-7500
www.palmerhousehiltonhotel.com

Did you know?
When Illinois became a state in 1818, it had a population of 34,620 people.
Illinois is now the sixth most populous state in the country with almost 11.5 million people.

Hilton Chicago

Overlooking Grant Park and Lake Michigan,
Hilton Chicago has served as one of the city's most
revered addresses since 1927. Meticulously
redesigned and restored, this historic Beaux-Arts hotel
offers 1,500 guestrooms and suites, exceptional
dining options, a 16,450 square foot athletic club,
and over 234,000 square feet of
meeting and event space.

720 S Michigan Ave, Chicago, IL 60605
(312) 922-4400
www3.hilton.com/en/hotels/illinois/hilton-chicago-CHICHHH/index.html

Threads and Beds
Retreat Center

www.threadsandbedsretreat.com

207 S. Buchanan St.
Danville, IL 61832
1-217-431-9202
reservations@threadsoftimefab.com

Welcome to Threads and Beds Retreat Center!
Our unique facility allows you to relax, explore your
creativity, and have a fantastic time sewing with
friends and fellow crafters. Our goal is to
provide you with the most spacious and gracious
accommodations you can find -- a facility specifically
designed for artistic endeavors of sewing,
quilting, and textile arts.

We look forward to hosting you and providing for
your artistic needs, both in our retreat center and in
the fabulous attached quilt shop, Threads of Time,
with more than 4,000 bolts of fabric, hundreds of the
newest notions, books, patterns, and fabulous displays.

- 10,000 sq. ft. of retreat area
- Three large sewing areas with sewing tables and chairs
- Sewing space for 42 sewists at a time
- Maximum of 36 overnight sewers
- Horn cutting tables, irons, and ironing-boards
- 7 Large Design Walls (8' x 6')
- Totally handicapped accessible, one-level facility with no stairs
- 7 individual restrooms, 4 shower rooms
- 3 Large kitchens & dining rooms
- Refrigerators, microwaves, toaster ovens & coffee pots
- Wireless Internet in dining areas
- Connected to Threads of Time, the region's premier quilt shop
- Online Registration

*"For the times of your life and
the fabric of the times . . ."*

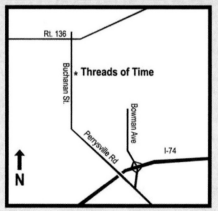

Did you know?
Chicago is home to the Chicago Water Tower and Pumping Station,
the only buildings to survive the Great Chicago Fire.

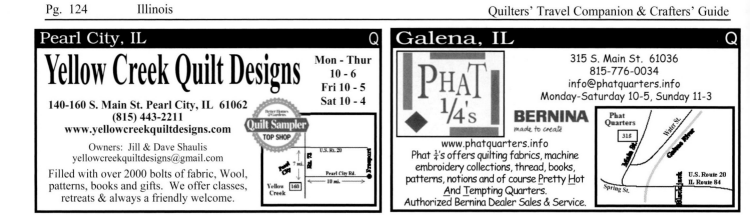

Northeastern Illinois

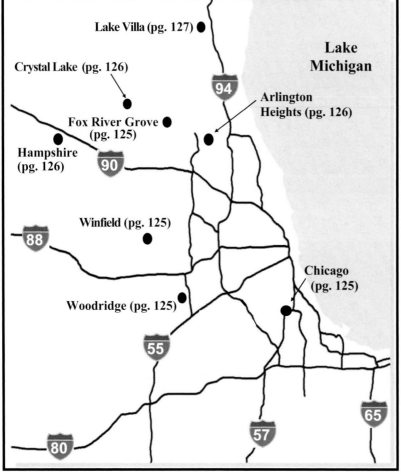

Lake Villa (pg. 127)

Crystal Lake (pg. 126)

Lake Michigan

94

Fox River Grove (pg. 125)

Arlington Heights (pg. 126)

Hampshire (pg. 126)

90

Winfield (pg. 125)

88

Chicago (pg. 125)

Woodridge (pg. 125)

55

65

80

57

Did you know?
Abraham Lincoln's first public office was as postmaster of New Salem, Illinois.

Did you know?
The first nuclear chain reaction took place in Illinois at the University of Chicago in 1942.

Notes

Illinois Shops

Q-Quilting ~ Y-Yarn ~ N-Needlework ~ R-Retreat ~ M-Museum

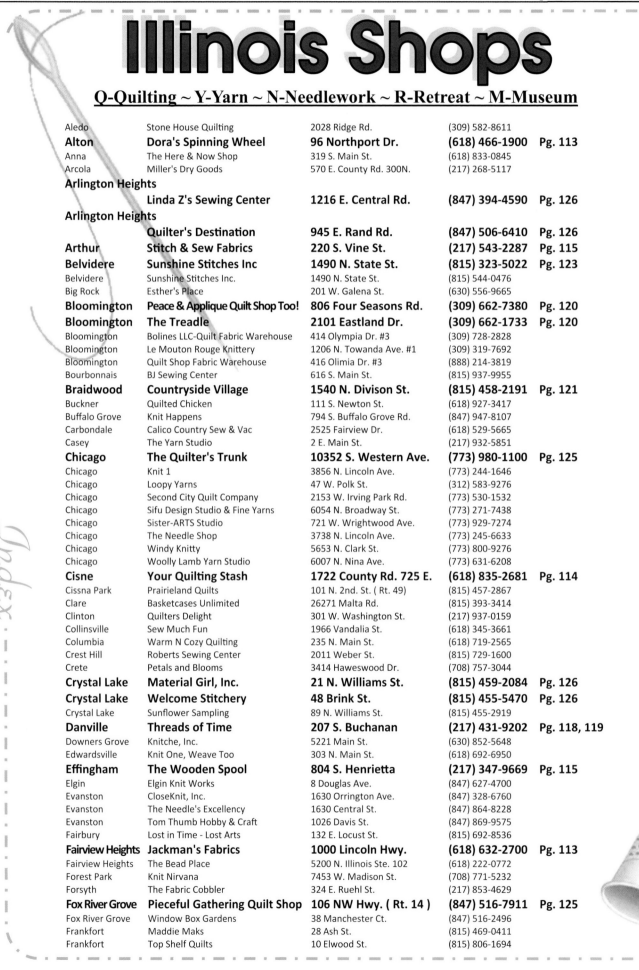

Aledo	Stone House Quilting	2028 Ridge Rd.	(309) 582-8611	
Alton	**Dora's Spinning Wheel**	**96 Northport Dr.**	**(618) 466-1900**	**Pg. 113**
Anna	The Here & Now Shop	319 S. Main St.	(618) 833-0845	
Arcola	Miller's Dry Goods	570 E. County Rd. 300N.	(217) 268-5117	
Arlington Heights				
	Linda Z's Sewing Center	**1216 E. Central Rd.**	**(847) 394-4590**	**Pg. 126**
Arlington Heights				
	Quilter's Destination	**945 E. Rand Rd.**	**(847) 506-6410**	**Pg. 126**
Arthur	**Stitch & Sew Fabrics**	**220 S. Vine St.**	**(217) 543-2287**	**Pg. 115**
Belvidere	**Sunshine Stitches Inc**	**1490 N. State St.**	**(815) 323-5022**	**Pg. 123**
Belvidere	Sunshine Stitches Inc.	1490 N. State St.	(815) 544-0476	
Big Rock	Esther's Place	201 W. Galena St.	(630) 556-9665	
Bloomington	**Peace & Applique Quilt Shop Too!**	**806 Four Seasons Rd.**	**(309) 662-7380**	**Pg. 120**
Bloomington	**The Treadle**	**2101 Eastland Dr.**	**(309) 662-1733**	**Pg. 120**
Bloomington	Bolines LLC-Quilt Fabric Warehouse	414 Olympia Dr. #3	(309) 728-2828	
Bloomington	Le Mouton Rouge Knittery	1206 N. Towanda Ave. #1	(309) 319-7692	
Bloomington	Quilt Shop Fabric Warehouse	416 Olimia Dr. #3	(888) 214-3819	
Bourbonnais	BJ Sewing Center	616 S. Main St.	(815) 937-9955	
Braidwood	**Countryside Village**	**1540 N. Divison St.**	**(815) 458-2191**	**Pg. 121**
Buckner	Quilted Chicken	111 S. Newton St.	(618) 927-3417	
Buffalo Grove	Knit Happens	794 S. Buffalo Grove Rd.	(847) 947-8107	
Carbondale	Calico Country Sew & Vac	2525 Fairview Dr.	(618) 529-5665	
Casey	The Yarn Studio	2 E. Main St.	(217) 932-5851	
Chicago	**The Quilter's Trunk**	**10352 S. Western Ave.**	**(773) 980-1100**	**Pg. 125**
Chicago	Knit 1	3856 N. Lincoln Ave.	(773) 244-1646	
Chicago	Loopy Yarns	47 W. Polk St.	(312) 583-9276	
Chicago	Second City Quilt Company	2153 W. Irving Park Rd.	(773) 530-1532	
Chicago	Sifu Design Studio & Fine Yarns	6054 N. Broadway St.	(773) 271-7438	
Chicago	Sister-ARTS Studio	721 W. Wrightwood Ave.	(773) 929-7274	
Chicago	The Needle Shop	3738 N. Lincoln Ave.	(773) 245-6633	
Chicago	Windy Knitty	5653 N. Clark St.	(773) 800-9276	
Chicago	Woolly Lamb Yarn Studio	6007 N. Nina Ave.	(773) 631-6208	
Cisne	**Your Quilting Stash**	**1722 County Rd. 725 E.**	**(618) 835-2681**	**Pg. 114**
Cissna Park	Prairieland Quilts	101 N. 2nd. St. (Rt. 49)	(815) 457-2867	
Clare	Basketcases Unlimited	26271 Malta Rd.	(815) 393-3414	
Clinton	Quilters Delight	301 W. Washington St.	(217) 937-0159	
Collinsville	Sew Much Fun	1966 Vandalia St.	(618) 345-3661	
Columbia	Warm N Cozy Quilting	235 N. Main St.	(618) 719-2565	
Crest Hill	Roberts Sewing Center	2011 Weber St.	(815) 729-1600	
Crete	Petals and Blooms	3414 Haweswood Dr.	(708) 757-3044	
Crystal Lake	**Material Girl, Inc.**	**21 N. Williams St.**	**(815) 459-2084**	**Pg. 126**
Crystal Lake	**Welcome Stitchery**	**48 Brink St.**	**(815) 455-5470**	**Pg. 126**
Crystal Lake	Sunflower Sampling	89 N. Williams St.	(815) 455-2919	
Danville	**Threads of Time**	**207 S. Buchanan**	**(217) 431-9202**	**Pg. 118, 119**
Downers Grove	Knitche, Inc.	5221 Main St.	(630) 852-5648	
Edwardsville	Knit One, Weave Too	303 N. Main St.	(618) 692-6950	
Effingham	**The Wooden Spool**	**804 S. Henrietta**	**(217) 347-9669**	**Pg. 115**
Elgin	Elgin Knit Works	8 Douglas Ave.	(847) 627-4700	
Evanston	CloseKnit, Inc.	1630 Orrington Ave.	(847) 328-6760	
Evanston	The Needle's Excellency	1630 Central St.	(847) 864-8228	
Evanston	Tom Thumb Hobby & Craft	1026 Davis St.	(847) 869-9575	
Fairbury	Lost in Time - Lost Arts	132 E. Locust St.	(815) 692-8536	
Fairview Heights	**Jackman's Fabrics**	**1000 Lincoln Hwy.**	**(618) 632-2700**	**Pg. 113**
Fairview Heights	The Bead Place	5200 N. Illinois Ste. 102	(618) 222-0772	
Forest Park	Knit Nirvana	7453 W. Madison St.	(708) 771-5232	
Forsyth	The Fabric Cobbler	324 E. Ruehl St.	(217) 853-4629	
Fox River Grove	**Pieceful Gathering Quilt Shop**	**106 NW Hwy. (Rt. 14)**	**(847) 516-7911**	**Pg. 125**
Fox River Grove	Window Box Gardens	38 Manchester Ct.	(847) 516-2496	
Frankfort	Maddie Maks	28 Ash St.	(815) 469-0411	
Frankfort	Top Shelf Quilts	10 Elwood St.	(815) 806-1694	

Frankfort	Yarns to Dye For	19 Ash St.	(815) 469-4906	
Freeport	Wall of Yarn	14 W. Stephenson St.	(815) 616-8402	
Galena	**Phat Quarter's, Inc.**	**315 S. Main St.**	**(815) 776-0034**	**Pg. 124**
Galena	Fiber Wild	304 S. Main St.	(815) 777-3550	
Galesburg	Knit 102	31 N. Kellogg St.	(309) 343-0965	
Galesburg	Quilting Bee	1580 E. Knox St. #1	(309) 343-2063	
Geneseo	Quilts-N-Blooms Quilt Shop	127 S. State St. Ste. 1	(309) 944-8739	
Geneva	Aunt Sassy's Quilts	11 N. 1st St.	(815) 787-8458	
Geneva	Designer's Desk	216 James St.	(630) 262-1234	
Geneva	Needle Things	426 S. 3rd St.	(630) 232-9915	
Gilson	**Wooden Eagle Barn**	**1291 Hwy. 150 E.**	**(309) 289-6880**	**Pg. 117**
Glen Ellyn	String Theory Yarn Co.	477 N. Main St.	(630) 469-6085	
Glen Ellyn	Tomorrow's Heirlooms	650 Roosevelt Rd. #103	(630) 790-1660	
Grant Park	Rocking Chair Quilts	301 S. Meadow St.	(815) 465-2428	
Grayslake	Quiltplay	1170 E. Washington St.	(847) 548-4967	
Grayville	Piece Time Quilt Shop	110 E. North St.	(618) 375-2800	
Hampshire	**Stitching on State**	**290 S. State St.**	**(847) 683-4739**	**Pg. 126**
Havana	**Ma's Got'a Notion**	**305 W. Main St.**	**(309) 543-6613**	**Pg. 117**
Herrin	The Yarn Shoppe	105 N. 16th St.	(618) 988-9276	
Highland	Rosemary's Fabric and Quilts	812 9th St.	(618) 654-5045	
Highland	The Machine Shop	518 Broadway	(618) 654-2233	
Highland Park	Magic Needle	463 Roger Williams Ave.	(847) 432-9897	
Highland Park	Mia Bella Yarn & Accessories	1815 St. Johns Ave.	(847) 748-8419	
Hillsboro	Stitcher's Station	1133 Vandalia Rd.	(217) 532-5984	
Hillsboro	The Quilt Traveler	423 S. Main	(217) 532-6900	
Hoopeston	**The Sewing Boutique**	**222 E. Main St.**	**(217) 283-7125**	**Pg. 120**
Jacksonville	**The Quilted Cow Emporium**	**60 E. Central Park**	**(217) 245-9190**	**Pg. 115**
Jacksonville	Times Square Sewing Complex	63 E. Central Park Plaza	(217) 245-5445	
Kewanee	**The Quilt Box**	**109 E. Third St.**	**(309) 854-9000**	**Pg. 121**
Knoxville	**Bent Needle Quilting and Embroidery**			
		506 Henderson Rd.	**(309) 335-6901**	**Pg. 120**
Knoxville	All Wound Up	221 E. Main St. #C	(309) 371-2723	
Knoxville	Sit-N-Knit Yarn Shop	236 E. Main St.	(309) 289-2379	
Lake Villa	**Sewing Source**	**122 E. Grand Ave.**	**(847) 356-5100**	**Pg. 127**
LaSalle	Quilting in the Valley	117 Gooding St.	(815) 410-5068	
Leaf River	Leaf River Quilt Company	6679 W. IL Rte. 72	(815) 738-2855	
Lemont	Inspired Needle LTD	315-B E. Illinois St.	(630) 243-9620	
Lincoln	Make It Sew	429 Pulaski St.	(217) 314-0915	
Lincoln	Serendipity Stitches	129 S. Kickapoo St.	(217) 732-8811	
Lisle	The Nook	4738 Main St.	(630) 968-0764	
Lockport	Betsy's	201 W. 10th St.	(815) 836-0470	
Lockport	Thimbles	940 S. State St.	(815) 836-8735	
Macomb	**Piece to Peace Treasures**	**1508 W. Jackson**	**(309) 836-5999**	**Pg. 116**
Mahomet	**A Quilting Bee**	**406 E. Main St.**	**(217) 714-1809**	**Pg. 117**
Marengo	The Fold	3316 Millstream Rd.	(815) 568-5320	
Maroa	Country Lace & Wood Creations	111 W. Main St.	(217) 794-5048	
Marshall	Merry Dragon Quilts	121 S. 6th St.	(217) 826-6000	
Moline	**Quilts by the Oz**	**5341 Ave. of the Cities**	**(309) 762-9673**	**Pg. 120**
Morris	**The Fabric Center**	**301 Liberty St.**	**(815) 942-5715**	**Pg. 122**
Morton	Ewe-Nique Yarns	110 E. Queenwood Rd.	(309) 266-9398	
Morton	The Quilt Corner	2037 S. Main St.	(309) 263-7114	
Mount Vernon	Quilts Plus	15833 N. Angling Ln.	(618) 237-1818	
Mt. Carmel	Caring Stitches Yarn	330 N. Market St.	(618) 262-5557	
Mt. Prospect	Mosaic Yarn Studio, Ltd.	109 W. Prospect Ave.	(847) 390-1013	
Mt. Zion	Stewart's Sewing Machines, Inc.	415 N. St. Hwy. 121	(217) 864-6142	
Mundelein	MADE Creative Fiber Arts Studio	25739 Hillview Ct.	(877) 479-9990	
Naperville	Gentler Times Stitching	124 S. Webster St. #102	(630) 637-0680	
Nashville	**Lee's Quilting & Craft Center**	**212 E. St. Louis St.**	**(618) 327-8898**	**Pg. 113**
Normal	**Sewing Studio**	**1503 E. College Ave. #C**	**(309) 452-7313**	**Pg. 120**
Northbrook	North Shore Needleworks	1512 Shermer Rd. #C	(847) 291-6550	
Northbrook	Quilter's Heaven	1747 Dundee	(847) 272-7245	
Northbrook	Three Bags Full Knitting Studio	1925-7 Cherry Ln.	(847) 291-9933	
Northfield	The Canvasback Ltd.	1747 Orchard Ln.	(847) 446-4244	
Oblong	**The Village Stitchery**	**108 E. Main St.**	**(618) 592-4134**	**Pg. 114**
Oneida	**Feed Mill Fabric and Quilting**	**246 West Hwy. St.**	**(309) 635-8283**	**Pg. 121**
Oquawka	**River Bank Fabrics & More**	**307 Schuyler St.**	**(309) 559-1070**	**Pg. 116**
Orangeville	Uniquely Yours Quilt Shop	12530 N. Oneco Rd.	(815) 789-4344	

Index

Orland Park	Country Cupboard	14314 Beacon Ave.	(708) 460-7779	
Oswego	Elemental Yarns	74 W. Van Buren ST.	(630) 636-9392	
Oswego	Prairie Stitches Quilt Shoppe	72 S. Main St.	(630) 554-9701	
Oswego	Woolkeeper	72 W. Van Buren St.	(331) 207-2855	
Pana	**The Fabric Patch**	**208 N. 2600 E. Rd.**	**(217) 561-1157**	**Pg. 114**
Paris	**Lori's Pins 'N Needles**	**1122 N. Main St.**	**(217) 465-5541**	**Pg. 120**
Pearl City	**Yellow Creek Quilt Designs**	**160 S. Main St.**	**(815) 443-2211**	**Pg. 124**
Pecatonica	Lucky 2B Quilting	421 Main St.	(815) 239-1026	
Pekin	Nonnie's Attic Fabric Shop	804 Derby St.	(309) 346-2125	
Peoria	Prairie Points	8851 N. Knoxville Ave.	(309) 692-4340	
Peoria	The Fiber Universe	305 SW Water St.	(309) 673-5659	
Peoria Heights	Sew Creative Peoria Heights	3905 N. Prospect Rd.	(309) 685-1739	
Petersburg	Sewing Seeds	111 E. Douglas	(217) 501-4768	
Plainfield	Elemental Yarns	24123 W. Lockport St.	(815) 729-7410	
Plainfield	Harvest House Quilting	24231 Apple Tree Ln.	(815) 609-5831	
Princeton	Quilter's Garden	527 S. Main St.	(815) 879-3739	
Quincy	**A to Z Quilting**	**826 State St.**	**(217) 223-9280**	**Pg. 116**
Quincy	**Sew What Shoppe**	**420 N. 24th**	**(217) 222-7458**	**Pg. 116**
Quincy	Knit Your Dreams	635 N. 66th St.	(217) 222-3335	
Rantoul	Kathy's Needle & I	1710 Grove Ave.	(217) 568-7852	
Richmond	Wool, Warp & Wheel	5605 Mill St.	(815) 678-4063	
Rochelle	Needles Quilting & Yarns	430 N. Lincoln Hwy.	(815) 384-2107	
Rochester	**Peace & Applique Quilt Shop**	**145 E. Main St.**	**(217) 498-6771**	**Pg. 115**
Rockford	**Quilter's General Store, Inc.**	**6903 Harrison Ave.**	**(815) 397-5160**	**Pg. 123**
Rockford	**Quilter's Haven**	**4616 E. State St.**	**(815) 227-1659**	**Pg. 123**
Rockford	It's For Quilting, etc. LLC	2252 New Milford School Rd.	(815) 874-0152	
Roscoe	Julieanne's Quilting & Sweet Things Shoppe	11718 N. Main St.	(815) 270-0119	
Salem	Barbaras Fabrics & Finds	105 N. Maple	(618) 548-0028	
Savoy	The Farm Ridge Quilt Shop	501 S. Dunlap #A	(217) 367-6067	
South Elgin	Twisted Stitch	218 Randall Rd.	(224) 238-3424	
Springfield	Knit Wits	3419 Chatham Rd.	(217) 698-6100	
Springfield	Nanncy's Knitworks	1305 Wabash Ave. Ste. D	(217) 546-0600	
Springfield	Sew Unique	1050 N. Grand Ave. W.	(217) 523-4293	
Springfield	Times Square Sewing Complex	3001 W. White Oaks Dr. #D	(217) 222-7458	
St. Charles	Sew Generously	3341 W. Main St. #5	(630) 444-1504	
St. Charles	Wool and Company	107 W. Main St.	(630) 444-0480	
Staunton	**Itch'n to be Stitch'n**	**111 W. Main St.**	**(618) 635-2429**	**Pg. 113**
Staunton	Main Street Mini Mall, Quilt Shop And More	124 E. Main St.	(618) 635-5509	
Sterling	Country at Heart Quilt Shop	1910 E. 4th St.	(815) 625-7484	
Sterling	Quilt Supplies for U	2503 Locust St.	(815) 622-9413	
Strasburg	Oliviers Country Creations	506 S. Walnut Rt. 32	(217) 644-2677	
Stronghurst	**Quilts & More**	**200 E. Nichols St.**	**(309) 924-2334**	**Pg. 116**
Towanda	Bolines at Indian Creek	6 Pepperwood Ct.	(309) 728-2828	
Urbana	**Sew Sassy**	**156 A Lincoln Sq. Mall**	**(217) 328-1591**	**Pg. 117**
Urbana	Klose Knit	311 W. Springfield Ave.	(217) 344-2123	
Virden	Quilting in Aisle 3	1525 N. Springfield St.	(217) 965-3014	
Washington	**Peddler's Way Quilt Company**	**127 Peddler's Way**	**(309) 444-7667**	**Pg. 121**
WAUCONDA	Unraveled	110 N. Main St.	(847) 865-0940	
West Frankfort	Calico Country Sewing Ctr.	310 S. Logan St.	(618) 932-2992	
West Frankfort	Leatta's Quilt Shop	307 S. Marion Rd.	(618) 932-2793	
West Frankfort	Sew Special Quilts	1810 E. Main St.	(618) 937-3974	
Westmont	Quiltfabric.com	818 Ogden Ave.	(630) 321-9051	
Westmont	T. L. D. Design Center & Gallery	26 E. Quincy St.	(630) 963-9573	
Westville	Cooke's Craft Cottage	11 Lyons Rd.	(217) 267-2088	
Wheaton	Craftique/Never Enough Knitting	119 N. Main St.	(630) 221-1007	
Wheaton	Lizzie's Yarn, Antiques & Gifts	300 S. Main St.	(630) 690-7945	
Winfield	**The Quilt Merchant**	**27 W. 209 Geneva Rd.**	**(630) 480-3000**	**Pg. 125**
Winnetka	The Classic Stitch	549 Chestnut St.	(847) 881-2930	
Winthrop Harbor	The Black Cat Stitchery	628 Sheridan Rd.	(224) 789-7224	
Wood River	Patchwork Plus	62 E. Ferguson Ave.	(618) 251-9788	
Woodridge	**Quilters Quest**	**7440-M Woodward Ave.**	**(630) 969-2205**	**Pg. 125**
Woodstock	That Quilt Shop, Inc.	1818 S Rose Farm Rd.	(815) 338-9353	
Woodstock	Woodstock Quilts	216 S. Seminary	(815) 338-1212	
Yorkville	Sewing Etc.	2661 N. Bridge St.	(630) 882-9328	

Notes

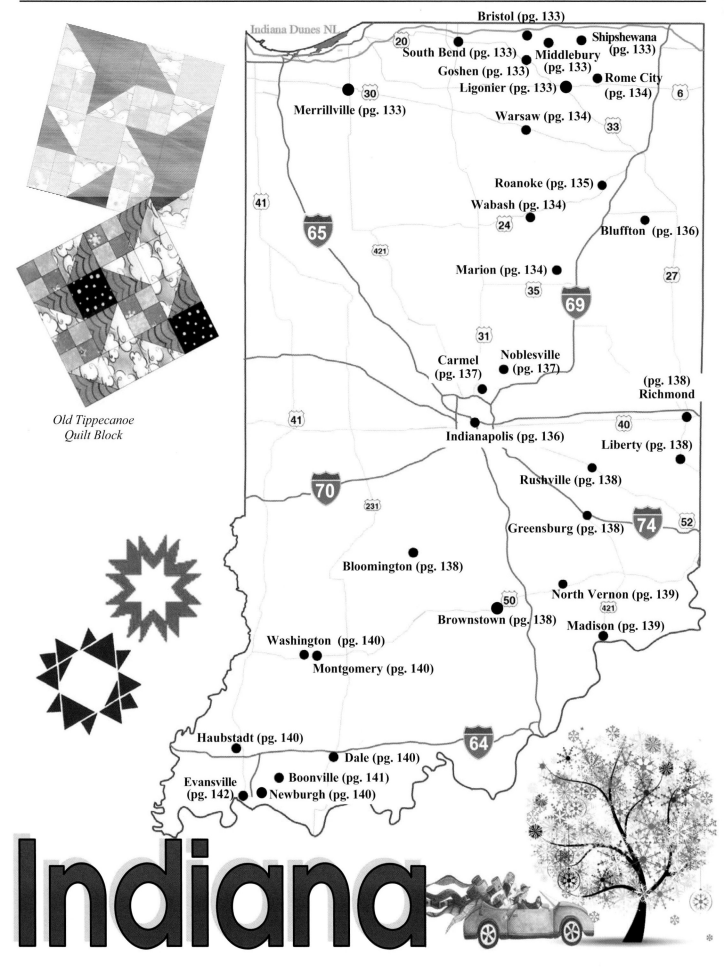

*Old Tippecanoe
Quilt Block*

Indiana Dunes NL

Bristol (pg. 133)

South Bend (pg. 133)

Shipshewana (pg. 133)

Middlebury (pg. 133)

Goshen (pg. 133)

Rome City (pg. 134)

Ligonier (pg. 133)

Merrillville (pg. 133)

Warsaw (pg. 134)

Roanoke (pg. 135)

Wabash (pg. 134)

Bluffton (pg. 136)

Marion (pg. 134)

Carmel (pg. 137)

Noblesville (pg. 137)

(pg. 138) Richmond

Indianapolis (pg. 136)

Liberty (pg. 138)

Rushville (pg. 138)

Greensburg (pg. 138)

Bloomington (pg. 138)

North Vernon (pg. 139)

Brownstown (pg. 138)

Madison (pg. 139)

Washington (pg. 140)

Montgomery (pg. 140)

Haubstadt (pg. 140)

Dale (pg. 140)

Evansville (pg. 142)

Boonville (pg. 141)

Newburgh (pg. 140)

Indiana

Did you know?
Most of the state's rivers flow south and west,
eventually emptying into the Mississippi. However, the
Maumee flows north and east into Lake Erie.

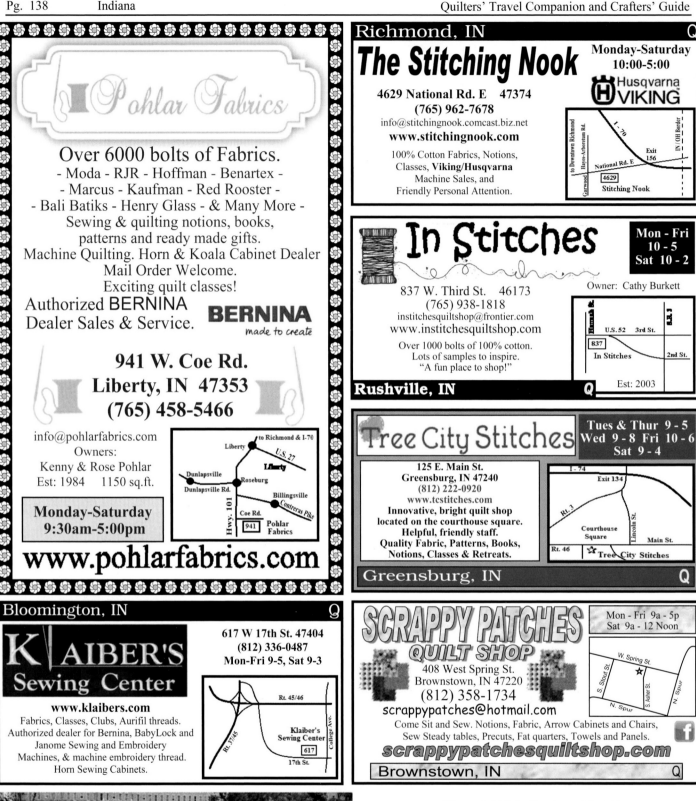

French Lick Springs Hotel

This massive hotel with its canary-yellow exterior
and gilded decor was first established in French Lick in
1845. Its Donald Ross golf course has made it a
destination for amateur players and professionals alike,
even playing host for a few PGA Championships.

8670 IN-56, French Lick, IN 47432
(888) 936-9360
www.frenchlick.com

Did you know?
True to its motto, "Cross Roads of America" Indiana has more miles of Interstate Highway per square mile than
any other state. The Indiana state Motto, can be traced back to the early 1800s. In the early years river traffic,
was a major means of transportation. The National Road, a major westward route, and the north-south Michigan
Road crossed in Indianapolis. Today more major highways intersect in Indiana than in any other state.

Plan

Notes

Indiana Shops

Q-Quilting ~ Y-Yarn ~ N-Needlework ~ R-Retreat ~ M-Museum

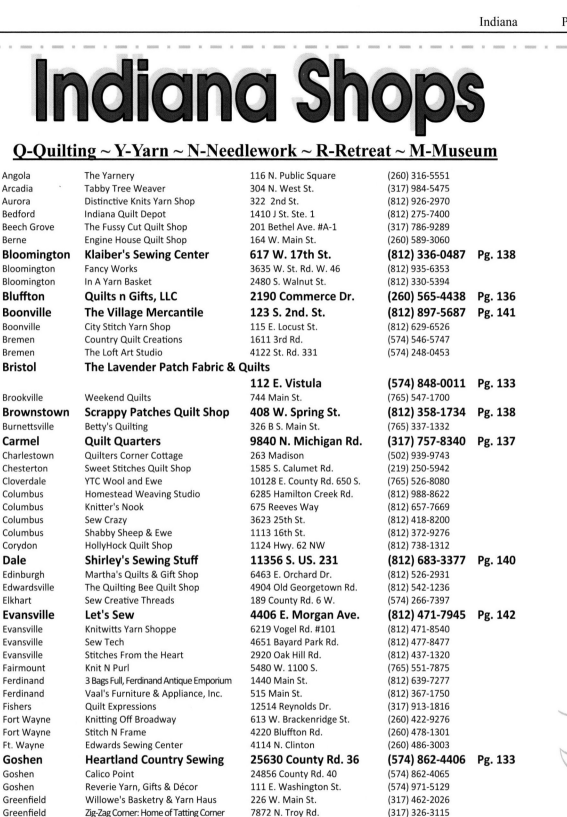

Angola	The Yarnery	116 N. Public Square	(260) 316-5551	
Arcadia	Tabby Tree Weaver	304 N. West St.	(317) 984-5475	
Aurora	Distinctive Knits Yarn Shop	322 2nd St.	(812) 926-2970	
Bedford	Indiana Quilt Depot	1410 J St. Ste. 1	(812) 275-7400	
Beech Grove	The Fussy Cut Quilt Shop	201 Bethel Ave. #A-1	(317) 786-9289	
Berne	Engine House Quilt Shop	164 W. Main St.	(260) 589-3060	
Bloomington	**Klaiber's Sewing Center**	**617 W. 17th St.**	**(812) 336-0487**	**Pg. 138**
Bloomington	Fancy Works	3635 W. St. Rd. W. 46	(812) 935-6353	
Bloomington	In A Yarn Basket	2480 S. Walnut St.	(812) 330-5394	
Bluffton	**Quilts n Gifts, LLC**	**2190 Commerce Dr.**	**(260) 565-4438**	**Pg. 136**
Boonville	**The Village Mercantile**	**123 S. 2nd. St.**	**(812) 897-5687**	**Pg. 141**
Boonville	City Stitch Yarn Shop	115 E. Locust St.	(812) 629-6526	
Bremen	Country Quilt Creations	1611 3rd Rd.	(574) 546-5747	
Bremen	The Loft Art Studio	4122 St. Rd. 331	(574) 248-0453	
Bristol	**The Lavender Patch Fabric & Quilts**			
		112 E. Vistula	**(574) 848-0011**	**Pg. 133**
Brookville	Weekend Quilts	744 Main St.	(765) 547-1700	
Brownstown	**Scrappy Patches Quilt Shop**	**408 W. Spring St.**	**(812) 358-1734**	**Pg. 138**
Burnettsville	Betty's Quilting	326 B S. Main St.	(765) 337-1332	
Carmel	**Quilt Quarters**	**9840 N. Michigan Rd.**	**(317) 757-8340**	**Pg. 137**
Charlestown	Quilters Corner Cottage	263 Madison	(502) 939-9743	
Chesterton	Sweet Stitches Quilt Shop	1585 S. Calumet Rd.	(219) 250-5942	
Cloverdale	YTC Wool and Ewe	10128 E. County Rd. 650 S.	(765) 526-8080	
Columbus	Homestead Weaving Studio	6285 Hamilton Creek Rd.	(812) 988-8622	
Columbus	Knitter's Nook	675 Reeves Way	(812) 657-7669	
Columbus	Sew Crazy	3623 25th St.	(812) 418-8200	
Columbus	Shabby Sheep & Ewe	1113 16th St.	(812) 372-9276	
Corydon	HollyHock Quilt Shop	1124 Hwy. 62 NW	(812) 738-1312	
Dale	**Shirley's Sewing Stuff**	**11356 S. US. 231**	**(812) 683-3377**	**Pg. 140**
Edinburgh	Martha's Quilts & Gift Shop	6463 E. Orchard Dr.	(812) 526-2931	
Edwardsville	The Quilting Bee Quilt Shop	4904 Old Georgetown Rd.	(812) 542-1236	
Elkhart	Sew Creative Threads	189 County Rd. 6 W.	(574) 266-7397	
Evansville	**Let's Sew**	**4406 E. Morgan Ave.**	**(812) 471-7945**	**Pg. 142**
Evansville	Knitwitts Yarn Shoppe	6219 Vogel Rd. #101	(812) 471-8540	
Evansville	Sew Tech	4651 Bayard Park Rd.	(812) 477-8477	
Evansville	Stitches From the Heart	2920 Oak Hill Rd.	(812) 437-1320	
Fairmount	Knit N Purl	5480 W. 1100 S.	(765) 551-7875	
Ferdinand	3 Bags Full, Ferdinand Antique Emporium	1440 Main St.	(812) 639-7277	
Ferdinand	Vaal's Furniture & Appliance, Inc.	515 Main St.	(812) 367-1750	
Fishers	Quilt Expressions	12514 Reynolds Dr.	(317) 913-1816	
Fort Wayne	Knitting Off Broadway	613 W. Brackenridge St.	(260) 422-9276	
Fort Wayne	Stitch N Frame	4220 Bluffton Rd.	(260) 478-1301	
Ft. Wayne	Edwards Sewing Center	4114 N. Clinton	(260) 486-3003	
Goshen	**Heartland Country Sewing**	**25630 County Rd. 36**	**(574) 862-4406**	**Pg. 133**
Goshen	Calico Point	24856 County Rd. 40	(574) 862-4065	
Goshen	Reverie Yarn, Gifts & Décor	111 E. Washington St.	(574) 971-5129	
Greenfield	Willowe's Basketry & Yarn Haus	226 W. Main St.	(317) 462-2026	
Greenfield	Zig-Zag Corner: Home of Tatting Corner	7872 N. Troy Rd.	(317) 326-3115	
Greensburg	**Tree City Stitches**	**125 E. Main St.**	**(812) 222-0920**	**Pg. 138**
Greenwood	Back Door Quilts	2503 Fairview Place Ste. W	(317) 882-2120	
Greenwood	Starstruck Cat Studio	3130 Meridian Parke Dr. #M	(317) 889-9665	
Griffith	Spinnin Yarns	145 N. Griffith Blvd.	(219) 924-7333	
Guilford	The Weavers Loft	24647 Zimmer Rd.	(812) 576-3904	
Haubstadt	**Quilts 'n Bloom**	**879 W. 1000 S.**	**(812) 768-6009**	**Pg. 140**
Indianapolis	**Quilts Plus**	**1748 E. 86th St.**	**(317) 844-2446**	**Pg. 136**
Indianapolis	**Accomplish Quilting**	**1746 E. 86th St.**	**(317) 470-1322**	**Pg. 136**
Indianapolis	Broad Ripple Knit	6510 N. Cornell Ave.	(317) 255-0540	
Indianapolis	Crimson Tate Modern Quilter	845 Massachusetts Ave. #A	(317) 426-3300	
Indianapolis	Knit Stop	3941 E. 82nd St.	(317) 595-5648	
Indianapolis	Mass Ave. Knit Shop	862 Virginia Ave.	(317) 638-1833	

Index

Indianapolis	The French Seam	9335 Castlegate Dr.	(317) 841-1810	
Jeffersonville	Grinny Possum Fiber Arts	326 Spring St.	(812) 284-9400	
Kokomo	Khadija Knit Shop	3712 S. Lafountain St.	(765) 453-4652	
La Porte	House of Stitches	1700 Lincolnway Place #4	(219) 326-0544	
Lafayette	River Knits Fine Yarns	926 Main St.	(765) 742-5648	
LaGrange	Homespun Treasures	205 E. Wayne St.	(260) 463-8499	
Lawrenceburg	Quilters Garden	84 E. High St.	(812) 539-4939	
Liberty	**Pohlar Fabrics**	**941 W. Coe Rd.**	**(765) 458-5466**	**Pg. 138**
Ligonier	**Zincks Fabric Outlet**	**1444 S. Lincolnway**	**(260) 894-3000**	**Pg. 133**
Lowell	Fox Farmhouse Quilting	15504 Morse St.	(219) 743-8570	
Lowell	K & S Sew-N-Quilt	304 E. Commercial Ave.	(219) 690-1695	
Madison	**L & L Yard Goods**	**1814 Taylor St.**	**(812) 273-1041**	**Pg. 139**
Madison	**Margie's Country Store**	**721 W. Main St.**	**(812) 265-4429**	**Pg. 139**
Madison	Fabric Shop	220 E. Main St.	(812) 265-5828	
Marion	**Quilter's Hall of Fame**	**926 S. Washington St.**	**(765) 664-9333**	**Pg. 134**
Merrillville	**Spyceware Sewing Center**	**1090 W. 84th Dr.**	**(219) 663-6973**	**Pg. 133**
Michigan City	Threadbenders Quilt Shop	906 Franklin St.	(219) 229-7845	
Middlebury	**The Quilt Shop**	**240 US. 20**	**(574) 825-9471**	**Pg. 133**
Middlebury	Pumpkinvine Quilting	500 Spring Valley Rd. #3	(574) 825-1151	
Mishawaka	Stone Soup Batiks	2520 Miracle Ln.	(574) 400-0258	
Mishawaka	The Quilting Loft	532 Lincolnway E.	(574) 252-0588	
Montgomery	**David V. Wagler's Quilts**	**4413 E. 200 N.**	**(812) 486-3836**	**Pg. 140**
Monticello	Krazy Lady Quilt Shop	1430 N. Main St.	(574) 583-0008	
Muncie	Cotton Candy Quilt Shoppe	5001 N. Wheeling Ave.	(765) 254-1584	
Muncie	Elegant Needleworks, Inc.	7500 N. Janna Dr.	(765) 284-9427	
Nappanee	Martin's Quilt Shop	25387 County Rd. 46	(574) 831-2256	
Nashville	The Clay Purl	58 E. Main #3	(812) 988-0336	
New Albany	Jan's Sewing Things	201 Hausfeldt Ln.	(812) 945-8113	
New Carlisle	Yarn & More	106 S. Filbert St.	(574) 654-3300	
New Castle	The Woolen Yurt	1435 N. Kennard Rd.	(765) 465-6101	
New Paris	Three Sisters Fabric	68276 Main St.	(574) 903-4847	
Newburgh	**Red Rooster Stitchery**	**10044 St. Rd. 662 W.**	**(812) 853-9657**	**Pg. 140**
Newburgh	Sheepskeins Yarn Shop	1109 Hwy. 662 W.	(812) 842-0200	
Noblesville	**Always In Stitches**	**1808 E. Conner St.**	**(317) 776-4227**	**Pg. 137**
Noblesville	Arbuckle's Railroad Place	1151 Vine St.	(317) 773-3985	
Noblesville	The Black Sheep Yarn and Fiberarts	1095 Conner St.	(317) 900-7117	
North Vernon	**Sharynn's Quilt Box**	**890 S. State St.**	**(812) 346-4731**	**Pg. 139**
Pekin	Craft Town Fabrics	3844 E Sheets Corner Rd.	(812) 967-8696	
Pendleton	The Trading Post for Fiber Arts	8833 S. 50 W.	(765) 778-3331	
Peru	The Knit Knack Shop	3378 W. 550 N.	(765) 985-3164	
Plainfield	Nomad Yarns	218 E. Main St.	(317) 742-7456	
Portland	Stickley's Quilt Shop	104 S. Harrison St.	(937) 417-2160	
Rensselaer	From The Needles Point	125 N. Front St.	(219) 866-5353	
Richmond	**The Stitching Nook**	**4629 National Rd. E.**	**(765) 962-7678**	**Pg. 138**
Richmond	Nancy's Fancys Sewing Corner	1446 NW 5th St.	(765) 939-0465	
Richmond	Ply Fiber Arts	921 E. Main St.	(765) 966-5648	
Roanoke	**Fabrics & Friends Quilt Shop LLC**	**126 W. 2nd St.**	**(260) 676-2149**	**Pg. 135**
Rochester	The Thread Shed	610 Main St.	(574) 223-4959	
Rockville	The Fiber Closet	120 S. Market St.	(765) 569-2953	
Rolling Prairie	Knitting in the Round	8353 N. 600 E.	(219) 778-4854	
Rome City	**Caroline's Cottage Cottons**	**195 Weston St.**	**(260) 854-3900**	**Pg. 134**
Rossville	Rossville Quilts & Mill House Retreat Center	356 W. Main St.	(765) 379-2900	
Rushville	**In Stitches**	**837 W. Third St.**	**(765) 938-1818**	**Pg. 138**
Seymour	Small Town Stitches	1129 W. Tipton St.	(812) 271-1663	
Shipshewana	**Lolly's Fabrics & Quilts**	**255 E. Main St.**	**(260) 768-4703**	**Pg. 133**
Shipshewana	**The Cotton Corner**	**350 S. Van Buren St.**	**(260) 768-7393**	**Pg. 133**
Shipshewana	**Yoder's Department Store**	**300 S. Van Buren St. State Rr. 5**		
			(260) 768-4887	**Pg. 133**

Notes

Shipshewana	Little Helpers Quilt Shop	1030 N. 1000 W.	(260) 768-4278	
Shipshewana	Rebecca Haarer Folk Arts & Antiques	165 Morton St.	(260) 768-4787	
Shipshewana	The D'Vine Gallery	310 N. Harrison St.	(260) 768-7110	
South Bend	**Stitch 'n Time Fabrics**	**2305 Miami St.**	**(574) 234-4314**	**Pg. 133**
South Bend	Erica's Craft & Sewing Center	1320 N. Ironwood Dr.	(574) 233-3112	
South Bend	Heckaman's Quilting & Yarns	63028 US. 31 S.	(574) 291-3918	
South Bend	Thyme to Sew	621 Lincolnway E.	(574) 855-2297	
Spencer	Unraveled Quilt Store	381 N. Fletcher Ave.	(812) 821-0309	
Spiceland	Stitches Quilt Shop	109 N. Pearl St.	(765) 987-1188	
St. Joe	The Big Red Barn	6205 St. Rd. 1	(260) 446-7997	
Terre Haute	River Wools	671 Wabash Ave.	(812) 238-0090	
Terre Haute	Wabash Valley Fabrics	1347 Wabash Ave.	(812) 232-0727	
Topeka	Sara's Attic	101 N. Main St.	(260) 593-2252	
Trafalger	Coffee Cup Quilting	7 Trafalger Sq. #A	(317) 878-5155	
Twelve Mile	The Scarlet Thread Quilt Co.	1974 E. 1000 S.	(574) 721-5899	
Union City	Home Place Sewing Shop	400 N. County Rd. 625 E.	(765) 584-7374	
Valparaiso	Cotton Cottage Quilts	831 E. Lincolnway	(219) 286-3929	
Valparaiso	Sheep's Clothing Knitting Supplies	60 W. Lincolnway	(219) 462-1700	
Versailles	The Quilter's Nook, Inc.	82 Hill St.	(812) 689-0980	
Vincennes	Atkinson Farm Yarns	1061 N. Atkinson Rd.	(812) 726-1306	
Wabash	**Heaven on Earth**	**4767 N. State Rd. 15**	**(765) 833-5461**	**Pg. 134**
Wabash	**Nancy J.'s Fabrics**	**1604 S. Wabash St.**	**(260) 563-3505**	**Pg. 134**
Wanatah	Scrapyard Quilting	10501 W. 1000 S.	(219) 733-9980	
Warsaw	**Lowery Sewing & Vacuum**	**707 E. Winona Ave.**	**(574) 267-8631**	**Pg. 134**
Washington	**The Stitching Post**	**401 E. Main St.**	**(812) 254-6063**	**Pg. 140**
Wawaka	Ragtime Rugs	1946 W. 1050 N.	(888) 724-7847	
Whiteland	Pattis Creative Felt	2367 E. 400 N.	(317) 403-5667	
Whitestown	Designer Sewing Center	8 S. Main St. #103	(317) 768-3023	
Zionsville	Persnickety Stitchers Inc.	58 N. Main St. #A	(317) 873-5010	
Zionsville	Village Yarn Shop	40 N. Main St.	(317) 873-0004	

Index

Notes

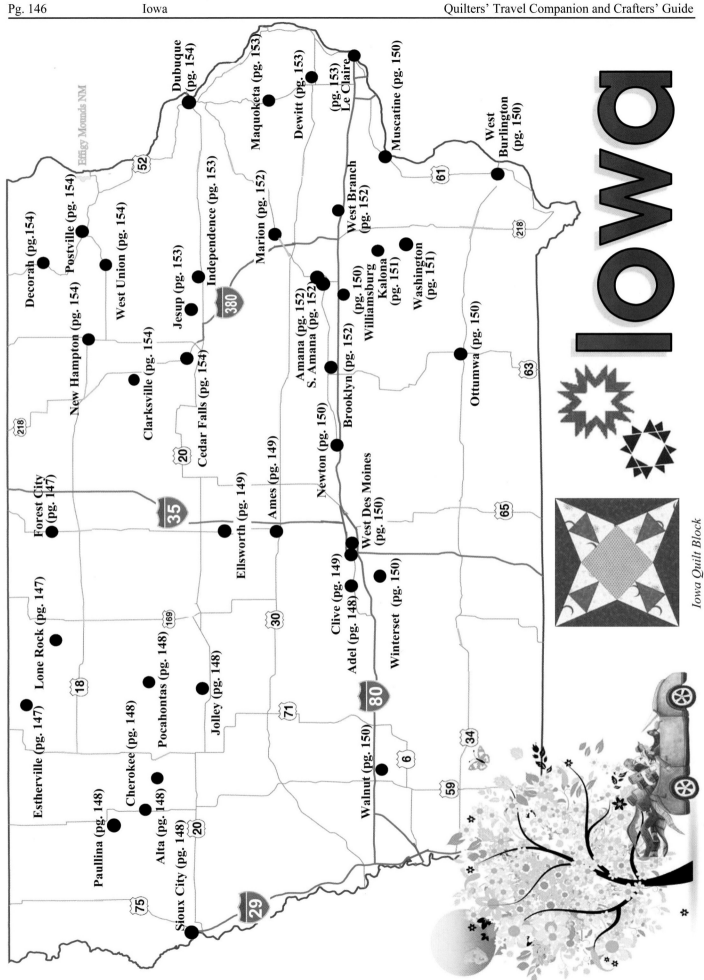

Effigy Mounds NM

Dubuque (pg. 154)

Maquoketa (pg. 153)

Dewitt (pg. 153)

(pg. 153)
Le Claire

Muscatine (pg. 150)

West
Burlington
(pg. 150)

Decorah (pg.154)

Postville (pg. 154)

West Union (pg. 154)

Independence (pg. 153)

Marion (pg. 152)

West Branch
(pg. 152)

Washington
(pg. 151)

Williamsburg
(pg. 150)

Kalona
(pg. 151)

New Hampton (pg. 154)

Jesup (pg. 153)

Clarksville (pg. 154)

Cedar Falls (pg. 154)

Amana (pg. 152)
S. Amana (pg. 152)

Brooklyn (pg. 152)

Ottumwa (pg. 150)

Forest City
(pg. 147)

Ellsworth (pg. 149)

Ames (pg. 149)

Newton (pg. 150)

West Des Moines
(pg. 150)

Lone Rock (pg. 147)

Pocahontas (pg. 148)

Jolley (pg. 148)

Clive (pg. 149)

Adel (pg. 148)

Winterset (pg. 150)

Estherville (pg. 147)

Cherokee (pg. 148)

Alta (pg. 148)

Paullina (pg. 148)

Walnut (pg. 150)

Sioux City (pg. 148)

Iowa Quilt Block

Did you know?
The highest double track railroad bridge in the world, the Kate Shelley Bridge, is located at Boone.

Did you know?
At 16 miles, East Okoboji is the longest
natural lake in the state.

Needle & Thread

On the Historic Square of Washington, Iowa

- Carefully selected, current, high quality quilting fabrics and sewing supplies.
- Your resource for: Batiks, Blenders, Backgrounds, Civil War, 1930's, Florals, Children.
- We love helping you choose your fabric.
- Kits unique to our store.
- A huge supply of fat quarters. Every Friday is Fat Quarter Friday (Buy 5 Fat Quarters, Get the 6th one free).
- Classes: Various Quilting Techniques, Block of the Month.

- We offer the complete line of *EverSewn* Sparrow series, the Hero embroidery machine, and accessories.

The *EverSewn* machine- *Is* perfection!

- We carry lots of antique Singer Featherweight machines and accessories.
- We service all makes and ages of machines.

Be inspired
Be encouraged
Develop your skills

Check out the various antiques while in our store.
Gift Certificates Available.
While you're here eat at the famous
Café Dodici restaurant
right on the square of our Historic Washington, IA.

Hours of Operation:
Tues, Wed, Fri 9:00-5:00, Thur 1:00-7:00, Sat 9:00-2:00

122 West Main Street Washington, IA 52353 ~ 319-591-2009

Email address for our free news letter: needleandthread@mail.com

Stitch N Sew Cottage

Kalona, IA   Q

207 4th St. Kalona, IA 52247
(319) 656-2923
stitchnsewc@yahoo.com

Custom made Quilts, Fabrics,
Notions, Quilting supplies,
3000+ Bolts, Books and Patterns.
Monday-Saturday 9:00am-5:00pm

Woodin Wheel

515 "B" Ave., P.O. Box 627 52247
(319) 656-2240
Katie@woodinwheel.com
www.woodinwheel.com
Over 300 New & Antique Quilts for Sale.
Sponsor of Annual Kalona Quilt Show & Sale.
Last Friday & Saturday of April.
Large selection of
Heartwood Creek by Jim Shore.

Monday - Saturday
9am - 5pm

Kalona, IA   Q

Willow Creek Quilting & Gifts

418 B Avenue,
Kalona, IA 52247
319-656-3939
willowcreekquilting@hotmail.com
Monday-Saturday 10:00-5:00

* Over 3000 bolts of quality quilt fabric
* Reproduction fabrics - Civil War & 30's
* Room dedicated to baby and kid fabrics
* A room full of models to inspire you
* Handmade ceramic buttons
* Kits galore!
* New sewing room for classes and group sewing

www.willowcreekquilting.com

Did you know?
Iowa is the only state name that starts with two vowels.

Iowa's longest and highest bridge crosses Lake Red Rock.

Iowa Shops

Q-Quilting ~ Y-Yarn ~ N-Needlework ~ R-Retreat ~ M-Museum

Adel	**Adel Quilting & Drygoods**	**909 Prairie St.**	**(515) 993-1170**	**Pg. 148**
Algona	Seams To Me	17 E. State St.	(515) 295-5841	
Alta	**The Quilt Shoppe**	**206 Main St.**	**(712) 284-2724**	**Pg. 148**
Amana	**Heritage Designs**	**614 46th Ave.**	**(319) 622-3887**	**Pg. 152**
Ames	**Quilting Connection**	**238 Main St.**	**(515) 233-3048**	**Pg. 149**
Ames	The Rose Tree Fiber Shop	2814 West St.	(515) 292-7076	
Ankeny	Knitting Next Door	704 SW Third St.	(515) 963-0396	
Ankeny	Quilter's Cupboard	706 SW 3rd St.	(515) 963-8758	
Aplington	Jen's Needleworks	900 Parriott	(319) 347-2793	
Arcadia	Arcadia Quilts	201 Gault St.	(712) 689-8888	
Atlantic	Something for You	501 Chestnut St.	(712) 243-4157	
Audubon	Country Quilting	1752 210th St.	(712) 563-3257	
Bellevue	JoQuilter Fabrics	128 S. Riverview Dr.	(563) 872-3473	
Bettendorf	Knit & Knot - A Yarn Boutique	3359 Devil's Glen Rd.	(563) 332-7378	
Bloomfield	Dutch Country Living	17192 Hwy. 2	(641) 722-3678	
Bondurant	Off the Rails Quilting	15 Main St. SE	(515) 967-3550	
Brooklyn	**Brooklyn True Value**	**118 W. Front St.**	**(641) 522-7712**	**Pg. 152**
Brooklyn	Brooklyn Fabric Company	116 Jackson St.	(641) 522-4766	
Burlington	Fiber Addicts	403 Jefferson St.	(779) 861-0195	
Burlington	The Sew 'N Sew Shop	3206 Division St.	(319) 752-5733	
Cantril	Dutchman's Store	103 Division St.	(319) 397-2322	
Carroll	The Quilt Shop & Yarn Basket	512 N. Adams St.	(712) 792-2890	
Cascade	The Quilting Tree	224 1st Ave. W.	(563) 852-7765	
Cedar Falls	**Crazy to Quilt Shop**	**707 W. 1st St.**	**(319) 277-1360**	**Pg. 154**
Cedar Falls	**Lulijune's Quilt Shop**	**14303 University Ave.**	**(319) 961-0705**	**Pg. 154**
Cedar Falls	Quilting Bug	7125 N. Union Rd.	(319) 266-1098	
Cedar Falls	The Sheep Baatique	602 State St. #E2	(319) 243-0435	
Cedar Rapids	Delve MIY	1011 3rd St. SE	(319) 200-4246	
Cedar Rapids	Inspired to Sew	1000 Old Marion Rd.	(319) 373-0334	
Cedar Rapids	R Rabbit's Mercantile	3260 Southgate Place SW	(319) 390-3373	
Cedar Rapids	Treasures From The Attic	2300 Grande Ave. SE	(319) 390-1929	
Cedar Rapids	West Side Sewing Machine Shop	4100 First Ave. NE	(319) 365-3075	
Centerville	Shabby Chic Boutique	211 E. State St.	(641) 895-0251	
Chariton	Cindy Lou's Gifts & Quilt Shop	907 Braden Ave.	(641) 774-1215	
Chariton	The Sampler	102 S. Grand	(641) 774-2116	
Charles City	Stitches	715 Kelly Mall	(641) 228-3383	
Cherokee	**Quilt 'N Kaboodle**	**420 W. Main St.**	**(712) 225-3600**	**Pg. 148**
Clarinda	Handcart Quilts & Barns	102 E. Washington	(712) 542-1290	
Clarksville	**Prairie Rose Fabrics**	**109 N. Main St.**	**(319) 278-4767**	**Pg. 154**
Clear Lake	Larson's Mercantile	323 Main Ave.	(641) 357-7544	
Clinton	Keeping You Sewing	226 4th Ave. S.	(563) 242-6135	
Clinton	Stitch 'N & Stuff	242 6th Ave. S.	(563) 243-2271	
Clive	**Creekside Quilting**	**9926 Swanson Blvd.**	**(515) 276-1977**	**Pg. 149**
Conrad	Hen and Chicks Studio	101 N. Main St.	(641) 366-3336	
Council Bluffs	Cut Up & Quilt	303 McKenzie Ave.	(712) 256-5550	
Cresco	Quilter's Garden	122 N. Elm St.	(563) 203-9266	
Decorah	**Blue Heron Knittery**	**300 W. Water St.**	**(563) 517-1059**	**Pg. 154**
Decorah	Red-Roxy Quilt Co.	415 W. Water St.	(563) 382-4646	
Denison	Wise Monkey Quilting	40 N. Main St.	(712) 393-7979	
Des Moines	Hill Vintage & Knits	432 E. Locust	(515) 288-2287	
Des Moines	Miller's Perfect Place	5255 NE 3rd St.	(515) 282-8605	
Des Moines	Stitch 'N Frame	7611 Douglas Ave. #110	(515) 270-1066	
Des Moines	Woodside Quilting	5360 NE 14th Ste. A	(515) 777-3500	
DeWitt	**Heartland Cottons**	**615 10th St.**	**(563) 659-6200**	**Pg. 153**
Dubuque	**The Cotton Cabin Quilt Shop**	**1075 Main St.**	**(563) 582-0800**	**Pg. 154**
Dubuque	Quilt Shack	3220 Dodge St. #106	(563) 556-3163	
Dubuque	Yarn Soup	1005 Main St.	(563) 587-8044	
Elkader	The Backstitch	108 S. Main St.	(563) 245-2967	
Ellsworth	**Mended Hearts Quilting & Boutique**			
		3212 330th St.	**(515) 836-4280**	**Pg. 149**

Estherville	**Homespun Quilt Shop**	**202 W. Central Ave.**	**(712) 362-5100**	**Pg. 147**
Estherville	**The Wooden Thimble**	**17 S. 6th St.**	**(712) 362-2561**	**Pg. 147**
Exira	Log Cabin Quilting	111 W. Washington	(712) 268-2487	
Fairfield	At Home Store	52 N. Main St.	(641) 472-1016	
Forest City	**The Quilted Forest**	**205 N. Clark St.**	**(641) 585-2438**	**Pg. 147**
Fort Dodge	Tillie's Quilts	17 S. 12th St.	(515) 576-6265	
Garner	Farm Chick Quilts	211 State St.	(641) 430-6341	
Glidden	Threads Etc.	126 Idaho	(712) 659-0113	
Greene	Dralle's Dept. Store	122 E. Traer St.	(641) 816-4158	
Hills	Inspirations	120 E. Main St.	(319) 679-2207	
Humeston	Snips of Thread Quilt Shop	124 S. Front St.	(515) 360-6901	
Independence	**Quilter's Quarters**	**213 First St. E.**	**(319) 334-4443**	**Pg. 153**
Independence	Stitcher's Hideway	115 First St. E.	(319) 332-1076	
Indianola	The Stitching Place	127 N. Buxtun	(515) 961-5162	
Iowa City	Fae Ridge Farm	5140 Rapid Creek Rd. NE	(319) 643-5873	
Iowa City	The Knitting Shoppe	2141 Muscatine Ave.	(319) 337-4920	
Iowa Falls	Iowa Falls Sewing Machine Co.	520 Washington Ave.	(641) 648-2379	
Jefferson	The Stitch	217 E. Licolnway	(515) 386-2014	
Jesup	**Merry's Stitchins**	**1923 Baker Rd.**	**(319) 827-6703**	**Pg. 153**
Jewell	Sew Bee It Quilt Shop	621 Main St.	(515) 290-0983	
Jolley	**Lee's Quilt Shed**	**2341 Inwood Ave.**	**(712) 297-8458**	**Pg. 148**
Kalona	**Stitch 'n Sew Cottage**	**207 4th St.**	**(319) 656-2923**	**Pg. 151**
Kalona	**Willow Creek Quilting & Gifts**	**418 B Ave.**	**(319) 656-3939**	**Pg. 151**
Kalona	**Woodin Wheel Antiques & Gifts**	**515 B Ave.**	**(319) 656-2240**	**Pg. 151**
Kalona	Kalona Quilt & Textile Museum	715 D Ave.	(319) 656-3232	
Keokuk	Quilt 'N Etc.	300 Main St. #750	(319) 524-1327	
Keosauqua	Bentonsport Quilt Company	21960 Hawk Dr.	(319) 288-1042	
Kirkville	Patchwork Peddlers Post	207 McCarroll St.	(641) 777-3302	
Klemme	Wash Tub Quilts	101 E. Main St.	(641) 587-2014	
Lake City	Towne Square Quilt Shoppe	103 E. Main St.	(712) 464-7477	
LaMotte	Irish Meadows Yarn Barn & Boutique	23477 Bellevue Cascade Rd.	(563) 543-1375	
Le Claire	**Expressions In Threads**	**208 S. Cody Rd.**	**(563) 289-1447**	**Pg. 153**
Lone Rock	**Sew and Sew**	**402 Front St.**	**(515) 925-3636**	**Pg. 147**
Lucas	Quilt With Us	100 E. Front St.	(641) 766-6486	
Mallard	The Quilter's Portable	607 Inman St.	(712) 425-3478	
Manchester	The Quiltmaker's Shoppe	110 E. Main St.	(563) 927-8017	
Maquoketa	**Hermes Auto & Upholstery**	**1325 E. Platt St.**	**(563) 652-2279**	**Pg. 153**
Marion	**Connie's Quilt Shop**	**785 Eighth Ave.**	**(319) 373-9455**	**Pg. 152**
Marion	Village Needlework	1129 7th Ave.	(319) 362-3271	
Monona	Suhdron Fabrics	120 W. Center St.	(563) 539-2135	
Montezuma	3 Sisters Fabric and Fashion	305 E. Main St.	(641) 623-5640	
Monticello	JT Hadherway Company	23004 150th Ave.	(319) 465-5090	
Mount Vernon	Helios Stitches N Stuff	221 1st St. NE	(319) 512-3323	
Mt. Pleasant	Quilter's Paradise	120 N. Main St.	(319) 385-1749	
Muscatine	**The Little Red Hen**	**612 Hope Ave.**	**(563) 262-5709**	**Pg. 150**
Muscatine	Neal's Vacuum & Sewing Center	309 E. 2nd. St.	(563) 263-4543	
Nevada	Block Party Studios Quilt Shop	1503 W. K Ave.	(800) 419-2812	
New Hampton	**Quilter's Window**	**101 E. Main St.**	**(641) 394-6900**	**Pg. 154**
New Hampton	Material Magic	22 E. Main St.	(641) 394-2461	
Newton	**Crazy Redhead Quilting**	**814 1st Ave. E.**	**(641) 787-9122**	**Pg. 150**
North Liberty	Common Threads	480 W. Zeller St.	(319) 626-3160	
Oelwein	Lou Ann's Quilt Garden & Retreat	21 E. Charles St.	(319) 283-5165	
Onawa	Susie's Quilts-N-More	904 Iowa Ave.	(712) 423-9625	
Orange City	Stitch Studio	104 Central Ave. NW	(712) 737-9800	
Osage	Debbie's Quilt Shop	605 Main St.	(641) 732-1474	
Osage	Ewe and Eye - Woolens and Such	3532 Lancer Ave.	(641) 832-2477	
Osage	The Stitchery Nook	635 Main St.	(641) 732-5329	
Osceola	Robinson's True Value	127 S. Main	(641) 342-2154	
Oskaloosa	Puppy Love Quilting	1516 A Ave. E.	(641) 569-9022	
Oskaloosa	Quilted Treasures & Retreats	3283 Merino Ave.	(641) 969-4444	
Ottumwa	**The Sewing House**	**220 E. Main St.**	**(641) 682-4995**	**Pg. 150**
Panora	Quilting Market	4926 Lynn Dr.	(641) 755-4151	
Paullina	**Prairie Woolens Quilt Shop**	**108 S. Main**	**(712) 229-0341**	**Pg. 148**
Pella	The Quilted Windmill	701 Franklin St.	(641) 628-3350	
Pocahontas	**Quilting on Main**	**229 N. Main**	**(712) 335-3969**	**Pg. 148**
Pocahontas	Ewe-Phoria Yarns	101 NW 7th St.	(712) 335-4910	
Postville	**Forest Mills Quilt Shop**	**650 Forest Mills Rd.**	**(563) 568-3807**	**Pg. 154**

Index

Richland	The Red Hen Shop	30847 323rd Ave.	(319) 456-2018	
Sioux Center	Roelof's Store	24 3rd St. NW	(712) 722-2611	
Sioux City	**Heart in Hand Dry Goods Co.**	**3011 Hamilton Blvd.**	**(712) 258-3161**	**Pg. 148**
South Amana	**Fern Hill Gifts & Quilts**	**103 220th Trail**	**(319) 622-3627**	**Pg. 152**
Spirit Lake	Quilt 'n' Stitches	816 Lake St.	(712) 336-2708	
Storm Lake	Inspired by Time Quilts	516 Lake Ave.	(712) 213-1100	
Story City	Udderly Quilts and More	324 Factory Outlet Dr.	(515) 231-9379	
Strawberry Point	Quilted Strawberry	107 Commercial St.	(563) 920-1449	
Tipton	The Fabric Stasher	505 E.Cedar St.	(563) 886-1600	
Tracy	B&B Creations Quilt Shop	305 Parker St.	(641) 949-6307	
Vincent	Mrs. T's Mercantile & Tea Room	100 Arthur St.	(515) 356-2230	
Walnut	**DR's Kalico Krafts**	**206 Antique City Dr.**	**(712) 784-3865**	**Pg. 150**
Washington	**Needle and Thread**	**122 W. Main St.**	**(319) 591-2009**	**Pg.151**
Waterloo	Three Oaks Knits	2827 University Ave.	(319) 883-8000	
Waukon	Queen Jean Quilting	802 2nd Ave. NW	(563) 217-0393	
Waverly	Fiberworks	108 E. Bremer Ave.	(319) 352-5464	
Waverly	The Moose Patch	205 E. Bremer Ave.	(319) 352-5040	
West Branch	**Cotton Creek Mill**	**113 W. Main St.**	**(319) 643-3554**	**Pg. 152**
West Burlington	**Ellen's Quilting Corner**	**123 Broadway St.**	**(319) 752-4288**	**Pg. 150**
West Des Moines				
	The Quilt Block	**325 5th St.**	**(515) 255-1010**	**Pg. 150**
West Des Moines	At the Heart of Quilting	315 5th St.	(515) 277-6497	
West Union	**One Block Over**	**322 E. Main St.**	**(563) 422-3822**	**Pg. 154**
West Union	Moonlight Stitching Studio	105 N. Vine St.	(563) 422-8212	
Williamsburg	**Rainbows and Calico Things**	**2811 240th St.**	**(319) 668-1977**	**Pg. 150**
Williamsburg	The Woolen Needle	225 W. Welsh St.	(319) 668-2642	
Winterset	**Heartland Fiber Company**	**112 N. 1st Ave.**	**(515) 468-8593**	**Pg. 150**
Winterset	Ben Franklin	72 W. Ct.	(515) 462-2062	
Winterset	Piece Works Quilt Shop	54 E. Ct.	(515) 493-1121	
Woodbine	Stitchin' Tree Quilts	3131 Hwy. 30	(712) 647-3161	

Index

Notes

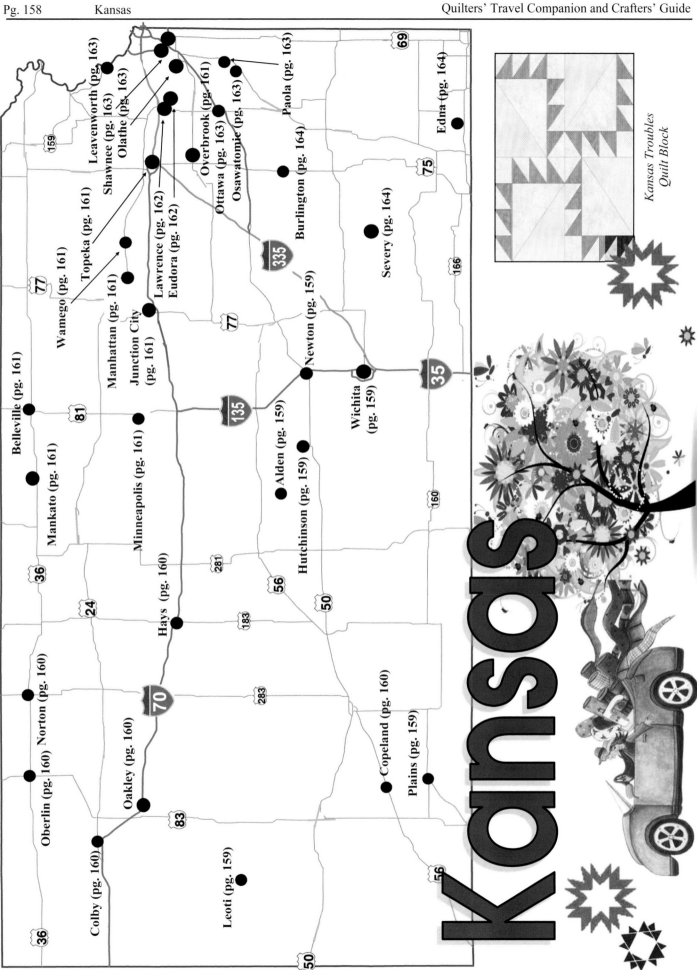

Kansas Troubles
Quilt Block

Leavenworth (pg. 163)
Shawnee (pg. 163)
Olathe (pg. 163)
Overbrook (pg. 161)
Osawatomie (pg. 163)
Ottawa (pg. 163)
Paola (pg. 163)
Edna (pg. 164)
Burlington (pg. 164)
Severy (pg. 164)
Topeka (pg. 161)
Wamego (pg. 161)
Lawrence (pg. 162)
Eudora (pg. 162)
Manhattan (pg. 161)
Junction City (pg. 161)
Belleville (pg. 161)
Mankato (pg. 161)
Minneapolis (pg. 161)
Newton (pg. 159)
Wichita (pg. 159)
Alden (pg. 159)
Hutchinson (pg. 159)
Hays (pg. 160)
Oberlin (pg. 160)
Norton (pg. 160)
Oakley (pg. 160)
Colby (pg. 160)
Copeland (pg. 160)
Plains (pg. 159)
Leoti (pg. 159)

Kansas

Did you know?
Kansas was a crucial battleground in the fight over slavery between 1858-1859
and was finally admitted as a free state in 1861, just before the Civil War.

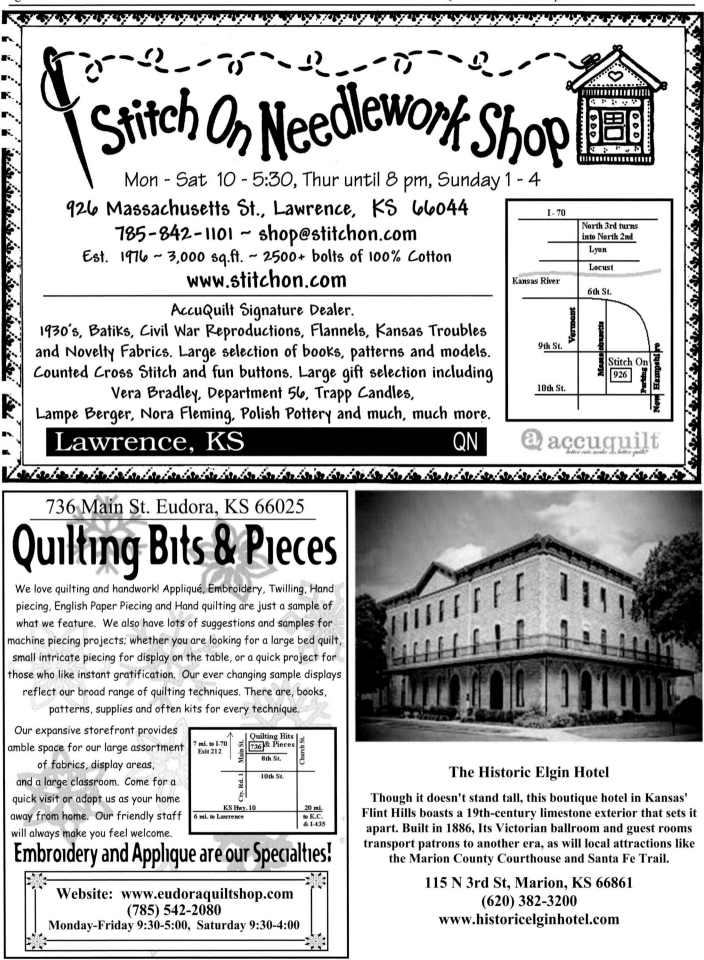

Notes

Kansas Shops

Q-Quilting ~ Y-Yarn ~ N-Needlework ~ R-Retreat ~ M-Museum

City	Shop	Address	Phone	Page
Abilene	Material Girls	306 N. Buckeye St.	(785) 263-7787	
Abilene	Shivering Sheep	308 N. Buckeye Ave.	(785) 263-7501	
Alden	**Prairie Flower Crafts**	**205 Pioneer St.**	**(620) 534-3551**	Pg. 159
Baldwin City	Quilters' Paradise	713 8th St.	(785) 594-3477	
Belleville	**Sew Country**	**1834 M St.**	**(785) 527-2332**	Pg. 161
Bennington	Kansas Troubles	103 N. Nelson St.	(785) 488-2120	
Bonner Springs	Sunflower Embroidery	207 Oak St.	(913) 422-4501	
Burlington	**Silver Threads & Golden Needles**			
		321 Neosho St.	**(620) 364-8233**	Pg. 164
Chanute	ThreadWorks	313 E. Main St.	(620) 431-7700	
Chapman	Lucky Charm Quilts	405 N. Marshall	(785) 922-6190	
Colby	**Colby Sew and Vac.**	**1015 Taylor Ave.**	**(785) 460-1900**	Pg. 160
Colby	**Quilt Cabin**	**1525 S. Range Ave.**	**(785) 462-3375**	Pg. 160
Conway Springs	Old Town Business	101 E. Spring St.	(620) 456-3225	
Copeland	**Sunflower Creations**	**23403 2 Rd.**	**(620) 668-5584**	Pg. 160
Edna	**The Quilters Patch**	**119 N. Marks Ave.**	**(620) 922-3129**	Pg. 164
Eudora	**Quilting Bits & Pieces**	**736 Main St.**	**(785) 542-2080**	Pg. 162
Eureka	Scrap Room	209 N. Main	(620) 583-7169	
Garden City	A Quilted Crow	902 Stone Creek Dr. # C	(620) 805-5073	
Garnett	Country Fabrics	108 E. 5th Ave.	(785) 448-0003	
Gove City	Gove City Yarns	319 Broad St.	(785) 938-2255	
Greensburg	Starla's Stitch 'N Frame	122 S. Main	(620) 723-3275	
Hays	**Quilt Cottage Co.**	**2520 Vine St.**	**(785) 625-0080**	Pg. 160
Hiawatha	Sunflower Quilt Shop	718 Oregon St.	(785) 742-4343	
Hillsboro	Kessler Kreations	112 S. Main St.	(620) 947-3138	
Holton	Quilting on the Square	400 Pennsylvania Ave.	(785) 364-4050	
Humboldt	Heavenly Kneads & Threads	724 Bridge St.	(620) 473-2408	
Hutchinson	**Country Fabrics**	**6411-D W. Morgan Rd.**	**(620) 662-3681**	Pg. 159
Hutchinson	Cottonwood Quilts	126 N. Main	(620) 662-2245	
Independence	Stella's Quilt-N-Fabrics	4530 County Rd. 6000	(620) 325-5378	
Junction City	**Quilter's Yard**	**722 N. Washington St.**	**(785) 307-0774**	Pg. 161
Kechi	Kechi Quilt Impressions	118 E. Kechi Rd.	(316) 616-8036	
Kiowa	Clark's Fabric Shop	605 Main St.	(620) 825-4985	
LaCrosse	A Quilt Corral	812 Main St.	(352) 266-7108	
Lawrence	**Stitch on Needlework Shop**	**926 Massachusetts St.**	**(785) 842-1101**	Pg. 162
Lawrence	Mea Bernina Sewing & Vacuum Center	2449 B Iowa St.	(785) 842-1595	
Lawrence	Sarah's Fabrics	925 Massachusetts	(785) 842-6198	
Lawrence	Yarn Barn of Kansas	930 Massachusetts St.	(785) 842-4333	
Leavenworth	**First City Quilts**	**200 S. 5th St.**	**(913) 682-8000**	Pg. 163
Leavenworth	3 Ladies Sewing Shop	421 Delaware St.	(913) 828-4003	
Leavenworth	Lac Quilt Shop	426 Miami St.	(913) 682-1916	
Leavenworth	Momo's Knitting Nook	518 Delaware St.	(785) 766-2214	
Leoti	**Prairie Flower Quilt Co.**	**102 S. Indian Rd.**	**(620) 375-2044**	Pg. 159
Lincoln	Joyce's Quilting & Fabrics	1837 E. Milo Dr.	(785) 524-4499	
Manhattan	**All About Quilts**	**8651 E. US. Hwy. 24**	**(785) 539-6759**	Pg. 161
Mankato	**Hidden Treasures Quilt Shop**	**101 N. Commercial**	**(785) 378-8020**	Pg. 161
Marion	Down on the Corner	162 W. Main St.	(620) 381-1577	
Marion	Sew What Quilt Shop	329 E. Main St.	(620) 382-2020	
McPherson	Oh Yarn It	221 S. Main St.	(620) 504-5001	
McPherson	Stitches Quilt Shop	102 S. Main St.	(620) 241-2986	
Meade	Green Acres Quilt Shop	140 W Carthage Hwy. 54	(620) 873-5125	
Minneapolis	**No Place Like Home Quilt Shop**	**204 W. 2nd St.**	**(785) 392-9065**	Pg. 161
Minneapolis	The Yarn Peddler	305 N. Rothsay Ave.	(785) 488-7776	
Newton	**Charlotte's Sew Natural**	**710 N. Main St.**	**(316) 284-2547**	Pg. 159
Norton	**Stitch Up A Storm**	**113 W. Main St.**	**(785) 874-5152**	Pg. 160
Oakley	**Smoky River Quilt Shoppe**	**307 Center Ave.**	**(785) 671-3070**	Pg. 160

Oberlin	Country Quilting & Keepsakes	310 W. Commercial	(785) 475-2411	Pg. 160
Olathe	Quilters' Haven	116 N. Clairborne Rd. #A	(913) 764-8600	Pg. 163
Osawatomie	Happy Crafters Quilt Shop	1935 Parker	(913) 755-4360	Pg. 163
Ottawa	Chris' Corner Quilt Shop	3593 Old Hwy. 59	(785) 242-1922	Pg. 163
Overbrook	Overbrook Quilt Connection	500 Maple	(785) 665-7841	Pg. 161
Overland Park	Addadi's Fabrics	9629 W. 87th St.	(913) 381-9705	
Overland Park	Fabric Recycles	9268 Metcalf	(913) 385-0614	
Overland Park	Harper's Fabrics	7918 Santa Fe Dr.	(913) 648-2739	
Overland Park	Quilted Memories	8015 Santa Fe Dr.	(913) 649-2704	
Overland Park	Yarn Shop & More	7212 W. 80th St.	(913) 649-9276	
Paola	Li'l Red Hen Quilt Shop	7 S. Agate St.	(913) 294-5230	Pg. 163
Phillipsburg	Quilting Fool	204 E. Union Rd.	(785) 543-2635	
Phillipsburg	The Quilt Bugs	205 W. E St.	(785) 543-7905	
Phillipsburg	The Shepherd's Mill	839 Third St.	(785) 543-3128	
Plains	Country Quiltin by Design	410 Grand Ave.	(620) 563-7757	Pg. 159
Riley	Oodles of Doodles Quilt Shop	109 S. Broadway	(785) 293-2580	
Salina	Emporium	1833 S. 9th St.	(785) 823-1515	
Salina	Yarns Sold and Told	148 S. Santa Fe Ave.	(785) 820-5648	
Seneca	The Quilt Basket	802 North St.	(785) 336-2133	
Severy	Needle in a Haystack	207 Q Rd.	(620) 736-2942	Pg. 164
Shawnee	Prairie Point Quilt & Fabric Shop	11950 Shawnee Mission Pkwy.	(913) 268-3333	Pg. 163
Spring Hill	The Quilted Sunflower	111 S. Main St.	(913) 592-0100	
Stockton	Stitch and Chatter	320 Main St.	(785) 415-2015	
Syracuse	Quilter's Stash	123 N. Main St.	(620) 384-5390	
Topeka	Stitching Traditions Quilt Shop	2900 SW Oakley Ave. Ste. H	(785) 266-4130	Pg. 161
Topeka	The Quilt Corner	332 Hillside	785-235-8911	
Topeka	Yak 'n Yarn	5331 SW 22nd Place	(785) 272-9276	
Troy	Out Back Quilt Shop	310 W. Locust	(785) 850-0375	
Wamego	Quilts & Crafts	806 4th St.	(785) 844-3531	Pg. 161
Wamego	The Wicked Stitch Yarn & Fiber	523 Lincoln St.	(785) 458-6100	
Wellington	Beehive Quilt Shop	122 N. Washington Ave.	(913) 259-3346	
Wichita	Hen Feathers Quilt Shop	110 N. Rock Rd.	(316) 652-9599	Pg. 159
Wichita	Picket Fence Quilt Co.	7011 W. Central # 129	(316) 558-8899	Pg. 159
Wichita	The Sewing Center	2407 W. 13th St.	(316) 832-0819	Pg. 159
Wichita	Attic Heirlooms	1705 W. Douglas	(316) 265-4646	
Wichita	Heart's Desire	3210 E. Douglas Ave.	(316) 681-3369	
Wichita	Heritage Hut Yarn	2820 E. Douglas Ave.	(316) 682-4082	
Wilson	Grandma J's	106 23rd St.	(785) 658-2225	
Winchester	Aunt Sadie's Quilt Shop	208 Winchester St.	(913) 774-7455	
Winfield	Field to Fabric Quilt Company	907 Main	(620) 229-8540	
Winfield	iYarn	915 Main	(620) 229-8381	

Notes

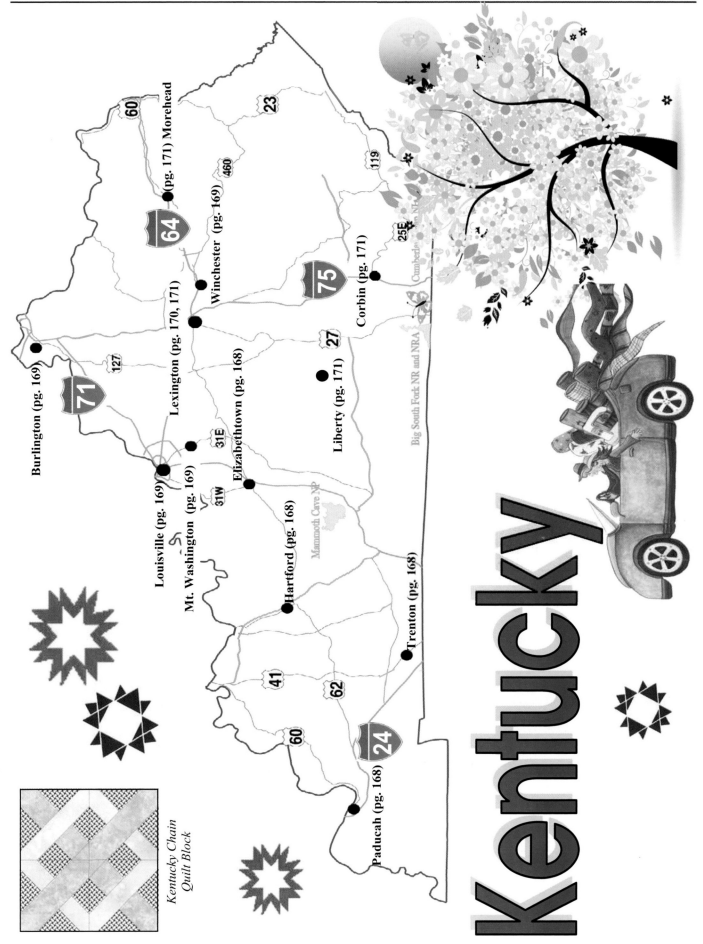

Morehead (pg. 171)

Winchester (pg. 169)

Lexington (pg. 170, 171)

Burlington (pg. 169)

Corbin (pg. 171)

Liberty (pg. 171)

Elizabethtown (pg. 168)

Louisville (pg. 169)

Mt. Washington (pg. 169)

Hartford (pg. 168)

Trenton (pg. 168)

Paducah (pg. 168)

Kentucky Chain
Quilt Block

Kentucky

Did you know?
The town of Corbin was the birthplace of old time movie star Arthur Lake
whose real surname was Silverlake: He played the role of Dagwood in the "Blondie" films of the
1930s and '40s. Lake's parents were trapeze artists billed as The Flying Silverlakes.

Did you know?
Mammoth Cave is the world's longest cave and was first promoted in 1816,
making it the second oldest tourist attraction in the United States.

Kentucky Shops

Q-Quilting ~ Y-Yarn ~ N-Needlework ~ R-Retreat ~ M-Museum

Ashland	Little Red Hen Quilt Shop	1653 Greenup Ave.	(606) 329-2400	
Ashland	The Craft Attic Quilt Shop	2027 Hoods Creek Pike	(606) 325-1212	
Bellevue	Knit On	301 Fairfield Ave.	(859) 291-5648	
Berea	Fiber Frenzy	137 N. Broadway #A	(859) 986-3832	
Berea	Log House Craft Gallery	200 Estill St.	(859) 985-3226	
Bowling Green	Crafty Hands	2910 B Scottsville Rd.	(270) 846-4865	
Bowling Green	Elegant Traditions	1326 State St.	(270) 781-8547	
Bowling Green	Kentucky Museum	1444 Kentucky St.	(270) 745-6082	
Bowling Green	The Kentucky Quilt Company	1575 Campbell Ln.	(270) 842-2434	
Burlington	**Cabin Arts**	**5878 N. Jefferson St.**	**(859) 586-8021**	**Pg. 169**
Clarkson	Sew Much More Sewing Center	120 W. Main St. 270-242-3349		
Corbin	**Fabric World & Quilting**	**33 Prestige Ln. S. US. Hwy. 25**		
			(606) 526-1799	**Pg. 171**
Crescent Springs	Knitwits A Contemporary Yarn Shop	620 Buttermilk Pike	(859) 341-2423	
Cynthiana	Purr-sonally Yours Quilt Shop	930 US. Hwy. 27 S. #B	(859) 234-0661	
Cynthiana	Tay's Cloth Peddler	121 E. Pike St.	(859) 234-1846	
Drodhead	Quilters' Haven	262 Bryant Ridge Rd.	(606) 256-1617	
Dry Ridge	The Quilt Box	470 E. Flynn Rd.	(859) 824-4007	
Eddyville	Yummee Yarn	242 Tanner Ave.	(270) 388-2021	
Elizabethtown	**Uniquely Yours Quilt Shop**	**2973 Rineyville Rd.**	**(270) 766-1456**	**Pg. 168**
Elizabethtown	Blueball Mountain Spindle & Needleworks	308 Central Ave.	(270) 763-3352	
Falmouth	Country Patchwork	101 W. Shelby St.	(859) 951-1118	
Frankfort	The Woolery	315 St. Clair St.	(502) 352-9800	
Georgetown	Birdsong Quilting and Crafts	401 Outlet Center Dr. Ste. 145	(502) 603-8088	
Grayson	Quilt Heaven	5306 S. State Hwy. 7	(606) 475-0091	
Greenup	Mom's Cotton Shop	2035 Ashland Rd.	(606) 473-2164	
Harlan	Berry Patch Quilt Shop	159 Albert Ln.	(606) 837-2236	
Harold	Blue Bee Quilting, Fabric & Gift Shop	228 Church Rd.	(606) 478-2583	
Hartford	**Quilts R Jewels Fabrics**	**483 Livermore Rd.**	**(270) 298-3507**	**Pg. 168**
Hartford	Omadarlings	222 Main St.	(270) 504-0092	
Jenkins	Vintage Rose Fabrics	1297 Hwy. 805	(606) 832-0311	
LaGrange	Friends and Fiber	106 E. Main St.	(502) 222-0658	
Lexington	**Quilter's Square**	**3301 Keithshire Way Ste. 109**		
			(859) 278-5010	**Pg. 171**
Lexington	**Sew-A-Lot Lexington Inc**	**2160 Sir Barton Way #148**	**(859) 264-7472**	**Pg. 170**
Lexington	Eye of the Needle	3344 Partner Pl. #10	(859) 278-1401	
Lexington	Magpie Yarn	513 E. High St.	(859) 455-7437	
Lexington	M's Canvashouse	131 Kentucky Ave.	(859) 253-1302	
Lexington	ReBelle Girls	225 Rosemont Garden	(859) 389-9750	
Lexington	The Stitch Niche INC	180 Moore Dr. Ste. B	(859) 277-2604	
Liberty	**The Quilters Trunk Sewing Center LLC**			
		694 S. Fork Creek Rd.	**(606) 787-7648**	**Pg. 171**
Louisville	**Among Friends Quilt Shop**	**9537 Taylorsville Rd.**	**(502) 261-7377**	**Pg. 169**
Louisville	Austin's Sewing Center	5640 Bardstown Rd.	(502) 239-2222	
Louisville	Beth's Needlepoint Nook	10246 Shelbyville Rd.	(502) 244-0046	
Louisville	Designs In Textiles	1234 S. Third St.	(502) 212-7500	
Louisville	Quilted Joy	10302 Bluegrass Pkwy.	(502) 718-7148	
Louisville	Sophie's Fine Yarn Shoppe	10482 Shelbyville Rd. Ste. 101	(502) 244-4927	
Louisville	The Cozy Quilter	12204 Shelbyville Rd.	(502) 742-2699	
Louisville	The Little Loomhouse	328 Kenwood Hill Rd.	(502) 367-4792	
Louisville	The Smocking Shoppe	3829 Staebler Ave.	(502) 893-3503	
Louisville	The Smocking Shoppe	169 S. English Station	(502) 409-9664	
Magnolia	The Jewell Box	10075 N. Jackson Hwy.	(270) 528-3087	
Mayfield	Backyard Fabric	421 State Rt. 893	(270) 345-2746	
Maysville	Apron Strings	52 W Second St.	(606) 584-7414	
McKee	Carroll's Quilts & Crafts	19282 Hwy. 2004	(606) 287-7018	
Monticello	Linda's Quilt Shop Etc.	627 Michigan Ave.	(606) 340-1812	
Morehead	**Calico Patch Quilt Shop**	**155 Bluebank Rd.**	**(606) 784-7235**	**Pg. 171**
Morehead	Quilter's Candy Shop	151 N. Main St.	(606) 356-0268	
Mt. Vernon	Heritage Crafts	2776 Lake Cumberland Rd.	(606) 256-9077	

Index

Mt. Washington	Busy Lady Quilt Shop	223 Delania Dr. #B	(502) 538-8800	Pg. 169
Murray	Murray Sewing Center	942A S. 12th St.	(270) 759-8400	
Murray	Red Bug Yarn & Gifts	102 S. 6th St.	(270) 761-2723	
Nicholasville	A Tangled Yarn and Lunabud Knits	605 N. Main St. #B	(859) 885-5426	
Nicholasville	Graphic Impressions	1090 High Point Dr.	(859) 881-0377	
Owensboro	Simple Stitches	102 W. Byers Ave.	(270) 698-8320	
Owensboro	Stychee Woman Studio	219 Williamsburg Sq.	(270) 686-7777	
Paducah	National Quilt Museum	215 Jefferson St.	(270) 442-8856	Pg. 168
Paducah	Calico Country Sewing Center	3401 Park Ave. Ste. 4	(270) 444-0301	
Paducah	Hancocks of Paducah	3841 Hinkleville Rd.	(270) 443-4410	
Paducah	Jefferson Street Studios	1149 Jefferson St.	(270) 217-3976	
Paducah	Must Stitch Emporium	109 S. 2nd St.	(270) 709-3331	
Paducah	Paper Pieces	502 N. 5th St.	(270) 534-5475	
Paducah	Quilt in a Day	119 N. 4th St.	(270) 442-2155	
Paducah	Quilters Alley	420 N. 4th St.	(270) 443-5673	
Rochester	Sue's Quilting & Fabric	223 Arndell Rd.	(270) 934-8401	
Russell	Janis Campbell Knitting Studio	424 Bluebird Dr.	(606) 494-2301	
Shelbyville	The Needle Nest	702 Washington St.	(502) 633-4701	
Smiths Grove	Psycho Granny's Quilt Shop and More	101 N. Main St.	(270) 202-1889	
Smith's Grove	Whittle's Fabrics	3858 Chalybeate Rd.	(270) 597-2987	
Somerset	Pauls Discount	1616 N. US. 2227	(606) 678-4405	
Trenton	Quilt and Sew at Golden Threads	115 S. Main St.	(270) 466-5000	Pg. 168
Whittley City	Agnes' Fabric Shop	66 N. Main St.	(606) 376-8773	
Winchester	Judy's Stitch In Time Quilt Shop	5839 Irvine Rd.	(859) 744-7404	Pg. 169

Index

Notes

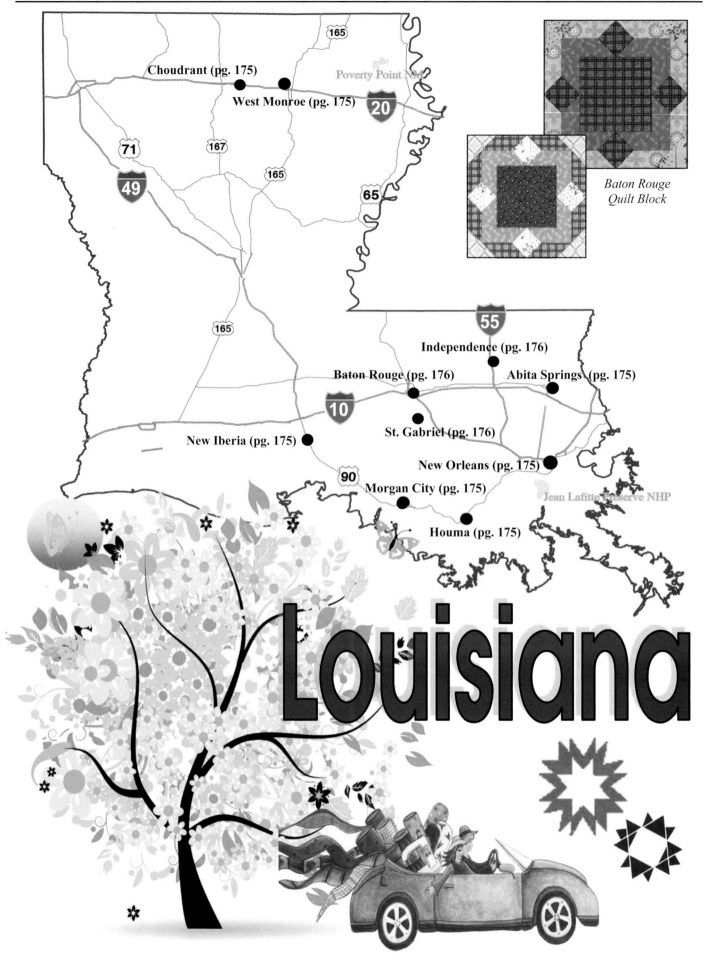

Choudrant (pg. 175)

West Monroe (pg. 175)

165

20

71

167

165

49

65

*Baton Rouge
Quilt Block*

165

55

Independence (pg. 176)

Baton Rouge (pg. 176)

Abita Springs (pg. 175)

10

St. Gabriel (pg. 176)

New Iberia (pg. 175)

New Orleans (pg. 175)

90

Morgan City (pg. 175)

Houma (pg. 175)

Poverty Point NM

Jean Lafitte Preserve NHP

Louisiana

Did you know?
Louisiana has 2,482 islands, covering nearly 1.3 million acres. Nationally, this ranks the state third in total islands and second in total island acreage.

Independence, LA   Q

Mama's Quilt Shop

15111 Catfish Farm Road   70443

985-878-6396

mamasquiltshop@yahoo.com
www.mamasquiltshop.com

We carry over 3000 Bolts of fabric including RJR, Benatex, Marcus Brothers, Andover, Moda, P&B, Northcott and many, many more.
<u>Best prices around!</u>

Fabrics, notions, books, classes and lots of inspiration at the "little quilt shop in the country."

**Hours: 9 am - 5 pm
Wed - Sat**

Cottage Creations

7222 Bayou Paul Rd.
St. Gabriel, LA 70776
225-642-8166
Owner: Daisy Comeaux
3000+ Bolts
Est: 2002

Where you can go for your complete quilting needs:
Fabrics, Notions, Books, Patterns and Classes.

Tuesday - Friday
10:30am - 5:00pm
Saturday
10:30am - 3:00pm

8 Minutes from Baton Rouge

The Quilt Corner
Inspiring Creativity

Baton Rouge, LA   Q

Quilting fabrics, books, patterns, notions & gifts. Local pattern designs. We specialize in LSU & Mardi Gras Fabrics. Newsletter

**Mon, Wed, Fri 10-5
Tues & Thur 10-6 Sat 10-2**

13521 Hooper Rd.
Baton Rouge, LA 70818
(225) 315-7285
Owner: Margaret Chair
info@quiltcorneronline.com
www.quiltcorneronline.com

Nottoway Plantation and Resort

The South's most magnificent remaining antebellum mansion, Nottoway Plantation splendidly overlooks the Great Mississippi River, and continues to entice visitors, from near and far, to take a step back in time to the days of glory and grandeur. With a natural backdrop of colorful gardens and two hundred-year-old oaks, Nottoway is the ultimate blend of Southern history and hospitality, and an exceptional choice.

**31025 LA-1, White Castle, LA 70788
(225) 545-2730
www.nottoway.com**

Louisiana Shops

Q-Quilting ~ Y-Yarn ~ N-Needlework ~ R-Retreat ~ M-Museum

City	Shop	Address	Phone	Page
Abita Springs	**Sew This!**	**70117 Hwy. 59 Ste. O**	**(985) 898-1112**	**Pg. 175**
Alexandria	Creative Quilting	2438 E. Texas Ave.	(318) 445-7793	
Alexandria	Stitched	1302 Texas Ave.	(318) 704-6188	
Baton Rouge	**The Quilt Corner**	**13579 Hooper Rd.**	**(225) 315-7285**	**Pg. 176**
Baton Rouge	My Sewing Shoppe	7630 Old Hammond Hwy.	(225) 218-2250	
Baton Rouge	The Elegant Needle	545 Saint Tammany St.	(225) 925-8920	
Baton Rouge	The Quilt Corner	13521 Hooper Rd.	(225) 315-7285	
Berwick	The Quilt Cupboard	101 Tournament Blvd.	(985) 354-0030	
Bossier City	Fabric Boutique	1701 Old Minden Rd. #11	(318) 742-0047	
Broussard	A&A Sewing Center	817 Albertson Pkwy. #N	(337) 837-3444	
Choudrant	**Hannah's Quilts & Crafts**	**402 St. Peter Loop Rd.**	**(318) 251-0314**	**Pg. 175**
Denham Springs	Mia's Fabric Café	34130 N. La Hwy. 16	(225) 271-4423	
DeRidder	Country Lane Cross Stitch & Frame Shop			
		2915 Glendale Rd.	(337) 463-2359	
Grand Cane	Homemade Quilts N More	8370 Hwy. 171	(318) 858-0092	
Houma	**The Quilting Niche'**	**1220 St. Charles St.**	**(985) 876-9077**	**Pg. 175**
Independence	**Mama's Quilt Shop**	**15111 Catfish Farm Rd.**	**(985) 878-6396**	**Pg. 176**
Jefferson	Quilted Owl	4600 Jefferson Hwy.	(504) 733-0993	
Lacombe	McNeedles	28120 Hwy. 190	(985) 882-7144	
Lafayette	Heirloom Creations	431 Rena Dr.	(337) 984-8949	
Lafayette	Lola Pink	121 Arnould Blvd.	(337) 456-2364	
Lafayette	Yarn Nook	321 Oil Center Dr.	(337) 593-8558	
Metairie	Accents Inc.	4500 Shores Dr. Ste. 103	(504) 888-2458	
Metairie	Gary's Arts Craft & Needlework	3109 18th St.	(504) 834-5258	
Morgan City	**The Quilt Cupboard**	**1010 8th St.**	**(985) 354-0030**	**Pg. 175**
New Iberia	**Emily's Closet**	**699 E. St. Peter St.**	**(337) 364-9404**	**Pg. 175**
New Orleans	**Mes Amis Quilt Shop**	**6505 Spanish Fort Blvd.**	**(504) 284-3455**	**Pg. 175**
New Orleans	Bette Bornside Company	2733 Dauphine St.	(504) 945-4069	
New Orleans	Chateau Sew & Sew	1115 St. Mary St.	(504) 533-9221	
New Orleans	Needle Arts Studio	5301 Canal Blvd.	(504) 832-3050	
New Orleans	Needlework Vault	1927 Sophie Wright	(504) 528-9797	
New Orleans	The Quarter Stitch	629 Chartres St.	(504) 522-4451	
New Orleans	Uptown Needle & CraftWorks	4610 Magazine St.	(504) 302-9434	
Pineville	Aunt Nell's Quilt Shop	1634 Hyland Park Dr.	(318) 640-5294	
Pitken	Country Yarns	182 Legg Loop	(318) 358-3386	
Ruston	Louisiana Quilt N More	1800 Trade Dr.	(318) 768-2662	
Ruston	Quilteroo's	1401 Farmerville Hwy.	(318) 255-0992	
Ruston	The Fabric Shop	100 Park Ave.	(318) 251-2400	
Shreveport	Cottage Quilts	9377 Mansfield Rd.	(318) 671-0331	
Shreveport	Hanging by a Thread	6505 Line Ave. #22	(318) 865-7878	
Slidell	All Stitched Up by Angela	1730 Front St.	(985) 288-505	
St. Francisville	Heirlooms Quilt Shoppe	7175 US. Hwy. 61	(225) 773-0032	
St. Gabriel	**Cottage Creations & Quilts**	**7222 Bayou Paul Rd.**	**(225) 642-8166**	**Pg. 176**
Sunset	J & B Quilting and Fabrics	988 Napoleon Ave.	(337) 662-1183	
West Monroe	**Quilt 'N Stitch**	**6049 Cypress St.**	**(318) 396-6020**	**Pg. 175**
Winnsboro	Sew Much More Quilting	607 Prairie St.	(318) 435-4044	
Youngsville	It's Sew Heavenly	220 Twin Lakes Dr.	(337) 856-8141	

Index

Notes

Maine

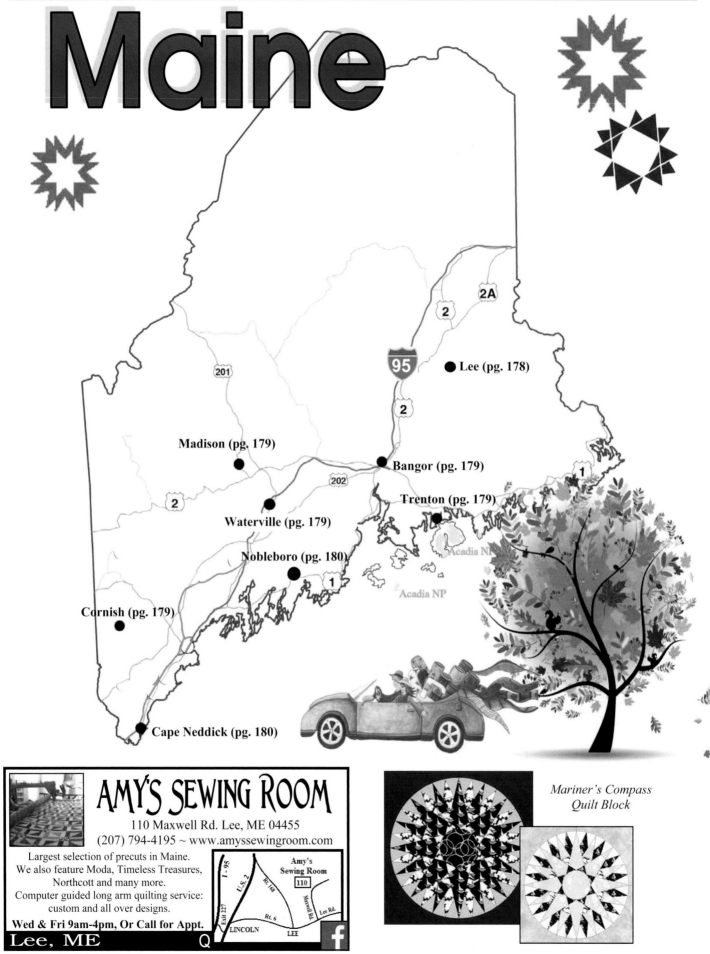

2A
2

95

● **Lee (pg. 178)**

201

2

Madison (pg. 179) ●

Bangor (pg. 179) ●

202

Trenton (pg. 179) ●

2

● **Waterville (pg. 179)**

1

Acadia NP

Nobleboro (pg. 180) ●

1

Acadia NP

Cornish (pg. 179) ●

● **Cape Neddick (pg. 180)**

Mariner's Compass
Quilt Block

Maine Shops

Q-Quilting ~ Y-Yarn ~ N-Needlework ~ R-Retreat ~ M-Museum

Auburn	Fabric Warehouse	104 Washington St.	(207) 784-7151	
Auburn	Quiltessentials	909 Minot Ave.	(207) 784-4486	
Augusta	Cozy Cottage Fabrics	173 Water St.	(207) 512-8531	
Bangor	**The Cotton Cupboard Quilt Shop**	**1213 Broadway**	**(207) 941-8900**	Pg. 179
Bangor	One Lupine Fiber Arts	170 Park St.	(207) 992-4140	
Bar Harbor	Bee's Inc	59 Cottage St.	(207) 288-9046	
Bar Harbor	Fabricate	64 Mt. Desert St.	(207) 288-5113	
Bath	Halcyon Yarn	12 School St.	(207) 442-7909	
Belfast	Fiddlehead Artisan Supply	64 Main St.	(207) 338-8422	
Belfast	Heavenly Socks Yarns	82 Main St.	(207) 338-8388	
Berwick	Mary's Yarn Nook	14 Wilson St.	(207) 337-3891	
Berwick	Village Quilt Shop	14 Wilson St.	(207) 451-0590	
Biddeford	Seacoast Sewing and Quilting	20 Edwards Ave.	(207) 283-3033	
Blue Hill	String Theory	132 Beech Hill Rd.	(207) 374-9990	
Bridgton	Michelle's	28 Forest Ave.	(207) 647-8828	
Camden	The Cashmere Goat	20 Bayview St.	(207) 236-7236	
Canton	Simply Sewing	32 Pinewoods Rd.	(207) 515-0721	
Cape Neddick	**Knight's Quilt Shop**	**1901 US. Rt. 1**	**(207) 361-2500**	Pg. 180
Chelsea	Mystic Maine Quilts	5 River Rd.	(207) 582-0312	
Cornish	**Bolt Fabrics**	**12 Main St.**	**(207) 625-4255**	Pg. 179
Cumberland	The Elegant Knitter at Goose Pond	176 Gray Rd.	(800) 340-2514	
Damariscotta	Attic Heirlooms	157 Main St.	(207) 712-9914	
Damariscotta	Pine Tree Yarns	74 Main St.	(207) 563-5003	
Farmington	Pins & Needles	157 Main St.	(207) 779-9060	
Freeport	Cotton Weeds Quilt Shop	15 Main St. #12	(207) 865-4600	
Freeport	Grace Robinson & Company	208 US. Rt. 1 Ste. 1	(207) 865-6110	
Freeport	Mother of Purl Yarn Shop	541 US. Rt. 1	(207) 869-5280	
Glenburn	Essentially Felt Studio & Fine Yarn	865 Pushaw Rd.	(207) 942-0365	
Greenville	Crazy Moose Fabrics	16 Pritham Ave.	(207) 695-3600	
Hallowell	Whipper Snappers	107 Water St.	(207) 622-3458	
Harmony	Bartlettyarns, Inc.	20 Water St.	(207) 683-2251	
Hope	Hope Spinnery	725 Camden Rd.	(207) 763-4600	
Houlton	Country Yarn Basket	224 B Rd.	(207) 532-9229	
Jonesport	Jolene's Originals	560 Mason Bay Rd.	(207) 497-2864	
Kennebunk	Camp Wool	42 Main St.	(207) 985-0030	
Kennebunk	The Ball and Skein	169 Port Rd. #14	(207) 967-4434	
Kennwbunk	Knit & Needlepoint	173 Port Rd.	(207) 967-4900	
Lee	**Amy's Sewing Room**	**110 Maxwell Rd.**	**(207) 794-4195**	Pg. 178
Limerick	Annie's Teeny Tiny Quilt Shop	54 Central Ave.	(207) 793-9988	
Litchfield	The Dorr Mill Store	2046 Hallowell Rd.	(207) 268-4581	
Lubec	Wags and Wool	83 Water St.	(207) 733-4714	
Madison	**The Fabric Garden**	**167 Lakewood Rd.**	**(207) 474-9628**	Pg. 179
Millinocket	Jandseau's Greenhouse	200 Iron Bridge Rd.	(207) 723-6332	
New Sharon	Imelda's Fabric & Designs	5 Starks Rd. #134	(207) 778-0665	
Nobleboro	**Maine-ly Sewing**	**48 Atlantic Hwy. US. Rt. 1**	**(207) 563-8445**	Pg. 180
Nobleboro	Alewives Fabrics	10 Main St.	(207) 563-5002	
North Edgecomb	On Board Fabrics	Rt. 27 Booth Bay Rd.	(207) 882-7536	
Norway	Fiber and Vine	402 Main St.	(207) 739-2664	
Norway	Sew Orchid Design	316 Main St.	(207) 739-2065	
Orrington	A Straight Stitch	177 River Rd.	(207) 989-1234	
Oxford	Oxford Mill End Store	971 Main St.	(207) 539-4451	
Portland	KnitWit Yarn Shop and Coffee Bar	247 A Congress St.	(207) 774-6444	
Portland	PortFiber	50 Cove St.	(207) 780-1345	
Portland	Z Fabrics	477 Congress St.	(207) 773-1331	
Rockland	Clementine	428 Main St.	(207) 596-3905	
Rockland	Over the Rainbow Yarn	18 School St.	(207) 594-6060	
Saco	Half Square Quilt Shop	15 Pepperell Sq.	(207) 494-7718	
Sanford	Sanford Sewing Machines	1923 Main St.	(207) 324-8375	
Shapleigh	Primitive Quarters	52 Jones Rd.	(207) 636-1571	
Skowhegan	Happy Knits	42 Court St.	(207) 474-7979	

Index

Skowhegan	Pinwheels Quilting	95 W. Front St.	(207) 474-1233
South Portland	Central Yarn Shop	868 Broadway Ave.	(207) 799-7789
Southwest Harbor	Quilt "n" Fabric	11 Seal Cove Rd.	(207) 244-1233
Stockton Springs	Purple Fleece	103 School St.	(207) 323-1871
Trenton	**Sewing by the Sea**	**11 Periwinkle Ln. / Bar Harbor Rd.**	
			(207) 664-2558 Pg. 179
Turner	Nezinscot Farm	284 Turner Center Rd.	(207) 225-3231
Verona Island	Searsport Rug Hooking	11 W. Side Dr.	(207) 249-0891
Waterville	**Yardgoods Center**	**60 W. Concourse**	**(207) 872-2118 Pg. 179**
Windham	Calico Basket Quilt Shop	31 Page Rd.	(207) 892-5606
Windham	Cashmere Cabin	119 Nash Rd.	(207) 892-4040
Windham	Rosemary's Gift and Yarn Shop	39 Roosevelt Tr.	(207) 894-5770
York	The Yarn Sellar	647 US. Rt. 1	(207) 351-1987
Houlton	Rather-B-Quilting	224 B Rd.	(207) 532-9229

NOTES

Grantsville (pg. 183)

Hagerstown (pg. 184, 185)

Towson (pg. 187)

Chesapeake City (pg. 186)

Frederick (pg. 183)

Aberdeen (pg. 186)

Columbia (pg. 186)

(pg. 186) Baltimore

Ellicott City (pg. 186)

(pg. 186) Catonsville

(pg.185) Gaithersburg

(pg. 186) Rock Hall

La Plata (pg. 187)

Prince Frederick (pg. 188)

Pocomoke City (pg. 188)

Annapolis Patch Quilt Block

Maryland

Hagerstown, MD   Q

The Prettiest Quilt Shop in Western Maryland!

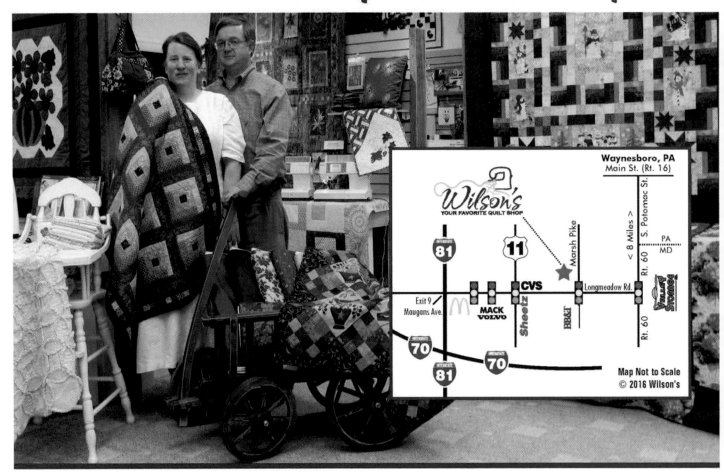

Wilson's Your Favorite Quilt Shop, offers:

- Only two miles from Interstate 81.

- 4000 bolts of fabric in a 4000 square foot store with 100 finished samples.

- Uniquely coordinated kits and bundles, books and patterns.

- Traditional quilts with embroidery machines.

- Lodging - go to our website ILuv2Quilt.com for our corporate rate recommendation.

Country Setting • Buses Welcome
Close to the Interstate • Easy-Off / Easy-On

YOUR FAVORITE QUILT SHOP

13516 Marsh Pike
Hagerstown, Maryland 21742
301.790.3526

Store Hours
Mon., Tues., Thurs., & Fri. 9 a.m. - 5 p.m.
Sat. 9 a.m. - 2 p.m. • Wed. CLOSED

ILuv2Quilt.com

Blog with over
500 quilts for
inspiration.

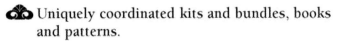

Don't go home without being able to say you were at Wilson's in Hagerstown!

The Maryland Inn

Built in 1772 and located right on Main Street in charming
downtown Annapolis, this red-brick inn has been a central meeting
place for national, state, and military visitors throughout its
history. Its restaurant, the Treaty of Paris, honors the agreement
that ended America's Revolutionary War in 1784.

16 Church Cir, Annapolis, MD 21401
(410) 263-2641
www.historicinnsofannapolis.com

Bear's Paw Fabrics

Est: 1996

We welcome you to the world of Bear's Paw Fabrics and BERNINA.

- Over 4000 beautiful cotton fabrics for the quilter or home sewist
- Books, notions, and patterns. Loads of samples.
- Authorized Bernina Dealer with the latest sewing & embroidery machines, software and accessories.

accuquilt
better cuts make better quilts

BERNINA
made to create

Towson, MD   Q

8812 Orchard Tree Lane   21286
410-321-6730
Owners: Doug and Judy Munro
www.bearspawfabrics.com

Mon-Fri 10:00-5:00
Sat 9:30-4:00
Sun 12:00-4:00

695 to Exit 29B (Loch Raven Blvd.)
right on Joppa Rd.
right on Orchard Tree Lane
5th store on left

A Different Sewing, Quilting & Embroidery Experience
We hope you can take the time to visit our conveniently located shop

---

MATERIAL Girls
Quilt Boutique

6750 Crain Hwy., Suites B/C,
LaPlata, MD 20646
301-392-9575
materialgirl@verizon.net

BERNINA+
made to create

Monday - Friday
9:30 - 6:00
Saturday 9:30 - 4:00

Join us on Facebook

We offer a wide selection of: Cotton, Flannel, Batiks,
Sewing Classes And So Much More!
Southern Maryland's Authorized Bernina Dealer.

La Plata, MD   Q

www.materialgirlsquilt.com

Did you know?

Fort Meade near Laurel became a base because a train engineer delivering soldiers to Meade knew only one Meade, the one in Maryland. He was not aware of Fort Meade, Florida. The confusion happened so often a second base was built in Maryland in an attempt to avoid the confusion.

Maryland Shops

Q-Quilting ~ Y-Yarn ~ N-Needlework ~ R-Retreat ~ M-Museum

City	Shop	Address	Phone	Pg.
Aberdeen	**Hoppin Bobbin**	**690 S Philadelphia Blvd. Ste. 100**	**(410) 272-2226**	**Pg. 186**
Annapolis	Cottonseed Glory, Inc.	4 Annapolis St.	410-263-3897	
Baltimore	**Lovelyarns**	**3610 Falls Rd.**	**(410) 662-9276**	**Pg. 186**
Baltimore	A Fabric Place	6324 Falls Rd.	(410) 828-6777	
Baltimore	Baltimore Museum of Art / Textile	Art Museum Dr.	(301) 396-6266	
Baltimore	The Stitching Post	67 Mellor Ave.	(410) 788-7760	
Baltimore	Woolworks Inc.	6117 Falls Rd.	(410) 377-2060	
Barnesville	Dancing Leaf Farm	21920 Beallsville Rd.	(301) 801-6995	
Berlin	A Little Bit Sheepish	2 S. Main St.	(410) 641-1080	
Bethesda	Astrid	509 Caesterbrook Rd.	(301) 229-5303	
Bethesda	Second Story Knits	4706 Bethesda Ave.	(301) 652-8688	
Catonsville	**Cloverhill Yarn Shop**	**77 Mellor Ave.**	**(410) 788-7262**	**Pg. 186**
Centreville	Peggy's Sewing Center	210 Pennsylvania Ave.	(410) 758-3827	
Chesapeake City	**Vulcan's Rest Fibers**	**106 George St.**	**(410) 885-2890**	**Pg. 186**
Columbia	**Spring Water Designs Quilting**	**9691 Gerwig Ln. Ste. G**	**(410) 381-0695**	**Pg. 186**
Columbia	All About Yarn	8970-G Rt. 108	(410) 992-5648	
Crofton	Tomorrow's Treasures	2110 Priest Bridge Dr. Ste. 12	(410) 451-0400	
Dickerson	A Paca Fun Farm	16707 Thurston Rd.	(301) 349-4111	
Easton	Lilies of the Field	335 N. Aurora St.	(410) 822-9117	
Eldersburg	Knitters Nest Yarn Shop	1431 Liberty Rd.	(410) 549-0709	
Ellicott City	**Ellicott City Sew Vac.**	**8480 Baltimore National Pike**	**(410) 465-6366**	**Pg. 186**
Fallston	Glory Bees Sewing Center	2112 Belair Rd. #5	(443) 981-3182	
Frederick	**Charlotte's Cottage Quilt Shop**	**122 N. E St.**	**(240) 815-6825**	**Pg. 183**
Frederick	The Knot House	129 E. Patrick St.	(334) 707-0528	
Frostburg	Frostburg Fiber Depot	9 W. Main St.	(240) 284-2154	
Fulton	Prints Charming	11711 E. Market Place	(301) 490-2342	

Funkstown	Y2 Knit	100 E. Baltimore St.	(301) 766-4543	
Gaithersburg	**Capital Quilts**	**15926 Louanne Dr.**	**(301) 527-0598**	Pg. 185
Glen Burnie	The Knitting Boutique	910 Cromwell Park Dr. #108	(410) 553-0433	
Grantsville	**Four Seasons Stitchery**	**116 Main St.**	**(301) 895-5958**	Pg. 183
Grantsville	Shady Grove Market & Fabrics	1493 Springs Rd.	(301) 895-5660	
Hagerstown	**Traditions at the White Swan**			
		16525 National Pike	**(301) 733-9130**	Pg. 185
Hagerstown	**Wilson's Your Favorite Quilt Shop**			
		13516 Marsh Pike	**(301) 790-3526**	Pg. 184
Hughesville	Michelle's Quilts	8132 Old Leonardtown Rd.	(301) 274-1919	
LaPlata	**Material Girls Quilt Boutique**			
		6750 Crain Hwy. Ste. B/C	**(301) 392-9575**	Pg. 187
Leonardtown	Crazy For Ewe	22715 Washington St.	(301) 475-2744	
Middletown	Kiparoo Farm Studio	3511 Bussard Rd.	(301) 371-7454	
Mount Airy	Patches Quilting & Sewing	308 S. Main St.	(301) 831-0366	
Oakland	Yoder's Fabrics	4166 Mason School Rd.	(301) 334-4965	
Ocean City	Salty Yarns	807 N. Boardwalk	(410) 289-4667	
Parkville	Needlecraft Corner	7905 E. Harford Rd.	(410) 668-3811	
Pocomoke City	**The Pincushion**	**151 Market St.**	**(410) 957-4766**	Pg. 188
Prince Frederick	**Calvert Quilt Shop**	**20 Industry Ln.**	**(410) 535-0576**	Pg. 188
Rock Hall	**Village Quilting**	**5701 Main St.**	**(410) 639-4101**	Pg. 186
Rockville	G Street Fabrics	5520 Randolph Rd.	(301) 231-8998	
Rockville	Woolwinders, A Knitting Salon	404 King Farm Blvd. Ste.150	(240) 632-9276	
Ruxton	Needles And Threads of Ruxton	7701 Bellona Ave.	(410) 828-7688	
Sandy Spring	SO Original	900 Olney Sandy Spring Rd.	(301) 774-7970	
St. Michaels	Frivolous Fibers	112 N. Talbot St.	(410) 822-6580	
Taneytown	Cedar Wool Farm	5001 Feeser Rd. W.	(410) 756-2393	
Timonium	Black Sheep Yarn Shop	9612 Deerco Rd.	(410) 628-9276	
Towson	**Bear's Paw Fabrics**	**8812 Orchard Tree Ln.**	**(410) 321-6730**	Pg. 187
Trappe	Quilt Vine	3987 Main St.	(410) 476-6166	
Westminster	Blue House Fabrics	410 E. Main St.	(443) 289-9347	
Westminster	Ewes-ful Fiber Arts	1191 Long Valley Rd.	(410) 876-0683	
White Marsh	Hooven Sewing Center	11550 Philadelphia Rd.	(410) 529-7943	
Woodsboro	Brookmere Alpacas	9610 Gravel Hill Rd.	(301) 845-4222	
Woodsboro	CIT Studios	208 N. Main St.	(301) 304-5854	
Woodsboro	Forestheart Studio	200 S. Main St.	(301) 845-4447	

Index

Notes

Massachusetts

Lighthouse Quilt Block

Willamstown (pg. 190)

Lowell (pg. 191)

Cambridge (pg. 191)

Chicopee (pg. 190)

Natick (pg. 192)

S. Egremont (pg. 190)

Sturbridge (pg. 191)

Charlton (pg. 191)

Westfield (pg. 190)

Dudley (pg. 191)

Franklin (pg. 192)

E. Longmeadow (pg. 191)

Lakeville (pg. 193)

W. Barnstable (pg. 193)

Minute Man NHP

Cape Cod NS

Did you know?
James Michael Curley was the first mayor of Boston to have a car. The license plate number was "576," the number of letters respectively in his name.
Today, the mayor of Boston's official car still has the same number on its license plate.

Omni Parker House

Founded in 1855, It's difficult to discuss the legacy of Boston without mention of the Parker House hotel. It's where Charles Dickens first recited "A Christmas Carol," where JFK held his bachelor party, and where culinary staples including Boston Cream pie and fluffy Parker House roll were born.

60 School St, Boston, MA 02108
(617) 227-8600
www.omnihotels.com

Massachusetts Shops

Q-Quilting ~ Y-Yarn ~ N-Needlework ~ R-Retreat ~ M-Museum

Acushnet	Perry Farm Patchworks	196 Perryhill Rd.	(508) 995-1555	
Adams	A Stitch In Time	45 Commercial St.	(413) 743-7174	
Arlington	Fabric Corner	783 Massachusetts Ave.	(781) 643-4040	
Auburn	Appletree Fabrics	850 Southbridge St.	(508) 832-5562	
Beverly	Sew Creative	14 Elliott St.	(978) 524-8848	
Beverly Farms	Yarns in the Farms	641 Hale St.	(978) 927-2108	
Bolton	The Quilted Crow	626 Main St.	(978) 266-9102	
Boston	Bead & Fiber	460 Harrison Ave.	(617) 426-2323	
Boston	Newbury Yarns, Inc.	164 Newbury St.	(617) 572-3733	
Boston	Stitch Boutique of Boston	231 Berkeley St.	(617) 236-4633	
Brewster	Quilt-ish of Cape Cod	1357 Main St.	(703) 403-9771	
Brewster	Town-Ho Needleworks	1912 Main St.	(508) 896-3000	
Brookfield	Knit Witts	56 Allen Rd.	(508) 867-9449	
Cambridge	**Cambridge Quilt Shop**	**95 Blanchard Rd.**	**(617) 492-3279**	**Pg. 191**
Cambridge	Gather Here	370 Broadway	(781) 775-9504	
Cambridge	Mind's Eye Yarns	22 White St.	(617) 354-7253	
Cambridge	The Knittin' Kitten	93 Blanchard Rd.	(617) 491-4670	
Canton	Ann's Fabrics	235 Turnpike St.	(781) 828-2201	
Charlton	**Charlton Sewing Center**	**12 Stafford St.**	**(508) 248-6632**	**Pg. 191**
Charlton	**The Fabric Stash**	**45 A Sturbridge, Rt. 20**	**(508) 248-0600**	**Pg. 191**
Chatham	A Great Yarn	894 Main St.	(508) 348-5605	
Chicopee	**Bayberry Quilt & Gift Shoppe**	**137 Sheridan St.**	**(413)-592-9653**	**Pg. 190**
Dennis	Yarn Hound	620 Rt. 6A	(508) 385-6951	
Dudley	**The Quilters Loft**	**26 Mill Rd.**	**(508) 949-9095**	**Pg. 191**
East Longmeadow	**Quilts & Treasures, Inc.**	**56 Shaker Rd.**	**(413) 525-4789**	**Pg. 191**
East Sandwich	Black Purls Yarn Shop	685 Rt. 6A	(508) 362-8880	
Eastham	Quilter's Palette	45 Ginger Plum Ln.	(508) 255-4038	
Eastham	Yarn Basket	4205 County Rd. Rt. 6	(508) 255-3557	

Index

Edgartown	Needleworks	12 N. Summer St.	(914) 238-8809
Essex	Hooked Knitting	8 Martin St. #3	(978) 768-7329
Fairhaven	Eva's Yarn Shop	42 Main St.	(508) 996-5648
Fall River	K G Krafts	260 New Boston Rd.	(508) 676-3336
Falmouth	Fabric Corner	12 Spring Bars Rd.	(508) 548-6482
Falmouth	Needleworks of Cape Cod	95 Davis Straits	(508) 495-0203
Franklin	**Emma's Quilt Cupboard and Sewing Center**		
		12 Main St.	**(508) 520-0234** Pg. 192
Franklin	Franklin Mill Store	305 Union St.	(508) 528-3301
Georgetown	Quilters' Quarters	59 North St.	(978) 352-2676
Gloucester	Coveted Yarn	127 Eastern Ave.	(978) 282-8809
Great Barrington	The Sewing Shop	323 Main St. #3	(413) 528-0118
Great Barrington	Wonderful Things	232 Stockbridge Rd.	(413) 528-2473
Greenfield	The Textile Co., Inc.	21 Power Sq.	(413) 773-7516
Hanover	American Folk Art & Craft Supply	1415 Hanover St. Rt. 139	(781) 871-7277
Hanover	Yarn's End	1112 Washington St.	(781) 924-5549
Harvard	The Fiber Loft (Bare Hill Studios)	9 Massachusetts Ave. Rt. 111	(978) 456-8669
Harwich	Adventures in Knitting	105 Rt. 137 #B	(508) 432-3700
Hatfield	The Yellow Quilt Shop	131 Main St. #107	(413) 203-6100
Hingham	Hingham Square Needlepoint	132 North St. 2nd Floor	(781) 836-5200
Hingham	Yarns in the Square	28 South St. Ste. 1	(781) 749-2280
Holden	The Sheep Shack	787 Main St.	(508) 829-5811
Hubbardston	Greenwood Hill Farm	59 Brigham St.	(978) 928-5175
Jamacia Plain	JP Knit & Stitch	461 Centre St.	(617) 942-2118
Lakeville	**Homestead Quilting and Fabrics**	**54 Main St. Rt. 105**	**(774) 419-3984** Pg. 193
Lenox	Colorful Stitches	48 Main St.	(413) 637-8206
Lowell	**The New England Quilt Museum**	**18 Shattuck St.**	**(978) 452-4207** Pg. 191
Marblehead	Marblehead Knits	152 Washington St.	(781) 990-1722
Marlborough	Wayside Sewing	1021 Boston Post Rd. E.	(508) 481-2088
Mashpee	Yarn Basket	681 Falmouth Rd.	(508) 477-0858
Melrose	Crosscut Sewing Co.	200 Green St.	(781) 620-1896
Merrimac	Red Barn Sewing & Yarn Center	116 W. Main St.	(978) 346-9292
Middleboro	Wool Patch	446 Wareham St.	(508) 923-6029
Nantucket	Erica Wilson Needle Works	25 Main St.	(508) 228-9881
Nantucket	Flock - A Nantucket Knit Shop	79 Orange St.	(508) 228-0038
Natick	**Fabric Place Basement**	**321 Speen St.**	**(508) 655-2000** Pg. 192
Natick	Iron Horse Farm	3 Pond St.	(508) 647-4722
Needham	Black Sheep Knitting	1500 Highland Ave.	(781) 444-0694
Needham	Creative Warehouse	220 Reservoir St. #10	(781) 444-9341
Newton	Knits & Pieces	8 Hale St.	(617) 969-8879
North Attleboro	Yarn It All	1 Bank St.	(508) 695-3331
North Billerica	Hub Mills Store	16 Esquire Rd. #2	(978) 408-2176
North Chelmsford	Aunt Margaret's	165 Princeton St.	(978) 251-2272
North Easton	Auntie Zaza's Fiber Works	104 Main St.	(774) 269-6899
Northampton	Northampton Wools Too	29 Pleasant St.	(413) 586-4331
Northampton	Webs America's Yarn Store	75 Service Center Rd.	(413) 584-2225
Orleans	Murray's Fabrics	11 Rt. 28	(508) 255-0653
Osterville	Christine's Osterville Needlepoint Shop Ltd.		
		846-A Main St.	(508) 428-4455
Palmer	Sew Bizzie Quilting	4109 Main St.	(413) 283-4422
Plymouth	Fancie Purls	170 Water St. #10	(508) 746-1746
Reading	Mary Rose's Quilts & Treasures	4 Brande Ct.	(781) 942-9497
Rehoboth	Loraine's Stitch 'n' Crafts	235 Winthrop St.	(508) 252-5640
Rockland	The Country Crafter	379 Liberty St.	(781) 421-6240
Salem	B. F. Goodstitch	18 Front St.	(978) 740-8986
Sandwich	Sew Pro	280 A Rt. 130 Bldg. 3	(508) 759-2222
Seekonk	The Calico Cottage Quilt Shop	1460 Rall River Ave. #10	(888) 403-5809
South Dartmouth	The Needleworker	1 Bridge St.	(508) 999-2477
South Egremont	**Brookside Quiltworks**	**2 Egremont Sheffield Rd.**	**(413) 528-0445** Pg. 190
South Grafton	Suzi's Fiber Cat	156 Main St.	(508) 839-3160
Sturbridge	**The Quilt and Cabbage**	**538 Main St.**	**(508) 347-3023** Pg. 191
Sturbridge	Sturbridge Quilting	559 Main St. #102	(508) 347-6500
Templeton	Heather Croft Quilt Shack	633 Patriots Rd.	(978) 939-1207
Tewksbury	Sew-Together Quilt Shop	2297 Main St.	(978) 203-0291
Townsend	Cobblestone Quilts	10 Elm St.	(978) 597-0091
Uxbridge	Pasa Yarns	175 Elmdale Rd.	(508) 278-2260
Vineyard Haven	The Heath Hen Yarn and Quilt Shop	455 State Rd.	(508) 693-6730
Vineyard Haven	Vineyard Knit Works	10 State Rd.	(508) 687-9163
Wakefield	Quilters Common	364 Main St. Rear	(781) 587-0360
Wales	Meeting House Fabric and Trim	83 Main St. Rt. 19	(413) 245-1235

Walpole	All About Quilts	958 Main St.	(508) 668-0145	
Walpole	Dee's Nimble Needles & Yarn Shop	15 West St.	(508) 668-8499	
Waltham	Island Yarn Co.	85 River St. #9	(781) 894-1802	
Wellesley	The Wellesley Needlepoint Collection	22 Grove St.	(781) 235-2477	
West Barnstable	**Tumbleweed Quilts**	**1919 Rt. 6A**	**(508) 362-8700**	**Pg. 193**
West Concord	Dabblers Hobbies & Café	119 Commonwealth Ave.	(978) 254-5798	
West Dennis	Cape Cod Quilts and Cottages	159 Main St.	(508) 760-4524	
West Newton	Putting on the Knitz	1282 Washington St.	(617) 969-8070	
West Springfield	Osgood Textile Co.	333 Park St.	(413) 737-6488	
Westfield	**The Spare Room**	**47 Southwick Rd.**	**(413) 642-6987**	**Pg. 190**
Westminster	Appleberry Fabrics	23 Village Inn Rd. #A	(978) 874-0400	
Westport	Sisters of the Wool	782 Main Rd.	(774) 264-9665	
Westport	Westport Yarns & Art Supplies	1099 State Rd.	(508) 994-7845	
Williamstown	**Karen's Quilting Corner**	**723 Cold Spring Rd.**	**(413) 884-6200**	**Pg. 190**
Winchester	Another Yarn	600 Main St.	(781) 570-2134	
Woburn	Marie's Sewing Center	300 Mishawum Rd.	(781) 935-5558	
Worcester	Knitscape	1116 Pleasant St.	(508) 459-0557	

Index

Notes

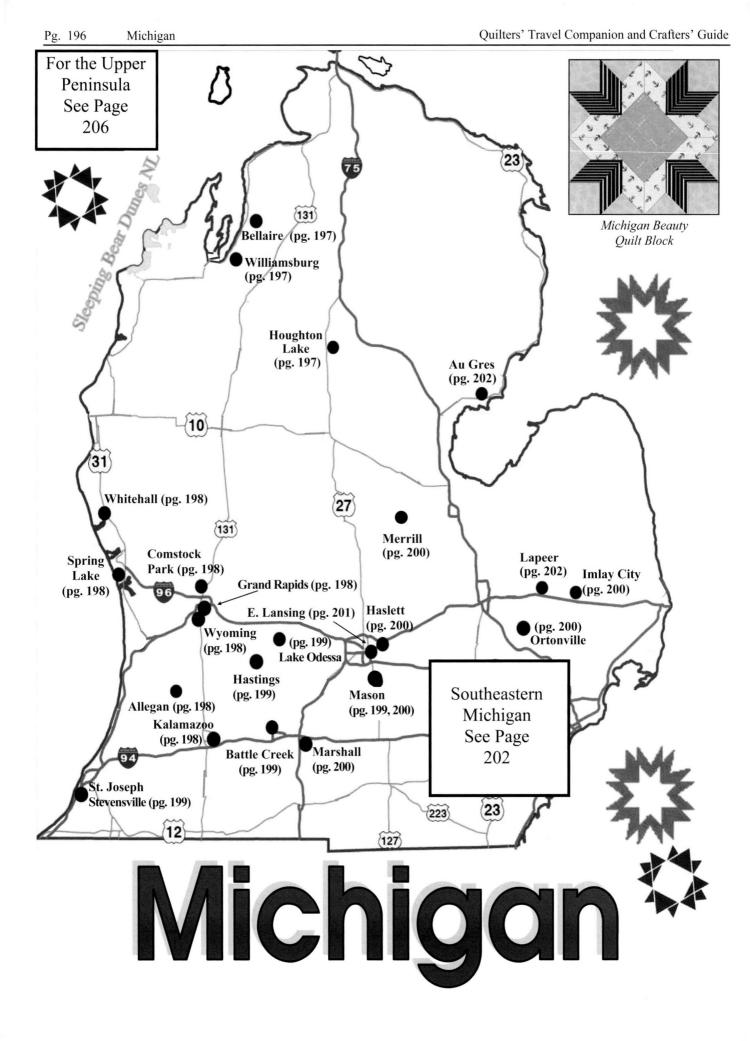

For the Upper
Peninsula
See Page
206

Sleeping Bear Dunes NL

*Michigan Beauty
Quilt Block*

Bellaire (pg. 197)

Williamsburg
(pg. 197)

Houghton
Lake
(pg. 197)

Au Gres
(pg. 202)

Whitehall (pg. 198)

Merrill
(pg. 200)

Lapeer
(pg. 202)

Imlay City
(pg. 200)

Spring
Lake
(pg. 198)

Comstock
Park (pg. 198)

Grand Rapids (pg. 198)

E. Lansing (pg. 201)

Haslett
(pg. 200)

(pg. 200)
Ortonville

Wyoming
(pg. 198)

(pg. 199)
Lake Odessa

Hastings
(pg. 199)

Mason
(pg. 199, 200)

Southeastern
Michigan
See Page
202

Allegan (pg. 198)

Kalamazoo
(pg. 198)

Battle Creek
(pg. 199)

Marshall
(pg. 200)

St. Joseph
Stevensville (pg. 199)

Michigan

Houghton Lake, MI   Q

AJ's Quiltery

4532 W. Houghton Lake Dr.
(989) 422-5276
ajsquiltery@i2k.com
www.ajsquiltery.com

Road Trip! AJ's got your back!
Fabrics, Kits, Patterns, Notions, and Books.
400+ bolts of wide backings. (West Location Only)

**NEW
SECOND
LOCATION**

**Mon-Sat 10:30-4:30
Winter hours:
Mon-Sat 10:30-4:00**

6230 W. Houghton Lake Dr.
(989) 302-8040
ajsquiltery@i2k.com

AJ's Quiltery West

Cousin's Quilt Shop
"The little shop with a big heart."

A wide selection of fabrics by many of the top designers. Valdani Threads. We also offer classes and weekend sewing events.

www.cousinsquiltshop.com

Wool Kits

Mon-Fri 10-5
Sat 10-3

BERNINA
made to create

Est: 2001   Find us on Facebook

Bellaire, MI   Q

**732 E. Cayuga St.
Bellaire, MI 49615
(231) 533-4661**
hartwig@torchlake.com
Owner: Carmen Hartwig

[map showing: to Charlevoix, Lake Michigan, U.S. 31, Torch Lake, Bellaire, M-88, Mancelona, M-72]

"A Quilter's Dream"

Renee's House of Quilting is situated in a 1912 farm house where every room is filled with wonderful fabrics such as florals, batiks and Asian fabrics. Major quilt fabric names like Hoffman, Timeless Treasures, Riley Blake, Benartex, Michael Miller and Moda grace our shelves. We've lots of purse patterns, jacket patterns and of course quilt patterns for you to choose from.

**Est: 2004
Owner:
Renee Savage**

We also carry gorgeous florals and terrific bright children's designs. The kitchen is just that, a kitchen, a place where we can meet and the men folk can have a cup of coffee and a cookie. Renee's husband Glenn does all the homemade cookies and cuts the fat quarters too! We are open year around & love to meet quilters from all over the country.

[map: to Hwy. 31- 5 mi., Turtle Creek Casino, Williamsburg Rd., Renee's Look for the Fuschia Mailbox, M-72 East, 8995 Shell]

**8995 M 72 East   49690
(231) 267-5895**

Mon - Fri 9:30 - 5:30
Sat 9:30 - 4

**NEW EXPANDED
SHOWROOM**

www.reneeshouseofquilting.net

Williamsburg, MI   Q

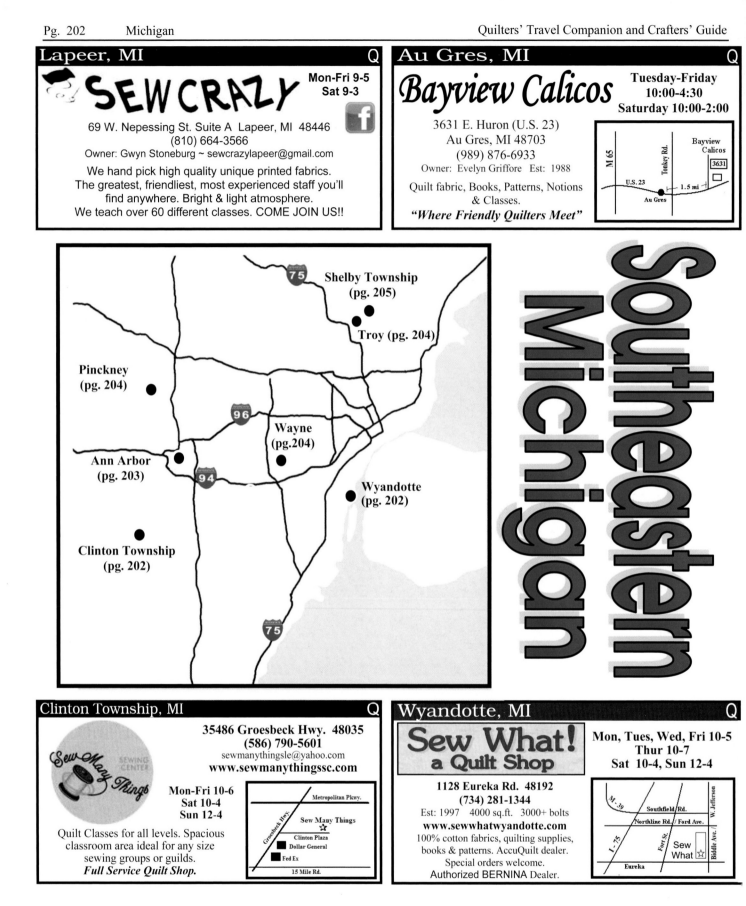

Shelby Township (pg. 205)

Troy (pg. 204)

Pinckney (pg. 204)

Wayne (pg.204)

Ann Arbor (pg. 203)

Wyandotte (pg. 202)

Clinton Township (pg. 202)

Southeastern Michigan

Did you know?
Spanning five miles between the upper and lower peninsulas of Michigan,
The Mackinac Bridge is one of the longest suspension bridges in the world.

Ann Arbor Sewing and Quilting Center

5235 Jackson Road, Ann Arbor, MI 48103

734-761-3094   www.annarborsewing.com

Open 7 days a week!

Hours: Monday-Friday 10:00 am-6:00 pm, Thursday 10:00 am-8:00 pm, Saturday 10:00 am-4:00 pm, Sunday 12:00 pm-4:00 pm.

Please call ahead to verify summer and holiday hours.

- Over 7000 bolts of exciting fabrics from top manufacturers: brights, batiks, novelty, traditional, modern, reproduction, flannel, cuddle, and more!
- Fabulous fabric room with wonderful lighting and lots of space
- Newest and coolest quilting and sewing notions
- Huge assortment of thread for machine quilting and embroidery
- Award winning service from factory trained technicians. Service and repair on ALL makes and models. FREE Estimates. 24 hour service available, see technician for details.
- Wide variety of classes, clubs and workshops
- Large selection of sewing, embroidery and quilting machines on display to test sew
- Authorized Koala and Horn cabinet dealer
- Buses welcome!

Celebrating 50
years in business!
1968-2018

Authorized Dealer for:

BERNINA
PFAFF

Husqvarna   VIKING

The Grand Hotel

Between Michigan's Upper and Lower Peninsulas, tiny Mackinac Island is home to this sprawling resort, overlooking crystal-clear Lake Huron. Five U.S. presidents have stayed at this majestic establishment, which opened in 1887, and has dazzled visitors with its lavishly decorated rooms, sublime service, and superlative front porch — the longest in the world at nearly 660 feet.

286 Grand Ave, Mackinac Island, MI 49757

(800) 334-7263

www.grandhotel.com

Notes

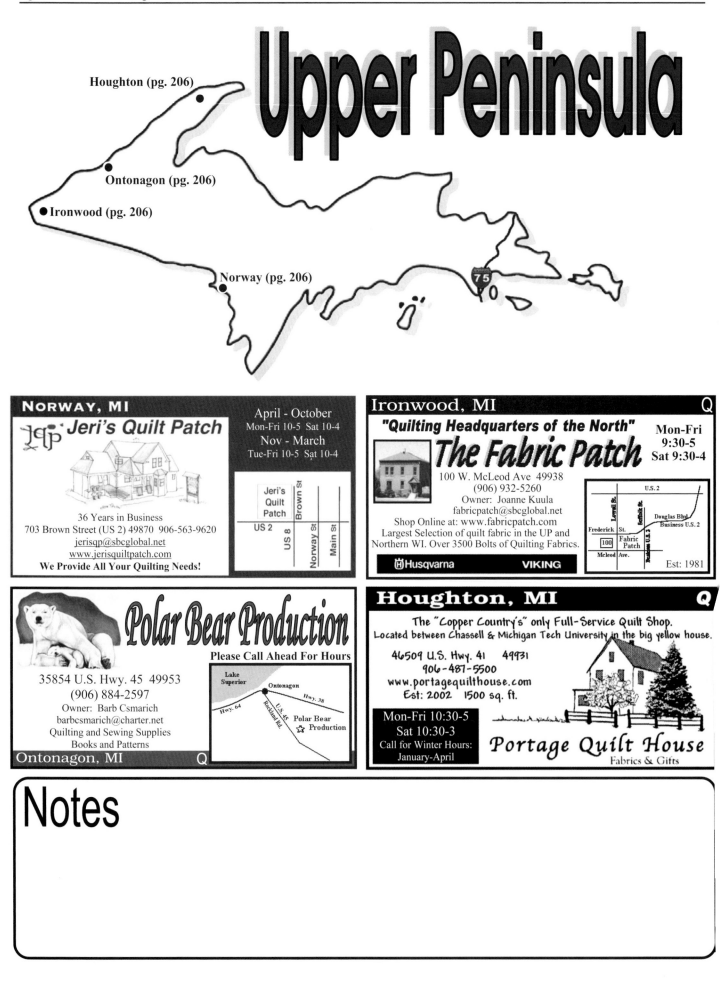

Notes

Michigan Shops

Q-Quilting ~ Y-Yarn ~ N-Needlework ~ R-Retreat ~ M-Museum

Ada	Clever Ewe	590 Ada Dr.	(616) 682-1545	
Ada	Peacock Alley Needlepoint	410 Ada Dr. SE	(616) 682-9854	
Adrian	Ann's By Design	118 W. Maumee St.	(517) 438-8459	
Alden	The Warm Fuzzy	9059 Helena Rd.	(231) 331-4000	
Allegan	**Sharon's Quilts & More**	**128 Hubbard St.**	**(269) 686-9579**	**Pg. 198**
Allegan	Marr Haven Wool Farm	772 39th St.	(269) 673-8800	
Alpena	Spruce Shadow Farms Yarn Shop	2328 US. 23	(989) 356-9434	
Alpena	Yarns to Go & Fabrics	127 N. Second Ave.	(989) 356-4119	
Ann Arbor	**Ann Arbor Sewing and Quilting Center**	**5235 Jackson Rd.**	**(734) 761-3094**	**Pg. 203**
Ann Arbor	Busy Hands Knitting & Gifts	306 S. Main St. Ste.1-C	(734) 996-8020	
Ann Arbor	Ophir Crafts / Ophir Yarn and Fiber	1522 N. Maple	(734) 794-7777	
Ann Arbor	Pink Castle Fabrics	1915 Federal Blvd.	(248) 885-6174	
Armada	A Knitter Hideaway	20805 33 Mile Rd.	(586) 784-9673	
Au Gres	**Bayview Calicos and Ceramics**	**3631 E. Huron Rd.**	**(989) 876-6933**	**Pg. 202**
Bad Axe	Backstreet Quilt Shop	110 E. Huron Ave.	(989) 375-4620	
Baldwin	Fabric Peddler	815 N. Michigan Ave.	(231) 745-4500	
Battle Creek	**Sew Unique Threads**	**7175 Tower Rd. #F**	**(269) 317-3022**	**Pg. 199**
Bay City	A Piece of Ewe	602 Saginaw St.	(989) 892-6400	
Bay City	Bonnie's Sewing Center	1200 N. Henry	(989) 439-1100	
Bay City	Bonnie's Sewing Center	3557 Wilder Rd.	(989) 686-8180	
Bay City	The Stitching Well	78 State Park Dr.	(989) 684-0231	
Bay City	Yarn Supply	3480 E. N. Union Rd.	(989) 667-5308	
Bellaire	**Cousin's Quilt Shop Bernina**	**732 E. Cayuga St.**	**(231) 533-4661**	**Pg. 197**
Benton Harbor	Quilters Joy	1041 Emerson Ave.	(269) 757-3036	
Berkley	Guildcrafters Quilt Shop	2600 W. 12-Mile Rd.	(248) 541-8545	
Berkley	Have You Any Wool	3455 Robina Ave.	(248) 541-9665	
Beulah	The Yarn Market	244 S. Benzie Blvd.	(231) 882-4640	
Big Rapids	Creative Loop	18841 Northland Dr.	(231) 629-8228	
Birmingham	Right Off The Sheep	359 S. Old Woodward Ave.	(248) 646-7595	
Birmingham	The Needleworks	725 S. Adams Rd.	(248) 645-1180	
Brighton	Creative Quilt Kits	10489 Grand River Rd. #B	(810) 225-2849	
Brighton	Ewe-Nique Yarns, Inc.	9864 E. Grand River	(810) 229-5579	
Bruce Township	Quilted Nine Patch	70941 Van Dyke	(586) 651-3937	
Burt Lake	Estelle Knit Shop	10249 E. W. Resort Rd.	(231) 881-0251	
Byron	Aspects of Wool	11955 E. Lovejoy Rd.	(810) 266-6563	
Cadillac	Northern Hearth Quilting & Sewing Center	115 N. Mitchell St.	(231) 942-4800	
Caledonia	Henny's Yarn Shop	131 E. Main St.	(616) 891-2406	
Caro	Back Alley Fibers	142 N. State St.	(989) 672-2144	
Caro	Catty Wampus Fabric Company	212 N. State St.	(989) 672-0090	
Carson City	Miner Road Fabrics	9617 S. Miner Rd.	(989) 584-2163	
Carson City	Seven Sisters Quilt Shop	210 West Main St	(989) 584-3300	
Cedar	Wool & Honey	9031 S. Kasson St.	(231) 228-2800	
Charlevoix	Hearts To Holly Quilt & Gift Shop	207 Ferry Ave.	(231) 547-2729	
Charlotte	Sweet Bee's Fabric	217 S. Cochran Ave.	(517) 543-1011	
Charlotte	The Hen House	211 S. Cochran Ave.	(517) 543-6454	
Charlotte	The Yarn Garden	111 W. Lawrence Ave.	(517) 541-9323	
Chesaning	The Silver Thimble	148 S. Chapman St .	(989) 326-0547	
Clare	Apple Tree Lane	522 N. McEwan	(989) 386-2552	
Clare	Surrey Rd. Quilt Shop	3681 E. Surrey Rd.	(989) 386-3043	
Clarkston	Basket Full of Yarn	5 S. Main St.	(248) 620-2491	
Clawson	PK Yarn Over Knit	25 S. Main St.	(248) 808-6630	
Clinton Township	**Sew Many Things**	**35486 Groesbeck**	**(586) 790-5601**	**Pg. 202**
Comstock Park	**Attic Window Quilt Shop**	**5363 Alpine NW**	**(616) 785-3357**	**Pg. 198**
Custer	Pig Patch Farm Quilts	3007 E. Hansen Rd.	(231) 757-2812	
Davison	Elaine's Yarns	219 E. Flint St.	(810) 653-9010	
Davison	Linda's Country Quilt Shop	3058 N. State Rd. #F	(810) 658-9051	
Dearborn	The Material Girls	1850 Grindley Park St.	(313) 561-1111	
East China	River Place Quilt and Sew	2000 River Rd.	(810) 329-9300	
East Jordan	Stonehedge Fiber Mill	2246 Pesek Rd.	(231) 536-2779	
East Lansing	**Country Stitches, Ltd.**	**2200 Coolidge Rd.**	**(517) 351-2416**	**Pg. 201**
East Lansing	Great Lakes Quilt Center	120 Linton	(517) 432-3800	
East Tawas	Ben Franklin	138 Newman St.	(989) 362-2751	
East Tawas	Tawas Bay Yarn Co., Inc.	1820 US. 23	(989) 362-4463	

Edwardsburg	Robin's Nest: Quilts & More	26848 US. Hwy. 12	(269) 663-3303	
Elk Rapids	Now & Then	126 River St.	(231) 264-5560	
Evart	Juneberry Cottage	147 N. Main St.	(231) 734-5863	
Ewen	Brambleberry, Inc.	134 Pine M-28 E.	(906) 988-2230	
Farmington	Artisan Knitworks	23616 Farmington Rd.	(248) 427-0804	
Farmington	Rocking Horse Designs in Cross Stitch	33305 Grand River Ave.	(248) 474-3113	
Farmington Hills	Fun With Fiber	33338 W. 12 Mile Rd.	(248) 553-4237	
Farwell	Elm Creek Ltd.	2609 W. Surrey Rd.	(989) 588-6061	
Fennville	Custom Quilts Unlimited, LLC	6184 Quilters Ct.	(269) 561-6214	
Fenton	Stitches 'N Things	14288 N. Fenton Rd.	(810) 629-3333	
Fife Lake	The Quilter's Clinic	108 W. State St.	(231) 879-4115	
Flint	Black Crow Primitives	4421 Richfield Rd.	(810) 845-6917	
Fort Gratiot	Sew Elegant Quilt Shoppe	3909 Pine Grove Ave.	(810) 982-6556	
Frankenmuth	Frankenmuth Woolen Mills	313 Rosstall St.	(989) 652-8121	
Frankenmuth	The Front Porch Quilt Shop	305 S. Franklin St.	(989) 652-8050	
Frankenmuth	Zeilinger Wool Co.	1130 Weiss St.	(989) 652-2920	
Gaylord	Delphine's Quilt Shop	114 N. Otsego Ave.	(989) 732-1252	
Gladwin	Yarn for Ewe	320 W. Cedar Ave.	(989) 709-5149	
Glen Arbor	The Yarn Shop	5873 Lake St.	(231) 334-3805	
Grand Blanc	Beyond the Rainforest	12830 S. Saginaw St. #E	(810) 953-0089	
Grand Blanc	Ewe to You Yarns	11225 S. Saginaw	(810) 344-2218	
Grand Blanc	Homestead Needle Arts	8185 Holly Rd. #4	(810) 694-3040	
Grand Haven	The Needlesmith	109 N. 7th St.	(616) 844-7188	
Grand Rapids	**Lakeshore Sewing**	**1971 E. Beltline NE**	**616) 365-8282**	**Pg. 198**
Grand Rapids	**Smith Owen Sewing & Quilting Center**			
		4051 Plainfield NE	**616-361-5484**	**Pg. 198**
Grand Rapids	A Grand Skein	2431 Eastern Ave. SE	(616) 551-1322	
Grand Rapids	Field's Fabrics	1695 44th St.	(616) 455-9330	
Grand Rapids	Field's Fabrics	3701 Plainfield Ave.	(616) 364-6505	
Grand Rapids	Field's Fabrics	3975 Lake Michigan Dr.	(616) 453-8381	
Grand Rapids	Gall Sewing & Vac Center	3933 Plainfield Ave.	(888) 363-1911	
Grand Rapids	Lamb Creek Farm Quilt & Fabrics	18701 E. Beltline NE	(989) 721-1778	
Grand Rapids	Queen Bee Quilt Shoppe	6522 Division Ave. S. #B	(616) 827-8911	
Grand Rapids	Stitched Studio Sewing Lounge	1144 E. Paris Ave. SE	(616) 214-8323	
Grass Lake	Rose's Quilts	11644 Morrissey Rd.	(734) 260-4198	
Grayling	Au Sable Fabrics & More	108 E. Michigan Ave.	(989) 745-2988	
Greenville	Forever Fabrics	117 W. Cass St.	(616) 225-8486	
Grosse Pointe	The Knotted Needle	20237 Mack Ave.	(313) 886-2828	
Grosse Pointe	The Wool & The Floss	397 Fisher Rd.	(313) 882-9110	
Hadley	Elaine's Quilty Shop	4600 Pratt Rd.	(810) 797-2242	
Hancock	Fiber Whims	210 Quincy St.	(906) 523-4048	
Harrison Township	City Knits	26050 Crocker Blvd.	(586) 469-9665	
Hart	A Sister's Act, LLC	55 S. State St.	(231) 301-8154	
Haslett	**Custom Quilt & Sewing Center**			
		5676 Okemos Rd.	**(517) 339-7581**	**Pg. 200**
Hastings	**Sisters Fabrics**	**218 E. State St.**	**(269) 945-9673**	**Pg. 199**
Hastings	Jami's Craft Supplies	130 E. State St.	(269) 945-4484	
Hastings	Walker Music & Textiles Co.	1450 W. M-43 Hwy. #1	(269) 804-6024	
Hesperia	Fanna's Mercantile	151 Spruce St.	(231) 854-0612	
Hessel	Pickle Point Inc.	138 Pickford Ave.	(906) 484-3479	
Hillman	Sandy Dee's Sewing Quilt Shop Fabric	1015 Hawley Rd.	(989) 379-2406	
Hillsdale	Laurie's Farmhouse Quilting	6551 Cambria Rd.	(517) 357-4478	
Hillsdale	Trevathan's Sweep & Sew Shoppe	47 N. Broad St.	(517) 437-5555	
Holland	Field's Fabrics	281 E. 8th	(616) 392-4806	
Holland	Flying Pig Yarn Shop	11975 E. Lakewood Blvd. Ste. 11	(616) 283-4162	
Holland	Garen Huis Yarn Studio	27 W. 9th St.	(616) 294-3492	
Holland	Pressing Matters Quilt Shop	399 E. 32nd St.	(616) 392-9700	
Houghton	**Portage Quilt House**	**46509 US. Hwy. 41**	**(906) 487-5500**	**Pg. 206**
Houghton	Sew Irresistible	407 Shelden Ave.	(906) 482-1722	
Houghton Lake	**AJ's Quiltery & Gifts**	**4532 W. Houghton Lake Dr. M-55**	**(989) 422-5276**	**Pg. 197**
Houghton Lake	Suze's Stitch'n	6230 W. Houghton Lake Dr.	(989) 422-6200	
Howard City	Mama's Cave Fabric Shop	9380 Jones Rd.	(231) 660-3937	
Howell	Stitch In Time	722 E. Grand River Ave.	(517) 546-0769	
Howell	The Stitchery	1129 E. Grand River	(517) 548-1731	
Imlay City	**The Pincushion**	**113 E. Third**	**(810) 724-7065**	**Pg. 200**
Imlay City	Stitchin' at the Barn	2648 S. Van Dyke Rd.	(810) 721-7037	
Indian River	The Quilt House	4819 S. Straits Hwy.	(231) 238-4339	
Interlochen	Inter Quilten	2323 M137	(231) 276-9100	
Ironwood	**The Fabric Patch Limited**	**100 W. McLeod Ave.**	**(906) 932-5260**	**Pg. 206**
Jackson	Dropped Stitch	1212 Wildwood Ave. Ste. C	(517) 768-8280	

Jackson	In Stitches	2618 Kibby Rd.	(517) 787-2566	
Jenison	Country Needleworks, Inc.	584 Chicago Ave.	(616) 457-9410	
Jenison	Field's Fabrics	550 Chicago Dr.	(616) 667-2800	
Jonesville	Quilt Around the Corner	107 Olds St. #5	(517) 826-5104	
Kalamazoo	**Bernina Sewing Center and Quilt Shop**	**4205 Portage Rd.**	**(269) 383-1244**	**Pg. 198**
Kalamazoo	**Lucy in the Sky Quilts**	**839 Gull Rd.**	**(269) 381-7242**	**Pg. 198**
Kalamazoo	Field's Fabrics	5401 Portage Rd.	(269) 383-4211	
Kalamazoo	Great Northern Weaving	451 E. D Ave.	(269) 341-9752	
Kalamazoo	Kalamazoo Sewing Center	Airview Plaza 5401 Portage Rd. Ste. 6	(269) 342-5808	
Kalamazoo	Quilts Plus	3314 Stadium Dr.	(269) 383-1790	
Kalamazoo	Stitching Memories	5401-3 Portage	(269) 552-9276	
Kentwood	Field's Fabrics	1695 44th St. SE	(616) 455-9330	
Lake City	Cardinal Creations, Inc.	7451 W. Blue Rd.	(231) 839-5570	
Lake Linden	Yarns And Threads	332 Calumet St.	(906) 296-9568	
Lake Odessa	**Friends Quilting Basket**	**1001 Fourth Ave.**	**(616) 374-3060**	**Pg. 199**
Lake Orion	Heritage Spinning & Weaving	47 E. Flint St.	(248) 693-3690	
Lake Orion	The Village Quilt Shoppe	3635 Baldwin Rd.	(248) 391-5727	
Lansing	Gall Sewing & Vac	428 Frandor Ave.	(517) 333-0500	
Lansing	Little Red Schoolhouse Yarn Shop	5002 W. Saginaw	(517) 321-6701	
Lansing	Sticks & Strings	1107 N. Washington Ave.	(517) 372-1000	
Lapeer	**Sew Crazy**	**69 W Nepessing St. #A**	**(810) 664-3566**	**Pg. 202**
Lathrup Village	Yarns and Knitting Machines	27208 Southfield Rd.	(800) 520-9276	
Leslie	Sittin' On Pins	110 S. Main St.	(517) 589-8802	
Lexington Hts	Victoria's Sewing and Heirloom Supplies	6894 Lakeshore Rd.	(810) 359-5940	
Livonia	Michigan Fine Yarns	37519 Ann Arbor Rd.	(734) 462-2800	
Ludington	Nautical Yarn	108 S. Rath Ave.	(231) 845-9868	
Macomb	Crafty Lady Trio	15401 Hall Rd.	(586) 566-8008	
Macomb	Time Remembered Quilting	16701 21 Mile	(586) 221-1954	
Manistee	Northern Spirits	389 River St.	(231) 398-0131	
Manistee	Sunrise Fabrics	354 River St.	(231) 398-3795	
Marine City	Quilting Dreams	256 S Water St.	(810) 420-0105	
Marlette	Sisters In Quilting	6407 Morris St.	(989) 635-0300	
Marquette	Alley Kat's Quilt Shop	623 W. Washington St.	(906) 315-0050	
Marquette	Merricks & Ben Franklin	100 Coles Dr.	(906) 226-9613	
Marshall	**Quilts at the Marshall House**	**100 Exchange St.**	**(269) 781-9450**	**Pg. 200**
Mason	**Keans Hallmark & Variety**	**406 S. Jefferson**	**(517) 676-5144**	**Pg. 199**
Mason	**Yards of Fabric**	**116 E. Ash St.**	**(517) 676-2973**	**Pg. 200**
Menominee	Quilter's Haven Ltd.	447 1st St.	(906) 864-3078	
Menominee	The Elegant Ewe	400 1st St.	(906) 863-2296	
Merrill	**Miles of Stitches**	**123 N. Midland**	**(989) 643-5566**	**Pg. 200**
Merrill	Twisted Warp & Skeins	105 N. Midland Rd.	(989) 643-0108	
Midland	Apple Valley Yarn Company	84 Ashman Cir.	(989) 832-2900	
Midland	Material Mart	86 Ashman Cir.	(989) 835-8761	
Midland	Park Bench Quilt Shop	1613 E. Wheeler St.	(989) 832-5722	
Milford	The Knitting Circle	400 N. Main St. #204	(248) 684-1915	
Millington	Quilted Hearts Quilting	6299 Millington Rd.	(989) 871-7425	
Mio	Stitches For You	422 S. Morenci Ave.	(989) 826-1890	
Monroe	Lake Erie Mercantile	15555 S. Telegraph Rd. #10	(734) 682-3945	
Montague	Quilted Memories	9919 US. Hwy. 31	(231) 893-0096	
Mt. Pleasant	Keepsake Quilts	4585 E. Pickard Rd. #K	(989) 317-8700	
Mt. Pleasant	Mt. Pleasant Sewing Center & Quilt Shop	1024 S. Mission	(989) 773-7403	
Muskegon	Abbi Mays Fabric Shop	2357 Holton Rd. #B	(231) 563-6861	
Muskegon	Apple Knits & Purls	2009 Lakeshore Dr.	(231) 780-5648	
Muskegon	Gall Sewing & Vac Center	1910 E. Apple Ave. #K	(231) 773-8494	
Muskegon	Lakeshore Sewing	1848 E. Sherman Blvd.	(231) 288-1263	
Newaygo	The New Ewe Yarn Shoppe & Quilting	59 W. State Rd.	(231) 652-5262	
Niles	Red Purl	207 N. 2nd St.	(269) 684-0411	
Norton Shores	Stitched Heart	186 E. Mount Garfield Rd.	(231) 798-3987	
Norway	**Jeri's Quilt Patch**	**703 Brown US. #2**	**(906) 563-9620**	**Pg. 206**
Ontonagon	**Polar Bear Production**	**35854 US. Hwy. 45**	**(906) 884-2597**	**Pg. 206**
Ortonville	**Mabelena Quilting Supplies & Comforts**	**470 Mill St.**	**(248) 627-9100**	**Pg. 200**
Ottawa Lake	Yarn Envy	4570 Sterns Rd. #1	(734) 856-1015	
Ovid	Elaine's Too	122 S. Main St.	(989) 834-2538	
Paradise	Village Fabrics & Crafts	32702 Hwy. M-123 W.	(906) 492-3803	
Perrinton	Calico Cupboard	4625 MacArthur	(989) 236-7728	
Petoskey	Cynthia's TOO! Yarn & Gifts	320 E. Mitchell St.	(231) 439-9221	
Pinckney	**Jennifer's Quilt Shop**	**149 N. Howell**	**(734) 878-6188**	**Pg. 204**
Pinconning	Bittersweet Quilt Shop & Home Décor	624 W. 5th St.	(989) 879-1900	

Index

Plainwell	Dancing Dogs Quilt Shop	119 N. Main St.	(269) 685-3647	
Plainwell	Stitching Bits & Bobs	211 E. Bannister St. #A9	(269) 685-9418	
Plymouth	Old Village Yarn Shop	42307 E. Ann Arbor Rd.	(734) 451-0580	
Port Huron	Mary Maxim, Inc.	2001 Holland Ave.	(810) 987-2000	
Port Huron	RMC Quilts	3561 Gratiot Ave.	(810) 985-3668	
Portland	Mo's Needle & Thread	120 Maple St.	(517) 647-5430	
Richland	Fabrications	8860 N. 32nd St.	(269) 629-0190	
Richmond	Sew Together	69295 Main St.	(586) 727-1555	
Riverdale	Sheila's Fabrics	11995 NW Monroe Rd.	(989) 833-7147	
Rochester	Skeins On Main	428 S. Main St.	(248) 656-9300	
Rockford	J T Stitchery	30 E. Bridge St. #A	(616) 866-2409	
Romeo	Labor of Love Yarn and fiber Arts	246 N. Main	(586) 246-4724	
Romeo	Sheep Stuff/Michigan Farm Woolies	6440 Boardman Rd.	(810) 798-2568	
Roscommon	Michigan Warm Hugs Quilts LLC	402 Lake St.	(989) 281-1621	
Royal Oak	Ewe-Nique Knits	515 S. Lafayette Ave. #E	(248) 584-3001	
Royal Oak	Ladybug Shoppe	210 W. 6th St.	(248) 545-3200	
Saginaw	Quilted Cottage	7075 Gratiot Rd. #4	(989) 790-3123	
Saginaw	Speedy Sew	3210 Tittabawassee Rd.	(989) 790-9048	
Saginaw	Stitch'n Time	7579 Gratiot Rd.	(989) 781-5209	
Saginaw	The Grand Emporium Knitting Studio	5880 State St.	(989) 792-1234	
Saginaw	The Little Yarn Shoppe	7075 Gratiot Rd. #4	(989) 274-8571	
Saline	The Quilting Season	7025 E. Michigan Ave. Ste. A3	(734) 429-2900	
Sault Ste. Marie	The Quilted Moose	1812 Ashmun St.	(906) 253-9886	
Schoolcraft	Big Island Quilt Co.	13228 S. 5th St.	(269) 679-3101	
Shelby Township	**Decorative Stitch**	**48814 Van Dyke**	**(586) 799-7507**	**Pg. 205**
Shelby Twp.	Sewing Products Co. Inc	50304 Schoenherr	(586) 566-4500	
Smiths Creek	The Charmed Quilter	7093 Main St.	(810) 367-2366	
South Haven	Calico Creations	70325 16th Ave.	(269) 637-5558	
South Haven	So South Haven	70920 County Rd. 388	(269) 637-0603	
South Lyon	Lake Street Mercantile	115 E. Lake St.	(248) 486-4410	
Southfield	Rachel's Needlepoint & Judaic Gifts	29260 Franklin Rd. #103	(248) 352-5622	
Spring Lake	**Field's Fabrics**	**212 W. Savidge St.**	**(616) 846-6040**	**Pg. 198**
St Ignace	Georgia B's Quilts	W 1044 Old Portage Trail	(906) 643-7726	
St. Charles	The Silver Thimble	200 S. Saginaw St.	(989) 865-5555	
St. Joseph	**Accomplish Quilting**	**810 Napier Ave.**	**(269)-556-2552**	**Pg. 199**
St. Joseph	At The Heart of Quilting	2603 S. Cleveland Ave. #2	(269) 408-8442	
St. Joseph	Ivelise's Yarn Shop	1601 Lake Shore Dr.	(269) 925-0451	
St. Louis	Common Threads Quilt Shop	109 N. Mill St.	(989) 681-5082	
Stockbridge	Quality Quilting	4983 Bird Rd.	(517) 851-6325	
Suttons Bay	Cherry Country Quilters	310 N. St. Joseph St.	(231) 271-0117	
Suttons Bay	Thistledown Shoppe	419 N. St. Joseph St.	(231) 271-9276	
Tapiola	Calico Bass Quilting Studio	20091 Aldrich Rd.	(906) 334-2441	
Tawas City	Cotton Patch Quilt Shop	685 N. McArdle Rd.	(989)-362-6779	
Tecumseh	The Quilt Patch	112 N. Evans St. #5	(517) 423-0053	
Tecumseh	Timeless Stitches	112 N. Evans St. Ste. 3	(517) 423-0808	
Temperance	Quilt Heaven	9030 Secor Rd. Ste. C	(734) 568-6607	
Three Rivers	Karen's Fabric Shop	57501 N. Main St.	(269) 279-9391	
Traverse City	Quilt-n-Bee Company	1425-G S. Airport Rd. W.	(231) 922-6766	
Traverse City	Yarn Quest	819 S. Garfield Ave.	(231)-929-4277	
Troy	**Front Porch Quilts**	**1790 Livernois**	**(248) 795-4876**	**Pg. 204**
Troy	Fabric Affair	4972 John R. Rd.	(248) 457-9320	
Troy	Needlepoint For You	1969 S. Blvd. W.	(248) 828-8020	
Vicksburg	Tanya's The Girl Garage	123 S. Main St.	(269) 720-8686	
Wakefield	Nanette's Knits & Gifts	501 Sunday Lake St.	(906) 364-4752	
Washington	Creative Corner Of Washington	66800 Van Dyke	(586) 752-7444	
Waterford	A Little Quilt Shop	5721 Elizabeth Lake Rd.	(248) 681-1107	
Wayne	**Bits 'N Pieces**	**34629 W. Michigan Ave.**	**(734)-641-4970**	**Pg. 204**
West Branch	Caroline's Sewing Room	3100 W. Houghton Ave.	(989) 345-9180	
West Branch	Crocker's Attic	3156 W. M-55	(989) 345-1780	
White Cloud	Quilt Something New	28 S. Charles St.	(231) 408-1309	
Whitehall	**The General Store**	**103 E. Colby St.**	**(231) 894-2164**	**Pg. 198**
Whitmore Lake	Forma	111 E. Northfield Church Rd.	(734) 761-1102	
Whitmore Lake	Whitmore Lake Yarn Company	9535 Main St.	(734) 449-9688	
Williamsburg	**Renee's House of Quilting**	**8995 M 72 E.**	**(231) 267-5895**	**Pg. 197**
Williamston	Knitters' Nook	120 High St.	(517) 899-6759	
Wyandotte	**Sew What**	**1128 Eureka Rd.**	**(734) 281-1344**	**Pg. 202**
Wyoming	**Lakeshore Sewing**	**1011 Gezon Pkwy. SW**	**(616) 531-5561**	**Pg. 198**
Wyoming	Gall Sewing & Vac Center	5316 Clyde Park Ave. SW #E	(616) 531-4373	
Wyoming	Threadbender Yarn Shop	2767 44th St. SW	(616) 531-6641	

Index

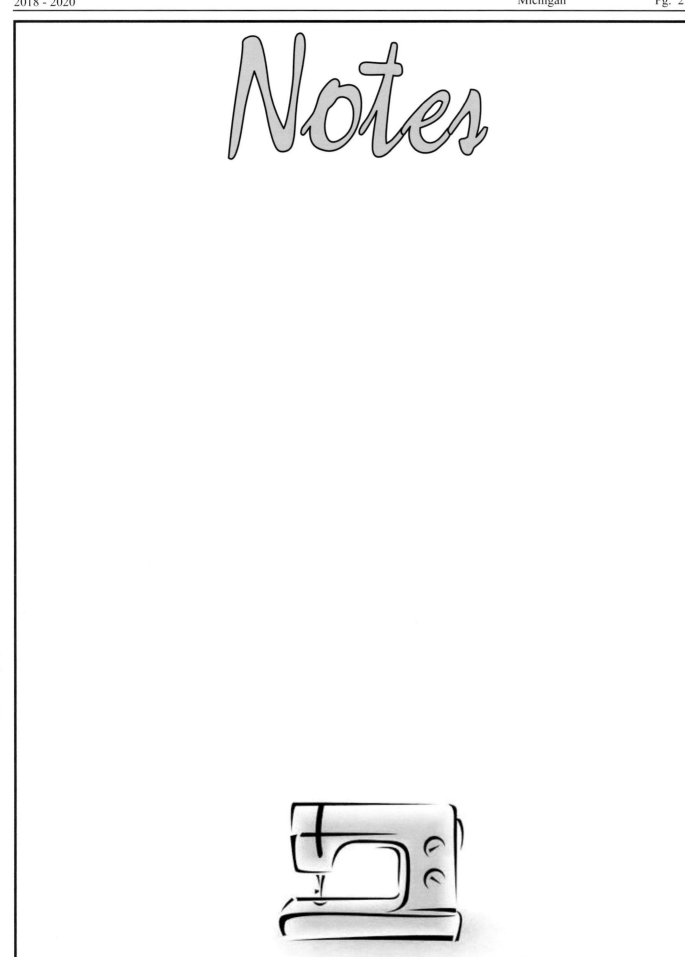

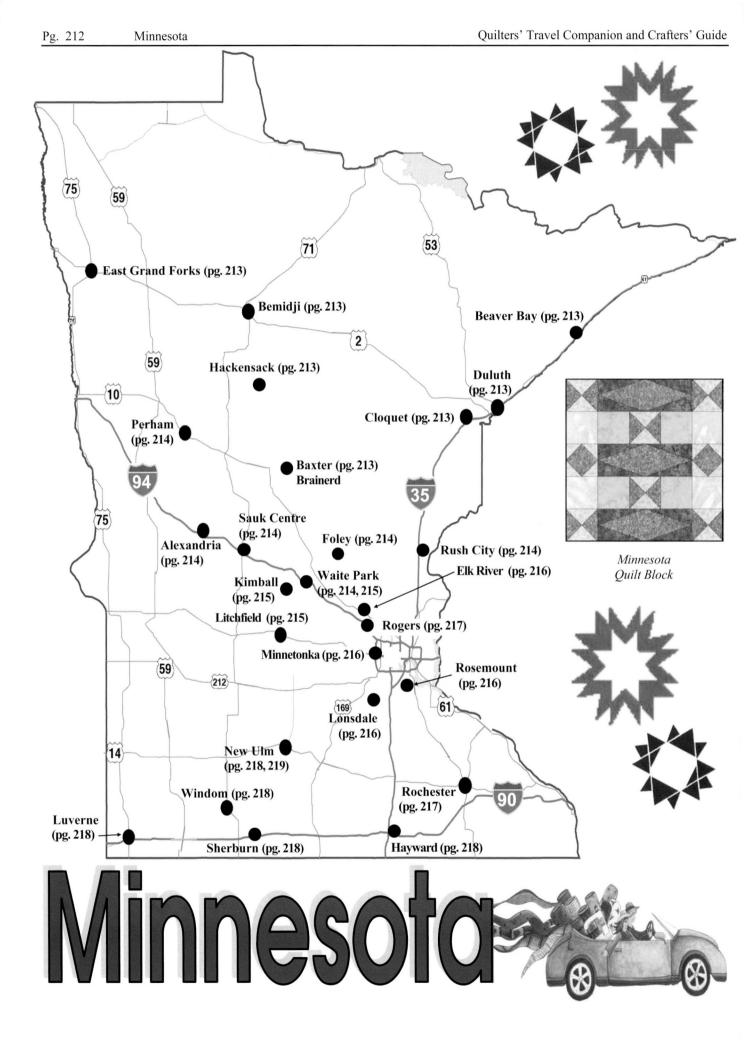

East Grand Forks (pg. 213)

Bemidji (pg. 213)

Beaver Bay (pg. 213)

Hackensack (pg. 213)

Duluth
(pg. 213)

Cloquet (pg. 213)

Perham
(pg. 214)

Baxter (pg. 213)
Brainerd

Sauk Centre
(pg. 214)

Foley (pg. 214)

Rush City (pg. 214)

Alexandria
(pg. 214)

Elk River (pg. 216)

Waite Park
(pg. 214, 215)

Kimball
(pg. 215)

Litchfield (pg. 215)

Rogers (pg. 217)

Minnetonka (pg. 216)

Rosemount
(pg. 216)

Lonsdale
(pg. 216)

New Ulm
(pg. 218, 219)

Windom (pg. 218)

Rochester
(pg. 217)

Luverne
(pg. 218)

Sherburn (pg. 218)

Hayward (pg. 218)

*Minnesota
Quilt Block*

Did you know?
The Mall of America in Bloomington is the size of 78 football fields --- 9.5 million square feet.

The Minneapolis Sculpture Garden is the largest urban sculpture garden in the country.

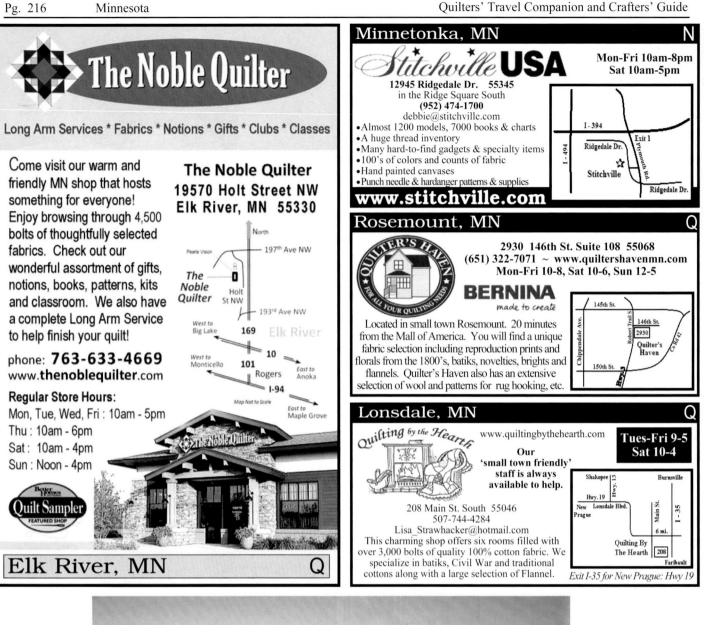

The St. James Hotel
The thriving wheat market in Red Wing during the early 1870s created a need for a comfortable place for tourists and businesses passing through, resulting in this 62-room hotel. Though it may not feel as extravagant as it did back in those days, it's still a storied spot for lodging in town.
406 Main St, Red Wing, MN 55066 - (651) 388-2846 - www.st-james-hotel.com

KNIT
NOTES

Minnesota Shops

Q-Quilting ~ Y-Yarn ~ N-Needlework ~ R-Retreat ~ M-Museum

City	Shop	Address	Phone	Page
Aitkin	Aitkin Quilts & Fabric	936 2nd St. NW	(218) 429-0057	
Aitkin	Pam's Patchwork Paradise	38 Miinesota Ave. S.	(218) 330-8700	
Aitkin	Sew Much & More	204 Minnesota Ave. N.	(218) 927-2914	
Albert Lea	Krafty Kat Kandy	2524 Bridge Ave.	(507) 320-8030	
Alexandria	**Dawn's Quilt Shop**	**522 Broadway St.**	**(320) 763-7011**	**Pg. 214**
Alexandria	Community Vacuum & Sewing	1321 Broadway St.	(320) 762-1412	
Anoka	Millie P's Quilt Shop	219 E. Main St.	(763) 421-0367	
Bagley	Gram's House Of Quilts & Gifts	22906 320th St.	(218) 694-3000	
Barrett	Quilting Etc.	308 2nd St.	(320)-528-2620	
Baxter	**Colorz Quilt Shop**	**14091 Baxter Dr. #112**	**(218) 825-9101**	**Pg. 213**
Baxter	The Cherrywood Store	14091 Baxter Dr. #112	(218) 829-0967	
Beaver Bay	**Quilt Corner**	**1007 Main St.**	**(218) 226-6406**	**Pg. 213**
Bemidji	**Willow Wood Market**	**23621 County Rd. 9**	**(218) 759-2310**	**Pg. 213**
Bemidji	Ann's Quilt Cottage	705 Washington Ave. S.	(218) 444-6387	
Bemidji	Bemidji Woolen Mills	301 Irvine Ave. NW	(218) 751-5166	
Bemidji	Quilting Keepsakes	8732 Country Club Rd. NE	(218) 751-5954	
Bird Island	Gathering Friends Quilt Shop	101 S. Main St.	(320) 365-4670	
Blackduck	Moon Pharmacy & Variety	17 Main St.	(218) 835-7740	
Blue Earth	Michele's Sewing	120 N. Main St.	(507) 526-3295	
Brainerd	A 2 Z Yarn	1001 Kingwood St. #115	(218) 454-0133	
Brainerd	Country Fabrics and Quilting	909 S. 6th St.	(218)-829-7273	
Brainerd	Utrinkets, LLC	617 Laurel St.	(218) 454-9276	
Buffalo	Detta's Spindle	209 9th St. NW	(763) 682-4389	
Buffalo	Silver Creek Cabin Yarn Cellar	3 Division St. E	(763) 684-0554	
Burnsville	Unwind Yarn Shop	14617 County Rd. 11	(952) 303-6617	

Cambridge	Quilterati	236 S. Adams St.	(763) 552-6080	
Cannon Falls	What in Yarnation	402 Mill St. W.	(507) 263-0005	
Circle Pines	Double Ewe Yarn Shop	9205 Lexington Ave. N. #3	(763) 795-9276	
Cloquet	**The Quilted Dog**	**274 Hwy. 33 N.**	**(218) 879-3577**	**Pg. 213**
Columbia Heights	Daisy Knits	819 49th Ave. NE	(763) 571-8724	
Cook	Cabin Quilting	227 1st St. SW	(218) 666-3146	
Coon Rapids	Anoka Fiber Works	4153 Coon Rapids Blvd.	(763) 479-9626	
Detroit Lakes	Hometown Crafts and Fabrics	824 Washington St.	(218) 844-5840	
Detroit Lakes	Red Pine Quilt Shop	915 Washington Ave.	(218) 844-5260	
Dodge Center	Redbrick Quilting and Crafts	110 W. Main St.	(507) 251-2103	
Duluth	**Yarn Harbor**	**4629 E. Superior St.**	**(218) 724-6432**	**Pg. 213**
Duluth	Creations Quilt Shop	2904 W. 3rd St	(218)-628-1687	
Duluth	Hannah Johnson Fabrics & Quilt Shop	4511 E. Superior St.	(218) 525-7800	
Eagan	Quilt Cove	1960 Cliff Lake Rd., Ste. 134	(651) 452-8891	
East Grand Fork	**Quilter's Eden**	**223 DeMers Ave.**	**(218) 773-0773**	**Pg. 213**
Elk Rapids	Wild Hare Rug Studio	204 River St.	(231) 409-7481	
Elk River	**The Noble Quilter**	**19570 Holt St. NW**	**(763) 633-4669**	**Pg. 216**
Excelsior	Lakeside Yarn	347 Water St.	(952) 401-7501	
Fergus Falls	Quilter's Cottage	1701 W. Lincoln Ave.	(218)-739-9652	
Floodwood	Hingeley Road Quilting	11284 Hwy. 2	(218) 476-3139	
Foley	**Quilts on Broadway**	**320 Dewey St.**	**(320) 968-9929**	**Pg. 214**
Fosston	Best Friends Quilting	808 Mark Ave. N.	(218) 435-2087	
Grand Marais	Crystal's Log Cabin Quilts	1100 W. Hwy. 61	(218) 387-3177	
Grand Marais	Raven's Beak Design	16 First Ave. W.	(218) 387-2621	
Grand Marais	That Little Red House	113 1st Ave. W.	(218) 387-1094	
Grand Rapids	50 Ewes & Counting	618 NW 5th Ave.	(218) 326-1894	
Grand Rapids	The Yarn Gallery	403 NW 1st Ave.	(218) 999-9922	
Granite Falls	Heather's Book Nook & Sew Much More	682 Prentice St. SE	(320) 564-0074	
Hackensack	**Piecemakers Quilt Shop**	**313 Hwy. 371**	**(218)-675-6271**	**Pg. 213**
Hastings	Rach-Al-Paca Farm	18495 Goodwin Ave.	(651) 485-7916	
Hawick	Not Just Yarns	15850 210th Ave. NE	(320) 276-8536	
Hayward	**Calico Hutch**	**20520 810th Ave.**	**(507) 377-1163**	**Pg. 218**
Hibbing	Knitting Knight	113 E. Howard St.	(218) 262-5764	
Hibbing	Quilts Around the Corner	12150 W. Hwy. 169	(218) 263-9078	
Hoffman	Nuts & Bolts Quilt Shop	213 1st St. N.	(320) 986-2447	
Hollandale	The Seed Room	103 Central Ave. S.	(507) 889-6351	
Hutchinson	Quilt Haven On Main	7 N. Main St.	(320) 587-8341	
International Falls	Studio 53	2030 2nd Ave. W.	(218) 285-9962	
International Falls	Up North Quilt Shop	4062 Hwy. 11	(218) 285-7704	
Iron	Terri's Treasures	8679 S. Iron Bowl Ln.	(218) 744-1935	
Isle	The Tinshack Co.	250 W. Main St.	(320) 676-1117	
Kasson	Kasson Variety	207 W. Main St.	(507) 634-6521	
Kimball	**Gone To Pieces Quilt Shop**	**70 S. Main St.**	**(320) 398-5300**	**Pg. 215**
Knife River	Playing With Yarn	276 Scenic Dr.	(218) 834-5967	
Lake City	Pumpkinberry Stitches	108 E Lyon Ave.	(651) 345-2573	
Lake City	Rather Bee Quilting	106 S. Lakeshore Dr.	(651) 345-3958	
Lanesboro	Cheryls Fabric Garden	108 Coffee St. E.	(507) 467-4466	
Lindstrom	Cottage Gifts / Miss Elsie's Yarnery	12760 Lake Blvd.	(651) 257-6199	
Litchfield	**DeAnn's Country Village Shoppe**			
		115 N. Sibley Ave.	**(320)-693-9113**	**Pg. 215**
Lonsdale	**Quilting By The Hearth**	**208 Main St. S.**	**(507) 744-4284**	**Pg. 216**
Luverne	**The Sewing Basket**	**204 E. Main**	**(507) 283-9769**	**Pg. 218**
Mable	Krazy Kwiltz	416 N. Maple Hwy. 44	(507) 493-5893	
Mahtomedi	Lavender Wool	110 Birchwood Ave.	(651) 426-8066	
Mahtomedi	Lila & Claudine's Yarn & Gifts	86 Mahtomedi Ave.	(651) 429-9551	
Mankato	Firefly Quilt Shop	1219 Caledonia St.	(507) 344-0441	
Mankato	Mary Lue's Yarn & Ewe	605 N. Riverfront	(507) 388-9276	
Maple Grove	Four Seasons Quilts	9708 63rd Ave. N.	(763) 557-5899	
Marshall	Fabrics Plus	307 W. Main St.	(507) 537-0835	
McGregor	Timeless Treasures Quilt Shop of McGregor	371 E. State Hwy. 210	(218) 768-2556	
Mendota Heights	Three Kittens Needle Arts	750 Main St. #112	(651) 457-4969	
Minneapolis	Cia's Palette - Fabric Essentials for Quilters	4155 Grand Ave. S.	(612) 823-5558	
Minneapolis	Crafty Planet	2833 Johnson St. NE	(612) 788-1180	
Minneapolis	Depth of Field Yarn	405 Cedar Ave.	(612) 340-0529	
Minneapolis	Digs	3800 Grand Ave. S.	(612) 827-2500	
Minneapolis	Ingebretsen's	1601 E. Lake St.	(612) 729-9333	
Minneapolis	Needlework Unlimited, Inc.	4420 Drew Ave. S.	(612) 925-2454	
Minneapolis	SR Harris Fabric Outlet	8865 Zealand Ave. N.	(763) 424-3500	
Minneapolis	Steven Be	3448 Chicago Ave.	(612) 259-7525	
Minneapolis	Textile Center	3000 University Ave. SE.	(612) 436-0464	

Minneapolis	The Wooly Red Rug	4630 Wentworth Ave.	(612) 964-1165	
Minnetonka	**Stitchville USA**	**12945 Ridgedale Dr.**	**(952) 474-1700**	**Pg. 216**
Montgomery	Quilter's Dream	116 1st St. S.	(507) 364-5130	
Moorhead	The Quilted Ladybug	420 Center Ave. #2	(218) 284-5239	
Moose Lake	Kathy's Country Square	100 Hillside Ter.	(218) 485-8231	
New London	The Giving Tree-Childrens Boutique	30 Main St. N.	(320) 354-4881	
New Ulm	**Sewing Seeds Quilt Company**	**1417 S State St.**	**(507) 354-8801**	**Pg. 218**
New Ulm	**The Thimble Box**	**10 N. Minnesota St.**	**(507) 354-6721**	**Pg. 219**
New Ulm	NadelKunst	212 N. Minnesota St.	(507) 354-8708	
New Ulm	Spinning Spools Quilt Shop	106 S. Minnesota	(507) 359-2896	
Northfield	Northfield Yarn	314 Division St. S.	(507) 645-1330	
Northfield	Reproduction Fabrics.com	105 E. 4th St. #205	(507) 664-1447	
Norwood Young America				
	The Quilting Grounds	224 W. Elm St.	(952) 467-2757	
Oklee	The Oklee Quilt Supply	128 S. Main St.	(218) 796-5151	
Park Rapids	Monika's Quilt & Yarn Shop	210 S. Main	(218) 732-3896	
Pequot Lakes	Mother Originals	29474 Hwy. 371 Po Box 878	(218) 568-6924	
Perham	**Bay Window Quilt Shop**	**116 2nd Ave. SW.**	**(218) 346-7272**	**Pg. 214**
Pine River	JJ's Trading Post	218 Barclay Ave.	(218) 587-2369	
Plymouth	Blue Bamboo	12865 Industrial Park Blvd.	(763) 744-1105	
Princeton	K & J Crafts	31351 Feldspar St. NW.	(763) 389-1937	
Princeton	Princeton Weaving and Fabrics	34301 Puma Street NW.	(763) 389-4156	
Prior Lake	Twisted Loop Yarn Shop	16210 Eagle Creek Ave.	(952) 240-8550	
Randall	The Old Creamery Quilt Shop	120 Superior Ave.	(320) 749-2420	
Robbinsdale	The Palette and Purl	4080 W. Broadway Ave. #125	(763) 535-6865	
Rochester	**The Quilting Cupboard**	**1611 N. Broadway**	**(507) 281-9988**	**Pg. 217**
Rochester	Hank & Purl's Creative Nook	1615 N. Broadway	(507) 226-8045	
Rochester	Kelleys Quality Sewing Center	3432 55th St. NW.	(507) 288-9051	
Rochester	Pine Needles Quilt Shop	1300 Salem Rd. SW, #250	(507) 226-8480	
Rochester	Westbrock Quilting	1815 75th St. Northwest	(507) 289-8219	
Rogers	**Quilted Treasures**	**14178 Northdale Blvd.**	**(763) 428-1952**	**Pg. 217**
Roseau	Quilt S'More	209 2nd Ave NE	(218) 463-3867	
Rosemount	**Quilter's Haven**	**2930 146th St, Ste 108**	**(651) 322-7071**	**Pg. 216**
Roseville	Twin Cities Quilting	1085 Dionne St.	(651) 340-8263	
Rush City	**Fabric, Fashions & More**	**485 S. Dana**	**(320) 358-3693**	**Pg. 214**
Sandstone	Quarry Quilts & Yarns, LLC	326 Quarry Place, #1	(320) 216-7639	
Sauk Centre	**Family Fabric Shop**	**306 Main Street S.**	**(320) 351-2739**	**Pg. 214**
Sauk Rapids	Bound In Stitches	2078 45th St. NE.	(320) 255-9021	
Shakopee	Eagle Creek Quilt Shop	333 2nd Ave W.	(952) 233-3774	
Sherburn	**Old Alley Quilt Shop**	**115 N. Main St., Hwy 4**	**(507) 764-4088**	**Pg. 218**
Silver Bay	Behind the Seams Quilt Shop	5715 Hwy. 1	(218) 226-3390	
St. Charles	Amish Market Sq.	I-90 & Hwy. 74	(507) 932-5907	
St. Cloud	Bonnie's Spinning Wheel	16 21st Ave. S.	(320) 253-2426	
St. Cloud	Carole's Country Knits	25636 County Rd. 74	(320) 252-2996	
St. Paul	The Yarnery	840 Grand Ave.	(651) 222-5793	
St. Paul	Treadle Yard Goods	1338 Grand Ave.	(651) 698-9690	
St. Peter	St. Peter Woolen Mill	101 W. Broadway	(507) 934-3734	
Stillwater	Darn Knit Anyway	423 S. Main St.	(651) 342-1386	
Stillwater	Sew with Me	1250 Frontage Rd. W. Hwy. 36	(651) 342-2126	
Taylors Falls	The Yarn Bank	406 Bench St.	(651) 465-6588	
Tower	North Country Quilts	303 Main St.	(218) 753-4600	
Wadena	Hometown Crafts and Fabrics	111 S. Jefferson St.	(218) 631-3141	
Wahkon	Country Caboose Quilts	108 S. Main St.	(320) 495-3658	
Waite Park	**Gruber's Quilt Shop**	**310 4th Ave. NE**	**(320) 259-4360**	**Pg. 214, 215**
Waite Park	At the Heart of Quilting	304 4th Ave. NE #2	(320) 259-7774	
Walker	Front Porch Quilts of Walker	613 Michigan Ave. W.	(218) 547-1122	
Warroad	Northern Exposure Quilts	210 Main Ave. NE	(218) 386-4809	
White Bear Lake	A Sheepy Yarn Shop	2185 3rd St.	(651) 426-5463	
White Bear Lake	Bear Patch Quilting Co.	2199 4th St.	(651) 429-1039	
Wilton	Sadie Rae's Quilt Shop	516 Whitetail Dr.	(218) 444-2387	
Windom	**Prairie Quilting**	**1293 Hale Pl.**	**(507) 831-2740**	**Pg. 218**
Winona	Bluffview Quilt Shop	1671 1/2 W. 5th St.	(507) 458-8539	
Winona	Yarnology	65 E. Third St.	(507) 474-9444	
Woodbury	Knit'n From The Heart	1785 Radio Dr.	(651) 702-0880	
Woodbury	Sew With Me Woodbury	1750 Weir Dr.	(651) 600-3258	
Worthington	Crafty Corner Quilt & Sewing Shoppe	1820 Oxford St.	(507) 372-2707	
Zumbrota	All in Stitches	308 S. Main St.	(507) 732-4101	
Zumbrota	Beelighted Fiber & Gifts	282 Main St.	(507) 732-4191	
Zumbrota	Ellison Sheep Farm	15775 Hwy. 60 Blvd.	(507) 732-5281	

Notes

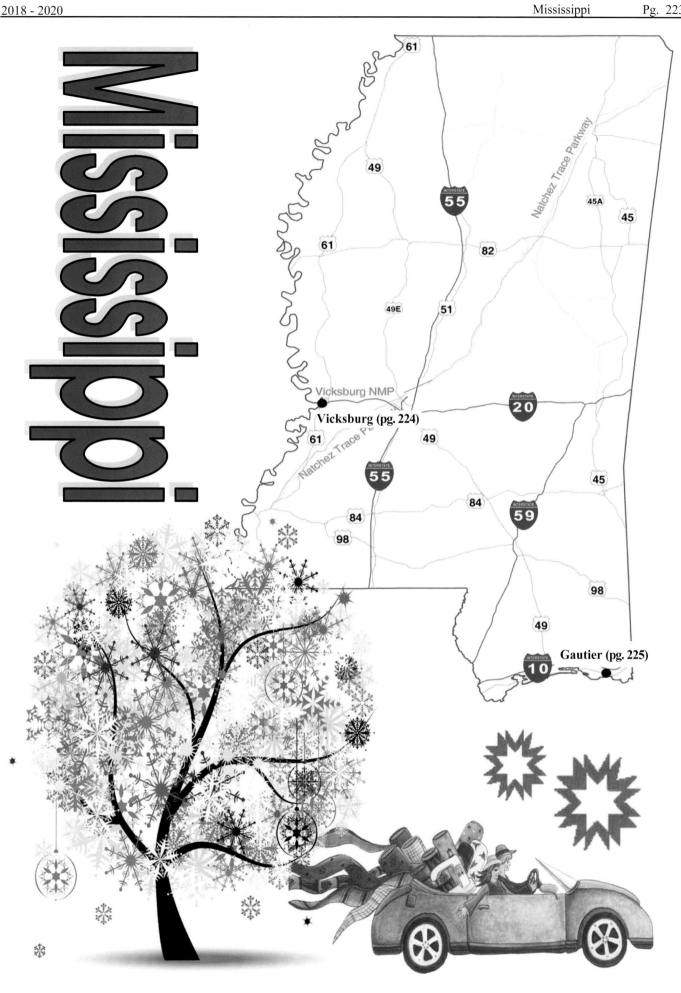

Vicksburg NMP

Vicksburg (pg. 224)

Gautier (pg. 225)

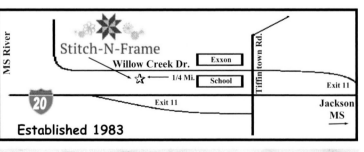

The White House Hotel

One of the only remaining grand hotels on the Mississippi Gulf Coast — built to accommodate travelers along the Gulf and Ship Island Railroad — the White House Hotel has plenty of history in Biloxi. Though it sat in disrepair for decades, the beautiful boutique property was finally renovated and reopened in 2014, with high-end amenities and a fantastic outdoor pool.

1230 Beach Blvd, Biloxi, MS 39530 - (228) 233-1230 - www.whitehousebiloxi.com

Mississippi Shops

Index

Q-Quilting ~ Y-Yarn ~ N-Needlework ~ R-Retreat ~ M-Museum

Ackerman	Main Street Fabrics	93 East Main St.	(662) 285-6241	
Bogue Chitto	The Cotton Patch	838 Auburn Dr. SW	(601) 823-1000	
Booneville	Quilt Gallery	1614 Hwy. 30 E.	(662) 728-3302	
Canton	P is for Primitive	141 W. Peace St.	(601) 859-4252	
Columbus	Figg Fabrics & Studio	59 Old Swan Ln.	(662) 549-4318	
Corinth	Treasure Chest Quilting & More	202 Hwy. 72 E.	(662) 594-1055	
Diamondhead	The French Knot	5401 Indian Hill Blvd.	(228) 255-3100	
Gautier	**Block Therapy Quilt Shop**	**4353 B Gautier Van Cleave Rd.**	**(228) 202-1493**	**Pg. 225**
Gulfport	Coastal Sew and Vac.	12100 Hwy. 49 N. Ste. 200	(228) 831-4771	
Hattiesburg	Stitch N Post	5039 Old Hwy. 11 #2	(601) 268-5545	
Laurel	Let's Make Something	1317 Hwy. 15 N. #E	(601) 340-3143	
Madison	The Cotton Blossom Fabric Shop	100 Depot Dr.	(601) 427-5214	
Oxford	Sit N Rock Quilting and Sewing Shop LLC	1502 W. Jackson Ave.	(662) 234-0800	
Ridgeland	Bernina Sewing Etc.	665 S. Pear Orchard Rd. #104	(601)-991-2120	
Ridgeland	The Southern Needle	500 Hwy. 51 N. #T	(601) 919-7118	
Senatobia	Cotton Treasures	218 E. Main St.	(662) 562-4422	
Tupelo	Heirlooms Forever	3112 Cliff Gookin Blvd.	(662) 842-4275	
Vicksburg	**Stitch - N - Frame**	**31 Willow Creek Dr.**	**(601) 634-0243**	**Pg. 224**
Wiggins	The Fabric Dock	2118 S. Azalea Dr.	(601) 928-1904	

Did you know?
Jackson is the state capital and largest city, with a population of around 175,000 people.
The state overall has a population of around 3 million people.
Mississippi is the 32nd most extensive and the 32nd most populous of the 50 United States.

Missouri

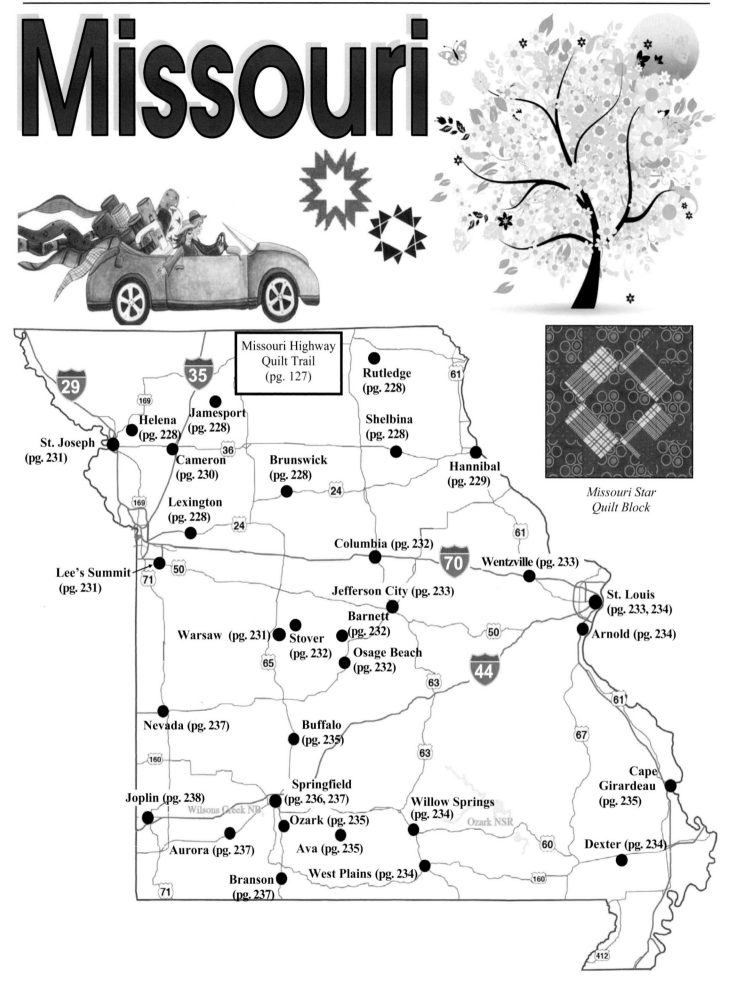

Missouri Highway
Quilt Trail
(pg. 127)

Rutledge
(pg. 228)

Helena
(pg. 228)

Jamesport
(pg. 228)

St. Joseph
(pg. 231)

Shelbina
(pg. 228)

Cameron
(pg. 230)

Brunswick
(pg. 228)

Hannibal
(pg. 229)

Lexington
(pg. 228)

Columbia (pg. 232)

Wentzville (pg. 233)

Lee's Summit
(pg. 231)

Jefferson City (pg. 233)

St. Louis
(pg. 233, 234)

Warsaw (pg. 231)

Stover
(pg. 232)

Barnett
(pg. 232)

Osage Beach
(pg. 232)

Arnold (pg. 234)

Nevada (pg. 237)

Buffalo
(pg. 235)

Cape
Girardeau
(pg. 235)

Joplin (pg. 238)

Springfield
(pg. 236, 237)

Willow Springs
(pg. 234)

Ozark (pg. 235)

Ava (pg. 235)

Dexter (pg. 234)

Aurora (pg. 237)

West Plains (pg. 234)

Branson
(pg. 237)

*Missouri Star
Quilt Block*

MISSOURI HIGHWAY 36
Quilt Trail

A Paradise of Patterns and Sew Much More

The Missouri Highway 36 Quilt Trail is full of inspiration—no matter if you're creating a masterpiece of your own or admiring someone else's.

The State For The Art

With 16 shops throughout 15 cities, the Missouri Highway 36 Quilt Trail runs through the northern portion of the state from Hannibal to St. Joseph. Featuring a wide variety of quilt shops, fabrics, notions, and expertise to explore, it's the perfect journey dedicated to the craft of quilting.

QUILTS ARE A WORK of heart!

Participating Quilt Shops

Bits & Pieces, Hannibal • By The Yard, Rayville
Cornerstone Fabric, Smithville • Crossroads Quilting,
Cameron • Cuts & Bolts, Chillicothe • Glenda's Sewing
Cupboard, St. Joseph • Hickory Stick Quilt Shop, Hannibal
Midwest Quilt Co, Shelbina • Missouri Star Quilt Co.,
Hamilton • Quilted Square, Kirksville • Rosie's
Quilts, Marceline • Sew Creative, Salisbury
Shearwood Quilts & Crafts, Jamesport
Sisters Fabric Farm, Lathrop
The Quilt Shoppe, Wheeling
Top Stitch Quilt Shop,
Helena

Passport Program

You'll find exciting new themes every year for the Highway 36 Quilt Trail Passport Program. Visitors can collect a free, unique pattern block—from each shop—and get their passport stamped. The program runs from April through October. Participants can submit their completed quilt top for the chance to win prizes. Check out our Facebook page for up to date information.

Cut From A Different Cloth

Dubbed "The Way of American Genius", the Quilt Trail is just one of the inspirations along Highway 36. Discover all its genius as you travel across the state—from the hometowns of American greats like A.T. Still (Kirksville), Mark Twain (Hannibal), Walt Disney (Marceline), and J.C. Penney (Hamilton) to the home of innovative ideas like sliced bread (Chillicothe) and the Pony Express (St. Joseph).

MISS⚬URI
enjoy the show

www.AmericanGeniusHighway.com/Quilt-Trail
START PLANNING YOUR GETAWAY AT
VISITMO.COM

Hilton President Kansas City

In 1928, this Kansas City establishment was the headquarters
for the Republican National Convention that would nominate
Herbert Hoover for President. Entertainers like Frank Sinatra
performed in the onsite Drum Room lounge, which is still
going strong thanks to the hotel's $45.5 million restoration.

**1329 Baltimore Ave, Kansas City, MO 64105
(816) 221-9490**

The Gateway Arch is a 630-foot monument in St. Louis. Clad in stainless steel and built in the form of an inverted, weighted catenary arch, it is the world's tallest arch, the tallest man-made monument in the Western Hemisphere, and Missouri's tallest accessible building

Did you know?
Missouri was the 24th state in the United States and became a state on August 10th, 1821.
It was also the birthplace of our the 33rd President, Harry S. Truman; born in Lamar on May 8, 1884.

LARGEST JELLY ROLL SELECTION IN CENTRAL MISSOURI
Huge selection of Precuts, Fat Quarter Bundles,
Kits, Wide Linings, Embroidery Blocks,
Books, Patterns and much more.
Quick Turn-around for Longarm
Computerized Machine Quilting Service

Special Quilts for Special People

Tuesday-Friday 9:00-5:00
Saturday 10:00-2:00
Monday By Appointment

Specialty Quilts
& Fabrics, LLC

Find us in our NEW BIGGER Location!
**2115 Industrial Dr.
Jefferson City, MO 65109
573-761-7313**
www.specialtyquilts.com

---

janie lou
QUILT. SEW. CREATE.
St. Louis, MO   Q

www.janielouquilts.com

Friendly, helpful shop full of
contemporary modern fabrics.
Large selection of Moda fabrics,
solids, Riley Blake, Robert Kaufman
and much much more.

124 W. Monroe Ave.
St. Louis, MO 63122
(636) 579-0120
Tues - Fri 10 - 5
Sat 10 - 4
Sun & Mon Closed

St. Louis, MO   Q

THE QUILTED FOX

SELECTED AS ONE OF THE TOP TEN FEATURED SHOPS 2001
QUILT SAMPLER MAGAZINE BY BETTER HOMES & GARDENS

6000 bolts of unique quilting fabrics
International, Asian, Australian, African and more.
Large selection of Kaffe Fassett and Amy Butler fabrics.
Books always 20% off

**M, W 10 - 5 T, Th 10 - 6:30
Fri & Sat 10 - 4:30 Sun 12 - 4**

10403 Clayton Rd. 63131   (314) 993-1181
info@quiltedfox.com   www.quiltedfox.com
Est: 1994   2500 sq. ft.   Owner: Louise L. Georgia

The Quilted Fox Enter At the
Blue Awning 2nd Floor
*Easy Access off & on the
highway Mail Orders always
welcome Handicap Accessible*

accuquilt

SusieQ Quilting

119 W. Pearce Blvd.
Wentzville, MO 63385

Susie Q
Quilting
119
Pearce Blvd.

About 1/2 mile N. of I-70 Exit 209

*Tues & Wed
10 - 5
Thurs 10-7
Fri & Sat
10 - 4*

*Contemporary
Quilt Shop
1000 + Bolts
Lots of brights
and batiks*

636-272-7455
www.facebook.com/Susie-Q-Quilting
www.susieqquilting.com

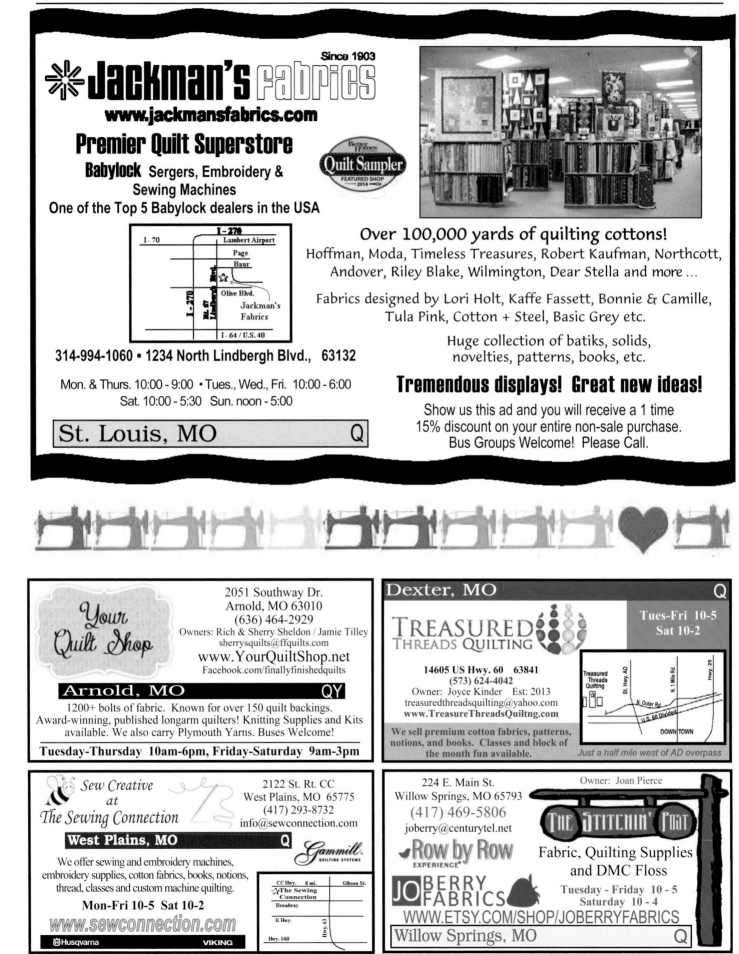

Missouri Shops

Q-Quilting ~ Y-Yarn ~ N-Needlework ~ R-Retreat ~ M-Museum

City	Shop	Address	Phone	Page
Arnold	**Your Quilt Shop**	**2051 Southway Dr.**	**(636) 464-2929**	**Pg. 234**
Arrow Rock	A Grand Yarn	302 Main St.	(660) 837-3111	
Aurora	**The Quilted Garden Fabric Shop**			
		620 McNatt Ave.	**(417) 678-1600**	**Pg. 237**
Ava	**Dogwood Quilting**	**808 S. Jefferson Ste. 1**	**(417) 683-4700**	**Pg. 235**
Ballwin	In Stitches Quilt Shop	14664 Manchester Rd.	(636) 394-4471	
Barnett	**Pleasant Valley Quilts**	**15050 Hopewell Rd.**	**(573) 378-4447**	**Pg. 232**
Beaufort	Gateway Quilt & Stuff	212 Fox Meadow Ln.	(314) 913-1197	
Billings	Fox Pen Quilting	154 NE Elm	(417) 695-3031	
Birch Tree	The Hideaway Quilt Shop	3217 W. 1st St.	(573) 292-1008	
Blue Springs	C C & Company	1701 W. Hwy. 40 #102	(816) 229-2950	
Blue Springs	Patchwork Pals Quilt Shop	1701 NW Burdette Crossing	(816) 622-8484	
Bolivar	Margie Pearl's House of Fabrics	4743 S. 131st Rd.	(417) 777-4913	
Bonne Terre	Cutt-N-Sew Quilt Shop	27 W. School St.	(573) 358-7887	
Boonville	Missouri Country Quilts	24298 Hwy. 98	(660) 537-3541	
Branson	**Quilts & Quilts**	**3500 N. Gretna Rd.**	**(417)-334-3243**	**Pg. 237**
Branson	**The Quilted Cow**	**18593 Business 13 Ste. 203**	**(417) 272-0000**	**Pg. 237**
Branson	Branson Sewing Center	4740 Gretna Rd.	(417) 320-6090	
Branson	Cecilia's Samplers	2652 Shepherd of the Hills Expy.	(417) 336-5016	
Branson	Homestead Fabrics & Woolens	2900 Green Mountain Dr. #205	(417) 239-6503	
Branson	Miss Kate's at Silver Dollar City	399 Silver Dollar Pkwy.	(417) 338-8216	
Branson	Silver Dollar City	399 Indian Point Rd.	(417) 338-8262	
Branson	The Fabric & Décor Shoppe	1828 W. 76th Country Blvd.	(417) 239-3900	
Brookfield	Hueffmeier's Fine Pine	27905 Hwy. FF	(660) 258-3244	
Brunswick	**Sew Sweet Quilt Shop**	**207 E. Broadway St.**	**(660) 548-3056**	**Pg. 228**
Buffalo	**Maw & Paw's Fabrics**	**800 S. Ash St.**	**(417) 345-4414**	**Pg. 235**
Butler	Rocking Chair Quilts	21 N. Main St.	(660) 200-2226	
Cameron	**Crossroads Quilting**	**1720 N. Walnut Ste. D**	**(816) 649-0550**	**Pg. 230**
Cape Girardeau	**The Sewing Basket**	**330 S. Kings Highway St.**	**(573) 339-0494**	**Pg. 235**
Carthage	The Country Store Quilt Shop	14426 Burr Oak Rd.	(417) 827-6626	
Cassville	Stitches	24493 St. Hwy. 76	(417) 858-2990	

Centerview	Hunter Heirloom Quilting	573 NW US. Hwy. 50	(660) 656-3325	
Centralia	Material Girl Quilt Shop	213 W. Sneed St.	(573) 682-1320	
Chillicothe	Cuts & Bolts Fabrics	24 S. Washington St.	(660) 240-0120	
Clinton	White Flower Quilt Shop	140 W. Jefferson St.	(660) 492-5379	
Columbia	**Satin Stitches Sewing & Embroidery**			
		705 D VanDiver Dr.	**573-817-0006**	**Pg. 232**
Columbia	Appletree Quilting Center	2541 Bernadette Dr.	(573) 446-2655	
Columbia	Hillcreek Fiber Studio	7001 S. Hill Creek Rd.	(573) 874-2233	
Columbia	Hillcreek Yarn Shoppe	601 Bus. Loop 70 W. Ste. 213C	(573) 449-5648	
Columbia	Quilt 4 U	908 Rain Forest Parkway Ste. E	(573) 443-7858	
Columbia	True Blewe Yarns & More	1400 Forum Blvd. #10	(573) 443-8233	
Dexter	**Treasured Threads Quilting**	**14605 US. Hwy. 60**	**(573) 624-4042**	**Pg. 234**
Doniphan	Current River Fabrics & Quilting	201 Washington St. #1	(573) 996-1888	
El Dorado Springs	Material Matters Quilting Shop	105 E. 54 Hwy.	(417) 876-2606	
Exeter	P-Dub's Quilt Stuff	12203 Hwy. 76	(417) 847-9276	
Fenton	Fenton Sew-N-Vac	180 A Gravois Bluffs Cir.	(636) 343-8088	
Florissant	Weaving Dept/Myers House	180 W. Dunn Rd.	(314) 921-7800	
Forsyth	Yarn Diva	10726 St. Hwy. 76	(417) 546-2037	
Fredericktown	Quilting on the Square	1390 Hwy. D.	(573) 944-0144	
Glenwood	Bri-Lee Quilting	16596 Johnson Dr.	(660) 216-4383	
Golden City	Golden Needle Quilt Shop	602 SE 115th Ln.	(417) 674-1815	
Granby	Heavenly Notions	217 N. Main St.	(417) 389-9472	
Hamilton	Missouri Star Quilt Co	306 N. Davis St.	(888) 571-1122	
Hannibal	**Bits & Pieces**	**221 N. Main St.**	**(573) 603-1279**	**Pg. 229**
Hannibal	**The Hickory Stick**	**326 N. Main St.**	**(573) 221-4538**	**Pg. 229**
Helena	**Top Stitch Quilt Shop**	**14000 Hwy. 169**	**(816) 369-2425**	**Pg. 228**
Higginsville	Quilters Harvest	1913 N. Main St.	(660) 584-3399	
Holts Summit	Rooster Creek Company	176 W. Simon Blvd.	(573) 896-8025	
Independence	Angelika's Yarn Store	500 N. Dodgion St.	(816) 461-5505	
Independence	Knitcraft Yarn Shop	215 N. Main St.	(816) 461-1248	
Independence	Rustic Yearnings	4621 S. Shrank Dr.	(816) 373-2423	
Jamesport	**Fabric Barn**	**21914 St. Hwy. 190**	**(660) 684-6720**	**Pg. 228**
Jamesport	Sue's Soft Stuff	205 S. Broadway	(660) 684-6205	
Jefferson City	**Specialty Quilts & Fabrics**	**2115 Industrial Dr.**	**(573) 761-7313**	**Pg. 233**
Joplin	**Bittersweet Quilts**	**8133 W. Hwy. 86**	**(417)-627-9555**	**Pg. 238**
Joplin	**The Fabric Merchant**	**120 S. Main St.**	**(417) 622-0012**	**Pg. 238**
Kahoka	DB's Quilter & Supplies	115 W. Main St. Ste. B	(660) 727-1208	
Kansas City	Modern Makers	3707 Summit	(816) 200-1396	
Kansas City	The Studio Knitting and Needlepoint	1121 W. 47th St.	(816) 531-4466	
Kingsville	Liberty Homestead	115 SW. 1991 Rd.	(816) 597-9402	
Kirksville	Quilted Square	511 S. Baltimore St. #10	(660) 665-7533	
Kirkwood	Kirkwood Knittery	10404 Manchester Rd.	(314) 822-7222	
Lamar	Blue Top Quilt Shop	61 SE First Ln.	(417) 681-0330	
Lathrop	Sisters Fabric Farm	6320 NE 272nd St.	(816) 528-3626	
Leadington	Country Home Quilters	120 Union St.	(573) 518-1981	
Lebanon	Buckles, Bobbins and Bolts	22476 Hwy. MM	(417) 588-3252	
Lees Summit	**Quilter's Station**	**3680 NE Akin Dr.**	**(816)-525-8955**	**Pg. 231**
Lees Summit	Zoelee's Fabrics	1329 NE Deer Valley Dr.	(816) 524-7217	
Lexington	**All About Quilting**	**912 Main St.**	**(816) 868-5246**	**Pg. 228**
Liberty	Old Mill Stitchery	131 S. Water St.	(816) 792-3670	
Liberty	Quilting Is My Therapy	2 E. Franklin St.	(816) 866-0126	
Liberty	Quilting Is My Therapy	2 E. Franklin	(816) 679-8810	
Linn	Quilts & More	102 S. 3rd St.	(573) 897-3933	
Macon	Ben Franklin	103 N. Rollins	(660) 385-5751	
Marceline	Rosie's Quilts & Things	11526 Long Branch Ave.	(660) 376-2593	
Memphis	Green Acres Sew & Vac	221 W. Grand Ave.	(660) 465-7131	
Mexico	Homestead Hearth	105 N. Coal St.	(573) 581-1966	
Mexico	Treasure Chest Yarn Shop & More	216 W. Monroe	(573) 581-8007	
Monroe City	Ben Franklin	100 S .Main	(573) 735-4395	
Mountain Grove	Ozarks Patchwork Peddler	106 E. 17th St.	(417) 926-0844	
Mountain View	Calico Cupboard Quilt Shop	116 N. Oak St.	(417) 934-6330	
Neosho	N Stitches/The Quilted Swan	108 W. Main St.	(417) 455-0999	
Nevada	**Nine Patch Quilt & Fabrics**	**129 E. Walnut St.**	**(417) 667-7100**	**Pg. 237**
New Florence	All N Stitches	352 Booneslick Rd.	(573) 564-4050	
Nixa	Lowlander Knitwear & Yarn Shop	512 E. Mt. Vernon St.	(417) 494-5006	
O'Fallon	O Sew Personal	1157 Bryan Rd.	(636) 294-7922	
Osage Beach	**Love to Sew Boutique**	**877 St. Hwy. 42-8**	**(573) 348-1972**	**Pg. 232**
Osceola	Brenda's Quilt Stop & More	785 SW Hwy. 54	(417) 876-9997	
Owensville	In the Niche	106 E. Peters Ave.	(573) 437-6124	

Index

Ozark	**Sew Simple Quilt Shoppe**	**5241 N. 17th St.**	**(417) 582-8383**	**Pg. 235**
Park Hills	Mad Monk's Fabric Warehouse	204 E. Main	(573) 431-1677	
Parkville	Peddler's Wagon	115 Main St.	(816)-741-0225	
Pierce City	The Thistle Quilt Shop & Fabric Store	102 W. Commercial St. #A	(417) 476-5844	
Pleasant Hill	Quilt Stop	431 N. Hwy. 7	(816) 987-2541	
Poplar Bluff	Country Fabrics	796 County Rd. 605	(573) 785-0821	
Poplar Bluff	Sew Much More	1103 Cherry St.	(573) 727-9898	
Potosi	Patches and Lace	201 E. High St.	(573) 438-6718	
Raymore	Creative Hands Quilt Shop	1907 W. Foxwood Dr.	(816) 331-1992	
Raytown	Show-Me Quilting	6221 Blue Ridge Blvd.	(816) 313-8225	
Rayville	By The Yard	16566 Hwy. C	(816) 470-6703	
Rock Port	Quilters Boutique LLC	300 W. US. Hwy. 136	(660) 744-2528	
Rockville	D barJ Quilts etc.	405 1st St.	(660) 598-2222	
Rogersville	One City Market	214 Beatie St.	(417) 753-7100	
Rolla	Melear Fabrics & Sew Much More	514 D Ft. Wyman Rd.	(573) 364-7134	
Rolla	Uniquely Yours	404 E. State Rt. 72	(573)-364-2070	
Rutledge	**Zimmerman's Store**	**29229 1st St.**	**(660) 883-5766**	**Pg. 228**
Saint Louis	Knitorious	3268 Watson Rd.	(314) 646-8276	
Salem	Melear Fabrics & Sew Much More	215 W. 4th St.	(573) 729-8900	
Salem	Quilter's Journey	1424 Hwy. 68	(573) 453-2100	
Salisbury	Sew Creative	407 E. Patterson	(660) 388-6287	
Sedalia	D & T Quilt Shop	3620 S. Marshall	660-826-4788	
Sedalia	Kaye's Fabrics	218 S. Ohio Ave.	(660) 827-5297	
Sedalia	Pa Pa Patch	500 S Kentucky Ave.	(660) 826-1109	
Seymour	Jan's Fabric & Quilt Shop	201 Commercial St.	(417) 935-4440	
Shelbina	**Midwest Quilt Company**	**102 Hall St.**	**(573) 588-7000**	**Pg. 228**
Sikeston	Quilting Fabrics & Crafts	620 S Kings highway St.	(573) 475-9393	
Springfield	**The Fabric Outlet**	**1333 S. Glenstone Ave.**	**(417) 881-4966**	**Pg. 237**
Springfield	**Merrily We Quilt Along**	**1718 S. Ingram Mill Rd.**	**(417) 890-9000**	**Pg. 236**
Springfield	Crinklelove	326 E. Commercial St.	(417) 310-6802	
Springfield	F.M. Stores	2814 S. Fremont	(417) 882-9244	
Springfield	Fabric Outlet	1241 E. Republic Rd.	(417) 889-0528	
Springfield	THE QUILT SAMPLER, INC.	1802A S. Glenstone Ave.	(417) 886-5750	
St. Charles	The Quilted Cottage	723 S. Main	(636) 757-3730	
St. Charles	Winston's Sewing Center	2772 Muegge Rd.	(636) 447-5554	
St. Clair	Yarn Farm	614 Pickles Ford Rd.	(636) 629-0567	
St. Joseph	**Glenda's Sewing Cupboard**	**18255 County Rd. 349**	**(816) 662-3105**	**Pg. 231**
St. Joseph	Around the Frame Quilting	2301 Frederick Ave. #1	(816) 273-5535	
St. Joseph	Keeping Good Company	114 S. 7th St.	(816) 364-4799	
St. Louis	**Jackman's Fabrics**	**1234 N. Lindbergh**	**(314) 994-1060**	**Pg. 234**
St. Louis	**Janie Lou**	**124 W. Monroe Ave.**	**(636) 579-0120**	**Pg. 233**
St. Louis	**The Quilted Fox**	**10403 Clayton Rd.**	**(314)-993-1181**	**Pg. 233**
St. Louis	Delve MIY	27 N. Gore	(314) 736-5815	
St. Louis	Hearthstone Knits	11429 Concord Village Ave.	(314) 849-9276	
St. Louis	Make It Sew	10206 Watson Rd.	(314)-966-4446	
St. Louis	Sign of the Arrow	9740 Clayton Rd.	(314) 994-0606	
St. Louis	The First and Last Stitch	8988 Manchester Rd.	(314) 961-8157	
St. Louis	The Needlepoint Clubhouse	717 N. New Ballas Rd.	(314) 432-2555	
Stockton	Creative Notions	211 East St.	(417) 276-4216	
Stover	**Stover Quality Quilting**	**606 N. Ash St.**	**(800) 521-4171**	**Pg. 232**
Stover	Nustyle Quilt Shop	309 W 4th St. Hwy. 52	(573) 377-2244	
Sullivan	Melear Fabrics & Sew Much More	256 S. Service Rd. W.	(573) 468-5255	
Valley Park	Merrily We Sew Along	932 Meramec Station Rd. Unit H	(636) 220-7738	
Viburnum	Seams Sew Sweet Designs	60 Walnut St.	(573) 244-3176	
Vienna	Leisure Time Sewing	410 8th St.	(573) 422-3500	
Warrensburg	Primitive Stitches	34 SW 365 Rd.	(660) 747-7787	
Warrensburg	Sew Good Quilting	126 SW 13 Hwy.	(660) 580-0033	
Warsaw	**City's Edge Quilt Shop and Sewing Center**			
		616 W. Main St.	**(660) 438-3177**	**Pg. 231**
Warsaw	Saltbox Primitive Woolens	30148 Dam Access Rd.	(660) 438-6002	
Washington	Bah! Yarns	106 Elm St.	(636) 390-2400	
Waynesville	The Thread Peddler	23470 Sage Rd.	(573) 774-2658	
Webb City	Stitch Space Yarn Shop	1715 S. Madison #G	(417) 673-2240	
Wentzville	**Susie Q Quilting**	**119 W. Pearce Blvd.**	**(636) 272-7455**	**Pg. 233**
West Plains	**The Sewing Connection**	**2124 State Rt. CC**	**(417) 293-8732**	**Pg. 234**
Weston	Florilegium	367 Main St.	(816) 746-6164	
Wheeling	The Quilt Shoppe	10650 Hwy. B	(660) 659-2469	
Willow Springs	**The Stitchin Post**	**224 E. Main St.**	**(417) 469-5806**	**Pg. 234**
Windsor	Country View Fabric Store	1291 SE 1300	(660) 647-2625	

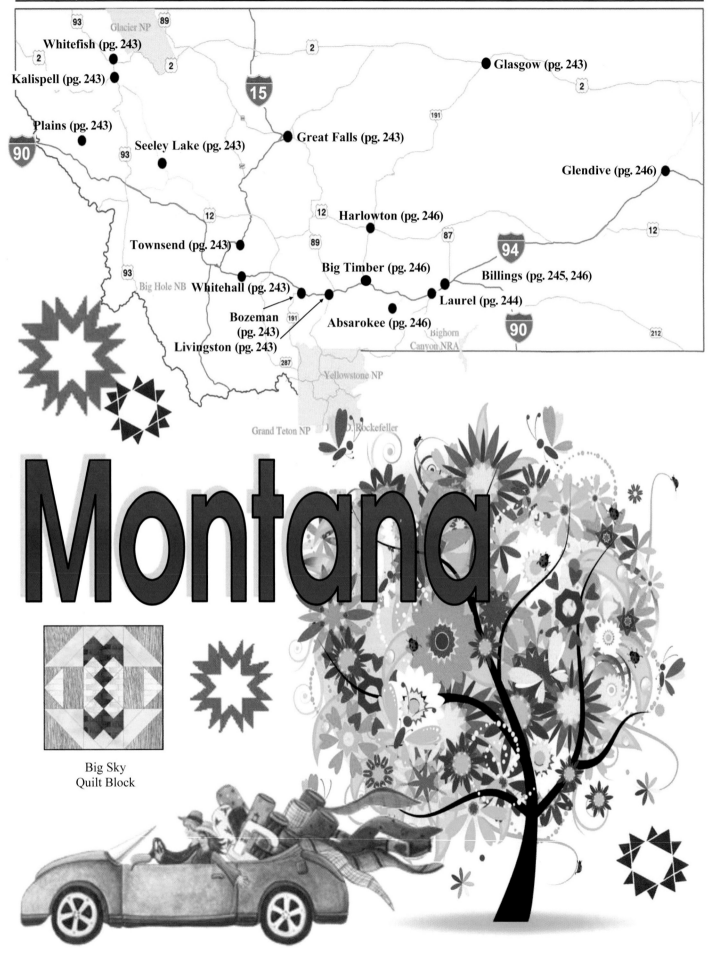

Whitefish (pg. 243)

Kalispell (pg. 243)

Plains (pg. 243)

Seeley Lake (pg. 243)

Glasgow (pg. 243)

Great Falls (pg. 243)

Glendive (pg. 246)

Harlowton (pg. 246)

Townsend (pg. 243)

Big Timber (pg. 246)

Billings (pg. 245, 246)

Whitehall (pg. 243)

Laurel (pg. 244)

Bozeman (pg. 243)

Absarokee (pg. 246)

Livingston (pg. 243)

Montana

Big Sky
Quilt Block

Livingston	**Back Porch Quilts**	**5237 US. Hwy. 89 S. #14**	**(406) 222-0855**	**Pg. 243**
Livingston	Thimbelina's Quilt Shop	118 N. B St. Ste. B	(406) 222-5904	
Malta	Gone to Pieces	137 S. 2nd St. E.	(406) 654-1649	
Missoula	Beads, Yarns & Threads	2100 Stephens Ave. Ste. 109	(406) 543-9368	
Missoula	Goin' Quilting	425 N. 5th St. W. #4	(406) 541-7111	
Missoula	Joseph's Coat	115 S. 3rd St. W.	(406) 549-1419	
Missoula	Kaye's Creative Knitting	9615 Old Mill Drill	(406) 721-5223	
Missoula	Selvedge Studio	509 S. Higgins Ave.	(406) 541-7171	
Missoula	The Confident Stitch	139 W. Front St.	(406) 540-4068	
Missoula	Timeless Quilts & Friends Quilt Shop	2412 River Rd. #F	(406) 542-6566	
Missoula	Vicki's Quilts Down Under	2425 W. Central Ave. #B	(406) 728-9446	
Philipsburg	Sew Unique Quilt Shop & Retreat	130 E. Broadway W. 1/2	(406) 491-3308	
Plains	**Mary Anne's Fabrics**	**100 Farmers St. #102**	**(406) 826-3777**	**Pg. 243**
Polson	All in Stitches	210 Main St.	(406) 883-3643	
Red Lodge	Quilt Lodge	517 S. Broadway	(406) 446-4234	
Seeley Lake	**Deer Country Quilts**	**3150 Hwy. 83 N.**	**(406) 677-2730**	**Pg. 243**
Shelby	Quilt With Class	131 4th Ave. S.	(406) 434-5801	
Shelby	The Creative Needle	325 Main St.	(406) 434-7106	
Sidney	Quilts & More	12653 County Rd. 352	(406) 482-3366	
Stevensville	Daydream Fabrics	304 Main St.	(406) 777-7195	
Sunburst	PM Quilting	307 2nd Ave. W.	(406) 937-2525	
Terry	Creative Cottage	415 S. Logan	(406) 635-5606	
Thompson Falls	The Quilting House	215 Woodland St.	(406) 827-4700	
Townsend	**Creative Closet**	**222 Broadway**	**(406) 266-4555**	**Pg. 243**
Townsend	JL Wright Trading Post	119 Broadway St.	(406) 266-3032	
West Yellowstone	Send it Home	30 Madison St.	(406) 646-7300	
White Sulphur Springs	Good Looks Unlimited	804 1st Ave. SE	(406) 547-2146	
Whitefish	**Whitefish Quilts and Gifts**	**131 Central Ave.**	**(406) 730-2207**	**Pg. 243**
Whitefish	Knit 'N Needle Yarn Shoppe	14 Lupfer Ave.	(406) 862-6390	
Whitefish	Quilt Kits To Go	903A Wisconsin Ave.	(406) 863-9773	
Whitehall	**The Dysfunctional Quilter**	**7 Sowden Ln.**	**(406) 287-9237**	**Pg. 243**
Whitehall	Cozy Mountain Quilts	12 N. Main	(406) 287-9984	
Wolf Point	Fabric Attic	224 Main St.	(406) 653-1506	

Index

Notes

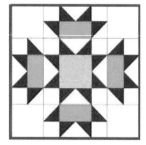

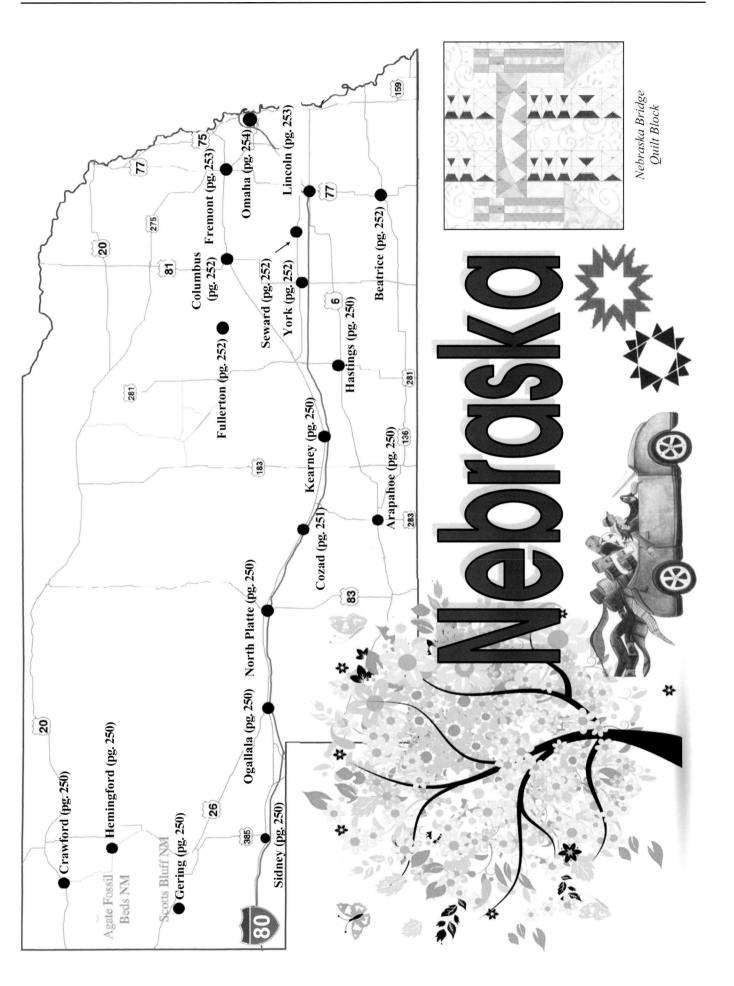

*Nebraska Bridge
Quilt Block*

Lincoln (pg. 253)

Omaha (pg. 254)

Fremont (pg. 253)

Columbus
(pg. 252)

Beatrice (pg. 252)

Seward (pg. 252)

York (pg. 252)

Hastings (pg. 250)

Fullerton (pg. 252)

Kearney (pg. 250)

Arapahoe (pg. 250)

Cozad (pg. 251)

North Platte (pg. 250)

Ogallala (pg. 250)

Sidney (pg. 250)

Crawford (pg. 250)

Hemingford (pg. 250)

Agate Fossil
Beds NM

Scotts Bluff NM

Gering (pg. 250)

Nebraska

Did you know?
The largest porch swing in the world is located in Hebron, Nebraska and it can sit 25 adults.
The Lied Jungle located in Omaha is the world's largest indoor rain forest.

Hotel Deco XV

As its name suggests, this Omaha landmark demonstrates the
unique Art Deco architecture found throughout the city. Inside,
things have been significantly modernized with neoclassic decor,
and the hotel's proximity to the city's historic Old Market make it
a highly desirable spot to stay. Hotel Deco XV was built in 1930
and boasts a prestigious placement on the National Register of
Historic Places list, as well as the distinction of
Omaha's only boutique luxury hotel.

1504 Harney St, Omaha, NE 68102
(402) 991-4981
www.hoteldecoomaha.com

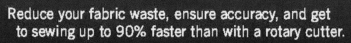

Nebraska Shops

Q-Quilting ~ Y-Yarn ~ N-Needlework ~ R-Retreat ~ M-Museum

City	Shop	Address	Phone	Page
Ainsworth	In Stitches on the Quilt Trail	216 N. Main	(402) 382-3282	
Alliance	Prairie Creations	5611 Madison Rd.	(308) 762-8365	
Arapahoe	**Wagner's Quilts & Conversation**	**404 Chestnut**	**(308) 962-8458**	**Pg. 250**
Auburn	Needles I	72896 638th Ave.	(402) 274-3339	
Auburn	The Fabric Fairie	900 Central Ave.	(402) 274-4454	
Beatrice	**Quilt Stitches**	**505 Court St. # B**	**(402) 223-1916**	**Pg. 252**
Blair	ACME Fabric & Quilt Co.	1716 Washington St.	(402) 533-1015	
Broken Bow	The Quilting Shack	518 E. Southeast St.	(308) 872-6221	
Chadron	Ta-Da! Quilt Shop	223 Main St.	(308) 432-3565	
Columbus	**Sew-What Needle Arts and Quilting**	**3415 21st St.**	**(402) 563-3900**	**Pg. 252**
Columbus	Claus'en Paus Quilt Shop	2510 13th St.	(402) 564-1618	
Columbus	Sew What Needle Arts & Quilting	3415 21st St.	(402) 563-3900	
Cozad	**Prairie Point Junction**	**124 E. 8th**	**(308) 784-2010**	**Pg. 251**
Crawford	**Pine Needle Quilt Shop**	**413 2nd St.**	**(308) 665-1107**	**Pg. 250**
Crawford	Stitches	120 McPherson St.	(308) 665-5069	
Fremont	**Country Traditions**	**330 N. Main**	**(402) 721-7752**	**Pg. 253**
Fremont	I Love Sewing	2948 N. Clarkson St. #B	(402) 727-7869	
Fullerton	**Calico Annie's Quilt Shop**	**210 Broadway**	**(308) 536-2925**	**Pg. 252**
Gering	**Prairie Pines Quilt Shop**	**1270 Tenth St. #B**	**(308) 436-5152**	**Pg. 250**
Grand Island	Fancy Girl Designs Quilt Shop	515 S. Webb Rd. Ste. C	(308) 380-6610	
Grand Island	Material Girl	3415 W. State St.	(308) 381-6675	
Gretna	The Quilted Moose	109 Enterprise Dr.	(402) 332-4178	
Hastings	**Calico Cottage**	**743 W. 2nd St.**	**(402) 463-6767**	**Pg. 250**
Hastings	Kitty Rose	237 N. St. Joseph Ave.	(402) 705-7747	
Hastings	The Plum Nelly & Julie's Xpressions	731 W. 2nd St.	(402) 462-2490	
Hebron	Sew Bee It Quilt Shop	341 Lincoln Ave.	(402) 768-6980	
Hemingford	**Pat's Creative**	**7355 Gage Rd.**	**(308) 487-3999**	**Pg. 250**
Humboldt	Creative Collectible Quilts and Crafts	332 E. Sq.	(402) 862-4001	
Imperial	New Generation Fabrics dba Prior's	525 Broadway	(308) 882-4354	
Kearney	**Quilters Cottage**	**2216 Central Ave.**	**(308) 237-2701**	**Pg. 250**
Kearney	Kearney Quality Sew & Vac.	712 E. 25th St.	(888) 801-2988	
Lincoln	**Cosmic Cow**	**6136 Havelock Ave.**	**(402) 464-4040**	**Pg. 253**
Lincoln	**International Quilt Study**	**1523 N. 33rd**	**(402) 472-6549**	**Pg. 253**
Lincoln	Crafthouse	3520 Village Dr. #600	(402) 261-4453	
Lincoln	Honey, Lace and More	4713 Hartley #2	(402) 261-3407	
Lincoln	Knit-Paper-Scissors	6701 Vanderslice Cir.	(402) 429-8029	
Lincoln	Sew Creative	5143 S. 48th St.	(402) 489-6262	
Lincoln	The Calico House	5221 S. 48th St. #4	(402) 489-1067	
Lincoln	The Yarn Shop	5221 S. 48th St. #6	(402) 489-9550	
Lincoln	Yarn Charm	4640 Bair Ave. #214	(402) 858-6300	
McCook	Sew Blessed	402 Norris Ave. #103	(308) 344-9389	
Mitchell	Brown Sheep Company	100662 County Rd. 16	(800) 826-9136	
Nebraska City	Sew Enchanting	616 1/2 Central Ave.	(402) 873-1009	
Nebraska City	The Sewing Basket	805 Central Ave.	(402) 873-3955	
Newman Grove	Betz's Little Shoppe	505 Hale Ave.	(402) 447-6048	
Norfolk	I Bee Quiltin	322 W. Norfolk Ave.	(402) 371-0045	
North Platte	**The Quilt Rack & Wool Cubby**	**101 W. Front St.**	**(308) 532-2606**	**Pg. 250**
North Platte	Prairie Hand Knits	508 S. Dewey St.	(308) 534-4272	
Ogallala	**Silver Thimble Sewing Center**	**108 N. Spruce St.**	**(308) 284-6838**	**Pg. 250**
Omaha	**AccuQuilt**	**8843 S. 137th Cir.**	**(888) 258-7913**	**Pg. 254**
Omaha	A Quilting Place	11019 I St.	(402) 884-2096	
Omaha	Country Sampler	11928 W. Center Rd.	(402) 333-6131	
Omaha	David M. Mangelsen's	3457 S. 84th St.	(402) 391-6225	
Omaha	For the Love of Stitching	2819 S. 125th Ave. #359	(402) 884-1104	
Omaha	ImagiKnit Yarn Shop	12100 W. Center Rd. #602	(402) 932-9525	
Omaha	More Sew For You, A Quilt Shop	14440 F St. #107	(402) 932-8217	
Omaha	Personal Threads Boutique	8600 Cass	(402) 391-7733	
Omaha	Sew Creative	2809 S. 125th Ave.	(402) 334-0121	
Omaha	The Quilt Studio	4429 S. 50th St.	(402) 934-4750	
Omaha	Village Needleworks	8707 Shamrock Rd.	(402) 391-1191	

Index

Omaha	Wooly Mammoth Yarn Shop	2806 S. 110th Ct.	(402) 932-2157	
O'Neill	Quilters Candy Shoppe	420 E. Douglas	(402) 336-1953	
Ralston	Bella Fiore Quilt Shop	7310 Harrison St.	(402) 592-6100	
Ralston	Reflections Framing	7314 Harrison St.	(402) 331-1740	
Red Cloud	The Sewing Box	422 N. Webster St.	(402) 746-3180	
Scottsbluff	Platte Valley Vac. & Sew	1804 Broadway	(308) 632-3734	
Scottsbluff	The Quilt Stop	1814 1st Ave.	(308) 632-7028	
Seward	**The Udder Store**	**636 Seward St.**	**(402) 646-1000**	**Pg. 252**
Seward	Weedy Creek Yarns	636 Seward St.	(402) 646-1000	
Shelby	Karens Kollectibles	150 E. Park St. #3	(402) 366-9333	
Sidney	**More Than Quilts**	**1044 Illinois St.**	**(308) 203-1600**	**Pg. 250**
Superior	Kitty Rose	336 N. Central	(402) 879-0151	
Superior	Quilter's Nook	214 N. Central Ave.	(402) 879-5431	
Valentine	The Quilting Cupboard	130 W. 4th St.	(402) 376-3702	
Wakefield	The Quilt Shop	314 Main St.	(402) 287-2325	
Wayne	Just Sew	512 E. 7th	(402) 375-4697	
West Point	Creative Notions	107 N. Main St.	(402) 372-2004	
York	**The Quilt Basket**	**718 N. Lincoln Ave.**	**(402) 362-5737**	**Pg. 252**

Index

Notes

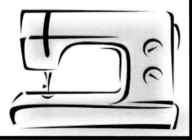

Lake Tahoe Quilt Block

Nevada

Reno (pg. 259)

Gardnerville (pg. 259)

Great Basin NP

Death Valley NM

Pahrump (pg. 259)

Las Vegas (pg. 258, 259)

Lake Mead NRA

Henderson (pg. 258)

Did you know?
The Reno Ice Pavilion is a 16,000-square-foot rink once dismantled and moved to
Reno from Atlantic City, New Jersey.

Nevada Shops

Q-Quilting ~ Y-Yarn ~ N-Needlework ~ R-Retreat ~ M-Museum

Battle Mountain	The Quilt Parlor	147 E. Front St.	(775) 635-2600	
Boulder City	Craft Cottage	1326 Wyoming	(702) 294-4465	
Carson City	Cagey Quilter	1010 S. Carson St.	(775) 883-5690	
Carson City	Sierra Sewing	911 Topsy Ln. #222	(775) 267-6694	
Carson City	The Yarn Niche	512 N. Curry St.	(775) 841-1975	
Carson City	The Yarn Niche	512 N. Curry St.	(775) 232-3303	
Fallon	The UnCommon Thread	1525 W. Williams Ave. #L	(775) 867-4225	
Fallon	Workman's Farms Crafts & Nursery	4990 Reno Hwy.	(775) 867-3716	
Fernley	A Stitch of Country	15 E. Main St. #1	(775) 835-0558	
Gardnerville	**The Quilt House**	**1328 Hwy. 395 #105**	**(775) 782-8845**	**Pg. 259**
Henderson	**QUILTIQUE**	**213 N. Stephanie St. #E**	**(702) 563-8600**	**Pg. 258**
Henderson	Quilt Tours of Las Vegas	2244 Heavenly View Dr.	(702) 647-8458	
Las Vegas	**Pocket Change Fabric**	**4317 Ivory Cir.**	**(702) 303-4923**	**Pg. 259**
Las Vegas	**The Christmas Goose**	**2988 S. Durango #109**	**(702) 877-1158**	**Pg. 258**
Las Vegas	Sew Little Time	6360 W. Sahara Ave.	(702) 450-6766	
Las Vegas	Sew Yeah Quilting	3690 N. Rancho Dr.	(702) 586-8687	
Las Vegas	Sin City Knit Shop	2165 E. Windmill Ln. #200	(702) 641-0210	
Las Vegas	Stitcher's Paradise	2550 S. Rainbow Blvd. E25	(702) 227-9735	
Las Vegas	Vac. & Sew Summerlin	2243 N. Rampart Blvd.	(702) 309-8787	
Mesquite	Simply Quilts & Crafts	190 E. Mesquite Blvd. #C	(702) 346-2180	
Minden	Fabric-Chicks Creative Oasis	1166 Annie Ct. #C	(775) 267-0204	
Minden	Pioneer Yarn Company	1653 Lucerne St. #B	(775) 392-3336	
Pahrump	**Bernina Sewing Center**	**4920 Pahrump Valley Blvd.**	**(775) 727-3633**	**Pg. 259**
Pahrump	The Quilted Dragon	2890 S. Yucca Terrace Ave.	(775) 751-9033	
Reno	**Stitch In Time**	**5000 Smithridge Dr. #A-15**	**(775) 829-9222**	**Pg. 259**
Reno	Going Batty Quilt Shop	9744 S. Virginia St. Ste. C	(775) 351-2424	
Reno	Jimmy Beans Wool	1312 Capital Blvd. #103	(775) 827-9276	
Reno	Mill End Fabrics	1745 Kuenzli St.	(775) 322-5844	
Reno	Sew-N-Such	2303 Kietzke Ln. Ste. 2	(775) 825-6677	
Reno	Sierra Sewing	8056 S. Virginia St.	(775) 823-9700	
Reno	Topaz Quilting & Embroidery	770 Smithridge Dr. #100	(775) 329-2197	
Reno	Windy Moon Quilts	440 Spokane St.	(775) 323-4777	
Sparks	Windy Moon Quilts	406 Pyramid Way	(775) 870-4031	
Winnemucca	Comfy Cozy Quilt and Gift Shop	1205 E. Winnemucca Blvd.	(775) 623-6674	
Winnemucca	Mad Hatter Quilt Shoppe	346 S. Bridge St.	(775) 623-2521	
Yerington	Sylvia's Quilters Quarters	120 Bovard St.	(775) 463-7036	
Yerington	The WorkShop in the Back	27 Broadway Ave.	(775) 463-9492	

Notes

New Hampshire

New England Star Quilt Block

Littleton (pg. 261)

Rumney (pg. 261)   Center Harbor (pg. 261)

Saint-Gardens NHS

Tilton (pg. 262)

Rochester (pg. 262)

Concord (pg. 262)   Portsmouth (pg. 262)

Keene (pg. 262)

Plaistow (pg. 262)

Pelham (pg. 262)

Golden Gese Quilt Shop

Concord, NH

Monday - Saturday 10 - 5
June, July, Aug
Monday - Friday 10 - 5
Saturday 10 - 1

All the latest fabrics and notions, Books, Patterns & Classes for new and interesting projects. We provide helpful assistance with all your projects.

22 Liberty St. Concord, NH 03301
(603) 228-5540
www.goldengesequilts.com

THE Quilting Corner

Tues - Fri 10 - 5
Sat 9 - 4

Where Inspiration Comes to Life!

322 W. Main St. # 110
Tilton, NH 03276
(603) 286-3437

www.quiltingcornernh.com

We offer Fabric, Books, Patterns, Kits, Notions, Gifts and Classes for all levels.

TILTON, NH   Q   Est: 2006

Keene, NH   Q

The Moses House Quilt Shop

391 West St. Keene, NH 03431
(603) 352-2312
Owner: Russ Moline
info@themoseshouse.com

We sell new and used machines.
Long arm machine sales & service.
Long arm quilting services.
Quilting frames. We are a Nolting Dealer.

Monday-Friday
10:00-1:00
Or by Appt.

Keene, NH   Q

NEW ENGLAND FABRICS
— & Decorating Center —

55 Ralston St., Keene, NH 03431
(603) 352-8683
www.newenglandfabrics.com
Tremendous Selection of Beautiful Fabrics for:
• Quilting • Apparel • Bridal • Draperies
• Slipcovers • Upholstery & More!
Plus Yarn & Sewing Machines
Central New England's Largest Fabric & Home Decorating Center!

Mon-Sat 9:30-5:30
Fri til 7
June, July, August
til 4 on Sat

---

70 Bridge St. #6
Pelham, NH 03076
Stone Cottage Square
603-635-9705
www.bnpquilts.com

Hours:
Mon 10 - 8
Tues 10 - 6
Wed 10 - 8
Thur 10 - 8
Fri 10 - 6
Sat 9 - 5
Sun 10 - 5

bits 'n pieces

fax 603-635-4524
Est: 2002   3000 sq.ft.
info@bnpquilts.com

OVER 7000 BOLTS

• Batiks
• Moda
• Flannels
• Florals
• Wilderness

• Novelties
• Patterns
• Kits
• Machine Quilting Services
• Much More

Handi Quilter
OFFICIAL RETAILER

elna

Plaistow, NH   Q

D&D Sewing

160 Plaistow Rd.
Plaistow Commons 03865
(603) 382-1122
Owners: Debbie & Dave Krauklin
dndkay@yahoo.com
www.ddsewing.com
Large Selection of Quilting, Sewing & Embroidery Supplies. PFAFF Sewing machines. Service on all brands. Classes.

Monday-Friday 10-5
Wednesday til 7
Saturday 9-4

Portsmouth, NH   Q

Portsmouth FABRIC Company

16th ANNIVERSARY
1979   2015

BERNINA
made to create

112 Penhallow St. 03801
(603) 436-6343
Fax: (603) 430-2943

Mon - Sat
9:30 - 5:30
Sun 12 - 5

www.portsmouthfabric.com

1100 sq.ft. with 7000 bolts of fabric.
An exceptional selection of quilting cottons-designer, ethnic, batik and handpainted. Rayons, silks and other fine garment fabrics. Patterns, buttons, fiber art magazines & books.

Rochester, NH   Q

The Fabric Garden

"Best Kept Secret in Town"

where fabrics are always in bloom

3 Stillwater Circle, Rochester, NH 03839
(603) 948-2869
Owner: Katrina Rhodes
www.myfabricgarden.com
Fabrics, Patterns, Kits, Notions, Classes
We also create custom quilts/items.

Wed 10am-6pm
Thurs- Sat
10am - 4pm
And by Appt.

Follow us
On Facebook

Did you know?
The highest wind speed recorded at ground level is at Mt. Washington, on April 12, 1934. The winds were three times as fast as those in most hurricanes.

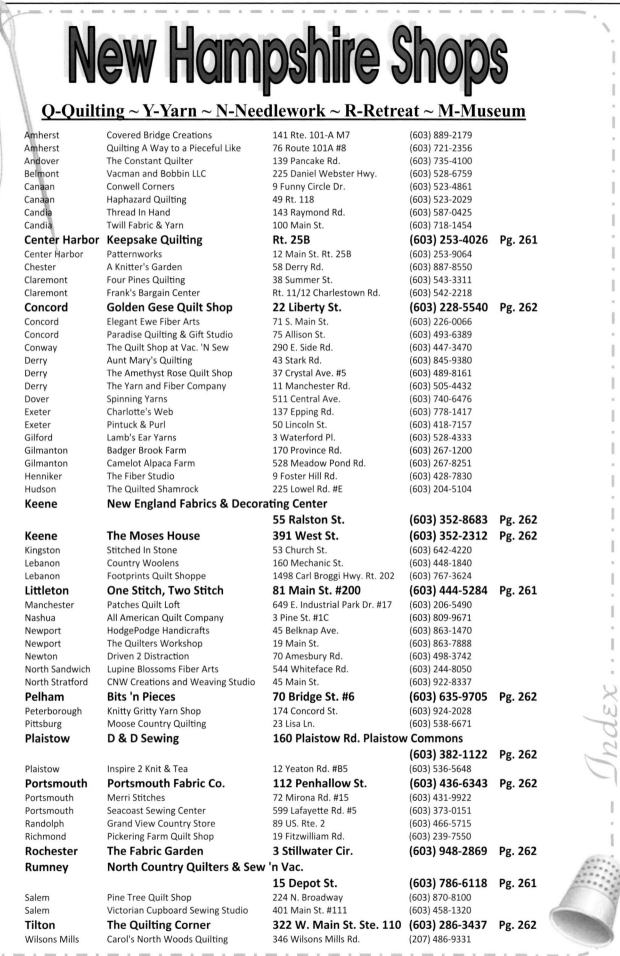

New Hampshire Shops

Q-Quilting ~ Y-Yarn ~ N-Needlework ~ R-Retreat ~ M-Museum

Amherst	Covered Bridge Creations	141 Rte. 101-A M7	(603) 889-2179	
Amherst	Quilting A Way to a Pieceful Like	76 Route 101A #8	(603) 721-2356	
Andover	The Constant Quilter	139 Pancake Rd.	(603) 735-4100	
Belmont	Vacman and Bobbin LLC	225 Daniel Webster Hwy.	(603) 528-6759	
Canaan	Conwell Corners	9 Funny Circle Dr.	(603) 523-4861	
Canaan	Haphazard Quilting	49 Rt. 118	(603) 523-2029	
Candia	Thread In Hand	143 Raymond Rd.	(603) 587-0425	
Candia	Twill Fabric & Yarn	100 Main St.	(603) 718-1454	
Center Harbor	**Keepsake Quilting**	**Rt. 25B**	**(603) 253-4026**	**Pg. 261**
Center Harbor	Patternworks	12 Main St. Rt. 25B	(603) 253-9064	
Chester	A Knitter's Garden	58 Derry Rd.	(603) 887-8550	
Claremont	Four Pines Quilting	38 Summer St.	(603) 543-3311	
Claremont	Frank's Bargain Center	Rt. 11/12 Charlestown Rd.	(603) 542-2218	
Concord	**Golden Gese Quilt Shop**	**22 Liberty St.**	**(603) 228-5540**	**Pg. 262**
Concord	Elegant Ewe Fiber Arts	71 S. Main St.	(603) 226-0066	
Concord	Paradise Quilting & Gift Studio	75 Allison St.	(603) 493-6389	
Conway	The Quilt Shop at Vac. 'N Sew	290 E. Side Rd.	(603) 447-3470	
Derry	Aunt Mary's Quilting	43 Stark Rd.	(603) 845-9380	
Derry	The Amethyst Rose Quilt Shop	37 Crystal Ave. #5	(603) 489-8161	
Derry	The Yarn and Fiber Company	11 Manchester Rd.	(603) 505-4432	
Dover	Spinning Yarns	511 Central Ave.	(603) 740-6476	
Exeter	Charlotte's Web	137 Epping Rd.	(603) 778-1417	
Exeter	Pintuck & Purl	50 Lincoln St.	(603) 418-7157	
Gilford	Lamb's Ear Yarns	3 Waterford Pl.	(603) 528-4333	
Gilmanton	Badger Brook Farm	170 Province Rd.	(603) 267-1200	
Gilmanton	Camelot Alpaca Farm	528 Meadow Pond Rd.	(603) 267-8251	
Henniker	The Fiber Studio	9 Foster Hill Rd.	(603) 428-7830	
Hudson	The Quilted Shamrock	225 Lowel Rd. #E	(603) 204-5104	
Keene	**New England Fabrics & Decorating Center**			
		55 Ralston St.	**(603) 352-8683**	**Pg. 262**
Keene	**The Moses House**	**391 West St.**	**(603) 352-2312**	**Pg. 262**
Kingston	Stitched In Stone	53 Church St.	(603) 642-4220	
Lebanon	Country Woolens	160 Mechanic St.	(603) 448-1840	
Lebanon	Footprints Quilt Shoppe	1498 Carl Broggi Hwy. Rt. 202	(603) 767-3624	
Littleton	**One Stitch, Two Stitch**	**81 Main St. #200**	**(603) 444-5284**	**Pg. 261**
Manchester	Patches Quilt Loft	649 E. Industrial Park Dr. #17	(603) 206-5490	
Nashua	All American Quilt Company	3 Pine St. #1C	(603) 809-9671	
Newport	HodgePodge Handicrafts	45 Belknap Ave.	(603) 863-1470	
Newport	The Quilters Workshop	19 Main St.	(603) 863-7888	
Newton	Driven 2 Distraction	70 Amesbury Rd.	(603) 498-3742	
North Sandwich	Lupine Blossoms Fiber Arts	544 Whiteface Rd.	(603) 244-8050	
North Stratford	CNW Creations and Weaving Studio	45 Main St.	(603) 922-8337	
Pelham	**Bits 'n Pieces**	**70 Bridge St. #6**	**(603) 635-9705**	**Pg. 262**
Peterborough	Knitty Gritty Yarn Shop	174 Concord St.	(603) 924-2028	
Pittsburg	Moose Country Quilting	23 Lisa Ln.	(603) 538-6671	
Plaistow	**D & D Sewing**	**160 Plaistow Rd. Plaistow Commons**		
			(603) 382-1122	**Pg. 262**
Plaistow	Inspire 2 Knit & Tea	12 Yeaton Rd. #B5	(603) 536-5648	
Portsmouth	**Portsmouth Fabric Co.**	**112 Penhallow St.**	**(603) 436-6343**	**Pg. 262**
Portsmouth	Merri Stitches	72 Mirona Rd. #15	(603) 431-9922	
Portsmouth	Seacoast Sewing Center	599 Lafayette Rd. #5	(603) 373-0151	
Randolph	Grand View Country Store	89 US. Rte. 2	(603) 466-5715	
Richmond	Pickering Farm Quilt Shop	19 Fitzwilliam Rd.	(603) 239-7550	
Rochester	**The Fabric Garden**	**3 Stillwater Cir.**	**(603) 948-2869**	**Pg. 262**
Rumney	**North Country Quilters & Sew 'n Vac.**			
		15 Depot St.	**(603) 786-6118**	**Pg. 261**
Salem	Pine Tree Quilt Shop	224 N. Broadway	(603) 870-8100	
Salem	Victorian Cupboard Sewing Studio	401 Main St. #111	(603) 458-1320	
Tilton	**The Quilting Corner**	**322 W. Main St. Ste. 110**	**(603) 286-3437**	**Pg. 262**
Wilsons Mills	Carol's North Woods Quilting	346 Wilsons Mills Rd.	(207) 486-9331	

Index

Notes

New Jersey

Delaware Water Gap NRA

Pequannock (pg. 265)

80 46

Morristown NHP

78 **Metuchen (pg. 265)**

22

202

1

9

195

Mt. Holly (pg. 265)

295

206

30

40

322

9

Trenton Quilt Block

New Jersey Shops

Q-Quilting ~ Y-Yarn ~ N-Needlework ~ R-Retreat ~ M-Museum

Allenhurst	Needles & Threads	411 Main St.	(732) 493-4300
Belleplain	North Country Knits	551 Hands Mill Rd.	(609) 861-0328
Bergenfield	Gone Stitching	31 S. Washington	(201) 385-2100
Berlin	Sam's Fabric Center	41 Clementon Rd. #120	(856) 767-2552
Brick	Crafty Fabrics	750 Mantoloking Rd.	(732) 920-6220
Bridgeton	Broad Meadows Country Fabrics	100 Mary Elmer Dr.	(856) 332-7269
Burlington	Just Make It Sew	306 High St.	(609) 386-4218
Burlington	Olde City Quilts	339 High St.	(609) 747-0075
Caldwell	Beyond Knits & Needles	339 Bloomfield Ave.	(973) 226-4242
Cape May	Fiber Arts Yarn Shop	315 Ocean St. #23	(609) 898-8080
Cape May	Stitch---by---Stitch	315 Ocean St. #9	(609) 898-9606
Carlstadt	Lion Brand Yarn Outlet	140 Kero Rd.	(201) 939-0611
Carteret	Sophisticated Stitchery	22 N. Whittier St.	(732) 969-0408
Clark	All About Ewe	5 Westfield Ave.	(732) 943-2763
Clifton	Where Victoria's Angels Stitch	658 Allwood Rd.	(973) 778-9827
Clinton	Aunt Jean's Handiworks	38 Center St.	(908) 713-0101
Collingswood	The Quilted Nest	807 Haddon Ave.	(856) 240-1410
Colts Neck	Chelsea Yarns	340 St. Rte. 34	(732) 637-8600
East Hanover	Sew Jersey	136 Rte. 10	(973) 585-7282
Edison	The Knit Kit	1996 State Hwy. 27 Ste. 7	(732) 287-8177
Englewood	Expression Yarn Shop	13 E. Ivy Ln.	(201) 569-4111
Fairfield	The Edwardian Needle	390 Fairfield Rd.	(973) 743-9833
Fanwood	Knit-a-Bit	42B S. Martine Ave.	(908) 322-3030
Forked River	Quilting Possibilities	918 Lacey Rd.	(609) 242-0033
Fort Lee	Pat's Yarn Boutique	807 Abbott Blvd.	(201) 224-7771
Freehold	Yarn Crafters	3333 US. Hwy. 9 N.	(732) 308-0181
Frenchtown	The Spinnery	33 Race St.	(908) 996-9004
Haddonfield	Assemble	417 N. Haddon Ave.	(856) 429-7573
Haddonfield	Hooked Fine Yarn Boutique	411 N. Haddon Ave.	(856) 428-0110
Haddonfield	Nimble Needle	50 D Tanner St.	(856) 354-8100
Harmony	The Blue Tulip Woolery	656 Harmony Brass Castle Rd.	(908) 859-6350
Hazlet	Moore Yarn	1366 Rte. 36	(732) 847-3665
Hillsborough	Swallow Hill Farm	583 Montgomery Rd.	(908) 369-7091
Hillsdale	Yarn Diva and More	428 Hillsdale Ave.	(201) 664-4100
Howell	Mouse Creek Quilts	2212 Rte. 9 S.	(732) 294-7858
Lakewood	Stitch N'Sew Center	123 E. County Line Rd.	(732) 363-2220
Lebanon	Budding Star Quilts	1271 Rt.22 E. Lebanon Plaza	(908) 236-7676
Livingston	Marji Nydick Needle Point	115 W. Mt. Pleasant Ave.	(973) 994-0770
Madison	The Blue Purl	60 Main St.	(973) 377-5648
Manasquan	House of Yarn and Needlecraft	227 Main St.	(732) 223-9788
Marlboro	Knit's Fabulous	130 S. Main St.	(732) 677-2020
Matawan	Creative Canvases Needlepoint	313 Broad St.	(732) 566-9300
Metuchen	**Needleworkers Delight**	**181 US. Hwy. 1 S.**	**(732) 388-4545** **Pg. 265**
Metuchen	The Brass Lantern	418 Main St.	(732) 548-5442
Midland Park	Close Knit	22 Paterson Ave.	(201) 891-3319
Midland Park	The Quilt Spot	25 Goffle Rd. #5	(201) 444-7182
Millville	Fiber Arts Café	501 N. High Cottage St.	(856) 669-1131
Mount Holly	**The Village Quilter**	**10 Charles St.**	**(609) 265-0011** **Pg. 265**
Mt. Holly	Woolbearers	90 High St.	(609) 914-0003
Mullica Hill	Needles & Pins Quilt & Fabric Shop	533 Mullica Hill Rd.	(856) 218-7467
North Plainfield	Fabric Land	855 Rte. 22	(908) 755-4700
North Plainfield	Prints Charming	717 Greenbrook Rd.	(908) 769-0278
Ocean City	Scrim Discovery Needle Work	924 Haven Ave.	(609) 398-6659
Ocean City	The Knitting Niche	1330 Asbury Ave.	(609) 399-5111
Pennington	Knit One Stitch Too	16 N. Main St.	(609) 737-2211
Pennington	Pennington Quilt Works	7 Tree Farm Rd. Suite 104	(609) 737-4321
Pequannock	**Acme Country Fabrics**	**24-26 Newark Pompton Tpke.**	
			(973) 696-1784 **Pg. 265**
Point Pleasant	Frame & Fiber	1004 Trenton Ave.	(732) 892-6207
Princeton	American Sewing & Vacuum Center	301 N. Harrison St.	(609) 921-2205
Princeton	Pins & Needles	8 Chambers St.	(609) 921-9075
Summit	Wool & Grace	102 Summit Ave.	(908) 277-1431

Vineland	The Pin Cushion	657 N. Delsea Dr.	(856) 682-5460
Voorhees	Needlepoints & Framing for U	2999 E. Evesham Rd. #11	(856) 424-7962
West Patterson	A Good Yarn	200 Browertown Rd.	(845) 913-6547
Westfield	Do Ewe Knit?	17 Elmer St.	(908) 654-5648
Westfield	Knit-a-Bit	66 Elm St. Ste. 2	(908) 301-0053
Wyckoff	Ridgewood Needlepoint	391 Clinton Ave.	(201) 612-7770

Index

Notes

New Mexico

Aztec (pg. 271)

Taos (pg. 271)

Santa Fe (pg. 271)

Corrales (pg. 271)

Las Vegas (pg. 271)

Edgewood (pg. 270)

Albuquerque (pg. 268, 269)

Alamogordo (pg. 268)

Lovington (pg. 268)

Carlsbad (pg. 268)

Las Cruces (pg. 268)

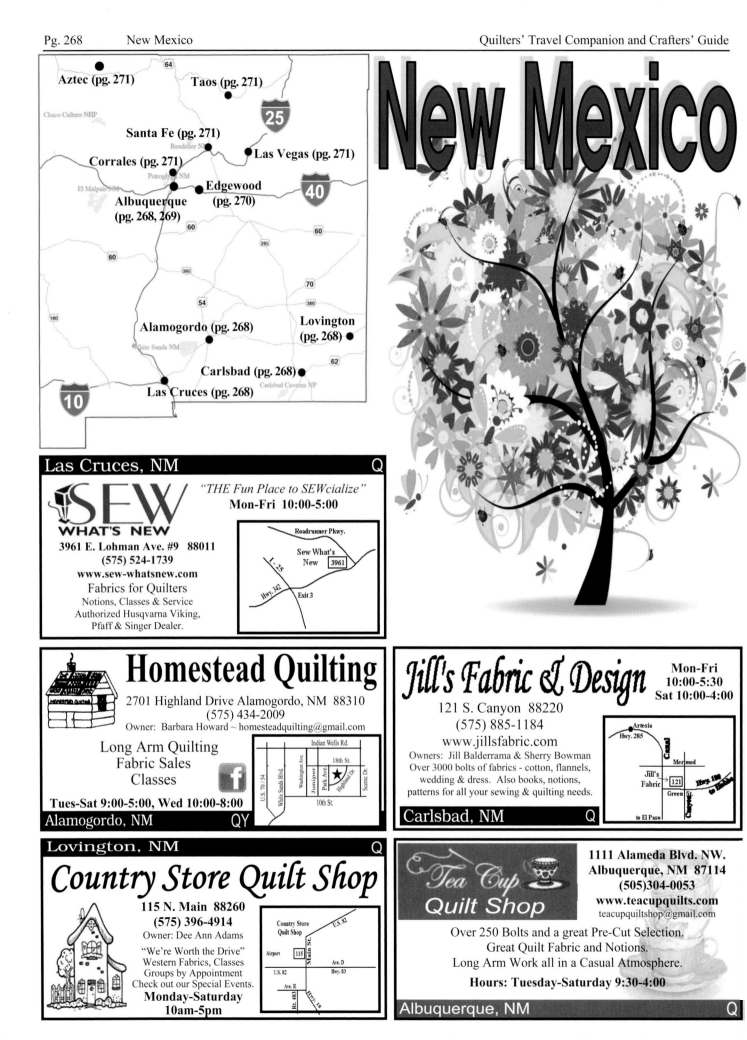

Did you know?
New Mexico is one of the four corners states.
Bordering at the same point with
Colorado, Utah and Arizona.

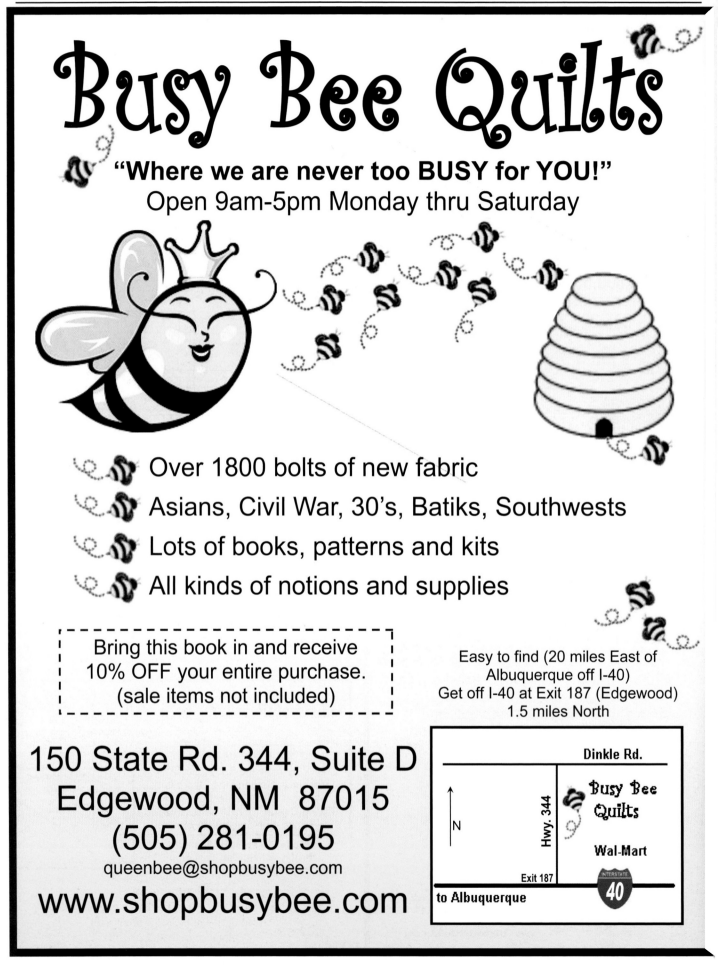

New Mexico Shops

Q-Quilting ~ Y-Yarn ~ N-Needlework ~ R-Retreat ~ M-Museum

Alamogordo	**Homestead Quilting**	**2701 Highland Dr.**	**(575) 434-2009**	**Pg. 268**
Albuquerque	**Ann Silva's Bernina Sewing Center**	**4520 Alexander Blvd. NE**	**(505) 881-5253**	**Pg. 269**
Albuquerque	**Hip Stitch**	**2320 Wisconsin St. NE**	**(505) 821-2739**	**Pg. 269**
Albuquerque	**Southwest Decoratives & Kokopeli Quilt CO.**			
		5711 Carmel Ave. NE #B	**(505) 821-7400**	**Pg. 269**
Albuquerque	**Tea Cup Quilt Shop**	**1111 Alameda Blvd.**	**(505) 304-0053**	**Pg. 268**
Albuquerque	**The Quilt Works**	**11117 Menaul Blvd. NE**	**(505) 298-8210**	**Pg. 269**
Albuquerque	Ryan's Sewing and Vacuum Center	5011 San Mateo Blvd. NE	(505) 237-8000	
Albuquerque	Stitchology	2400 Rio Grande Blvd. NW	(505) 242-3288	
Albuquerque	The Stitcher's Garden	2801 Eubank Blvd. NE Ste. I	(505) 881-6601	
Albuquerque	The Yarn Store at Nob Hill	120 Amherst Dr. NE	(505) 717-1535	
Angel Fire	Turquoise Angel Quilt Shop	3382 Mountain View Blvd.	(575) 377-2266	
Arroyo Seco	Weaving Southwest	487 State Rd. 150	(575) 758-0433	
Aztec	**Quilt it! Ya Ya Fabric and Quilt Store**	**201 S. Church Ave.**	**(505) 334-9566**	**Pg. 271**
Carlsbad	**Jill's Fabric & Design**	**121 S. Canyon**	**(575) 885-1184**	**Pg. 268**
Carlsbad	Cotton Patch Quilts	223 S. Canyon St.	(575) 628-0633	
Carlsbad	Granny's Quilt Barn	1811 Jewel St.	(575) 885-5276	
Clovis	The Sewing Basket	1605 N. Prince St.	(575) 762-9082	
Corrales	**Quilts Ole**	**3923 Corrales Rd.**	**(505) 890-9416**	**Pg. 271**
Deming	Sew-N-Sew	609 E. Florida St.	(575) 546-8085	
Edgewood	**Busy Bee Quilts**	**150 State Rd. 344 #D**	**(505) 281-0195**	**Pg. 270**
Edgewood	Edgewood Yarns & Fibers	95 State Rd. 344 #2	(505) 286-8900	
Espanola	Espanola Valley Fiber Arts Center	325 Paseo de Onate	(505) 747-3577	
Farmington	Quilted Threads	5501 Evergreen Dr.	(505) 325-4490	
Gallup	Gallup Service Mart Vac & Sewing Center	104 W. Coal Ave.	(505) 722-9414	
Hobbs	Got 2 Sew LLC.	209 W. Broadway #16	(575) 393-2739	
Las Cruces	**Sew What's New**	**3961 E. Lohman Ave. # 9**	**(575) 524-1739**	**Pg. 268**
Las Cruces	Be Sew Creative	1601 E. Lohman Ave.	(575) 523-2000	
Las Vegas	**Thread Bear**	**1813 Plaza St.**	**(505) 425-6263**	**Pg. 271**
Los Alamos	Atomic City Quilts	1247 Central Ave. #C	(505) 662-1416	
Los Lunas	Gathering Stitches	643 Hwy. 314 NW	(505) 916-0458	
Los Ojos	Tierra Wools	91 Main St.	(575) 588-7231	
Lovington	**Country Store Quilt Shop**	**115 N. Main**	**(575) 396-4914**	**Pg. 268**
Mora	Mora Valley Spinning Mill & Tapetes de Lana	298 State Hwy. 518	(575) 387-2247	
Raton	Patchwork Phoenix	228 S. 1st St.	(575) 445-8000	
Rio Rancho	Enchanted Creations	1447 32nd Cr. SE	(505) 892-8916	
Roswell	Calico Cow Quilt Shop	311 N. Main	(575) 623-8647	
Roswell	Sew Easy Sewing	200 E. College Blvd.	(575) 623-3774	
Ruidoso	A Quilting Stitchuation	1715 Sudderth Dr.	(575) 315-0541	
Ruidoso	Martha's Fabric Shop	101 Vision Dr.	(575) 630-2231	
Santa Fe	**Santa Fe Quilting**	**3018 A Cielo Ct.**	**(505) 473-3747**	**Pg. 271**
Santa Fe	Jennifer Day Studios	1240 Camino de Cruz Blanca	(505) 660-8656	
Santa Fe	Looking Glass Yarns and Gifts	1807 2nd St. Ste. 2	(505) 995-9649	
Santa Fe	Ryan's Sewing & Vacuum Center	1607 St. Michaels Dr.	(505) 820-1100	
Santa Fe	Yarn & Coffee	1836-B Cerrillos Rd.	(505) 780-5030	
Silver City	Aunt Judy's Attic	1950 Hwy. 180 E.	(575) 388-1620	
Silver City	Yada Yada Yarn	621 N. Bullard St.	(575) 388-3350	
Taos	**Taos Adobe Quilting**	**102 Teresina Lane**	**(575) 751-3219**	**Pg. 271**
Taos	Mooncat Fiber	120 Bent St. Ste. B	(575) 758-9341	
Taos	Needlepoint de Taos	216 Paseo Del Pueblo Norte	(505) 751-1615	
Taos	Vortex Yarns	216 B Paseo del Pueblo Norte	(575) 758-1241	

Notes

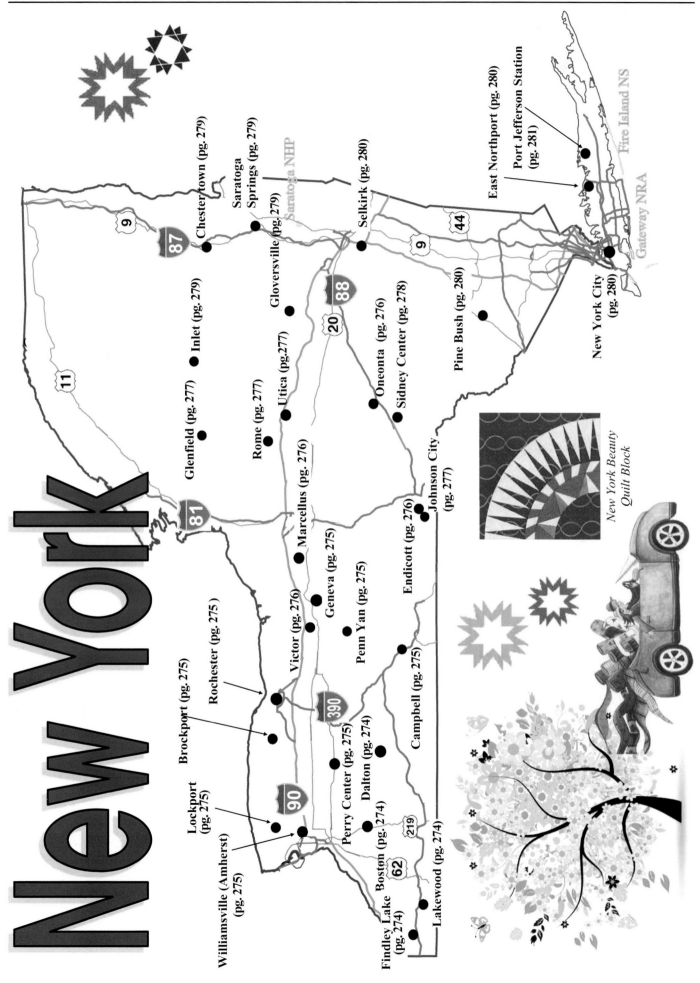

New York

New York Beauty
Quilt Block

Chestertown (pg. 279)

Saratoga
Springs (pg. 279)

Saratoga NHP

Selkirk (pg. 280)

East Northport (pg. 280)

Port Jefferson Station
(pg. 281)

Fire Island NS

Gateway NRA

Inlet (pg. 279)

Gloversville (pg. 279)

New York City
(pg. 280)

Pine Bush (pg. 280)

Glenfield (pg. 277)

Rome (pg. 277)

Utica (pg.277)

Oneonta (pg. 276)

Sidney Center (pg. 278)

Marcellus (pg. 276)

Johnson City
(pg. 277)

Endicott (pg. 276)

Geneva (pg. 275)

Penn Yan (pg. 275)

Victor (pg. 276)

Campbell (pg. 275)

Rochester (pg. 275)

Brockport (pg. 275)

Perry Center (pg. 275)

Dalton (pg. 274)

Lockport
(pg. 275)

Williamsville (Amherst)
(pg.275)

Boston (pg. 274)

Lakewood (pg. 274)

Findley Lake
(pg. 274)

Did you know?
The first capital of the United States was New York City. In 1789 George Washington took his oath as president on the balcony at Federal Hall.

Ivy Thimble Quilt & Gift Shop

www.ivythimble.com

**11 Framark Dr.
Victor, NY 14564
(585) 742-2680**

Int. Rt. 90 (thruway)
Exit 45   Exit 44
Main St.   Rt. 96
School St. | Ivy ☆Thimble | St. Rt. 332
Framark Dr.

**Mon - Thurs
9 - 5
Fri & Sat
9 - 4**

Victor, NY   Q

We're not just a Quilt Shop!

We're your hometown full-service quilt shop!
Our fun-loving and knowledgeable staff invites
you to stop in and visit us soon.
We offer you over 3,500 bolts of high quality fabric,
a great selection of patterns and books and we now
offer Longarm Quilting Services.

Patchwork Angels Quilt Shop

**307 W. Main St. Endicott, NY 13760
(607) 748-0682
www.PatchworkAngels.com**
Owner: Rose Oswald ~ info@PatchworkAngels.com

**Mon, Thur, Fri 11 - 8
Tues & Wed 11 - 5
Sat 9:30 - 4**
Sundays during scheduled
classes & retreats

Namticoke Ave. | Main St.
Patchwork Angels
307 | Vestal Ave. | McKinley Ave.
Vestal Pkwy. | Rt. 434

Located in the Union District of Endicott. Fine
Quilting Fabrics, Notions & Patterns. We specialize
in weekend quilting retreats. Auth. Janome Dealer.

Endicott, NY   Q

Country Fabrics & Quilts

**6187 State Hwy. 23 Oneonta, NY 13820
(607) 432-9726**
Tues-Fri 9:00-4:00, Mon & Sat 9:00-1:00
Over 4000 bolts of cotton fabrics plus notions,
books, & patterns at yester-year prices.
Custom machine and hand quilting.
2 miles off of I -88

The Plaza

This elegant hotel in midtown Manhattan is the height of New
York City extravagance. The distinguished establishment has
treated guests to the finest amenities since 1907, providing
a butler for each floor, and serving refined tea in the Palm
Court, with its marble columns and stained-glass ceiling.

**768 5th Ave, New York, NY 10019
(212) 759-3000
www.theplazany.com**

Notes

The Fieldstone House

"A quilter's dream come true"

1884 Wheat Hill Rd. Sidney Center, NY 13839

(607) 369-9177

Proprietors: Jane & Allan Kirby

fieldstonehouse@frontiernet.net

Shop is filled to capacity with more than 20,000+ bolts of current favorites & past treasures!

This outstanding selection includes many of your favorite designs from . . .

Andover • Alexander Henry • Bali Fabrications • Benartex • Clothworks • Elizabeth's Studio
Hoffman • In the Beginning • Kaffe Fassett • Kona Bay • Lakehouse • Makower • Marcus Brothers
Michael Miller • Moda • Northcott • P&B • Robert Kaufman • RJR • Red Rooster
Timeless Treasures .... and more.

Hours: Monday-Saturday 11am-4pm Sunday-Call for Hours
Other hours available upon request.
Closed Occasionally for Quilt Shows and Family Events

We recommend calling in advance.

---

www.fieldstonehousefabrics.com

Visit our website for a list of quilt shows we vend…
or contact us for a list of quilt show dates/locations.

Did you know?
Rochester is known as both the Flour City and the Flower City.

Notes

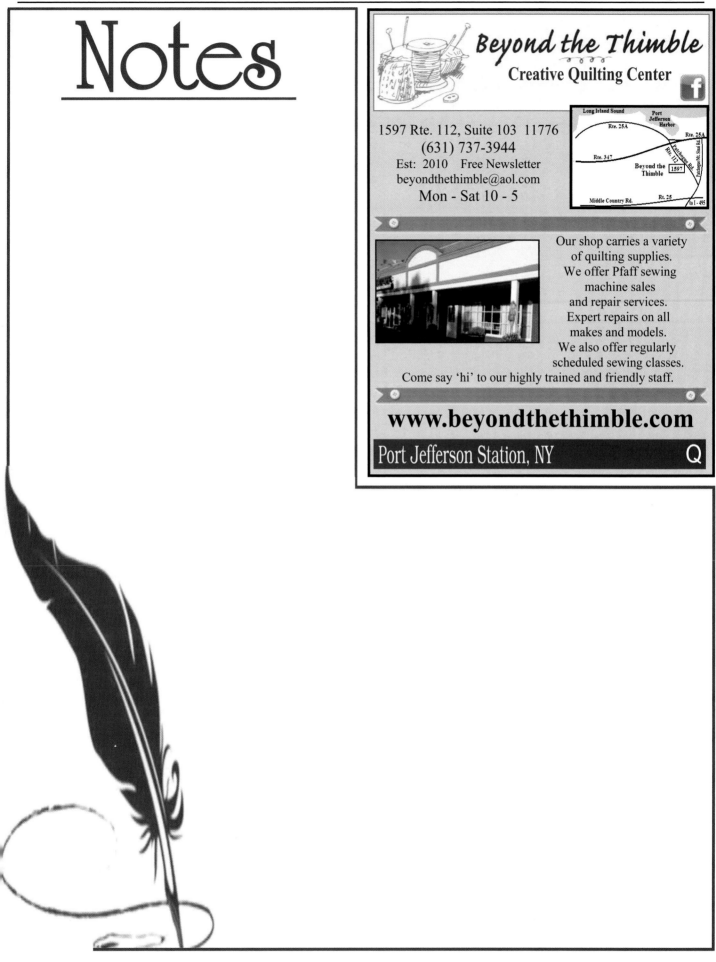

New York Shops

Q-Quilting ~ Y-Yarn ~ N-Needlework ~ R-Retreat ~ M-Museum

Addison	Back Yard Quilter	108 Front St.	(607) 359-4479
Addison	Sew What? Fabric Shoppe	11597 County Rt. 119 #102	(607) 359-4308
Afton	Sew Clever	195 Hwy. 41 S.	(607) 639-2460
Akwesasne	Dreamcrafter Quilt Shop	1422 State Rte. 37	(518)-358-4285
Alfred Station	Alfred Knitting Studio	16 S Main St.	(607) 587-8002
Altamont	The Spinning Room	190 Main St.	(518) 861-0038
Altona	Maw & Paw's Fabrics	4954 Military Tpke.	(518) 236-5762
Amherst	Amherst Museum	3755 Tonawanda Creek Rd.	(716) 689-1440
Arcade	Creekside Fabrics & Quilts & Yarns	237 Main St.	(585) 492-4226
Auburn	All Tied Up Yarns	14 State St.	(315) 258-9276
Bath	Farm Fresh Fabrics	8825 St. Rt. 53	(607) 329-1906
Beacon	Beetle and Fred	171 Main St.	(845) 440-8867
Beacon	Clay Wood & Cotton	133 Main St.	(845) 481-0149
Big Flats	The Witches Stitches	18 Canal St.	(607) 358-4016
Bohemia	Ladybug Stitches, Inc.	840 Lincoln Ave. Unit 8	(631) 244-0001
Boston	**Quilt Farm**	**5623 Feddick Rd.**	**(716) 941-3140** Pg. 274
Bouckville	The Gingham Patch	3490 Pratts Rd.	(315) 893-7750
Brockport	**Country Treasures Quilt Shop**	**61 Main St.**	**(585) 637-5148** Pg. 275
Brocton	Wool Gathering	7 W. Main St.	(716) 792-9665
Brooklyn	Argyle Yarn Shop	288 Prospect Park W.	(347) 227-7799
Brooklyn	B & E Yarn	784 Manhattan Ave.	(718) 383-8907
Brooklyn	Brooklyn General Store	128 Union St.	(718) 237-7753
Brooklyn	Feza Yarns	161 Jamaica Ave.	(800) 684-3392
Brooklyn	La Casita Yarn Shop Café	253 Smith St.	(718) 963-0369
Brooklyn	Needles & Knots	2942 Ave. R	(718) 265-9600
Brooklyn	Sew Beary Special	1025 E. 28th St.	(718)-951-3973
Brooklyn	sm Stitches	335 Ave. U	(917) 325-4435
Brooklyn	Stitch Therapy	180 Lincoln Place	(718) 398-2020
Buffalo	Elmwood Village Fabrics	543 Franklin St.	(716) 881-2866
Buffalo	Elmwood Yarn Shop	1639 Hertel Ave.	(716) 834-7580
Burdett	Graceful Arts Fiber Studio	4760 Rte. 414	(607) 546-8344
Caledonia	Chestnut Bay Quilting	262 North St.	(585) 538-4420
Caledonia	The Woolery on Main Street	3127 Main St.	(585) 538-9898
Campbell	**Sew Pieceful Quilt Shoppe**	**5541 County Rte. 125**	**(607) 583-4968** Pg. 275
Canandaigua	Expressions in Needleart	110 S. Main St.	(585) 394-4870
Canandaigua	Liberty Cottage	4390 Middle Cheshire Rd.	(585) 393-1070
Candor	Pucky Huddle Delight	71 Owego Rd.	(607) 659-7743
Canton	The Celtic Knot	17 Main St.	(315) 714-3206
Cattaraugus	Hand Dyed Fabrics by Lori	9868 Leon Rd.	(716) 257-5671
Chatham	Foofsique Quilting Emporium	437 Rte. 295	(518) 392-3111
Chatham	The Warm Ewe	31 Main St.	(518) 392-2929
Chestertown	**Country Girl Crafts & Quilts**	**6328 Main St.**	**(518) 494-2299** Pg. 279
Chestertown	Chester Yarn Boutique	5797 State Rte. 8	(518) 494-4334
Cobleskill	The Yardstick	147 Barnerville Rd. #1	(518) 234-2179
Cold Spring Harbor	Loop on Main	143 Main St.	(631) 659-3810
Cooperstown	Sybil's Yarn Shop	1037 State Hwy. 166	(607) 286-7603
Corning	Wooly Minded	91 W. Market St. #102	(607) 973-2885
Cornwall	Cornwall Yarn Shop	227 Main St.	(845) 534-0383
Cornwall on Hudson	Hudson Valley Quilt & Sew	1 Idlewild Ave. #2	(845) 534-7300
Croton-on-Hudson	Pinwheels	2006 Albany Post Rd.	(914) 271-1045
Cuddebackville	Bonnie's Kozy Knit	300 Rte. 211	(845) 754-0700
Dalton	**The Journey Quilt Company**	**3 N. State St.**	**(585) 476-2630** Pg. 274
Dansville	Material Rewards	10160 Sandy Hill Rd.	(585) 335-2050
Delmar	Amelia's Garden	340 Delaware Ave.	(518) 439-4614
Depew	Sew on Sew Forth	6152 Transit Rd.	(716) 684-4880
Dewittville	Martha's Quilt Barn	7145 Walker Rd.	(716) 753-3786
Dundee	The Fabric Shop	12 Main St.	(607) 243-7052
East Amherst	Patchwork Garden Quilt Shop	6281 Transit Rd.	(716) 810-9088
East Aurora	Aurora Sewing Center	659 Main St.	(716) 652-2811
East Aurora	The Carriage Quilt Shoppe	586 Main St. Ste. 4	(716) 655-4561
East Aurora	The Woolly Lamb	712 Main St.	(716) 655-1911
East Aurora	Vidler's 5 & 10 Store	690 Main St.	(716) 652-0481

Index

East Northport	**Pieceful Quilting**	**3027 Jericho Turnpike**	**(631) 670-6254**	**Pg. 280**
East Rochester	Patricia's Fabric House	333 W. Commerical St.	(585) 248-2362	
East Rochester	The Village Yarn & Fiber Shop	350 W. Commercial St.	(585) 586-5470	
East Syracuse	Pick Your Stitch	6701 Manlius Center	(315) 437-0962	
Eden	Marie's Sewing Center	8386 N. Main St.	(716) 992-4364	
Ellenburg Center	Lost Sheep Quilt Shop	7270 Star Rd. Rte. 190	(518) 594-3253	
Ellicottville	Ellicottville Quilt Shop	19 Jefferson St.	(716) 699-2065	
Ellisburg	The Old Creamery Quilting	12022 State Rt. 193	(315) 846-5393	
Elmira	Malley's In The Yarn	729 Kinyon St.	(607) 732-4034	
Endicott	**Patchwork Angels Quilt Shop**	**307 W. Main St.**	**(607) 748-0682**	**Pg. 276**
Endicott	Cornucopia Yarns	2909 Watson Blvd.	(607) 748-3860	
Endwell	Yarns N' More	2605 E. Main St.	(607) 786-9276	
Evans Mills	Josiphina's Quilting Patch	25600 State Rt. 342	(315) 221-3880	
Evans Mills	The Old Tattered Flag	29098 NY Rt. 37	(315) 767-8313	
Fairport	Sew Creative	650 Whitney Rd.	(585) 388-0230	
Fayetteville	A Stitcher's Garden	7070 Cedar Bay Rd.	(315)-449-2181	
Flushing	Cook Arts & Crafts	8009 Myrtle Ave.	(718) 366-6085	
Flushing	Sandy's Knit 'N' Needles	15403B Union Tpke.	(718) 380-0370	
Fly Creek	Heartworks Quilts & Fabrics	6237 Rt. #28	(607) 547-2501	
Fulton	The Robin's Nest Quilt Shop & More	11 W. Broadway	(315) 598-1170	
Geneva	**Quilty Pleasures**	**492 Exchange St.**	**(315) 325-4248**	**Pg. 275**
Geneva	Yarn Shop of Geneva	513 Exchange St.	(315) 789-7211	
Genoa	Fingerlakes Woolen Mill	1193 Stewart's Corners Rd.	(315) 497-1542	
Ghent	Turose	330-B County Rd. 21-C	(518) 672-0052	
Glenfield	**Sew Crazy Fabric Shop**	**5146 State Rte. 12**	**(315) 376-7630**	**Pg. 277**
Glens Falls	Patti's Quilting & Fabrics	485 Glen St.	(518) 409-4533	
Glenville	The Joyful Quilter	19 Glenridge Rd. Unit A	(518) 399-0128	
Gloversville	**Gloversville Sewing Center**	**385 S. Main St.**	**(518) 725-4919**	**Pg. 279**
Granville	Village Yarn Shop	4 E. Main St.	(518) 796-3188	
Greene	Creative Threads	604 Jackson Hill Rd.	(607) 656-8883	
Greenwich	Yarn	99 Main St.	(518) 791-8067	
Groton	Sew Beautifully Creative Quilt Shop	190 Cayuga St.	(607) 351-5873	
Hamburg	Embraceable Ewe	213 Main St.	(716) 646-6674	
Hammondsport	Finger Lakes Fiber & Art Emporium	67 Shether St.	(607) 569-3530	
Hampton Bays	Rainbow Yarns & Needlecraft Shoppe	13 Ponquogue Ave.	(631) 728-3085	
Harpursville	Quilted Crow	54 Cafferty Rd.	(607) 648-8956	
Hartsdale	Hartsdale Fabrics	275 S. Central Ave.	(914) 428-7780	
Hicksville	Gone Sewin	161 D Levittown Pkwy.	(516) 342-1127	
Hilton	Amelia's Fabric & Yarn Shoppe	7 Upton St.	(585) 392-1192	
Hopewell Junction	Out of the Loop	2593 Rte. 52 #5	(845) 223-8355	
Hudson Falls	Knit Wit Kreations	265 Main St.	(518) 747-4010	
Huntington	Knitting Corner	718 New York Ave.	(631) 421-2660	
Huntington	Knitting Garden	49 Green St.	(631) 923-3222	
Hyde Park	Deer Hill Farm Cross Stitching	1164 Rte. 9 G Ste. 5	(845) 229-0246	
Inlet	**Crazy Moose Quilt Shop**	**115 Rt. 28**	**(315) 357-5092**	**Pg. 279**
Islip	Sew What's New	400 Main St.	(631) 277-4215	
Ithaca	Homespun Boutique	314 E. State St.	(607) 277-0954	
Ithaca	Knitting Etc.	2255 N. Triphammer Rd.	(607) 277-1164	
Ithaca	Quilters Corner	518 W. State St.	(607) 266-0850	
Jamaica	Smiley's Yarn Store	92-06 Jamaica Ave.	(718) 849-9873	
Jamesville	Yarn Cupboard	6487 E. Seneca Trpk.	(315) 399-5148	
Johnson City	**Southern Tier Sewing Center**	**800 Valley Plaza Dr.**	**(607) 797-7022**	**Pg. 277**
Katonah	Katonah Yarn Co.	120 Bedford Rd.	(914) 977-3145	
Kaueonga Lake	Knit One Needlepoint Too	140 Lake St.	(845) 583-5648	
Lakewood	**Quilters' Haven**	**167 W Fairmount Ave. Rte. 394**		
			(716) 763-0342	**Pg. 274**
Lancaster	Simple Pleasures & Homespun Treasures	5300 William St.	(716) 359-5038	
Larchmont	Etui Fiber Arts	2106 Boston Post Rd.	(914) 341-1426	
Larchmont	Silver Canvas Ltd.	12 Chatsworth Ave.	(914) 834-4868	
Larchmont	Stitch By Stitch	1971 Palmer Ave.	(914) 834-1886	
Locke	Grisamore Farms	749 Cowan Rd.	(315) 497-1347	
Lockport	**Marie's Sewing Center**	**6310 Robinson Rd.**	**(716) 434-2583**	**Pg. 275**
Lockport	Heartland Quilt Shop	34 Main St.	(716) 433-3188	
Malverne	Basic Stitches	298 Hempstead Ave.	(516) 887-3524	
Manhattan	Elizabeth Yarns Store	15 Elizabeth St. #21	(917) 217-9570	
Manlius	In-Stitches	206 E. Seneca St.	(315) 692-4090	
Marathon	The Fabric Patch	5 W. Main St.	(607) 849-3611	
Marcellus	**Patchwork Plus**	**2532 Cherry Valley Tpke.**	**(315) 673-2208**	**Pg. 276**
Mattituck	Altman's Needle & Fiber Arts	195 Love Ln.	(631) 298-7181	

Mayville	Yarn Cottage at Red Brick Farm	5031 W. Lake Rd.	(716) 753-5696	
Medina	A Knitters Corner	111 W. Center St.	(585) 798-5648	
Merrick	Needlepaint Nook	76 N. Merrick Ave.	(516) 623-0250	
Middletown	American Needleworks	10 North St.	(845) 699-6405	
Miller Place	Knitters Knitche	745 Rte. 25A	(631) 849-4684	
Millerton	Copper Star Alpaca	132 Carson Rd.	(518) 592-1414	
Mohawk	The Pincushion Patch	3659 State Rte. 168	(315) 868-8586	
Monroe	Everything You Needle	59 Forest Rd. #301	(845) 783-1494	
Montauk	Purl By The Sea	25 Pocahontas Ln.	(631) 668-7875	
Montgomery	Montgomery Mills Inc.	23 Factory St.	(845) 457-9241	
Mt. Kisco	Pins & Needles	159 Lexington Ave.	(914) 666-0824	
Mumford	Old Mill Shoppe at the Genesee Country Inn	948 George St.	(585) 538-2500	
Naples	Carriage House Quilts	201 N. Main St.	(585) 374-9580	
Naples	Winderwood Country Store	1669 State Rte. 245	(585) 554-3554	
Nesconset	Keep Me In Stitches	127 Smithtown Blvd. #14	(631) 724-8111	
New Hartford	Sew Wilde Quilt	3987 Oneida St.	(315) 765-0157	
New Paltz	White Barn Farm Sheep & Wool	815 Albany Post Rd.	(914) 456-6040	
New York	B&J Fabrics	525 7th Ave. 2nd Floor	(212) 354-8150	
New York	Downtown Yarns	45 Ave. A	(212) 995-5991	
New York	Knitting 321	321 E. 75th St.	(212) 772-2020	
New York	Knitty City	208 W. 79th St.	(212) 787-5896	
New York	Lion Brand Yarn Studio	34 W. 15th St.	(212) 243-9070	
New York	Loop of the Loom	227 E. 87th St.	(212) 722-2686	
New York	Paron Fabrics	206 W. 40th St.	(212) 768-3266	
New York	Purl Patchwork	147 Sullivan St.	(800) 597-7875	
New York	Purl Soho	459 Broome St.	(212) 420-8796	
New York	Rita's Needlepoint	150 E. 79th St.	(212) 737-8613	
New York	Seaport Yarn	181 Broadway 5th Floor	(212) 220-5230	
New York	String Yarns NYC	144 E. 74th St.	(212) 288-9276	
New York	The Yarn Co.	2274 Broadway #1C	(212) 787-7878	
New York	Vardhman Inc.	269 W. 39th St.	(212) 840-6950	
New York City	**Annie & Company**	**1763 2nd Ave.**	**(212) 360-7266**	**Pg. 280**
New York City	Gotham Quilts	40 W. 37th St. #603	(212) 220-3958	
Newcomb	Aunt Polly's Material Girls	3 Hudson River Dr.	(518) 582-2260	
Niagara Falls	Auntie's Attic Quilt Shop	1995 Military Rd.	(716) 297-3636	
Niagara Falls	Quiltmakers and Friends	6404 Packard Rd.	(716) 297-4067	
North Syracuse	Sheep Thrills Yarn Company	503 N. Main St.	(315) 458-0048	
North Tonawanda	Raveloe Fibers	7296 Schultz Rd.	(716) 695-7464	
North Tonawanda	Teddy Bear Fabrics	64 Webster St.	(716) 692-4756	
Norwich	Sew Nice	6142 State Hwy. 12	(607) 334-2477	
Nyack	Knitting Nation	30 N. Broadway	(845) 348-0100	
Nyack	The Quilt Tree	9 S. Broadway	(845) 353-1501	
Oakland Gardens	Sew Time Sewing	7835 Springfield Blvd.	(718) 776-1900	
Oceanside	The Knitting Store, LLC	2 Poole St.	(516) 442-0722	
Old Forge	Old Forge Hardware	104 Fulton St.	(315) 369-6100	
Oneonta	**Country Fabrics & Quilts**	**6187 St. Hwy. 23**	**(607) 432-9726**	**Pg. 276**
Oxford	Shadeyside Farm	109 Brown Rd.	(607) 843-8243	
Oyster Bay	The Knitted Purl	80 South St.	(516) 558-7800	
Parrishville	Handiworks Quilt Shop	20 Picketville Rd.	(315) 265-2670	
Patchogue	112 Sewing Supplies, Inc.	142 Rte. 112	(631) 475-8282	
Pawling	Quilt Basket	4D Oak St.	(845) 227-7606	
Pawling	The Yarn & Craft Box	24 Charles Coleman Blvd.	(845) 855-1632	
Pearl River	The Stitchery	49 E. Central Ave.	(845) 735-4534	
Peekskill	Cozy Corner Yarn Shop	116 Washington St.	(914) 737-0179	
Penn Yan	**Golden Lane Fabrics**	**3732 State Rte. 14A**	**(315) 536-8342**	**Pg. 275**
Penn Yan	Country Quest	2358 Bellona Station Rd.	(315) 536-4878	
Penn Yan	Weaver View Farms	386 State Rte. 14	(315) 781-2571	
Perry Center	**The Quilter's Daughter**	**2817 State Rte. 246**	**(585) 770-4926**	**Pg. 275**
Pine Bush	**Quilter's Attic**	**118 Maple Ave.**	**(845) 744-5888**	**Pg. 280**
Pittsford	The Yarne Source	7 Schoen Place	(585) 662-5615	
Plainview	The Fabric Mill	219 S. Service Rd.	(516) 465-6400	
Port Chester	Nimble Thimble	21 Putnam Ave.	(914) 934-2934	
Port Jefferson	The Knitting Cove	218 E. Main St.	(631) 473-2121	
Port Jefferson Station				
	Beyond the Thimble	**1597 Rte. 112 #103**	**(631) 737-3944**	**Pg. 281**
Port Washington	Knitting Place	191 Main St. #4	(516) 944-9276	
Queensbury	The Yarn Angel	318 Ridge St.	(518) 761-2031	
Randolph	Yarn for Ewe	129 Main St.	(716) 267-2070	
Red Hook	Hudson Valley Sheep & Wool CO.	190 Yantz Rd.	(845) 758-3130	
Red Hook	The Village Fabric Shoppe	7578 N. Broadway #4	(845) 758-8541	
Remsen	Woolhaven Yarn & Fiber Shop	10071 Bardwell Mills Rd.	(315) 794-3769	

Rensselaer Falls	Susan's Stitches	216 B Rensselaer St.	(315) 344-5043	
Rhinebeck	The Knitting Garage at Stickles	13 E. Market St.	(845) 876-3206	
Richville	Hart Country Fabrics	115 County Rte. 20	(315) 287-3250	
Ripley	Concord Quilting Studio	9009 Old Rte. 20	(716) 753-6996	
Rochester	The Bobbin Case	1784 Monroe Ave.	(585) 244-7780	
Rochester	**Quilting With Margaret**	**1115 E. Main St.**	**(505) 780-5030**	**Pg. 275**
Rockville Centre	Lazy Daisy Stitchery	218 Merrick Rd.	(516) 764-7500	
Rome	**Stash Away Quilt Shoppe**	**1249 Erie Blvd. W.**	**(315) 533-7611**	**Pg. 277**
Rome	Carol's Crafts	1245 Erie Blvd. W.	(315) 336-3785	
Rome	Sweethearts Stamps and Stitches	304 N. George St.	(315) 337-6279	
Roslyn	Knit	1353 Old Northern Blvd.	(516) 625-5648	
Rushford	The Barefoot Quilter	9005 Main St.	(585) 437-2241	
Salem	Fiber Kingdom	137 E. Broadway	(518) 854-7225	
Salem	Simple Pleasures Yarns	588 Chamberlain Mill Rd.	(518) 854-9543	
Salem	The Quilting Beaver	217 Main St.	(518) 854-8120	
Sandy Creek	Mary's Needleart Supplies	Rt. 11 S.	(315) 387-5903	
Saratoga Springs	**KC Framing and Fabrics**	**67 Davidson Dr.**	**(518) 580-9055**	**Pg. 279**
Saratoga Springs	Common Thread Saratoga	508 Broadway	(518) 583-2583	
Saratoga Springs	Gloversville Sewing Center	426 Maple Ave.	(518) 584-2695	
Saugerties	Pinewoods Farm Wool Shop	71 Phillips Rd.	(845) 246-2203	
Saugerties	The Prefect Blend Yarn and Tea Shop	50 Market St.	(845) 246-2876	
Savannah	Springlake Fabrics	4250 Wolcott Spring Lake Rd.	(315) 594-8485	
Schenectady	Quiltbug	3637 Carman St.	(518) 280-2586	
Schenectady	The Homespun Heart	1029 Roberta Rd.	(518) 356-0165	
Schuylerville	The Yarn Shop at Foster Sheep Farm	460 W. River Rd.	(518) 338-6679	
Selkirk	**Log Cabin Fabrics**	**1145 Rte. 9 W.**	**(518) 767-2040**	**Pg. 280**
Sherman (Findley Lake)	**Fabric Outlet Barn & Needle in a Haystack Retreat**			
		3141 North Rd.	**(814) 882-0411**	**Pg. 274**
Sidney Center	**The Fieldstone House**	**1884 Wheat Hill Rd.**	**(607) 369-9177**	**Pg. 278**
Skaneateles	Elegant Needles	7 Jordan St.	(315) 685-9276	
Snyder	Have Ewe Any Wool?	4551 Main St.	(716) 839-7800	
Sodus	The Quilting Bee	10 Maple Ave.	(315) 553-2383	
South Glens Falls	Adirondack Quilts	22 5th St.	(518) 615-0134	
South Hampton	Hildreth's Dept. Store	51 Main St.	(800) 462-1842	
Springville	Fabric Cottage	33 Pearl St.	(716) 592-4350	
Staten Island	Crafting on the Plaza with M&M	1194 Hyland Blvd.	(718) 442-0859	
Staten Island	The Naked Sheep	4038 Victory Blvd.	(718) 477-9276	
Staten Island	Wild & Wooly Needlepoint	18 New Dorp Ln.	(718) 987-7000	
Sterling	Maplegrove Wool Boutique	1275 State Rt. 104A	(315) 947-5408	
Syracuse	Calico Gals	3906 New Court Ave.	(315) 445-0617	
Syracuse	Seams Possible Quilt Shoppe	1201 W. Genesee St.	(315) 314-7829	
Tarrytown	Flying Fingers Yarn Shop	15 Main St.	(914) 631-4113	
Tivoli	Fabulousyarn	54 A Broadway	(845) 757-4322	
Troy	Eastside Weavers	1 Carlyle Ave.	(518) 274-1931	
Troy	Lansingburgh Yarn Depot	366 Grange Rd. Rte. 142	(518) 233-1052	
Troy	Pookie's Fabrics	615 Pawling Ave.	(518) 272-6479	
Tupper Lake	Affordable Quilting	85 Broad St.	(518) 359-8086	
Utica	**Tiger Lily Quilt Company**	**809 Court St.**	**(315) 735-5328**	**Pg. 277**
Verona	Liberty Ridge Yarns	6175 Greenway Lowell Rd.	(315) 337-7217	
Victor	**Ivy Thimble Quilt & Gift Shop**	**11 Framark Dr.**	**(585) 742-2680**	**Pg. 276**
Walton	A Quilt of Many Colors	137 Stockton Ave.	(607) 510-4033	
Warwick	Sewcology, Inc.	19 West St.	(845) 987-8435	
Waterloo	Waterloo Woolens	13 W. Main St.	(315) 539-3288	
Watertown	Just Threads	22440 Swan Rd.	(315) 782-1674	
Watkins Glen	Fiber Arts in the Glen	315 N. Franklin St.	(607) 535-9710	
Wayland	Pollywogs	7 Bush Ave.	(585) 728-5667	
Webster	Café Sewciety Quilts	2126 Empire Blvd.	(585) 347-4852	
Weedsport	Lucky Frog Fabrics	2762 E. Brutus St.	(315) 834-3006	
West Danby	Susan's Spinning Bunny	311B Tupper Rd.	(607) 564-7178	
Westfield	Wool Works	7265 Martin Wright Rd.	(716) 326-2848	
White Plains	White Plains Sewing	200 Hamilton Ave.	(914) 682-0595	
Williamsville	Aurora Sewing Center	8575 Main St.	(716) 204-8350	
Williamsville (Amherst)	**Sew What?**	**6816 Main St.**	**(716) 632-8801**	**Pg. 275**
Windham	The Patchwork Co.	5326 State Rte. 23	(518) 734-6838	
Woodridge	Needlepoint Gallery & More	51 Broadway	(845) 434-1834	
Worchester	The Quilt Zoo	88 Main St.	(607) 397-9047	
Wynantskill	Martha's Treasures Boutique	22 Main Ave.	(518) 221-2736	
Yaphank	Long Island Livestock Co.	125 Gerard Rd.	(631) 680-6721	
York	Mt. Pleasant Quilting Company	2877 Mt. Pleasant Rd.	(585) 243-0767	
Yorktown Heights	Fabric Mart-NY	2019 Crompond Rd.	(914) 962-3328	

Index

Notes

Did you know?
The Statue of Liberty is a colossal neoclassical sculpture on
Liberty Island in New York Harbor in New York City, in the United States. The copper statue,
esigned by Frédéric Auguste Bartholdi, a French sculptor, was built by Gustave Eiffel and dedicated on
October 28, 1886. It was a gift to the United States from the people of France.
The statue is of a robed female figure representing Libertas, the Roman goddess, who bears a torch and a
tabula ansata upon which is inscribed the date of the American Declaration of Independence, July 4, 1776.
A broken chain lies at her feet. The statue is an icon of freedom and of the United States,
and was a welcoming sight to immigrants arriving from abroad.

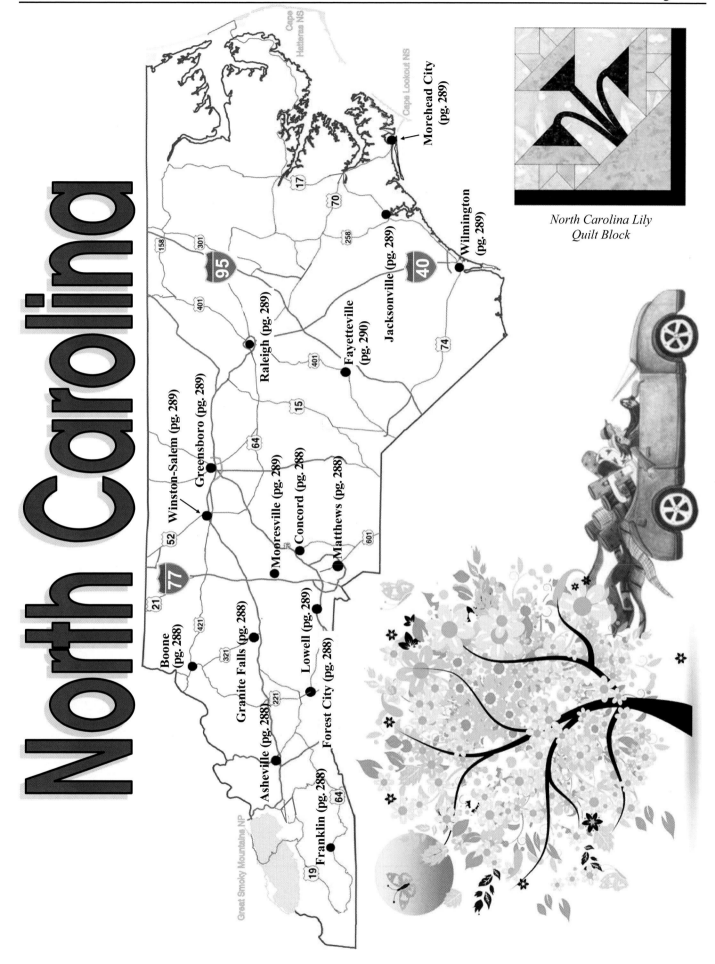

North Carolina

Morehead City (pg. 289)

Wilmington (pg. 289)

Jacksonville (pg. 289)

Fayetteville (pg. 290)

Raleigh (pg. 289)

Greensboro (pg. 289)

Winston-Salem (pg. 289)

Mooresville (pg. 289)

Concord (pg. 288)

Matthews (pg. 288)

Boone (pg. 288)

Granite Falls (pg. 288)

Lowell (pg. 289)

Forest City (pg. 288)

Asheville (pg. 288)

Franklin (pg. 288)

North Carolina Lily
Quilt Block

The Inn on Biltmore Estate

Built in 1895 and one of Asheville's finest hotels, the Inn sits on the grounds of Biltmore Estate, the Châteauesque-style mansion built by George and Edith Vanderbilt. The gorgeous setting, complete with pool, fine-dining restaurant, and an envy-inducing library might make you feel like you are American royalty, just like the Vanderbilt's.

1 Antler Hill Rd, Asheville, NC 28803
(828) 225-1600
www.biltmore.com

North Carolina Shops

Q-Quilting ~ Y-Yarn ~ N-Needlework ~ R-Retreat ~ M-Museum

City	Shop	Address	Phone	Page
Ahoskie	Southern Purls	606 NC 561 E .	(252) 287-8469	
Andrews	Valleytown Quilt Shop	955 Main St.	(828) 321-2800	
Angier	Sew There!	27 E. Depot St.	(919) 331-2499	
Apex	DownTown Knits Yarns & Teas	122 N. Salem St.	(919) 249-5638	
Asheville	**Ashville Cotton Company**	**1378 Hendersonville Rd.**	**(828) 277-4100**	**Pg. 288**
Asheville	Asheville Custom Framing	856 Merrimon Ave.	(828) 252-8001	
Asheville	Asheville NC Home Crafts	1 Page Ave. Ste. 134A	(828) 350-7556	
Asheville	Earth Guild	33 Haywood St.	(828) 255-7818	
Asheville	Purls Yarn Emporium	10 Wall St.	(828) 253-2750	
Asheville	The Knitting Diva	61 Merrimon Ave. Ste. 13	(828) 247-0344	
Asheville	Yummi Yarns	18 Brook St. #105B	(828) 575-2094	
Belmont	Quilted Thimble Cottage	26 N. Main St. #2	(704) 266-6445	
Black Mountain	Periwinkles	102 Cherry St.	(828) 664-1700	
Blowing Rock	Unwound Yarn	1132 Main St. #105	(828) 295-5051	
Boone	**Sew Original**	**1542-G 421 S.**	**(828) 264-1049**	**Pg. 288**
Boone	**The Quilt Shop, Inc.**	**2348 Hwy. 105**	**(828) 263-8691**	**Pg. 288**
Bunn	The Broken Needle	219 NC Hwy. 98 E.	(919) 497-0828	
Burnsville	The Scrap Basket	208 W. Blvd.	(828) 208-0077	
Burnsville	Yummiyarns	17 W. Main St.	(828) 678-9890	
Candler	Friends & Fiberworks	19 Westridge Market Place	(828) 633-2500	
Cary	Cary Quilting Company	935 N. Harrison Ave.	(919) 238-9739	
Cary	Warm 'n Fuzzy	200 S. Academy St. #140	(919) 380-0008	
Chapel Hill	Chapel Hill Needlepoint	1705-A Legion Rd.	(919) 929-3999	
Chapel Hill	Yarns Etc.	1322 Fordham Blvd. #4	(919) 928-8810	
Charlotte	Charlotte Yarn	1235 E. Blvd.	(704) 373-7442	
Charlotte	Cottage Yarn	7717 Matthews Mint Hill Rd.	(704) 545-8440	
Charlotte	Lee's Sewing Center	7888-D Rea Rd.	(704) 542-8760	
Charlotte	Po's Point	6700 Fairview Rd. #106	(704) 553-8777	
Charlotte	The Fibre Studio at Yarns to Dye For	658 Griffith Rd. #107	(704) 614-4745	
Clayton	Sew Happy Fabrics	100 Pecan Ln. #101	(919) 359-8500	
Concord	**We're Sew Creative**	**8637 Concord Mills Rd.**	**(704) 971-0351**	**Pg. 288**
Davidson	The Needlecraft Center	102 S. Main St.	(704) 892-8988	
Denver	A Tangled Yarn Shop	3692 N. Hwy. 16 #4	(704) 966-1300	
Dillsboro	Yarn Corner	64 Front St.	(828) 586-3420	
Dunn	Memories in Stitches	214 E. Broad St.	(910) 292-2391	
Durham	Cozy	770 Ninth St.	(919) 286-3400	
Elizabeth City	B & P Yarn Hut	1249 US. 17 #3	(252) 333-3276	
Elizabeth City	Quilts & More	1092 Commissary Rd.	(252) 338-9500	
Elkin	Circle of Friends Yarn Shop	120 W. Main St.	(336) 526-3100	
Fayetteville	**Loving Stitches**	**7076 Ramsey St.**	**(910) 630-3912**	**Pg. 290**
Fayetteville	All Things By Hand	25 Market Sq.	(910) 703-8585	
Fayetteville	Crafts, Frames & Things, Inc.	108 Owen Dr.	(910) 485-4833	
Fletcher	Foam & Fabrics Outlet	3049 Hendersonville Rd.	(828) 684-0801	
Fletcher	Quilters On The Go	235 St. John Rd.	(828) 692-6100	
Forest City	**Schoolhouse Quilts**	**399 Sunset Memorial Rd.**	**(828) 245-9774**	**Pg. 288**
Franklin	**A Stitch in Time**	**23 Macon Center Dr.**	**(828) 524-3300**	**Pg. 288**
Franklin	Sassy Stitches	106 W. Palmer St.	(828) 349-8912	
Franklin	Sew Creative	91 Highlands Rd.	(828) 524-5221	
Franklin	Silver Threads & Golden Needle	41 E Main St.	(828) 349-0515	
Fuquay Varina	Lone Star Mercantile	1501 N. Main	(919) 557-0202	
Gastonia	Mary Jo's Cloth Store, Inc	401 Cox Rd.	(704) 861-9100	
Gastonia	Things Remembered Framing & Unique Gifts	3805 S. New Hope Rd.	(704) 824-0473	
Granite Falls	**The Cotton Quilt**	**4900 Troy Rd.**	**(828) 726-6786**	**Pg. 288**
Greensboro	**Studio Stitch**	**3215 Battleground Ave.**	**(336) 288-9200**	**Pg. 289**
Greensboro	Calla Lily Quilts	2921 Battleground Ave. #E	(336) 763-0528	
Greensboro	Gate City Yarns	231 S. Elm St.	(336) 370-1233	
Greensboro	McKinney Sewing	1710 Battleground Ave.	(336) 274-6793	
Greensboro	Studio Stitch	3715 Battleground Ave.	(336) 288-9200	

Greensboro	Ye Olde Forest Quilters	107 Creek Ridge Rd. #H	(336) 339-5190	
Greenville	Sewing Creations	2508 Charles Blvd.	(252) 321-0829	
Harrisburg	The Quilter's Station	8401 Live Oak Rd.	(704) 455-5236	
Hayesville	Just Stitchin	321 Hwy. 64 W.	(828) 644-3368	
Hayesville	Two Busy Hands	68 Sanderson St.	(828) 371-4030	
Henderson	Yarny & Sassy	131 S. Garnett St.	(252) 432-5601	
Hendersonville	Beginnings Quilt Shop	1032-C Greenville Hwy.	(828) 693-6622	
Hendersonville	Sandy's X-Stitch On The Go	918 Kanuga Rd.	(828) 693-4499	
Hendersonville	The Wool Room	630 Boxcar St.	(828) 692-7373	
Hendersonville	Yarns To Dye For	927 Greenville Hwy.	(980) 475-4705	
Hickory	Lee Sewing Center	2361 US. Hwy. 70 SE	(828) 327-6888	
Hickory	Wildskeins Yarn Co.	131 NC Hwy. 127 SE	(828) 322-9276	
Highlands	Needlepoint of Highlands	210 N. 5th St.	(828) 526-3901	
Hillsborough	Hillsborough Yarn Shop	114 S. Churton St.	(919) 732-2128	
Huntersville	Knit One Stitch Too	9709 Sam Furr Rd. #C	(704) 655-9558	
Icard	Strings N Things	7718 Old NC #10	(828) 397-3861	
Jacksonville	**All About Quilting**	**3736 Henderson Rd.**	**(910) 577-9200**	**Pg. 289**
Kannapolis	Ben Franklin Crafts	875 Cloverleaf Plaza	(704) 788-7921	
Kernersville	Maggies Crochet	705 Graves St.	(336) 992-0054	
King	Papanana	145 Retail Cir.	(336) 983-0400	
Kings Mountain	Carolina Cotton Company	227 S Battleground Ave.	(704) 750-4164	
Kitty Hawk	Knitting Addiction, LLC	3708 N. Croatan Hwy. #2	(252) 255-5648	
Lenoir	Chix with Stix	108 Main St. NW	(828) 758-0081	
Lenoir	The Last Stitch	2018 Connelly Springs Rd.	(828) 244-2537	
Lewisville	Sewingly Yours	1329 Lewisville Clemmons Rd.	(336) 766-8271	
Lexington	The Stitchin' Magician	110 G Cotton Grove Rd.	(336) 247-1206	
Lowell	**Sew Much Fun!**	**831 S. Church St.**	**(704) 824-1961**	**Pg. 289**
Madison	Stitch Party Studio	124 W. Murphy St.	(336) 427-7144	
Manteo	Shoreline Handw0rks	4250 Maritime Woods Dr.	(252) 473-2271	
Matthews	**Quilt Patch Fabrics**	**1017 Stallings Rd.**	**(704) 821-7554**	**Pg. 288**
Mebane	The Twisted Knitter	109 N. Third St.	(919) 563-2468	
Mooresville	**Quilters Loft Co.**	**109 Professional Park Dr. #103**		
			(704) 662-8660	**Pg. 289**
Morehead City	**The Quilted Butterfly**	**110 Little 9 Rd.**	**(252) 222-0787**	**Pg. 289**
Morganton	Morganton Sewing Center	128 N. Sterling St.	(828) 439-8050	
Morganton	Osuzannah's Yarn on Union	130 W. Union St.	(828) 430-3300	
Mount Airy	Creative Sewing Machines	247 N. Main St.	(336) 786-7074	
Mount Airy	Oopsy Daisy Fabric Boutique	411 N. Main	(336) 648-8161	
Mt. Airy	What's Needlin' Ewe	300 N. Main St.	(336) 789-5648	
Murphy	Bless My Stitches Quilt Shop	498 Hill St.	(828) 835-4900	
New Bern	Mill Outlet Village	3915 ML King Jr. Blvd.	(252) 633-5675	
New Bern	New Bern Fabric Center	1218 S. Glenburnie Rd.	(252) 633-4780	
New Bern	Sewing on the River	127 Market St.	(252) 671-0611	
New Bern	Sewing Solutions	1505 S. Glenburnie Rd. #G	(252) 633-1799	
Newton	Our Home Quilt Shop	1094 N. Rankin Ave.	(828) 461-8723	
North Wilkesboro	Gloria Sews	303 10th St.	(336) 818-0940	
North Wilkesboro	Sew Blessed Quiltworks	201 Sparta Rd. #A	(336) 818-0852	
Pinehurst	Moore than Needlepoint	850 Linden Rd.	(910) 295-3727	
Plymouth	Yearning for Yarn	109 W. Water St.	(252) 793-2500	
Raleigh	**Bernina World of Sewing**	**6013 Glenwood Ave.**	**(919) 782-2945**	**Pg. 289**
Raleigh	Admit Ewe Knit	8320 Litchford Rd. Ste. 146	(919) 876-4640	
Raleigh	Great Yarns Inc.	1208 Ridge Rd.	(919)-832-3599	
Raleigh	My Sewing Shoppe	5910 Duraleigh Rd. #139	(919) 784-9300	
Raleigh	Needlepoint.com	3811 Hillsborough St.	(888)-769-7446	
Raleigh	Thread Waggle Quilting	8521 Cantilever Way	(919) 576-9897	
Raleigh	Wish Upon A Quilt	8817 Westgate Park Dr. #104	(919) 782-6363	
Richlands	The Tail Spinner	109 N. Wilmington St.	(910) 324-6166	
Rockwell	Andersons Sew & So	10104 Old Beatty Ford Rd.	(704) 279-3647	
Saluda	Knitcality	55 Robin Ln.	(828) 749-3640	
Sanford	Find X Designs	719 Carthage St.	(919) 774-4700	
Shelby	Lee's Sewing Center	114 W. Graham St.	(704) 487-5224	
Siler City	Against His Will Gallery and Studio	117 E. Second St.	(919) 742-1122	
Southern Pines	Bella Filati Yarns	277 NE Broad St.	(910) 692-3528	
Southport	Angelwing Needleworks	507 N. Howe St.	(910) 454-9163	
Spruce Pine	Fabrics in The Fray	2601 Hwy. 19 E. #2	(828) 467-3991	
Statesville	foothill fiberarts	107 E. Broad St.	(704) 871-1030	
Statesville	JS Quilt and Craft Shop	1250 Northside Dr.	(704) 871-1939	
Statesville	Needle and Thread	101 S. Center St.	(704) 838-1100	
Stedman	A Row Of Purls	175 E. 1st St.	(910) 483-3678	
Swansboro	The Salty Sheep Yarn Shop	101 W. Church St. #4	(910) 325-0018	

Wake Forest	Creative Threads	992 Durham Rd.	(984) 235-1208	
Wake Forest	Quilt Lizzy	12223 Hampston Way #100	(919) 570-0777	
Wake Forest	Quilts Like Crazy	1241 S Main St. Ste. 8	(919) 562-3425	
Wake Forest	Whatever's Quilted	11829 Retail Dr.	(888) 546-0665	
Warrenton	Quilt Lizzy	110 E. Macon St.	(252) 257-7117	
Washington	Cotton Fields Quilt Shop	3751 Wharton Station Rd.	(252) 948-0372	
Waxhaw	Tangles Knitting on Main	200 W. North Main St.	(704) 243-7150	
Waynesville	J Creek Fabrics	3391 Dellwood Rd.	(828) 400-0276	
Waynesville	Quilters Quarters	1510 Dellwood Rd.	(828) 926-0803	
Weaverville	5 Little Monkeys Quilt and Sew	32 N. Main St.	(828) 484-7200	
Wendell	Ladybug's Cottage Inc.	5 N. Main St.	(919) 365-3636	
Wilmington	**Fran's Sewing Circle**	**5751 Oleander Dr. Unit 5**	**(910) 397-9399**	**Pg. 289**
Wilmington	Bay Country Boutique	104 Travelers Ct.	(910) 392-9469	
Wilmington	Mill Outlet Village	515 S. College Rd.	(910) 392-0287	
Wilmington	Quilting-N-Crafts-N-Things	1616 Shipyard Blvd. #16	(910) 444-4503	
Wilmington	Sew Happins Creative Studio	413 S. College Rd. Units 11-12	(910) 399-4935	
Wilmington	Yarns of Wilmington Needlepoint Too	3401 1/2 Wrightsville Ave.	(910) 791-2157	
Winston Salem	Village Fabric Shop	114 R Reynolda Village	(336) 779-6155	
Winston-Salem	**Sew Original**	**3358 Robinhood Rd.**	**(336) 760-1121**	**Pg. 289**
Winston-Salem	Fox in the Hen's House Quilt & Knit	5365 Robinhood Rd.	(336) 922-5894	
Winston-Salem	Knit One Smock Too, Inc.	4003-A Country Club Rd.	(336) 765-9099	
Woodleaf	Little Country Quilt Shop	840 Parks Rd.	(704) 278-1773	

Index

Notes

North Dakota

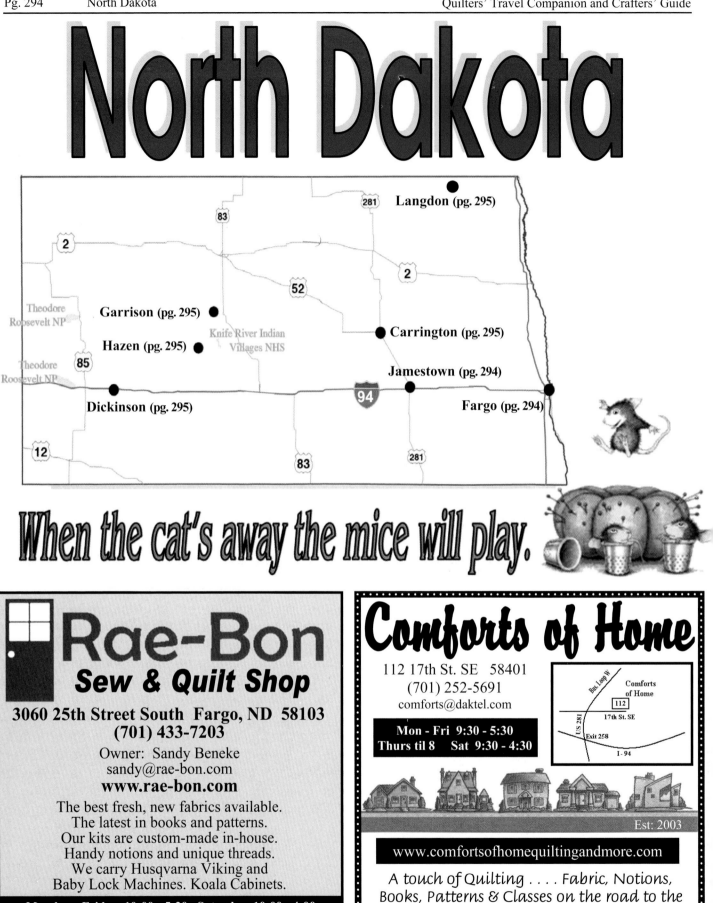

Langdon (pg. 295)

Garrison (pg. 295)

Hazen (pg. 295)

Carrington (pg. 295)

Jamestown (pg. 294)

Dickinson (pg. 295)

Fargo (pg. 294)

Theodore Roosevelt NP

Theodore Roosevelt NP

Knife River Indian Villages NHS

When the cat's away the mice will play.

Dakota Gold Quilt Block

Notes

North Dakota Shops

Q-Quilting ~ Y-Yarn ~ N-Needlework ~ R-Retreat ~ M-Museum

Bismarck	Bismarck Sewing & Quilting	1300 Skyline Blvd.	(701) 258-5139	
Bismarck	J & R Vacuum & Sewing, The Quilt Shop	223 E. Main Ave.	(800) 371-5515	
Bottineau	Simple Threads Quilt Shop	120 11th St. W.	(701) 228-2180	
Arrington	**Designer Fabrics**	**6711 Hwy. 200**	**(701) 652-3535**	**Pg. 295**
Devils Lake	Quilt Essential	206 5th St. NE	(701) 662-3634	
Dickinson	**Dakota Sew and So**	**2797 3rd Ave. W.**	**(701)-225-1408**	**Pg. 295**
Enderlin	Stone Ridge Quilting	13991 54th St. SE	(701) 437-2013	
Fargo	**Rae-Bon Sew and Quilt Shop**	**3060 25th St. S.**	**(701) 433-7203**	**Pg. 294**
Fargo	Modern Textiles	17 S. 7th St.	(701) 566-8749	
Fargo	Prairie Yarns	2607 S. University Dr.	(701) 280-1478	
Garrison	**This That 'N More**	**62 N. Main St.**	**(701) 463-2671**	**Pg. 295**
Garrison	Merry Moose Quilt Shoppe	11 N. Main	(701) 463-2199	
Hazen	**Quilts From the Heart & More**	**213 1st Ave. NW**	**(701) 748-3999**	**Pg. 295**
Hettinger	Buffalo Creek Quilt Shop	218 S. Main St.	(701) 567-2277	
Jamestown	**Comforts of Home**	**112 17th St. SE**	**(701) 252-5691**	**Pg. 294**
Langdon	**Sew On & Sew North**	**706 3rd St.**	**(701) 256-2526**	**Pg. 295**
Mandan	Sewing Machines Plus!	322 West Main St.	(701) 663-9025	
Mayville	Sew Batik	879 W. Main St.	(877) 235-5025	
Minot	Bernina Plus	104 S. Main St.	(701) 837-5638	
Minot	Good Vibrations Quilt Shop	213 7th St. SE	(701) 839-5645	
Minot	Prairie Rose Quilt Shop	1500 53rd Ave. SW	(701)-852-2835	
Minot	The Yarn Stash	107 Central Ave. W.	(701) 839-4099	
Oakes	Quilt-n-Sew, LLC	514 Main Ave.	(701) 742-2642	
Rugby	Theresa's Quilting Lodge	510 S. Main Ave.	(701) 881-1111	
Valley City	Quilted Ceiling	316 Central N.	(701) 845-4926	
Wishek	Rumpelquiltskin	18 N. 5th St.	(701) 452-6100	

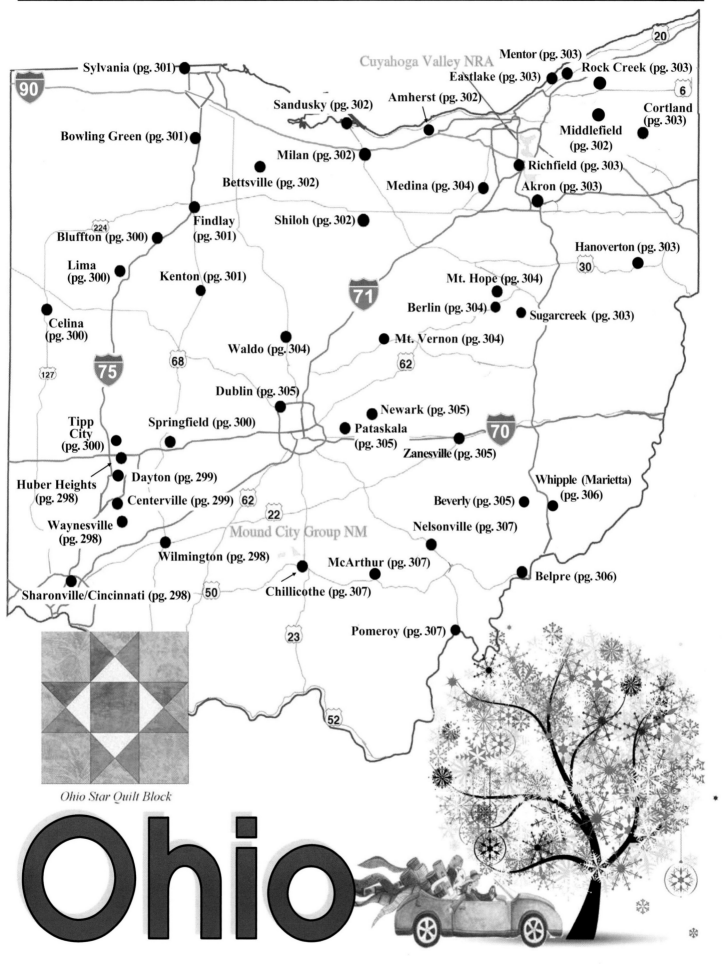

Sylvania (pg. 301)

Mentor (pg. 303)

Rock Creek (pg. 303)

Eastlake (pg. 303)

Cuyahoga Valley NRA

Sandusky (pg. 302)

Amherst (pg. 302)

Cortland (pg. 303)

Middlefield (pg. 302)

Bowling Green (pg. 301)

Milan (pg. 302)

Richfield (pg. 303)

Bettsville (pg. 302)

Medina (pg. 304)

Akron (pg. 303)

Findlay (pg. 301)

Shiloh (pg. 302)

Bluffton (pg. 300)

Hanoverton (pg. 303)

Lima (pg. 300)

Kenton (pg. 301)

Mt. Hope (pg. 304)

Berlin (pg. 304)

Sugarcreek (pg. 303)

Celina (pg. 300)

Waldo (pg. 304)

Mt. Vernon (pg. 304)

Dublin (pg. 305)

Tipp City (pg. 300)

Springfield (pg. 300)

Newark (pg. 305)

Pataskala (pg. 305)

Whipple (Marietta) (pg. 306)

Huber Heights (pg. 298)

Dayton (pg. 299)

Zanesville (pg. 305)

Centerville (pg. 299)

Beverly (pg. 305)

Waynesville (pg. 298)

Nelsonville (pg. 307)

Belpre (pg. 306)

Mound City Group NM

Wilmington (pg. 298)

McArthur (pg. 307)

Sharonville/Cincinnati (pg. 298)

Chillicothe (pg. 307)

Pomeroy (pg. 307)

Ohio Star Quilt Block

Ohio

The Golden Lamb Inn
Established in 1803, The Golden Lamb holds the title of oldest hotel in Ohio, and it also happens to house the state's oldest restaurant as well. Twelve American presidents have paid visits to Lebanon, and stayed at the historic, colonial-style establishment.
27 S Broadway St, Lebanon, OH 45036
(513) 932-5065 - www.goldenlamb.com

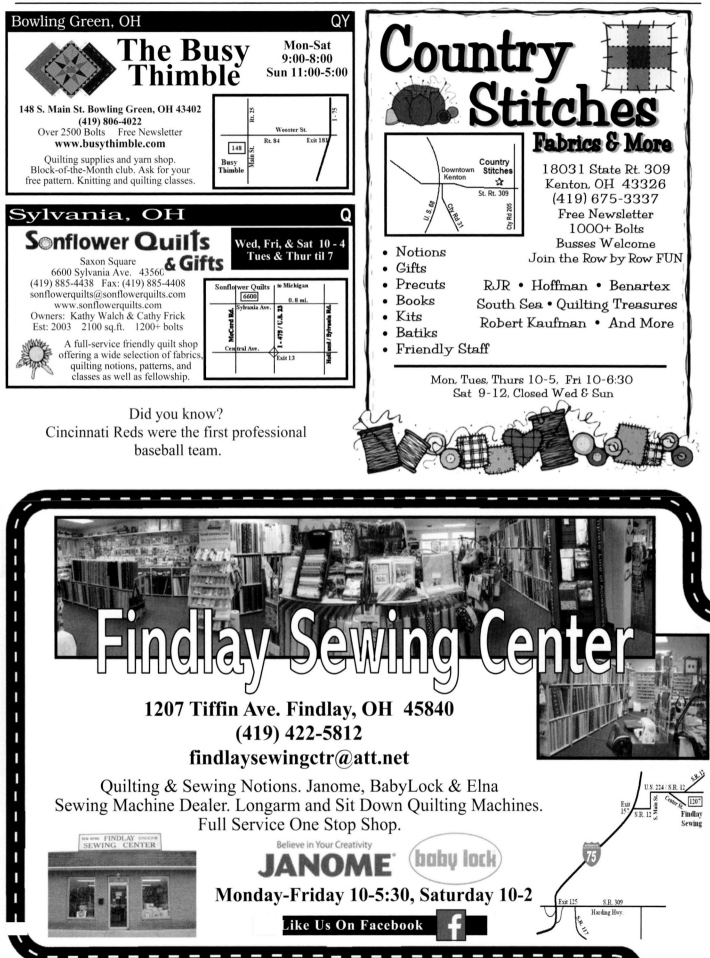

I ♥ Quilting

Did you know?
Ohio was the birthplace of many U.S. presidents,
including Ulysses S. Grant, Rutherford B. Hayes,
James A. Garfield, Benjamin Harrison,
William McKinley, William Howard Taft,
And Warren G. Harding.

Ohio Shops

Q-Quilting ~ Y-Yarn ~ N-Needlework ~ R-Retreat ~ M-Museum

Akron	**Ohio Star Quilts**	**2383 S. Main St. C101**	**(330) 644-6100**	**Pg. 303**
Akron	Blueberry Hill Stitchery	880 Mull Ave. #101	(330) 864-9688	
Albany	Fiber FUN Studio	28743 Gaston Rd.	(740) 698-0101	
Amherst	**Mom's Sewing Basket**	**1907 Cooper Foster Park Rd.**	**(440) 984-1444**	**Pg. 302**
Apple Creek	Pine Tree Fabric	12464 Western Rd.	(330) 857-3651	
Arcanum	Smith Merchants and Quilterie	109 W. George St.	(937) 692-6300	
Archbold	Sauder's Village--Threads of Tradition	22611 State Rt. 2	(419) 445-9610	
Ashland	Suzie Homemaker Fabrics n More	508 Claremont Ave.	(419) 752-9020	
Athens	Dairy Barn Arts Center	8000 Dairy Ln.	(740) 592-4981	
Aurora	The Knit Shop	226 S. Chillicothe Rd.	(330) 562-7226	
Avon	French Creek Fiber Arts	36840 Detroit Rd.	(440) 934-1236	
Beavercreek	Fiberworks	1350A N. Fairfield Rd.	(937) 429-9276	
Beavercreek	Stitching Cottage	1263 N. Fairfield Rd.	(937) 320-9055	
Bellefontaine	Coblentz Crafts and Fabrics	5451 County Rd. 25	(937) 468-2081	
Bellefontaine	Sewing & Yarn Shop	118 N. Main St.	(937) 592-1885	
Belpre	**Neff's Country Loft**	**2514 Washington Blvd.**	**(740) 423-1965**	**Pg. 306**
Belpre	Sew Happy Quilting Traditions	407 Washington Blvd.		
Berea	Abigayle's Quiltery	591 W. Bagley Rd.	(440) 239-9000	
Berlin	**Gramma Fannie's Quilt Barn**	**4363 State Rt. 39**	**(330) 893-3243**	**Pg. 304**
Berlin	**Helping Hands Quilt Shop**	**4818 Main St.**	**(330) 893-2233**	**Pg. 304**
Berlin	Country Craft Cupboard	4813 E. Main St.	(330) 893-3163	
Berlin	Spector's Plain & Fancy Fabrics	4900 Oak St.	(330) 893-3898	
Bettsville	**The Door Mouse**	**5047 W. State Rd. 12**	**(419) 986-5667**	**Pg. 302**
Beverly	**Jacob's Ladder Quilting Shop**	**131 5th St.**	**(740) 410-1175**	**Pg. 305**
Bexley	Betty's Yarn Shop	2451 Elm Ave.	(614) 231-7168	
Big Prairie	Yarn & Bead Shop	9049 Township Rd. 1043	(330) 496-3574	
Bluffton	**Forever In Stitches**	**120 N. Main St.**	**(419) 358-0656**	**Pg. 300**
Boardman	Bernina Store & Sew Much More	7081 West Blvd.	(330) 726-9396	
Boardman	The Flaming Ice Cube Knit Shop	1499 Boardman-Canfield Rd.	(330) 726-4766	
Boardman	With Needle in Hand	7330 Southern Blvd. Ste. 5	(330) 758-8122	
Bowling Green	**The Busy Thimble**	**148 S. Main St.**	**(419) 806-4022**	**Pg. 301**
Brecksville	Crochet Innovations	7660 Chippewa Rd. Rte. 82	(440) 838-4455	
Broadview Heights	Crafty Ewe Inc.	8035 Broadview Rd.	(440) 838-1600	
Broadview Heights	Soft 'n Sassy Yarn and Fiber Arts	8047 Broadview Rd.	(440) 746-9650	
Brunswick	Carol's Fabric Shop	1325 N. Carpenter Rd.	(330) 225-4436	
Bryan	Jack's Sew & Vac.	122 N. Main St.	(419) 636-4914	
Bryan	Quilt Shoppe	6537 State Rte. 15	(419) 636-2900	
Canal Winchester	The Laughing Ewe	360 W. Waterloo St.	(614) 829-7450	
Canfield	Village Quilts	17 W. Main St.	(330) 533-0545	
Canton	Angelic's A Quilters Haven	3095 Cleveland Ave. SW	(330) 484-5480	
Canton	Bare Naked Wools	211 15th St. NW	(330) 453-7867	
Canton	Little Creek Needleworks	4205 Whipple Ave. NW #B	(234) 360-3257	
Celina	**Linda's Sew 'n So**	**216 W. Fayette St.**	**(419) 586-2324**	**Pg. 300**
Celina	The Quilterie	126 S. Main St.	(419) 586-0910	
Centerville	**Sew-A-Lot**	**232 N. Main St.**	**(937) 433-7474**	**Pg. 299**
Chagrin Falls	The Artful Yarn	100 N. Main St. #230	(440) 321-9754	
Chesterland	The Quilted Thimble	12628 Chillicothe Rd. #F	(440) 729-2259	
Chillicothe	**Creations Sew Clever**	**192 S. Paint St.**	**(740) 775-1957**	**Pg. 307**
Chillicothe	Old Town Fabric Shop	56 W. Water St.	(740) 779-9898	
Chillicothe	Quilts and Quackers	915 Betts Ln.	(740) 773-3434	
Cincinnati	A Stitch Above	7754 Camargo Rd.	(513) 271-2712	
Cincinnati	Absolutely Needlepoint	7117 Miami Ave.	(513) 561-7999	
Cincinnati	Fiberge, Knits & Bolts	6200 Montgomery Rd.	(513) 351-1251	
Cincinnati	Hank, a yarn boutique	2651 Observatory Ave. Ste. 101	(513) 386-9869	
Cincinnati	Homegrown Homesewn	5761 Springdale Rd. #L	(513) 401-9747	
Cincinnati	Silk Road Textiles	6106 Hamilton Ave.	(513) 541-3700	
Cincinnati	Stitches n Such	16 Village Sq.	(513) 733-3999	
Cleveland	Davie Hyman Designs	123 N. Lake St.	(216) 536-3295	
Cleveland	Fine Points	12620 Larchmere Blvd.	(216) 229-6644	
Cleveland	Flaming Ice Café and Knit Shop	140 Public Sq.	(216) 263-1111	
Cleveland Heights	Susan Yarns	2132 S. Taylor Rd.	(216) 321-2687	

Cleveland Heights	Wool & Willow Needlepoint	3475 Fairmount Blvd.	(216) 791-7952	
Coldwater	Coldwater Ben Franklin	840 E. Main St.	(419) 678-2321	
Columbus	Cross My Heart Ltd.	1141 Kenny Centre	(614) 442-0820	
Columbus	Dabble & Stitch	211 E. Arcadia Ave.	(614) 407-4987	
Columbus	Quilt Trends	6155-J Huntley Rd.	(614) 841-7845	
Columbus	Sew to Speak	4610 N. High St.	(614) 267-3011	
Columbus	The Yarn Shop	1125 Kenny Centre Mall	(614) 457-7836	
Cortland	**Quilters Fancy**	**124 N. High St.**	**(330) 637-3106**	**Pg. 303**
Cortland	Olive Grace Studios An Eccentric Quilt Shop			
		2627 1/2 Youngstown Kingsville Rd.	(330) 637-0800	
Coshocton	Mercantile on Main	603 Main St.	(740) 622-5956	
Creston	Moonstruck Farm & Fiber	9874 Cleveland Rd	(330) 435-6669	
Cuyahoga Falls	Harps & Thistles Yarn Emporium	129 Portage Tr.	(234) 208-9482	
Dayton	Busy Beaver Arts & Crafts	3445 Dayton-Xenia Rd.	(937) 429-3920	
Dayton	Park Avenue Needlepoint	41 Park Ave.	(937) 298-5776	
Dayton	**Sew-A-Lot**	**2270 Mamisburg-Centerville Rd.**	**(937) 433-9191**	**Pg. 299**
Dayton	Strings Attached	225 N. Main St.	(937) 221-9585	
Defiance	The Fifth Stitch	300 Clinton St.	(419) 782-0991	
DeGraff	Rollicking Hills Fiber Designs	486 E. Miami St.	(937) 585-5161	
Dover	Anything Sews	209A E. Ohio Ave.	(330) 365-9707	
Dublin	**Red Rooster Quilts**	**48 Corbins Mill Dr.**	**(614) 734-9007**	**Pg. 305**
Dublin	Knitting Temptations	35 S. High St.	(614) 734-0618	
Dublin	Quilt Beginnings	6591 Sawmill Rd.	(614) 799-2688	
Dublin	What's The Point	126 S. High St.	(614) 717-9008	
Eastlake	**Mara's Fabric & Gifts**	**35003 Vine St.**	**(440) 942-7849**	**Pg. 303**
Elmore	Crafty Needle	364 Rice St.	(419) 862-0333	
Englewood	The Rabbit Hutch Yarn Shop	5 N. Walnut St.	(937) 540-9292	
Fairfield	Seams Sew Easy Quilt Shop	2326 Mack Rd.	(513) 860-1373	
Fairlawn	I of the Needle	2858 W. Market St. #H	(330) 867-0005	
Fairlawn	The Designing Woman	137 Ghent Rd.	(330) 835-9400	
Fairview Park	Annas Sewing Center	22250 Lorain Rd.	(440) 716-8884	
Findlay	**Findlay Sewing Center**	**1207 Tiffen Ave.**	**(419) 422-5812**	**Pg. 301**
Findlay	Craft Gallery	406 Walnut St.	(419) 422-7980	
Franklin	Wooly Bully Yarn Company	135 S. Main St.	(937) 748-1002	
Georgetown	Schoolhouse Quilts	118 N. Main St.	(937) 378-4828	
Glendale	Stitches Quilt Shop	16 Village Sq.	(513) 733-3999	
Glouster	The Brass Thimble	83 High St.	(740) 517-8670	
Goshen	Quilt Cabin	1703 St. Rte. 28	(513) 722-7332	
Hamilton	Lambikins Hideaway Yarn & Stitchery	217 S. B St.	(513) 895-5648	
Hanoverton	**Serendipity Quilt Shop**	**7346 State Rt. 9**	**(330) 223-1102**	**Pg. 303**
Hillsboro	Margaret's Memories	220 W. Beech St.	(937) 402-4097	
Huber Heights	**Sulphur Grove Quilt Shop**	**7340 Taylorsville Rd.**	**(937) 233-7021**	**Pg. 298**
Jeromesville	Country Charm Fabrics	14 South St.	(419) 368-6403	
Kenton	**Country Stitches Fabrics & More**	**18031 State Rt. 309**	**(419) 675-3337**	**Pg. 301**
Lakewood	River Color Studio	1387 Sloane Ave.	(216) 228-9276	
Lakewood	Stitch Cleveland	18117 Detroit Rd.	(216) 220-4808	
Lancaster	Farmer's Country Store	540 N. High St.	(740) 654-4853	
Lancaster	Lunn Fabrics	317 E. Main St.	(740) 654-2202	
Lancaster	Pleasant Mountain Stitchery	743 N. Pierce Ave.	(740) 652-9688	
Leetonia	Amish Quilt Shop	41658 Kelly Park Rd.	(330) 482-3230	
Lima	**Heavenly Stitches**	**2696 Greely Chapel Rd.**	**(419) 979-0218**	**Pg. 300**
Lodi	Black Locust Farm	110 Bank St.	(330) 948-9276	
Louisville	AnnaLouisa's Needle Arts	1408 N. Chapel St.	(330) 875-5300	
Loveland	The Quilter's Studio of Loveland	535 W. Loveland Ave.	(513) 683-3666	
Lucasville	Stippling Stitches Quilt Shop	1179 Owensville Rd.	(740) 259-5111	
Ludlow Falls	Fabric Crafts By Rosalie	2810 Ohio 48	(937) 698-4066	
Madeira	Fiberlicious	8157 Camargo Rd.	(513) 561-8808	
Manchester	The Quilt Barn	250 Reed Cemetery Rd.	(937) 549-4900	
Marietta	Dad's Primitives Work Bench	268 Front St.	(740) 374-9722	
Marietta	Quilter's Corner	400 Tennis Center Dr.	(740) 373-6150	
Marion	Spin A Yarn Fiber Garden	187 W. Center St.	(740) 382-6969	
Mason	Main Street Yarns	126 W. Main St.	(513) 204-0078	
Mason	Martha's Heirlooms	306 W. Main St.	(513) 229-7340	
Maumee	Quilt Foundry	234 W. Wayne St.	(419) 893-5703	
McArthur	**McArthur Quilt Shop**	**118 W. Main**	**(740) 596-2345**	**Pg. 307**
Medina	**Little Red Quilt House**	**3616 Ridge Rd.**	**(234) 248-4492**	**Pg. 304**
Mentor	**Quilts & Sew Forth**	**7406 Center St.**	**(440) 266-1601**	**Pg. 303**
Miamisburg	The Little Shop of Stitches	79 S. Main St.	(937) 384-0804	
Middleburg Heights	Pins & Needles Sewing Shoppes	5937 Mayfield Rd.	(440) 243-6400	

Index

Middlefield	The Craft Cupboard	14275 Old State Rd.	(440) 632-5787	Pg. 302
Middlefield	Tiny Stitches Quilt Shop	14277 Old State Rd.	(440) 632-9410	
Middletown	Complete Quilting	6585 Terhune Dr.	(513) 217-0193	
Milan	**The Sewing Connection**	**11001 US. Rt. 250 N. B-2**	**(419) 499-9393**	Pg. 302
Millersburg	Chestnut Ridge Sewing	3647 St. Rt. 39	(330) 893-3359	
Millersburg	Miller's Dry Goods	4500 State Rt. 557	(330) 893-9899	
Millersburg	Somewhere Sewing	11004 County Rd. 320	(330) 674-1677	

Millersburg (Berlin)

	Zinck's Fabic Outlet	4568 State Rd. 39	(330) 893-7225	Pg. 304

Millersburg (Mt. Hope)

	Lone Star Quilt Shop	7700 County Rd. 77	(330) 674-3858	Pg. 304
Minster	Paper and Yarn	56 W. 4th St.	(419) 628-1300	
Mogadore	The Spider's Web Fabric Shop	2123 Martin Rd.	(330) 594-7119	
Mt. Vernon	**Paw Patch Quilt Shop**	**444 Columbus Rd. Ste. E**	**(740) 397-9450**	Pg. 304
Nelsonville	**Nelsonville Quilt Co.**	**52 W. Washington St.**	**(740) 753-3343**	Pg. 307
New Albany	The Knitting Nomad	4101 Audley Rd.	(614) 939-9935	
New Waterford	Embroidered 4 You & Yarn 2	5577 State Rte. 7	(330) 457-0351	
Newark	**Bunny's Sew Fine Fabrics**	**28 Price Rd.**	**(740) 366-1433**	Pg. 305
Newark	Lola's Alpaca Shop	2653 Swans Rd. NE	(740) 345-2199	
Newton Falls	Elsie's Custom Creations	139 1/2 Windham Rd.	(330) 609-9376	
North Canton	Artists Gallery Yarn	1142 S. Main St.	(330) 494-8838	
North Olmsted	Anna's Sewing Center	24357 Lorain Rd.	(440) 716-8884	
Northfield	Memory Lane Quilting	512 W. Aurora Rd.	(330) 468-2831	
Oberlin	Ginko Gallery & Studio	19 S. Main St.	(440) 774-3117	
Oberlin	Smith's Knitshop	250 W. College St.	(440) 774-2371	
Parma	Quilter's Source	6683 State Rd.	(440) 843-2464	
Pataskala	**Calico Cupboard Quilt Shop**	**74 Oak Meadow Dr.**	**(740) 927-2636**	Pg. 305
Pataskala	Quilt Store Next Door	365 S. Main St.	(614) 382-8008	
Pepper Pike	Ewes d'Bleu Yarns of Distinction	30559 Pinetree Rd. Ste. 206	(216) 319-6559	
Perrysburg	Ribbonry	119 Louisiana Ave.	(419) 872-0073	
Perrysburg	Yarn Cravin	146 E. 2nd St.	(419) 872-9276	
Piqua	In the Patch Designs	408 N. Main St.	(937) 552-7912	
Piqua	The Tapestry Angel	516 Spring St.	(937) 773-6352	
Pomeroy	**The Fabric Shop**	**110 W. Main St.**	**(740) 992-2284**	Pg. 307
Powell	Louise's Needleworks	23 W. Olentangy St.	(614) 436-3905	
Richfield	**The Polka Dot Pincushion**	**3807 Brecksville Rd. Ste. 8**	**(330) 659-0233**	Pg. 303
Richfield	Cornerstone Yarns	4174 Wheatley Rd.	(330) 659-2669	
Rock Creek	**The Quilting Block**	**4150 State Rte. 45**	**(440) 563-9386**	Pg. 303
Salem	Knit Wit Knits	645 E. State St.	(330) 337-5648	
Sandusky	**M & E Quilt Shoppe**	**279 E. Market St.**	**(419) 502-9123**	Pg. 302
Sardinia	Ohio Valley Natural Fibers	8541 Louderback Rd.	(937) 446-3045	
Sebring	Heidi and Lana	222 N. 15th St.	(330) 257-9292	
Sharonville	Keepsakes Framing & Floral	11423 Lebanon Rd.	(513) 563-6845	

Sharonville (Cincinnati)

	Sew Ezy Sewing Studio	11427 Lebanon Rd.	(513) 563-7474	Pg. 298
Shiloh	**Country Fabrics**	**6142 Ganges 5 Points Rd.**	**(419) 896-3785**	Pg. 302
Shreve	Noah's Landing	7575 Brown Rd.	(330) 496-9065	
South Amherst	Quilts & Kreations	101 E. Main St.	(440) 986-4132	
South Point	Quilts And Things	207A Solida Rd.	(740) 377-4551	
Springboro	Wooly Bully Yarn Company	135 S. Main St.	(937) 748-1002	
Springfield	**Creative Fires**	**1525 Progress Dr.**	**(937) 327-9420**	Pg. 300
St. Clairsville	From Past to Present Quilt Shop	139 W. Main St.	(740) 526-9371	
Stow	Sew déjà vu	1608 Norton Rd.	(330) 653-5598	
Strongsville	Just Stitching	13211 Prospect Rd.	(440) 572-9777	
Sugarcreek	**Carlisle Fabrics**	**108 E. Main St.**	**(330) 852-2264**	Pg. 303
Sugarcreek	Carlisle Fabric	108 E. Main St.	(330) 852-2264	
Sugarcreek Township	Crafters Lodge	6056 Wilmington Pike	(937) 470-2649	
Sylvania	**Sonflower Quilts & Gifts**	**6600 Sylvania Ave. Ste. 3E**	**(419) 885-4438**	Pg. 301
Thompson	Crows on The Ledge	15815 Thompson Rd.	(440) 479-8480	
Tipp City	**Tippecanoe Weaver & Fibers Too**	**17 N. 2nd St.**	**(937) 667-5358**	Pg. 300
Toledo	Stitch	4024 N. Holland Sylvania Rd. #10	(419) 517-7092	
Toledo	Yarn Co.	4434 Secor Rd.	(419) 474-6744	
Trenton	Valley Quilts	104 E. State St.	(513) 988-2560	
Troy	In The Patch Designs	210 E. Main St.	(937) 552-7912	

Index

Uniontown	Sue Spargo Folk-Art Quilt	3755 Boettler Oaks Dr. #B	(330) 899-9454	
University Heights	JEllen's House of Fabric	2171 S. Green Rd.	(216) 860-4116	
Vandalia	Fiber and Fusion Studio	11180 N. Dixie Dr.	(937) 602-3248	
Vermillion	Clare's Stitching Post	682 Main St.	(440) 967-0826	
Wadsworth	Sally's Shop	141 College St.	(330) 334-1996	
Wadsworth	The Fabric Peddler	139 College St.	(330) 336-1101	
Waldo	**Serendipitee Quilt Shop**	**7143 Waldo-Delaware Rd.**	**(740) 726-2900**	**Pg. 304**
Warren	Just Quilt It Inc.	171 Folsom St. NW	(330) 469-6956	
Waynesville	**Fabric Shack Stores**	**99 S. Marvin Ln.**	**(513) 897-0092**	**Pg. 298**
Waynesville	Katherine's Web	174 S. Main St.	(937) 728-0126	
West Milton	Wertz Variety Store	6 N. Miami St.	(937) 698-5212	
Whipple (Marietta)				
	The Quilted Work	**320 Stanleyville Narrows Rd.**	**(740) 373-0579**	**Pg. 306**
Wilmington	**Cotton Junky Quilt Shop**	**110 W. Main St.**	**(937) 366-6302**	**Pg. 298**
Worthington	Sew To Speak	752 High St.	(614) 547-7380	
Zanesville	**A Touch of Thread Quilting Center**			
		2885 E. Pike St. (Rte. 40)	**(740) 454-8372**	**Pg. 305**
Zanesville	**Nonna's Quilting Nook**	**1004 Beverly Ave.**	**(740) 450-2626**	**Pg. 305**
Zanesville	The Alpacas of Spring Acres Farm Store	3390B Big B Rd.	(740) 796-2195	

Index

Notes

Boise City (pg. 312)
64
Guymon (pg. 312)

Sand Springs (pg. 314)
Stillwater (pg. 313)   Tulsa (pg. 314)
Stilwell (pg. 314)
Guthrie (pg. 314)
Oklahoma City (pg. 313)
40
Chickasha (pg. 313)   Allen (pg. 314)
35   McAlester (pg. 314)
Altus (pg. 313)
44   Chickasaw NRA
Antlers (pg. 314)

Road to Oklahoma
Quilt Block

I'd Rather Bee Quilting !

Astoria (pg. 321)
Cannon Beach (pg. 321)
Tillamook (pg. 321)
Cloverdale (pg. 321)
Newport (pg. 321)
Waldport (pg. 320)
Florence (pg. 320)
Eu (pg
Coos Bay (pg. 320)
Bandon (pg. 320)

Oklahoma Shops

Q-Quilting ~ Y-Yarn ~ N-Needlework ~ R-Retreat ~ M-Museum

City	Shop	Address	Phone	Page
Ada	Santa Fe Depot Quilt Shop	425 W. Main	(580) 436-2886	
Allen	**Prairie Notions Fabric Shop**	**701 E Gilmore**	**(580) 857-2831**	**Pg. 314**
Altus	**Johnson's Vacuum Shop & Sewing**	**105 W. Commerce**	**(580) 477-1398**	**Pg. 313**
Alva	Fabrics & More Etc.	413 Barnes Ave.	(580) 327-0240	
Antlers	**Betsy's Quilts & Fabric Shop**	**419580 E. 1930 Rd.**	**(580) 298-5821**	**Pg. 314**
Ardmore	Ardmore Creative Sewing Center	320 N. Commerce St. #10	(580) 223-6655	
Ardmore	Key Grocery & Quilts	116 E. Broadway St.	(580) 223-8821	
Atoka	Blessed Quilting and Fabric	207 W. 6th St.	(580) 364-7306	
Barnsdall	Red Barn Quilting	99 County Rd. 2285	(918) 847-2544	
Bartlesville	Carrico's Creative Corner	20873 N. 4040 Rd.	(918) 333-8933	
Bixby	The Log Cabin Quilt Shop	14803 E. 171st S.	(918) 366-6902	
Blanchard	Beth's Quilting Quarters	114 N. Main St.	(405) 485-3880	
Boise City	**Pam's Variety Fabrics**	**23 E. Main**	**(580) 544-2989**	**Pg. 312**
Cache	Quilt N Bee	506 SW C Ave.	(580) 429-2400	
Checotah	Sew Many Quilts Quilt Shoppe	427332 E. 1050 Rd.	(918) 473-4318	
Chickasha	**Steelman Framing, Gifts & Sew Much More**	**410 Chickasha Ave.**	**(405) 224-2036**	**Pg. 313**
Chickasha	Bush Family Affair	401 W. Chickasha Ave. #202	(405) 224-2280	
Claremont	Cotton Cottage	331 N. Davis Ave.	(918) 607-0831	
Duncan	Deb's Sew Biz	427 S. Hwy. 81	(580) 255-2843	
Edmond	David's Yarn	16526 N. Pennsylvania Ave.	(405) 562-1839	
El Reno	K's Quilting Studio	107 S. Bickford Ave.	(405) 422-2707	
Frederick	Thayer Rags Fabric Center	108 W. Grand Ave.	(580) 335-3380	
Gore	Fabric Patch	305 S Main St.	(918) 489-5163	
Guthrie	**Sooner Quilts**	**7821 S. Sooner Rd.**	**(405) 282-2070**	**Pg. 314**
Guthrie	Cross Stitch Haven	117 1/2 W. Harrison	(405) 466-8210	
Guthrie	Sealed With a Kiss	109 E. Oklahoma	(405) 282-8649	
Guthrie	Weavery At Indian Meridian	624 S. Henney Rd.	(405) 822-8927	
Guymon	**Cheryl's Quilt Corner**	**1608 N. Ellison**	**(580) 338-3677**	**Pg. 312**
Hennessey	Prairie Quilt	101 S. Main St.	(405) 853-6801	
Jay	Keepin' U N Stitches	705 N. 4th St.	(918) 253-2455	
Lawton	Morning Star Quiltworks	916 SW E. Ave.	(580) 248-9200	
Mannford	Reddik's Country Living Store	140 Evans Ave.	(918) 865-2470	
McAlester	**Country Fabrics & Quilts**	**5819 S. Hwy. 69**	**(918) 423-0933**	**Pg. 314**
Moore	Country Collections by Hart	113 W. Main	(405) 799-0773	
Nash	Stash to Stitches Quilting	14077 Hwy. 132	(580) 839-2555	
Norman	L & B Yarn Co.	425 W. Grey	(405) 310-3636	
North Miami	Cotton Pickin' Quilts	612 Nebraska	(918) 542-2836	
Oklahoma City	**Buckboard Quilts**	**5025 Brettshire Way**	**(405) 751-3885**	**Pg. 313**
Oklahoma City	**Oklahoma Quiltworks**	**9323 N. Pennsylvania**	**(405) 842-4778**	**Pg. 313**
Oklahoma City	**Sew N Sews**	**5125 N. Portland**	**(405) 942-2700**	**Pg. 313**
Oklahoma City	**The Savage Quilter**	**6903 N. May Ave.**	**(405) 840-1466**	**Pg. 313**
Oklahoma City	Heartland Needleworks	3160 W. Britton Rd. Ste. B	(405) 748-5999	
Owasso	The Knitting Nook	12500 E. 86th St. N. #106	(918) 272-6665	
Pauls Valley	The Gallery	204 W. Paul Ave.	(405) 207-9527	
Pawhuska	The Tangled Thread	230 E. 6th St.	(918) 287-4826	
Ponca City	Completely Quilted	315 E. Grand Ave.	(580) 718-9300	
Prague	Gwen's Unwind & Sew Shop	1408 N. Klabzuba	(405) 831-3514	
Ripley	Nancy's Trunk	9211 W. Main	(405) 413-5037	
Sand Springs	**Quilt Nuts**	**216 N. Main St.**	**(918) 613-9341**	**Pg. 314**
Sand Springs	Sweet Pea's Quilt Company	17427 W. 9th St. S.	(918) 245-7987	
Sand Springs	The Little Quilt Shop	1 W. 41st St. Ste. H	(918) 245-1339	
Sapulpa	Quilt Styles	18 S. Water	(918) 224-6299	
Shawnee	WonderArc Quilt Shop	26 W. MacArthur St.	(405) 550-0613	
South Bixby	The Log Cabin	14803 E. 17th St.	(918) 366-6902	
Stillwater	**Sew N Sews**	**211 N. Perkins Rd.**	**(405) 707-0700**	**Pg. 313**
Stillwater	The Quilting Post	717 S. Main St.	(405) 624-0303	
Stilwell	**Front Porch Fabrics**	**10 W. Chestnut**	**(918) 797-2206**	**Pg. 314**

Index

Tul
Tuls
Tuls
Tuls
Tuls
Tuls
Tuls
Wat
Woo
Yuk

Est: 1988

Hours
Monday-Saturday
10:00-5:00
Sunday
Noon-4:00

Retreat Center Upstairs

See our ad in the retreat section of this book.

640 2nd St. SE, Hwy. 101 Bandon, OR 97411

(800) 347-9021

Owners: Michelle Hoffman ~ michelle@forget-me-knots.net
Fax: (541) 347-9021   2500 sq.ft.   2000 Bolts

A unique & charming shop specializing in quilting, kits, embroidery supplies, silk ribbon embroidery. Supplies, patterns, books, classes & a large selection of 100% cottons.

On-line store now available

www.forget-me-knots.net

Wenz-daze Quilter's Emporium

wenz-dazequiltingfabric.com

Florence, OR   QN

Homey atmosphere, Novelty, and Flannels, 100% Cotton. We also have Quilting Notions, Patterns, Books, Embroidery Supplies, Wool Felt and many samples to inspire you. Handi Quilter, HQ16, Avanté Sales & Service.

1745 15th St. 97439
541-997-3293

Charley & Cyndie Wenz
Est: 2008   1500 sq.ft.
wenz-daze@charter.net
Online Newsletter

Winter Hours:
Tuesday- Saturday 10-5
Memorial Day - Labor Day
Monday-Saturday 10-5

Did you know?
At 11,239 feet Mount Hood stands as the tallest peak in Oregon. Mount Hood is a dormant volcano.

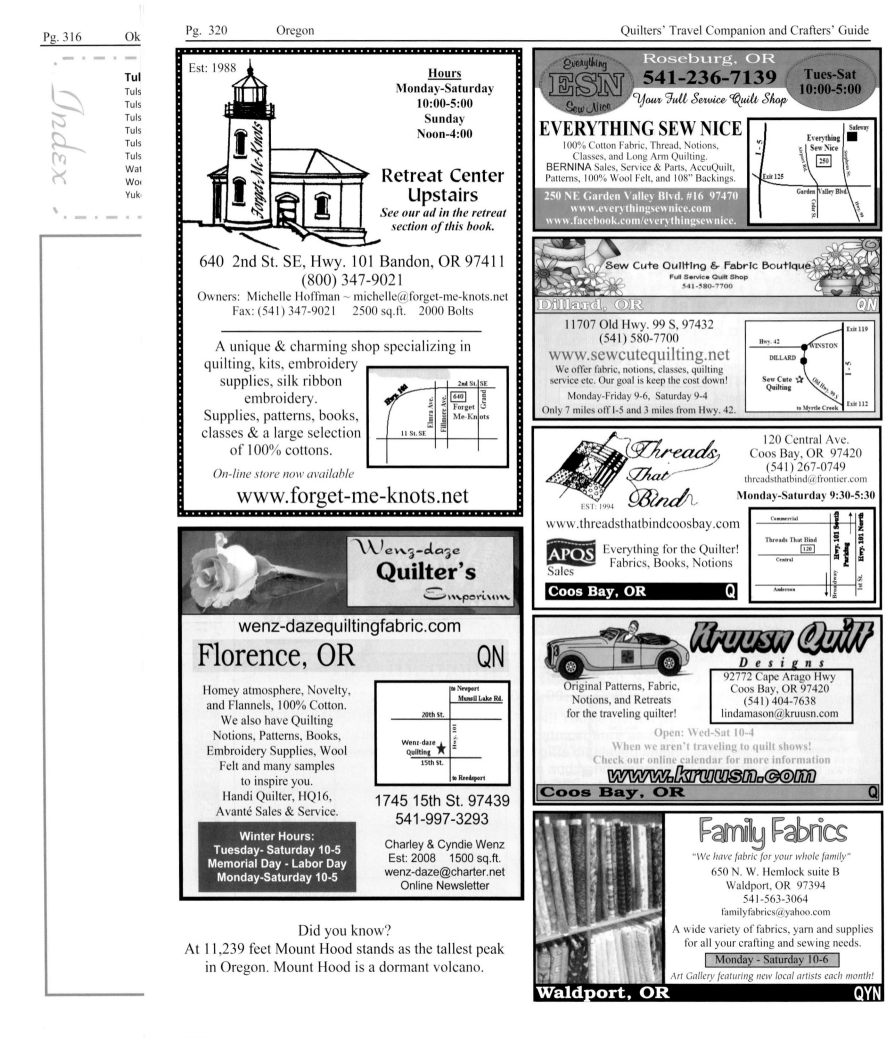

Cloverdale, OR   Q

B J's Fabrics & Quilts

Open 7 Days
10am-5pm

34365 B Hwy 101 S.
(877) 690-5267 ~ (503) 392-6195
BJsfabrics@embarqmail.com
www.BJsFabricsquilts.com

Owner: Barbara Lewis   Over 4000 bolts of fabric.
Hwy. 101 from the North-2 miles south of
Cloverdale, turn left past the 90 mile marker, then left
again at the 2nd driveway. Hwy. 101 from the South-
¼ mile from the Pacific City Turn-off, turn right after
BJ's Fabrics & Quilts State sign, left at 2nd driveway.

Map: Cloverdale, 2 mi., BJ's Fabrics, Hwy 101, Pacific City

LATIMER QUILT
& TEXTILE CENTER

2105 Wilson River Loop   97141
(503) 842-8622
latimertextile@centurylink.net
www.latimerquiltandtextile.com

April - October
Mon - Sat 10 - 5 Sun 12 - 4
November - March
Tues - Sat 10 - 4

An active textile museum, dedicated to
the preservation and promotion of the
textile arts… weaving, spinning, quilting,
history, research, education & exhibits.
Handcrafted gift items for sale.
- - - - - - - - - - - - - - - -
We are located one block east of
Shilo Inn off Hwy. 101

Tillamook, OR   *Exhibits change every two months.*   QY

Cannon Beach, OR   Q

CENTER DIAMOND

1065 S. Hemlock
P.O. Box 997, Cannon Beach, OR   97110
(888) 305-0854 or (503) 436-0833
Owner: Julie Walker
centerdiamond@aol.com
Est: 1994 1500 sq.ft.

Over 3000 bolts of the most gorgeous 100%
cotton fabrics. Books, patterns, notions & gifts.

www.centerdiamond.com

7 Days a Week 10 - 5   *Located 1 block from the beach.*

Astoria, OR   QNY

Homespun Quilts

108 10th St. Astoria, OR 97103
(800) 298-3177 or (503) 325-3300
www.homespunquilts.com

Quality cotton fabrics
for quilting and sewing.
Wool felt and books,
Patterns, notions and Yarn.

Bernina Dealer and
authorized repair.

Mon-Sat 10:00-5:00

Map: Columbia River, 10th St., 108 Homespun Quilts, Marine Dr., West to Hwy. 101 (Seaside), East to Hwy. 30 (Portland)

QUILTER'S COVE

www.quilterscove.net
Quilt Shop with a great beachy feel!

Where you come to be "Sew" inspired with
Fabric, Books, and Hundreds of Patterns, notions & gifts.
We feature Landscapes, Batiks, Fish, Nautical, & Beachy.

Mon - Sat 10 - 5
Sun   11 - 4

Conveniently located on
Hwy 101 and US 20,
Next to JC Market

27 N. Coast Hwy.
Newport, OR 97365
866-43-QUILT or 541-265-2591
Owners: Holly Nevins &
Judy Muller

Newport, OR   Q

Jane's Fabric Patch

1110 Main Ave. 97141
(503) 842-9392
fabric@pacifier.com
Owner: Jane Wise
Est: 1981   5000+ Bolts
www.janesfabricpatch.com

Mon - Fri 9 - 5
Sat 10 - 4
Summer - Sundays &
Holidays 11 - 3

Coastal Retreat.
Multi-faceted Quilt shop.
Large fabric selection, creative,
knowledgeable and friendly ideas
and assistance.
"Janome Machine Dealer"

Map: Main Ave., Pacific, 9th St., 10th St., 11th St., Jane's Fabric Patch 1110

Tillamook, OR   Q

Beaverton, OR   Q

Aloha Sewing & Vacuum

Monday-Friday
9:00-6:00
Saturday
9:00-5:00

18335 SW Tualatin Valley Hwy. 97003
(503) 649-6050
alohavacnsew@hotmail.com
www.alohavacnsew.com

It's Sew Easy to get hooked on our large selection
of unique Fabrics while inspiring your creativity
with Brother and Elna Sewing & Embroidery
Machines. Lifetime lessons with purchase. We
continually offer a variety of classes and clubs to inspire
creations on your new machine.

Map: Exit 64, U.S. 26, 185th, Aloha Vac N Sew, Exit 69, Tualatin Valley Hwy, Hwy. 8, Hwy 217, Exit 2, Farmington Rd., Hwy. 10, Beaverton-Hillside Hwy.

Pine Needles

McKenna Ryan's Shop & Showroom
Located in Historic Milwaukie

Appliqué Patterns, Fabric, Laser Cut Kits,
Notions & In-Store Exclusives!

Visit Our Shop!

1915 SE Jefferson Street
Portland, OR 97222

800·728·2278 · www.pineneedles.com

Timberline Lodge

Timberline Lodge is perched on the south side of
Mt. Hood, with the peak looming in the background.
Some might recognize its exterior, which was used
as a location for the Overlook Hotel in The Shining,
but today, it's a popular destination for skiers.
Timberline Lodge was dedicated September 28,
1937, by President Franklin D. Roosevelt.
The National Historic Landmark sits at an elevation
of 5,960 feet.

27500 E Timberline Road, OR 97028
(503) 272-3311
www.timberlinelodge.com

Oregon Shops

Q-Quilting ~ Y-Yarn ~ N-Needlework ~ R-Retreat ~ M-Museum

Albany	Bolts to Blocks	133 Broadalbin SW	(541) 704-0386	
Albany	Fine Fiber Studio	101 SE Jefferson St.	(541) 917-3251	
Ashland	Sew Creative Ashland	115 E. Main St.	(541) 482-1665	
Ashland	The Websters	11 N. Main St.	(541) 482-9801	
Astoria	**Homespun Quilts**	**108 10th St.**	**(503) 325-3300**	**Pg. 321**
Astoria	Astoria Fiber Arts Studio	1296 Duane St.	(503) 325-5598	
Athena	**Highland Quilts**	**312 E. Main**	**(541) 969-6178**	**Pg. 318**
Aurora	Beyond Art	21497 Hwy. 99 NE	(503) 678-2633	
Aurora	Speckled Hen Quilts	25455 NE Boones Ferry Rd.	(503) 678-3368	
Baker City	Treasure Every Stitch Quilt Shop	2101 Main St. #108	(541) 523-9499	
Bandon	**Forget-Me-Knots**	**640 2nd St. SE Hwy. 101**	**(800) 347-9021**	**Pg. 320**
Bandon	The Wool Company	990 2nd St. SE	(541) 347-3912	
Beaverton	**Aloha Sewing & Vacuum**	**18335 SW Tualatin Valley Hwy.**		
			(503) 649-6050	**Pg. 321**
Beaverton	For Yarn's Sake	11767 SW Beaverton Hillsdale Hwy.	(503) 469-9500	
Beaverton	Mill End Retail Store	4955 NW Western Ave.	(503) 646-3000	
Beaverton	Montavilla Sewing Center	4955 SW Western	(503) 619-6619	
Beaverton	Nitro Knitters	10047 SW Nimbus Ave.	(503) 372-9318	
Beaverton	Quilters Corner Store	12580 SW Broadway	(503) 644-5678	
Bend	**B J's Quilt Basket**	**20225 Badger Rd.**	**(541) 383-4310**	**Pg. 318**
Bend	**Sew Many Quilts**	**2550 NE. Hwy. 20 Ste. 140**	**(541) 385-7166**	**Pg. 318**
Bend	QuiltWorks	926 NE Greenwood Ave.	(541) 728-0527	
Brookings	By My Hand	1109 Chetco Ave.	(541) 412-0917	
Brookings	Country Keepsakes	800 Chetco Ave.	(541) 469-6117	

Brownsville	Brownsville Stitching Parlor	113 Spaulding Ave.	(541) 466-3660	
Brownsville	Yankee Dutch Quilting & Dry Goods	140 Spaulding Ave.	(541) 466-3662	
Cannon Beach	**Center Diamond**	**1065 S. Hemlock**	**(503) 436-0833**	**Pg. 321**
Cannon Beach	Coastal Yarns	131 W. 2nd St.	(503) 436-1128	
Clatskanie	The Bag Ladies Yarn Shop	265 E. Columbia River Hwy.	(503) 728-9276	
Clatskanie	The Quilted Dandelion	75 S. Nehalem St. #B	(503) 728-0626	
Cloverdale	**B J's Fabrics & Quilts**	**34365 B Hwy. 101 S.**	**(503) 392-6195**	**Pg. 321**
Coos Bay	**Kruusn Quilt Designs**	**92772 Cape Arago Hwy.**	**(541) 404-7638**	**Pg. 320**
Coos Bay	**Threads That Bind**	**120 Central Ave.**	**(541) 267-0749**	**Pg. 320**
Coos Bay	My Yarn Shop	264 B Broadway	(541) 266-8230	
Corvallis	Friendship Crossing	211 SW 2nd St.	(541) 758-4152	
Corvallis	Stash	110 SW 3rd St.	(541) 753-9276	
Creswell	Mountain Shadow Ranch	83207 Rodgers Rd.	(541) 206-4893	
Dallas	Grandma's Attic Sewing Emporium	167 SW Court St.	(503) 623-0451	
Dillard	**Sew Cute Quilting and Fabric Boutique**			
		11707 Old Hwy. 99 S.	**(541) 580-7700**	**Pg. 320**
Drain	The Fabric Farm	438 W. B Ave.	(541) 315-7171	
Eugene	**Piece by Piece Fabrics**	**62 W. 13th Ave.**	**(541) 743-0266**	**Pg. 319**
Eugene	Eugene Textile Center	1510 Jacobs Dr.	(541) 688-1623	
Eugene	Glimakra USA	1471 Railroad Blvd. #5	(541) 246-8679	
Eugene	Mindy's Needlepoint Factory	296 E. 5th Ave. #227	(541) 344-7132	
Eugene	Soft Horizons Fibre	412 E. 13th Ave.	(541) 343-0651	
Eugene	Stick + String	965 Tyinn #11	(541) 683-6670	
Eugene	The Knit Shop	2821 Oak St.	(541) 434-0430	
Florence	**Wenz-daze Quilter's Emporium**	**5045 Hwy. 101**	**(541) 997-3293**	**Pg. 320**
Florence	Happy Kampers Yarn Barn	88878 Hwy. 101	(541) 997-9414	
Forest Grove	Needles in the Grove	2813 Pacific Ave. #D	(503) 206-2254	
Fossil	Fossil Mercantile Company	555 Main St.	(541) 763-4617	
Garibaldi	Swift Stitches	101 11th St.	(971) 265-1090	
Gilchrist	Dragonfly Yarn & Gifts	138315 Hwy. 97 N.	(541) 771-2248	
Grants Pass	Bead Merchant & Yarn Supply	300 SW 6th St.	(541) 471-0645	
Grants Pass	Jordan Fabrics	1590 NE 7th St. #C	(541) 476-0214	
Grants Pass	Plaza Quilting & Sewing Center	311 SE 6th St.	(541) 479-5757	
Grants Pass	Unique Lee Yours	3921 Highland Ave.	(541) 476-6229	
Gresham	Feather Your Nest	126 N. Main Ave.	(971) 220-0936	
Gresham	Montavilla Sewing Center	971 NE Kelly Ave.	(503) 661-2102	
Halfway	Quilts Plus	280 S. Main St.	(541) 742-5040	
Happy Valley	Quilting Delights	12117 SE Stevens Ct.	(503) 658-1600	
Hermiston	The Material Girl Quilt Shop	1565 N. 1st St. #7	(541) 289-2555	
Hillsboro	Black Sheep at Orenco	6154 NE Brighton St.	(971) 732-5391	
Hood River	E.T.C.--Every Thread Counts	514 State St.	(541) 386-5044	
Hood River	Knot Another Hat	202 New Yasui	(541) 308-0002	
Independence	Ladies of Liberty Mercantile	130 C St.	(503) 837-0676	
Jefferson	Janice Jenney Studios	13364 Marlatt Rd. S.	(541) 327-9886	
Jefferson	The Purple Frog Quilt Shop	890 N. 2nd St.	(541) 327-3764	
John Day	Skeins	516 S. Canyon Blvd.	(541) 575-5648	
Joseph	Cattle Country Quilts	203 N. Main St. #2	(541) 432-6669	
Joseph	The Sheep Shed	3 S. Main St.	(541) 432-7000	
Keizer	The Cotton Patch	4475 River Rd. N.	(503) 463-1880	
Klamath Falls	Circle of Yarns	815 Main St.	(541) 884-9276	
Klamath Falls	Quilting Sisters	26654 Rocky Point Rd.	(541) 356-2218	
Klamath Falls	Willing Hands	921 Klamath Ave.	(541) 882-3002	
La Grande	Claudson's Sew & Soak	1401 Adams Ave.	(541) 963-6402	
La Grande	La Grande Quilt Shop	1107 Washington Ave.	(541) 663-1817	
La Pine	**Homestead Quilts and Gallery**	**51425 Hwy. 97**	**(541) 536-2360**	**Pg. 318**
Lafayette	Mix Fabrics	392 Third St.	(503) 537-8101	
Lake Oswego	The Pine Needle	429 First St.	(503) 635-1353	
Lakeview	Goose Tracks, Quilting & Fabric Arts	728 N. 2nd St.	(541) 947-0299	
Langlois	Wild Rivers Wool Factory	48443 Hwy. 101	(541) 348-2033	
Lebanon	**Finally Together Quilters**	**54 W. Ash St.**	**(541) 258-6006**	**Pg. 319**
Lebanon	Knitty Gritty Yarn Store	285 S. Main St.	(541) 936-4677	
Manzanita	T-Spot Yarns, Teas and Chocolates	144 Laneda Ave.	(503) 368-7768	
McMinnville	Boersma's Knitting Basket	309 Baker St.	(503) 472-4611	
McMinnville	Boersma's Sewing Center	203 NE Third St.	(503) 472-4611	
McMinnville	Oregon Knitting Company	309 N. Baker St.	(971) 261-9608	
Medford	Cottage Quilts Sew Creative Studio	1310 A Center Dr.	(541) 500-8071	
Medford	Fasturn Junction	3859 S. Stage Rd.	(541) 772-8430	
Medford	Jennie's Yarn Shop	30 N. Central Ave.	(541) 499-6295	
Medford	Top Stitch	1596 Biddle Rd.	(541) 608-7722	
Merrill	Tater Patch Quilts	109 E. Front St.	(541) 798-5955	

Index

Milton Freewater	Oregon Trail Yarn	1112 S. Main St.	(541) 310-1857	
Milwaukee	Mill End Store	9701 SE. McLoughlin Blvd.	(503) 786-1234	
Molalla	Canby Quilt & Fabric	12012 S. Wildcat Rd.	(503) 829-8057	
Molalla	Stitches 301	301 N. Molalla Ave.	(503) 320-5192	
Mount Vernon	Shiny Thimble Quilt Studio	100 E. Main St.	(541) 932-4111	
Mt. Angel	Sassie's Yarn Barn	585 Birch St.	(503) 845-6748	
Mulino	Mill Barn Quilter's & Mercantile	26412 S. Hwy. 213	(503) 759-5282	
Myrtle Creek	Rustic Rooster Quilt Shop	137 First Ave.	(541) 863-5329	
Myrtle Creek	Sew Cute Quilting & Fabric Boutique	11707 Old Hwy. 99 S.	(541) 580-7700	
Newberg	Pacific Wool and Fiber	2505 Portland Rd. (Hwy. 99 W.)	(503) 538-4741	
Newport	**Quilter's Cove**	**27 N. Coast Hwy. 101**	**(541) 265-2591**	**Pg. 321**
Newport	Quilter's Cottage	1460 N. Coast Hwy. 101	(541) 265-4248	
Newport	Yarn For All Seasons	3101 SE Ferry Slip Rd.	(541) 867-3411	
Ontario	Charm Shack Quilt Shop	222 S. Oregon St.	(541) 889-3085	
Oregon City	Knit-A-Bit	16925 Beckham Rd.	(503) 631-4596	
Pendleton	Thimbles Fabric-N-More	1849 Westgate Place	(541) 278-7910	
Philomath	**Janni Lou Creations**	**1243 Main**	**(541) 929-3795**	**Pg. 319**
Port Orford	Quilter's Corner	335 W. 7th	541-332-0502	
Portland	**Pine Needle Designs**	**1915 SE Jefferson St.**	**(800) 728-2278**	**Pg. 322**
Portland	A Common Thread	15495 SW Sequoia Pkwy. #140	(503) 624-7440	
Portland	Acorns & Threads	4475 SW Scholls Ferry Rd. #158	(503) 292-4457	
Portland	Bolt Neighborhood Fabric Boutique	2136 NE Alberta St.	(503) 287-2658	
Portland	Close Knit	2140 NE Alberta St.	(503) 288-4568	
Portland	Cool Cottons	2417 SE Hawthorne Blvd.	(503) 232-0417	
Portland	Dublin Bay Knitting Co.	1227 NW 11th Ave.	(503) 223-3229	
Portland	Fabric Depot	700 SE 122nd Ave.	(503) 252-9530	
Portland	Fiber Rhythm Craft & Design	3701 SE Milwaukee Ave. #F	(503) 236-7318	
Portland	Gossamer	2418 E. Burnside St.	(503) 233-4807	
Portland	Happy Knits	1620 SE Hawthorne Blvd.	(503) 238-2106	
Portland	In Stitches Needlepoint	2361 NW Westover Rd.	(503) 226-0814	
Portland	Knit Purl	1101 SW Alder	(503) 227-2999	
Portland	Knitting Bee	18305 NW W. Union Rd. #E	(503) 439-3316	
Portland	Knittn' Kitten	7530 NE Glisan St.	(503) 255-3022	
Portland	Modern Domestic	1408 NE Alberta St.	(503) 808-9910	
Portland	Montavilla Sewing Center	8326 SE Stark St.	(503) 254-7317	
Portland	Montavilla Sewing Center	700 SE 122nd Ave	(503) 262-6734	
Portland	Needle Art Closet	4231 NE Broadway St.	(503) 288-3992	
Portland	Northwest Wools	3524 SW Troy St.	(503) 244-5024	
Portland	Pearl Fiber Arts	428 NW 11th Ave.	(503) 227-7746	
Portland	Pendleton Woolen Mill Store	8500 SE McLoughlin Blvd.	(503) 535-5786	
Portland	Pioneer Quilts	3101 SE Courtney	(503) 654-1555	
Portland	The Naked Sheep Knit Shop	2142 N. Killingsworth	(503) 283-2004	
Portland	Twisted	2310 NE Broadway St.	(503) 922-1150	
Portland	Yarnia Custom Yarn Shop	3773 SE Belmont St.	(503) 939-5338	
Portland	Yarntastic, Fiber Arts	6802 SE Milwaukie Ave.	(971) 302-7137	
Prairie City	Quilts and Beyond	209 N. McHaley St.	(541) 820-4777	
Prineville	The Quilt Shack	1211 NW Madras Hwy.	(541) 447-1338	
Redmond	High Mountain Fabric Quilt Shop	1542 S. Hwy. 97	(541) 548-6909	
Redmond	Material Girl Fabrics	307 NW 7th St.	(541) 923-1600	
Riddle	Etcetera Needlework Shop	120 Main St.	(541) 874-3571	
Roseburg	**Everything Sew Nice**	**250 NE Garden Valley Blvd. #16**		
			(541) 236-7139	**Pg. 320**
Roseburg	Country Lady Quilt Shop	611 & 613 SE. Jackson St.	(541) 673-1007	
Roseburg	Jackson St Fiber Arts	970 NW Garden Valley Blvd.	(541) 672-9276	
Roseburg	Knotty Lady Yarns	632 SE Jackson St.	(541) 673-2199	
Roseburg	Lydia's Quilt and Crafts Studio	960 W. Harvard	(541) 391-6661	
Salem	Discover Quilting	910 Commercial St. SE	(971) 304-7349	
Salem	Tangled Purls	2290 Commercial St. SE Ste. 140	(503) 339-7556	
Salem	Teaselwick Wools	1313 Mill St. SE	(971) 304-7050	
Sandy	Designer Yarn	38871 Proctor Blvd.	(503) 826-0123	
Sandy	Paradise Quilts & Fabrics	39400 Pioneer Blvd. #7	(503) 668-3106	
Seaside	Creative Beginnings	620 S. Holladay Ste. 1	(503) 738-9580	
Silver Lake	Desert Rose Quilt Shop	65458 Hwy. 31	(541) 576-3530	
Silverton	Apples to Oranges	204 E. Main St.	(503) 874-4901	
Sisters	**The Stitchin' Post**	**311 W. Cascade St.**	**(541) 549-6061**	**Pg. 319**
Sisters	Pieceful Expressions Quilt	204 W. Adams Ave. #102	(541) 549-8354	
Springfield	**Jean Marie's Fabrics**	**110 Main St.**	**(541) 746-0433**	**Pg. 319**
Springfield	**Something to Crow About**	**4227C Main St.**	**(541) 746-3256**	**Pg. 319**
Stayton	Quilt-N-Stitch	395 N. 3rd Ave.	(503) 767-4240	
StHelens	Mo's Art, Hook & Needle	400 Columbia Blvd.	(503) 366-9276	

Sutherlin	Chicks and a Rooster	460 S. Comstock St.	(541) 860-8140	
Sweet Home	Seamingly Creative	1245 Main St.	(541) 367-8934	
Terrebonne	Quilter's Attic	8154 11th St. #1	(541) 548-8119	
The Dalles	The Whole Ball of Yarn	421 E. 2nd St.	(541) 506-9276	
Tillamook	**Jane's Fabric Patch**	**1110 Main Ave.**	**(503) 842-9392**	**Pg. 321**
Tillamook	**Latimer Quilt & Textile Center**	**2105 Wilson River Loop**	**(503) 842-8622**	**Pg. 321**
Toledo	Goin To The Dogs	281 N. Main St.	(541) 336-1141	
Union	Knitabob	156 S. Main St.	(541) 562-2276	
Waldport	**Family Fabrics**	**650 NW Hemlock Ste. B**	**(541) 563-3064**	**Pg. 320**
Warren	Fibers & Stitches	58093 Columbia River Hwy.	(503) 397-5536	
West Linn	Hollyhill Quilt Shoppe	1914 Willamette Falls Dr. #160	(503) 607-0600	
West Linn	Wool 'N Wares Yarn Shop	21540 Willamette Dr.	(503) 657-7470	
Wheeler	Creative Fabrics	475 Hwy. 101	(503) 368-5900	
Wilsonville	Sewn Loverly, The Fabric Store	8502 SW Main St. #100	(971) 224-5712	
Woodburn	Woodburn Sew & Vac.	1585 N. Pacific Hwy.	(503) 981-6921	
Yamhill	The Quilted Hill	7601 NE Blackburn Rd.	(503) 662-4052	
Zig Zag	Cast One On	70140 E. Hwy. 26	(503) 622-0105	

Index

Notes

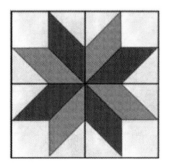

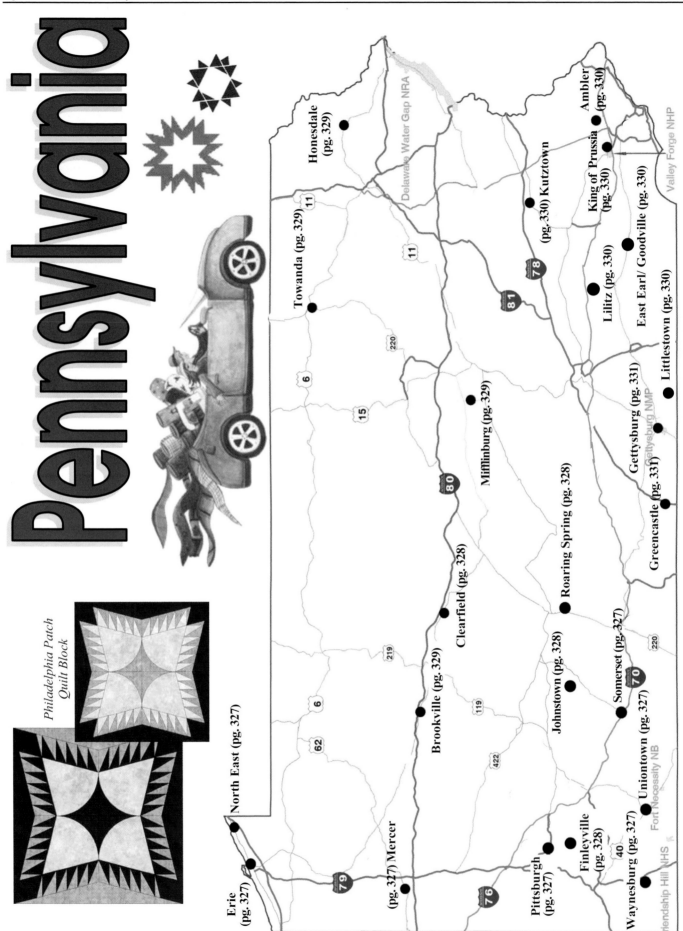

Pennsylvania

Philadelphia Patch
Quilt Block

Honesdale
(pg. 329)

Towanda (pg. 329)

Kutztown

Ambler
(pg. 330)

King of Prussia
(pg. 330)

(pg. 330) Kutztown

East Earl/ Goodville (pg. 330)

Lilitz (pg. 330)

Littlestown (pg. 330)

Valley Forge NHP

Delaware Water Gap NRA

Mifflinburg (pg. 329)

Gettysburg (pg. 331)

Gettysburg NMP

Roaring Spring (pg. 328)

Greencastle (pg. 331)

Clearfield (pg. 328)

Johnstown (pg. 328)

Somerset (pg. 327)

Brookville (pg. 329)

North East (pg. 327)

Uniontown (pg. 327)

Fort Necessity NB

Finleyville
(pg. 328)

Waynesburg (pg. 327)

Friendship Hill NHS

Mercer

(pg. 327) Mercer

Pittsburgh
(pg. 327)

Erie
(pg. 327)

North East, PA   Q

107 Clay St. #3 North East, PA 16428
(814) 725-2275
cpqshop@gmail.com
www.calicopatchquiltshop.com
www.facebook.com/calicopatchquiltshop

CALICO PATCH QUILT SHOP

1600+ Bolts, Books,
Notions, Classes and a Large Selection of
Extra Wide Backing.

Tues, Wed, Fri, Sat 10am-4pm, Thur 12pm-6pm

Mercer, PA   Q

The Gallery of Fabric

116 N. Pitt St. 16137
(724) 662-0464
thegalleryoffabric@zoominternet.net
www.thegalleryoffabric.com

Est: 1995
Owners Sandy & Frank Lord offer
A full service sewing and quilting shop
with over 6000 bolts of discounted fabrics.
500 Batiks, Lots of friendly service, Classes,
HandiQuilter and Janome sales and service.

Tue-Fri 10am-5pm, Sat 10am-4pm

Pittsburgh, PA   Q

Piecing It Together

Mon - Sat 10 - 5
Thur til 6

3458 Babcock Blvd. Pittsburgh, PA 15237
(412) 364-2440
Owners: Johanna Blanarik
Est: 1986   1200 sq.ft.
piecingittogether@comcast.net
www.piecingittogether.biz

Complete line of quilting supplies, 100%
cotton fabrics, books, notions, patterns, and
classes. Lots of samples. Personal & friendly.

Waynesburg, PA   Q

175 Wade St. #D Waynesburg, PA 15370
(724) 833-9147
Owner: Linda Jones ~ ljanejo@windstream.net
Tue-Fri 10-5, Sat 10-3

We offer a wide variety of
Fabrics, Patterns, Notions,
Books, Thread, Classes
and Much More!

Like us on
Facebook

PINE TREE
QUILT SHOP, LLC

73 W. Main St. Uniontown, PA 15401
724-438-1765
www.sew-special.biz
Tue, Wed, Fri 9-5, Thurs 9-8,
Sat 9-4, Closed Sun & Mon

Sew Special
"the answer place
for everything sewing"

Fayette County's Only Authorized Dealer

Husqvarna **PFAFF**
VIKING Perfection starts here.™

Fabrics, threads and notions.
Classes for both beginners and
experienced quilters.

Uniontown, PA   Q

Erie, PA   Q

Millcreek Sewing & Fabric

6044 Peach St. Erie, PA 16509
814-866-8227   Est: 1998
www.millcreeksew.com

baby lock

FOR THE LOVE OF SEWING

Mon - Sat 10 - 5

Look for the White Picket Fence
"Just to see the
Marvelous Samples,
It's Worth the Trip!"
Tri State Leader in
Batiks and blenders
Friendly, Knowledgeable
Staff

Just minutes
off I-90 between the
6th and 7th lights.

www.sewingboxquiltshop.com

The Sewing Box QUILT SHOP

JANOME
WHAT'S NEXT
Mon-Wed & Sat 10am-5pm
Thur & Fri 10am-6pm

¼ mile. from exit 110 off PA Turnpike
2,000+ Bolts of Fabric. Great variety of Books,
Patterns & Notions. Authorized Janome Dealer.
Come and be inspired.

311 Georgian Place Somerset, PA 15501
(814) 701-2635

Somerset, PA   Q

Historic Hotel Bethlehem
Soldiers who fought in World War I stopped to rest and
recover at this iconic hotel in Bethlehem, which dates back to
1741. Its distinguished visitors include several former
presidents, movie stars like Shirley Temple, and figures
including Amelia Earhart and the Dalai Lama.
437 Main St, Bethlehem, PA 18018   (610) 625-5000
www.hotelbethlehem.com

Quilters Corner

Finleyville, PA   **Q**

6101 State Route 88 Ste. 1
Finleyville, PA 15332
724-348-8010

Shop Hours:
Monday thru Saturday 10am - 5pm
Thursday till 9pm

Explore our extensive selection of both traditional
and contemporary fabrics with over 7000 bolts to browse.
Classes for all skill levels from beginner to advanced.
Consult with our friendly, knowledgeable staff.
Visit our website for the latest shop information,
online shopping and directions to visit our shop.
Be sure to sign up for our online newsletter to get
all the latest Quilters Corner news!

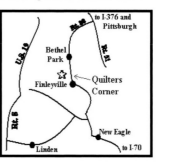

www.quilterscorner-pa.com

Quilt Sampler
FEATURED SHOP
2009

We are your premier quilt shop in South-Western Pennsylvania.

Johnstown, PA   **Q**

Schraders Fabrics by Barb

Monday-Saturday
9:00-5:00

2078 Bedford St.   15904
(814) 266-3113
www.schradersfabricsbybarb.com
Owners: Barb & Bill Schrader
barb.js.100@hotmail.com

Huge Selection of Quality Quilter's Flannels,
Shannon Cuddle, Panels, Moda, Henry Glass,
Benartex, Stonehenge, Quilters Cottons. King
Tut Thread. AccuQuilt Signature Dealer.

Quilt Peddler

M, W, F, 10-5
T, Th 10-6
Sat 10-3

620 Lamberd Ave.
Johnstown, PA 15904
(814) 262-9656
www.thequiltpeddlerllc.com
Owner: Lugene Shaver ~ quiltped@gmail.com
3000+ bolts, Quilting supplies, Classes
Handi Quilter Dealer.

Johnstown, PA   **Q**

Country Beefers

125 Lock Mt. Rd. 16673
(814) 224-4818
Owners: Louann Ferraro
ctrybee@embarqmail.com

Roaring Spring, PA   **Q**

Cotton fabrics, homespuns, books, craft
patterns, notions, stencils.
Also country gift items, small antiques,
Yankee & Village Candles.

Monday - Friday 10:00 - 4:30
Saturday 10:00 - 2:00

Clearfield, PA   **Q**

Quilters Stash Plus

Tues-Fri
10am-5pm
Sat 10am-3pm

500 Turnpike Ave. 16830
(814) 765-2162
Est: 2013   2000+ Bolts
quiltersstashplus@gmailcom
www.quiltersstashplus.com
Easy to find off Interstate 80.

Find us on
Facebook

We specialize in Modern & Bright Colors and Contemporary
Fabrics. Classes. Notions, Purse finding supplies.

Did you know?
Independence Hall and the Liberty Bell belong today to the city of Philadelphia, which purchased the
property for $70,000 from the Commonwealth of Pennsylvania in 1816.

Did you know?
Hershey is considered the Chocolate Capital
of the United States.

Notes

Pennsylvania Shops

Q-Quilting ~ Y-Yarn ~ N-Needlework ~ R-Retreat ~ M-Museum

Airville	Country Variety Store	209 W. Telegraph Rd.	(717) 862-3140	
Allentown	Allentown Sewing Outlet	725 N. 15th St.	(610) 434-8777	
Allentown	Quiltery	2030 Whitehall Ave.	(610) 439-8948	
Allentown	Springtown Textile Co.	950 W. Hamilton	(610) 439-8811	
Allentown	Tucker Yarn Co.	950 W. Hamilton St.	(610) 434-1846	
Allison Park	The Quilt Company	3940 Middle Rd.	(412) 487-9532	
Altoona	Frye's Sweeping and Sewing Center	1400 Valley View Blvd.	(814) 943-5001	
Altoona	Moore Stitches	1635 E. Pleasant Valley Blvd.	(814) 943-2977	
Ambler	**The Round Bobbin Quilt Shop**	**1126-B Horsham Rd.**	**(215) 367-5596**	**Pg. 330**
Bedford	Firesong Studio	201 W. Penn St.	(814) 623-0776	
Bedford	Mary's Quilt Shop	113 W. Pitt St.	(814) 310-2278	
Bedford	Sewing Solutions	6068 Business 220	(814) 623-2413	
Bedford	Unique Stiches Quilt Shop	127 E Pitt St.	(814) 623-2070	
Bellefonte	Third Bay Quilt Shop	105 Rabbit Hill Rd.	(814) 355-7108	
Belleville	Mary Lee's Fabric Shop	3510 W. Main St.	(717) 935-2691	
Bensalem	The Quilt Academy	3671 Hulmerville Rd.	(215) 245-2011	
Berwyn	FrouFrou	601 Lancaster Ave.	(610) 296-8597	
Bethlehem	The Knitter's Edge	1601 W. Broad St.	(610) 419-9276	
Bird in Hand	Log Cabin Quilt Shop	2679 Old Philadelphia Pike	(717) 393-1702	
Bird-in-Hand	The Quilt and Fabric Shack	3137 Old Philadelphia Pike	(717) 768-0338	
Bird-In-Hand	Labadie Looms	2572 Old Philadelphia Pike	(717) 291-8911	
Bradford	Keeping Ewe In Stitches	82 Main St.	(814) 368-7321	
Bradford	Little Fabric Garden	25 Main St.	(814) 362-6070	
Bridgeville	Kid Ewe Knot	429 Washington Ave.	(412) 257-2557	
Bridgewater	Covered Bridge Needlearts	300 Bridge St.	(724) 775-4440	
Bristol	Ye Olde Cross Stitchery	119 Pond St.	(215) 785-0870	
Brookville	**Heirloom Quilting and Antiques**	**1225 Rt. 36 N.**	**(814) 849-8739**	**Pg. 329**
Brookville	Spin-A-Yarn	360 Main St.	(814) 849-2512	
Bryn Mawr	Creative Way Needlepoint	849 W. Lancaster Ave.	(610) 525-2366	
Cambridge Springs	Country Stitichin/Smokin Needles	516 Venango Ave.	(814) 398-8623	
Chadds Ford	A Garden of Yarn	18 Old Ridge Village	(610) 459-5599	
Chadds Ford	Busy Lizzy	387 Spring Mill Rd.	(610) 388-5878	
Chambersburg	Yarn Basket	150 Falling Spring Rd.	(717) 263-3236	
Christiana	The Quilt Ledger	326 N. Bridge St.	(610) 593-7300	
Clarion	B'ewe'tiful Knits Yarn Boutique	22586 Rte. 68	(814) 229-1598	
Clearfield	**Quilter's Stash Plus**	**500 Turnpike Ave.**	**(814) 765-2162**	**Pg. 328**
Conneaut Lake	The Craft Patch	11073 St. Hwy. 18	(814) 382-6110	
Coudersport	Yarn at Olga's	107 E. 2nd St.	(814) 260-9966	
Covode	Autumn House Farm	1001 Locust Rd.	(724) 286-9596	
Cranberry Township	Amy Baughman's Sewing Center	20215 Rte. 19 #106	(724) 779-1390	
Danville	Swisher's Yarn Basket	327 Ferry St.	(570) 275-9276	
Denver	Burkholder Fabrics	2155 W. Rte. 897	(717) 336-6692	
Dover	The Finishing Stitch	4103 Carlisle Rd.	(717) 467-8274	
Doylestown	Byrne Sewing Connection	422 E. Butler Ave.	(215) 230-9411	
Doylestown	Forever Yarn	15 W. Oakland Ave.	(215) 348-5648	
Duncansville	Connie's Collectibles & Quilt Shop	469 Fort of Ten Rd.	(814) 695-2786	
Duncansville	Delightful Ewe	1381 Old Rte. 220 N.	(814) 696-0331	
East Berlin	Manning's Hand Weaving	1132 Green Ridge Rd.	(717) 624-2223	
East Berlin	Woolgatherings	529 W. King St.	(717) 259-0924	
East Earl	**Zincks Fabric Outlet**	**1564 Main St.**	**(717) 445-6123**	**Pg. 330**
East Earl	Family Farm Fabrics	1121 Main St.	(717) 354-2086	
East Petersburg	Threads Needlework	2019C Miller Rd.	(717) 435-8245	
East Stroudsburg	Mountain Knits & Pearls	114 Washington St. Ste. 100	(570) 424-7770	
Easton	At Piece Quiltery	2210 Corriere Rd. #F	(610) 438-4630	
Ebensburg	Creative Fabrics & Quilt Shop	3135 New Germany Rd. #25	(814) 419-8227	
Effort	The Country Quilterie	2783 Rte. 115	(570) 620-9707	
Emmaus	Conversational Threads Fiber Arts Studio	6 S. 4th St.	(610) 421-8889	
Emmaus	The Needle Art Studio	63 S. 7th St.	(610) 967-2138	
Ephrata	Piece by Piece Quilt Shop	22 N. State St. #201	(717) 738-6983	
Ephrata	West Earl Woolen Mill	130 Cocalico Creek Rd.	(717) 859-2241	
Erie	**Millcreek Sewing & Fabric**	**6044 Peach St.**	**(814) 866-8227**	**Pg. 327**
Erie	Burning the Midnight Oil Quilts	8845 Wattsburg Rd.	(814) 825-9000	

Erie	Cultured Purl	3141 W. 26th St.	(814) 836-7875	
Erie	Kelly's Sewing Corner	3330 W. 26th St. Village W. #15	(814) 838-7158	
Erie	Rustic & Refined	2598 W. 8th St.	(814) 838-1710	
Erie	Stitchin' Stuff	3734 W. 12th St.	(814) 838-8591	
Erie	Ta Da Quilting Studio	3628 W. 12th St.	(814) 520-5774	
Evans City	Little Foot Quilt Shoppe	115 W. Main St.	(724) 482-6334	
Everett	Eweknit	22 N. Spring St.	(814) 348-1020	
Exton	The Quilt Block	95 E. Welsh Pool Rd.	(610) 363-0404	
Falls Creek	Amy's Yarn Boutique	394 Slab Run Rd.	(814) 371-4300	
Fayetteville	The Sew'n Place	6195 Chambersburg Rd.	(717) 352-3050	
Finleyville	**Quilters Corner**	**6101 State Rt. 88**	**(724) 348-8010**	**Pg. 328**
Fleetwood	Quilting Friends	1412 N. Richmond Rd.	(610) 944-7475	
Fogelsville	Althouse's Sewing Center	2371 Packhouse Rd.	(610) 285-6597	
Forbes Road	Raggz Fiber Art	118 General St. #A	(724) 600-5550	
Frazer	Fireside Stitchery	490 Lancaster Ave.	(610) 889-9835	
Gettysburg	**Needle and Thread**	**2215 Fairfield Rd.**	**(717) 334-4011**	**Pg. 331**
Glen Mills	The Strawberry Sampler	364 Wilmington Pike A-2	(610) 459-8580	
Glenshaw	The Quilting Needle	3394 Saxonburg Blvd. #550	(412) 767-5500	
Glenside	Stitchers' Dream	221 S. Easton Rd.	(215) 885-3780	
Goodville	Obie's Country Store	1585 Main St.	(717) 445-4616	
Greencastle	**Stitch-N-Time**	**14472 Molly Pitcher Hwy.**	**(717) 597-0051**	**Pg. 331**
Greencastle	Marian's Fabrics	15021 Molly Pitcher Hwy.	(717) 597-3266	
Greensburg	The Stitch in Time Shoppe	801 N. Greengate Rd. Ste. 370	(724) 836-0611	
Greensburg	Zara's Place	161 Old 30 Plaza #11	(724) 420-5673	
Halifax	Coughlin Homespun Yarns	3293 Peters Mountain Rd.	(717) 896-9066	
Hamburg	Yarns R Us	700 B S. 4th St.	(610) 562-5629	
Hanover	Danner's Bernina Shoppe	551 Beck Mill Rd.	(717) 637-4685	
Harmony	Darn Yarn Needles and Thread	253 D Mercer St.	(724) 473-0983	
Harrisburg	Knitters Dream	2340 Mockingbird Rd.	(717) 599-7665	
Havertown	Needle Me	12 E. Eagle Rd.	(610) 446-4004	
Havertown	Stash	2120 Darby Rd.	(484) 416-3649	
Hawley	The Gentle Arts	8 Silk Mill Dr.	(570) 352-3352	
Hershey	Hershey Museum of American Life	63 W. Chocolate Ave.	(717) 534-3439	
Honesdale	**Mountain Quiltworks**	**20 Grandma's Ln.**	**(570) 253-9510**	**Pg. 329**
Huntington	Hindman's Fabrics	11569 Hartslog Valley Rd.	(814) 627-4195	
Indiana	Sheep Thrills	244 Lower Twolick Dr.	(724) 465-2617	
Indiana	Yarns	1136 Philadelphia St.	(724) 349-3240	
Intercourse	Lancaster Yarn Shop	3519 Old Philadelphia Pike	(717) 768-8007	
Intercourse	The Old Country Store	3510 Old Philadelphia Pike	(717) 768-7101	
Intercourse	Zook's Fabric Store	3535 Old Philadelphia Pike	(717) 768-8153	
Jenkintown	Stephanie's Yarn & Needlepoint	319 Old York Rd.	(215) 635-2132	
Jersey Shore	Inspirations Quilt Shop	701 Allegheny St.	(570) 398-7399	
Johnstown	**Quilt Peddler**	**620 Lamberd Ave.**	**(814) 262-9656**	**Pg. 328**
Johnstown	**Schrader's Fabrics by Barb**	**2078 Bedford St.**	**(814) 266-3113**	**Pg. 328**
King of Prussia	**Steve's Sewing, Vacuum & Quilting**			
		314 S. Henderson Rd.	**(610) 768-9453**	**Pg. 330**
Kingston	Gosh Yarn It	303 Market St.	(570) 287-9999	
Kittanning	Claypoole's Fabrics	592 Claypoole Rd.	(724) 297-3860	
Knox	Countryside Quilts	6361 Canoe Ripple Rd.	(814) 797-2434	
Kutztown	**Wooden Bridge Dry Goods**	**195 Deysher Rd.**	**(610) 683-7159**	**Pg. 330**
Lahaska	Twist Knitting & Spinning	5743 Deysher Rd.	(215) 794-3020	
Lancaster	Oh Susanna	2204 Marietta Ave.	(717) 393-5146	
Lancaster	Pennsylvania Farm Museum	2451 Kissel Hill Rd.	(717) 569-0401	
Lancaster	Stitches Unlimited	721 Olde Hickory Rd.	(717) 560-9416	
Lancaster	The Heritage Center Museum	5 W. King St.	(717) 299-6440	
Lancaster	The Speckled Sheep	713 Olde Hickory Rd.	(717) 435-8359	
Landisville	Flying Fibers	329 Main St.	(717) 898-8020	
Lebanon	Martin's Fabric Barn	2799 E. Cumberland St.	(717) 274-5359	
Lederach	Just Cross Stitch	690 Harleysville Pike	(215) 513-9373	
Leechburg	Common Threads	1121 State Rte. 356	(724) 236-0196	
Leechburg	Farmhouse Fabrics	786 Schenley Rd.	(724) 845-2745	
Lewisburg	The Village Stitchery	5762 Old Turnpike Rd.	(570) 966-8711	
Lewistown	Marty's Quilt Shop	135 Nolan Dr.	(717) 953-9947	
Ligonier	Bo Peep Fine Yarns	221 W. Main	(724) 238-4040	
Ligonier	Kathy's Kreations	141 E. Main St.	(724) 238-9320	
Limerick	Just Cross Stitch	308 W. Ridge Pike	(610) 409-9373	
Lititz	**Weaver's Dry Goods**	**108 W. Brubaker Valley Rd.**	**(717) 627-1724**	**Pg. 330**
Lititz	Ball & Skein Shop	2 E. 28th Division Hwy.	(717) 625-4280	
Littlestown	**Simply Stashing Fabric & Quilts**	**1897 Hanover Pike**	**(717) 359-4121**	**Pg. 330**

Index

Lower Burrell	The Sewing Store	103 Macbeth Dr.	(724) 334-1985	
Loysville	Wise Dry Goods	5683 Sherman Valley Rd.	(717) 789-4308	
Manheim	Stitch & Craft	2957 Lebanon Rd.	(717) 664-4230	
Mansfield	Yorkshire Meadows Knitting & Spinning Shop			
		9646 N. Elk Run Rd.	(570) 549-2553	
Marchand	Silverbrook Fiber Arts & Sheepskins	16040 Rt. 119 Hwy. N.	(724) 286-3317	
Martinsburg	Traditions	2327 Curryville Rd.	(814) 793-3980	
Marysville	Smile Spinners	1975 Valley Rd.	(717) 957-4225	
McMurray	Sew Much Fun	242 E. McMurray Rd.	(724) 942-9425	
Meadville	Fiberworks	910 Market St.	(814) 333-1228	
Meadville	Yarn Vault	940 Park Ave.	(814) 758-8837	
Mercer	**The Gallery of Fabric**	**116 N. Pitt St.**	**(724) 662-0464**	**Pg. 327**
Midland	Create A Stitch	17 7th St.	(724) 643-4833	
Mifflinburg	**Verna's Fabrics**	**1430 Red Bank Rd.**	**(570) 966-2350**	**Pg. 329**
Mifflinburg	Hoover's Bernina Sew	2282 Beaver Rd.	(570) 966-3822	
Monongahela	The Memory Tree & Yarn Branch	1015 Chess St.	(724) 258-6758	
Monroeville	Creative Stitches Café	2644 Mosside Blvd.	(412) 646-4736	
Mount Pleasant	Quilt Patch	806 W. Main St.	(724) 887-4160	
Muncy	Muncy Historical Society & Museum of History			
		40 N. Main St.	(570) 546-5917	
Murrysville	Little Country Cross Stitch	4403 Old William Penn Hwy.	(724) 325-4770	
Nazareth	The Kraemer Yarn Shop	240 S. Main St.	(610) 759-4030	
New Castle	Log House	134 Mohawk School Rd.	(724) 667-8444	
New Cumberland	Half Moon Handwerks	214 3rd. St.	(717) 774-3020	
New Enterprise	Zimmernan's Bernina Sewing Shop	208 Flitch Rd.	(814) 766-9942	
New Holland	Brubaker's Sewing Center	20 N. Robert Ave.	(717) 354-8332	
New Holland	Cedar Lane Dry Goods	204 Orlan Rd.	(717) 354-0030	
New Hope	Gazebo Plus	7 Village Row	(215) 862-0740	
Newburg	Esh's Store	16285 Cumberland Hwy.	(717) 530-5305	
Newtown	Knit in Newtown	10 S. State St. #3	(267) 685-0794	
Newtown Square	Slip Knot	3719 W. Chester Pike	(610) 359-9070	
North East	**Calico Patch Quilt Shoppe**	**107 Clay St. #3**	**(814) 725-2275**	**Pg. 327**
North East	Super Stitch	110 E. Main St.	(888) 525-9724	
Oakdale	Tonidale Yarn & Needlecraft Corner	1050 Montour Church Rd.	(412) 788-8850	
Oakmont	Yarns by Design	622 Allegheny River Blvd.	(412) 794-8332	
Oley	All Things Ewesful	3240 W. Philadelphia Ave.	(484) 491-1330	
Oley	Ladyfingers Sewing Studio	6375 Oley Turnpike	(610) 689-0068	
Palmerton	The Quilted Crow	413 Delaware Ave.	(610) 900-4700	
Penns Park	Knitting to Know Ewe	2324 Second St. Pike	(215) 598-9276	
Perkasie	Lillie's Yarns	1000 E. Walnut St. #204	(215) 258-1259	
Philadelphia	Hidden River Yarns	4358 B Main St.	(215) 920-2603	
Philadelphia	Loop Yarn	1914 South St.	(215) 893-9939	
Philadelphia	Nangellini	832 S. St.	(215) 413-5001	
Philadelphia	Rittenhouse Needlepoint	1737 Chestnut St. #201	(215) 563-4566	
Philadelphia	Rosie's Yarn Cellar	2017 Locust St.	(215) 977-9276	
Philadelphia	Yarnphoria	1016 Pine St.	(215) 923-0914	
Phoenixville	Purls of Wisdom	2208 Kimberton Rd.	(610) 933-5010	
Pine Grove Mills	Stitch Your Art Out	235 E. Pine Grove Rd.	(814) 238-4151	
Pittsburgh	**Piecing It Together**	**3458 Babcock Blvd.**	**(412) 364-2440**	**Pg. 327**
Pittsburgh	Airport Sewing Center	13 W. Prospect	(412) 922-1000	
Pittsburgh	Beehive NeedleArts	671 Washington Rd.	(412) 343-4630	
Pittsburgh	Dyed in the Wool	3458 Babcock Blvd.	(412) 364-0310	
Pittsburgh	Gloria Horn Sewing Studio	300 Castle Shannon Blvd.	(412) 344-2330	
Pittsburgh	Knit One	2721 Murray Ave.	(412) 421-6666	
Pittsburgh	Natural Stitches	6401 Penn Ave.	(412) 441-4410	
Pittsburgh	Needle Point Breeze	6734 Reynolds St.	(412) 361-6380	
Pittsburgh	Quilters Depot	4160 Library Rd.	(412) 308-6236	
Punxsutawney	Lydia's Quilt Shop	56 Stuchell Ln.	(814) 938-8488	
Reading	Stitch 'N Stuff	3646 Pottsville Pike	(610) 929-2464	
Rebersburg	Main Street Yarn	121 E. Main St.	(814) 349-2611	
Red Lion	Grim Hollow Stitchery	1040 Grim Hollow Rd.	(717) 244-3220	
Richboro	Stitch Inn Works	10 Stable Mill Trail	(215) 962-9456	
Roaring Spring	**The Country Beefers**	**125 Lock Mt. Rd.**	**(814) 224-4818**	**Pg. 328**
Ronks	Dutchland Quilt Patch	2851A Lincoln Hwy. E	(717) 687-0534	
Ronks	Family Farm Quilt	3511 W. Newport Rd.	(717) 768-8375	
Ronks	Quilt Shop at Millers	2811 Lincoln Hwy. E	(717) 687-8439	
Saegertown	The Needleworks	16408 Hwy. 86	(814) 783-0040	
Sarver	Kimberlys' Quilting & Pittsburg Sewing Center			
		102 Eastown Rd.	(724) 524-1110	
Sayre	Friendship Star Quilt Shop	131 Center St.	(570) 886-2296	

Sayre	Mary's General Store	927 W. Lockhart St.	(570) 888-2320	
Seven Valleys	Sweitzer's Countryside Fibers & Gifts	7335 Yellow Church Rd.	(717) 428-2909	
Sewickley	The Porcupine Needlepoint Shop	404 Beaver St.	(412) 741-3380	
Sewickley	Yarns Unlimited	435 Beaver St.	(412) 741-8894	
Shippensburg	Rocky Turf General Store	949 Mud Level Rd.	(717) 532-3977	
Shiremanstown	The Colonial Yarn Shop	7 Front St. Ste. 100	(717) 763-8016	
Skippack	Yarnings	4007 Skippack Pike	(610) 584-6216	
Slippery Rock	Fabric Sewing Center	537 New Castle Rd.	(724) 794-3076	
Smicksburg	SuzyB Knits	52 Clarion St.	(814) 257-8326	
Somerset	**The Sewing Box Quilt Shop**	**311 Georgian Place**	**(814) 701-2635**	**Pg. 327**
Spring Grove	Painted Spring Farm Alpacas	280 Roth Church Rd.	(717) 891-8060	
Spring Mills	The Knitters Underground	532 Lower Georges Valley Rd.	(814) 422-8612	
Strasburg	HodgePodge	14 E. Main St.	(717) 687-8951	
Stroudsburg	American Ribbon's Quilt Shop	925 Ann St.	(570) 421-7470	
Stroudsburg	Pocono Sew & Vac.	567 Main St.	(570) 421-4580	
Swarthmore	Finely A Knitting Party	104 Park Ave.	(610) 328-7210	
Sweet Valley	118 Fabrics & More	1205 St. Rt. 118	(570) 477-3166	
Towanda	**Shores Quilt Stop**	**1003 Golden Mile Rd.**	**(570) 265-4444**	**Pg. 329**
Towanda	Country Thread Shed	54 Mountain Lake Rd.	(570) 265-4124	
Troy	Perry's Patches & Quilting	29 Painter Lick Dr.	(570) 297-4558	
Union City	Bee Happy Quilting	16412 State Hwy. 8	(814) 694-2126	
Uniontown	**Sew Special**	**73 W. Main St.**	**(724) 438-1765**	**Pg. 327**
Warren	Sew Kreative	111 Madison Ave.	(814) 723-8356	
Wayne	Stitch Haus	110 S. Wayne Ave.	(610) 688-2726	
Waynesboro	Itchin' 2 Stitch	204 S. Potomac St.	(888) 492-3719	
Waynesboro	The Knitting Cottage	6810 Iron Bridges Rd.	(717) 762-1168	
Waynesburg	**Pine Tree Quilt Shop**	**175 Wade St. #D**	**(724) 833-9147**	**Pg. 327**
West Reading	Yarn Gallery	628 Penn Ave.	(610) 373-1622	
West Warren	Super Stitch 2	1056 Pennsylvania Ave.	(814) 726-2501	
Willow Street	Legacy Yarn Co.	2611 Willow Street Pike N.	(717) 464-7575	
Womelsdorf	In Stitches Quilt & Fabric	4017 Conrad Weiser Pkwy.	(610) 589-2625	
York	Uncommon Threads	2025 Springwood Dr.	(717) 699-1600	

Index

Notes

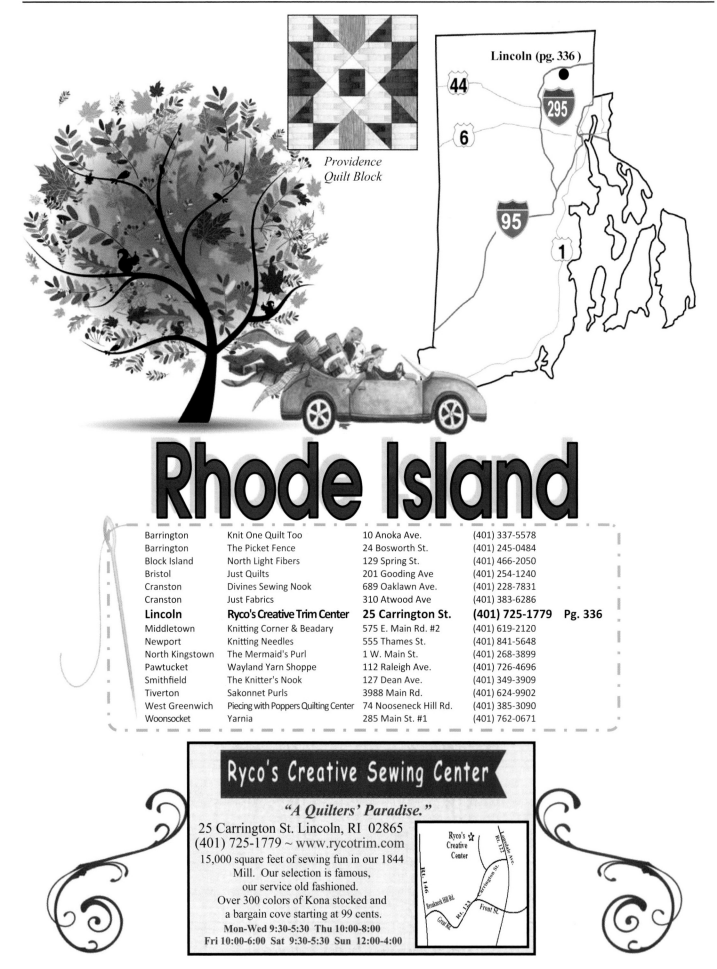

*Providence
Quilt Block*

Lincoln (pg. 336)

Rhode Island

Barrington	Knit One Quilt Too	10 Anoka Ave.	(401) 337-5578	
Barrington	The Picket Fence	24 Bosworth St.	(401) 245-0484	
Block Island	North Light Fibers	129 Spring St.	(401) 466-2050	
Bristol	Just Quilts	201 Gooding Ave	(401) 254-1240	
Cranston	Divines Sewing Nook	689 Oaklawn Ave.	(401) 228-7831	
Cranston	Just Fabrics	310 Atwood Ave	(401) 383-6286	
Lincoln	**Ryco's Creative Trim Center**	**25 Carrington St.**	**(401) 725-1779**	**Pg. 336**
Middletown	Knitting Corner & Beadary	575 E. Main Rd. #2	(401) 619-2120	
Newport	Knitting Needles	555 Thames St.	(401) 841-5648	
North Kingstown	The Mermaid's Purl	1 W. Main St.	(401) 268-3899	
Pawtucket	Wayland Yarn Shoppe	112 Raleigh Ave.	(401) 726-4696	
Smithfield	The Knitter's Nook	127 Dean Ave.	(401) 349-3909	
Tiverton	Sakonnet Purls	3988 Main Rd.	(401) 624-9902	
West Greenwich	Piecing with Poppers Quilting Center	74 Nooseneck Hill Rd.	(401) 385-3090	
Woonsocket	Yarnia	285 Main St. #1	(401) 762-0671	

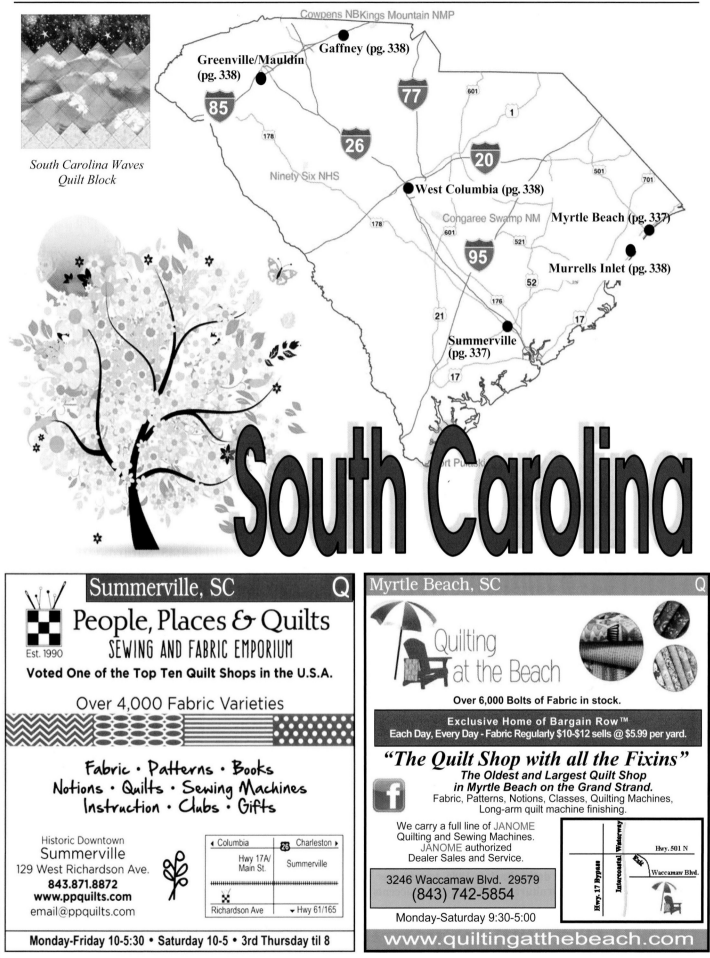

South Carolina Waves Quilt Block

Cowpens NB Kings Mountain NMP

Gaffney (pg. 338)

Greenville/Mauldin (pg. 338)

West Columbia (pg. 338)

Ninety Six NHS

Congaree Swamp NM

Myrtle Beach (pg. 337)

Murrells Inlet (pg. 338)

Summerville (pg. 337)

South Carolina

South Dakota

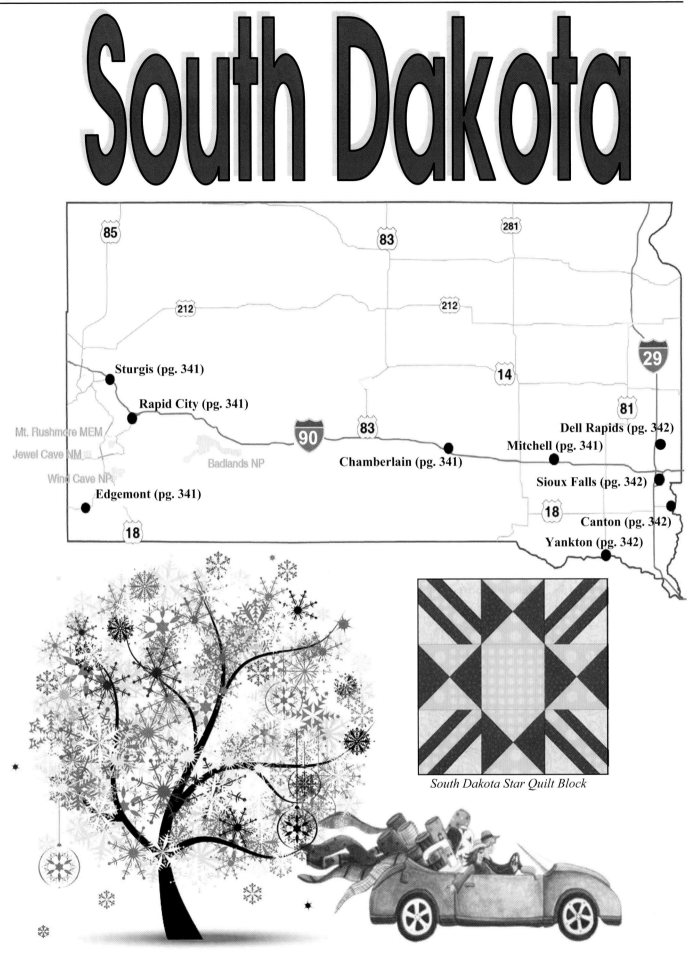

Sturgis (pg. 341)

Rapid City (pg. 341)

Chamberlain (pg. 341)

Dell Rapids (pg. 342)

Mitchell (pg. 341)

Sioux Falls (pg. 342)

Edgemont (pg. 341)

Canton (pg. 342)

Yankton (pg. 342)

South Dakota Star Quilt Block

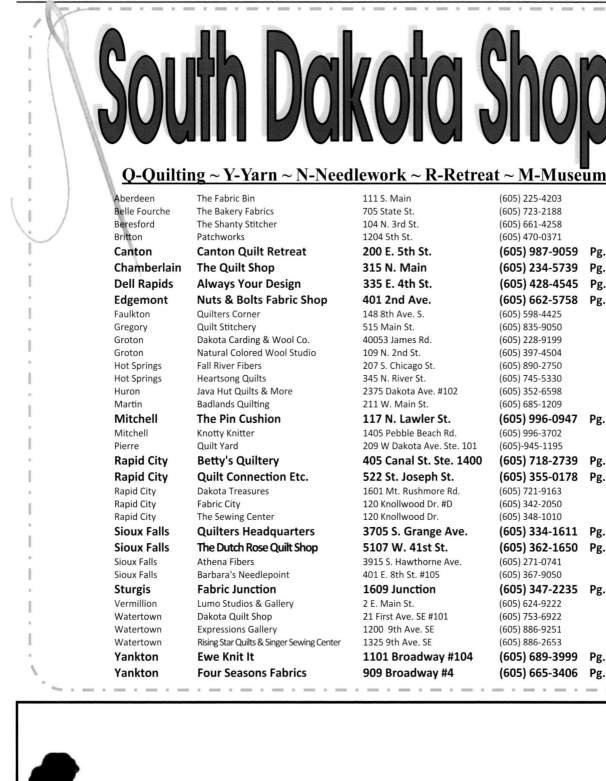

South Dakota Shops

Q-Quilting ~ Y-Yarn ~ N-Needlework ~ R-Retreat ~ M-Museum

City	Shop	Address	Phone	Page
Aberdeen	The Fabric Bin	111 S. Main	(605) 225-4203	
Belle Fourche	The Bakery Fabrics	705 State St.	(605) 723-2188	
Beresford	The Shanty Stitcher	104 N. 3rd St.	(605) 661-4258	
Britton	Patchworks	1204 5th St.	(605) 470-0371	
Canton	**Canton Quilt Retreat**	**200 E. 5th St.**	**(605) 987-9059**	**Pg. 342**
Chamberlain	**The Quilt Shop**	**315 N. Main**	**(605) 234-5739**	**Pg. 341**
Dell Rapids	**Always Your Design**	**335 E. 4th St.**	**(605) 428-4545**	**Pg. 342**
Edgemont	**Nuts & Bolts Fabric Shop**	**401 2nd Ave.**	**(605) 662-5758**	**Pg. 341**
Faulkton	Quilters Corner	148 8th Ave. S.	(605) 598-4425	
Gregory	Quilt Stitchery	515 Main St.	(605) 835-9050	
Groton	Dakota Carding & Wool Co.	40053 James Rd.	(605) 228-9199	
Groton	Natural Colored Wool Studio	109 N. 2nd St.	(605) 397-4504	
Hot Springs	Fall River Fibers	207 S. Chicago St.	(605) 890-2750	
Hot Springs	Heartsong Quilts	345 N. River St.	(605) 745-5330	
Huron	Java Hut Quilts & More	2375 Dakota Ave. #102	(605) 352-6598	
Martin	Badlands Quilting	211 W. Main St.	(605) 685-1209	
Mitchell	**The Pin Cushion**	**117 N. Lawler St.**	**(605) 996-0947**	**Pg. 341**
Mitchell	Knotty Knitter	1405 Pebble Beach Rd.	(605) 996-3702	
Pierre	Quilt Yard	209 W Dakota Ave. Ste. 101	(605)-945-1195	
Rapid City	**Betty's Quiltery**	**405 Canal St. Ste. 1400**	**(605) 718-2739**	**Pg. 341**
Rapid City	**Quilt Connection Etc.**	**522 St. Joseph St.**	**(605) 355-0178**	**Pg. 341**
Rapid City	Dakota Treasures	1601 Mt. Rushmore Rd.	(605) 721-9163	
Rapid City	Fabric City	120 Knollwood Dr. #D	(605) 342-2050	
Rapid City	The Sewing Center	120 Knollwood Dr.	(605) 348-1010	
Sioux Falls	**Quilters Headquarters**	**3705 S. Grange Ave.**	**(605) 334-1611**	**Pg. 342**
Sioux Falls	**The Dutch Rose Quilt Shop**	**5107 W. 41st St.**	**(605) 362-1650**	**Pg. 342**
Sioux Falls	Athena Fibers	3915 S. Hawthorne Ave.	(605) 271-0741	
Sioux Falls	Barbara's Needlepoint	401 E. 8th St. #105	(605) 367-9050	
Sturgis	**Fabric Junction**	**1609 Junction**	**(605) 347-2235**	**Pg. 341**
Vermillion	Lumo Studios & Gallery	2 E. Main St.	(605) 624-9222	
Watertown	Dakota Quilt Shop	21 First Ave. SE #101	(605) 753-6922	
Watertown	Expressions Gallery	1200 9th Ave. SE	(605) 886-9251	
Watertown	Rising Star Quilts & Singer Sewing Center	1325 9th Ave. SE	(605) 886-2653	
Yankton	**Ewe Knit It**	**1101 Broadway #104**	**(605) 689-3999**	**Pg. 342**
Yankton	**Four Seasons Fabrics**	**909 Broadway #4**	**(605) 665-3406**	**Pg. 342**

Index

Notes

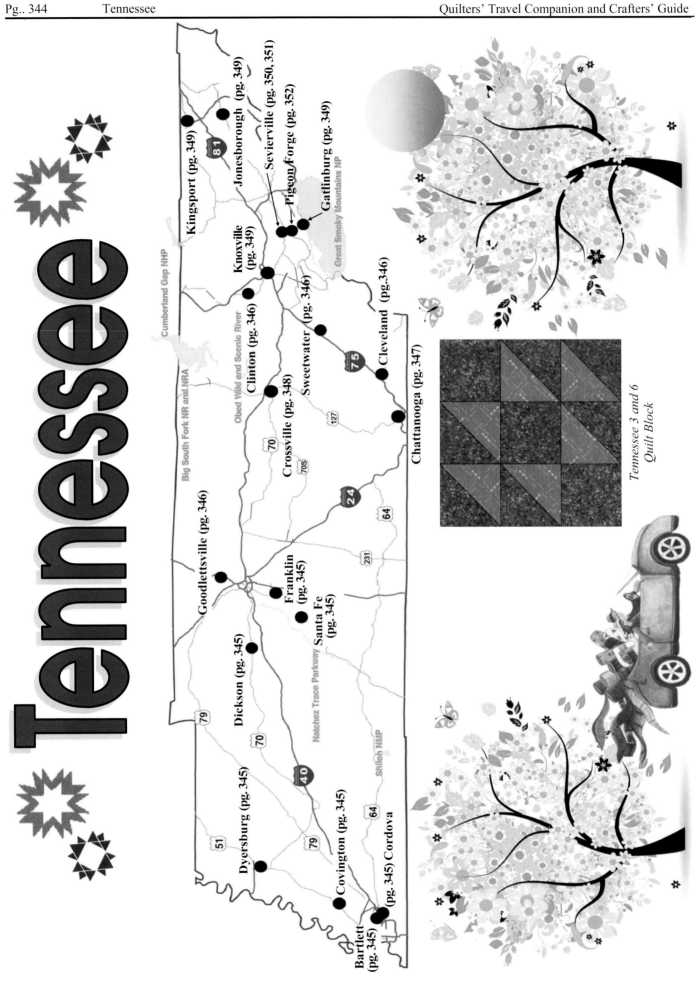

Tennessee

Kingsport (pg. 349)

Jonesborough (pg. 349)

Sevierville (pg. 350, 351)

Pigeon Forge (pg. 352)

Gatlinburg (pg. 349)

Great Smoky Mountains NP

Cumberland Gap NHP

Knoxville (pg. 349)

Clinton (pg. 346)

Sweetwater (pg. 346)

Cleveland (pg. 346)

Obed Wild and Scenic River

Big South Fork NR and NRA

Crossville (pg. 348)

Chattanooga (pg. 347)

Goodlettsville (pg. 346)

Franklin (pg. 345)

Santa Fe (pg. 345)

Dickson (pg. 345)

Natchez Trace Parkway

Shiloh NMP

Dyersburg (pg. 345)

Covington (pg. 345)

(pg. 345) Cordova

Bartlett (pg. 345)

Tennessee 3 and 6
Quilt Block

Did you know?
The first guide dog for the blind in the U.S.
lived in Nashville with her owner
Morris Frank. "Buddy" was trained in
Switzerland by The Seeing Eye,
the first organization
to train guide dogs.

My soul is fed with needle and thread.

Notes

Little Blessings
QUILT SHOP

4351 Hwy. 127 N. Crossville, TN
blessings4u@volfirst.net

931-707-7724
www.littleblessing.net

Owners: Robert & Julia Ranney

"Where we are always wrapped up in Quilting"

- Large selection of quality 100% cotton quilting fabric and growing
- Featuring the Newest Patterns & Books
- Large selection of quilting & sewing notions
- Friendly knowledgeable Staff
- Comfortable classroom
- Classes for all skill levels
- Longarm Quilting Services

Crossville, TN   Q

an authorized PFAFF dealer
Machine Sales & Service

Monday - Friday 9:30 - 5, Sat 9:30 - 3
Winter hours: December 1 - March 1
Monday - Friday 9:30 - 4, Sat 9:30 - 3

Iva's

MACHINE QUILTING
& SEWING CENTER

1020 Old Knoxville Highway
Sevierville, TN 37862

www.ivaquilts.com

info@ivaquilts.com

(865) 428-8008

Over 7,000 bolts of top-name
fabrics and PreCuts!
Large assortment of patterns, books,
notions, machine accessories and More...
Charms, Jelly Rolls, Layer Cakes,
Honey Buns & Turn Overs.
We offer Machine Quilting Services and
Rental of our Longarm Machines.

| Monday-Friday 9:00-5:00 |
| Saturday 9:00-4:00 |

Peabody Hotel

Though it was built in 1869 and hosted guests including
Andrew Johnson and William McKinley, this elegant
Memphis hotel became a true cornerstone of the downtown
area after a grand reopening ceremony in 1981. Today it's
most famous for its feathered residents, the "Peabody
Ducks," who live on the rooftop and make daily treks to the
lobby to swim in the hotel fountain.
a tradition since the 30s.

149 Union Ave, Memphis, TN 38103
(901) 529-4000
www.peabodymemphis.com

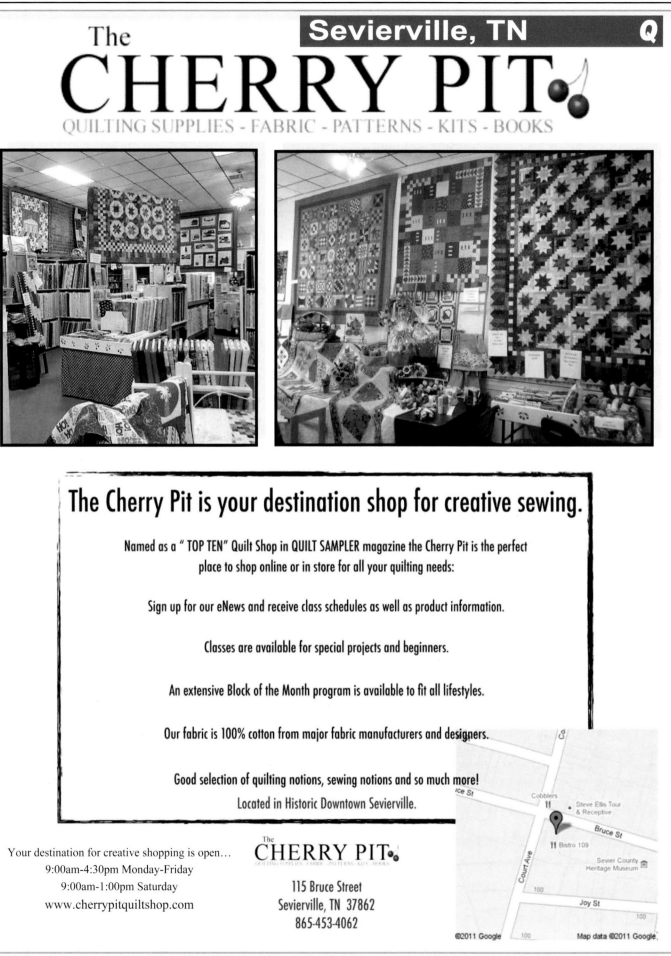

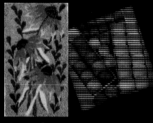
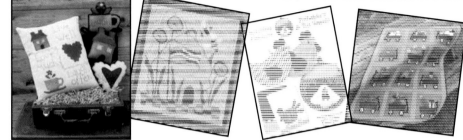
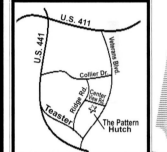

Tennessee Shops

Q-Quilting ~ Y-Yarn ~ N-Needlework ~ R-Retreat ~ M-Museum

Bartlett	**Klassy Katz**	**6022 Stage Rd.**	**(901) 213-0099**	**Pg. 345**
Blountville	Quilted Blessings Quilt Shop	3218 Hwy. 126	(423) 323-7700	
Brentwood	Bernina Sewing Machine Station	91 Seaboard Ln. #102	(615) 373-1600	
Brentwood	Bliss Yarns	127 Franklin Rd. #170	(615) 370-8717	
Brentwood	Nashville Needleworks	7020 Church St. E. #5	(615) 377-6336	
Brighton	The Discerning Quilter	1700 Old Hwy. 51 S. Ste.	(901) 837-6938	
Bristol	Skeins & Things	1537 Southside Ave.	(423) 764-2144	
Chapel Hill	Silver Threads & Golden Needles	130 S. Horton Pkwy.	(931) 364-2886	
Charlotte	Three Creeks Farm	365 Peabody Rd.	(615) 789-5943	
Chattanooga	**Ready Set Sew**	**3444 Ringgold Rd.**	**(423) 629-6411**	**Pg. 347**
Chattanooga	Bernina Sew N Quilt Studio	5950 Shallowford Rd. Ste. A	(423) 521-7231	
Chattanooga	Genuine Purl	140 N. Market St.	(423) 267-7335	
Chattanooga	Pins & Needles Quilt Shop	6425 Hixson Pike #1	(423) 668-8734	
Chattanooga	Spool--BadAss Quilters Society	1420 McCallie Ave.	(423) 602-8526	
Clarksville	Absolutely Fun Sewing	2068 Wilma Rudolph Blvd. #C	(931) 802-5800	
Clarksville	Yarn Asylum	2535 Madison St. #A	(931) 919-5171	
Cleveland	**Hyderhangout**	**219 1st St. NE**	**(423) 715-2908**	**Pg. 346**
Cleveland	Lana's Quilts & Sew Much More	189 Godfrey Ln. SE	(423) 715-1880	
Cleveland	Time to Sew	2328 Treasure Dr. #A-10	(423) 310-6117	
Clinton	**Museum of Appalachia**	**2819 Andersonville Hwy.**	**(865) 494-7680**	**Pg. 346**
Clinton	**Sew Unique Fabric Store**	**403 Hillcrest St.**	**(865) 457-5070**	**Pg. 346**
Clinton	The Clinch River Yarn Company	725 N. Charles G. Seivers Blvd.	(865) 269-4528	
Columbia	The Needle Nest	601 W. 7th St.	(931) 381-9910	

Cookeville	All Points Needleworks	368 Tommy Dodson Hwy.	(931) 239-5910	
Cookeville	Country Patchworks	283 S. Lowe Ave.	(931) 526-7276	
Cookeville	Spring Creek Quilts	3900 Cookeville Hwy.	(931) 498-3473	
Cookeville	T's Yarn Barn	1120 England Dr.	(931) 526-6410	
Cordova	**Quiltsmiths**	**1150 Dexter Ln. # 103**	**(901) 624-9985**	**Pg. 345**
Cosby	Holloway's Country Home	3892 Cosby Hwy.	(423) 487-3866	
Covington	**The Stitching Store**	**887 Hwy. 51 S.**	**(901) 476-2030**	**Pg. 345**
Crossville	**Little Blessings Quilt Shop**	**4351 Hwy. 127 N.**	**(931) 707-7724**	**Pg. 348**
Crossville	The Yarn Patch	1771 Peavine Rd. #102	(931) 707-1255	
Dandridge	Mom & Megg Quilt Shop	1105 B Banner St.	(515) 559-4608	
Dayton	The Sewing Shop	280 2nd Ave. Unit 4	(423) 775-0882	
Dickson	**Granny B's Quilt Shop**	**189 Beasley St.**	**(615) 441-3884**	**Pg. 345**
Dickson	SPO Sewing Center	115 W. Christi Dr.	(615) 740-8774	
Dickson	Yarn Frenzy	107 Myatt St.	(615) 446-3577	
Dyersburg	**Stitchery Quilt Shoppe**	**2675 Lake Rd. #D**	**(731)-285-2332**	**Pg. 345**
Englewood	Katy's Fabric	17 Main St.	(423) 887-5725	
Fayetteville	Hooked On Quilting	8 Elkton Pike	(931) 433-1886	
Franklin	**Stitcher's Garden**	**209 S. Royal Oaks Blvd. #223**	**(615) 790-0603**	**Pg. 345**
Franklin	The Joy of Knitting	209 S. Royal Oaks Blvd. #223	(615) 925-2745	
Gatlinburg	**Mountain Stitches by Susan**	**601 Glades Rd. #13**	**(865) 436-0077**	**Pg. 349**
Gatlinburg	Maple's Tree	639 Parkway #1	(865) 436-4602	
Gatlinburg	Smoky Mountain Spinnery	466 Brookside Village Way #8	(865) 436-9080	
Georgetown	R & M Yarns	8510 Hwy. 60	(423) 961-0690	
Germantown	Bumbletees Fabrics	2219 S. Germantown Rd. #E	(901) 755-9701	
Germantown	Rainbow Yarn & Fibers	1980 Exeter Rd.	(901) 753-9835	
Goodlettsville	**Accomplish Quilting**	**855 Springfield Hwy. Ste. 109**	**(615) 756-9556**	**Pg. 346**
Goodlettsville	Sewing Machines Etc.	808 Meadowlark Ln.	(615) 859-9900	
Greenback	Mountain Creek Quilt Shop	6588 US. Hwy. 411 S.	(865) 856-0805	
Harriman	Loose Threads	1211 S. Roane St. #5	(865) 882-5588	
Harrogate	Cosby's Fabric & Crafts	662 Patterson Rd.	(423) 869-5599	
Hohenwald	Main Street Fabric and Flowers	101 E. Main St.	(931) 796-3451	
Hohenwald	The Quilter's Shack	1220 Columbia Hwy.	(931) 306-3204	
Huntington	Mockingbird Threadworks	19703 E. Main St.	(731) 986-8111	
Jackson	Sew Carefree	2078 Hollywood Dr. #A	(731) 736-3996	
Jackson	Sew Many Ideas	405 Vann Dr. #D	(731) 668-8099	
Jamestown	Fabrics N Quilts	847 Old Hwy. 127 S.	(931) 752-7539	
Jasper	Sew Notions	4571 Main St. #C	(423) 939-0550	
Johnson City	Bernina in Stitches	408 S. Roan St. #100	(423) 283-0456	
Johnson City	Cross Stitch & Crafts	240 E. Main St. #200	(423) 610-0441	
Johnson City	Yarntiques	410 E. Watauga Ave.	(423) 232-2933	
Jonesborough	**Tennessee Quilts**	**114 Boone St.**	**(423) 753-6644**	**Pg. 349**
Jonesborough	Pioneer Quilting	732 Mill Springs Rd.	(423) 753-7154	
Kingsport	**Heavenly Stitches Quilt Shoppe**	**4219 Ft Henry Dr. #100**	**(423) 406-1401**	**Pg. 349**
Kingsport	Carriage House	528 E. Market St.	(423) 247-9091	
Kingston Springs	Ewe & Company	407 N. Main St.	(615) 952-0110	
Knoxville	**Dizzy Divas Fabric Shop**	**4752 Centerline Dr.**	**(865) 474-9921**	**Pg. 349**
Knoxville	Gina's Bernina Sewing Center	10816 Kingston Pike	(865) 966-5941	
Knoxville	Kat Lover's Pur-Fect Quilting and Fabric Shop	813 Kermit Dr.	(865) 687-5293	
Knoxville	Loopville	5204 Kingston Pike Ste. 3	(865) 584-9772	
Knoxville	Mammaw's Thimble Fabric & Quilt Shop	4319 Papermill Dr.	(865) 588-8818	
Knoxville	MidSouth Sewing	7240 Kingston Pike	(865) 249-6381	
Knoxville	Sewing Machines ETC	8419 Kingston Pike	(865) 690-7770	
Knoxville	The Yarn Haven	464 N. Cedar Bluff Rd.	(865) 694-9900	
Lafollette	The Quilt Patch	2221 Jacksboro Pike Ste. C4	(423) 562-4420	
Lynnville	Stitchin Station	155 Mill St.	(931) 309-7301	
Maryville	Hook & Needle	113 W. Harper Ave.	(865) 268-5003	
Maryville	Twisted Sisters	3426 Sevierville Rd.	(865) 980-0950	
McMinnville	B J's custom Quilting & Fabric	1202 Sparta St.	(931) 473-8141	
Memphis	Amy's Golden Strand	3808 Summer Ave.	(901) 458-6109	
Memphis	Sew Memphis	2075 Madison Ave. Ste. 6	(901) 244-6224	
Memphis	Yarniverse	709 S. Mendenhall Rd.	(901) 818-0940	
Murfreesboro	Absolutely Fun Sewing	2705 Old Fort Pkwy. Ste. L	(615) 295-2998	
Murfreesboro	Country Cupboard	325 N. Front St.	(615) 895-1632	
Murfreesboro	Knaughty Knitter	423 N. Walnut St.	(615) 217-4966	
Murfreesboro	MidSouth Sewing	266 River Rock Blvd.	(615) 893-1800	
Murfreesboro	Quilt Connection	1011 #A Memorial Blvd.	(615) 867-0210	
Nashville	Nutmeg Fabric & Yarns	1006 Fatherland St. #204	(615) 419-2661	
Nashville	Stitchin' Post	2811 Columbine Pl.	(615) 383-3672	
Oak Ridge	Atomic Fibers	103 W. Tennessee Ave.	(865) 272-5263	

Index

Ooltewah	Chattanooga Quilt Shop	5711 Main St.	(423) 648-2842	
Pigeon Forge	**The Pattern Hutch**	**926 Center View Rd.**	**(865) 428-1361**	**Pg. 352**
Pigeon Forge	Dixie Darlin Inc.	3355 Butler St.	(865) 453-3104	
Powell	Stitches 'N' Stuff Fabric Shoppe	7553 Barnett Way	(865) 512-9109	
Rogersville	Sunny Side Yarns on Depot	207 S. Depot St.	(423) 272-9276	
Santa Fe	**The Quilting Frame**	**5990 Leipers Creek Rd.**	**(931) 682-3746**	**Pg. 345**
Sevierville	**Iva's Machine Quilting**	**1020 Old Knoxville Hwy.**	**(865) 428-8008**	**Pg. 350**
Sevierville	**The Cherry Pit**	**115 Bruce St.**	**(865) 453-4062**	**Pg. 351**
Sevierville	**The Lodge at Douglas Lake**	**1280 Flat Creek Rd.**	**(615) 268-7781**	**Pg. 350**
Sevierville	Terri's Yarns and Crafts	927 Dolly Parton Pkwy.	(865) 453-7756	
Smithville	Country Lane Quilts	930 Vaughn Ln.	(615) 215-8696	
Smithville	Sew Clever Fabrics & More	105 W. Main St.	(615) 597-8521	
Smyrna	Stitcher's Playhouse	540 Rock Springs Rd.	(615) 355-1309	
Sparta	Simply Southern Quilts	12 Liberty Sq.	(931) 836-3271	
Spring Hill	The Dancing Bobbin Quilt Shop	5326 Main St.	(931) 486-2380	
Springfield	The Fabric Shop	508 S Main St.	(615) 382-5600	
Sweetwater	**Whistlestop Quilt Retreat**	**134 Head of Creek Rd.**	**(423) 271-6380**	**Pg. 346**
Tazewell	Mountain Hollow Farm	559 Vancel Rd.	(423) 869-8927	
Tennessee Ridge	Yards-N-Yarns	2235 S. Main St.	(931) 721-4008	
Tullahoma	Quilting Dreams	114 SW Atlantic St.	(931) 393-3870	
Tullahoma	Threaded Needle	209 SE Atlantic St.	(931) 455-8543	

Index

Notes

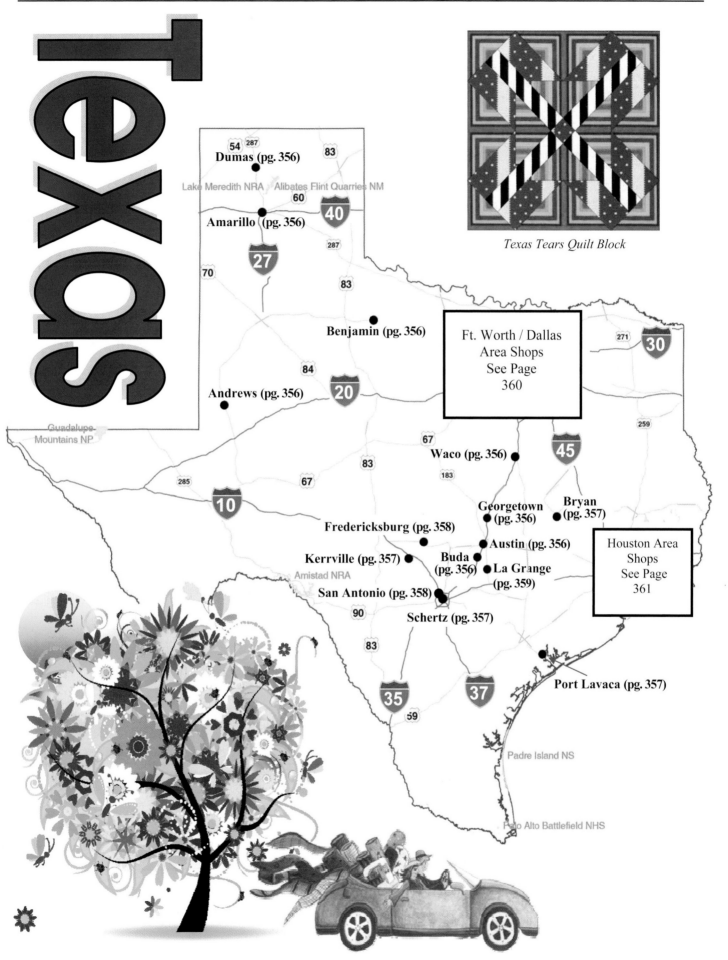

Texas Tears Quilt Block

Dumas (pg. 356)

Amarillo (pg. 356)

Benjamin (pg. 356)

Ft. Worth / Dallas
Area Shops
See Page
360

Andrews (pg. 356)

Waco (pg. 356)

Georgetown
(pg. 356)

Bryan
(pg. 357)

Fredericksburg (pg. 358)

Austin (pg. 356)

Houston Area
Shops
See Page
361

Kerrville (pg. 357)

Buda
(pg. 356)

La Grange
(pg. 359)

San Antonio (pg. 358)

Schertz (pg. 357)

Port Lavaca (pg. 357)

Longhorns

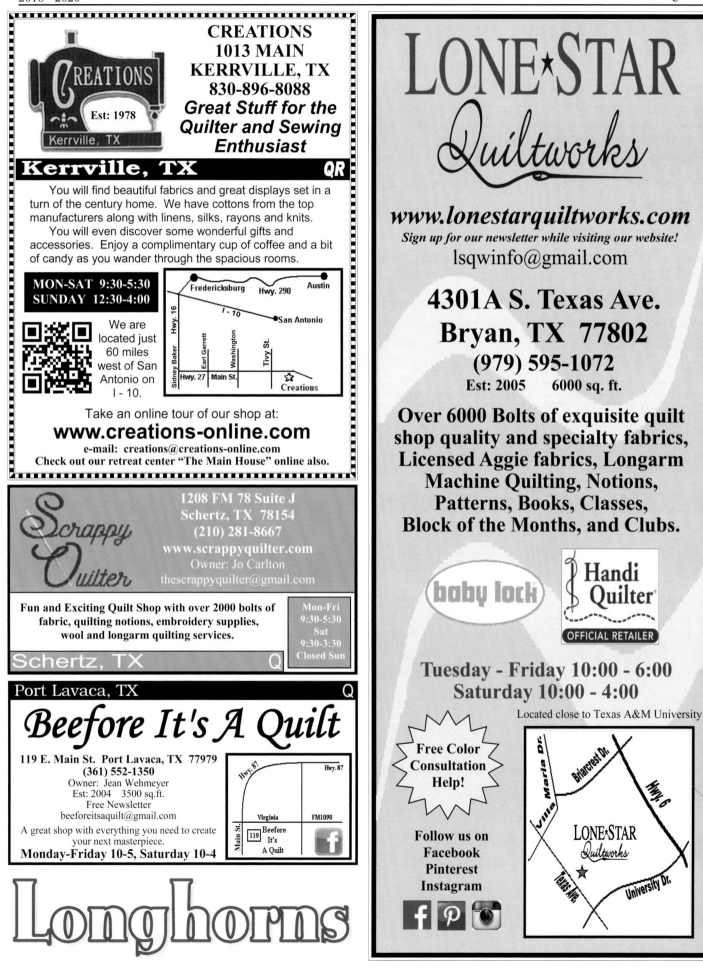

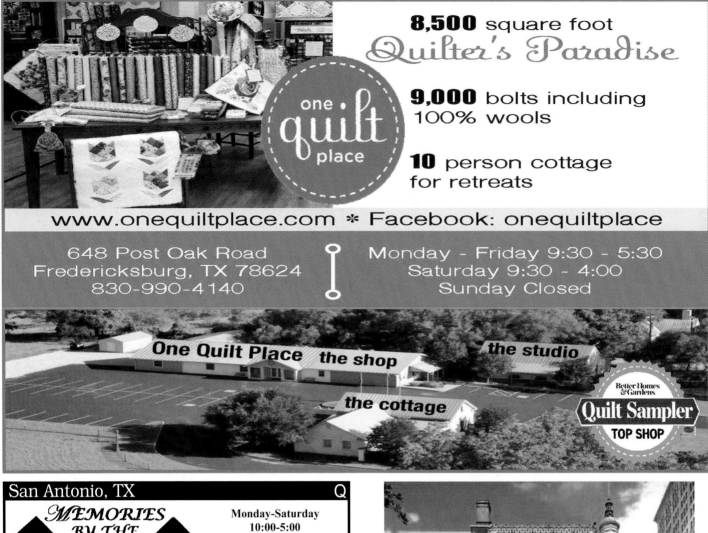

The Adolphus

The founder of the Anheuser-Busch company, Adolphus
Busch, is responsible for this Dallas landmark, which opened
in 1912. The Beaux Arts–style building, though rumored to
have a haunted 19th floor, welcomed big band entertainers,
presidents including Jimmy Carter and Ronald Reagan, and
even Queen Elizabeth II and Prince Philip.

1321 Commerce St, Dallas, TX 75202
(214) 742-8200 - www.adolphus.com

Don't let our name fool you...
Texas is our location, but our reach is worldwide!

In our museum you'll find...

✪ Three spacious galleries with room to step back and admire great quilt art in our beautifully restored 19th century buildings. Four changing exhibitions are scheduled each year.

✪ *Quilts...History in the Making*, our 13 by 85 foot outdoor mural featuring 15 colorful quilts.

✪ *Grandmother's Flower Garden*, a period "town garden" typical of the area between 1893-1930.

✪ The Museum Store with collectible quilts and unique quilt-themed products for sale.

✪ Space for educational lectures and special presentations.

✪ The Pearce Memorial Library and Material Culture Study Center.

You're also invited to join us as a Museum member at a level that's right for you...or schedule a trip for your guild! We'd love to welcome you!

Check our website for all the details!
www.TexasQuiltMuseum.org

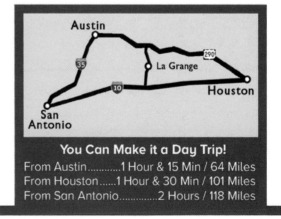

You Can Make it a Day Trip!
From Austin............1 Hour & 15 Min / 64 Miles
From Houston......1 Hour & 30 Min / 101 Miles
From San Antonio.............2 Hours / 118 Miles

Texas Quilt Museum • 140 West Colorado • La Grange, Texas • 78945
phone 979.968.3104 • fax 979.968.6010 • email projects@texasquiltmuseum.org
www.TexasQuiltMuseum.org

Fort Worth & Dallas Area

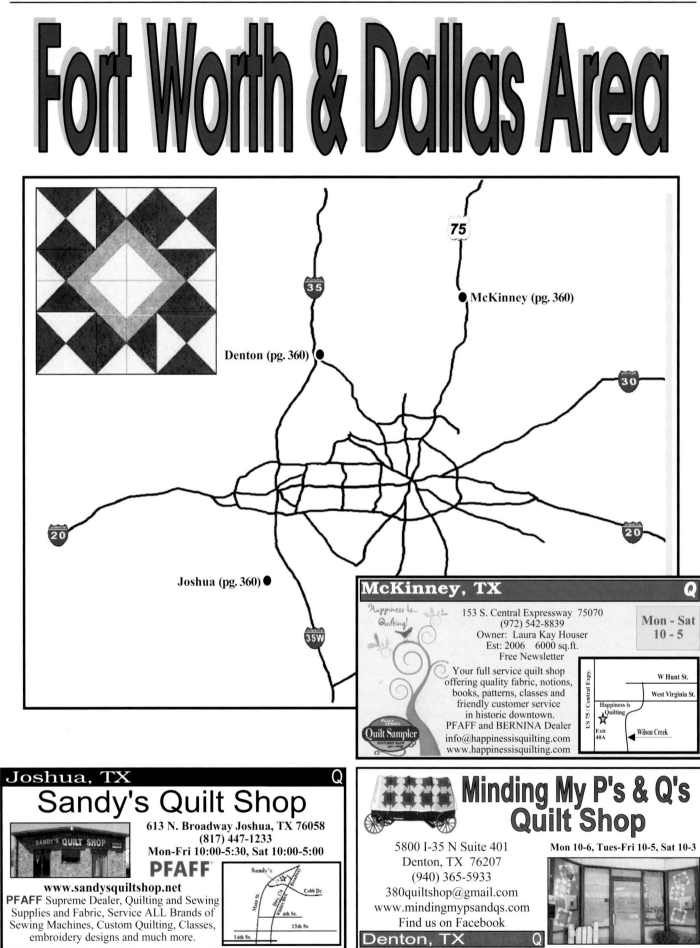

75

● McKinney (pg. 360)

35

Denton (pg. 360) ●

30

20

20

Joshua (pg. 360) ●

35W

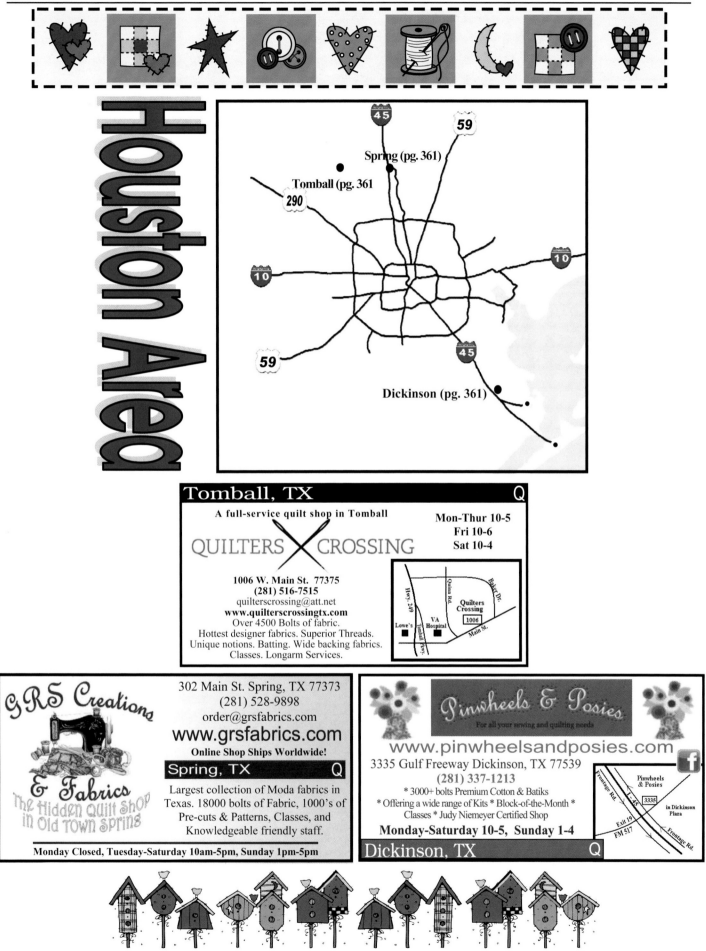

Houston Area

Spring (pg. 361)

Tomball (pg. 361)

290

59

10

10

59

45

45

Dickinson (pg. 361)

Tomball, TX   Q

A full-service quilt shop in Tomball

QUILTERS CROSSING

Mon-Thur 10-5
Fri 10-6
Sat 10-4

1006 W. Main St. 77375
(281) 516-7515
quilterscrossing@att.net
www.quilterscrossingtx.com
Over 4500 Bolts of fabric.
Hottest designer fabrics. Superior Threads.
Unique notions. Batting. Wide backing fabrics.
Classes. Longarm Services.

Map: Hwy. 249, Quinn Rd., Baker Dr., Quilters Crossing 1006, Lowe's, VA Hospital, Tomball Pkwy., Main St.

GRS Creations & Fabrics
The Hidden Quilt Shop in Old Town Spring

302 Main St. Spring, TX 77373
(281) 528-9898
order@grsfabrics.com
www.grsfabrics.com
Online Shop Ships Worldwide!

Spring, TX   Q

Largest collection of Moda fabrics in
Texas. 18000 bolts of Fabric, 1000's of
Pre-cuts & Patterns, Classes, and
Knowledgeable friendly staff.

Monday Closed, Tuesday-Saturday 10am-5pm, Sunday 1pm-5pm

Pinwheels & Posies
For all your sewing and quilting needs

www.pinwheelsandposies.com
3335 Gulf Freeway Dickinson, TX 77539
(281) 337-1213
* 3000+ bolts Premium Cotton & Batiks
* Offering a wide range of Kits * Block-of-the-Month *
Classes * Judy Niemeyer Certified Shop

Monday-Saturday 10-5, Sunday 1-4

Dickinson, TX   Q

Map: Frontage Rd., I-45, 3335, Exit 19, FM 517, Pinwheels & Posies in Dickinson Plaza, Frontage Rd.

Texas Shops

Q-Quilting ~ Y-Yarn ~ N-Needlework ~ R-Retreat ~ M-Museum

Abilene	Yarnies	2506 S. 7th St.	(325) 455-5463	
Alvin	Quilter's Corner	219 W. House St.	(281) 489-4925	
Amarillo	**Pam's Quilting Corner**	**204 S. Western St.**	**(806) 373-7777**	**Pg. 356**
Amarillo	**Sisters' Scraps**	**6018 SW 33rd Ave.**	**(806) 372-0660**	**Pg. 356**
Amarillo	Stitch N Knit	5501 Floyd Ave.	(806) 355-8811	
Andrews	**The Sewing Cottage**	**102 S. Main St.**	**(432) 524-7409**	**Pg. 356**
Arlington	The Stitch Niche	2425 W. Arkansas Lane	(817) 277-4281	
Athens	The Needle Niche	905 E. Tyler	(903) 670-3434	
Austin	**Honey Bee Quilt Store**	**9308 Anderson Mill Rd. #300**		
			(512) 257-1269	**Pg. 356**
Austin	A Quilter's Folly	8213 Brodie Ln. #100	(512) 899-3233	
Austin	European Knits	3431 N. Hills Dr. #116-J	(512) 345-0727	
Austin	Gauge Knits	5406 Parkcrest Dr.	(512) 371-9300	
Austin	Hill Country Weavers	1701 S. Congress Ave.	(512) 707-7396	
Austin	Me & Ewe	4903 Woodrow Ave.	(512) 220-9592	
Austin	Northwest Sewing Center	5448 Burnet Rd. #1	(512) 459-3961	
Austin	Sew Much More	3010 W. Anderson Ln. #J	(512) 452-3166	
Austin	Stitch Lab	1000 S. 1st St.	(512) 440-0712	
Austin	The Needle Works	4401 Medical Pkwy.	(512) 451-6931	
Austin	Yarnbow	1310 Ranch Rd. 620 S. b202	(512) 535-2332	
Azle	Ladybug Quilt and Fabric	217 W. Main St.	(817) 455-8983	
Ballinger	The Quilt Shop in Ballinger	712 Hutchings Ave.	(325) 365-3230	
Bandera	Gone Quiltin'	1115 Cedar St.	(830) 796-4360	
Bay City	BJ's Quilt Shop	3020 4th St.	(979) 429-0164	
Beaumont	Sew What Bernina	4136 Dowlen Rd.	(409) 892-7574	
Beaumont	Strings and Things	229 Dowlen Rd.	(409) 225-5185	
Benjamin	**Front Porch Quilts**	**111 E. Hayes**	**(940) 454-2000**	**Pg. 356**
Blanco	Uptown Blanco Textile Studio	317 Main St.	(830) 833-1579	
Blessing	Quilt Fabric -N- More	688 Farm Rd. Hwy. 616	(361) 588-6500	
Boerne	Ewe & Eye	512 River Rd.	(830) 249-2083	
Boerne	Sew It Fabulous	1026 N. Main St.	(830) 331-2886	
Borger	Material Girlz	101 Broadmoor St.	(806) 273-2311	
Brady	Serenity Quilts of Many Colors	2018 S. Bridge St.	(325) 597-3102	
Bridgeport	A & K Quilting & Fabric	12103 FM 2210 E.	(940) 748-2060	
Bronte	The Wool 'N' Cotton Shop	503 S. State St.	(325) 659-2000	
Bryan	**Lone Star Quiltworks**	**4301A S. Texas Ave.**	**(979) 595-1072**	**Pg. 357**
Buda	**B & B Quilting**	**410 E. Loop St.**	**(512) 312-2299**	**Pg. 356**
Burkburnett	The Stitching Depot	316 E. 3rd St.	(940) 569-0804	
Burleson	Country Stitches Quilt Shop	426 SW Wilshire Blvd.	(817) 426-5981	
Camp Wood	Suzie Q Quilts	508 S. Nueces St.	(830) 597-6310	
Canton	Sew N' Sew	22390 E. Hwy. 64	(903) 567-4640	
Carrollton	A & L Needlecraft & Frame Shop	1106 S. Elm St.	(972) 245-1829	
Carrollton	The Old Craft Store	1110 W. Main St.	(972) 242-9111	
Carthage	The Whistling Chicken Quilt Shop	450 W. Panola St.	(903) 690-9992	
Castroville	The Quilt Shop	1314 Constantinople	(830) 538-3100	
Cedar Hill	Corner Square Quilts	702 Cedar St.	(972) 293-0088	
Cedar Park	Sew Crazy	601 E. Whitestone Blvd.	(512) 259-2988	
Celeste	Quilt Mercantile	215 Hwy. 69 N.	(903) 568-8739	
Cisco	JT Ranch Quilt Shop	706 Conrad Hilton	(254) 442-1940	
Cleburne	Fancy Stitches	106 N. Pendell St.	(817) 641-4761	
Clifton	Quilting Cousins	603 South Ave. G	(254) 675-0010	
Clute	So and Sew	88 Flag Lake Dr.	(979) 299-3445	
Clyde	Feathered Star	107 Oak	(325) 893-4699	
College Station	Pruitt's Fabric	318 George Bush Dr.	(979) 693-9357	
Colleyville	Quilter's Dream	6409 Colleyville Blvd.	(817) 481-7105	
Comfort	The Loom Room	402 7th St.	(830) 995-5299	
Comfort	The Tinsmith's Wife	405 7th St	(830) 995-5539	
Conroe	Quilter's Quarters	3301 W. Davis Ste. B	(936) 756-7200	
Copperas Cove	Nedlewerkes on Main	100 Cove Terrace Shopping Ctr.	(254) 542-6335	
Corpus Christi	Darling Rose	3202 Reid Dr.	(361) 271-1771	
Corpus Christi	Heirloom Elegance	4343 Kostoryz Rd.	(361) 852-4247	

Corpus Christi	Knotty Girl Fiber Arts Studio	3230 Reid Dr.	(361) 906-9276	
Corpus Christi	Knotty Girls Knit	3230 Reid Dr.	(361) 906-9276	
Dallas	Creative Stitches and Gifts	12817 Preston Rd. #137	(214) 361-2610	
Dallas	Golden D'or Fabrics	10795 Harry Hines Blvd.	(214) 351-2339	
Dallas	Holley's Yarn Shoppe	5211 Forest Ln. Ste. 115	(972) 503-5648	
Dallas	Needlepoint This!	4420 Lovers Ln.	(214) 363-6377	
Dallas	Quilters Connection	9658 Plano Rd.	(214) 343-1440	
Dallas	Sew Let's Quilt It	7989 Belt Line Rd. #170	(972) 661-0044	
Dallas	Urban Spools Sewing Lounge	1152 N. Buckner Blvd. #121	(214) 324-5755	
Dallas	White Rock Weaving Center	9533 Losa Dr. Ste. 2	(214) 320-9276	
Dallas	Yarn and Stitches	15615 Coit Rd. Ste. 206	(972) 239-9665	
Decatur	Stitchin' Nook	115 W. Main St.	(817) 220-1210	
Denton	**Minding My P's & Q's Quilt Shop**			
		5800 I-35 N. Ste. 401	**(940) 365-5933**	**Pg. 360**
Denton	Material Girl Quilt Shop	1800 N. Carroll Blvd. #102	(940) 484-2500	
Dickinson	**Pinwheels and Posies**	**3335 Gulf Freeway**	**(281) 337-1213**	**Pg. 361**
Dripping Spring	The Sated Sheep	100 Commons Rd. #5	(512) 829-4607	
Dripping Springs	Valli & Kim	700 W. Hwy. 290	(512) 858-4433	
Dumas	**Down Home Quilts**	**102 E. 7th St. Ste. A**	**(806) 934-4041**	**Pg. 356**
Duncanville	Ben Franklin Apothecary	302 N. Main St.	(972) 298-1147	
Edinburg	Bela's Needle Works	2502 S. Closner	(956) 287-9882	
El Campo	Cedar Chest Quilt Shoppe	121 S Mechanic	(979) 578-8929	
El Paso	Bernina of El Paso	1809 Trawood Dr.	(915) 599-1909	
El Paso	Mayaluna Yarns	5024 Doniphan Ste. 10	(915) 585-7779	
El Paso	Mundo de Papel	3417 Alameda Ave.	(915) 351-0250	
Fort Worth	Berry Patch Fabrics	4913 S. Hulen	(817) 346-6400	
Fort Worth	Cabbage Rose Quilting and Fabrics	3000 Montgomery St.	(817) 377-3993	
Fort Worth	Jennings Street Yarns	217 S. Jennings Ave.	(817) 878-2740	
Fort Worth	Suddenly Sewing	3529 W. Heritage Trace Pkwy. #173	(817) 741-5400	
Fort Worth	The French Knot	4706 Bryce Ave.	(817) 731-3446	
Fredericksburg	**One Quilt Place**	**648 Post Oak Rd.**	**(830) 990-4140**	**Pg. 358**
Fredericksburg	Fredericksburg Pie Company and Quilts			
		108 E. Austin St.	(830) 990-6992	
Fredericksburg	Sandy Jenkins Designs	203 E. Austin St.	(830) 997-9863	
Fredericksburg	Stonehill Spinning	104-A E. Ufer St.	(830) 990-8952	
Friendswood	Cross Stitch Country	2503 Cobblers Way	(281) 332-6962	
Friendswood	Marie's Yarn Shop	210 Dawn	(281) 482-8546	
Gainesville	Pass Time Fabrics	105 W. California St.	(940) 668-1747	
Garrison	Love Bug Fabric and Quilting	169 N. US. Hwy. 59	(936) 347-2130	
Georgetown	**Poppy Quilt 'N Sew**	**3010 Williams Dr. Ste. 156**		
			(512) 863-6108	**Pg. 356**
Georgetown	A Sheep At The Wheel Yarn Co.	3010 Williams Dr. #162	(737) 444-6969	
Georgetown	Fiber Arts Republic	170 Young Ranch Rd.	(512) 868-8695	
Georgetown	The Knitting Cup	708 S. Rock St.	(512) 869-2182	
Giddings	All Around the Block Quilt Shop	979 N. Leon	(979) 542-2782	
Giddings	Gerline's Quilt Shoppe	1383 County Rd. 205	(979) 542-3318	
Giddings	Meme's Quilts	1695 Country Rd. 119	(979) 540-8162	
Gonzales	Craft Crossing	525 St. Joseph St.	(830) 203-5303	
Graham	The Quilt Box	1033 4th St.	(940) 282-9406	
Granbury	Houston St. Mercantile	126 N. Houston St.	(817) 279-0425	
Granbury	Yarns Extrodinare	120 N. Houston St.	(817) 707-1012	
Grand Prairie	Knitting Fairy	2100 N. State Hwy. 360 #1904	(214) 412-2889	
Grandview	Heritage Arts Texas	10740 County Rd. 102	(817) 866-2772	
Grapevine	Must Love Fabric	1451 S. Hwy. 114 W. Ste. 502	(817) 488-6764	
Harlingen	GOB Quilts	108 E. Jackson St.	(956) 648-9709	
Harlingen	Judy's Stitchery Nook	1046 N. 77 Sunshine Strip #2	(956) 421-2654	
Harwood	Omi'z Quilting Haus	1097 County Rd. 234	(210) 865-5823	
Hemphill	CedarSix Mile Quilting	203 Worth St.	(409) 787-4076	
Henrietta	Aunt Pam's Closet	101 W. Gilbert	(940) 631-7101	
Hewitt	Wrapped in Quilts	935 Vail Highlands	(254) 666-5226	
Horseshoe Bay	Nan's Needlework	100 Bunny Run Ln. #205	(830) 598-4560	
Houston	Buttons N Bows	14070 Memorial Dr.	(281) 496-0170	
Houston	Chandail Needlework	2015 G W. Gray	(713) 524-6942	
Houston	Chaparral Needlework Shop	3701 W. Alabama St. #300	(713) 621-7562	
Houston	Georgia's Custom Quilting	8315 Cheswick	(281) 620-9550	
Houston	High Fashion Fabric Center-Quilter's Corner			
		3101 Louisiana St.	(713) 528-7299	
Houston	It's A Stitch	1980 Westheimer Rd. #D	(281) 584-0019	
Houston	Merribee Needlearts	12682 Shiloh Church Rd.	(281) 440-6980	
Houston	Nancy's Knits	5300 N. Braeswood Blvd. #30	(713) 661-9411	

Index

City	Shop	Address	Phone	
Houston	Needle House	2815 Bammel Ln.	(713) 522-9704	
Houston	Nimblefingers	12456 Memorial Dr.	(713) 722-7244	
Houston	QuiltWorks	9431 Jones Rd.	(281) 890-3550	
Houston	Stitches in Time	1850 Fountain View Dr.	(713) 975-9778	
Houston	Tea Time Quilting	1046 Tulane St.	(713) 861-7743	
Houston	Thimble Fingers Sewing Studio	14505 Memorial Dr.	(281) 493-1941	
Huffman	The Quilt Room	11515 FM 1960 Ste. B	(281) 324-9018	
Humble	It's a Stitch	9574 FM 1960 Bypass	(281) 446-4999	
Huntsville	Fabric Carousel	1101 12th St.	(936) 295-8322	
Hurst	Richland Sewing Center	850 W. Pipeline Rd.	(817) 590-4447	
Hurst	Sew It Up	740 Grapevine Hwy.	(817) 514-6061	
Italy	Suzzett's Fabric, Quilts & More LLC	200 Hamrock Rd.	(214) 797-0393	
Jacksonville	Heart & Home	102 E. Commerce St.	(903) 258-2937	
Jasper	Lake Area Quilts	8484 US. Hwy. 96 S.	(409) 384-3878	
Jefferson	Quilter's Corner	1102 FM 2208 Rt. 4	(903) 665-3385	
Jewett	A Cowgirl Quilt Shop	299 County Rd. 915	(903) 626-4808	
Jonestown	Happy Ewe	18360 FM1431 Ste. B	(512) 284-7408	
Joshua	**Sandy's Quilt Shop**	**613 N. Broadway**	**(817) 447-1233**	**Pg. 360**
Joshua	Batiks Galore	7301 CR 912	(817) 556-2200	
Katy	Quilt 'n Sew Studio	829 S. Mason Rd. Ste. 224	(281) 398-0670	
Katy	Sew Special Quilts	21800 Katy Freeway Ste. 100	(281) 717-8033	
Katy	Yarntopia	2944 S. Mason Rd. #J	(281) 392-2386	
Kerrville	**Creations**	**1013 Main St.**	**(830) 896-8088**	**Pg. 357**
Kerrville	Hometown Crafts and Gifts	841 Junction Hwy.	(830) 896-5944	
Kingwood	Quilts & Creations	23858 Hwy. 59 N.	(832) 644-5696	
Kountze	Jae's of the Big Thicket	7616 Old Honey Island Rd.	(409) 246-4462	
La Grange	**Texas Quilt Museum**	**140 W. Colorado**	**(979) 968-3104**	**Pg. 359**
La Grange	The Quilted Skein	126 W. Colorado	(979) 968-8200	
La Porte	Painted Pony N Quilts	1015 S. Broadway St.	(281) 471-5735	
Lake Jackson	Calico Cat Sewing Center	107 W. Way, #5-6	(979) 285-9277	
Lakeway	The Cotton Cupboard	1607 Ranch Rd. 620 N. #100	(512) 294-2776	
Lampasas	Fatty Corners Quilts	406 E. 3rd St.	(512) 556-5704	
Lampass	Lakadaisies	7548 N. US. HWY. 281	(512) 556-3019	
Lancaster	The Sassy Spinster	125 Historic Town Sq.	(972) 218-5335	
League City	Park Avenue Yarns	260 Park Ave.	(832) 932-0300	
Lewisville	Aidaworks	1140 W. Main St.	(972) 436-5999	
Lewisville	Quilt Country	701 S. Stemmons #90	(972) 436-7022	
Livingston	Jean's Corner at Feeder's Supply	712 N. Jackson St.	(936) 327-8817	
Llano	Buckaroo Blankets	103 E. Main St.	(325) 248-6701	
Llano	The Country Quilt Shop	100 E. Exchange Pl.	(325) 248-0300	
Lockhart	Calico Crossing	215 W. Market St.	(512) 398-2422	
Longview	Sharman's Sewing Center	112 A Johnston St.	(903)-753-8014	
Longview	Stitches 'N Stuff	7793 US. Hwy. 259 N.	(903) 663-3840	
Lubbock	Cottage Fabrics	3412 82nd St.	(806) 797-7397	
Lubbock	Pocket Full of Stitches	4523 50th St.	(806) 792-1761	
Lubbock	RahRah's Fabrics & Quilting	3412 82nd St.	(806) 792-1885	
Lufkin	Bove Sewing Center	501 E. Lufkin Ave.	(936) 634-5323	
Luling	HollyDee Quilts	405 E. Davis St.	(830) 875-5432	
Marquez	Country Living Quilts	1816 County Rd. 427	(936) 396-2889	
McAllen	Rio Bravo Fabric Store	1510 Beaumont	(956) 686-0291	
McKinney	**Happiness Is Quilting**	**153 S. Central Expwy.**	**(972) 542-8839**	**Pg. 360**
Mckinney	Linda's Electric Quilters	2001 Central Cir.	(972)-542-4000	
McKinney	McKnittey	1007 W. Hunt St.	(844) 562-5648	
McKinney	Stitched with Love	500 N. Custer Rd. #110	(972) 540-5355	
McKinney	The Quilt Asylum	153 S. Central Expwy.	(972) 562-2686	
Medina	Little Cottage Quilt Shop	14076 St. Hwy. 16	(830) 589-2502	
Mesquite	Pieced Together Studio	205 W. Main St.	(972) 270-0961	
Mesquite	Thomas Sewing Center	1515 N. Town E. Blvd. Ste. 133	(972) 681-3996	
Mesquite	Watt A Find	910 W. Kearney St. #D	(972) 896-4088	
Midland	Patches & Scraps	2420 W. Illinois	(432) 695-9961	
Midland	The Stitching Post	4610 N. Garfield St. #B4	(432) 697-1241	
Midlothian	Quilts 'n More	211 W. Ave. F	(972) 723-8669	
Mineola	Stitchin' Heaven	1118 N. Pacific St.	(800) 841-3901	
Missouri City	Little Stitches Sewing Center	3340 FM 1092 #130	(281) 403-1564	
Montgomery	Montgomery Quilt Company	312 A John A. Butler	(832) 580-9445	
Nacogdoches	Bove Sewing Center	1122 N. University Dr.	(936) 569-7663	
Navasota	WC Mercantile	201 E Washington Ave.	(936) 825-3378	
Nederland	Sew Much More Sewing Center	1336 Boston Ave.	(409) 853-4387	
New Braunfels	Lucky Ewe Yarn	2327 Gruene Lake Dr. #C	(830) 620-0908	
New Braunfels	Oak Leaf Quilts	225 S. Seguin Ave.	(830) 629-0774	
New Braunfels	Sew Little Time Bernina	625 W. San Antonio St.	(830) 626-8463	
New Braunfels	The Quilt Haus	651 N. Business 35 #510	(830) 620-1382	

New Waverly	Mohair and More	231 Gibbs St.	(936) 661-8022	
Oakalla	Threadheads	28625 FM 963	(512) 556-4739	
Odessa	Betty's Bobbin Box	2734 N. Grandview	(432) 550-0093	
Paige	Yarnorama	130 Gonzales St.	(512) 253-0100	
Palestine	Sew-What	619 W. Oak St.	(903) 729-2889	
Pantego	Peggy's Quilt Studio	2410 C Superior Dr.	(817) 275-4155	
Pantego	Sew Fabricated	2899 W. Pioneer Pkwy.	(817) 795-1925	
Paris	Sew Much More	2400 Stillhouse Rd.	(903) 784-6342	
Perryton	K's	1622 S. Fordham St.	(806) 435-2708	
Pittsburg	Quilters Playhouse	1880 FM 3384	(903) 855-1429	
Plainview	Cindy's Country Quilt Shoppe	633 N. Ash	(806) 296-5888	
Plano	Best of Bernina Plano	340 Coit Rd. #500	(972) 578-9227	
Plano	Compusew	3237 Independence Pkwy.	(972) 596-5628	
Plano	Fabric Fanatics	624 Haggard St. #706	(972) 881-7750	
Plano	Not Your Mama's Quilt Store	4152 W. Spring Creek Pkwy. #156	(972) 612-2641	
Plano	The Woolie Ewe	1301 Custer Rd. #328	(972) 424-3163	
Plano	Threads That Bind	3100 Independence Pkwy. #204	(972) 867-5700	
Port Lavaca	**Beefore It's A Quilt**	**119 E. Main St.**	**(361)-552-1350**	**Pg. 357**
Richmond	CJ's Quilt Shop	5529 FM 359 #E	(832) 222-2033	
Richmond	Quilters Cottage	920 FM 359	(281) 633-9331	
Rockport	Golden Needles & Quilts	701 N. Allen St.	(361) 729-7873	
Rockwall	Texas Quiltworks	212 E. Rusk	(972) 771-9952	
Rosenburg	3 Sisters Quilt shop	801 2nd St.	(281) 932-9786	
Round Rock	Austin's Sewing & Vacuum	1401 S. IH 35 Ste. 170	(512) 310-7349	
Saginaw	Sew So Easy Quilt Shop	734 S. Saginaw Blvd.	(817) 306-1002	
Salado	A Sewing Basket	560 N. Main St. #6	(254) 947-5423	
Salado	The Salado Yarn Company	22 N. Main	(254) 947-0888	
San Angelo	Chandler Cottage	1821 Knickerbocker Rd.	(325) 227-6985	
San Angelo	The Fiber Co-op	7024 Orient Rd.	(325) 262-5447	
San Antonio	**Memories By The Yard**	**8015 Mainland**	**(210) 520-4833**	**Pg. 358**
San Antonio	Creative Sewing Center	11777 W. Ave.	(210) 344-0791	
San Antonio	Cross Stitch Plus	2267 NW Military Hwy. #113A	(210) 342-8252	
San Antonio	InSkein Yarns	8425 Bandera Rd Ste.128	(210) 334-0200	
San Antonio	Las Colchas	110 Ogden St.	(210) 223-2405	
San Antonio	Mesquite Bean Fabrics	6708 N. New Braunfels	(210) 973-5705	
San Antonio	Sew Special Quilts--Bernina	5139 N. Loop 1604 W. #110	(210) 698-6076	
San Antonio	Stitches from the heart	5123 N. Loop 1604 W. #109	(210) 479-2600	
San Antonio	Unraveled - The Chic Yarn Boutique	815 E. Rector #104A	(210) 251-4451	
San Antonio	Yarn Barn of San Antonio	1615 McCullough Ave.	(210) 826-3679	
San Antonio	Yarnivore	2357 NW Military Hwy.	(210) 979-8255	
Santa Anna	Country Quilting and More	803 Ave. B	(325) 348-3771	
Savoy	Savvy Quilters	113 W. Hayes	(903) 965-2023	
Schertz	**The Scrappy Quilter**	**1208 FM 78 #J**	**(210) 281-8667**	**Pg. 357**
Seagoville	Fabrics 4 You	1501 N. Kaufman St.	(972) 287-3800	
Seymour	Mrs. Sew 'n Sew	713 N. Charles St.	(940) 256-2017	
Shiner	The Square Quilter	807 North Ave. D	(361) 594-8022	
Silsbee	The Vintage Owl	110 East Ave. H	(409) 373-2069	
Slaton	Quilts-n-More	121 S. 9th St.	(806) 828-3222	
Smithville	Making Memories Quilt Shop	1004 Nichols St.	(512) 575-7040	
Snyder	Nana Bear's Notions	2513 College Ave.	(325) 436-0211	
Sour Lake	The Quiter's Studio	640 Hwy. 105 E	(409) 445-2024	
Spring	**GRS Creations & Fabrics**	**302 Main St.**	**(281) 528-9898**	**Pg. 361**
Spring	3 Stitches	7822 Louetta Rd.	(281) 320-0133	
Spring	ABC Stitch Therapy	16712 Champion Forest Dr.	(281) 205-7507	
Spring	Cupcake Quilts	219 Gentry St. #A	(281) 528-2929	
Spring	Texas Quilt Machines	2311 Sciaaca Rd.	(281) 793-1777	
Spring	The Social Knitwork	26511 Keith St.	(281) 630-4144	
Spring	Twisted Yarns	702 Spring Cypress Rd. Ste. A	(281) 528-8664	
Stafford	Quilt Your Own	11925 Southwest Frwy.	(281) 795-7635	
Stafford	Quilter's Emporium	11925 Southwest Frwy. Ste. 11	(281) 491-0016	
Stephenville	Deb's Flying Needle	1495 W. South Loop	(254) 965-7577	
Sugar Land	It Seams To Be Sew...	13134 Dairy Ashford Rd. #300	(281) 302-6059	
Sweet Home	Sweet Home Stitching Post	7159 FM 531	(361) 293-6733	
Taylor	E-Jay's Trunk	220 E 4th St. Ste. C.	(512) 352-6350	
Terrell	Quilter's Apprentice	1100 E. Moore Ave.	(972) 563-3830	
Texarkana	The Yarn Garden	3423 New Boston Rd.	(903) 223-9276	
Texas City	Cactus Quilts	1811 6th St. N.	(409) 965-9778	
The Woodlands	iPurl	3335 College Park Dr. Ste. 450	(936) 242-1031	
Tomball	**Quilters Crossing**	**1006 W. Main St.**	**(281) 516-7515**	**Pg. 361**
Tomball	Needle & Thread	112 Commerce St. #1	(281) 357-0215	
Trinity	Heavenly Threads Quilt Shop	334 Prospect Dr.	(936) 594-1237	

Index

Troup	All Those Quilts	159 County Rd. 4924	(903) 842-2044
Tyler	A Nimble Thimble	1813 Capital Dr. #300	(903) 581-4926
Tyler	Crafts & Quilting, Etc.	715 S. College Ave.	(903) 533-1771
Tyler	Granny's Needle Haus	6004 S. Broadway Ave.	(903) 561-4637
Tyler	Quilting Barn	11334 St. Hwy. 64E	(903) 566-3518
Tyler	Rose Path Weaving Inc.	13161 County Rd. 461	(903) 882-3234
Tyler	Sharman's Sewing Center	6005 S. Broadway Ave.	(903) 581-5470
Victoria	Past Times Needlepoint	105 W. Santa Rosa St.	(361) 572-0088
Victoria	Quilters Patch	205 N. Star Dr. #Q	(361) 578-0380
Victoria	Silver Threads	104 Kelly #D	(331) 442-2412
Waco	**Simply Fabrics**	**6408 Gholson Rd.**	**(254) 829-7119 Pg. 356**
Waco	Homestead Fiber Arts	608 Dry Creek Rd.	(254) 754-9680
Waco	Tomorrow's Quilts	800 Lake Air Dr.	(254) 741-6988
Waxahachie	Common Threads Quilting	315 S. Rogers St.	(972) 935-0510
Weatherford	Quilting Around	806 Palo Pinto St.	(817) 599-7810
Webster	Fabrics Etcetera	571 W. Bay Area Blvd.	(281) 338-1904
Whitesboro	Kaleidoscope Quilt Shop	114 E. Main St.	(903) 564-4681
Wichita Falls	The Enchanted Quilt	1813 9th St.	(940) 689-0990
Wimberley	Ply! Yarn, Art & Handwovens	14015 Ranch Rd. #4	(512) 406-1719
Wimberley	Wimberley Stitch Studio	490 FM 2325	(512) 808-0490
Wimberly	The Old Oaks Ranch	601 Old Oaks Ranch Rd.	(512) 847-8784
Winnie	My Sister's Closet	1743 Orchid Ln.	(409) 338-4837
Winters	Bee's Quilting and Gifts	106 S. Main St.	(325) 754-4624
Wolfforth	Red Barn Ranch	18311 County Rd. 1640	(806) 863-2276
Wylie	Blue Ribbon Quilt Shoppe	102-C N. Ballard Ave.	(972) 941-0777
Yorktown	Seams Like Home, A Little Fabric Store	441 W. 5th	(361) 564-9455

Utah

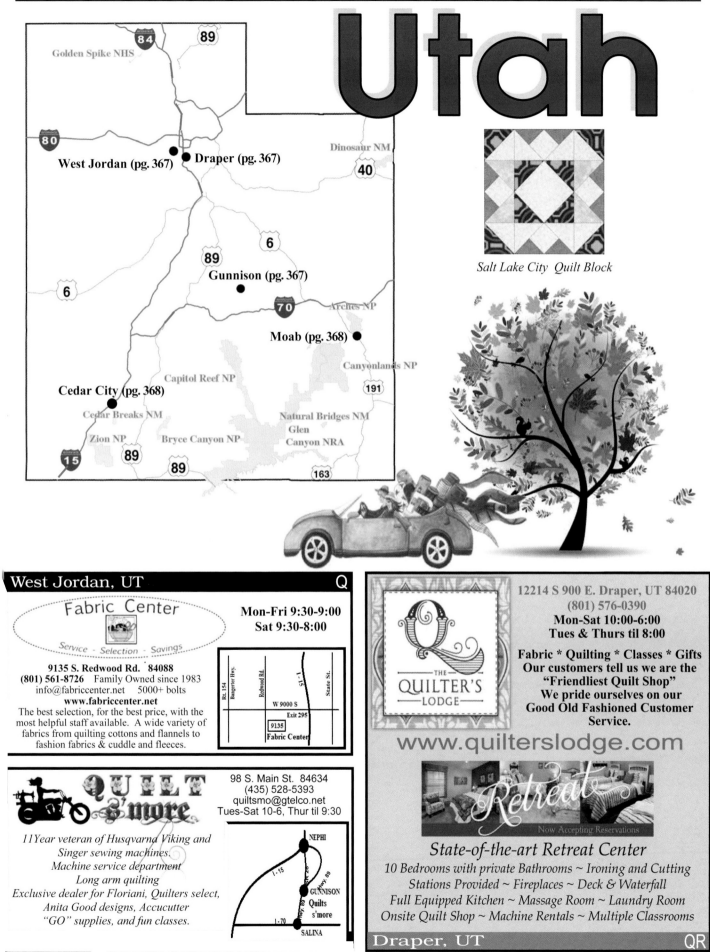

Salt Lake City Quilt Block

West Jordan (pg. 367)   **Draper (pg. 367)**

Gunnison (pg. 367)

Moab (pg. 368)

Cedar City (pg. 368)

Utah Shops

Q-Quilting ~ Y-Yarn ~ N-Needlework ~ R-Retreat ~ M-Museum

City	Shop	Address	Phone	Page
American Fork	Nuttall's Bernina & Fabrics	53 W. Main	801-756-2223	
American Fork	The Quiltmakers	285 E. Main St.	(801) 763-7167	
American Fork	The Sewing Basket	51 S. 100 E.	(801) 980-9150	
Blanding	We're In Stitches	259 N. 100 W. #19-3	(435) 678-3305	
Bountiful	Brooks Fabrics	220 N. Main	(801) 295-2941	
Bountiful	Quilter's Attic	2155 S. Orchard Dr.	(801) 292-1710	
Brigham City	Village Dry Goods	92 S. Main	(435) 723-1315	
Cedar City	**4everQuilting**	**921 S. Main St.**	**(435) 363-1940**	**Pg. 368**
Cedar City	Stitching It Up	117 N. Main St.	(435) 586-6300	
Cedar City	The Yarn Bard	770 W. Industrial Rd. #18	(435) 531-8789	
Clearfield	Sew N Save	1475 S. State St.	(801) 825-2177	
Cottonwood Heights	Elaine's Quilt Block	6970 S. 3000 E.	(801) 947-9100	
Delta	Mom's Crafts and Fabrics	313 S. 100 W.	(435) 864-3325	
Draper	**The Quilter's Lodge**	**12214 S. 900 E.**	**(801) 576-0390**	**Pg. 367**
Escalante	Cross Stitch & More	55 S. 200 E.	(435) 826-4628	
Ferron	Pat's Sew 'n' Stuff	30 E. Main	(435) 384-2620	
Gunnison	**Quilt S'More**	**98 S. Main St.**	**(435) 528-5393**	**Pg. 367**
Heber City	Isabel's Yarn Shop	650 W. 100 S.	(435) 657-9544	
Highland	Just Sew	11073 N. Alpine Hwy. # 101	(801) 492-7929	
Hurricane	Main Street Quilt Cottage	130 S. Main St.	(435) 635-4748	
Hyde Park	Adorn It	3419 N. US. Hwy. 91	(435) 563-1100	
Kaysville	K & H Quilt Shoppe	250 W. 200 N. Ste. 4	(801) 444-4375	
Lindon	Kate's Quilting Block	62 W. 450 N.	(801) 796-1533	
Logan	Knit Unique	27 N. Main	(435) 787-2616	
Logan	My Girlfriends Quilt Shoppe	1115 N. 200 Ste. 230	(435) 213-3229	
Logan	Stylish Fabrics	138 N. Main St.	(435) 752-4186	
Midvale	Mormon Handicraft	1110 E. Fort Union Blvd. #4M	(801) 561-8777	
Midway	My Girlfriend's Quilt Shoppe	6 W. 200 S.	(435) 654-2844	
Moab	**It's Sew Moab**	**40 W. Center St.**	**(435) 259-0739**	**Pg. 368**
Moab	Desert Thread	29 E. Center St.	(435) 259-8404	
Mona	E-Z P-Z Quilt & Sew	327 W. 300 S.	(435) 655-5356	
Murray	Nuttall's Bernina & Fabrics	4742 S. 900 E.	(801) 262-6665	
Ogden	My Heritage Fabrics	1843 Valley Dr.	(801) 621-2202	
Ogden	Shepherd's Bush	220 24th St.	(801) 399-4546	
Ogden	The Needlepoint Joint	241 Historic 25th St.	(801) 394-4355	
Orem	American Quilting	426 W. 800 N.	(801) 802-7841	
Park City	Davidene's Quilt Shop	7132 N. Silver Creek Rd. #A	(435) 649-9639	
Park City	Wasatch and Wool Yarns	1635 W. Redstone Center G130	(435) 575-0999	
Payson	Morganson's Sew Forth	51 S. Main	(801) 465-9133	
Providence	The Quilt House	135 S. 100 E.	(801) 752-5429	
Provo	Daines Cotton Shop	164 W. 500 N.	(801) 373-6210	
Provo	Harmony Sew Knit Learn	315 E. Center St.	(801) 615-0268	
Provo	Heindselman's Yarn, Needlework & Weaving	176 W. Center St.	(801) 373-5193	
Richfield	Christensen's	39 N. Main St.	(435) 896-6466	
Richfield	Julia's Shoppe	350 S. 100 E.	(435) 896-1821	

Richfield	Knit N Craft	5 N. Main St.	(435) 896-8133
Richfield	Rather Bee Quiltin	25 N. Main St.	(435) 896-8354
Riverton	My Sister's Quilt	12544 S Pasture Rd.	(801) 810-3999
Riverton	Nuttall's Bernina	1849 W. 12600 S.	(801) 446-7958
Roosevelt	Miss Annie's Quilt Shoppe	165 E. 100 S.	(435) 722-3111
Salem	Gracie Lou's Quilts	446 N. State Rd. 198	(801) 423-1339
Salina	Cotton Tree Quilt Co.	315 W. Main St.	(435) 896-7111
Salt Lake City	And Sew On	1625 W. 700 N. #H	(801) 355-0553
Salt Lake City	And Sew On	2037 E. 3300 S.	(801) 467-6465
Salt Lake City	Blazing Needles	1365 S. 1100 E.	(801) 487-5648
Salt Lake City	Bohemiam Yarn & Imports	3194 S. 1100 E.	(801) 486-0075
Salt Lake City	Craft Center for Fine Stitchery	1920 E. Fort Union Blvd.	(801) 944-4994
Salt Lake City	Elaine's Quilt Block	6970 S. 3000 E.	(801) 947-9100
Salt Lake City	Needlepoint & Other Things	2020 E. 3300 S. #25	(801) 485-2512
Salt Lake City	The Wool Cabin	2020 E. 3300 S. #11	(801) 466-1811
Sandy	Daines Cotton Shop	9441 S. 700 E.	(801) 572-1412
Sandy	Gingerbread Antiques and Yarn	8540 S. 700 E.	(801) 255-5666
Sandy	Heartfelt Hobby & Crafts	407 S. 1100 E.	(801) 233-9028
Sandy	Quilt Quilt Quilt	11 E. Main St.	(801) 255-2666
Sandy	Quilts on the Corner	208 E. Main St.	(801) 503-7012
Santa Clara	The Clover Patch	2721 Santa Clara Dr.	(435) 986-9070
Springville	Corn Wagon Quilt Company	303 E. 400 S.	(801) 491-3551
St. George	Dave's Bernina	691 E. St. George Blvd.	(435) 656-1498
St. George	Mormon Handicraft	735 S. Bluff	(435) 628-4495
St. George	Mother Superior's FAB Fabrics	87 E. 2580 S.	(435) 256-6420
St. George	Quilted Works	140 N. 400 W. # A7	(435) 674-2500
St. George	Scrap Apple Quilts	144 W. Brigham Rd. #23	(435) 628-8226
Sunset	Nuttall's Bernina Sewing Center	2465 N. Main St. #3	(801) 773-6625
Tooele	Yard Sale Fabrics & Gift	60 S. Main St.	(435) 843-0139
Vernal	Quilted Hens	38 S. 600 W.	(435) 789-2411
West Jordan	**Fabric Center**	**9135 S. Redwoood Rd.**	**(801) 561-8726 Pg. 367**
West Jordan	Floyd & Lizzie's Quilt Shop	2263 W. 7800 S.	(801) 255-4130
West Jordan	Kamille's	1100 W. 7800 S.	(801) 282-0477
West Jordan	Knittin Pretty	1393 W. 9000 S.	(801) 676-9933
West Jordan	Pine Needles	1100 W. 7800 S. #29S	(801) 233-0551
West Jordan	The Quilt Shop	9135 S. Redwood Rd.	(801) 568-7720

Grand America Hotel

The towering Grand America Hotel, consisting of 24 floors and 775 rooms, stands out against the mountainous backdrop in downtown Salt Lake City. The impressive Grand Spa is equipped with a salon, massage services, and indoor pool, but outdoorsy guests can enjoy nearby national parks and the area's many ski resorts, like Snowbasin.

555 Main St, Salt Lake City, UT 84101
(801) 258-6000
www.grandamerica.com

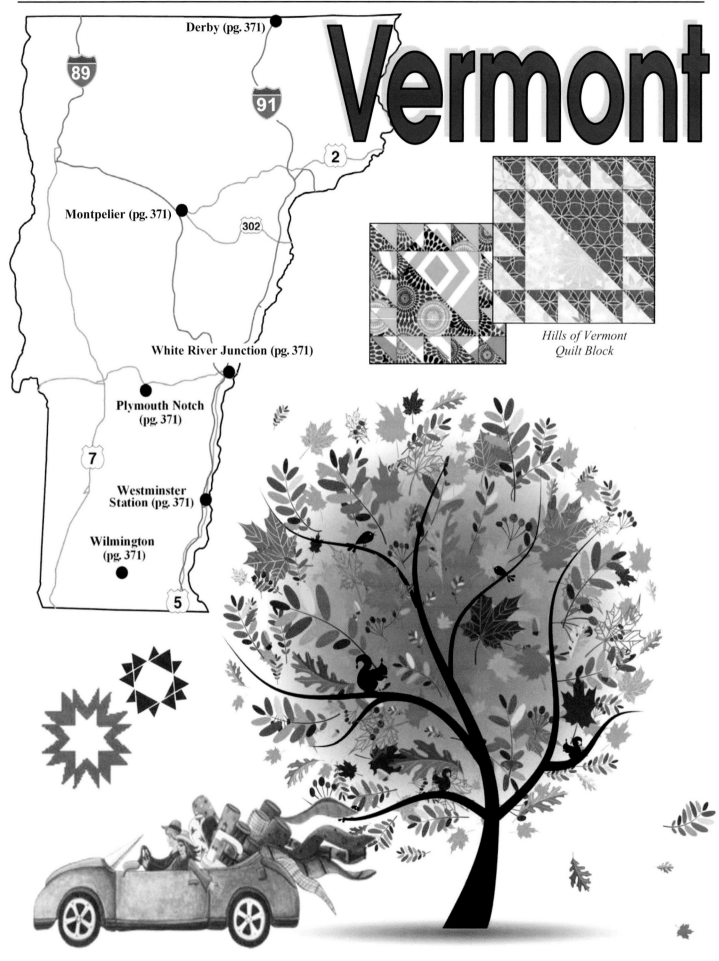

Derby (pg. 371)

89

91

2

Montpelier (pg. 371)

302

White River Junction (pg. 371)

Plymouth Notch
(pg. 371)

7

Westminster
Station (pg. 371)

Wilmington
(pg. 371)

5

*Hills of Vermont
Quilt Block*

Vermont

Inn at Shelburne Farms
This hotel and sustainable working farm in Shelburne, VT began as
an agricultural estate in the late 1800s. Today, the property
invites guests to stay on the grounds during warm-weather months,
where they can swim in nearby Lake Champlain,
play lawn games, stroll the gardens,
and enjoy fresh farm suppers at the Inn Restaurant.
1611 Harbor Rd, Shelburne, VT 05482   (802) 985-8498
www. shelburnefarms.org

Q-Quilting ~ Y-Yarn ~ N-Needlework ~ R-Retreat ~ M-Museum

Arlington	Battenkill Stitchery	6350 Vermont Rte. 7A	802-362-0654	
Bennington	The Scarlett Creation	626 Main St.	(802) 447-3794	
Brattleboro	Hand Knits	56 Elliot St.	(802) 579-1799	
Bristol	Yarn & Yoga LLP	25 Main St. #A	(802) 453-7799	
Chester	Country Treasures	12 Common St.	(802) 875-4377	
Chester	Log Cabin Quilting	3864 Flamstead Rd.	(802) 886-1671	
Colchester	Sunny Laurel Sisters	3424 Roosevelt Hwy.	(802) 872-5363	
Derby	**Country Thyme Vermont**	**60 Rte. 111**	**(802) 766-2852**	**Pg. 371**
Dorset	In Stitches Fine Needlepoint	3041 Rte. 30	(802) 867-7031	
Essex Junction	Yankee Pride	9 Main St.	(802) 872-9300	
Fairfax	Pine Ledge Fiber Studio	103 Ledge Rd.	(802) 849-2876	
Fairlee	Barnyard Quilting	232 US. Rt. 5 N.	(802) 333-3566	
Graniteville	God's Little Acres Alpaca Farm	64 Orchard Terrace	(802) 522-6741	
Jamaica	Margie's Muse	3779 Vermont Rte. 30	(802) 874-7201	
Londonderry	Waterwheel Quilt Shop	6795 Vermont Rte. 100	(802) 824-5700	
Lyndonville	Sewin' Love Fabric Shoppe	101 Depot St.	(802) 427-3070	
Middlebury	Cacklin' Hens	383 Exchange St.	(802) 388-2221	
Middlebury	Vermont Yarn Co. & Field Farm	2571 Rte. 7 S.	(802) 388-9665	
Montgomery Center	Mountain Fiber Folk	188 Main St.	(802) 326-2092	
Montpelier	**A Quilter's Garden**	**342 River St. Rte. 302**	**(802) 223-2275**	**Pg. 371**
Montpelier	The Knitting Studio	112 Main St.	(802) 229-2444	
Newport	Ewe-Forium	79 Coventry St.	(802) 334-9955	
Norwich	Northern Nights Yarn Shop	Corner of Elm & Main St.	(802) 649-2000	
Peacham	Snowshoe Farm	520 The Great Rd.	(802) 592-3153	
Plainfield	Vermont Yarn Shop	858 E. Hill Rd.	(802) 454-1114	
Plymouth	**Plymouth Notch Historic District**			
		3780 Rte. 100 A	**(802) 672-3773**	**Pg. 371**
Poultney	Stitchy Women	144 Main St.	(802) 287-4114	
Proctorsville	Six Loose Ladies	7 Depot St.	(802) 226-7373	
Putney	Green Mountain Spinnery	7 Brickyard Ln.	(802) 387-4528	
Rutland	Green Mountain Fibers Yarn Store	2559 Woodstock Ave.	(802) 775-7800	
Shelburne	Must Love Yarn	2438 Shelburne Rd.	(802) 448-3780	
South Duxbury	Singing Spindle Spinnery	701 Vermont Rte. 100	(802) 244-8025	
St. Albans	What A Yarn	54 N. Main St.	(802) 393-0121	
Stowe	Stowe Fabric & Yarn	37 Depot St.	(802) 253-6740	
Stowe	The Wooden Needle	56 Park St.	(802) 253-3086	
Troy	Vermont Quilter's Schoolhouse	6529 Vermont Rte. 100	(802) 744-4023	
Waitsfield	Shades of Winter Yarn Shop	5123 Main St.	(802) 496-9040	
West Dover	Ugly Duckling Yarn	114 Rte. 100	(802) 464-6300	
West Glover	The Merlin Tree	2093 Barton Rd.	(802) 754-6433	
Westminster Station			**(802) 722-4743**	**Pg. 371**
	Quilt-a-way Fabrics	**190 Back Westminster Rd.**		
Weston	Wits End Woolens	468 Moses Pond Rd.	(802) 375-4190	
White River Junction				
	Hen House Fabric	**246 Holiday Dr. #2**	**(802) 295-4436**	**Pg. 371**
Williston	Northeast Fiber Arts Center	7531 Williston Rd.	(802) 288-8081	
Williston	Quilting With Color	21 Taft Corners Shopping Center	(802) 876-7135	
Wilmington	**Norton House, A Quilters Paradise**			
		30 W. Main St.	**(802) 464-7213**	**Pg. 371**
Woodstock	Whippletree Yarn Shop	7 Central St.	(802) 457-1325	
Worcester	The Wool Shed at Frostbite Falls Farm	3 Hancock Brook Rd.	(802) 223-2456	

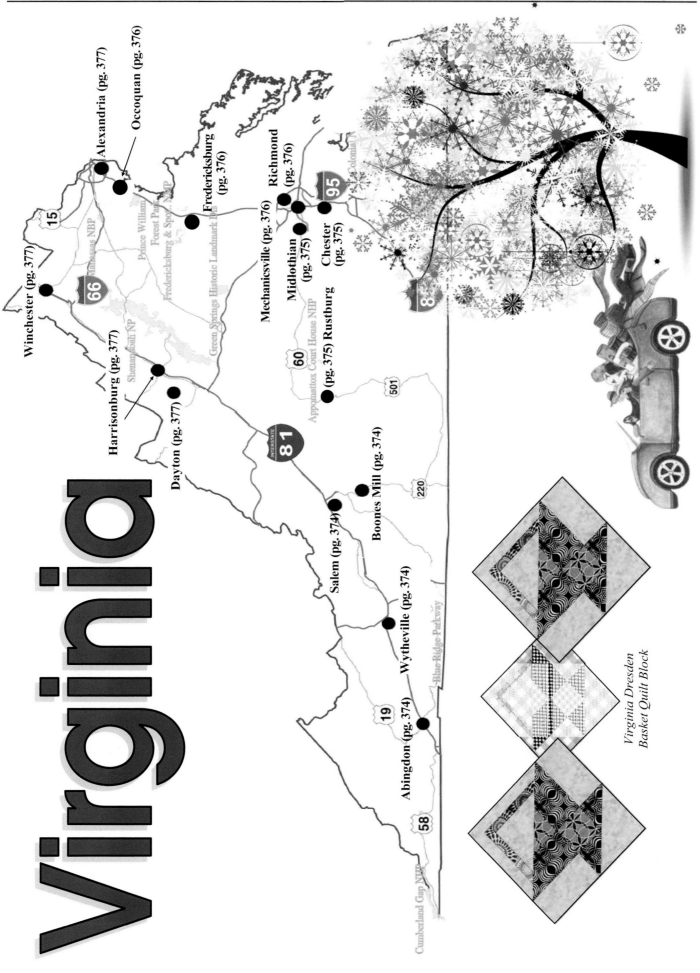

Virginia Dresden Basket Quilt Block

Virginia

Winchester (pg. 377)
Alexandria (pg. 377)
Occoquan (pg. 376)
Fredericksburg (pg. 376)
Richmond (pg. 376)
Mechanicsville (pg. 376)
Midlothian (pg. 375)
Chester (pg. 375)
Rustburg (pg. 375)
Harrisonburg (pg. 377)
Dayton (pg. 377)
Salem (pg. 374)
Boones Mill (pg. 374)
Wytheville (pg. 374)
Abingdon (pg. 374)

Notes

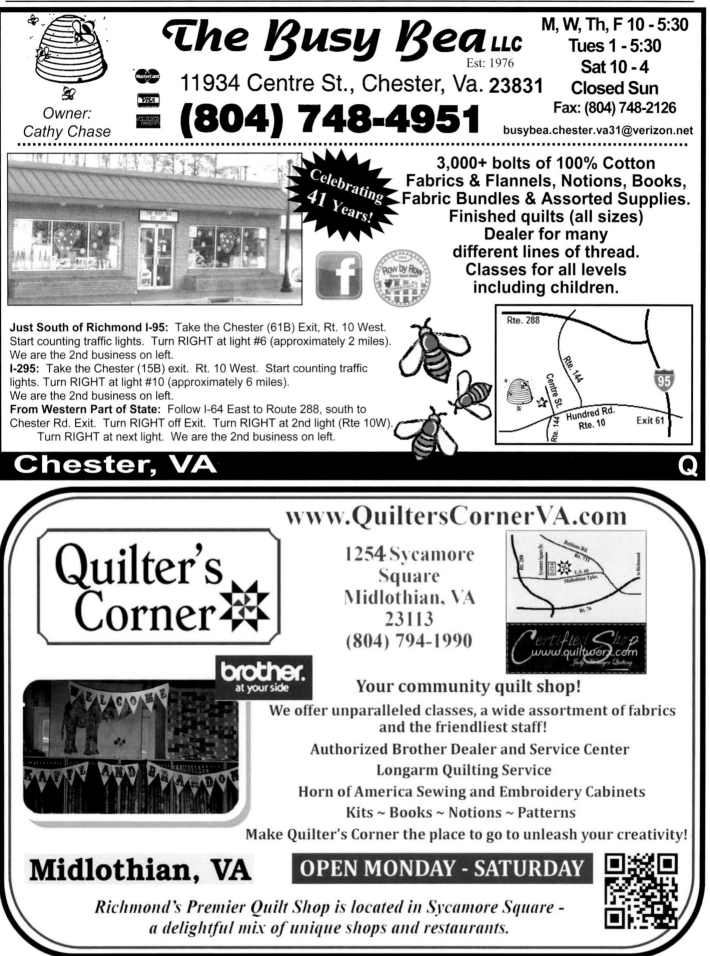

The Jefferson Hotel
Richmond is home to this Spanish Baroque–style hotel, opened in 1895 by Lewis Ginter, who enlisted the architects that designed the New York Public Library and Henry Frick House in New York. Several U.S. presidents as well as stars like the Rolling Stones, Dolly Parton, and Elvis Presley have stayed here while visiting.
101 W Franklin St, Richmond, VA 23220   (888) 918-1895   www.jeffersonhotel.com

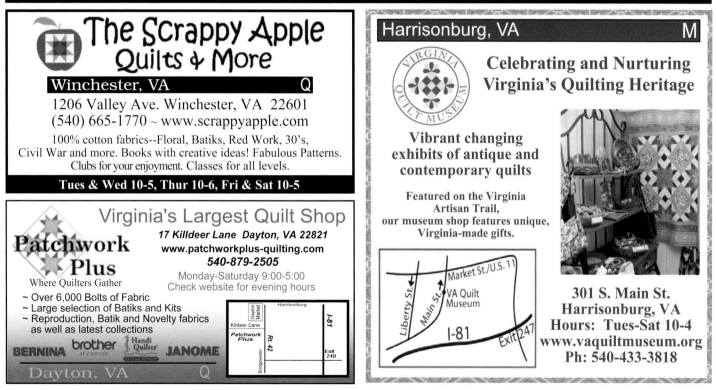

Did you know?
Opened in 1964, the Chesapeake Bay Bridge-Tunnel is 18 miles long
and has two bridges and two mile-long tunnels.
It extends over the mouth of Chesapeake Bay and connects the cities of Cape Charles and Norfolk.

Virginia Shops

Q-Quilting ~ Y-Yarn ~ N-Needlework ~ R-Retreat ~ M-Museum

Abingdon	**Jeannine's Fabrics & Quilt Shop**	**414 W. Main St.**	**(276) 628-9586**	**Pg. 374**
Abingdon	A Likely Yarn	213 Pecan St.	(276) 628-2143	
Abingdon	Plumb Alley Stitchery	117 W. Main St.	(276) 628-1181	
Abingdon	Virginia Highlands Quilt Shop	25066 Lee Hwy.	(276) 628-6442	
Alexandria	**Fabric Place Basement**	**6660 Richmond Hwy.**	**(703) 660-6661**	**Pg. 377**
Alexandria	Artistic Artifacts	4750 Eisenhower Ave.	(703) 823-0202	
Alexandria	Bonny's Sewing & Fabric	5515 Cherokee Ave. #101	(703) 451-8480	
Alexandria	Del Ray Fabrics	209 E. Mason Ave.	(571) 312-7991	
Alexandria	Fibre Space	1219 King St.	(703) 664-0344	
Alexandria	Hillin Hall Variety Store	7902 Fort Hunt Rd.	(703) 765-4110	
Alexandria	In Stitches Needlework	8800-F Pear Tree Ct.	(703) 360-4600	
Arlington	Waste Knot Needlepoint	4502 Lee Hwy.	(703) 807-1828	
Ashburn	Sew Magarbo	44933 George Washington Blvd. #110		
			(703) 375-9739	
Bedford	Hearthside Quilts	207 E. Depot St.	(800) 451-3533	
Blacksburg	Mosaic	880 University City Blvd.	(540) 961-4462	
Blacksburg	The New River Fiber Co.	102 Roanoke St. E.	(540) 200-5554	
Boones Mill	**Boone's Country Store**	**2699 Jubal Early Hwy.**	**(540) 721-2478**	**Pg. 374**
Burke	Yarn Barn	9413-C Old Burke Lake Rd.	(703) 978-2220	
Capron	Quilter's N Friends	17293 Pinopolis Rd.	(434) 658-4564	
Centreville	G Street Fabrics	5077 Westfields Blvd.	(703) 818-8090	
Charlottesville	Cottonwood	2035 Barracks Rd.	(434) 244-9975	
Charlottesville	Laughing Sheep Yarns	188 Zan Rd.	(434) 973-0331	
Charlottesville	Magpie Knits	114 E. Main St. #A	(434) 296-4625	
Charlottesville	Mangham Wool and Mohair Farm	901 Hammocks Gap Rd.	(434) 973-2222	
Charlottesville	Threads	2246 Ivy Rd. #9	(434) 295-3575	
Chesapeake	A Different Touch	1107 S. Military Hwy. #B	(757) 366-8830	
Chesapeake	Tidewater Sew-vac.	237 S. Battlefield Blvd.	(757) 484-1837	
Chesapeake	Your Crochet Connection	1105 Shore Rd.	(757) 487-5578	
Chester	**The Busy Bea**	**11934 Centre St.**	**(804) 748-4951**	**Pg. 375**
Chesterfield	Stitch by Stitch Quilt Shop	6501 Centralia Rd.	(804) 318-9571	
Chincoteague Island	Carodan Farm Wool Shop	7151 Horseshoe Dr.	(757) 336-0536	
Covington	Sew Many Quilts	431 W. Main St.	(540) 962-0023	
Crewe	Rose Patch Creations	125 W. Carolina Ave.	(434) 645-7780	
Culpeper	145 Art & Design Studio	122 E. Davis St.	(540) 825-5620	
Culpeper	Dog House Yarns and More	708 Sunset Ln.	(540) 825-3585	
Dayton	**Patchwork Plus**	**17 Killdeer Ln.**	**(540) 879-2505**	**Pg. 377**
Dillwyn	Yarn Barn of Andersonville	5077 Andersonville Rd.	(434) 983-1965	
Fairfax	Nature's Yarns	11212 Lee Hwy.	(703) 273-3596	
Fairfax	The Quilt Patch	10381 Main St.	(703) 273-6937	
Fairfax	The Quilters Studio	9600 Main St. #L	(703) 261-6366	
Fairfield	The Quiltery	5499 N. Lee Hwy.	(540) 377-9191	
Floyd	Schoolhouse Fabrics	220 N. Locust St.	(540) 745-4561	
Floyd	Wooly Jumper Yarns	202 S. Locust St.	(210) 745-5648	
Fredericksburg	**The Crazy Cousin**	**4131 Plank Rd.**	**(540) 786-2289**	**Pg. 376**
Fredericksburg	Old Town Yarnery	433 Elm St.	(540) 287-2101	
Fredericksburg	Untangled Purls	2561 Cowan Blvd.	(540) 479-8382	
Gainesville	Quilting Cellar	4198 Stepney Dr.	(703) 354-2061	
Gloucester	Field's Quilting and Crafts	6568 Main St.	(804) 693-6120	
Great Falls	Jinny Beyer Studio	776-F Walker Rd.	(703) 759-0250	
Hampton	Phoebus Needlework	13 E. Mellen St.	(757) 723-1558	
Hampton	Tidewater Sew-Vac.	2040 Coliseum Dr.	(757) 826-1801	
Harrisonburg	**Virginia Quilt Museum**	**301 S. Main St.**	**(540) 433-3818**	**Pg. 377**
Harrisonburg	Ragtime Fabrics	926 W. Market St.	(540) 434-5663	
Harrisonburg	Sew Classic Fabrics	121 Carpenter Ln.	(540) 421-3309	
Haymarket	Needle in the Haymarket	15125 Washington St. #316	(703) 659-1062	
Haymarket	Oh Sew Persnickety Fabrics & Threads	15125 Washington St. #116	(571) 222-7759	
Irvington	Village Needlepoint of Irvington	4395 Irvington Rd.	(804) 438-9500	
Kenbridge	Keeping You In Stitches	118 S. Broad St.	(434) 676-4000	
LaCrosse	Country Cross Stitch	2220 Hall Rd.	(434) 636-5556	
Louisa	The Fabric Hut and Gift Gallery	203 W. Main St.	(540) 967-1630	
Lynchburg	Backstitches	100 Wayne Dr.	(434) 385-0185	
Lynchburg	Quilted Expressions	3622 Old Forest Rd.	(434) 385-6765	

City	Shop	Address	Phone	Page
Manassas	Suzzie's Quilt Shop	10370 Portsmouth Rd.	(703) 368-3867	
McLean	Vienna Quilt Shop	6819 Elm St.	(703) 281-4091	
Meadows of Dan	Greenberry House	12206 Squirrel Spur Rd.	(276) 952-2444	
Mechanicsville	**Millstone Quilts**	**8074 Flannigan Mill Rd.**	**(804) 779-3535**	**Pg. 376**
Middleburg	Stitch Middleburg	112 W. Washington St.	(540) 687-5990	
Midlothian	**Quilter's Corner**	**1245 Sycamore Square Dr.**	**(804) 794-1990**	**Pg. 375**
Millboro	Echo Valley Fiber	541 Deerfield Rd.	(540) 968-0529	
Moneta	The General Store	213 Scruggs Rd.	(540) 721-3009	
Montvale	Bargain Barn Fabrics	11600 W. Lynchburg-Salem Trpk.	(540) 947-2894	
Mount Jackson	Country Quilters	5555 Main St.	(540) 477-9511	
Narrows	Ms. Audre's Fabric and Fellowship	206 Main St.	(540) 358-2516	
Nassawadox	Teresa's Quilts	7401 Railroad Ave.	(757) 710-0644	
Newport News	Nancy's Calico Patch	896 J. Clyde Morris Blvd.	(757) 596-7397	
Newport News	The Loom Room	83 Queens Ct.	(757) 599-3889	
Newport News	Tidewater Sew-Vac.	996J Clyde Morris Blvd.	(757) 595-7850	
Newport News	Village Stitchery	97 Main St. #102	(757) 599-0101	
Nokesville	Daffodil Quilts & Fibers	13059 Fitzwater Dr.	(703) 594-0386	
Norfolk	Baa Baa Sheep	754 W. 22nd St.	(757) 802-9229	
Norfolk	Fabric Hut	828 E Little Creek Rd.	(757) 588-1300	
Norfolk	Tidewater Sew-Vac.	7525 Tidewater Dr. Ste. 34	(757) 587-3136	
North Chesterfield	Material Things	9930 Hull St. Rd.	(804) 276-3689	
Occoquan	**Yarn Cloud**	**204 Washington St.**	**(571) 408-4236**	**Pg. 376**
Portsmouth	Tidewater Sew-Vac.	701 Airline Blvd Ste. A	(757) 399-2417	
Pound	Fabric House	8424 W. Main St.	(276) 796-4500	
Purcellville	Webfabrics Showroom	116 N. Bailey Ln.	(540) 751-2069	
Purcellville	Two Rivers Yarns	221 E. Main St. #201	(240) 457-0410	
Radford	Sew Biz	92 Harvey St.	(540) 639-1138	
Richmond	**Quilting Adventures**	**6943 Lakeside Ave.**	**(804) 262-0005**	**Pg. 376**
Richmond	Blue Crab Quilt Company	3991 Deep Rock Rd.	(804) 755-4499	
Richmond	Chadwick Heirlooms	12501 Patterson Ave.	(804) 285-3355	
Richmond	Jermie's	5701 Grove Ave.	(804) 282-8021	
Richmond	Knitting B	8801 Three Chopt Rd. #L	(804) 484-6005	
Richmond	The Stitching Studio	5615 Patterson Ave.	(804) 269-0355	
Roanoke	Mosaic Yarn	3117 Franklin Rd. SW #5	(540) 685-2285	
Roanoke	Yarn Explosion	5227 Airport Rd. NW	(540) 206-2638	
Rocky Mount	The Crooked Stitch	390 Franklin St.	(540) 420-7129	
Rustburg	**Threads Run Thru It**	**40 Exchange Dr.**	**(434) 821-3000**	**Pg. 374**
Saint Paul	Sweet Dreams Quilts & Crafts	16610 Broad St.	(276) 762-0408	
Salem	**Quilting Essentials**	**405 Apperson Dr.**	**(540) 389-3650**	**Pg. 374**
Sperryville	Knit Wit Yarn Shop	12018 Lee Hwy.	(540) 987-8251	
Stafford	Bonny's Sewing And Fabric	2789 Jefferson Davis Hwy. #105	(540) 288-2022	
Staunton	Rachel's Quilt Patch	40 Middlebrook Ave.	(540) 886-7728	
Stephens City	Cloth Peddler Quilt Shop	5330 Main St.	(540) 868-9020	
Stephens City	We Keep You In Stitches	5387 Main St.	(540) 869-4684	
Stuart	Quilted Colors	107 N. Main St.	(276) 694-3020	
Suffolk	Tidewater Sew-Vac.	1574 Holland Rd.	(757) 539-0009	
Tappahannock	Sew Happy	158 Prince St.	(804) 443-2154	
The Plains	Hunt Country Yarns	6482 Main St.	(540) 253-9990	
Topping	2 B's Quilt Shop	2324 Greys Point Rd.	(804) 758-2642	
Virginia Beach	Tidewater Sew Vac.	2401 Sea Board Rd. Ste. 100	(757) 486-2996	
Virginia Beach	Dyeing To Stitch	5312 Kemps River Dr. #102	(757) 366-8740	
Virginia Beach	Sarah's Thimble	2245 W Great Neck Rd. #5	(757) 481-1725	
Virginia Beach	The Yarn Club	240 Mustang Trail Ste. 8	(757) 486-5648	
Virginia Beach	Tidewater Sew-Vac.	1352 Fordham Dr. Ste. 102	(757) 479-3950	
Virginia Beach	Tidewater Sew-Vac.	315 N. Great Neck Rd.	(757) 340-3481	
Warrenton	Kelly Ann's Quilting	9 S. 5th St.	(540) 341-8890	
Warrenton	Yarnia of Old Town	92 Main St. Ste. 103	(540) 878-2039	
Waynesboro	Cross Stitch Station	1500 W. 11th St.	(540) 943-7742	
Waynesboro	JJ's Knitting Knook	3396 Stuarts Draft Hwy.	(540) 337-3770	
White Stone	Dirt Woman Fiber Arts	577 Rappahannock Dr.	(804) 725-7525	
White Stone	Sew Lovelee	85 First St.	(804) 577-7272	
Williamsburg	The Stitching Well at Haus Tirol	1915 Pocohantas Trail	(757) 220-0313	
Williamsburg	Tidewater Sew-Vac.	551 Merrimac Tr. Ste. E	(757) 220-8710	
Winchester	**The Scrappy Apple, Quilts & More**	**1206 Valley Ave.**	**(540) 665-1770**	**Pg. 377**
Winchester	Knit 1. Purl 2	20 W. Boscawen St.	(540) 662-6098	
Winchester	Never Enough Yarn	393 Millwood Ave.	(540) 665-1800	
Wise	Clapboard House	207 Main St.	(276) 328-4470	
Woodstock	Shenandoah Sew & Vac.	498 N. Main St.	(540) 459-1888	
Wytheville	**Batiks Etc. & Sew What Fabrics**	**460 E. Main St.**	**(276) 228-6400**	**Pg. 374**

Index

Notes

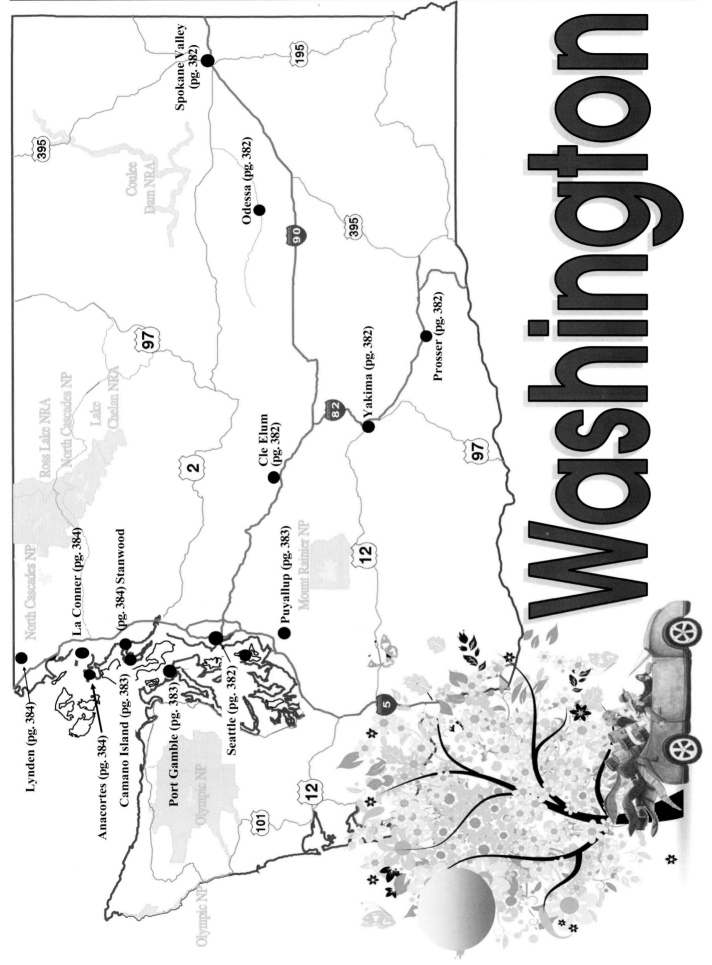

The Quilting Bee inc.

BERNINA
JANOME
baby lock

"Where lasting friendships are pieced together"

16002 E. Broadway Ave. Spokane, WA 99037
(509) 928-6037 or (888) 928-6037
manager@quiltingbeespokane.com

❖ Authorized BERNINA, JANOME and Baby Lock Dealer
❖ Accuquilt Signature Dealer
❖ Machine Service & Repair All Makes
❖ 6000+ Bolts of Fabric, Kits, Notions
❖ Machine Embroidery Supplies
❖ Quilting Classes for ALL Levels
❖ Row by Row Experience Participant

Shop Hours
M&F 10:00-8:00
Tues, Wed, Thur
10:00-6:00
Sat 10:00-5:00
2nd Sun
12:00-5:00

www.quiltingbeespokane.com

Odessa, WA   Q

EXPERIENCE Quilts!

4 W. 1st Ave. Odessa, WA 99159
(509) 982-2012
www.experiencequilts.com
Est: 2013 Free Newsletter
experiencequilts@gmail.com
NOT JUST ANOTHER
SMALL TOWN QUILT SHOP!
Mon-Fri 10am-5pm, Sat 10-4

Rt. 28
Rt. 21
Alder St.
Experience Quilts!
☆
1st Ave.
to I-90

Stitch n' Quilt

8405 Ahtanum Rd.
Yakima, WA 98903
(509) 945-2560
Owner: Jolou Catron
stitchnquiltjl@gmail.com

Custom made quilts, nice selection for kids, long arm services. Happy fabrics, Down on the Farm, wildlife, horses. Notions too.

Tues-Fri 10am- 5pm, Sat 10am-2pm

W. Valley Mall Rd.
Exit 36
AIRPORT
I-82
Occidental Ave.
8405 Stitch n' Quilt
Ahtanum Rd.
86th Ave.
Main St.

Yakima, WA   Q

The Sewing Basket & The Quilted Country Inn

1108 Wine Country Rd.
Prosser, WA 99350
(509) 786-7367
www.prossersewingbasket.com
Owner: Marilyn Dalstra
prossersewingbasket@earthlink.net

The Sewing Basket
Wine Country Rd.
Grant Ave.
Wine Ctry Rd.
Yakima River
7th St.
6th St.
☆

Our quilt shop and retreat center are right next door to each other. We've just expanded our store to accommodate 12,000+ Bolts of cotton fabric, Notions & Patterns.
Or plan your next retreat at our wonderful center with 6 bedrooms, 4 bathrooms and a newly remodeled kitchen.
Enjoy the relaxing view out over the Yakima River.
Call today for rates and to schedule your retreat!

Monday - Saturday
10:00 - 5:30

Ruby's in Cle Elum

116 E. 1st St • Cle Elum, WA • 98922
Phone: 509.674.2296 Fax: 509.674.2416
www.rubysstore.com

FABRIC - YARN - EMBROIDERY
♦ Baby Lock Sales and Service
♦ Janome Sales and Service
♦ Long Arm Quilting
♦ Scrapbooking - paper, stickers and more
♦ Precuts - Jelly Rolls, Layer Cakes, Charm Packs and Fat Quarters.
♦ Batting - by the Yard or Roll

Sew What? retreat
See Our Ad In The Retreat Section!

Tuesday-Friday 10:00am-5:00pm
Monday & Saturday 10:00am-4:30pm

Show this ad for 15% off regularly priced items!

Seattle, WA   Q

UNDERCOVER QUILTS
QUILTS - FABRICS - NOTIONS

98 Virginia St. Seattle, WA 98101
(800) 469-6511 or (206) 622-6382
Owner: Linda Hitchcock ~quilts@serv.net
www.undercoverquilts.com

Fabrics, Kits, Patterns, Notions, Gifts and Supplies. Exclusive Quilting Patterns.
New and Antique American Made Quilts.
Mon-Sat 10:00-6:00, Sun 10:00-5:00

Virginia St.
Stewart St.
Pine St.
Pike St.
Union St.
98 Undercover Quilts
Pike Place Market
1st Ave.
2nd Ave.
3rd Ave.
I-5
Exit 165

The Quilt Barn
Serving Quilters since 1980

2102 E. Main #102, Puyallup, WA 98372
(253) 845-1532

Regular Business Hours:
Mon. thru Fri. 10-6 p.m. Sat 10-5 p.m. Sun. 12-4 p.m.

Check out our new online store at: **www.quiltbarn.com**

Visit us on Facebook

❖ **Over 12,000 bolt selection of 100% fine cotton quilting fabrics ~ specializing in brights, batiks, novelty prints and flannels**
❖ **Complete quilting supplies and notions**
❖ **Large selection of books and patterns**
❖ **Friendly and knowledgeable staff**
❖ **Open 7 day a week**

From Hwy 167: Going south, follow signs to Hwy 410. Take 1st exit (Traffic Ave). At stop sign, turn right and go 1 ¼ miles. We are on the left.

From I-5: Take the hwy 512 exit. Take Pioneer exit. At stop sign turn right. Make left at 15th. then right at E. Main. We are on the right.

Port Gamble, WA   QN

Quilted Strait
Quilting and Needlework Supplies

Open 7 Days
10am - 5pm

32280 Puget Way   98364
1-855-GOQUILT
info@quiltedstrait.com
www.quiltedstrait.com

1 ½ miles from the Hood Canal Bridge on Hwy. 104 on the Kitsap Peninsula.

Quilt Sampler FEATURED SHOP

Our 100 year old building is full of quilts for inspiration and more than 4000 bolts of quilting fabrics. Our eclectic inventory includes batiks, Asian inspired fabrics, flannels and contemporary prints as well as supplies for embroidery, needle felting, wool applique and a wide variety of flosses and thread.

Camano Island, WA   QR

Over the Rainbow
where a world of color awaits you...

33 years!

Owner: Laura Van Divier
Est: 2001   23,000+ Bolts
lauraotr@msn.com
www.overrainbow.com
Wide Variety, Fun Novelty Fabrics, Quirky Gift Items.
Exit 212 off I-5

Mon-Sat 9am-12pm

Retreat Center too! See Retreat Section.

740 Michael Way
Camano Island, WA98282
(360) 387-2366

The Historic Davenport Hotel

Opened in 1914, The Davenport is Washington's grandest hotel. Whether it's the soaring architecture, award-winning amenities, rich history, or simply its proximity to nearby Spokane attractions, The Historic Davenport Hotel has welcomed film stars, explorers, writers, politicians and other luminaries for more than 100 years.

10 S Post St, Spokane, WA 99201
(509) 455-8888
www.davenporthotelcollection.com

Washington Shops

Q-Quilting ~ Y-Yarn ~ N-Needlework ~ R-Retreat ~ M-Museum

Aberdeen	Quilt Harbor	208 S. Broadway St.	(360) 532-1200	
Allyn	Allyn Knit Shop	16590 Hwy. 3	(360) 275-4729	
Almira	Nana's Quilts & More	318 W. Maple Ave.	(509) 639-2648	
Anacortes	**In Stitches Quilt Shoppe**	**820 Commercial Ave.**	**(360) 293-2146**	**Pg. 384**
Anacortes	Fabrics Plus	608 Commercial Ave.	(360) 293-7641	
Arlington	The Quiltmaker's Shoppe	315 N. Olympic Ave.	(360) 435-3993	
Bainbridge Island	Churchmouse Yarns & Teas	118 Madrone Ln.	(206) 780-2686	
Bainbridge Island	Esther's Fabrics	181 Winslow Way E #D	(206) 842-2261	
Battle Ground	Country Manor Fabrics	7702 NE 179th	(360) 573-6084	
Bellevue	Pacific Fabrics & Crafts	1645-140th Ave. NE	(425) 747-3551	
Bellevue	QuiltWorks Northwest	121 A 107th Ave. NE	(425) 453-6005	
Bellingham	Apple Yarns Inc.	2925 Newmarket Place #104	(360) 756-9992	
Bellingham	Fabric-Etc	1633 Birchwood Ave.	(360) 671-5277	
Bellingham	J & J's Needle Art	436 W. Bakerview Rd. #109	(360) 676-9090	
Bellingham	Kori's Fabric Creations	4300 Alice St.	(360) 671-7570	
Bellingham	Northwest Handspun Yarns	1401 Commercial St.	(360) 738-0167	
Bellingham	Spincycle Yarns	1318 Bay St.	(360) 752-0783	
Bellingham	Two Thimbles Quilt Shop	1805 Cornwall Ave.	(360) 715-1629	
Birch Bay	Beach Basket Yarn & Gifts	7620 Birch Bay Dr.	(360) 371-0332	
Bonney Lake	Ben Franklin Crafts	21121 Hwy. 410	(253) 862-6822	
Bothell	Keepsake Cottage Fabrics	818 238th St. SE	(425) 486-3483	
Bothell	Mad Cow Yarn	17171 Bothell Way NE	(206) 397-4898	
Bothell	Martingale & Company	19021 120th Ave. NE #102	(425) 368-1387	
Bremerton	Pacific Fabrics & Crafts	4214 Wheaton Way	(360) 479-4214	
Buckley	Front Porch Quilts	832 Main St.	(360) 761-7185	
Camano Island	**Over the Rainbow**	**740 Michael Way**	**(360) 387-2366**	**Pg. 383**
Cashmere	Cashmere Cottage Yarn	102 A Maple St.	(509) 782-0382	
Castle Rock	The Quilt Nest	105 Cowlitz St. W.	(360) 274-4663	
Centralia	Loose Ends Fiber Arts	401 N. Tower Ave.	(360) 669-0280	
Centralia	Whalen Quilt Works	404 S. Tower #5	(360) 807-1255	
Chehalis	Ewe & I	566 N. Market Blvd.	(360) 345-1506	
Chehalis	Sister's Fabric Shop	476 N. Market	(360) 748-9747	
Chehalis	Yarn & Things	545 N. Market Blvd. Ste. 5	(360) 748-2134	
Chelan	3 Wild Sheep Yarn Company	210 E. Woodin Ave.	(509) 888-0285	
Chelan	Woven Threads	136 E. Woodin Ave. #B	(509) 682-7714	
Chewelah	Akers United Drug	N. 406 Park	(509) 935-8441	
Clarkston	Patrick's Craft Shoppe	860 6th St.	(509) 758-2110	
Cle Elum	**Ruby's Store**	**116 E. 1st St.**	**(509) 674-2296**	**Pg. 382**
Colfax	Palouse River Quilts	S. 101 Main St.	(509) 397-2278	
Colville	E-Z Knit Fabrics	165 N. Main St.	(509) 684-2644	
Dayton	Jacci's Yarn Basket	242 E. Main St.	(509) 382-2526	
Deer Park	Ed & Jean's Quilt Shop	22 S. Vernon St.	(509) 276-6678	
Deer Park	Sew-Into-Quilts	110 W. Crawford St.	(509) 276-2035	
Des Moines	All Points Yarn	21921 Marine View Dr. S.	(206) 824-9276	
Des Moines	Carriage Country Quilts	22214 Marine View Dr. S.	(206) 878-9414	
Duvall	The Quilter's Garden	15705 Main St. NE	(425) 844-1621	
Eatonville	Alice's Reflection Farm	31801 79th Ave. Court E.	(253) 380-5511	
Edmonds	All Wound Up Yarn Shop	18521 76th Ave. W #109	(425) 245-5104	
Ellensburg	Yarn Folk	304 N. Pearl	(509) 304-4588	
Elma	Elma Variety and Quilt Shop	325 W. Main St.	(360) 482-2411	
Eltopia	In the Sticks Quilt Shop	790 Fir Rd.	(509) 531-9988	
Enumclaw	Cow Lick Quilts n' Crafts	38125 303rd Ave. SE	(360) 825-5433	
Ephrata	The Fabric Patch	220 10th Ave. SW	(509) 754-8280	
Everett	Great Yarns	4023 Rucker Ave.	(425) 252-8155	
Everett	Loving Stitches Quilt Shop & Fine Baskets			
		2916 Hewitt Ave.	(425) 252-7777	
Everett	The Needle and I	4727 Evergreen Way	(425) 259-3013	
Everett	The Needlepointer	2517 Colby Ave.	(425) 252-2277	
Fife	Firwood Farm Alpacas	8002 48th St. E.	(253) 926-2582	
Freeland	Island Fabrics	1592 Main St. #220	(360) 331-7313	
Friday Harbor	Island Wools	140 B First St.	(360) 370-5648	
Gig Harbor	Harbor Quilt Garden	7716 C Pioneer Way	(253) 358-3856	
Gig Harbor	Rainy Day Yarns	3200 Tarabochia St.	(253) 514-6890	
Gig Harbor	Vintage Knits Wool Shoppe	6212 34th St. NW	(253) 265-1235	

Index

Grand Coulee	Kissed Quilts	301 Main St.	(509) 386-5715	
Ilwaco	Purly Shell Fiber Arts	157 Howerton St. #B	(360) 642-3044	
Issaquah	APQS Northwest	1315 NW Mall St. #4	(425) 243-3502	
Issaquah	Gossypium Quilt Shop	355 NW Gillman Blvd Ste. 102	(425) 557-7878	
Issaquah	Threadneedle Street	485 Front St. N Ste. B	(425) 391-0528	
Kelso	Paisley Duck Quilting and Design	404-E S. Pacific Ave.	(360) 703-3279	
Kennewick	Sandy's Fabrics & Machines	24 N. Benton St.	(509) 585-4739	
Kennewick	Sheep's Clothing	3311 W. Clearwater Ave. # B-120	(509) 734-2484	
Kent	Makers' Mercantile	18437 E. Valley Hwy.	(425) 251-1239	
Kent	Running Stitch Fabric	213 1st Ave. S.	(253) 277-2248	
Kettle Falls	Red Rooster	41 Enzyne Ln.	(509) 738-4418	
Kirkland	Quality Sewing & Vacuum Centers	13501 100th Ave. NE	(425) 821-1747	
Kirkland	Serial Knitters Yarn Shop	8427 122nd Ave. NE	(425) 242-0086	
La Conner	**Pacific Northwest Quilt & Fiber Arts Museum**			
		703 2nd. St.	**(360) 466-4288**	**Pg. 384**
La Conner	Jennings Yarn & Needlecraft	106 S. First St.	(360) 466-3177	
Lakewood	Yorkshire Yarns	6122 Motor Ave. SW	(253) 589-9276	
Langley	Knitty Purls	210 First St.	(360) 331-2212	
Leavenworth	Dee's Country Accents	917 Commercial St.	(509) 548-5311	
Leavenworth	Leavenworth Quilt Co.	11007 Hwy. 2	(509) 888-8807	
Lind	Crazy Quilter	316 N. I St.	(509) 677-3335	
Longview	Longview Sewing & Fabric	1113 Vandercook Way	(360) 578-2628	
Longview	Momma Made It	2121 8th Ave.	(360) 636-5631	
Lopez Island	Island Fibers	4208 Port Stanley Rd.	(360) 468-2467	
Lynden	**Calico Country**	**1722 Front St.**	**(360) 354-4832**	**Pg. 384**
Lynden	Folktales	1885 Kok Rd.	(360) 354-0855	
Lynden	Tangled Threads Quilt Shop	202 6th St.	(360) 318-1567	
Lynden	Wear On Earth	8150 Washington 539	(360) 318-8657	
Marysville	Loving Stitches Quilt Shop	306 State Ave.	(360) 659-4006	
Metaline Falls	Sweet Creek Creations	219 E. 5th Ave.	(509) 446-2429	
Mossyrock	Kathy's Kountry Fabrics	121 Ajlune Rd.	(360) 983-8171	
Mt. Vernon	WildFibers	706 S. 1st St.	(360) 336-5202	
Mukilteo	Peacock & Periwinkle	11700 Mukilteo Speeway, Ste. 201	(425) 232-1355	
Northgate	Quality Sewing & Vacuum Centers	842 NE Northgate Way	(206) 363-1634	
Oak Harbor	Quilters Workshop	601 SE Pioneer Way	(360) 675-7216	
Ocean Shores	Beach Tyme Quilts	873 Pt. Brown Ave. NW #2	(360) 289-7917	
Odessa	**Experience Quilts!**	**4 W. 1st Ave.**	**(509) 982-2012**	**Pg. 382**
Olympia	Canvas Works	525 Columbia St. SW	(360) 352-4481	
Olympia	The Black Sheep Yarn Boutique	2615 Capital Mall Dr. SW #3B	(360) 350-0470	
Omak	Needlelyn Time	9 N. Main St.	(509) 826-1198	
Onalaska	Heavenly Quilts & Fabrics Redeemed	266 Carlisle Ave.	(360) 978-6300	
Othello	Dianna's Knitting & Embroidery	1970 W. Bench Rd.	(509) 488-2563	
Packwood	Packwood Spirits-Cabin Quilts	13042 US. Hwy. 12	(360) 494-5781	
Palouse	Grammy G's Tresures & Notions	124 W. Main St.	(509) 878-1660	
Pasco	Jackie's NeedleArt Mania	4807 Lobelia Ct.	(509) 582-9900	
Pasco	Janean's Bernina	6303 Burden Blvd. #C	(509) 544-7888	
Pomeroy	Rather-Be's Quilting Shop	382 Hwy. 12 E.	(509) 843-6162	
Port Angeles	Cabled Fiber Studio	125 W. 1st St.	(360) 504-2233	
Port Angeles	Sleepy Valley Quilt Co.	1017 E. Front St.	(360) 452-5227	
Port Angeles	Viking Sew & Vac.	707 E. 1st	(360) 457-3077	
Port Gamble	**Quilted Strait**	**32280 Puget Way**	**(360) 930-8145**	**Pg. 383**
Port Gamble	The Artful Ewe	32180 Rainier Ave. NE	(360) 643-0183	
Port Orchard	A Good Yarn Shop	1140 Bethel Ave. #101	(360) 876-0377	
Port Townsend	Creative Union Fabrics	112 Kala Sq. Pl. #3	(360) 379-0655	
Port Townsend	Diva Yarn	940 Water St.	(360) 385-4844	
Poulsbo	Amanda's Art-Yarn	18846 Front St. NE #E	(360) 779-3666	
Poulsbo	B's Fabric Fun & Sewing	19467 Viking Ave. NW	(360) 930-8210	
Poulsbo	Sawdust Hill Alpaca Farm	25448 Port Gamble Rd. NE	(360) 286-9999	
Poulsbo	The Quilt Shoppe	19020 Front St. NE	(360) 697-7475	
Prosser	**The Sewing Basket & The Quilted Country Inn**			
		1108 Wine Country Rd.	**(509) 786-7367**	**Pg. 382**
Puyallup	**The Quilt Barn**	**2102 E. Main #102**	**(253) 845-1532**	**Pg. 383**
Puyallup	The Quilting Fairy	13507 Meridian E. #O	(253) 845-0462	
Redmond	Ben Franklin Crafts	15756 Redmond Way	(425) 883-2050	
Renton	Knittery	601 S. Grady Way #C	(425) 228-4694	
Republic	Wisherwood Gallery and Yarn Studio	1003 S. Clark Ave.	(509) 775-0441	
Richland	Needful Needlecrafts	1515 Wright Ave. #D	(509) 539-4918	
Richland	Quiltmania	1442 Jadwin Ave. #C	(509) 946-7467	
Richland	White Bluff's Quilt Museum	294 Torbett St.	(509) 943-2552	
Rochester	Cathy's Classy Quilts	6835 183rd Ave. SW	(360) 339-2120	

Seattle	**Undercover Quilts from the USA**			
		98 Virginia St.	**(206) 622-6382**	**Pg. 382**
Seattle	Acorn Street Yarn Shop	2818 NE 55th St.	(206) 525-1726	
Seattle	Bad Woman Yarn	1815 N. 45th St. #215	(206) 547-5384	
Seattle	Fiber Gallery	7000 Greenwood Ave. N.	(206) 706-4197	
Seattle	Little Knits	3200 Ariport Way S. Bldg. 8 Ste. 110	(206) 535-7720	
Seattle	Seattle Yarn	5633 California Ave. SW	(206) 935-2010	
Seattle	So Much Yarn	1525 First Ave. #4	(206) 443-0727	
Seattle	Tea Cozy Yarn	5816 24th Ave. NW	(206) 783-3322	
Seattle	The Needle & I	540 NE Northgate Way #D	(206) 724-0695	
Seattle	The Weaving Works	6514 Roosevelt Way NE	(206) 524-1221	
Sedro Woolley	Cascade Fabrics	824 Metcalf St.	(360) 855-0323	
Sequim	Karen's Quilt Shop	271 S. 7th Ave. #26	(360) 681-0820	
Shelton	Fancy Image Yarn	591 SE Arcadia Rd.	(360) 426-5875	
Snohomish	Quilting Mayhem	1118 First St.	(425) 533-2566	
Spokane	Haberdashery Needlework	600 W. Garland Ave.	(509) 326-2587	
Spokane	Paradise Fibers	225 W. Indiana	(888) 320-7746	
Spokane	Quilt Patch Lane	413 W. Hastings Rd.	(509) 467-0133	
Spokane	Quilted Posies	6412 N. Monroe	(509) 474-9394	
Spokane	Regal Fabrics & Gifts	5620 S. Regal St. #8	(509) 242-3731	
Spokane	Sew E-Z, Too	603 W. Garland	(509) 325-6644	
Spokane	Sew Uniquely You	10220 N. Nevada #10	(509) 467-8210	
Spokane	The Cozy Quilt	8108 N. Division	(509) 464-2425	
Spokane Valley	**Quilting Bee**	**16002 E. Broadway Ave.**	**(509) 928-6037**	**Pg. 382**
Spokane Valley	Charming Lulu	1300 N. Mullan	(509) 340-9256	
Spokane Valley	Hattie's Quilt Shop	13817 E. Sprague #4	(509) 279-2150	
Stanwood	**Cotton Pickins'**	**8718 270th St. NW**	**(360) 629-4771**	**Pg. 384**
Stanwood	PinchKnitter Yarns	8712 271st. St.	(360) 939-0769	
Stanwood	Quilter's Coop	15102 W. Lake Goodwin Rd.	(855) 926-8102	
Tacoma	Artco Crafts	5401-401 6th Ave.	(253) 759-9585	
Tacoma	Calico Threads	2727 N. Pearl St.	(253) 759-4415	
Tacoma	Fibers Etc.	705 Opera Alley #301	(253) 572-1859	
Tacoma	Parkland Parish Quilt Co.	12152 Pacific Ave. S.	(253) 531-4309	
Tacoma	Trains & Fabrics	1315 S. 23rd	(253) 779-0219	
Tumwater	Ruby Street Quiltworks	100 Ruby St. SE	(360) 236-0596	
Twisp	The Quilting Hive	309 N. Hwy. 20	(509) 997-7020	
University Place	Shibori Dragon	7025 27th St. W #1	(253) 582-7455	
Vancouver	A Quilt Forever	9317 NE Hwy. 99 Ste. M	(360) 949-7880	
Vancouver	Art and Sew'l	2727 E. Evergreen	(360) 904-7157	
Vancouver	Fiddlesticks Quilt Shop	2701 NE 114TH Ave. #1	(360) 718-7103	
Walla Walla	Grandma's Sewing Room	901 W. Rose	(590) 240-2425	
Walla Walla	Stash Fabrics	25 W Main St.	(509) 526-5141	
Walla Walla	Thread and Bolts	326 Newtown Rd.	(509) 526-3873	
Walla Walla	Walla Walla Sew & Vac.	102 E. Main St.	(509) 529-7755	
Washougal	Wooly Wooly Wag Tails Yarn	982 E St.	(360) 835-9649	
Waterville	Yesteryear Quilting	107 W. Locust	(509) 745-9306	
Wenatchee	K1P2 Yarn	1012 Springwater Ave.	(509) 888-0337	
Wenatchee	Needlework, Linen & More	1425 Westpoint Pl.	(509) 667-8977	
Wenatchee	The Attic Window Quilt Shoppe	4 S. Wenatchee Ave.	(509) 888-2006	
Westport	Yarn N Darn Things	2172 Washington 105	(360) 267-0281	
Winthrop	3 Bears Café & Quilts	414 Riverside Ave.	(509) 996-8013	
Yakima	**Stitch n' Quilt**	**8405 Ahtanum Rd.**	**(509) 945-2560**	**Pg. 382**
Yakima	Ann's Quilts and Things	3504 Ahtanum Rd.	(509) 965-2313	
Yakima	Sandy's Sewing Center	404 W. Chestnut Ave.	(509) 901-7792	
Yakima	The Quilters Café	910 Summitview #1A	(509) 452-8666	
Yakima	Viking Sewing Center	5643 Summitview Ave.	(509) 966-3430	
Yelm	Gee Gee's Quilting	601 Yelm Ave. W.	(360) 458-5616	

Index

Notes

*West Virginia Star
Quilt Block*

Morgantown (pg. 388)

Fairmont
(pg. 389)

Parkersburg (pg. 389)

Jane Lew (pg. 388)

Elkins (pg. 388)

50

220

33

79

Huntington
(pg. 389)

19

Hurricane
(pg. 389)

Gauley River NRA

219

60

Lansing (pg. 389)

77

64

New River Gorge NR

Bluestone NSR

Princeton (pg. 389)

81

West Virginia Shops

Q-Quilting ~ Y-Yarn ~ N-Needlework ~ R-Retreat ~ M-Museum

City	Shop	Address	Phone	Page
Barboursville	WV Quilt	642 Main St. #101	(304) 302-5400	
Beckley	Itchin' 2 Be Stitchin'	612 N Eisenhower dr.	(304) 252-4575	
Bluefield	Bluefield Yarn Company	313 Federal St.	(304) 800-4229	
Bridgeport	The Nest	601 S. Virginia Ave.	(304) 848-2444	
Buckhannon	Helen's Hen House	36 N. Spring St.	(304) 472-1723	
Buckhannon	The Stitching House	255 King Schoolhouse Rd.	(304) 472-8188	
Charleston	Kanawaha City Yarn Co.	5132-A MacCorkle Ave.	(304) 926-8589	
Clarksburg	Classic Quilt Shop	1236 E. Pike St.	(304) 326-6969	
Danville	Town Square Fabrics	28 Town Sq.	(304) 369-6269	
Elkins	**Elkins Sewing Center**	**300 Davis Ave.**	**(304) 636-9480**	**Pg. 388**
Elkins	Yarn & Co.	R.R. 4	(304) 636-3760	
Fairmont	**Sew Chic**	**348 Meadowdale Rd.**	**(304) 366-4135**	**Pg. 389**
Gilbert	Valice's Quilt Shop	Rte. 52 Main St.	(304) 664-3217	
Hillsboro	Deb Ann's Fabrics	37 Hill St.	(304) 653-4150	
Huntington	**Sew Many Blessings**	**1925 Adams Ave.**	**(304) 429-0050**	**Pg. 389**
Hurricane	**Quilts by Phyllis**	**2943 Putnam Ave.**	**(304) 562-7404**	**Pg. 389**
Jane Lew	**Quilter's Garage**	**6385 Main St.**	**(304) 805-2140**	**Pg. 388**
Lansing	**Quilts & More**	**632 Milroy Grose Rd.**	**(304) 658-3606**	**Pg. 389**
Lewisburg	Country Road Yarn House	107 N. Court St.	(304) 667-4797	
Martinsburg	All About Fabric Quilt Shop	248 N. Queen St.	(304) 263-6800	
Morgantown	**Country Roads Quilt Shop**			
		709 Beechurst Ave. #27	**(304) 241-5645**	**Pg. 388**
Morgantown	Sew Special South	120 High St.	(304) 212-5366	
Morgantown	The Needlecraft Barn	162 Chancery Row Ste. #1	(304) 296-3789	
Moundsville	Finishing Touches Quilt Shop	308 Jefferson Ave.	(304) 810-4089	
Moundsville	Theresa's Fabrics	264 Jefferson Ave.	(304) 845-4330	
Parkersburg	**Bolts & Quarters Quilt Shop**			
		1809 Dupont Rd. Ste. 1	**(304) 428-4933**	**Pg. 389**
Parkersburg	Market Street Yarn & Crafts	615 Market St.	(304) 865-9276	
Parkersburg	Sew Creative	617 Market St.	(304) 422-6454	
Peterstown	Quilting Essentials	Rte. 2	(304) 753-5832	
Princeton	**The Sewing Gallery**	**431 Rogers St.**	**(304) 487-6700**	**Pg. 389**
Rainelle	Marie's Fabric & Crafts	705 Main St.	(304) 438-5500	
Reedsville	Eleanor's Quilts & Fabric Shop	399 N. Robert Stone Way	(304) 864-6330	
Shepherdstown	Yarnability / Sewinclined	207S Princess St.	(304) 876-8081	
Sistersville	Quintilla's Fabrics	946 Allen Run Rd.	(304) 758-2890	
St.Albans	Village Sampler	86 Olde Main Plaza	(304) 722-0123	
Summersville	The Quilt Shoppe	521 Main St.	(304) 872-0959	

Notes

Wisconsin

Milwaukee's Own Quilt Block

St. Croix Falls (pg. 400)

Rice Lake (pg. 400)

Saint Croix NSR

Lower Saint Croix NSR

Stanley (pg. 400)

Withee (pg. 400)

Wausau (pg. 398)

Sturgeon Bay (pg. 399)

Eau Claire (pg. 400)

Marshfield (pg. 399)

Tigerton (pg. 399)

Green Bay (pg. 398)

Fairchild (pg. 400)

Wisconsin Rapids (pg. 399)

Waupaca (pg. 398)

Appleton (pg. 398)

Onalaska (pg. 396)

Endeavor (pg. 397)

Plymouth (pg. 398)

Sparta (pg. 395)

La Crosse (pg. 395)

Reedsburg (pg. 397)

West Bend (pg. 397)

Cedarburg (pg. 392)

Viroqua (pg. 395)

Lodi (pg. 394)

Waunakee (pg. 394)

Sun Prairie (pg. 392)

Elm Grove (pg. 393)

Spring Green (pg. 395)

Fennimore (pg. 394)

Madison (pg. 397)

Evansville (pg. 392)

West Allis (pg. 392)

Platteville (pg. 394)

Clinton (pg. 392)

Salem (pg. 392)

Racine (pg. 392)

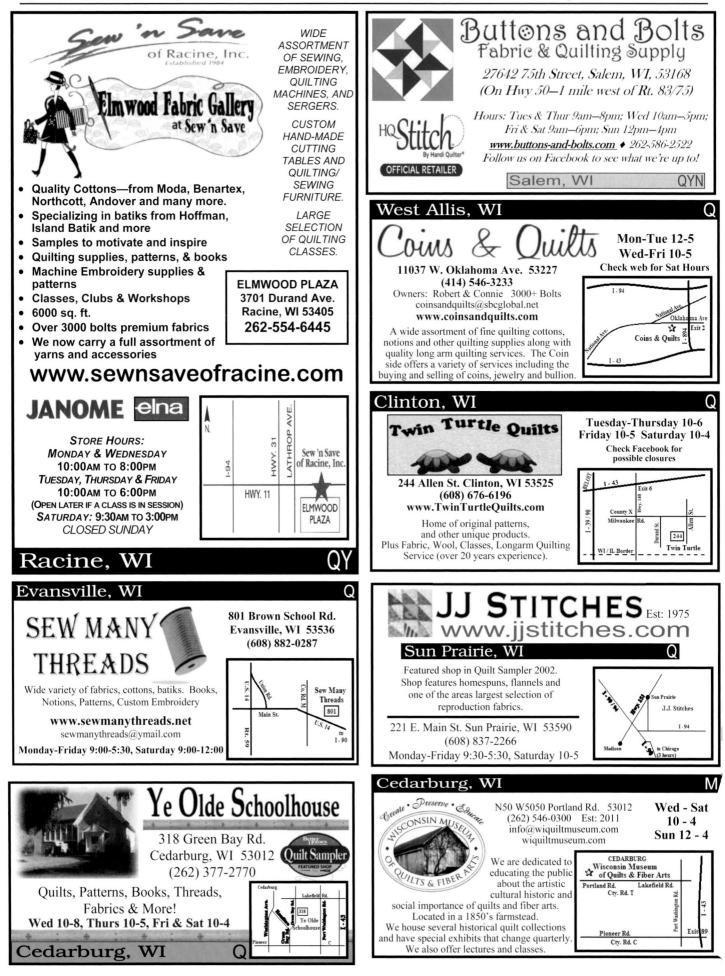

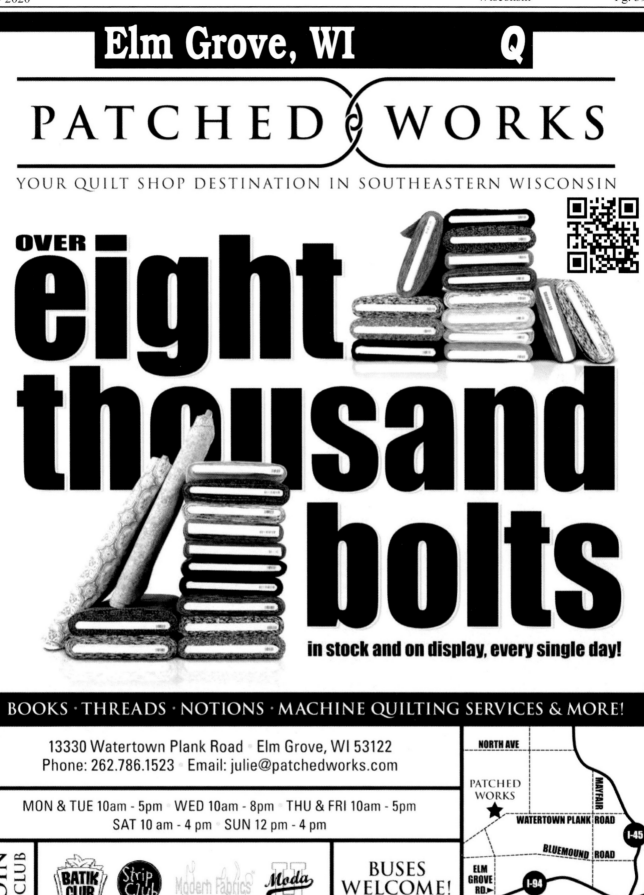

117 F. S. Dr. Viroqua, WI 54665
(608) 637-7002
Owner: Carol Melcher
carol@quiltobsession.com

Mon - Fri 9 - 5
Sat 9 - 4

LaCrosse
35 mi.
Hwy 14
Viroqua
Madison

Est: 1999

Great selection of 100% cotton fabrics, books,
patterns, notions, wool felt, DMC floss and yarn.
Bus Tours Welcome.
Long Arm Quilting Services Available.

Viroqua, WI   **QN**

RIVER ROAD *QUILT SHOP*
at Nelson Flag

2501 South Ave.
La Crosse, WI 54601
(608) 788-2990
www.nelsonflag.com

Mon-Fri 9a-6p, Sat 10a-5p
Sun 12p-4p

Jackson St.
State Rd.
South Ave.
West Ave.
U.S. 14 61
WI MN Border
Horton St.
2501
River Road
Quilt Shop

Family owned neighborhood Quilt Shop
on the Great River Road.
Two shops in one Gifts & Garden
in front, Fabric in back.

La Crosse, WI   **Q**

Sparta, WI   **QNR**

Quilt CORNER

219 N. Water St. 54656
(608) 269-1083
contactus@quiltcorner.net
www.quiltcorner.net

A Large 2 Story House that is ALL
Quilt Shop! We have over 5000 bolts
of Fabric, Wool, DMC Floss and a large
selection of premade items including
Totes, Quilts and More.
Check out our sale room and everything
to help you with your next big project.
Handi Quilter Dealer
And Quilt Clubs.

Mon - Fri 9 - 5, Sat 9 - 3

Notes

Country Sampler & 2nd Story

Recognized by Quilt Sampler® in 2000
Phone 608-588-2510
Open Daily 10am-5pm
Sunday Noon-4pm

You can sign up on our website for our weekly email
newsletter. This is what keeps you in the loop of
what's new, our coming events, Girl Clubs and if we
are traveling where you can find us.

www.sgcountrysampler.com

The Shop is unique in many ways but the fact that
the owner has her own fabric line produced by
Baum and Windham Textiles in New Jersey
makes things even more interesting.

Our in-house Shop Girl
Design Team is responsible
for many of our new patterns
that use the reproduction
fabric I design for Windham.
Farmhouse Living is the
newest. We host our classes
and Girl Gatherings such as
Grand Olde Flag, Summer
Camp, Primitives Stitch
Camp and Boxwood &
Berries in our spacious
SchoolRoom. Plan a visit at
our Guest House-2nd story.
(We sleep seven.) Rates are
$65 plus tax per person
per night.

You'll be inspired by our Seasonal Quilt
Collections and Reproduction Cross Stitch
Samplers. Everything is creatively showcased with
amazing signature Farmhouse décor that fits into
your everyday home style.

U.S. Hwy. 14
COUNTRY SAMPLER
133 E. Jefferson
★   Jefferson Street
U.S. Hwy. 23
Downtown Spring Green

113 E. Jefferson St. Spring Green, WI 53588
Fax: (608) 588-3530 ~ stchgirl@yahoo.com

Onalaska, WI   Q

Traditional *with a Twist!*

Olive Juice Quilts, LLC is a quirky quilt shop in Onalaska, WI that offers a wide variety of fabrics, patterns, notions, BERNINA and Baby Lock sewing and embroidery machines, sewing cabinets, classes, clubs, and events!

1258 County Road PH | Onalaska, WI 54650
(608) 782-3257
www.olivejuicequilts.com

mon - sat 10 - 5 | thurs 10 - 8 | Closed Sundays

The Pfister Hotel

Built in 1893, this Milwaukee jewel is the height of
luxury in this Midwestern state. An extensive
collection of Victorian artwork adorns the walls,
bringing more magic to the Romanesque Revival
design. Each year, the hotel's Artist-in-Residence
program allows guests to experience the works of a
current Milwaukee artist in a gallery on the first
floor, just about the only sight that could top the
views of nearby Lake Michigan.

424 E Wisconsin Ave, Milwaukee, WI 53202
(414) 273-8222
www.thepfisterhotel.com

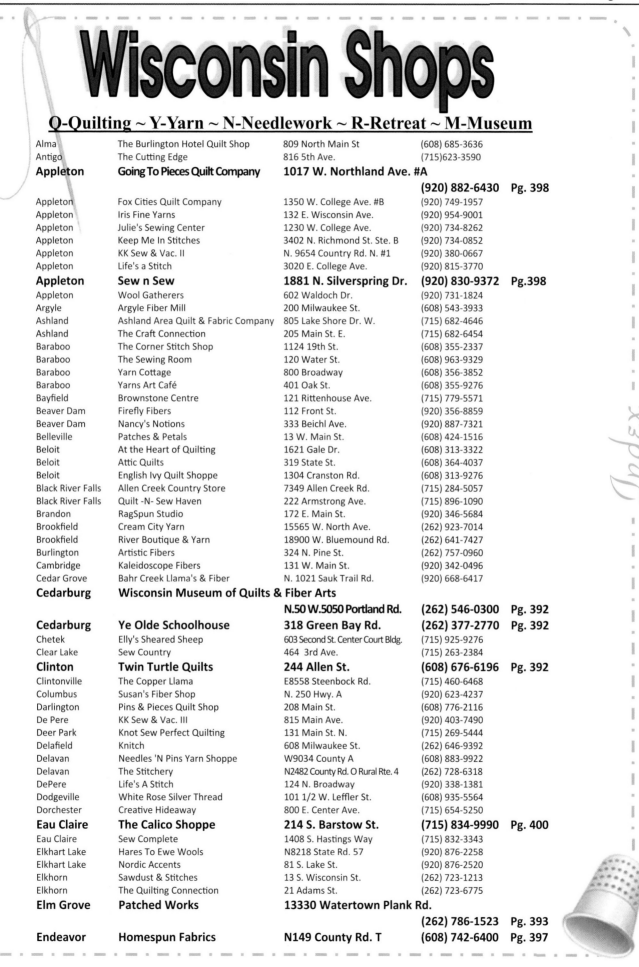

Wisconsin Shops

Q-Quilting ~ Y-Yarn ~ N-Needlework ~ R-Retreat ~ M-Museum

Alma	The Burlington Hotel Quilt Shop	809 North Main St	(608) 685-3636	
Antigo	The Cutting Edge	816 5th Ave.	(715)623-3590	
Appleton	**Going To Pieces Quilt Company**	**1017 W. Northland Ave. #A**		
			(920) 882-6430	**Pg. 398**
Appleton	Fox Cities Quilt Company	1350 W. College Ave. #B	(920) 749-1957	
Appleton	Iris Fine Yarns	132 E. Wisconsin Ave.	(920) 954-9001	
Appleton	Julie's Sewing Center	1230 W. College Ave.	(920) 734-8262	
Appleton	Keep Me In Stitches	3402 N. Richmond St. Ste. B	(920) 734-0852	
Appleton	KK Sew & Vac. II	N. 9654 Country Rd. N. #1	(920) 380-0667	
Appleton	Life's a Stitch	3020 E. College Ave.	(920) 815-3770	
Appleton	**Sew n Sew**	**1881 N. Silverspring Dr.**	**(920) 830-9372**	**Pg.398**
Appleton	Wool Gatherers	602 Waldoch Dr.	(920) 731-1824	
Argyle	Argyle Fiber Mill	200 Milwaukee St.	(608) 543-3933	
Ashland	Ashland Area Quilt & Fabric Company	805 Lake Shore Dr. W.	(715) 682-4646	
Ashland	The Craft Connection	205 Main St. E.	(715) 682-6454	
Baraboo	The Corner Stitch Shop	1124 19th St.	(608) 355-2337	
Baraboo	The Sewing Room	120 Water St.	(608) 963-9329	
Baraboo	Yarn Cottage	800 Broadway	(608) 356-3852	
Baraboo	Yarns Art Café	401 Oak St.	(608) 355-9276	
Bayfield	Brownstone Centre	121 Rittenhouse Ave.	(715) 779-5571	
Beaver Dam	Firefly Fibers	112 Front St.	(920) 356-8859	
Beaver Dam	Nancy's Notions	333 Beichl Ave.	(920) 887-7321	
Belleville	Patches & Petals	13 W. Main St.	(608) 424-1516	
Beloit	At the Heart of Quilting	1621 Gale Dr.	(608) 313-3322	
Beloit	Attic Quilts	319 State St.	(608) 364-4037	
Beloit	English Ivy Quilt Shoppe	1304 Cranston Rd.	(608) 313-9276	
Black River Falls	Allen Creek Country Store	7349 Allen Creek Rd.	(715) 284-5057	
Black River Falls	Quilt -N- Sew Haven	222 Armstrong Ave.	(715) 896-1090	
Brandon	RagSpun Studio	172 E. Main St.	(920) 346-5684	
Brookfield	Cream City Yarn	15565 W. North Ave.	(262) 923-7014	
Brookfield	River Boutique & Yarn	18900 W. Bluemound Rd.	(262) 641-7427	
Burlington	Artistic Fibers	324 N. Pine St.	(262) 757-0960	
Cambridge	Kaleidoscope Fibers	131 W. Main St.	(920) 342-0496	
Cedar Grove	Bahr Creek Llama's & Fiber	N. 1021 Sauk Trail Rd.	(920) 668-6417	
Cedarburg	**Wisconsin Museum of Quilts & Fiber Arts**			
		N.50 W.5050 Portland Rd.	**(262) 546-0300**	**Pg. 392**
Cedarburg	**Ye Olde Schoolhouse**	**318 Green Bay Rd.**	**(262) 377-2770**	**Pg. 392**
Chetek	Elly's Sheared Sheep	603 Second St. Center Court Bldg.	(715) 925-9276	
Clear Lake	Sew Country	464 3rd Ave.	(715) 263-2384	
Clinton	**Twin Turtle Quilts**	**244 Allen St.**	**(608) 676-6196**	**Pg. 392**
Clintonville	The Copper Llama	E8558 Steenbock Rd.	(715) 460-6468	
Columbus	Susan's Fiber Shop	N. 250 Hwy. A	(920) 623-4237	
Darlington	Pins & Pieces Quilt Shop	208 Main St.	(608) 776-2116	
De Pere	KK Sew & Vac. III	815 Main Ave.	(920) 403-7490	
Deer Park	Knot Sew Perfect Quilting	131 Main St. N.	(715) 269-5444	
Delafield	Knitch	608 Milwaukee St.	(262) 646-9392	
Delavan	Needles 'N Pins Yarn Shoppe	W9034 County A	(608) 883-9922	
Delavan	The Stitchery	N2482 County Rd. O Rural Rte. 4	(262) 728-6318	
DePere	Life's A Stitch	124 N. Broadway	(920) 338-1381	
Dodgeville	White Rose Silver Thread	101 1/2 W. Leffler St.	(608) 935-5564	
Dorchester	Creative Hideaway	800 E. Center Ave.	(715) 654-5250	
Eau Claire	**The Calico Shoppe**	**214 S. Barstow St.**	**(715) 834-9990**	**Pg. 400**
Eau Claire	Sew Complete	1408 S. Hastings Way	(715) 832-3343	
Elkhart Lake	Hares To Ewe Wools	N8218 State Rd. 57	(920) 876-2258	
Elkhart Lake	Nordic Accents	81 S. Lake St.	(920) 876-2520	
Elkhorn	Sawdust & Stitches	13 S. Wisconsin St.	(262) 723-1213	
Elkhorn	The Quilting Connection	21 Adams St.	(262) 723-6775	
Elm Grove	**Patched Works**	**13330 Watertown Plank Rd.**		
			(262) 786-1523	**Pg. 393**
Endeavor	**Homespun Fabrics**	**N149 County Rd. T**	**(608) 742-6400**	**Pg. 397**

Ettrick	Christa's Yarn & Crafts	W14271 County Rd. C	(608) 525-2757	
Evansville	**Sew Many Threads**	**801 Brown School Rd.**	**(608) 882-0287**	**Pg. 392**
Fairchild	**Sew Country Quilt Shop**	**S. 14375 Sperber Rd.**	**(715) 456-4516**	**Pg. 400**
Fall Creek	Yard Work	133 S. State St.	(715) 877-3885	
Fennimore	**Quilt Peddler**	**4420 US. Hwy. 18 E.**	**(608) 822-6822**	**Pg. 394**
Fish Creek	Red Sock Yarns	9331 Spring Rd.	(920) 868-5700	
Fond du Lac	The Knitting Room	28 N. Main St.	(920) 906-4800	
Fond Du Lac	The Woolgatherers	35 N. Main St.	(920) 907-0510	
Fort Atkinson	The Quilt Patch	W. 3352 Lower Hebron Rd.	(262) 593-8462	
Fox Point	The Knitting Knook	6858 N. Santa Monica Blvd.	(414) 540-4080	
Frederic	Fibre Functions Yarns	682 263rd Ave.	(715) 472-8276	
Gordon	Kunert Kreations	9586 E. County Y	(715) 376-4722	
Grafton	Grafton Yarn Store	1300 14th Ave.	(262) 377-0344	
Green Bay	**Silver Thimble Quilt & Yarn Shoppe**			
		2475 University Ave.	**(920) 468-1495**	**Pg. 398**
Green Bay	Julie's Sewing Center	933 Anderson Dr. #D	(920) 965-0680	
Green Bay	My Favorite Quilt Shop	1550 Dousman St.	(920) 965-2085	
Green Bay	Patricia Knits	1437 Traeger St.	(920) 499-2325	
Green Bay	Patti's Yarn Shop	1512 Main St.	(920) 433-9276	
Green Bay	Quilting Divas Sewing Boutique	445 Cardinal Ln. #108	(920) 434-9980	
Green Bay	The Stitching Bee	2304 Velp Ave.	(920) 434-6884	
Hartford	Main St. Yarn Shop	59 N Main St.	(262) 673-2203	
Hartford	Sheeping Beauty Fibre Arts	W533 State Rd. 33	(920) 927-3481	
Hayward	Northwoods Craft & Variety	10550 Main St.	(715) 634-4909	
Hayward	River's Edge Antiques & Quilt Loft	10103 State Rd. 27	(715) 634-0706	
Horicon	Knitty Gritty Shop	W5346 Wisconsin 33	(920) 485-0549	
Janesville	A Quilt Lovers Shoppe	1604 S. Crosby Ave.	(608) 754-6497	
Janesville	Dragonfly Yarnshop	1327 N. Wright Rd.	(608) 757-9228	
Janesville	Quilt Central	1800 Humes Rd. #120	(608) 563-4415	
Jefferson	Tea and Textiles Quilt Shop	107 S. Main St.	(920) 674-9017	
Juneau	J & A Stitches	N3914 Welsh Rd.	(920) 696-3827	
Kaukauna	Kaukauna Vacumms & Sewing Center	132 W. Wisconsin Ave.	(920) 403-7490	
Kenosha	Fiddlehead Yarns	7511 26th Ave.	(262) 925-6487	
La Crosse	**River Road Quilt Shop**	**2501 South Ave.**	**(608) 788-2990**	**Pg. 395**
La Crosse	Crosse Stitchery	205 Pearl St.	(608) 782-7008	
Ladysmith	Heartlight Quilt Shop	213 W. Lake Ave.	(715) 532-5333	
Ladysmith	Northwoods Fiber Arts	105 Miner Ave. E.	(715) 532-5858	
Lodi	**Village Creek**	**123 S. Main St.**	**(608) 592-5793**	**Pg. 394**
Madison	Electric Needle	4281 W. Beltline Hwy.	(608) 422-5449	
Madison	Gayfeather Fabrics	1521 Williamson St.	(608) 294-7436	
Madison	Lynn's Craftshop	5928 Odana Rd.	(608) 274-1442	
Madison	**Quintessential Quilts Sewing Center**			
		4261 Lien Rd.	**(608) 242-8555**	**Pg. 397**
Madison	The Knitting Tree	2636 Monroe St.	(608) 698-5199	
Madison	Wisconsin Craft Market	148 Westgate Mall	(608) 271-6002	
Manitowoc	Fabric Creations	912 S. 8th St.	(920) 482-0545	
Manitowoc	The Shaggy Sheep	828 S. 8th St.	(920) 682-3152	
Marinette	Pine Street Quilts	801 Marinette Ave. #2	(715) 735-9806	
Marshfield	**Quilt Kits & Beyond**	**S. 549 W. Mann Rd.**	**(715) 384-8004**	**Pg. 399**
Mauston	Mielke's Fiber Arts	N. 4826 21st Ave.	(608) 350-0600	
Mayville	Loose Ends Yarn Shop	40 S. Main St.	(920) 387-9960	
Menasha	Primitive Gatherings	850 Racine St.	(920) 722-7233	
Mercer	Cheri's Fabric to Quilt	5244 N. US. Hwy. 51	(715) 476-0111	
Milton	Joslyn's Fiber Farm	5738 E. Klug Rd.	(608) 868-3224	
Milton	KJ Craft	8303 N. Oak Ridge Dr.	(608) 868-4900	
Milton	Loose Threads Quilt & Yarn	8005 N. Milton Rd.	(608) 868-7912	
Milwaukee	Fiberwood Studio	2709 N. 92nd St.	(414) 302-1849	
Milwaukee	French Knots II	8585 N. Port Washington Rd.	(414) 351-2414	
Milwaukee	Midwest Yarn	3385 S. Kinnickinnic Ave.	(414) 979-9276	
Minocqua	Around the Block Quilt Shop	9785 State Hwy. 70	(715) 356-1427	
Minocqua	The 13th Colony and Elizabeth's Woolery	7735 Hwy. 51 S.	(715) 358-6600	
Mishicot	Lisa's Photo Quilting & More	418 E. Main St.	(920) 755-4217	
Monroe	Orange Kitten Yarns	1620 11TH St.	(608) 328-4140	
Montello	Anne's Fiber Expressions	N. 1513 State Rd. 22	(608) 297-7254	
Montello	Teapot Quilt Cottage	505 Main St.	(608) 297-7849	
Monticello	Quilter's Compass	201 N. Main St	(608) 938-4334	
Mt. Horeb	Blackberry Ridge Woolen Mill	3776 Forshaug Rd.	(608) 437-3762	
Mt. Horeb	The Cat and Crow	205 E. Main St.	(608) 437-1771	
Mt. Horeb	Witchery Stitchery	103 E. Front St.	(608) 437-8635	
Mukwonago	Quilt-agious	109 Lake St.	(262) 363-3066	

Neenah	Yarns by Design	123 W. Wisconsin Ave.	(920) 727-0530	
Nekoosa	Knitwise Yarns & Fiber Arts Gallery	421 County Rd. G	(715) 886-1030	
New Glarus	Rainbow Fleece Farm	W7181 Hustad Valley Rd.	(608) 527-5311	
New Holstein	Bleating Heart Haven	W1993 Thede Rd.	(920) 286-0971	
New Richmond	A Little Piece of Mind	464 Park Ave.	(715) 246-7314	
New Richmond	Doyle's Farm & Home	560 Deere Dr.	(715) 246-6184	
Oak Creek	Just 4 Ewe	8615 S. Market Pl.	(414) 768-9276	
Oakfield	Quilter's Finishing Touch	W7791 Highbridge Rd.	(920) 583-6110	
Oakfield	Stitches 'N Tyme	203 S. Main St.	(920) 583-2625	
Oconomowoc	Ben Franklin Crafts	1083 Summit Ave.	(262) 567-0271	
Onalaska	**Olive Juice Quilts**	**1258 County Rd. PH**	**(608) 782-3257**	**Pg. 396**
Onalaska	Baskets of Yarn	2026 Rose Ct.	(608) 783-1402	
Osceola	Earthsong Fibers	1782 40th Ave.	(715) 268-5298	
Oshkosh	Quilt Essentials	1928 S. Washburn St.	(920) 230-3680	
Osseo	The Quilting Nook & More	13712 7th St.	(715) 864-0742	
Platteville	**Hidden Quilts**	**85 W. Main St.**	**(608) 348-4977**	**Pg. 394**
Plover	Antoinette's Quilt Shop	3046 Village Park Dr.	(715) 544-6076	
Plymouth	**The Sewing Basket**	**426 E. Mill St.**	**(920) 892-4751**	**Pg. 398**
Portage	The Welcome Home Sew-N-Vac.	118 E. Cook St.	(608) 566-1663	
Prairie du Chien	Front Porch Quilts	216 N. Marquette Rd.	(608) 326-4371	
Prairie du Chien	The Pickett Fence	100 W. Blackhawk Ave.	(608) 326-4593	
Prescott	Forever Gifts Boutique & Quilt Shop	220 Broad St.	(715) 262-2369	
Racine	**Elmwood Fabric Gallery**	**3701 Durand Ave.**	**(262) 554-6445**	**Pg. 392**
Reedsburg	**Quintessential Quilts**	**940 E. Main St.**	**(608) 524-8435**	**Pg. 397**
Rhinelander	Sew Smart	2185 Lincoln St.	(715) 362-8321	
Rice Lake	**Busy Bobbin**	**234 N. Wilson Ave.**	**(715) 234-1217**	**Pg. 400**
Richfield	Sew Many Pieces	1717 Wolf Rd. #A	(262) 628-9505	
Ripon	Bungalow Quilting and Yarn	646 W. Fond Du Lac St.	(920) 517-1910	
Ripon	Holly & Ivy	319 Watson St.	(920) 748-1233	
River Falls	Riverside Quilting	117 E. Pine St.	(715) 425-1754	
Roberts	Color Crossing	201 N. Vine St.	(715) 749-3337	
Salem	**Buttons and Bolts Fabric & Quilting Supply**			
		27642 75th St.	**(262) 586-2522**	**Pg. 392**
Sand Creek	Heart Blossom Design	N13430 County Rd. I	(715) 658-1333	
Seymour	The Crabbe Reader Book Store & Yarn Shop	214 S. Main St.	(920) 833-9504	
Sheboygan	My Sister's Quilt Shoppe	2707 S. Business Dr.	(920) 457-4787	
Sheboygan Falls	Magpie's Cottage	308 Pine St.	(920) 467-9978	
Solon Springs	The Little Gift House	9234 E. Main St.	(715) 378-4170	
Sparta	**Quilt Corner**	**219 N. Water St.**	**(608) 269-1083**	**Pg. 395**
Sparta	Yarn Stash	112 N. Water St.	(608) 269-5648	
Spooner	Northwind Book & Fiber	205 Walnut St.	(715) 635-6811	
Spooner	Thimbles Quilt Shop	237 Walnut St.	(715) 635-6040	
Spring Green	**Country Sampler**	**133 E. Jefferson St.**	**(608) 588-2510**	**Pg. 395**
Spring Green	Nina's Department & Variety Store	143 E. Jefferson St.	(608) 588-2366	
St. Croix Falls	**Pins "N" Needles**	**126 N. Washington**	**(715) 483-5728**	**Pg. 400**
St. Germain	Just Yarnin'	446 C Hwy. 70 E.	(715) 479-9276	
St. Germain	Sutter's Gold 'n Fleece	9094 County Rd. O	(715) 479-7634	
Stanley	**Pine Hollow, The Country Shop**	**N. 14085 Fernwall Ave.**	**(715) 644-3591**	**Pg. 400**
Stanley	**Sew N Sew Quilts and Fabric**	**36360 County Hwy. MM**	**(715) 644-5563**	**Pg. 400**
Stevens Point	Herrschners	2800 Hoover Rd.	(715) 341-8686	
Stevens Point	Wisconsin Wool Exchange	1009 First St.	(715) 295-0975	
Stoughton	Woodland Studios	195 E. Main St.	(608) 877-8007	
Sturgeon Bay	**Barn Door Quilt Shop**	**154 N. 3rd Ave.**	**(920) 746-1544**	**Pg. 399**
Sturgeon Bay	Apple Hollow Fiber Arts	732 Jefferson St.	(920) 746-7815	
Sturgeon Bay	Spin	108 S. Madison Ave.	(920) 746-7746	
Sun Prairie	**J. J. Stitches**	**221 E. Main St.**	**(608) 837-2266**	**Pg. 392**
Sun Prairie	Prairie Junction	227 E. Main St.	(608) 837-8909	
Superior	Country Schoolhouse Quilt Shop	2104 E. 5th St.	(715) 398-0150	
Thayne	Thayne True Value - Beyond Bolts	120 Patersen Pkwy.	(307) 883-2464	
Thiensville	My Material Matters Quilt Shop	219 N. Main St.	(262) 292-8218	
Thorp	Bolts of Fun Quilt Shop	102 E. Stanley St.	(715) 773-0018	
Tigerton	**Pinery Patches**	**N4647 Hwy. 45**	**(715) 535-2277**	**Pg. 399**
Tomah	Bear Creek Fibers	27686 Holly Ave.	(608) 374-4078	
Tomahawk	Sew Pieceful Quilting	118 W. Wisconsin Ave.	(715) 453-7126	
Two Rivers	Intertwined Yarn Shop	1623 Washington St.	(920) 793-2241	
Two Rivers	The Quilt Shop of Two Rivers	1623 Washington St.	(920) 889-5229	
Valders	Hidden Valley Farm & Woolen Mill	14804 Newton Rd.	(920) 758-2803	
Viroqua	**Quilt Basket 'N' Creations**	**117 FS Dr. #C**	**(608) 637-7002**	**Pg. 395**

Index

Viroqua	Ewetopia Fiber Shop	102 S. Main St.	(608) 637-3443	
Viroqua	Kindred Threads	E4621A Norwegian Hollow Rd.	(608) 606-0679	
Washington Island	Sievers School of Fiber Arts	986 Jackson Harbor Rd.	(920) 847-2264	
Waukesha	Frank's Sewing Center	2140 W St. Paul Ave. #L	(262) 547-7774	
Waunakee	**Mill House Quilts**	**100 Baker St.**	**(608) 849-6473**	**Pg. 394**
Waupaca	**Sew n Sew**	**112 S. Main**	**(715) 256-1071**	**Pg. 398**
Wausau	**The Quilting Workshop**	**312 S. First Ave.**	**(715) 848-5546**	**Pg. 398**
Wausau	Black Purl	1102 3rd St.	(715) 843-7875	
Wausau	Grants March Quilting Mercantile	1220 Merrill Ave.	(715) 298-1112	
Wausau	Sew Smart	2907 Rib Mountain Dr.	(715) 845-9675	
Wausau	The Needle Workshop	312 1st Ave.	(715) 848-5545	
West Allis	**Coins & Quilts**	**11037 W. Oklahoma Ave.**	**(414) 546-3233**	**Pg. 392**
West Bend	**Royce Quilting**	**840 S. Main St.**	**(262) 338-0597**	**Pg. 397**
West Bend	Quilt Factory	5046 S. Oak Rd.	(262) 338-0054	
West Bend	Xpressions Yarn & Bead Boutique	264 N. Main St.	(262) 306-1300	
West Salem	Salem Stitchery N Knittery	W 4253 Hwy. B	(608) 786-1961	
Whitehall	Pammy's Patchwork Playhouse	N40684 County Rd. E	(715) 694-2142	
Whitehall	Renee's Stitchery & Boutique	36237 West St.	(715) 538-2238	
Whitewater	Kari's Country Sew Unique	12524 E. County Rd. N.	(262) 473-2049	
Whitewater	Woodland Quilts	147 W. Main St.	(262) 473-2978	
Wisconsin Rapids				
	The Cotton Thimble	**540 Daly Ave.**	**(715) 424-1122**	**Pg. 399**
Withee	**Brubaker Sewing & Furniture**	**N14590 County Hwy. 0**	**(715) 229-2851**	**Pg. 400**
Woodruff	Hidden Talents	9404 County Rd. J	(715) 358-3787	

NOTES

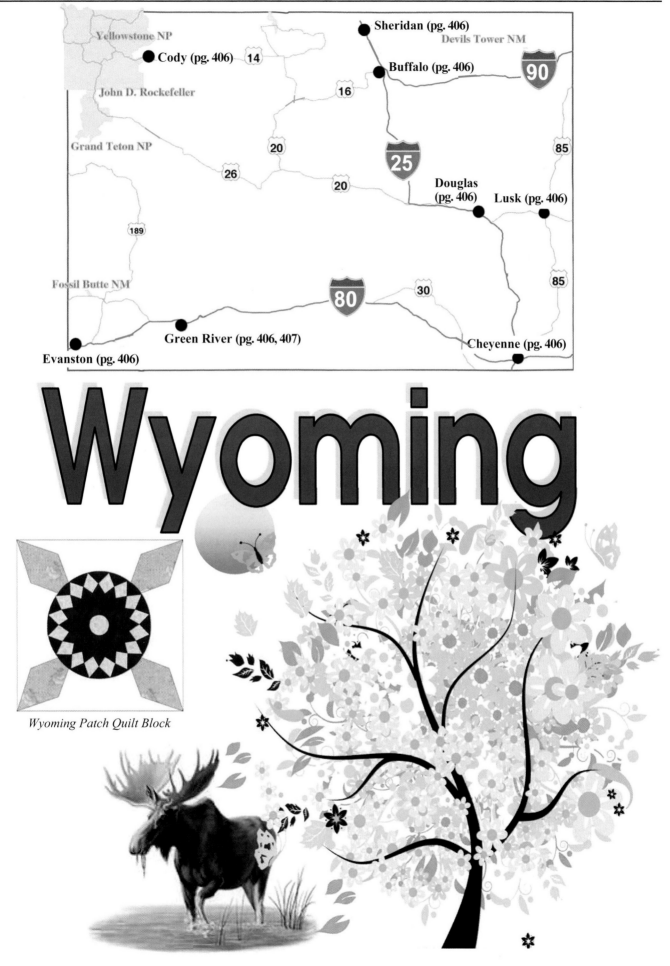

Wyoming Patch Quilt Block

Old Faithful Inn

You might not expect to find a hotel within the confines of
Yellowstone National Park, but this rustic, log cabin–style resort
has been in business here since 1904. It's considered to be the
largest log structure in the world, consisting of 327 rooms,
a stone fireplace, and a full-service restaurant for visitors to
enjoy while they're taking in the natural sights.

1 Grand Loop Rd, Yellowstone National Park, WY 82190
(307) 344-7901
www.yellowstonenationalparklodges.com

Notes

Wyoming Shops

Q-Quilting ~ Y-Yarn ~ N-Needlework ~ R-Retreat ~ M-Museum

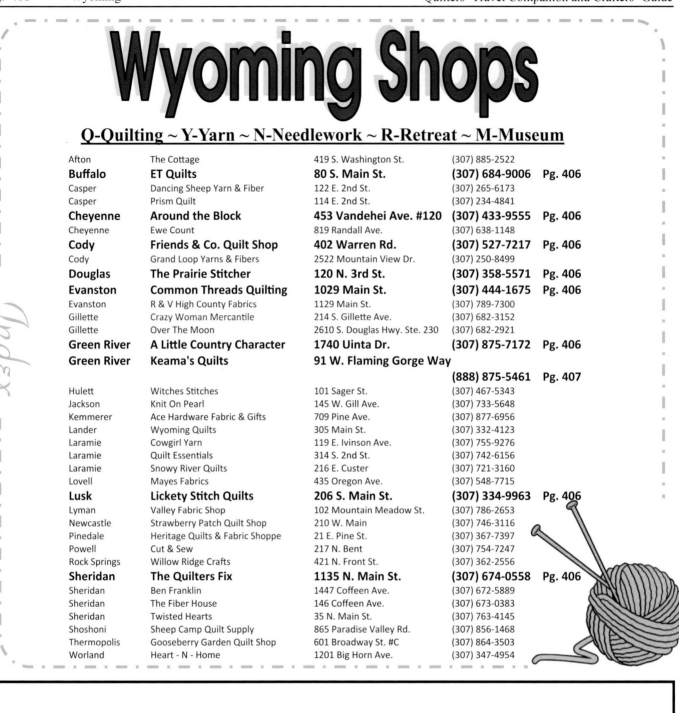

City	Shop	Address	Phone	Page
Afton	The Cottage	419 S. Washington St.	(307) 885-2522	
Buffalo	**ET Quilts**	**80 S. Main St.**	**(307) 684-9006**	**Pg. 406**
Casper	Dancing Sheep Yarn & Fiber	122 E. 2nd St.	(307) 265-6173	
Casper	Prism Quilt	114 E. 2nd St.	(307) 234-4841	
Cheyenne	**Around the Block**	**453 Vandehei Ave. #120**	**(307) 433-9555**	**Pg. 406**
Cheyenne	Ewe Count	819 Randall Ave.	(307) 638-1148	
Cody	**Friends & Co. Quilt Shop**	**402 Warren Rd.**	**(307) 527-7217**	**Pg. 406**
Cody	Grand Loop Yarns & Fibers	2522 Mountain View Dr.	(307) 250-8499	
Douglas	**The Prairie Stitcher**	**120 N. 3rd St.**	**(307) 358-5571**	**Pg. 406**
Evanston	**Common Threads Quilting**	**1029 Main St.**	**(307) 444-1675**	**Pg. 406**
Evanston	R & V High County Fabrics	1129 Main St.	(307) 789-7300	
Gillette	Crazy Woman Mercantile	214 S. Gillette Ave.	(307) 682-3152	
Gillette	Over The Moon	2610 S. Douglas Hwy. Ste. 230	(307) 682-2921	
Green River	**A Little Country Character**	**1740 Uinta Dr.**	**(307) 875-7172**	**Pg. 406**
Green River	**Keama's Quilts**	**91 W. Flaming Gorge Way**	**(888) 875-5461**	**Pg. 407**
Hulett	Witches Stitches	101 Sager St.	(307) 467-5343	
Jackson	Knit On Pearl	145 W. Gill Ave.	(307) 733-5648	
Kemmerer	Ace Hardware Fabric & Gifts	709 Pine Ave.	(307) 877-6956	
Lander	Wyoming Quilts	305 Main St.	(307) 332-4123	
Laramie	Cowgirl Yarn	119 E. Ivinson Ave.	(307) 755-9276	
Laramie	Quilt Essentials	314 S. 2nd St.	(307) 742-6156	
Laramie	Snowy River Quilts	216 E. Custer	(307) 721-3160	
Lovell	Mayes Fabrics	435 Oregon Ave.	(307) 548-7715	
Lusk	**Lickety Stitch Quilts**	**206 S. Main St.**	**(307) 334-9963**	**Pg. 406**
Lyman	Valley Fabric Shop	102 Mountain Meadow St.	(307) 786-2653	
Newcastle	Strawberry Patch Quilt Shop	210 W. Main	(307) 746-3116	
Pinedale	Heritage Quilts & Fabric Shoppe	21 E. Pine St.	(307) 367-7397	
Powell	Cut & Sew	217 N. Bent	(307) 754-7247	
Rock Springs	Willow Ridge Crafts	421 N. Front St.	(307) 362-2556	
Sheridan	**The Quilters Fix**	**1135 N. Main St.**	**(307) 674-0558**	**Pg. 406**
Sheridan	Ben Franklin	1447 Coffeen Ave.	(307) 672-5889	
Sheridan	The Fiber House	146 Coffeen Ave.	(307) 673-0383	
Sheridan	Twisted Hearts	35 N. Main St.	(307) 763-4145	
Shoshoni	Sheep Camp Quilt Supply	865 Paradise Valley Rd.	(307) 856-1468	
Thermopolis	Gooseberry Garden Quilt Shop	601 Broadway St. #C	(307) 864-3503	
Worland	Heart - N - Home	1201 Big Horn Ave.	(307) 347-4954	

Notes

Alberta Shops

Barrhead	Freedom to Knit	Site 9 RR #1	(780) 674-5141
Barrhead	Homestead Fabric & Quilting	Site 3 RR3	(780) 674-6022
Beaver Lodge	Around the Block	1040 1St. Ave.	(780)-354-3423
Blackfalds	Peaceful Patch Quilt Shoppe	Bay 2 5049 Parkwood Rd.	(403) 600-0025
Blairmore	A Nest of Needles Wool Shop	12921 20 Ave.	(403) 564-4041
Brooks	Deanna's Quilted Garden	114 2nd St. W.	(403) 362-6606
Brooks	Kalm Quilting and Fabrics	114 2nd St. W.	(403) 362-6722
Calgary	A Sewing Sensation	3832 19th St. NW	(403) 288-8288
Calgary	Along Came Quilting	6432 1A St. SW	(403) 253-4419
Calgary	Beehive Yarn & Needle	333 36 Ave. SE	(403) 243-3699
Calgary	Gina Brown's Fine Yarns & Needlecraft	107 5718 1A St. SW	(403) 255-2200
Calgary	Knit One Chat Too	509 1851 Sirocco Dr. SW	(403) 685-5556
Calgary	My Sewing Room Inc.	148 8228 Macleod Trail SE	(403) 252-3711
Calgary	Out of Hand	12 6449 Crowchild Tr. SW	(403) 217-4871
Calgary	Pudding Yarn	1516 6th St. SW	(403) 244-2996
Calgary	Stash Needle Art Lounge	1309 9th Ave. SE	(403) 244-2996
Calgary	Stitching at Hearthside	1978 Kensington Rd. NW	(403) 266-1034
Calgary	The Loop	1978 Kensington Rd. NW	(403) 457-3020
Calgary	Traditional Pastimes	7 Parkdale Cres. NW	(403) 286-9421
Calgary	Traditional Stitches	261051 Bearspaw Rd.	(866) 208-9650
Camrose	Quilting From the Heart	4811 50 St.	(780) 679-5492
Camrose	Sewing Center Inc.	4944 50th St.	(780) 672-2732
Canmore	The Sugar Pine Company	#1 737 Tenth St.	(403) 678-9603
Canmore	Yarn & Co.	105 717 9th St.	(403) 707-7121
Cardston	Imagination Unlimited	257 Main St.	(403) 653-2633
Caroline	Beaver Creek Merchantile	355018 Range Rd. 62	(403) 722-2050
Carstairs	Custom Woolen Mill	R.R. # 1	(403) 337-2221
Claresholm	3B Quilting	25 Saddle Mountain Rd.	(403) 625-4821
Coaldale	Chicken Feed Quilts	1401 20 Ave.	(403) 345-4048
Cochrane	Addie's Creative Fabrics	420 1st St. W.	(403) 932-1500
Cochrane	The Stitching Corner by NyGaBe	208 1 St. W.	(403) 932-3390
Cold Lake	Quilted Gems	5214 50 Ave.	(780) 594-5200
Cold Lake	Your Sewing Store	5006 50th Ave.	(780) 564-0026
Coleman	Cozy Corner	7801 17th Ave.	(403) 562-2699
Coleman	Timber Bear Batiks	8013 22 Ave.	(403) 562-7662
Crooked Creek	Country Stitches Quilts & Fabrics	R.R. 1 Site 5	(780) 957-2446
De Winton	Shuttleworks, Ltd.	Site 5 RR 1	(403) 938-1099
Delburne	Country Quilting & More	2206 20 St.	(403) 749-3330
Drayton Valley	Stitches & Dreams	5128 51 St.	(780) 514-5051
Drumheller	Spoolz Quilt Shop	342 Center St.	(403) 823-5828
Edmonton	Earthly Goods Quilting Corner	4115 106 St.	(780) 433-7179
Edmonton	Quilter's Dream	10736 124 St. NW	(780) 452-0102
Edmonton	Quilter's Dream	4359 99 St. NW	(780) 496-9375
Edmonton	River City Yarns	16956 111 Ave.	(780) 477-9276
Edmonton	Sew Divine	13632 82 St.	(780) 476-8877
Edmonton	Sparrow Studioz Quilting & Gallery	9532 87 St.	(780) 463-4242
Edson	Quilter's Quarters	4823 4th Ave.	(780) 723-6043
Edson	Runaway Quilting	301 50th St.	(780) 723-8084
Forestburg	The What Not Shop	5104 47 Ave.	(780) 582-2110
Fort McMurray	Suzy Q's Quilt Shop	10012 Franklin Ave.	(780) 743-2992
Ft. Saskatchewan	Kountry Knits & Sewing Centre	10103 100 Ave.	(780) 998-1635
Grande Prairie	Avenue Crafts & Gifts	10012 100th Ave.	(780) 532-8480
Grande Prairie	Cotton Candy Quilts & Sewing	12405 99th St.	(780) 532-2202
High River	Chinook Fabrics	149 MacLeod Tr.	(403) 652-3145
Hinton	The Hen House Textile Co.	105 211 Pembina Ave.	(780) 865-7147
Innisfail	Wawa's Quilts	5028 49 St.	(403) 597-3067
Irma	Creative Klutter	4907 50th St.	(780) 754-2227
Irma	Like It Never Was	5008 50 St.	(587) 281-3025
Killam	Crafty Creations	5007 50 St.	(780) 385-2153
Lacombe	The Crafty Lady	5009 50th St.	(403) 782-7238
Lamont	L.A. Sewing Centre	5028 50 Ave.	(780) 895-2599
Lethbridge	Knitting Time	1240 2nd Ave. A N.	(403) 320-5648
Lethbridge	Sewing Lane	2020A Mayor Magrath Dr. S.	(403) 320-9700
Lethbridge	The Fabric Addict	1021 3 Ave. S.	(403) 394-1440
Lethbridge	Village Crafts	1419 3rd Ave. S.	(403) 320-1817

Lloydminster	B & H Fabrics LTD-CC	4010 So. Ave. Bay 2	(780) 871-2830
Lloydminster	Country Quilts & Stitches	5014 48 St.	(780) 875-6661
Mannville	Village Treasures	5009 50 St.	(780) 763-2202
Medicine Hat	Crazi Quilters Lair	902 Kingsway Ave. SE	(403) 487-5114
Milk River	Stitch in Time	207 Main St. NW	(403) 647-3931
Mundare	The Chicken Coop	5103 50 St.	(780) 764-3727
Okotoks	Rumpled Quilt Skins	64 N. Railway St.	(403) 938-6269
Olds	Craig's	5102 50th Ave.	(403) 556-3717
Olds	The Quilting Bee	5026 51st St.	(403) 507-8825
Olds	The Stitchery	Site 1 R.R. 2 Olds	(403) 556-6221
Peace River	Seams Easy	10003 A 102 Ave.	(780) 624-2750
Pincher Creek	Dragons Heart Quilt Shop	656 Main St.	(403) 904-4040
Red Deer	Nuts for Bolts etc.	1428 TWP 381 R.R. 1	(403) 588-2445
Red Deer	Sew You're Quilty	5127 48 St.	(403) 343-0089
Rocky Mountain House			
	Country Quilts	Corner of Hwy. 11/22 S.	(403) 845-6648
Rocky Mountain House			
	Twisted Barn	RR 2 Site 14	(403) 845-5050
Sherwood Park	Lori's Country Cottage	250 130 Broadway Blvd.	(780) 464-9697
Slave Lake	Patchwork Fabrics	220 2nd Ave. NW	(780) 849-6464
Spruce Grove	Woodland Quilting Co.	323 McLeod Ave.	(780) 962-2599
St. Albert	Quiltessential Co.	100 McKenney Ave.	(780) 418-7845
St.Paul	Yvonne's Gone Quilting	5556 50th Ave.	(780) 645-5580
Stettler	Caroline's Homespun Seasons	5008 50 St.	(403) 742-0295
Stettler	Hardanger House	4708 52 St.	(403) 742-2749
Stony Plain	Pam's Woolly Shoppe	4812 50 Ave.	(780) 963-1559
Stony Plain	Sewing With Class	3806 49th Ave.	(780) 963-5992
Strathmore	Cotton & Candy Quilt Shop	55 Wheatland Tr. 2	(403) 934-3832
Sundre	That'll Do Quilting & Gifts	R.R. 1 Site 22	(403) 638-4317
Swan River	Fabriculous	520 Main St.	(204) 734-5662
Three Hills	The Fabric Nook at Three Hills Pharmacy	422 Main St.	(403) 443-5551
Tofield	Snow Goose Quilting	5311 50 St.	(780) 662-2022
Vegreville	The Quilt Rack	5008 50 St.	(780) 632-7890
Vermilion	Extraordinary Extras	4420 Railway Ave.	(780) 853-6626
Westlock	Just Purl Crafts & Gifts	10211 100 St.	(780) 307-8299
White Court	Sew Right	5106 50th St.	(780) 778-5717
Winfield	Country Stitches Fabrics & Quilting	2 Ave. E.	(780) 682-2666

Index

Notes

Atlantic Provinces

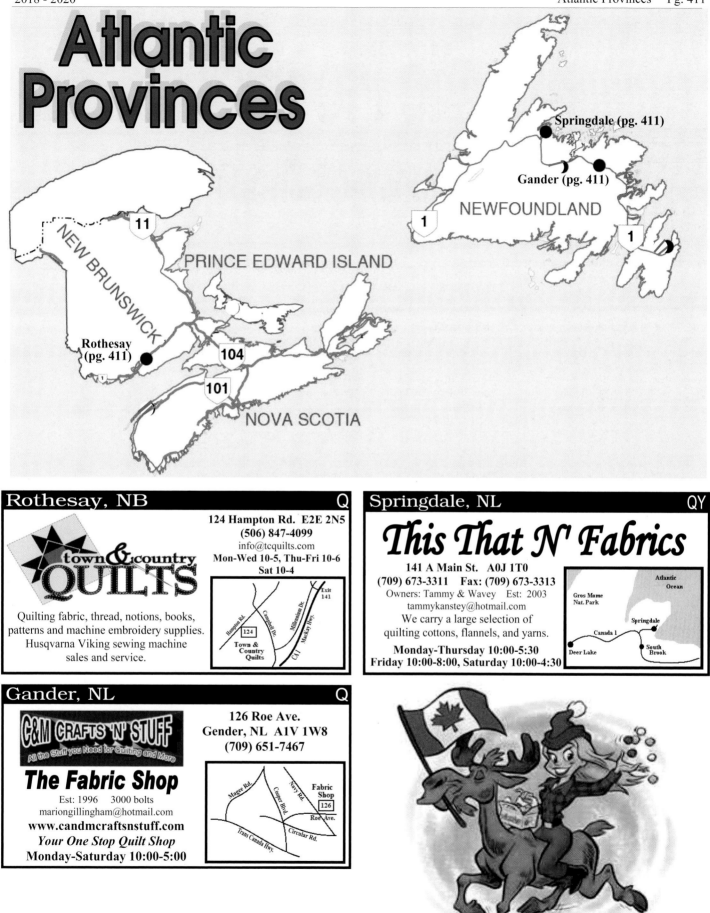

Springdale (pg. 411)

Gander (pg. 411)

NEWFOUNDLAND

1

1

NEW BRUNSWICK

PRINCE EDWARD ISLAND

11

Rothesay
(pg. 411)

104

101

NOVA SCOTIA

Atlantic Provinces

Q-Quilting ~ Y-Yarn ~ N-Needlework ~ R-Retreat ~ M-Museum

New Brunswick Shops

Blacks Harbor	Cricket Cove	836 Main St.	(506) 456-3897
Campbellton	Camille Sewing Center	36-A Roseberry St.	(506) 753-3229
Fredericton	Country Crafts and Curtains	334 York St.	(506) 454-2572
Fredericton	Cricket Cove	647 McLeod Ave.	(506) 450-5648
Glenwood	River Gallery and Textile Studio	7310 Rte. 102	(506) 468-9004
Harvey	Briggs & Little Woolen Mills	3500 Rte. 635	(506) 366-5438
Moncton	Because You Count	164 Collishaw St.	(506) 856-8282
Moncton	Cricket Cove	303 Mountain Rd.	(506) 384-7920
Moncton	The Fabric Cupboard	22 Brandon St.	(506) 855-3800
New Maryland	The Christmas Crab Quiltery	572 New Mryland Hwy.	(506) 459-6180
Port Elgin	Spruce It Up Quilt Shop	2063 Upper Cape Rd. Rte. 960	
			(506) 538-7888
Riverview	The Covered Bridge Quiltery	630 Pinewood Rd.	(506) 386-2888
Rothesay	**Town & Country Quilts**	**124 Hampton Rd.**	**(506) 847-4099** **Pg. 411**
St. Andrews	Cricket Cove	8 King St.	(506) 456-3897
St. Andrews	Sew Natural	391 Queen St.	(506) 529-4735
St. John	Cricket Cove	Brunswick Square 39 King St.	
			(506) 642-2797

Newfoundland Shops

Carmanville	C & M Crafts 'N' Stuff	49 Howells Ave.	(709) 534-2173
Gander	**The Fabric Shop**	**126 Roe Ave.**	**(709) 651-7467** **Pg. 411**
Gander	The Needle Nook	35 B Armstrong Blvd.	(709) 256-8358
Grand Falls	Fabric Boutique	114 Main St.	(709) 489-7384
Port Aux Basques	Material World	Grand Bay Mall	(709) 695-9595
Springdale	**This That N' Fabrics**	**141 A Main St.**	**(709) 673-3311** **Pg. 411**
St. John's	Cast On Cast Off	685 Water St. W.	(709) 739-7318
St. John's	Fiberlilly	10 Highland Dr.	(709) 138-4499
St. John's	Sewing World	Hamlyn Road Plaza. Unit. #52	(709) 747-4100
St. John's	Wool Trends	238 Hamilton Ave.	(709) 726-3242

Index

Nova Scotia Shops

Amherst	Hooking Rugs	33 Church St.	(902) 667-0560
Amherst	Mrs. Pugsley's Emporium	50 Victoria St. E.	(902) 661-4260
Avonport	Avonport Discount Fabrics	12725 Old Hwy. 1	(902) 542-3247
Baddeck	Baadeck Yarns	16 Chebucto St.	(902) 295-3303
Bedford	Makinso	848 Basinview Dr.	(902) 425-1660
Bridgewater	Atlantic Fabrics	2304 Hwy. 325 R.R. #7	(902) 527-2212
Dartmouth	Atlantic Fabrics	114 Woodlawn Rd.	(902) 434-7220
Dartmouth	Dartmouth Yarns	122 Portland St.	(902) 422-9276
Digby	A Needle Pulling Thread Quilt Shop	3 Warwick St.	(902) 378-7845
Digby County	Panier d'Art	464 Comeauville	(902) 769-3457
Greenwood	Altantic Fabrics	Greenwood Mall	(902) 765-0600
Halifax	L.K. Yarns	5545 Young St.	(902) 431-9633
Head of Jeddore	Jeddore Variety	8990 Hwy. 7	(902) 889-2360
Lower Sackville	From Ewe to You	546 Sackville Dr.	(902) 252-9665
Lunenburg	The Mariner's Daughter	107 Montague St.	(902) 634-3263
Mahone Bay	Have a Yarn	583 Main St.	(902) 624-0569
Mahone Bay	Suttles and Seawinds	466 Main St.	(902) 624-8375
New Glasgow	Atlantic Fabrics	980 E. River Rd.	(902) 752-1234
Sidney	Quilting on the Mira	89 Disco St.	(902) 539-6340
Tatamagouche	Tatamagouche Yarn & Co.	317 Main St.	(902) 548-2589
Upper Tantallon	The Purkle Frog Sewing School	5288 St. Margaret's Bay Rd.	(902) 826-1829
Wolfville	Gaspereau Valley Fibres	830 Gaspereau River Rd.	(902) 542-2656
Yarmouth	K&K Fashion Design	610 Main St.	(902) 742-0139

Prince Edward Island Shops

Breadalbane	The Master's Pieces	3664 Dixon Rd. RR 4	(902) 621-0569
Charlottetown	Leisure World/Owls Hollow	95 Capital Dr.	(902) 894-8800
Charlottetown	Quilting B and More	95 Capital Dr.	(902) 628-1998
Cornwall	Glen Valley Custom Knits	43 Bonavista Dr.	(902) 628-6365
Kensington	Sew Blessed Quilters	18 Andrews Dr.	(902) 836-4110
O'Leary	Fabric, Crafts 'n More	538 Main St.	(902) 859-1888
Summerside	Bargain Fabric Outlet	11 MacMurdo Rd. RR	(902) 887-2189
Summerside	Trailside Yarn Shoppe	122 Waugh Rd. RR	(902) 836-4780

Notes

Vanderhoof (pg. 415)

97

16

Kamloops (pg. 415)

1

Nanaimo (pg. 415)

British Columbia

"O Canada" is the national anthem of Canada. The song was originally commissioned by Lieutenant Governor of Quebec Théodore Robitaille for the 1880 Saint-Jean-Baptiste Day ceremony; Calixa Lavallée composed the music, after which words were written by the poet and judge Sir Adolphe-Basile Routhier. The lyrics were originally in French and an English version was created in 1906. Robert Stanley Weir wrote in 1908 another English version, which is the official and most popular version, one that is not a literal translation of the French. Weir's lyrics have been revised twice, taking their present form in 1980, but the French lyrics remain unaltered. "O Canada" had served as a de facto national anthem since 1939, officially becoming Canada's national anthem in 1980 when the Act of Parliament making it so received Royal Assent and became effective on July 1 as part of that year's Dominion Day celebrations.

British Columbia Shops

100 Mile House	Dancing Quilts	195 Birch Ave. #2	(250) 395-4227
100 Mile House	Little Wool Shop	330 Birch Ave.	(250) 395-8816
Abbotsford	A Great Notion QuiltWorks	32526 George Ferguson Way	(604) 853-8930
Abbotsford	On The Lamb Yarns Ltd.	32660 George Ferguson Way	(604) 226-6175
Aldergrove	Langley Yarns & Crafts	256 St.	(604) 856-3636
Armstrong	Pleasant Valley Quilting	3495 Pleasant Valley Rd.	(250) 546-0003
Armstrong	The Twisted Purl Yarn Studio	2541 Pleasant Valley Blvd.	(778) 442-5455
Burnaby	Burnaby Sewing Centre	6190 Kingsway Ave.	(604) 437-1633
Burnaby	The Needle and I Quilt Shop	7870 6th St.	(778) 397-8001
Burns Lake	Yarn and Sew On	870 Hwy. 16 W.	(250) 692-0080
Campbell River	Island Sewing Centre	2231 S. Island Hwy.	(778) 418-2232
Campbell River	Needle & Arts Center	990 Shoppers Row	(250) 287-8898
Campbell River	Red Barn Quilt Shop	1100 Homewood Rd.	(250) 286-3600
Campbell River	Sew 'N' Sew Fabrics	58 C Adams Rd.	(250) 923-6065
Castlegar	Jean's Material Things	343 Columbia Ave.	(250) 304-2337
Chilliwack	Aunt Debbie's Knit and Stitch	5616 Vedder Rd.	(604) 824-7790
Chilliwack	Chilliwack Wool & Craft Shop	45717 Ontario Ave.	(604) 795-9281
Chilliwack	Countryfolk Fabrics & Gifts	45802 Luckakuck Way	(604) 824-5643
Chilliwack	Hamels Fabrics	5843 Lickman Rd.	(604) 846-4350
Clearwater	Greenscapes Art and Craft	733 Clearwater Village Rd.	(250) 674-3562
Comox	Huckleberry's Fabrics, Inc.	1930 Ryan Rd.	(250) 339-4059
Comox	Village Yarn Shoppe	190 Port Augusta St. 30	(250) 339-2474
Coquitlam	Fabricana Imports	1348 United Blvd.	(604) 524-5454
Coquitlam	Poco Sewing & Vacuum Ltd	547 Linton St.	(604) 941-7633
Coquitlam	Quilted Treasures	1140 Austin Ave.	(604)-936-4778
Courtenay	Red Barn Quilt Shop	2175 Cliffe Ave.	(250) 338-6634
Courtenay	Uptown Yarns	206 307 Fifth St.	(250) 338-1940
Cranbrook	Sugar Town Quilt Co.	338 King St.	(778) 517-3011
Cranbrook	The Cotton Tree Quilt Shop	38 Cranbrook St. N.	(250) 426-3358
Creston	Blanket Maker Quilt Shop	1011 Canyon ST.	(250) 402-9043
Creston	The Needle and Quill	125 12th Ave. N.	(250) 428-9976
Dawson Creek	Quilting B Fabric Shop	913 B 102 Ave.	(250) 784-1990
Delta	Crafty Creations	6425 120 St.	(778) 438-3008
Delta	The Quilted Bear	4869 Delta St.	(604) 940-7051
Duncan	Black Sheep Quilt Shop	180 Trunk Rd.	(250) 737-1600
Duncan	Creative Quilting	5859 York Rd.	(250) 746-8033
Duncan	Ingrid's Yarn & Needlework	133 Craig St.	(250) 709-9699
Duncan	Kaleidoscope Quilt Company	4715 Trans Canada Hwy.	(778) 455-4715
Duncan	The Loom	4705 Trans-Canada Hwy.	(250) 746-5250
Falkland	Falkland Store Ltd.	5744 Hwy. 97 N.	(250) 379-2465
Fernie	Heaven Boutique	672C 2nd Ave.	(250) 423-6652
Fort Nelson	Ye Olde Quilt Shoppe	1161 Sikanni Rd. Mile 295	(250) 774-2773
Fort Saint John	Piece By Peace Quilts	9919 103 Ave.	(250) 787-0060
Gibsons	Carola's Quilt Shop	1161 Sunshine Coast Hwy.	(604) 886-1245
Grand Forks	Caba's Quilting Cottage	7578 8th St.	(250) 442-2875
Grand Forks	Heart N' Sole Quilts	325 75th Ave.	(250) 442-0661
Grand Forks	Lynden Tree Yarns	7375 2nd St.	(250) 442-2203
Invermere	Villa Skein	4884 D Althalmer Rd.	(604) 200-2346
Kamloops	**Heather's Fabric Shelf**	**1800 Tranquille Rd. Unit 15**	**(250) 376-7630** **Pg. 415**
Kamloops	Bead Connections	1320 Trans Canada Hwy. W.	(250) 372-1300
Kamloops	Katja's Quilt Shoppe	1967 E. Trans Canada Hwy.	(250) 851-0324
Kelowna	Art of Yarn	3003 Pandosy St.	(250) 717-3247
Kelowna	Cottage Quilting	2000 Spall Rd.	(250) 860-1120
Kelowna	Hummingbird Cottage Craft	1525 Geen Road	(250) 765-4862
Kelowna	Kelowna Yarn & Needlecrafts	1751 Harvey Ave.	(250) 860-8801
Kelowna	Linda's Quilt Shoppe	948 McCurdy Rd.	(250) 491-9770
Kimberley	Sew Creative Chalet	260 Spokane St.	(250) 427-3393
Ladysmith	Main Street Yarn	524 1st Ave.	(250) 924-1000
Langford	Cloth Castle	786 Goldstream Ave. Hwy. 1A	(250)-478-2112
Langley	88 Stitches	21183 88 Ave.	(604) 888-6689
Lytton	Lytton Knittin'	336 Main St.	(778) 254-0036
Maple Ridge	Once Upon A Sheep	22188 Lougheed Hwy.	(604) 463-8296
Mission	Bent Needle Fabrics	33167 N. Railway St.	(604) 287-1114
Mission	Trendy or What Knot Yarns	33118 A 1st Ave.	(604) 287-5668
N Vancouver	Stitch and Bobbin	2065 Old Dollarton Rd.	(604) 982-0088
Nanaimo	**Snip & Stitch Sewing Centre**	**4047 Norwell Dr.**	**(250) 756-2176** **Pg. 415**
Nanaimo	Future Dreams Needlework Shoppe	693 Montague Rd.	(250) 754-4359
Nanaimo	Mad About Ewe Fine Yarns	321 Wesley St.	(250) 754-0785
Nanaimo	Serge and Sew	6750 N. Island Hwy.	(250) 390-3602
Nelson	Maplerose	390 Baker St.	(250) 352-5729
Nelson	Shannon's Fabrics Ltd.	560 Baker St.	(250) 352-6104

New Denver	Sew Much More	304 6th Ave.	(250) 551-6509
North Vancouver	Urban Yarns	3111 Highland Blvd.	(604) 984-2214
Oyama	Batik Corner Fabric	14450 Middlebench Rd.	(250) 548-0038
Parksville	Sweet Pea Quilting	1209 East Island Hwy.	(250) 586-1050
Parksville	The Wool Shop	281 E. Island Hwy.	(250) 248-3821
Pemberton	Bog Fabrics	1355 Aster St.	(604) 894-6164
Penticton	Knotty Knitter	416 Main St.	(250) 493-1033
Penticton	Poppins Quilt Parlour	350 Main St.	(250) 493-1815
Port Alberni	Kismet Quilts	5334 Argyle St.	(250) 723-6605
Port Alberni	Pincushion	3218 3rd Ave.	(250) 723-8831
Port Moody	Black Sheep Yarns	88 Crant St.	(778) 355-9665
Prince George	Kathy's Quilt Shop	1260 4th Ave.	(250) 960-1021
Prince George	Prince George Sewing Center	1210 5th Ave.	(250) 563-1533
Prince George	Top Drawer Yarn Studio	1685 Third Ave.	(250) 596-9276
Pritchard	Di-Versity Quilting Supplies	2144 Nordkinn Rd.	(250) 577-3494
Qualicum Beach	Let's Knit	211 Second Ave. W.	(250) 594-3608
Quesnel	Expressions by Ewe	222 McNaughton Ave.	(250) 992-8896
Quesnel	Quilted Accents	1706 Lawlor Rd.	(250) 747-2366
Quesnel	R & R Sewing Center	158 Davie St.	(250) 992-9777
Richmond	Fabricana & Interior Delights	4591 Garden City Rd.	(604) 273-5316
Richmond	Imagine Craft Co.	4311 Hazelbridge Way	(604) 270-9683
Richmond	Steveston Crafts 'N More	3471 Moncton St.	(604) 272-3824
Richmond	Wool & Wicker	12051 2nd Ave.	(604) 275-1239
Salmon Arm	Intwined Fibre Arts	81 Hudson Ave. NE	(778) 489-1090
Salmon Arm	The Sewing Basket	168 Macleod St.	(250) 832-3937
Salmon Arm	Thread & Paper	650 Trans Canada Hwy. NE	(250) 832-3937
Salt Spring Island	Stitches Fiber Art Supplies	127 Rainbow Rd.	(877) 537-8985
Salt Spring Island	Stitches Quilts & Yarns	120 Hereford Ave.	(250) 537-8985
Sechelt	Fibre Expressions Quilt Shop	5679 Cowrie St	(604) 885-6677
Sechelt	Sew Easy	5755 Cowrie St.	(604) 885-2725
Sidney	In Sheeps Clothing	9711 Fifth St.	(250) 656-2499
Smithers	Fabrications	3892 3rd Ave.	(250) 847-3250
South Surrey	Penelope Fibre Arts	16055 8th Ave.	(778) 292-1282
Summerland	Cherry Tree Quilts	10105 Main St.	(250) 494-1314
Surrey	A Great Notion QuiltWorks	19289 Langley ByPass	(604) 575-9028
Surrey	Castle's Sewing Centre	18543 Fraser Hwy.	(604) 574-5333
Surrey	Tom's Sewing Center	8338 120th St.	(604) 507-2841
Surrey	Valley Yarn	6758 188th St.	(604) 576-4222
Taylor	Windy Willow Fabrics	Collins Rd. Mile 30	(250) 789-9248
Terrace	Cotton Pick n' Quilt Patch	4632 Davis Ave.	(250) 638-1335
Terrace	Fabricland	4717 Lakels Ave.	(250) 635-2164
Trail	Allan's Sewing Center	1268 Pine Ave.	(250) 368-8485
Twin Bays	Twin Bays Knit Shop	10278 Hwy. 3A	(250) 223-8290
Vancouver	Baaad Anna's	2667 Hastings St. E.	(604) 255-2577
Vancouver	Birkeland Bros. Wool Ltd.	3573 Main St.	(604) 874-4734
Vancouver	Dressew Supply Ltd.	337 W. Hastings St.	(604) 682-6196
Vancouver	Fibre Art Studio	1610 Johnson St.	(604) 688-3047
Vancouver	Gina Brown's Yarn	3424 W. Broadway	(604) 734-4840
Vancouver	Spool of Thread	649 E. 15th Ave.	(604) 879-3031
Vancouver	Sweet Georgia Yarns	408 E. Kent Ave.	(604) 569-6811
Vancouver	The Cloth Shop	1551 Johnston St.	(604) 224-1325
Vancouver	Three Bags Full Knit Shop	4458 Main St.	(604) 874-9665
Vancouver	Urban Yarns	4437 W. 10th Ave.	(604) 228-1122
Vancouver	Wet Coast Wools	2923 W. 4th Ave.	(604) 568-0011
Vancouver	Wool is Not Enough	1683 E. 13th Ave.	(778) 549-5696
Vanderhoof	**Quilters Corner in the Vanderhoof Dept Store**		
		2465 Burrard Ave.	**(250) 567-2311** **Pg. 415**
Vanderhoof	Quilters Nook	185 W. Stewart St.	(250) 567-2828
Vernon	A Twist of Yarn	3915 31st St.	(250) 549-4200
Victoria	Aurelia Wool & Weaving	5012 Old W. Saanich Rd.	(250) 378-2468
Victoria	Bee Hive Wool Shop	1700 Douglas St.	(250) 385-2727
Victoria	Bib n' Tucker Quilting	1006 Craigflower Rd.	(250) 386-6512
Victoria	Button & Needlework Boutique	614 View St.	(250) 384-8781
Victoria	Buttons N Bows	2867 Foul Bay Rd.	(250) 592-7924
Victoria	Calico Cupboard	5134 Cordova Bay	(250) 658-2722
Victoria	Capitol Iron	1900 Store St.	(250) 385-9703
Victoria	Satin Moon Quilt Shop	825 Fort St.	(250) 383-4023
West Kelowna	Tyjo's Fabrics	822 Montigny Rd.	(778) 755-0103
West Vancouver	Knit and Stitch Shoppe	2460 A Marine Dr.	(604) 922-1023
Williams Lake	Ibea's Quilting & Craft Galore	30 3rd Ave. N.	(250) 392-7748

Index

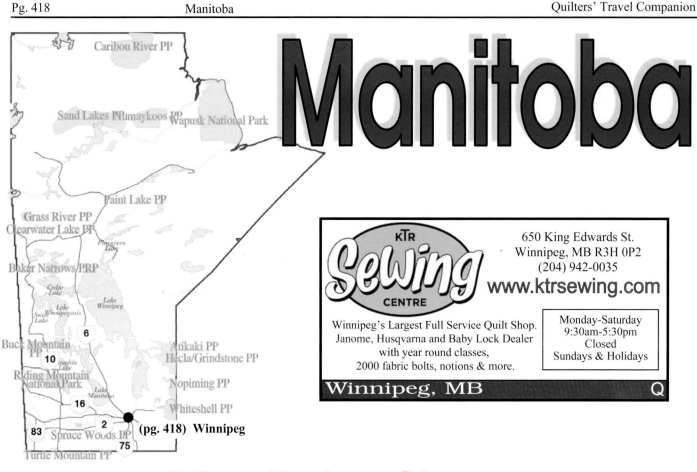

(pg. 418) Winnipeg

Manitoba Shops

Q-Quilting ~ Y-Yarn ~ N-Needlework ~ R-Retreat ~ M-Museum

Brandon	Lasting Image	708 B 10th St.	(204) 727-1777
Brandon	The Knit 2 Scrap 2 Store Inc.	215 6th St. #1	(204) 717-5272
Carman	Kathy's Fabrics	2 1st Ave. SW	(204) 745-3074
Grunthal	Oma's Quilt Shop	Box 961	(204) 434-6747
Morden	Quilters' Den	565A Stephen St.	(204) 822-3105
Oakville	Prairie Knits Sian Taris	112 2nd St.	(800) 841-0633
Winnipeg	**KTR Sewing Centre**	**650 King Edward St.**	**(204) 942-0035** Pg. 418
Winnipeg	Keystone Quilts	15 1599 Dugaid Rd.	(204) 667-5833
Winnipeg	Red River Co Op Store	850 Dakota St.	(204) 254-6516
Winnipeg	Sheena's Gallery	953 St. Mary's Rd.	(204) 255-3534
Winnipeg	Wolseley Wool	162 Lipton St.	(204) 772-5648

Notes

Northwest Territories

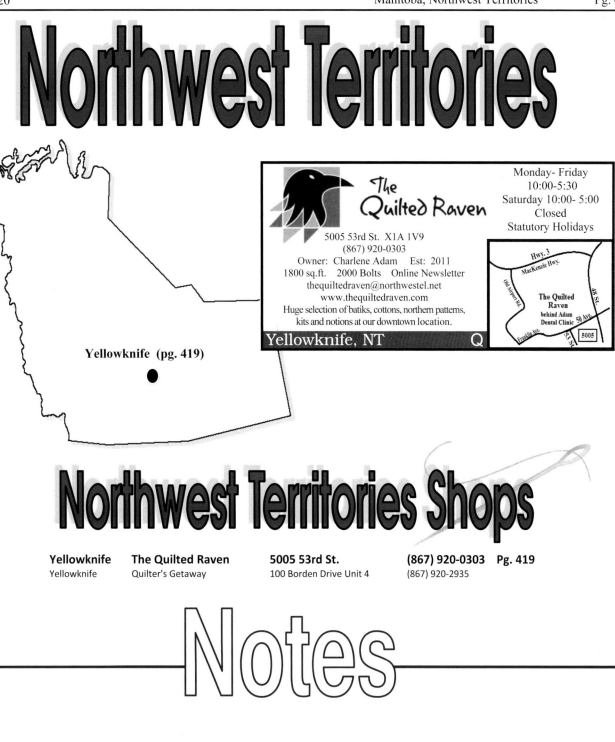

Yellowknife (pg. 419)

The Quilted Raven

5005 53rd St. X1A 1V9
(867) 920-0303
Owner: Charlene Adam   Est: 2011
1800 sq.ft.   2000 Bolts   Online Newsletter
thequiltedraven@northwestel.net
www.thequiltedraven.com
Huge selection of batiks, cottons, northern patterns,
kits and notions at our downtown location.

Yellowknife, NT   Q

Monday- Friday
10:00-5:30
Saturday 10:00- 5:00
Closed
Statutory Holidays

Northwest Territories Shops

Yellowknife	**The Quilted Raven**	**5005 53rd St.**	**(867) 920-0303**	**Pg. 419**
Yellowknife	Quilter's Getaway	100 Borden Drive Unit 4	(867) 920-2935	

Notes

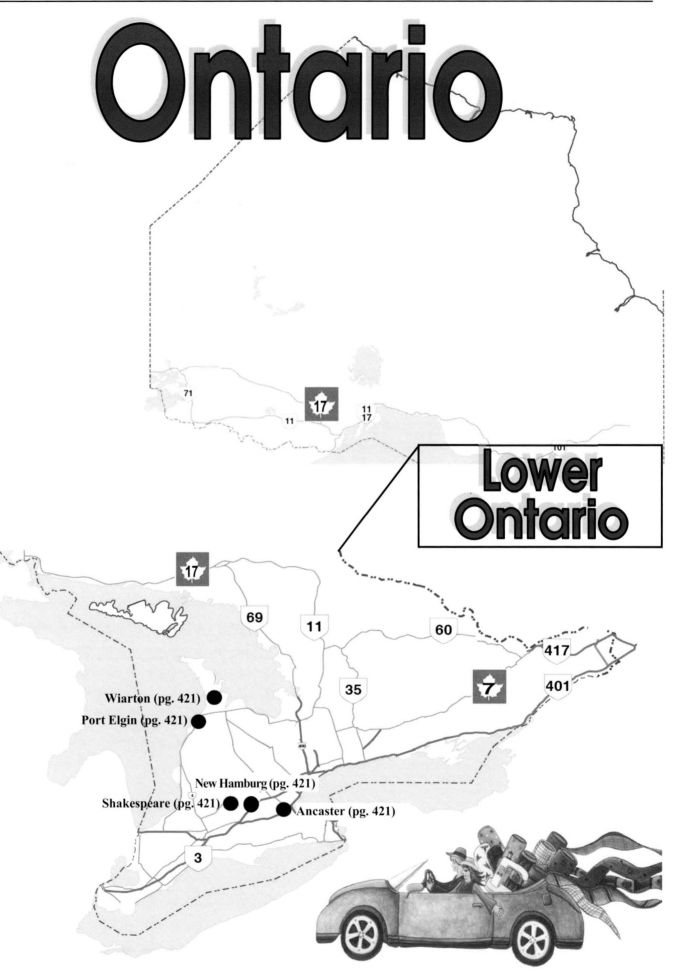

Ontario

Lower
Ontario

71

17

11

11
17

101

17

69

11

60

417

35

7

401

Wiarton (pg. 421)

Port Elgin (pg. 421)

400

New Hamburg (pg. 421)

Shakespeare (pg. 421)

Ancaster (pg. 421)

3

Ontario Shops

Q-Quilting ~ Y-Yarn ~ N-Needlework ~ R-Retreat ~ M-Museum

Acton	The Needle Gnome	43 Mill St. E.	(519) 853-5245
Alliston	Alliston Yarns, Crafts & Gifts	21B Young St.	(705) 434-0880
Alliston	Lilac Lane Quilts	180 Parson Rd. #27	(705) 435-2746
Almonte	Textile Traditions	87 Mill St.	(613) 256-3907
Almonte	The Quilting Quarters	24 Mill St.	(613) 256-4248
Amherstburg	Rose Cottage Quilt Shoppe	580 Middle Side Rd.	(519) 730-1172
Amprior	Sew Inspired	106 John St. N.	(613) 623-0500
Ancaster	**The Quilt Rack**	**356 Wilson St. E.**	**(905) 304-0180 Pg. 421**
Ancaster	The Needle Emporium	420 Wilson St. E.	(905) 648-1994
Arkona	Quilts 'n Things	43 Ann St.	(519) 518-6228
Athens	Sit N Knit	15 Mill St.	(613) 349-7919
Aurora	Needles & Knits	15040 Yonge St.	(905) 713-2066
Aurora	Yarn Crate	99 Lewis Honey Dr.	(647) 828-7940
Barrie	Eliza's Button & Yarn	250 Bayview Dr. #2	(705) 725-8536
Barrie	HummingBird Sewing	19 Hart Dr. #102	(705) 726-4510
Barrie	Lens Mill Store	364 Vincent St.	(705) 722-5467
Barrie	Simcoe Sew & Quilt	4 Cedar Pointe Dr. #E1	(705) 737-3777
Barrie	True North Yarn Co.	15 Cedar Pointe Dr. #7	(888) 304-4418

Beamsville	The Quilted Cardinal	4516 Mountainview Rd.	(905) 563-3939
Belleville	Fun With Stitches	1963 Old Hwy 2. RR#2	(613) 966-4715
Belleville	Kraft Village	191 Dundas St. E.	(613) 966-9964
Bethany	From the Heart Quilt Shop	1436 Hwy. 7A	(705) 277-2934
Blenheim	Pastime Pieces	11175 Brush Line	(519) 676-5059
Blyth	Stitches With A Twist	404 Queen St.	(519) 523-9449
Bolton	Odd's & Sod's	43 Queen St. N.	(647) 546-4415
Bowmanville	Sewing Essentials	51 B King St. E.	(905) 623-2404
Bowmanville	Soper Creek Yarns	80 King St. W.	(905) 623-2336
Bowmanville	Why Knot Knit	114 Scugog St.	(905) 623-9703
Bracebridge	Muskoka Yarn Connection	295 Wellington St.	(705) 645-5819
Bracebridge	The Muskoka Quilting Co.	181 Manitoba St.	(705) 645-4446
Brampton	Arts and Crafts 4 You	118 Inspire Blvd.	(416) 723-6312
Brampton	Brampton Sew & Surge	289 Rutherford Rd. S. #7	(905) 874-1564
Brantford	Brantford Fabrics	128 Nelson St. #3	(519) 304-8220
Brantford	Red Red Bobbin	495 Mt. Pleasant Rd.	(519) 770-3580
Brighton	Knowledge and Needles	190 Smith St.	(613) 475-4843
Brighton	The Robbins Nest	53 Main	(613) 475-0578
Brockville	Taylor Sewing Centre	7712 Kent Blvd.	(613) 342-3153
Brockville	Woolly Lamb	56 Louis St.	(613) 342-5343
Brussels	Country Quilting	84849 Ethel Line RR #3	(519) 887-9456
Burlington	Johanne's Knit N Stitch	2049A Mount Forest Dr.	(905) 332-5565
Burlington	SewEtc	4155 Fairview St.	(905) 639-5525
Burlington	Spun Fibre Arts	4155 Fairview Ave. #2	(905) 681-7786
Burlington	Village Square Quilt Shop	422 Pearl St.	(905) 681-2256
Campbellford	Your # 1 Sewing Center	62 Bridge St. E.	(705) 653-5642
Carleton Place	The PickleDish Quilt Shop & Studio	24 Lake Ave. W.	(613) 212-8770
Carleton Place	The Real Wool Shop	142 Franktown Rd.	(613) 257-2714
Carlisle	A Juggling Ewe	306 Carlisle Rd.	(905) 570-3765
Casselman	Tric-O-Knit	68 Lafleche Blvd.	(613) 764-9992
Chatham	Put It Together Quilt Shoppe	15 Maple Leaf Dr.	(519) 354-1110
Chesterville	Flair With Fabrics	3 King St.	(613) 448-9032
Cobourg	The Stitch Witch	884 Division St.	(905) 372-5145
Cochrane	NeedleWorks Studio Canada	142 3rd Ave.	(705) 272-6701
Coldwater	The Purple Sock	13 Coldwater Rd.	(705) 686-3455
Collingwood	Grey Heron Natural Designs	65 Simcoe St. #1	(705) 444-0370
Combermere	Quilters Curve	39072 Combermere Rd.	(613) 756-6262
Cookstown	Country Concessions	1 Dufferin St.	(705) 458-4546
Corbeil	The Cottage Quilter	64 Shady Ln.	(705) 752-1496
Creemore	Creemore House of Stitches	3 Caroline St. W.	(705) 466-6363
Dresden	Shelley's Painted Treasures and Quilt Shop	462 St. George S.	(519) 683-4244
Dryden	Fabric Fusion	123 Queen St.	(807) 223-2164
Dryden	The Quilting Trunk	187 Grand Trunk Ave.	(807) 223-4739
Dundas	Feathering Quilt Shop	33 King St. E. #5	(905) 570-2055
Dundas	The Cotton Mill Threadworks	2 Crowly Court	(905) 628-5267
East Millbrook	The Quilter's Bolt	30 King St.	(705) 932-2120
Elliot Lake	The Knitting Room	11 Columbia Walk	(705) 578-2630
Elmira	Busy Bee Quilts	9 Arthur St. S.	(519) 669-3441
Elmira	Quilter's Nine Patch	384 Arthur St. S.	(519) 669-9511
Elora	Yarn Bird	22 Mill St. W.	(519) 846-0003
Espanola	Black Sheep Yarns	289 James St.	(705) 578-2630
Espanola	Cindy Bee's Quilt Shoppe	70 McCulloch Dr.	(705) 869-2548
Essex	Sewcraft Quilting Fabrics & More	106 Talbot St. N.	(519) 776-1100
Etobicoke	Signature Yarns	181 Shaver Ave. N.	(416) 795-5500
Exeter	Kalidoscope of Quilts	355 Main St.	(519) 235-4004
Fenelon Falls	The Crafty Ewe	8A Water St.	(705) 878-2766
Fenelon Falls	The Lil Wee Quilt Shoppe	18 Francis St. E.	(705) 887-4848
Fergus	Undercover Quilts and More!	223 St. Andrew St. E.	(519) 843-3930
Fonthill	Rose's Fine Yarns	67 Canboro Rd.	(905) 892-2222
Fonthill	Rose's Fine Yarns of Niagara	67 Canboro Rd.	(905) 892-2222
Fonthill	The Quilting Bee	155 Hwy. 20	(905) 892-7926
Forest	My Favourite Store	3-85 King St. E.	(519) 786-2791
Georgetown	Georgetown Yarn & Crafts	170 Guelph St.	(905) 877-1521
Georgetown	The Hobby Horse	RR #5 12707 9th Line	(905) 877-9292
Georgetown	The Sewing Café	118 Mill St. #C	(905) 873-0043
Groe Bay	Freshisle Fibers	6 Doc Strain Dr.	(705) 282-3205
Guelph	All Strung Out	36 Quebec St.	(226) 820-3766
Guelph	Greenwood Quiltery	275 Woolwich	(519) 822-2790
Guelph	Sew Fancy	328 Speedvale Ave. E. Ste. #110	(519) 824-4127
Guelph	Triangle Sewing Centre	386 Woolwich St.	(519) 822-9910
Haliburton	Fibersden	2253 Harburn Rd.	(705) 457-2804
Haliburton	Janknits Studio	214 Highland St.	(705) 457-4000

Hamilton	Handknit Yarn Studio	144 James St. N.	(905) 393-5976
Hamilton	Needlework	174 James St. N.	(905) 667-5663
Hamilton	Project Fleece	144 James St. N.	(905) 541-6032
Harrow	Sue2Knits	12045 3rd Conscession W.	(519) 738-0579
Harrowsmith	Wilton Creek Fabrics	4909 Hwy. 38	(613) 372-1972
Hawkesbury	Fabric Box	371 Main St. E.	(613) 632-7172
Hawkesbury	Heartworks Quilt Shop	371 Main St. E.	(613) 632-7172
Huntsville	Sheep Strings	3 Main St. W.	(705) 788-2832
Ignace	Gail's Stitches	210 Main St.	(807) 934-0999
Ilderton	The Marsh Store	10266 Ilderton Rd.	(519) 666-3330
Ingersoll	Kraft Korner	123 Thames St.	(519) 485-2525
Ingersoll	Stitch-It Central	189 Thames St.	(519) 303-1563
Jackson's Point	The Quilting Gnome	954 Lake Dr.	(905) 722-4200
Jordan Village	Stitch	3799 Main St.	(905) 562-1505
Kanata	The Running Stitch	462 Hazeldean Rd.	(613) 836-5908
Kemptville	Kemptville Fabric Shoppe	31 Clothier St. E.	(613) 258-4437
Kenora	Born To Quilt	506 First St. S.	(807) 468-1847
Kilworthy	Gateway Fibreworks	1396 Beiers Rd.	(705) 687-5222
Kincardine	Retail Dry Goods	R.R. #5	no phone
Kingston	Fibre and Fleece	78 Dalgleish Ave.	(613) 542-7846
Kingston	Garden Thyme Quilt & Gift Emporium	1080 Gardiner's Rd.	(613) 384-8028
Kingston	Knit Traders of Kingston	725 Gardiners Rd.	(613) 384-3951
Kingston	Stitch by Stich	550 Days Rd. #1	(613) 389-2223
Kingston	Wool on Wellington	157 Wellington St.	(613) 549-5546
Kitchener	Creative Sisters Quilt Studio	321 Lancaster St. W.	(519) 584-2130
Kitchener	Woolverine	93 King St. W.	(519) 749-0248
Lakefield	Happenstance Books & Yarn	44 Queen St.	(705) 652-7535
Leamington	A Stitch in Time	30 Mill St. W.	(519) 322-4690
Lindsay	Aberdeen's Wool Company	228 Kent St. W.	(705) 928-5417
Lindsay	Appleseed Quiltworks	19 William St. N.	(705) 324-0385
Lindsay	Bolts & Bobbins	33 Midland Dr.	(705) 324-9868
Linwood	Retail Dry Goods	7546 Rd. 116 RR#1	no phone
Little Current	Needle Box	26 Water St. E.	(705) 368-3010
London	Cornerstone Quilts & More	1700 Hyde Park Rd.	(519) 518-0110
London	Joyce's Sewing Shop	325 Wortley Rd.	(519) 433-5344
London	Knit Stitch	609 Richmond St.	(519) 601-7024
London	Krafty Kennedys	2711 Dingman Dr.	(519) 681-0015
London	London Yarns	1890 Hyde Park Rd. #F	(519) 474-0403
London	Needles & Pins Inc.	205 Oxford St. E. #103	(519) 642-3445
London	The Wool Boutique	900 King St.	(519) 854-0372
London	Thread & Eye	962 Leathorne St. #1	(519) 685-1444
Markdale	Quilters' Line	57 Main St. W.	(519) 986-2244
Maxwell	Threads That Bind	408016 Hwy. 4 Unit 2	(519) 922-1010
Meaford	Purrsonally Yours	35 Sykes St. N.	(519) 538-4283
Meaford	The Fabric Shoppe	35 Sykes St. N.	(519) 538-3955
Midland	Mom's Tangled Threads	559 Bay St.	(705) 528-0909
Milton	Main St. Yarns	1264 Main St. E.	(905) 693-4299
Mississauga	Gitta's Petit Point	271 Lakeshore Rd. E.	(905) 274-7198
Mississauga	Ruti's Needlebed	10 Thomas St.	(905) 821-9370
Mississauga	Three Crafty Grannies	6700 Montevideo Rd.	(416) 272-7012
Mississauga	Linda's Craftique	237 Lakeshore Rd. E.	(905) 274-4115
Mt. Brydges	Sew Creative	22486 Adelaide Rd.	(519) 264-2177
Nepean	Sew for It!	418 Moodie Dr.	(613) 820-2201
Nepean	Wool-Tyme	90 Colonnade Rd. S.	(613) 225-9665
New Hamburg	**Quilting by Design**	**337 Waterloo St.**	**(519) 390-1155** Pg. 421
New Hamburg	Heart "N Home Creations	115 A Peel St.	(519) 662-4962
New Liskeard	The Quilting Barn	097460 Jelly Rd.	(705) 647-0081
Newcastle	Annie's Quilt Shop	816 Regional Rd. 17	(905) 987-1779
Newmarket	Serenity Knits	525 Brooker Ridge	(905) 710-3283
Newmarket	The Quilt Store	17817 Leslie St. # 40	(905) 853-7001
Newmarket	Unwind: Yarn House	234 Main St. S.	(905) 954-1153
Newton	E and E'S Cloth and Creations	4463 Perth Line 72	(519) 595-8569
Niagra Falls	Country Road Cross Stitch	6666 Garner Rd.	(905) 356-0816
North Gower	Loghouse Cottage	7383 4th Line Rd.	(613) 227-7266
Nuestadt	Have You Any Wool	500 Mill St.	(519) 799-5881
Oakville	The Wool Bin	332 Kerr St.	(905) 845-9512
Orangeville	Sew Jax	28 Mill St.	(519) 940-0001
Orillia	Purl 3 Orillia	425 West St. N.	(705) 325-4334
Orillia	Thimbles & Things	1282 Brodie Dr.	(705)-326-9357
Orleans	Quilty Pleasures	2211 St. Joseph Blvd.	(613) 834-3044
Orleans	Wool N' Things	1439 Youville Dr. Unit 20	(613) 841-8689

Index

Oshawa	Ruby Pearl Quilts	500 King St. W. #8	(905) 436-3535	
Oshawa	Sew Have Fun	133 Taunton Rd. W.	(905) 728-7397	
Oshawa	The Wool Queen	182 Simcoe St. S.	(905) 725-8543	
Oshawa	Ultimate Sewing Centre	191 Bloor St. E.	(905) 436-9193	
Oshawa	Wool on William	5 William St.	(905) 914-7706	
Otonabee	River of Yarn	353 Kent's Bay Rd.	(705) 295-1131	
Ottawa	Calico Expressions by Ellen	280 Slater St.	(613) 233-9219	
Ottawa	Yarns Etc.	368 Dalhousie St. #4	(613) 884-0064	
Owen Sound	Riverside Yarns	136 10th St. E	(519) 371-4311	
Paris	Heirloom Treasures Creative Sewing Studio	132 Governors Rd. E.	(519) 774-5164	
Parry Sound	Parry Sound Sewing Centre	53 James St.	(705) 746-8030	
Perth	janie h. knits	528 Glen Tay Rd.	(613) 326-0626	
Perth	Perth Fabrics Crafts 'n More	14 Gore St. E.	(613) 267-7990	
Perth	Unraveled	9 Wilson St. E.	(613) 485-0747	
Petawawa	Algonquin Sewing Center	2096 Petawawa Blvd.	(613) 732-4789	
Peterborough	Needle Works and Your #1 Sewing Center	186 George St. N.	(705) 742-3337	
Peterborough	Needles in the Hay	385 Water St.	(705) 740-0667	
Petrolia	Country Yarns	2776 LaSalle Line RR # 3	(519) 882-8740	
Pickering	Elizabeth Dillinger Studio & Designs	1735 Bayly St. #7C	(905) 420-1101	
Pickering	Log Cabin Yardage	955 Brock Rd.	(416) 818-1393	
Pickering	The Knit Kabin	3230 Salem Rd.	(905) 686-9060	
Picton	Needle In A Haystack	76 Main St.	(613) 476-7048	
Picton	Picton Fabric World	261 Main St.	(613) 476-6397	
Picton	Rosehaven Yarn Shop	187 Main St.	(613) 476-9092	
Port Elgin	**Shoreline Quilts**	**728 Goderich St.**	**(226) 453-4040**	**Pg. 421**
Port Elgin	Doc Knits	651 Goderich St.	(519) 832-6486	
Port Hope	Cozy Quilts	121 Toronto Rd.	(905) 885-5777	
Port Hope	The Black Lamb	198 Victoria St. N.	(905) 885-0190	
Port Perry	Never Enough Wool	26 Water St.	(905) 985-0030	
Powassan	FibreChick	309 Chiswick Line	(705) 498-3555	
Prescott	We R Quilts	253 King St. W.	(613) 925-0110	
Red Lake	Gail's Stitches	281 Hwy. 105	(807) 727-3161	
Renfrew	Dolan's Fabric Shop & Yarn	172 Raglan St. S.	(613) 432-6434	
Renfrew	Valley Needleworx	2-94 Plaunt St. S.	(613) 431-4739	
Richmond	Country Quilter	3444 McBean St.	(613) 838-5541	
Richmond Hill	Knitter's Attic	10119 Yonge St.	(905) 508-5637	
Rideau Ferry	Sew Crafty	1068 Rideau Ferry Rd.	(613) 264-1547	
Rosemont	The Knitting Basket	1 Jamieson Dr.	(705) 434-4255	
Russell	Quilters Barn & Gifts	1087 Concession St. #102	(613) 496-2276	
Sarnia	Ewe Are Special Wool Shoppe	1059 Briarfield Ave.	(519) 337-1289	
Sarnia	Feather Your Nest	138 Front St. N.	(519) 336-1617	
Sarnia	Heaven Is Handmade	250 Christina St. N. #D	(519) 491-9276	
Sault Ste. Marie	Life's A Stitch	516 Queen St. E.	(705) 254-3339	
Sault Ste. Marie	Shabby Motley Handcraft	365 Queen St. Lower	(705) 575-9276	
Scarborough	Creative Yarns	269 Ellesmere Rd.	(416) 331-8085	
Seaforth	The Cotton Harvest Quilt Shop	60 Main St. S.	(519) 600-1646	
Selkirk	Wee Folks Heirloom Sewing & Quilt Shoppe	108 Blue Water Pkwy.	(905) 776-1929	
Shakespeare	**The Quilt Place**	**3991 Perth Rd. #107**	**(519) 625-8435**	**Pg. 421**
Shelburne	Cobwebs and Caviar	147 Main St. W.	(519) 306-3000	
Shelburne	The Wool & Silk Co.	138 Main St. W.	(519) 925-6194	
Simcoe	The Quilting Corner	603 Ireland Rd.	(519) 426-6705	
Sioux Lookout	Dori's Sewing Studio	3 Loon Lake Rd	(807) 737-3674	
Sioux Lookout	Northern Knits	299 Ogemah Rd.	(807) 737-1241	
Smiths Falls	Knit Knackers Yarn Warehouse	12 Russell St.	(613) 371-7731	
St Thomas	Little Red Mitten	86 Talbot St	(519) 207-2880	
St. Catharines	Kindred Spirits	211 Martindale Rd.	(905) 397-9500	
St. Catharines	Kismet Wool Shop	8 Queenston St.	(905) 685-8642	
St. Jacobs	Quilt Essentials	1340 King St. N.	(519) 664-2060	
St. Marys	Hyggeligt Fabrics	144 Queen St. E.	(519) 284-1508	
St. Mary's	Simply Sew	97 Queen St. E.	(519) 284-0856	
Stittsville	Mad about Patchwork	2477 Huntley Rd.	(613) 838-0020	
Stoney Creek	Gifts from Eighth and Mud	232 Eighth Rd. E.	(905) 308-6188	
Stoney Creek	Tii Casa	286 Barton St.	(905) 930-9596	
Stouffville	Ann's Fabrics & Sewing Centre	6350 Main St.	(905) 640-5635	
Stouffville	Homespun Designs Quilt Shoppe & More	86 Ringwood Dr. #37	(905) 642-9836	
Stratford	Close Knit	76 Wellington St.	(519) 508-5648	
Stratford	Ye Olde Fabric Shoppe	327 Erie St.	(519) 273-5773	
Sturgeon Falls	Diane's Creative Elements	196 Front St. Hwy. 17 W.	(705) 753-4545	
Sudbury	Country Quilter	1191 Lansing Ave.	(705)-524-6235	
Sudbury	Sweet Yarns	947 Lorne St.	(705) 586-4648	
Tara	Karen's Country Fabrics	117538 Grey Road #3 RR #4	(519) 376-4839	

Tecumseh	Joy Quilts	11886 Tecumseh Rd. E. Unit #6	(519) 735-2295
Thessalon	The Creative Basket	210 Main St.	(705) 842-3806
Thunder Bay	Caryll's Yarns	809 Victoria Ave. E.	(807) 625-9276
Thunder Bay	Circle of Friends Quilt Shoppe	218 Tupper St.	(807) 344-2625
Thunder Bay	Threads in Time	426 E. Victoria Ave.	(807) 626-9023
Tilsonburg	Cherished Pieces	133 Broadway St.	(519) 842-2658
Toronto	Eweknit	832 Bloor St. W.	(416) 530-4438
Toronto	Knit - O - Matic	1378 Bathurst St.	(416) 653-7849
Toronto	Knitting Place	1738 Avenue Rd.	(416) 787-8100
Toronto	Ladee Bee Yarn & Beads	3079 B Dundas St. W.	(416) 605-0811
Toronto	PassionKnit Ltd.	3232 Yonge St.	(416) 322-0688
Toronto	Purple Purl	1162 Queen St. E.	(416) 463-1162
Toronto	Romni Wools, Ltd.	658 Queen St. W.	(416) 703-0202
Toronto	Sew Sisters Quilt Shop	3961 Chesswood Dr.	(416) 633-8800
Toronto	Sew'N Knit'N Serge Outlet	15 Gower St.	(416) 752-1828
Toronto	The Wool Mill	2170 Danforth Ave.	(416) 696-2670
Toronto	The Workroom	1340 Queen St. W.	(416) 534-5305
Toronto	Wool Gathering	12 Advance Rd.	(647) 785-5394
Toronto	Yarns Untangled Inc.	86 Nassau St.	(647) 895-2633
Trenton	Andjareenas Place	60 Carrying Place Rd.	(613) 394-4990
Trenton	Pine Ridge Knit & Sew	17477 Hwy. 2	(613) 392-1422
Uxbridge	On The Lamb	66 Brock St. W.	(905) 852-1944
Uxbridge	Quilters Cupboard	202 Brock St. E.	(905) 862-0666
Vankleek Hill	QuiltBees	22 Main St. E.	(613) 307-1222
Vankleek Hill	Sue's Quilting Studio	7951 County Rd. 10 W.	(613) 678-3256
Virgil	Modern Bee - Fabrics and Yarns	1507 Niagara Stone Rd.	(905) 468-8190
Waterdown	Green Acres Alpaca Farm	59 Mill St. N.	(905) 690-6050
Waterford	Quilt Junction	121 Alice St.	(519) 443-7222
Waterloo	Len's Mill Store	130 Moore Ave. S.	(519) 743-4672
Waterloo	Shall We Knit?	11 Willow St.	(519) 725-9739
West Lorne	Heather Bell's Sewing Studio	24846 Pioneer N.	(519) 768-1284
Whitby	Kniterary	124 Dundas St. W.	(905) 668-8368
Whitby	Kniterary & Hedgehog Stitchery	124 Dundas St. W.	(905) 668-8368
Whitby	Whitby Fabrics Sewing Centre	601 Dundas St. W.	(905) 668-4821
Wiarton	**Mother's Fabric**	**603 Berford St.**	**(519) 534-4004 Pg. 421**
Windsor	Ella Quilts	12056 Tecumseh Rd. #C	(519) 739-1122
Windsor	Knit One Sew Too	3703 Walker Rd.	(519) 966-7444
Windsor	Quilting Confections	3393 Country Rd. 42	(519) 250-8888
Woodbridge	The Enchanted Needle	3850 Steeles Ave. W. #5	(905) 264-9265
Woodstock	Country Patchworks	515533 11th Line RR #3	(519) 537-8753
Wyoming	Stitcharie	569 Broadway St.	(519) 845-0768
Wyoming	Stitcharie	569 Broadway St.	(519) 845-0768
Yanker	Anwyn Yarn Studio	Box 4034	(613) 766-1422

Index

Notes

Alma	Le Petit Point Enr.	726 Ouest Gagne	(418) 668-9254
Anjou	La Cigale Brodeuse	6610 Blvd. des Galeries d' Anjou	(514) 355-3883
Aylmer	Le Tricot	135 Ave. Frank Robinson	(819) 682-7997
Bassin	Depanneur De La Montagne	2979 Chemin De La Montagne	(418) 937-2326
Beaconsfield	Le Coin Artisanal	454 A Boul. Beaconsfield	(514) 505-3075
Bronmont	Les Alpagas De La Ferme Norli	25 Ch. De Magog	(450) 534-2305
Brossard	Les Laines Saute Mouton	2144 Boul Lapiniere	(450) 671-1155
Cap St. Ignace	Boutique Alpagas Csi	1547 Rte. Des Pommiers	(418) 241-3674
Champlain	Creation Mamzelle Bibine	1230 Notre Dame	(819) 244-2710
Chateauguay	Laine Et Tricot Solange	190 Du Boise	(450) 699-4932
Chicoutimi	Atelier L.T.	1897 Des Tulipes	(418) 690-3015
Chicoutimi	Boutique Bee-La	44 Rue Price Est.	(418) 690-2995
Cowansville	Boutique Meli-Melo	140 Rue Principale	(450) 931-1965
Donaconna	Aspirateurs R.G. Inc.	325 De L'Eglise	(418) 285-2552
Drummondville	Bout. De Laine Pingouin Enr.	1165 Jean De Lalonda	(819) 478-0496
Gatineau	Artisan Knots	11 Emile Zola	(819) 661-0161
Gatineau	Les Ateliers Quilt et Coton	110 Georges St. #15	(819) 617-6777
Gatineau	Tricot Darquise	825 Boul.Maloney Est. #7	(819) 893-9393
Gatuneau	Magifil	317 Boul.St-Joseph	(819) 595-3694
Granby	Le Centre De Couture Et	77 Robinson Sud.	(450) 375-1821
Grand Mere	Tissue Berthiaume	526 6Eme Ave.	(819) 538-4521
Jonquiere	L'Artisane	2016 Rue St. Familie	(418) 695-4476
Kahnawake	Calico Cottage Quilt & Gift Shop	Rt. 132 E.	(450) 632-7070
Lac Aux Sables	Julie Belanger	523 Principale	(514) 945-0178
L'Ancienne - Lorette	L'atelier de Penelope	1368B Rue Saint-Jaques	(418) 634-0050
Laval	Laine Et Couture Crystel	1600 Boul. Le Carbusier, Local 90	(514) 686-8445
Laval	Le Café Tricot	2708 Concorde Est. #C	(450) 933-4555
Lavel	Artfil	1773 Boul. Cure Labelle	(514) 307-3388
Lavel	Centre de Couture Gema	3270 Boul. St. Martin	(450) 682-4112
Lebel Quevillon	Magasin General Levesque	62 Place Quevillon Cp. 340	(819) 755-4111
Lemoyne	Fibre Detours	1515 Rue St. Thomas	(514) 553-1603
L'Lle Perrot	Marie Mode Tricot	200 Grand Blvd.	(514) 901-0708
Loretteville	Multi-Laine Loretteville	10143 De L'Hopital	(418) 842-1286
Magog	Boutfils	580 Demasse Bastilien	(819) 432-5927
Mont Royal	La Tricotheque Mtl.	1789 Boul. Graham	(514) 508-1789
Montreal	A La Lainerie Lepine Limitee	3884 Rue Jean-Talon Est	(514) 721-2440
Montreal	Laine Et Couture Décor	7275 Sherbrook Est.	(514) 351-2544
Montreal	Les Tricots Knitwits	6900 Decarie Blvd. #3110	(514) 342-9332
Montreal	Louise Diamond	3442 Rue De Bordeaux	(514) 526-1927
Montreal	Mouline Yarns	5317 Rue Sherbrooke Quest	(514) 935-4401
Montréal	Salle de Couture & Tricot Lounge	6260 Saint-Hubert	(514) 276-2547
Nicolet	La-Julie Factrie	3010 Rang Bas De La Riviere	(819) 293-7652
Outremont	Le Foulard Reconfort	258 Chemin Cote St. Catherine	(514) 576-8153
Pointe-Claire	Les Lainages du Petit Mouton	295 B Boul St. Jean	(514) 694-6268
Quebec	La Dauphine	1487 Chemin St. Foy	(418) 527-3030
Riviere Du Loup	Salon De Couture L'Oiseau Bleu	272 Lafontaine	(418) 862-4006
Roberval	La Maison De La Laine	910 Boul. St. Joseph	(418) 275-4248
Rosemere	Centre De Couture Gema	239 Boul. Cure-Labelle	(450) 437-9562
Rouyn Noranda	Tric. & Art. Ce-Laur	14 Perreault Est	(819) 762-4177
Shawinigan	Artisanat De La Mauricie	6523 Boul. Royal	(819) 539-5590
Sherbrooke	Au Grenier Des Perles	76 12E Ave. Sud.	(819) 791-3009
Sherbrooke	Tricot The Serre	201 Jacques-Cartier Sud.	(819) 575-1410
St. Adele	Au P'Tit Brin De Laine	1332 Boul De St. Adele #100	(450) 229-2221
St. Adele	La Juste Laine Au Juste Prix	1125 Claude Gregoire	(450) 229-2006
St. Andre Avelin	Boutique D'Arts Textiles	57 Pue Principale	(819) 983-1164
St. Bruno	Biscotte E Cie	1315 Roberval #100	(450) 482-1513
St. Eustache	Tricotine & Cie.	112 Rue St. Laurent	(514) 234-1701
St. Gervais	Boutique Du Travailleur	192 Principale	(418) 887-6608
St. Hubert	Basylvie	5310 Rue Begin	(450) 445-2277
St. Hubert	Boutique Fil D'Arts Ns	6250 Boul. Cousineau	(450) 676-7364
St. Hubert	Club Tissus Rive - Sud	1651 Boul. Des Promenades	(514) 983-1203
St. Jerome	Artisanat Du Nord	711 St. Georges	(450) 438-0860
St. Jerome	Artisanat Paule	550B St. Georges	(450) 432-4779
St. Julie	Boutique Laine Et Laine	1681 B Principale	(450) 922-6116
St. Prime	Petit Marche De St. Prime	1113 Rue Principale	(418) 902-3018
St. Sauveur	Pur Laine Etc. Engr.	328 Pue Principale	(450) 744-1949
St. Vallier	Alpagas Analuka	304 Chemin D'Azur	(418) 804-0646
Sutton	Mont Tricot	20 K Rue Principale Nord	(450) 538-8040
Thetford Mines	Tricots Huguette	87 Rue Gangeau	(418) 335-2223
Tingwick	Poule De Laine	21 Jutras	(819) 359-2516
Trois Rivieres	Pompon Laine Café	667 Rue Bonaventure	(819) 841-3223
Val D'Or	Les Tricots De Sandrine	1190 5Eme Rue	(819) 825-6622

Saskatchewan Shops

Carlyle	Sew & Sews Quilt & Fabric Shop	117 Main St.	(306) 453-2562
Duck Lake	Mami's Country Quilts	253 Front St.	(306) 467-4453
Foam Lake	Quiltworks Studio Quilt Shop	323 Main St.	(306) 272-4420
Frontier	Sweet Material Things	112 2nd Ave. W.	(306) 296-2025
Humboldt	Saskatchewan Haus of Stitches	626 Main St.	(306) 682-0772
Kindersley	Veronica's Sewing Supplies	100 Main St.	(306) 463-4505
Maidstone	Quilt Paradise	202 Main St.	(306) 893-2802
Maple Creek	Cat's Meow Quilts & Gifts	200 Jasper St.	(306) 662-2180
Maple Creek	Main Street Mercantile	111 Maple St.	(306) 662-4440
Melfort	Quarter Inch Quilt Shop	202 Main St.	(306) 752-2290
Moose Jaw	Heather's Quilting Palette	361 Main St. N.	(306) 693-1393
Moose Jaw	Karen's Buttons 'n' Bows	138 Fairford St. W.	(306) 692-7001
Moose Jaw	Passionknit	1048 6th Ave. NW	(306) 692-7917
Moose Jaw	Quilters Haven	422 Main St. N.	(306) 693-8523
Moose Jaw	Stitchers Nook	50 Stadacona St. W.	(306) 692-5377
Moose Jaw	The Quilt Patch	35 High St. E.	(306) 692-3360
Moosomin	Shirley's Sewing Room	506 Main St.	(306) 435-3633
Nipawin	Sew Materialistic	223 C 3Rd St. N.	(306) 862-9789
Outlook	Broderick Garden Centre	420 Saskatchewan Ave. E.	(306) 867-8999
Prince Albert	Beth's Yarn & Needlecraft	909A Central Ave.	(306) 764-6910
Regina	Accent Stitchery, Framing & Gifts	4907 Albert St.	(306) 584-7010
Regina	Cindy-rella's Sewing & Quilting	1230 St. John St. #2	(306) 585-2227
Regina	Golden Willow Fibres	3104 13th Ave.	(306) 791-1930
Regina	Peachtree Heirlooms Quilt Shop	140 Albert St.	(306) 569-1552
Saskatoon	440 Quilt Shop	440 4th St. E.	(306) 242-4404
Saskatoon	Periwinkle Quilting	2105 8th St. E. 105	(306) 933-3072
Saskatoon	Periwinkle Quilting & Beyond	912 Broadway Ave.	(306) 933-3072
Saskatoon	Prairie Lily Knitting	7 1730 Quebec Ave.	(306) 665-2771
Saskatoon	The Sewing Machine Store	294 Venture Crescent	(306) 652-6031
Saskatoon	The Wool Emporium	2605 Broadway Ave.	(306) 374-7848
Saskatoon	Unique Textiles Studio	1022 Louise Ave.	(306) 653-4977
Spiritwood	Pipers Lake Quilt Shop	229 Main St.	(306) 883-3455
Swift Current	Sowen Quilt Shop	3 405 N. Service Rd. W.	(306) 773-0151
Unity	Ilene's Quilting Plus	120 3rd Ave. E.	(306) 228-2288
Warman	Prairie Chicks Quilting	110 Central St.	(306) 934-1972
Wolseley	Tiger Lily Quilts	402 Garnet St.	(306) 698-4000
Yorkton	Colette's Sewing Machines Plus	206 Smith St. E.	(306) 782-3520

Index

Yukon Shops

Whitehorse	Bear Paw Quilts	2093 2nd Ave.	867-393-2327
Whitehorse	Itsy-Bitsy Yarn Store	125 1116 Front St.	(438) 862-6608

For the most up-to-date information
www.quilterstc.com OR www.crafterstc.com

Quilt Name:

_____

_____

Date Started:

_____

Date Completed:

_____

Source, Book, Pattern or Original:

_____

_____

Finished Size:

_____

Quilted By:

_____

_____

Created For:

_____

_____

Notes:

_____

_____

_____

_____

_____

_____

Additional Notes……..

_____

_____

_____

_____

_____

_____

_____

_____

Photos and Sketches……..

Quilt Name:
_____
_____

Date Started:
_____

Date Completed:
_____

Source, Book, Pattern or Original:
_____
_____

Finished Size:
_____

Quilted By:
_____

Created For:
_____
_____

Notes:
_____
_____
_____
_____
_____
_____

Fabrics and Supplies…...

Additional Notes……..
_____
_____
_____
_____
_____
_____
_____
_____
_____

Photos and Sketches……..

Quilt Name:

Date Started:

Date Completed:

Source, Book, Pattern or Original:

Finished Size:

Quilted By:

Created For:

Notes:

Fabrics and Supplies…...

Additional Notes……..

Photos and Sketches……..

Fabrics and Supplies…...

Additional Notes……..

Photos and Sketches……..

Quilt Name:

_____
_____

Date Started:

Date Completed:

_____

Source, Book, Pattern or Original:

_____
_____

Finished Size:

_____

Quilted By:

_____
_____

Created For:

_____
_____

Notes:

_____
_____
_____
_____
_____
_____

Fabrics and Supplies…...

Additional Notes……..

_____
_____
_____
_____
_____
_____
_____
_____
_____

Photos and Sketches……..